WINE GLOBALIZATION

In this anthology, editors Kym Anderson and Vicente Pinilla have gathered together some of the world's leading wine economists and economic historians to examine the development of national wine industries before and during the two waves of globalization. These empirically based chapters analyze developments in all key wine-producing and consuming countries using a common methodology to explain long-term trends and cycles in wine production, consumption and trade. The authors cover topics such as the role of new technologies, policies and institutions, as well as exchange rate movements, international market developments, evolutions in grape varieties and wine quality changes. The final chapter draws on an economic model of global wine markets, to project those markets to 2025 based on various assumptions about population and income growth, real exchange rates and other factors. All authors of the book contributed to a unique global database of annual data back to the mid-nineteenth century.

Kym Anderson is a Professor of Economics and foundation Executive Director of the Wine Economics Research Centre at the University of Adelaide in South Australia. He is also Professor of Economics at the Australian National University in Canberra. He is a cofounder and vice-president of the American Association of Wine Economists, and a coeditor of its *Journal of Wine Economics*. His previously compiled compendium of global wine data *(Global Wine Markets, 1961 to 2009: A Statistical Compendium)* has been extended to cover 1860 to 2016 for this book.

Vicente Pinilla is Professor of Economic History at the University of Zaragoza. He is Editor of *Historia Agraria* and Director of the Center for Depopulation and Rural Development Areas Studies. He belongs to the Editorial Board of the Rural History in Europe Series. He is the author of *Peaceful Surrender: The Depopulation of Rural Spain in the Twentieth Century*, and is an editor of the books *Agriculture and Economic Development in Europe since 1870*, *Markets and Agricultural Change in Europe from the 13th to the 20th Century* and *Natural Resources and Economic Growth: Learning from History*.

Wine Globalization

A New Comparative History

Edited by

KYM ANDERSON

University of Adelaide and
Australian National University

and

VICENTE PINILLA

Universidad de Zaragoza

CAMBRIDGE
UNIVERSITY PRESS

CAMBRIDGE
UNIVERSITY PRESS

University Printing House, Cambridge CB2 8BS, United Kingdom

One Liberty Plaza, 20th Floor, New York, NY 10006, USA

477 Williamstown Road, Port Melbourne, VIC 3207, Australia

314-321, 3rd Floor, Plot 3, Splendor Forum, Jasola District Centre, New Delhi - 110025, India

79 Anson Road, #06-04/06, Singapore 079906

Cambridge University Press is part of the University of Cambridge.

It furthers the University's mission by disseminating knowledge in the pursuit of education, learning and research at the highest international levels of excellence.

www.cambridge.org
Information on this title: www.cambridge.org/9781107192928
DOI: 10.1017/ 9781108131766

First published 2018

A catalogue record for this publication is available from the British Library

Library of Congress Cataloging in Publication data
Names: Anderson, Kym, editor. | Pinilla, Vicente, 1959– editor.
Title: Wine globalization : a new comparative history / edited by Kym Anderson (University of Adelaide and Australian National University) and Vicente Pinilla (Universidad de Zaragoza).
Description: New York, NY: Cambridge University Press, 2018. | Includes bibliographical references and index.
Identifiers: LCCN 2017044978 | ISBN 9781107192928 (hardback)
Subjects: LCSH: Wine industry. | International trade.
Classification: LCC HD9370.5.W557 2018 | DDC 381/.456632–dc23
LC record available at https://lccn.loc.gov/2017044978

ISBN 978-1-107-19292-8 Hardback
ISBN 978-1-316-64275-7 Paperback

Contents

Figures

Tables

Contributors

Julian M. Alston is a Distinguished Professor in Agricultural and Resource Economics and Director of the Robert Mondavi Institute's Center for Wine Economics at the University of California, Davis, where he leads projects on the economics of production and consumption of grapes and wine and related policies. He is a Fellow of the American Association of Wine Economists.

Kym Anderson is George Gollin Professor of Economics and Executive Director of the Wine Economics Research Centre at the University of Adelaide in Adelaide, South Australia, Professor of Economics at the Australian National University in Canberra, and a Research Fellow of the London-based Centre for Economic Policy Research. His research interests include international trade and economic development as well as the economics of agriculture, food and wine.

Willem H. Boshoff is Associate Professor of Economics at Stellenbosch University, South Africa. His research interests are in business cycles and industrial organization. He has published on long-term cycles in agricultural production and competition policy problems in agriculture. He is also a director of an economics consultancy firm based in Stellenbosch.

Jean-Michel Chevet has been a Researcher in Economic History at France's Institute National de la Recherche Agronomique (INRA). Currently he works at CERVIN at the Institut des Sciences de la Vigne et du Vin (ISVV) in Bordeaux. His work focusses on the history of the agricultural revolutions in England and France and of winegrowing, especially as it relates to technology and climate change.

Alessandro Corsi is an Associate Professor of Agricultural Economics at the University of Turin, Italy. His main recent research fields are agricultural labor markets and pluri-activity, wine economics, the market of organic products and the functioning of the alternative food networks. He has published more than 100 scientific articles, books, book chapters, and papers.

Giovanni Federico is a Professor of Economic History, Department of Economics and Management, University of Pisa, and formerly Professor of Economic History at the European University Institute in Florence, Italy. He is Editor of the *European Review of Economic History* and President of the European Historical Economics Society. He is the author of *Feeding the World: An Economic History of World Agriculture* (2005).

Eva Fernández is an Associate Professor in Economic History in the Social Sciences Department of Carlos III University in Madrid, Spain. Her research fields include markets and institutions in the wine sector of Spain and France in the nineteenth and twentieth centuries, agricultural policy and its determinants in developed countries, regional productivity of agriculture, agricultural cooperatives, and religion and its effects on wealth.

William Foster (PhD in agricultural and resource economics from the University of California at Berkeley) is a Professor in the Department of Agricultural Economics at the Pontificia Universidad Católica de Chile in Santiago. His research interests are rural development, economic geography, welfare impacts of agricultural and food policy, and the Chilean wine industry.

Johan Fourie is Associate Professor of Economics at Stellenbosch University, South Africa. His PhD was awarded best dissertation prize at the World Economic History Congress in 2015. Fourie is editor of *Economic History of Developing Regions*, cofounder of the African Economic History Network and Director of the Laboratory for the Economics of Africa's Past.

Eric Giraud-Héraud, an Economist, is Research Director at France's Institute National de la Recherche Agronomique (INRA) and the Scientific Director of the Institute of Vine and Wine Sciences (ISVV) in Bordeaux. His research interests include the economics of food supply chains (industrial organization) and consumer behavior (experimental auctions) connected to corporate social responsibility.

Pedro Lains is Research Professor at the Institute of Social Sciences, University of Lisbon and Visiting Professor at Católica-Lisbon School of Business and Economics, Portugal. His latest coauthored book is

An Economic History of Portugal, 1143–2000 (Cambridge University Press, 2016), and his latest coedited book is *An Agrarian History of Portugal, 1000–2000* (2017).

James T. Lapsley is a semiretired wine historian. He is an Adjunct Associate Professor with the Department of Viticulture and Enology, University of California, Davis. He works as an academic researcher on wine and grape economics and history at the University of California's Agricultural Issues Center.

Charles C. Ludington is Teaching Associate Professor of History at North Carolina State University in the United States and Marie Sklodowska Curie Senior Research Fellow at University College Cork in Ireland. His first book, *The Politics of Wine in Britain: A New Cultural History*, was published in 2013. He is currently working on a book about the role of Irish merchants in the development of Bordeaux wines in the eighteenth century.

Pablo Martinelli (PhD from the European University Institute, 2012) is currently an Assistant Professor of Economic History at Universidad Carlos III de Madrid. His main research areas are the role of agriculture in economic development and quantitative agricultural history. His published contributions deal with the role of geography, rural inequality, and conflict in Italian economic history.

Ana María Mateu is a Researcher at Argentina's Consejo Nacional de Investigaciones Científicas y Técnicas (CONACYT) and a Professor of History at the Universidad Nacional de Cuyo, Mendoza. She has published *Una antología histórica sobre el desarrollo de la industria vitvinícula argentina* (2008) and, with Steve Stein, the edited volume *Vinos y Competitividad Agroindustrial: Un largo camino* (2011).

Lewis S. McLean is a postgraduate student at the Department of Economics at Stellenbosch University, South Africa. He conducts microeconometric research on South African social and economic issues, especially development, education, health, and labor. He has also conducted research in business cycle economics and the measurement of policy uncertainty.

Oscar Melo is an Associate Professor in the Department of Agricultural Economics, Pontificia Universidad Catolica de Chile. He holds a PhD and MSc in agricultural and resource economics from the University of Maryland, College Park. His research interests are water economics, climate change, quality and regulation, economic valuation, and agricultural trade and development.

Giulia Meloni is a Robert M. Solow Post-Doctoral Fellow at the Cournot Centre, Paris, and a Senior Researcher at the Centre for Institutions and Economic Performance (LICOS) at the University of Leuven, Belgium. She holds a PhD from the University of Leuven and a bachelor's degree from LUISS University, Rome. She has published on political economy, European agriculture, product standards and wine economic history.

Vicente Pinilla is Professor in Economic History at the University of Zaragoza, Spain, and a Research Fellow of the Instituto Agroalimentario de Aragón (IA2). His research interests include international trade in agricultural products, long-term agricultural changes, environmental history and migration. He was Vice-Rector of Budget and Economic Management of the University of Zaragoza from 2000 to 2004.

Eugenio Pomarici is Associate Professor of Agricultural Economics at the University of Padua, Italy. His main recent research fields are sustainability, wine industry structure analysis and wine policy. He is Past President of the OIV Economy and Law Commission and Coeditor in Chief of the *Wine Economics and Policy* journal. He has published more than 100 scientific works.

Olena Sambucci is a Postdoctoral Scholar in the Department of Agricultural and Resource Economics at the University of California, Davis. Her research focusses on the economics of adoption and use of precision vineyard technology. She has done extensive research on the structure of the US grapegrowing industry, with emphasis on the production and pricing of wine grapes.

Roberta Sardone is a Senior Researcher at CREA-PB in Rome. Her research interests are focussed on the structural and economical evolution of Italian agriculture and analysis of the European Union's Common Agricultural Policy for wine and tobacco. She is also an expert on the EU's budget, institutional framework and decision-making processes. Since 2009, she has edited the *Yearbook of Italian Agriculture*, published since 1947.

Steve Stein (PhD in History from Stanford University) is Senior Professor of History at the University of Miami in Florida. He is coeditor with Ana María Mateu of *El vino y sus revoluciones: Una antología histórica sobre el desarrollo de la industria vitvinícula argentina* (Mendoza, 2008), the first comprehensive historical treatment of the Argentine wine industry.

Karl Storchmann is a Clinical Professor in the Economics Department of New York University. Previously (2000–2005), he was a Lecturer in

Yale University's Department of Economics and an Associate Professor of Economics at Whitman College (2005–2010). He is a Cofounder and Managing Editor of the *Journal of Wine Economics* and Cofounder and Vice-President of the American Association of Wine Economists. His research interests cover a wide range of applied microeconomics in addition to wine.

Daniel A. Sumner is Director of the University of California's Agricultural Issues Center and Distinguished Professor in Agricultural and Resource Economics, University of California, Davis. He has family roots in the Californian grape and wine industry. He is a Fellow of the Agricultural and Applied Economics Association and former Chair of the International Agricultural Trade Research Consortium.

Johan Swinnen is Professor of Economics and Director of the Centre for Institutions and Economic Performance (LICOS) at the University of Leuven in Belgium and a Visiting Scholar at the Center for Food Security and the Environment (FSE) at Stanford University in California. He has published widely on agricultural and food policies, political economy, institutional reform, trade, global value chains, and technical standards.

Nick Vink has been Professor of Agricultural Economics and Chair of the Department at Stellenbosch University since 1996. His research encompasses structural change in South African and African agriculture, land reform, trade, and wine economics. He serves as a Nonexecutive Director on the Board of the South African Reserve Bank.

Gavin Williams is an Emeritus Fellow of St Peter's College, Oxford University, United Kingdom. He is interested in social theories and the empirical study of politics, political economy, societies, and histories. He was the recipient of the 2014 African Studies Association UK Distinguished Africanist Award.

Glyn Wittwer is a Professorial Fellow and Deputy Director of the Centre of Policy Studies at Victoria University in Melbourne, Australia. He specializes in multiregional dynamic modeling of national economies and their resource base, in addition to modeling global wine markets. His latest edited volume is *Economic Modeling of Water: The Australian CGE Experience* (2012).

Preface

At the start of this century, two scholarly efforts were being undertaken simultaneously on opposite sides of the world. One was a wine economics workshop sponsored by the University of Adelaide's Centre for International Economic Studies (CIES), as part of the Eleventh Australian Wine Industry Technical Conference. That conference was held in Adelaide, South Australia during 7–11 October 2001, immediately preceding the Twenty-Sixth World Congress of the Office Inernational de la Vigne et du Vin, 11–18 October, Adelaide. Half of the CIES wine economics workshop was set aside to review wine market developments in the major wine-producing and/or wine-consuming regions of the world. Following the workshop, authors revised and updated those papers for a volume aimed at providing a comprehensive and contemporary picture of the impacts of the second globalization wave on the world's wine markets (*The World's Wine Markets: Globalization at Work*, edited by Kym Anderson, Edward Elgar 2004). While many of the chapters provided a brief historical overview by way of background, the main focus of that book was on the dramatic changes since the late 1980s. All chapters were informed by a new annual database assembled to assist that project, which has since been updated as K. Anderson and S. Nelgen, *Global Wine Markets, 1961 to 2009: A Statistical Compendium* (University of Adelaide Press, 2011, freely available as an ebook at www.adelaide.edu.au/press/titles/global-wine).

The other scholarly exercise was taking place at the University of Zaragoza in Spain, where economic historians were assembling global wine data in order to analyze an aspect of the first wave of globalization, namely the rise and fall of Spain as a wine exporter in the century prior to World War II. That led to a paper by V. Pinilla and M. I. Ayuda ('The Political Economy of the Wine Trade: Spanish Exports and the International Market, 1890–1935', *European Review of Economic History* 6: 51–85, 2002) and also the beginnings of a global wine database for that period that has since been made available as V. Pinilla, 'Wine Historical Statistics: A Quantitative Approach to its Consumption, Production and Trade, 1840–1938' (AAWE Working Paper 167, August 2014, freely available at www.wine-economics.org).

Meanwhile, Kym Anderson undertook an analysis of the economic development of Australia's wine industry from its beginning in the 1830s. Comprehensive though that study was (available as K. Anderson, *Growth and Cycles in Australia's Wine Industry: A Statistical Compendium, 1843 to 2013*, University of Adelaide Press, 2015, freely available at www.adelaide.edu.au/press/titles/austwine), it was incomplete because at that time there was not a comparable set of pre-1961 annual data available for the other pertinent wine-producing countries, nor global wine production, consumption and trade totals, against which to compare Australian trends and industry cycles. Hence the comparative approach, as illustrated in the edited volume by Hatton, O'Rourke and Williamson on *The New Comparative Economic History* (MIT Press, 2007), was confined in that study mostly to the years since 1960.

A natural next step for both of us was to get together and entice others to join us in a comparative assessment of national and global wine market developments over both the first and second globalization waves, as well as in the intervening 'lost' decades that included two world wars and the Great Depression. There was no funding available for the project as a whole, but each contributing author was able to self-fund or assemble some local funds to cover research assistant time and travel costs. Subsets of us met on the sidelines of several international meetings, including the annual conferences of the American Association of Wine Economists in Mendoza (26–30 May 2015) and Bordeaux (25–28 June 2016), the triennial congress of the International Association of Agricultural Economists in Milan (9–14 August 2015) and a follow-on workshop at Castello di Verrazzano in Tuscany (16–17 August 2015).

Crucially, all participants agreed to contribute national data to expand on the post-1960 data previously compiled by Anderson and the pre-1939 data assembled by Pinilla. We added data from secondary sources so as to cover the world, and aimed to go back at least to 1835 when the first wave of globalization began. In the end, we included some data back as far as the 1660s for South Africa and even to the 1320s in the case of Britain, but for many of the less wine-focused countries the series did not start until the late nineteenth century, and some series had years missing, such as during the two world wars. We therefore interpolated to fill gaps in the most important series covering volumes of wine production, exports and imports so as to be able to estimate global totals for those key variables back to 1860.

As the editors and compilers of the global database (K. Anderson and V. Pinilla, *Annual Database of Global Wine Markets, 1835 to 2016*, freely available in Excel at the University of Adelaide's Wine Economics Research Centre, www.adelaide.edu.au/wine-econ/databases), we wish to record our grateful thanks to the research assistants who helped assemble that database, and the ebook that makes those data more accessible for the general reader (K. Anderson, S. Nelgen and V. Pinilla, *Global Wine Markets, 1860 to 2016: A Statistical Compendium*, University of Adelaide Press, 2017, www.adelaide.edu.au/press). Those assistants include Alexander Holmes and Thithi Nguyentran at Adelaide and Adrián Palacios at Zaragoza. Funding support also is gratefully acknowledged, including from Wine Australia and the University of Adelaide's EU Centre for Global Affairs and its Faculty of the Professions, and the Ministry of Science and Innovation of Spain (project ECO2015-65582) and the Government of Aragon through the Research Group Agri-food Economic History (Nineteenth and Twentieth Centuries).

Last but certainly not least, we are immensely grateful to each of the contributors to this multiauthored study, not only for their painstaking efforts in assembling data and preparing their analytical narrative but also for their energy and enthusiasm throughout the project and their willingness to attend its workshops at their own expense and meet our various deadlines.

Abbreviations and Acronyms

AOC	Appellation d'origine contrôlée (of France)
AWBC	Australian Wine and Brandy Corporation
CAP	Common Agricultural Policy (of the EU)
CMO	Common Market Organization (of the EU)
COMECON	Council for Mutual Economic Assistance (among communist countries, 1949–1991)
DO	Denominaciones de Origen (of Spain)
DOC	Denominazione di Origine Controllata (of Italy)
DOCG	Denominazione di Origine Controllata e Garantita (of Italy)
DWI	German Wine Institute
EEC	European Economic Community
EC	European Commission
EFTA	European Free Trade Association
EU	European Union
FAO	Food and Agriculture Organization (of the United Nations)
FDI	foreign direct investment
fob	free on board (a ship, for exporting)
FTA	free trade agreement
GATT	General Agreement on Tariffs and Trade (now part of WTO)
GI	geographical indication
ha	hectares
IGT	Indicazione Geografica Tipica (of Italy)
INDO	Instituto Nacional de Denominaciones de Origen (of Spain)
ISO	International Standards Office
KL	kilolitres

KWV	Ko-operatiewe Wijnbouwersvereniging van Zuid-Afrika Beperkt (Cooperative Wine Farmers' Association of South Africa)
LAL	litres of alcohol
ML	million litres
OIV	Office International de la Vigne et du Vin (the Paris-based International Organization of Vine and Wine)
ONIVINS	Office National Interprofessionelle des Vins
PDO	protected designation of origin
PGI	protected geographical indication
RCA	(index of) 'revealed' comparative advantage
SAWIS	South Africa Wine Information and Systems
VDQS	Vin Délimité de Qualité Supérieure
VQPRD	Vin de Qualité Produit dans une Région Déterminée
WFA	Winemakers' Federation of Australia
WIC	Wine Institute of California
WINZ	Wine Institute of New Zealand
WSET	Wine and Spirit Education Trust (of the United Kingdom)
WSTA	Wine and Spirit Trade Association (of the United Kingdom)
WTO	World Trade Organization
Z.A.R.	Zuid-Afrikaansche Republiek (South African Republic, an independent country during 1852–1902 before becoming part of the Union of South Africa in 1910 [together with Cape Colony and Orange Free State], which was renamed the Republic of South Africa in 1961)

Technical Terms and Units

Definitions of *Wine*

Wine is defined variously by international organizations, including the United Nations (FAO CODE 0564; SITC 112.12; Harmonised System Tariff Heading 2204), and refers to beverage wines of fresh grapes of all qualities, including still, sparkling and fortified wines.

Beverage wine is sometimes divided in international trade data into the following three subcategories:

Bottled still wine (Harmonised System Tariff Heading 220421): Still grape wines traded in containers of two litres or less;

Bulk (or other) wine (Harmonised System Tariff Heading 220429): Still grape wines traded in containers exceeding two litres; and

Sparkling wine (Harmonised System Tariff Heading 220410): All sparkling grape wines, including from champagne.

Nonbeverage wine refers to grape wine used for distillation or for industrial uses.

Table wine refers to unfortified still beverage wine (that is, excluding sparkling as well as high-alcohol fortified wines and wines that are distilled or put to industrial uses).

Some alcoholic beverages made from products other than grapes also are called wine (as with rice wine, for example, which is common in Asia). They are not included in the wine data in the present study, but are included in total alcohol consumption data.

Units of measurement

Abbreviation	Definition	Conversion
ha	hectare	10,000 square metres or 2.471 acres
t	tonne	1,000 kilograms or 2,205 pounds
kt	kilotonne	1,000 tonnes
L	litre	1,000 millilitres or 0.26417 US gallons or 0.21997 Imperial gallons
LAL	litres of alcohol	Assumed 12% for wine and 4.5% for beer, while the volume of spirits (typically around 40% alcohol) is normally quoted in LAL
KL	kilolitre	1,000 litres or 10 hectolitres
ML	megalitre	1 million litres
US$	US dollar	
US$m	million US dollars	
1 million	1,000,000	
1 billion	1,000,000,000	

Measures used for most-common variables

Variable	*Unit (per year)*
Grape vine area	'000 ha of bearing vines
Grape yield	Tonnes of grapes/ha or KL of wine/ha
Volume of wine production	ML
Volume of wine consumption	ML
Wine consumed per capita or per adult	L
Beer consumed per capita or per adult	L
Spirits consumed per capita (alcohol content)	LAL
Alcohol consumed per capita or per adult	LAL
Volume of wine exports and imports	ML
Value of wine exports and imports	current $US million
Unit value of wine exports and imports	current $US/L
Adult population	People 15 years or older

Boundaries and Names of Countries

Nation-states change their borders and names from time to time, and many of today's 190-plus countries have changed in one or both of those respects during the past two centuries. In the present study, we follow the usual tradition of comparative historians in adopting the current name and current border of each country. That has required careful disaggregation of national data in many cases. Where that has not been possible, authors have made clear to what subregion particular data refer (e.g., England or Great Britain rather than all of the United Kingdom).

PART I

OVERVIEW

1

Introduction

Kym Anderson and Vicente Pinilla

Winemaking is really quite a simple business; only the first 200 years are difficult.
The late Baroness Philippine de Rothschild
(vigneron in France, California and Chile)

This book has a dual purpose: as a study to help those associated with the wine industry understand evolving market opportunities and challenges in the wake of globalization, and as a single industry case study to help society understand some of globalization's myriad impacts on businesses, consumers and governments.

Globalization is inherently disruptive, whether due to technological changes in transportation and communication services or to governmental regulatory or trade policy reforms. A lowering of the cost of goods, services, capital, labour, tourists, information or ideas moving across geographic borders raises average incomes, alters producer technologies and consumer preferences, and changes relative prices of products and primary inputs, exchange rates, and comparative advantages of nations. Societies and their governments wish to know not only about benefits from change but also whether such disruptions lead to losses for significant groups. Indeed, the latter is one of the motivating forces behind much research on globalization's various impacts.

WHY FOCUS ON WINE?

Globalization is especially disruptive to markets for goods based on capital-intensive perennial crop production and processing, because both investments and disinvestments in such activities adjust rather sluggishly to altered incentives (Dixit and Pindyck 1994). That is one reason why this is an ideal industry case study, because modern winegrape growing and winemaking are among the most capital intensive of all primary production, processing and marketing activities – especially at the premium end of the quality spectrum. Even traditional winegrowing by small farm businesses using labour-intensive methods cannot easily switch in and out of production as profits change.

Another reason for focusing on wine is that global production and consumption were concentrated in a very small number of just European countries at the start of the first globalization wave: in 1860, the top five countries accounted for 81 percent of global wine production, and the next three also were European and added another 7 percent. That concentration meant there was great potential for the growth in high-income countries' incomes, as a result of globalization, to lead to wine consumption growth in new or underdeveloped markets.

Yet the first globalization wave that ended at the outbreak of World War I seemed to affect global wine markets very little except in one important respect, namely, the transfer of the tiny phylloxera insect from the United States to Europe. That insect devastated the majority of Europe's vineyards. It led to French vignerons investing hugely in nearby Algeria, whose share of global wine markets rose from 0.1 percent in 1870 to 8 percent of production and more than 40 percent of exports by 1910. But if colonial Algeria is thought of as part of France (as the French government did prior to 1962), then the share of global wine production that was exported was no higher at the end of the first globalization wave – nor indeed in 1960 – than it was in 1860, at around 5 percent.

By contrast, exports as a share of global wine production grew from 5 percent to 15 percent between 1960 and 1990, and then to 40 percent by 2012. In the past half-century of globalization, wine has switched from being one of the world's least-traded agricultural products to one of the most traded internationally. This has been an unprecedented boom for consumers everywhere. There have been huge improvements in the quality and diversity of wines available to middle-income consumers in an ever-expanding number of countries, at very affordable prices.

Not all winegrowers have benefitted, though. The rapid expansion in wine exports from the Southern Hemisphere since 1990 has put additional pressure on European producers, who, since the early 1960s, have been facing declining demand in their domestic markets. More recently, winegrowers in some newly exporting countries have been struggling to retain competitiveness too, while others (e.g., in New Zealand and the United States) have been enjoying high wine and hence grape prices. Meanwhile, all exporters are examining demand developments in Asia, especially China, in the hope of benefitting from that region's emerging import growth while also noting

China's rapid expansion in domestic vineyards and wine production since the late 1990s.

Boom–slump cycles are normal in the wine industry. The latest national production cycles clearly did not all coincide, suggesting that unique national features contribute to those cycles in addition to common developments in markets abroad. To what extent was that the case in earlier periods? What lessons can be learnt from the past about why the wine industry in some countries grew while it stagnated or took off later in others? How does the extent of wine's globalization in recent decades compare/contrast with that in the first globalization wave?[1] And what happened to wine markets in those intervening decades of slow global output and trade growth that were punctuated by two world wars and the Great Depression?

More specifically, why did it take until quite recently for temperate New World countries with ideal winegrape growing conditions to develop a comparative advantage in wine? Most were net importers of wine prior to 1900, even though ocean transport costs were falling rapidly and Europe's vineyards were devastated by phylloxera from the 1870s.[2] What about producers in formerly planned economies of Eastern Europe and the CIS, and those in Islamic North Africa: to what extent might some of them rebuild their former competitiveness?

With these types of questions in mind, the purpose of this present study is to report on a comparative research project aimed at providing a series of empirically based analytical narratives for key countries and regions that shed light on why each national wine market developed as it did in the lead-up to and during the first and second globalization waves and in the decades between them; how the timing, length and amplitude of its wine cycles compared with those in other countries; and how it affected wine market developments elsewhere.

[1] Globalization of the wine industry had been slowly progressing for eight millennia, but with very little product trade. The cultivation of *Vitis vinifera* grapes (by far the most suitable for winemaking) began around 6000 BC in or near the Caucasus region. It spread west to the eastern Mediterranean from 2500 BC and spread north into much of Europe by 400 AD. It then took another 1,100 years before spreading to Latin America from the 1520s, South Africa by 1655, Australia by 1788 and California and New Zealand by 1820 (Unwin 1991). But it involved mostly the transfer of vine cuttings and grape and wine production knowhow rather than trade in wine, since wine deteriorated quickly prior to the use of corked bottles, which only began to be used from the 1700s (Johnson 1989, pp. 195–8).

[2] Phylloxera began to spread in France in 1864, in Austria-Hungary, Portugal, Switzerland and Turkey during 1871–1873, in Spain in 1875, Italy in 1879 and Germany in 1881. France took the longest to recover, because its scientists first had to find a cure. Certainly some regions of numerous New World countries also suffered from phylloxera outbreaks, but later and with much less damage than in Europe (Unwin 1991, p. 284; Campbell 2004).

For most of the past two millennia, grape wine has been a European product. Most production was for home consumption and sale in local markets, with very little crossing national borders. Europe's imperial expansionism from 1500 led to the emergence of winegrape production in some colonies, but again mostly for local consumption by European emigrants or, in the case of South Africa's Western Cape, to resupply crews of passing European ships. The first wave of globalization, from the 1830s to World War I, might have stimulated intercontinental trade in wine as it did for so many other goods, but it did so only slightly: apart from vineyard expansion in North Africa, the product remained almost exclusively European, plus minor exports to European colonies.[3] Even within Europe, wine remained a luxury product in the nonproducing countries, where it accounted for only a tiny fraction of alcohol consumption. It took until the second globalization wave, which accelerated from 1990, before intercontinental trade in wine expanded – which it then did so spectacularly, albeit unevenly, and which led to the democratization of wine consumption in many more countries.[4]

AIM OF THIS BOOK

The present study seeks to explain why wine's geographic spread was so delayed, why its belated takeoff has been so dramatic in a few producing countries and why consumption of wine is spreading to a far larger set of countries and to far more than just their most-affluent consumers. Lessons from those varying experiences provide a basis for looking forward and anticipating future developments. The book therefore finishes with a chapter that employs a model of global wine markets to project them to 2025 for nonpremium, commercial premium and super-premium wines. It begins in Chapter 2, though, with an overview of global wine market developments over the past 150+ years, of the contributions of major wine countries to those developments, and of the impacts they have had on numerous other wine-producing and -consuming countries.

3 In the 1920s, Europe still accounted for 95 percent of global wine production and exports (counting Algeria as part of France) and more than 90 percent of global wine consumption and imports.

4 According to FAO data, grapes were the world's most valuable horticultural crop until 2001 (when tomatoes surpassed them), half of which go into wine production. Economic integration in Europe began soon after World War II, as did North Atlantic trade; and European postwar emigration to former European colonies spread an interest in wine. But a disinterest among newly independent developing countries during the 1960s and 1970s in trading with Western Europe, and the prolonging of communism until the end of the 1980s and early 1990s (apart from China, where reforms started a decade earlier), meant that the second globalization wave accelerated from around 1990.

Improving our understanding of these trends is of obvious interest to producers of wine and of competing and complementary consumer goods and services, but its value is much broader. True, winegrapes are grown on less than 0.2 percent of the world's cropland, and wine accounts for well under 1 percent of global retail expenditure. Nor is wine a rapid-growth industry: the volume of global wine production is no higher now than it was in the early 1960s, and wine's share of global alcohol consumption has more than halved over that half-century, to just 15 percent by volume and 21 percent by (tax-inclusive retail) value. But to millions of investors and hundreds of millions of consumers, wine provides a far more fascinating product than its shares of global production or expenditure might suggest.

Wine also provides an intriguing case study of globalization at work. In addition to the rapid rise in the share of wine production that is traded internationally, there has been a surge also of foreign investment in and mergers and takeovers of wineries large and small. The extremely wide ranges of prices at which vineyards and wines are sold makes winegrapes and wineries leaders in the agricultural and agribusiness sectors in terms of finding market niches through product differentiation, quality upgrading and sophisticated marketing. And the fact that even small winegrowers have been able to move beyond producing a standardized commodity over which they have no market power intrigues producers of other farm products seeking to graduate from being just a price-taking primary producer to becoming a value-adding actor in up to three sectors (by adding processing and possibly on-premise retailing and tourism services).

Wine's globalization has brought major economic gains to participants and regions in the countries where production is expanding, although – as noted at the outset – not without some pain to those traditional European producers whose competiveness has been threatened by declining domestic demand and rising New World competition. In the past six decades, winegrowers have seen the volume of domestic per capita consumption fall by two-fifths in Portugal, two- thirds in France, and by a whopping three-quarters in Italy and Spain. The associated fall in winegrape prices has led to a three-fifths decline in these countries' combined grapevine bearing area, from 6.5 million ha in the late 1960s to just above 2.5 million today. For those countries' growers, it added insult to injury to see wines from New World upstarts suddenly invading what they perceived as 'their' export markets. Meanwhile, for Eastern European producers, that New World onslaught came at the same time as they were struggling to adjust to their transition from communism's central planning.

Those less able or unwilling to adjust understandably were upset by the emergence of New World exporters. For example, at the beginning of the new millennium, Maurice Large, a winemaker and president of the Union Interprofessionelle des Vins du Beaujolais, likened Australian wine to Coca-Cola and called the consumers who purchased it 'philistines'; and a report commissioned by the French Ministry of Agriculture in 2001 concluded, 'Until recent years wine was with us, we were the centre, the unavoidable reference point. Today, the barbarians are at our gates: Australia, New Zealand, the United States, Chile, Argentina, South Africa.'

Traditional consumers of fine wines are concerned too. They worry that what for centuries has been characterized as a largely cottage industry – with colourful, passionate personalities and a wide variety of wines that differ across regions from year to year because of the vagaries of weather or the vigneron's experimentation – will soon be difficult to distinguish from any other globalized industry producing for the masses. Similar concerns are expressed for ancillary industries associated with wine tourism, since boutique wineries are the lifeblood of such regional tourism.

New World winegrowers also are not immune to hardship. On the contrary, they too have faced severe downturns in the past, and some have felt such pain once again during the current globalization wave. What is different this time is that, with wine now traded internationally so much more than ever before, each country's adjustments impact far more on other countries' wine markets, and far faster, than previously. Indeed, with 40 percent of global wine exports now shipped in bulk containers, prices can adjust within minutes of new information on supplies or demands becoming available. These dramatic developments raise a raft of questions, answers to many of which are empirical.

WHAT DIFFERENTIATES THIS BOOK FROM OTHERS?

A unique feature of the present study is that its contributors have assembled the world's first comprehensive annual database of national and global wine markets back to the start of the first globalization wave (Anderson and Pinilla 2017). Data for forty-seven individual countries and for five regional groups of remaining countries allow regional and global totals to be estimated for each variable. Those forty-seven countries have accounted for 96 percent of global wine production and exports and more than 90 percent of global consumption and imports since 1860.[5] With this new

[5] The new database is outlined in this book's appendix. Further details, including sources and interpolations, are included in Anderson, Nelgen and Pinilla (2017).

empirical resource, contributors have been able to complement and add value to the many national and global wine histories currently available.[6] They have also been able to not only add analysis of an extra fifteen years of developments since an earlier study to which several of them contributed (Anderson 2004), but also extend their empirically based insights back an extra hundred-plus years.

The academic economists and historians contributing national studies to this volume have adopted a common methodology to describe and seek to explain long-run trends and cycles in national wine markets in the context of what is happening in the rest of the world. Their analyses are comparative across long time periods, across regions within their country of focus and relative to what is affecting other sectors and hence macroeconomic variables in their country. Among the topics they explore are the roles of new technologies, and of policies, institutions, real exchange rate movements and international market developments. Other topics are wine's evolving share of total alcohol consumption and evolutions in winegrape varieties, wine styles and wine qualities.

The fifteen country or regional chapters are preceded by a global overview (Chapter 2), and the study concludes with model projections of global wine markets to 2025 based on various assumptions about population and income growth, real exchange rate developments, changes in trade policies, and trends in production technologies and consumer preferences (Chapter 18).

We aimed to go back to at least 1835, when the first wave of globalization began (O'Rourke and Williamson 2002, 2004). That is also just before California, South Australia, Victoria and New Zealand began commercial winegrape production. A few chapters had access to data allowing them to go back further (Portugal to 1750, South Africa to the 1660s and Britain to the 1320s), but for many of the other countries the data are only sporadic until late in the nineteenth century. We therefore interpolated to fill gaps in the most important series (volumes of wine production, exports and imports) so as to be able to estimate global totals for those key variables

[6] Many histories have been written about the wine industry in wine-producing countries, and about wine and other alcohol consumption (mainly in high-income countries). Fewer studies have covered the history of international trade in wine, and even fewer have focused on the extent to which wine has been 'globalized' relative to other industries/ products. Among the many popular books on the history of global wine markets and trade are Francis (1972), Johnson (1989), Unwin (1991), Phillips (2000, 2014), Campbell and Guibert (2007), Nye (2007), Rose (2011), Simpson (2011) and Lukacs (2012). See also Anderson (2004).

back to 1860. We chose that time because that was when globalization accelerated, thanks to Gladstone's tariff cuts, the treaty between Britain and France and the subsequent freeing of trade in other parts of Europe.

Of course, over such a long time frame, national borders were changing. We follow the convention of other comparative historians in using current boundaries. For example, Alsace and Lorraine are counted as part of France even though they were folded into Germany from 1871 to 1918. We also count European colonies as separate countries during the imperial period. Importantly, Algeria is considered as a separate trading entity preindependence. It also means the colonies that came together to form the Federation of Australia in 1901 are treated as if the Federation also existed in the nineteenth century.[7]

WHAT HAVE WE LEARNT?

Even though each nation's experiences involved unique features that affected their globalization, it is possible to highlight some general findings. Almost all of today's wine-focused countries experienced a mixture of positive and negative effects on various groups of wine producers, traders and/or consumers. The selection of influences summarized in the following relate to the international transmission of insect pests, technological improvements and their international transfer, trade costs, commercial policies operating at the border of customs territories, excise taxes and other domestic (behind-the-border) regulations plus promotional campaigns affecting domestic wine and other alcoholic beverage consumption, real exchange rate movements and institutional changes. This section also points to the multiple convergences that have occurred in the world's wine markets during the first and/or second globalization waves. The final section of the chapter draws out some of the implications of these findings.

International Transmission of Insect Pests

Perhaps the biggest disrupter to global wine markets over the past 150 years was the infestation of the phylloxera insect into Europe.[8] It also appeared

[7] The number of countries with greater than 100,000 inhabitants was 132 in 1835, but it halved over the next sixty years and was as few as fifty-one in 1912. By 1922, when the Austria-Hungary and Ottoman empires had collapsed, there were sixty-six countries. That number had risen to seventy-six by 1950, 136 by 1970, 163 by 1990 and 182 by 2011 – or 195 if UN member countries with less than 100,000 inhabitants are included (Griffiths and Butcher 2013).

[8] This was not the only pest or disease imported across the Atlantic as globalization proceeded, of course. See, for example, Crosby (2003) and Nunn and Qian (2010).

in other continents, but later and hence was less damaging because France had by that time found a solution to the problem. France was hit first, in the mid-1860s. Being by far the world's biggest consumer and producer of wine (accounting for two-fifths of both), other countries were immediately impacted through the sudden increase in France's demand for imports. Especially affected were low-quality wines, since it was the south of France that was impacted first and most in volume terms. That created a boom for countries most competitive in that segment of the market, especially Spain but also Italy and (in the form of raisins for rehydrating) Greece. It also stimulated a boom in vineyard and winery investment in nearby North Africa, most notably Algeria, which subsequently led to seven decades of sustained exports from that region back to France. That boom, however, had major adverse effects on those countries that initially expanded to supply exports to pest-ridden France, as mentioned later in the section on trade policies.

Technological Improvements and Their International Transfer

The international transfer of vine cuttings and grape and wine production know-how has been going on for millennia. It served as a substitute for trade in wine itself, including in the New World, where wines produced from local plantings gradually substituted for imports in domestic markets following European settlement.

Once a solution to phylloxera was found and successfully adopted toward the end of the nineteenth century in France (using resistant American rootstocks in place of European ones), that technology was quickly taken up in other countries as they became infected. In some cases, American rootstocks were used as a preventative method, along with strict quarantine protocols, to insure against infestation.

There is always potential to improve on traditional production, processing, entrepreneurship and marketing, be that by trial and error of practitioners over the generations or via formal investment in private and public research and development (R&D). New World wine-producing countries have been more dependent on developing new technologies and less on terroir than have producers in Europe, although both sets of countries have made major R&D investments – and expanded complementary tertiary education in viticulture, oenology and wine business and marketing – over the past half-century (Giuliana, Morrison and Rabellotti 2011).

The capacity to transfer such new technologies to other countries has been greatly accelerated over recent decades, through two mechanisms.

One is the emergence of fly-in, fly-out viticulturalist and winemaker consultants from both Old World and New World wine-producing countries (Williams 1995). The decline in airfares has made it far more affordable for young professionals to work in both hemispheres each year, doubling their vintage experiences and learning and spreading new technologies quickly. The other mechanism is via foreign direct investment, including joint ventures: by combining two firms' technical and marketing knowledge, the latest technologies can be diffused to new regions more rapidly.

How important modern technologies are relative to terroir in determining wine comparative advantage is a moot point. One study suggests terroir is not as dominant as is commonly assumed – even in regions as established as Bordeaux (Gerguad and Ginsburg 2008). A recent book by Lewin (2010) begins its section on wine regions with the New World rather than the Old World, to emphasize the point that wines almost everywhere are manipulated by winemakers as they endeavour to make use of available knowledge to produce the products most desired by their customers. What they choose to produce is increasingly being affected by how they can maximize profits through satisfying consumer demand, rather than by what they prefer to make with their available resources.

New technologies in agriculture have long tended to be biased in favour of saving the scarcest factor of production, as reflected in relative factor prices. Hayami and Ruttan (1985) emphasize that the focus of R&D investments thus has been driven in part by changes in factor prices, and in particular by the rise in real wages. That has resulted in the development and/or adoption of labour-saving technologies such as mechanical harvesters and pruners for vineyards and superfast bottling/labelling equipment for wineries in viticultural land-abundant, labour-scarce countries such as Australia. The adoption of labour-saving technologies has helped countries with the highest and fastest-rising real wages retain their comparative advantage in what traditionally had been (at least at the primary stage) a labour-intensive industry. This in turn means labour-intensive producers in poorer countries need to find sources of comparative advantage other than just low wages in order to remain internationally competitive.

Trade Costs

Despite declining transport and communication costs during the nineteenth century, trade costs – both domestic and international – continued to matter a lot throughout the first globalization wave for all but the most expensive wines. In Europe, those costs began to fall as railways were built, so that regions such as the south of France could profitably ship some of their wines to Paris. But exports to Britain and Northwest Europe continued to be confined mainly to premium wines.

In the case of the settler economies of the New World, trade costs mattered so much that the majority of export earnings of each of them came from just two primary products throughout most of the decades to World War I. In none of those countries was their wine of sufficient value per litre or per tonne to make it profitable to export very much. In the case of Argentina, it wasn't even profitable to ship wine from Mendoza to Buenos Aires until the trans-national railway came into operation in 1885, before which most of the wine consumed in that country had to be imported from Europe.

High trade costs explain why New World wine producers didn't benefit from the phylloxera devastation in Europe during the first globalization wave. Even before Algerian production came on stream, they were unable to compete with France's neighbours in supplying the desired low-priced, nonpremium wines needed to replace the temporary loss in production capability in the south of France – let alone afterwards once France erected barriers to imports from all but North Africa. The European and Algerian supply responses were so rapid that wine prices in France rose for only a few years in the 1870s before steadily falling over the three decades to World War I (Simpson 2004, figure 6).

By contrast, as ocean transport, air travel and communication costs fell further during recent decades, trade costs eased greatly as a constraint on wine exports, especially for producers in the Southern Hemisphere. They fell further as the technology for storing wine in 24,000 litre bladders improved enough to allow safe, long-distance bulk shipping of wine in twenty-foot containers. As a result, around 40 percent of wine is so exported now, up from 30 percent early this century. This is a return to what was done in the nineteenth century, when all but fine wine was exported in large barrels rather than bottles[9] – except the transport cost per litre and time involved are far less now than during that first globalization wave.

Commercial Policies Operating at the Border

A milestone in wine's globalization was Gladstone's cuts to tariffs on Britain's wine imports in 1860–1862. Britain and Russia were the two largest wine-importing countries in the 1840s, each spending an

9 Even in the case of wine exports from Bordeaux to Britain, all but one-fifth were shipped in barrels rather than bottles during the latter half of the nineteenth century (Simpson 2004, figure 3).

average of US$4.3 million per year. By the 1860s, when the value of Russia's wine imports was 10 percent higher, Britain's was almost eight times higher. The growth in imports from France was at the expense of imports of fortified wines from Spain, Portugal and South Africa, which for many decades had enjoyed preferential access to the British market.

Wine trade surged again following the infestation of phylloxera in France. The main supplier was Spain, from the late 1860s, followed by Italy from the late 1870s, and then Portugal and (in the form of raisins for rehydrating) Greece in the 1880s. However, that trade shrank when France imposed during the 1890s a series of ever-higher tariffs on those imports and introduced labelling regulations that required wine made from raisins to be so labelled (which reduced greatly its saleability). The volume of global exports did not fall, though, as France allowed investors in Algeria duty-free access to the French market for the next six-plus decades until Algeria became independent in 1962. If those shipments across the Mediterranean are considered internal French trade, the rest of the world's exports amounted to just 5 percent of global production over the 100 years to 1960.

Protectionist tariffs also were important in reversing the nineteenth-century growth in wine imports from Europe by Argentina: they allowed Mendoza to subsequently supply most of the wine consumed in Buenos Aires thanks to the new transnational railway that opened in 1885.

Tariff protection in the Australian colonies inhibited nineteenth-century wine imports not only from Europe but also from neighbouring colonies, until those colonies joined to form a federation of Australian states in 1901. From that time, trade was made free between states, but protectionist barriers remained against foreign imports, as they did in New Zealand when it too became an independent country at that time. As in Argentina, such protection assisted the local industry but shielded it from the cool winds of competition that would have stimulated more innovation and quality improvement.

Following World War I, Australia provided an export bounty on fortified wines, and Britain provided preferential access to its market for such wine. Together those measures assisted returning soldiers who took up grape growing in warm irrigated regions. Those trade policies were abandoned following World War II, however, and Australia's wine exports shrunk to a trickle for the next four decades. In other words, those support policies had done nothing to make Australian producers more internationally competitive. On the contrary, they eroded the country's reputation as a supplier of still wine exports that had been evolving over the quarter-century prior to World War I.

When Russia took over neighbouring countries and formed the Union of Soviet Socialist Republics (USSR) in 1922, the wine trade of countries such as Georgia, Moldova, Ukraine and Uzbekistan switched from being international to internal. COMECON, a trading arrangement between the USSR and Eastern European countries, former Yugoslavia and others from 1949 to 1991, also played an important role: it gave preferential access to Soviet markets for exporters of wine from such countries as Bulgaria, Hungary, Macedonia and Romania. Once the Soviet Union dissolved in 1991, however, exports from those countries shrunk.

In Asia, trade policies have long inhibited wine imports, as a way of protecting not local vignerons (there are very few) but rather local beer and spirits producers. When Hong Kong decided to eliminate its tariffs on wine in 1996, imports surged. So too have China's imports since it agreed to a lower its wine tariffs as part of its accession to the World Trade Organization at the end of 2001. Subsequent bilateral free trade agreements (FTAs) between China and Chile (2005), New Zealand (2008) and Australia (2015) have provided producers in those countries with even greater access to the burgeoning Chinese market. Similar bilateral FTAs also have been signed between those wine-exporting countries and Japan and Korea over the past decade or so.

Excise Taxes and Other Domestic Influences on Wine Consumption

Wine and other alcohol consumption per capita tends to increase as incomes rise, but only up to a point. In a study of patterns across all countries from 1961 to 2015, Holmes and Anderson (2017a) find that the national average volume of wine and other alcohol consumed peaks at about the real per capita income level of Western Europe in 1990. They also find that expenditure on wine peaks but at a slightly higher average income level as consumers raise the quality of their purchases, and it declines at a slower rate as incomes rise further than does the volume consumed. Furthermore, that study shows there is a wide range across countries in both the average volume of alcohol consumed and the shares of wine and other beverages in the alcohol mix. Clearly there are other influences on consumption per capita than just income levels.

One of those other influences is excise taxes (plus the import taxes discussed previously). They vary hugely across countries and are frequently adjusted by governments over time. The rates tend to favour consumption of the most-common beverage produced locally, and so are relatively low or zero on wine in wine-producing countries and high in wine-importing countries that are focused on beer or spirits production locally (Anderson 2010, 2014). That necessarily inhibits convergence in national alcohol mixes that a lowering of trade costs would otherwise encourage.

Governments influence wine and other alcohol consumption also through numerous other means besides altering consumer prices with taxes. In Britain in 1860, Gladstone was keen to encourage wine consumption, as he perceived it to be more civilizing than spirits or beer consumption. So while lowering tariffs on wine imports, he also reformed retail licencing regulations to reduce the competitive strength of ale and gin providers. Annual wine consumption per capita in Britain rose from 1.1 litres in the 1860s to 2.3 litres in the 1870s. But it fell back to 1.1 litres by 1913 and stayed well below 2 litres through to the mid-1960s. Then in the 1970s the British government stimulated wine consumption once again when it allowed retailing of wine through food supermarkets. Consumption per capita climbed to 11 litres by 1990 and to 21 litres by 2004. Similar dramatic rises in wine sales have occurred in Ireland and other Northwest European wine-importing countries over the past four decades. But the opposite occurred in the Soviet Union, where, in an attempt to curb excessive drinking, the government limited wine and other alcohol production and imports. That included pulling out a large minority of USSR vines in the latter 1980s, just before the Union dissolved in 1991.

In France, the government actively promoted domestic wine consumption from 1931, when wine prices were at an historic low. By 1934, consumption in France peaked at 170 litres per capita. Today it is now less than one-quarter of that – another reminder that the influence of such disrupters are not permanent.

Lobby groups seeking to influence governments, as well as consumers directly, have had major influences on alcohol consumption from time to time. Prohibition in the United States is the best-known example (1920–1934), but partial prohibitions in many other jurisdictions also resulted from very concerted lobbying by temperance movements from the mid-nineteenth century (Briggs 1986; Phillips 2014). Recently there have been active anti-alcohol lobbies in most high-income countries, seeking temperance on health and road-safety grounds. The World Health Organization also has been active, supporting that movement with information and analysis on alcohol trends worldwide. Undoubtedly this has been contributing to the decline over recent decades in high-income countries' per capita consumption of alcohol, and hence of wine, at least in traditional wine-consuming countries.

Of course, *which* wines consumers choose is affected by advertising, critics' ratings, consumer reviews and the like. Occasionally, a publicity stunt can have an influence too, perhaps the most famous being the so-called Judgement of Paris. In 1976, an English wine merchant, Stephen Spurrier, organized a blind tasting for French wine judges of top Californian and French red and white wines. The result caused a sensation because the Californian wines were ranked higher (Taber 2005). This was a major milestone in raising consumer perceptions in favour of New World wines. Likewise, a broadcast of the CBS *60 Minutes* television progam in 1991 publicized a so-called 'French Paradox', suggesting the French people have a relatively low incidence of coronary heart disease because of their diet, in which wine is integral. And the Chinese boom in wine consumption was catalyzed by Premier Li Peng affirming in 1997 the health virtues of red wine.

Real Exchange Rate Movements

Being blessed with a climate and abundant land suitable for wine production is a necessary but not sufficient condition for a country to be competitive in national and global wine markets. Especially in the presence of high international transport costs, it has been common for natural resource–abundant New World countries to be competitive in only a handful of primary products, and wine was rarely one of them prior to 1990. This was especially so during eras of boom in other industries. Such booms could be supply-driven (e.g., a domestic discovery of minerals) or demand-driven (a rise in the price of another exportable). Both types of economic booms strengthen the country's real exchange rate, which weakens the competitiveness of that country's producers of other tradable goods (Corden 1984; Freebairn 2015).

For countries subject to cycles in the value of their currency, and in the absence of sufficient offsetting government intervention (e.g., through a sovereign wealth fund), its wine (and any other tradable) industry is likely to be subject to cycles in profitability too. This has been one of the contributors to fluctuating fortunes in wine and other agricultural industries in Australia over the past 180 years, for example (Anderson 2017). This destabilizing macroeconomic influence on the wine industry has increased in importance since the moves by numerous countries in the 1980s to more flexible exchange rate regimes. Countries in the Eurozone, however, have instead been subject to movements not in their national currency but rather in the value of the Euro since its creation in 2000.

Institutional Changes

Perhaps the most important institutional innovation following the first globalization wave was the progressive introduction in France of regulations aimed at reducing grape and wine fraud and thereby boosting consumer confidence in wine. A by-product of the myriad restrictions on grape growing and winemaking that have accumulated is that producer flexibility and innovativeness are reduced. Cross-regional blending also is disallowed. With the formation of the European Economic Community (EEC) and now the European Union (EU), these French regulations have largely become EU-wide regulations (Meloni and Swinnen 2013). One consequence is that there is very little wine firm concentration in Western Europe, the main exceptions being in Champagne (where major brands developed, even if they depend on many small grape-growers), in Bordeaux (where negotiants have traditionally served as middlemen between the chateaux and the importer abroad) and in Portugal (where English firms have managed the export trade in port).

This predominance of small firms in Europe contrasts markedly with the high degree of firm concentration in much-less-regulated New World countries. The four largest firms in terms of domestic sales in Europe is in the 10 to 20 percent range whereas in the New World it is in the 50 to 80 percent range (Anderson Nelgen and Pinilla 2017, table 42). The latter's large firms can exploit economies of huge scale in viticulture, oenology and wine marketing. They naturally have become multinational, using not just their production expertise but also their knowledge of market niches globally to deliver to those markets at lowest cost from anywhere in the world. They are thereby well suited to selling into the supermarket retailing system, which is why it was New World firms that initially dominated the burgeoning sales of commercial premium wine in Britain, Ireland and other wine-importing countries of Northwest Europe during the current globalization wave.

Summary of Convergences

Convergence is a theme that comes up frequently in the chapters that follow, as in many comparative economic history projects. They are highlighted in the next chapter, but can be summarized as convergences in the following:

- EU and New World aggregate shares of global (excluding intra-EU) wine exports
- Per capita wine production in the EU and New World

- Per capita wine consumption, and wine's share of alcohol consumption, in Europe's wine-exporting countries (and Argentina) on the one hand and both Northwest Europe and the New World on the other hand
- Wine comparative advantage indexes of the EU and New World
- Technologies for grape-growing, winemaking and, somewhat less rapidly, wine business and marketing

IMPLICATIONS FOR PRODUCERS, CONSUMERS AND RESEARCHERS

One of the strongest themes that emerges from comparing the nature and timing of national histories of wine industry developments is that there is at least one silver lining for almost every cloud that comes across part of the world's wine markets. Perhaps the most striking example from the first globalization wave is the fact that Spain (and to a lesser extent Italy and Greece) was a beneficiary of the damage done to France's vineyards by phylloxera in the 1870s and 1880s (Pinilla and Ayuda 2002). In the current globalization wave, a clear example is the downturn in Australian wineries' international competitiveness over the past decade because of the real exchange rate appreciation associated with that country's massive mining boom: it enabled wine exporters in several other countries to expand their sales in third countries at Australia's expense (Anderson and Wittwer 2013).

As for consumers, the point was made earlier that the globalization of wine over recent decades has been an unprecedented boom for consumers everywhere, with huge improvements in the quality and diversity of wines available and at very affordable prices. The fear of some that increasing globalization of the wine trade would result in the homogenization of the world's wines has not materialized. Firm concentration within the global wine market started from a very low base, and is still very low compared with even beer and spirits let alone the world's soft drink industry. True, the New World's large-volume, low-end commercial premium wines sold in supermarkets are not sophisticated, but these days they are free of serious technical faults and are a low-cost way for new wine consumers to begin to explore the world of wine.

With increasing affluence comes an increasing demand for many things, including product variety. Over time, new consumers will gradually differentiate more between grape varieties, wine styles and not just countries of origin but regions within them. With the help of wine critics, these new consumers will increasingly discriminate between brand names and labels within brands. The preference for differentiated products, and the infinite scope for experimentation by vignerons, will ensure that there will always be small- and medium-sized wineries alongside the few large corporate labels.

The forces of globalization, together with the expansion in premium wine-grape supplies as winegrowers upgrade, will spur more mergers, acquisitions or alliances among wineries across national borders. The success of their corporate wine labels in the global marketplace will in turn provide a slipstream within which astute smaller operators can also thrive. The popularity of cult wines shows that small and medium enterprises can do well in the age of mass marketing and consolidated winemaking and retailing giants, provided small wineries work hard on marketing and distribution to ensure their differentiated product is in demand.

A final word on future research areas. Despite our best efforts at compiling pertinent data, our global database still has important gaps, especially pre-1961, when United Nations data began to be collected more systematically. There are more gaps on consumption than production data, and on competing beverages than on wine itself. A supplementary effort to also assemble consumer expenditure and price data, to match the consumer volume data, has been made by Holmes and Anderson (2017b). However, for econometric analysis it would be helpful to have longer historical time series on beverage expenditures. That would enable the reestimation of price and income elasticities of demand for wine and other beverages, extending the work of, for example, Selvanathan and Selvanathan (2007) to include also soft drinks. It would also enable econometricians to better explain changes in the volumes and values of consumer spending on the various alcoholic beverages, thus going beyond the work of, for example, Colen and Swinnen (2016) on beer. Producer price data also would be very helpful, as would comparable firm-level producer performance data. Then it would be possible to estimate the relative importance of determinants of export growth, as has been done increasingly over the past decade for other industries (Bernard et al. 2012).

Clearly plenty of scope remains for future research in this space, but at least this volume lays down much more solid empirical foundations than have hitherto been available as a springboard for such cliometric research.

REFERENCES

Anderson, K. (ed.) (2004), *The World's Wine Markets: Globalization at Work*, Cheltenham, UK: Edward Elgar.

(2010), 'Excise and Import Taxes on Wine vs Beer and Spirits: An International Comparison', *Economic Papers* 29(2): 215–28, June.

(2014), 'Excise Taxes on Wines, Beers and Spirits: An Updated International Comparison', Working Paper No. 170, American Association of Wine Economists, October.

(2017), 'Sectoral Trends and Shocks in Australia's Economic Growth', *Australian Economic History Review* 57(1): 2–21, March.

(with the assistance of N.R. Aryal) (2015), *Growth and Cycles in Australia's Wine Industry: A Statistical Compendium, 1843 to 2013*, Adelaide: University of Adelaide Press. Also freely available as an ebook at www.adelaide.edu.au/press/titles/austwine and as Excel files at www.adelaide.edu.au/wine-econ/databases/winehistory/

Anderson, K. and S. Nelgen (2011), *Global Wine Markets, 1961 to 2009: A Statistical Compendium*, Adelaide: University of Adelaide Press. Also freely available as an ebook at www.adelaide.edu.au/press/titles/global-wine and as Excel files at www.adelaide.edu.au/wine-econ/databases/GWM

Anderson, K., S. Nelgen and V. Pinilla (2017), *Global Wine Markets, 1860 to 2016: A Statistical Compendium*, Adelaide: University of Adelaide Press. Also freely available as an ebook at www.adelaide.edu.au/press/

Anderson, K. and V. Pinilla (with the assistance of A. J. Holmes) (2017), *Annual Database of Global Wine Markets, 1835 to 2016*, freely available in Excel files at the University of Adelaide's Wine Economics Research Centre, at www.adelaide.edu.au/wine-econ/databases

Anderson, K. and G. Wittwer (2013), 'Modeling Global Wine Markets to 2018: Exchange Rates, Taste Changes, and China's Import Growth', *Journal of Wine Economics* 8(2): 131–58.

Bernard, A. B., J. B. Jensen, S. J. Redding and P. K. Schott (2012), 'The Empirics of Firm Heterogeneity and International Trade', *Annual Review of Economics* 4(1): 283–313.

Briggs, A. (1986), *Wine for Sale: Victoria Wines and the Liquor Trade, 1860–1984*, Chicago: University of Chicago Press.

Campbell, C. (2004), *Phylloxera: How Wine Was Saved for the World*, London: HarperCollins.

Campbell, G. and N. Guibert (eds.) (2007), *The Golden Grape: Wine, Society and Globalization, Multidisciplinary Perspectives on the Wine Industry*, London: Palgrave Macmillan.

Colen, L. and Swinnen, J. (2016), 'Economic Growth, Globalisation and Beer Consumption', *Journal of Agricultural Economics* 67(1): 186–207.

Corden, W. M. (1984), 'Booming Sector and Dutch Disease Economics: Survey and Consolidation', *Oxford Economic Papers* 36(3): 359–80, November.

Crosby, A. W. (2003), *The Columbian Exchange: Biological and Cultural Consequences of 1492*, Westport, CT: Praeger.

Dixit, A. and R. S. Pindyck (1994), *Investment Under Uncertainty*, Princeton, NJ: Princeton University Press.

Francis, A. D. (1972), *The Wine Trade*, London: Adams and Charles Black.

Freebairn, J. (2015), 'Mining Booms and the Exchange Rate', *Australian Journal of Agricultural and Resource Economics* 59(4): 533–48.

Gerguad, O. and V. Ginsburg (2008), 'Natural Endowments, Production Technologies and the Quality of Wines in Bordeaux: Does Terroir Matter?' *Economic Journal* 118(529): F142–57, June. Reprinted in *Journal of Wine Economics* 5(1): 3–21, 2010.

Giuliana, E., A. Morrison and R. Rabellotti (eds.) (2011), *Innovation and Technological Catch-up: The Changing Geography of Wine Production*, Cheltenham, UK: Edward Elgar.

Griffiths, R. D. and C. R. Butcher (2013), 'Introducing the International System(s) Dataset (ISD), 1816–2011', *International Interactions* 39(5): 748–68. Data Appendix is at www.ryan-griffiths.com/data/

Hayami, Y. and V. W. Ruttan (1985), *Agricultural Development: An International Perspective*, Baltimore, MD: Johns Hopkins University Press.

Holmes, A. J. and K. Anderson (2017a), 'Convergence in National Alcohol Consumption Patterns: New Global Indicators', *Journal of Wine Economics* 12(2): 117–48.

Holmes, A. J. and K. Anderson (2017b), 'Annual Database of National Beverage Consumption Volumes and Expenditures, 1950 to 2015', Wine Economics Research Centre, University of Adelaide, at www.adelaide.edu.au/wine-econ/databases/

Johnson, H. (1989), *The Story of Wine*, London: Mitchell Beasley.

Lewin, B. (2010), *Wine Myths and Reality*, Dover: Vendange Press and San Francisco: Wine Appreciation Guild.

Lukacs, P. (2012), *Inventing Wine: A New History of One of the World's Most Ancient Pleasures*, New York: W. W. Norton.

Meloni, G. and J. Swinnen (2013), 'The Political Economy of European Wine Regulations', *Journal of Wine Economics* 8(3): 244–84.

Nunn, N. and N. Qian (2010), 'The Columbian Exchange: A History of Disease, Food, and Ideas', *Journal of Economic Perspectives* 24(2): 163–88, Spring.

Nye, J. V. C. (2007), *War Wine, and Taxes: The Political Economy of Anglo-French Trade, 1689–1900*, Princeton, NJ: Princeton University Press.

O'Rourke, K. H. and J. C. Williamson (2002), 'When Did Globalisation Begin?' *European Review of Economic History* 6(1): 23–50.

O'Rourke, K. H. and J. C. Williamson (2004), 'Once More: When Did Globalisation Begin?' *European Review of Economic History* 8(1): 109–17.

Phillips, R. (2000), *A Short History of Wine*, London: Penguin. Revised edition published in 2015 as *9000 Years of Wine (A World History)*, Vancouver: Whitecap.

(2014), *Alcohol: A History*, Chapel Hill: University of North Carolina Press.

Pinilla, V. and M. I. Ayuda (2002), 'The Political Economy of the Wine Trade: Spanish Exports and the International Market, 1890–1935', *European Review of Economic History* 6: 51–85.

Rose, S. (2011), *The Wine Trade in Medieval Europe 1000–1500*, London and New York: Bloomsbury.

Selvanathan, S. and E. A. Selvanathan (2007), 'Another Look at the Identical Tastes Hypothesis on the Analysis of Cross-Country Alcohol Data', *Empirical Economics* 32(1): 185–215.

Simpson, J. (2004), 'Selling to Reluctant Drinkers: The British Wine Market, 1860–1914', *Economic History Review* 57(1): 80–108.

Simpson, J. (2011), *Creating Wine: The Emergence of a World industry, 1840–1914*, Princeton, NJ: Princeton University Press.

Taber, G. M. (2005), *Judgment of Paris: California vs France and the Historic Paris Tasting that Revolutionized Wine*, New York: Simon and Schuster.
Unwin, T. (1991), *Wine and the Vine: An Historical Geography of Viticulture and the Wine Trade*, London and New York: Routledge.
Williams, A. (1995), *Flying Winemakers: The New World of Wine*, Adelaide: Winetitles.

2

Global Overview

Kym Anderson and Vicente Pinilla

This chapter begins by first discussing the types of indicators of globalization typically sought and the subset to be used in this study as prescribed by available data. It then examines trends in those selected globalization indicators for three time periods: the first globalization wave from 1860 (when our comprehensive global data series begin) to World War I; the interwar and immediate post–World War II years; and the period from 1960 but especially from 1990 when the second globalization wave accelerated. The chapter then summarizes the contributions of different countries to global wine production, consumption and trade volumes and values. Attention focuses on long-run trends not only in those extensive indicators but also in intensive ones (e.g., vineyard share of total crop area; wine production per capita or per dollar of gross domestic product [GDP]). As well, key reasons behind contributions to or major turning points in those trends are highlighted. For wine-exporting countries, those include shifters in the domestic wine supply curve (disease outbreaks, changes in technologies), in the domestic wine demand curve (growth in population or incomes, changes in preferences) or in demand for the country's wine exports (e.g., due to a change in real exchange rates). They also could include movements along those curves due to, for example, changes in producer, consumer or trade taxes or subsidies or in other regulatory policies.

CONCEPTUALIZING WINE GLOBALIZATION INDICATORS

There are two dominant views among historians about globalization (which is due to the lowering of the cost of goods, services, capital, labour, information and ideas moving across geographic borders, for example because of technological revolutions in transport or communications or the lowering of governmental barriers to such movements). On the one hand, 'world historians' think of it as the spreading to more countries of production, consumption and trade of a product, in our case, wine. Cliometricians (or quantitative economic historians), on the other hand, criticize this concept as too loose, pointing out that a geographic spreading of production could occur because of the raising of protectionist trade barriers, which they would view as an antiglobalization policy development.[1] The growth of trade is also not considered a sufficient condition to speak of globalization.[2] They instead look for explicit indicators of international economic integration such as the convergence across countries of product and factor prices. That stricter criterion poses difficulties in this case, though, because of the very heterogeneous nature of wine, winegrapes, vineyards and grapegrower and winemaker skills.[3]

The only prices that have been available for many decades across many countries are the unit values of national wine exports and imports, and even those border prices are averages over often widely varying wine styles and qualities – and they tell us nothing about prices inside national borders, which are affected by myriad government regulations, producer subsidies and consumer taxes (Anderson 2010, 2014b). Declines in wine import tariffs are poor indicators of wine globalization, again because of the wide range of wine prices and the common use of a complex system of specific rather than *ad valorem* tariffs on particular types of wines, not to mention the common substitution of nontariff protectionist measures and other forms of producer assistance when tariffs are lowered (Anderson and Jensen 2016; Bianco et al. 2016).

Domestic prices too are difficult to pin down, and not only because of product heterogeneity. Many grapegrowers make their own wine (and some wineries lease vineyards) so their winegrapes are not priced in a market; many wineries sell their wines at their cellar door, where taxes may not be paid; other domestic sales are subject to often complex excise tax structures in addition to value-added taxes (VAT) or goods and services taxes (GST); and increasingly wine is sold through supermarkets, which occasionally

1 Some seminal globalization books by cliometricians include O'Rourke and Williamson (1999), Bordo, Taylor and Williamson (2003), Findlay and O'Rourke (2007) and Hatton, O'Rourke and Williamson (2007). An early contribution by a world historian is Pomeranz (2000).

2 See on this topic the discussion between O'Rourke and Williamson (2002, 2004) and Flynn and Giráldez (2004).

3 Sale prices of established vineyards within developed countries can range in price between \$10,000 and \$2+ million per hectare, and retail prices of new wines can range from as little as \$2 to thousands of dollars per 750 ML bottle.

discount certain wines to varying extents so that a recommended retail price even for a single homogeneous branded wine overstates the average selling price to an unknown extent.

There are, however, various other partial indicators that can be used to measure the degree of globalization of the world's wine markets. Given that wine production and consumption had been confined mostly to southern Europe and east of the Mediterranean Sea before the mid-nineteenth century, one could be growth in global per capita production and consumption of wine beyond those traditional producing regions. An increase in the number of countries contributing significantly to global wine production might be another, although as cliometricians have pointed out, that would also happen if protectionist barriers were raised. The latter would not be the cause if the number of countries contributing significant shares to global wine exports or consumption also rose, though. Another indicator is a rise in the share of global wine production that is exported. Yet another at the national level is an increase in two-way trade, that is, growth in the share of imported wines in domestic consumption even in wine-exporting countries. Convergence across countries in the share of wine in national alcohol consumption (or, more broadly, in the national mix of alcoholic beverages) also could be a consequence of increasing globalization, as preferences homogenize.

One of the ways in which wine globalization began was via the spread of vine cuttings. That continues to happen, as new wine regions develop and their terroir is explored by growers through the planting of different winegrape varieties. Data have recently been assembled to capture that diffusion during the current globalization wave.

With these concepts in mind, the next section examines empirical evidence of globalization in the world's wine markets in aggregate, and the following section summarizes national contributions to those global developments and their effects on national wine markets – detailed analyses of which are the subject of the subsequent chapters.

GLOBALIZATION INDICATORS: EMPIRICAL EVIDENCE

The global per capita production of wine averaged 9 litres per year in the 1860s. It fell back to 8 litres during the worst of the vineyard damage due to phylloxera but had returned to 9 litres just prior to World War I.[4] Since then,

[4] For details of phylloxera's impact, see this book's Chapters 3, 4 and 16 in particular, as well as Campbell (2004).

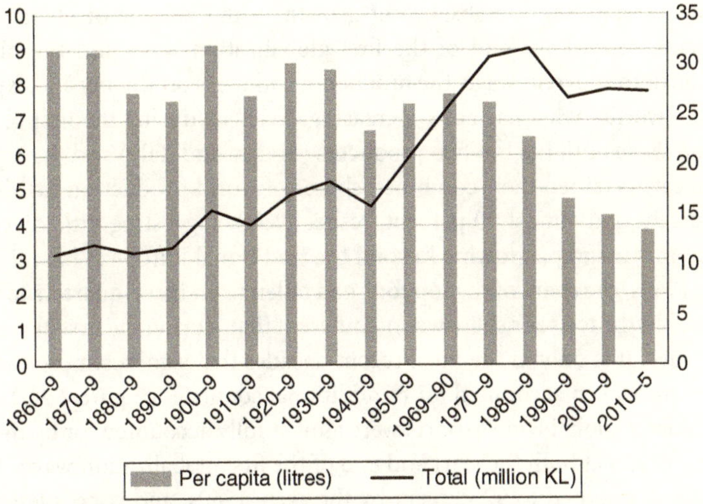

Figure 2.1 Total and per capita wine production in the world, 1860 to 2015 (litres on left axis, million KL on right axis).
Source: Compiled from data in Anderson and Pinilla (2017).

it has steadily fallen, though, to 8.5 litres in the interwar period, 7.5 during 1950 to 1979, 6.5 in the 1980s, 4.5 during 1990 to 2009 and 3.8 in 2010 to 2015. As for aggregate annual global wine production, it did not grow during most of the first globalization wave, thanks to the devastating effect of phylloxera, rising only in the first decade of the twentieth century. During the interwar period, it was about 50 percent higher than during 1860 to 1900, and then it doubled in the four decades to the mid-1980s. However, since the acceleration in the 1990s start of the current globalization wave, it has fallen by about one-eighth, returning it to the level of the 1960s (Figure 2.1). That is, the industry has been shrinking in global volume terms.

The expansion during the first globalization wave is also indicated by the volume of wine production per million dollars of real GDP globally, which rose from 10 litres in 1870 to 18 in 1913. But it fell steadily as the global economy expanded post–World War II, from 3.6 in 1950 to 2.1 in 1970, 1.0 in 1990 and 0.4 litres in 2014 (Anderson and Pinilla 2017).

What these data do not disclose, though, is the unquantifiable but widely acknowledged increase in the average quality of wines being produced, starting in the early 1800s (Johnson 1989, ch. 36; Lukaks 2012, pp. 127–40) but especially since the 1980s. Unfortunately, there is no way to estimate trends in their average real producer or consumer prices, though, nor in grapegrower or winery profits.

Notwithstanding the absence of growth in the volume of global wine production until the end of the first globalization wave and the output decline in the current wave, the number of countries producing and exporting the world's wine has been increasing. Even so, during the first globalization wave both the top two producers (France and Italy) and the top ten producers retained their combined shares of world production (at almost 60 percent and almost 90 percent, respectively), suggesting little diversification in winegrape growing beyond the traditional European base. By the early 1960s, the share of the top four had fallen from three-quarters to two-thirds, but the top ten's share was no different than during the first globalization wave. It is only in the most recent decades that significant production shares have been accounted for by additional countries (Figure 2.2(a)).

Similarly, global wine exports were almost fully accounted for by the top ten exporters at both the start and end of the first globalization wave. Their share had dropped to 92 percent by the early 1960s, and is now less than 89 percent (Figure 2.2(b)). Again this suggests not much increase in diversification of exporting countries during the first globalization wave, but somewhat more in the second wave.

The graphs in Figure 2.2 do not disclose the ranking of the countries that are doing the producing and exporting, though. As will become clear in the next section, there was some shuffling in the ordering as well as some new entrants into those top ten listings. Spain was the first supplier able to respond to the sudden need by phylloxera-ridden France for wine imports, which boosted the share of global production exported from an historical average of around 5 percent to 12 percent in the early 1880s. But once French vignerons' massive investments in Algerian vineyards and wineries began to generate exports, France reerected its barriers to the imports of wine and raisins it had been buying from other southern European countries – while allowing Algeria (in a customs union with France since December 1884) duty-free access to the French market. Algeria almost exactly substituted for those other exporters, hence the trend share of global wine production that was exported remained flat at about one-eighth until around 1970.[5] In short, most of the increase in the export share of global production was evidently a response to production shortfalls due to disease rather than to globalization drivers (although there was some increase in wine exports to northern Europe and the Americas in the 1880s). How much

[5] If Algeria were to be treated as part of France, by subtracting its exports (which went almost exclusively to France) from the world total, then the trend share of global production exported is only 5 percent instead of 10 percent during 1900 to 1962 (when Algeria gained its independence) – see the dashed line in Figure 2.3(a), and Chapter 16 of this volume.

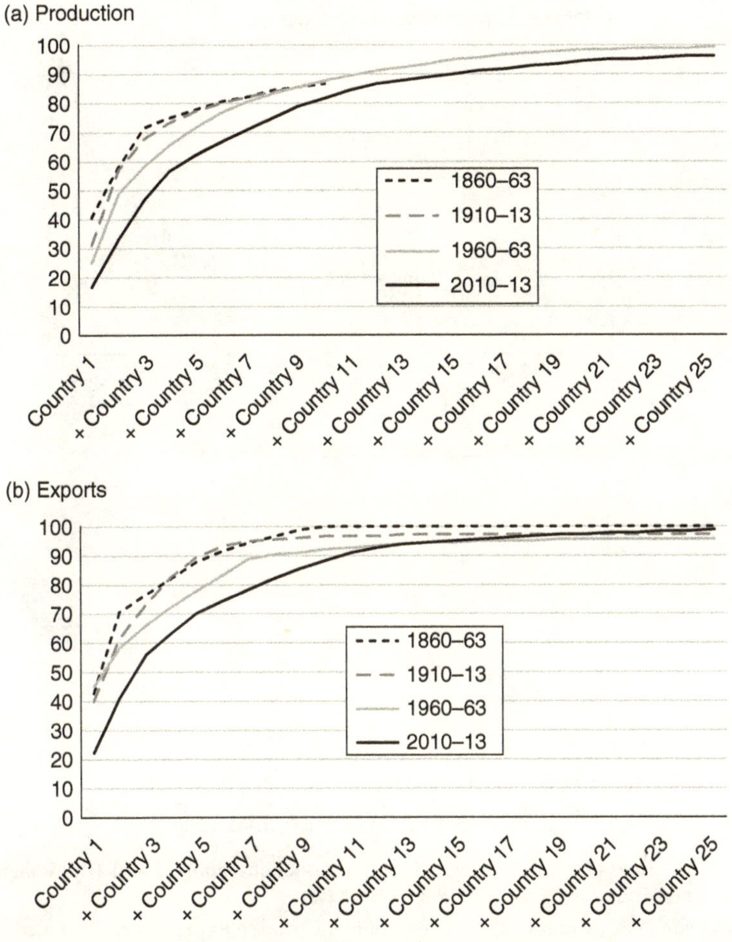

Figure 2.2 Cumulative national shares of global volume of wine production and exports, top twenty-five countries, 1860 to 2013 (%).
Source: Compiled from data in Anderson and Pinilla (2017).

if any investment in and wine exports from Algeria would have happened without the phylloxera outbreak is a moot point.

That share of output exported then rose moderately for two decades, before rising very rapidly over the subsequent twenty-five years (Figure 2.3(a)). The moderate rise in the export share of global wine production during the 1970s and 1980s was no more than a by-product of a faster decline in wine consumption than in production in the traditional wine-consuming countries of France, Italy and Spain: their combined annual consumption fell by 4 billion litres over those two decades while their annual exports

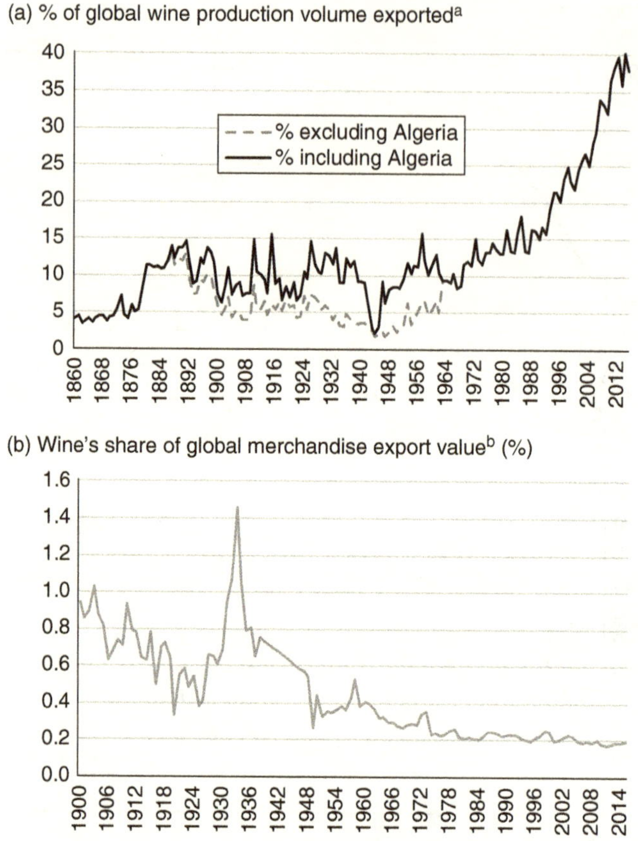

Figure 2.3 Share of volume of global wine production exported and wine's share of global merchandise export value, 1860 to 2015 (%).

[a] The dashed line assumes Algeria is part of France and so its exports are excluded from the world total.

[b] Data for 1939–47 are not available, so a straight line is inserted from 1938 to 1948.

Source: Compiled from data in Anderson and Pinilla (2017).

rose by 2 billion litres. Global annual exports were only 1.1 billion litres higher, though, indicating that exports from the rest of the world fell over this period immediately preceding the second globalization wave.

How does the extent of international trade in wine compare with that for other products? Having been never more than 15 percent before 1990, and no more than 5 percent before the phylloxera outbreak in the final quarter of the nineteeth century, the share of global production exported for wine was lower than that for other farm products, the average of which has been estimated to be 10 to 15 percent during 1900 to 1938 and 15 to 30 percent during 1950 to 1990 (Aparicio, Pinella and Serano 2009, p. 57). The trebling in wine's share since 1980 to around 40 percent (Figure 2.3(a)) puts it at the higher end of the spectrum[6] – as it should be for a heterogeneous, highly differentiated product group whose primary ingredient (winegrapes) can be grown profitably in a very small share (currently less than 0.5 percent) of the world's cropping land.

Data on the *value* of wine exports are available globally only from 1900, when it represented almost 1 percent of all merchandise exports. That share gradually halved over the first three decades of the twentieth century, before rising rapidly in the 1930s when other merchandise exports shrunk around the world as a consequence of protectionist responses to the Great Depression. The temporary reversal was due once more to Algeria, whose share of global wine export volume rose sixfold, from one-sixth of the world total in 1920 to two-thirds by 1933. Wine's share of world merchandise exports returned to 0.4 percent in the 1950s, but once Algeria became independent in 1962 that share halved again over the next two decades. With the sudden surge in wine exports from the latter 1980s, however, wine's share of the value of world merchandise exports has held steady at 0.2 percent during the current globalization wave (Figure 2.3(b)).

Turning to consumption developments, the top five wine-consuming countries accounted for 66 percent of global wine consumption in 1869–73, and that rose to 75 percent by 1909–13 – and the top seven's share rose from 70 percent to 80 percent. The top seven's share had declined only slightly by 1959–63, to 77 percent, indicating very little change over that half-century. In the next half-century, to 2009–13, that share fell far more, to just 61 percent (with the top five's share falling from 69 percent to 51 percent). Again, this evidence from Anderson and Pinilla (2017) is not consistent with the first globalization wave spreading consumption geographically, and is consistent with that happening in the second wave. Further corroboration of that finding is provided in Figure 2.4. It shows that during the first globalization wave, there was almost no change in the distribution of countries across five size categories of per capita wine consumption.

Of course, wine is not the only beverage that is becoming more globalized. Beer traditionally was produced and sold locally. However, with technological advances and exploitation of economies of scale through mergers and acquisitions of what have become multinational companies, beer brands are becoming nearly as global and concentrated as carbonated soft

[6] According to the Global Trade Analysis Project (GTAP) database (Walmsley, Aguiar and Narayanan 2012), global exports as a percentage of global production in 2007 was just 11 percent for agricultural and food products, compared with 42 percent for nonfarm primary products and 31 percent for other manufactured goods (www.gtap.agecon.purdue .edu/databases/v8/default.asp).

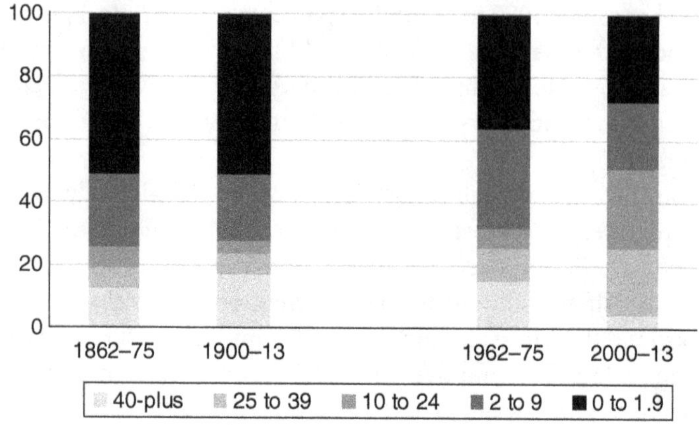

Figure 2.4 Shares of all forty-seven countries within various ranges of average per capita wine consumption levels,[a] 1862 to 2013 (%).

[a] The blocks shown in each column refer to ranges of national wine consumption in litres per capita per year. There are data for only forty-seven individual countries (in addition to five residual regions) in the Anderson and Pinilla (2017) database.

Source: Compiled from data in Anderson and Pinilla (2017).

drinks (Swinnen 2011).[7] As part of that, beer is increasingly being traded across national borders: in 1960 only 1.5 percent of the world's recorded beer production was exported, but by 2015 that share had increased five-fold to 7.5 percent (Anderson and Pinilla 2017). Most of the world's spirits too are produced by a small number of multinationals and are very highly traded globally. Unlike wine company outputs, production by both beer and spirits conglomerates are not affected by seasonal weather variations, and both invest heavily in marketing their brands.

In the 1960s, all three beverages had a similar share of the global recorded alcohol market (measured in litres of alcohol, or LAL). In the subsequent three decades, the share of wine in that overall market halved, and is now just one-third of the shares of beer and spirits, which are each a bit over 40 percent (Figure 2.5(a)). Total recorded alcohol consumption per capita in the world has traced a flat trend since 1960 (at around 2.9 LAL per year), but wine consumption has fallen from 0.9 LAL in 1960 to 0.4 LAL in 2015 while beer has risen from 0.7 to 1.2 LAL and spirits consumption per capita has been maintained at around 1.2 LAL (Figure 2.5(b)).

[7] According to Euromonitor International, the world's top eight alcoholic drinks companies are all beer firms, with a combined share of global alcohol sales value of 45 percent from 2010 to 2014.

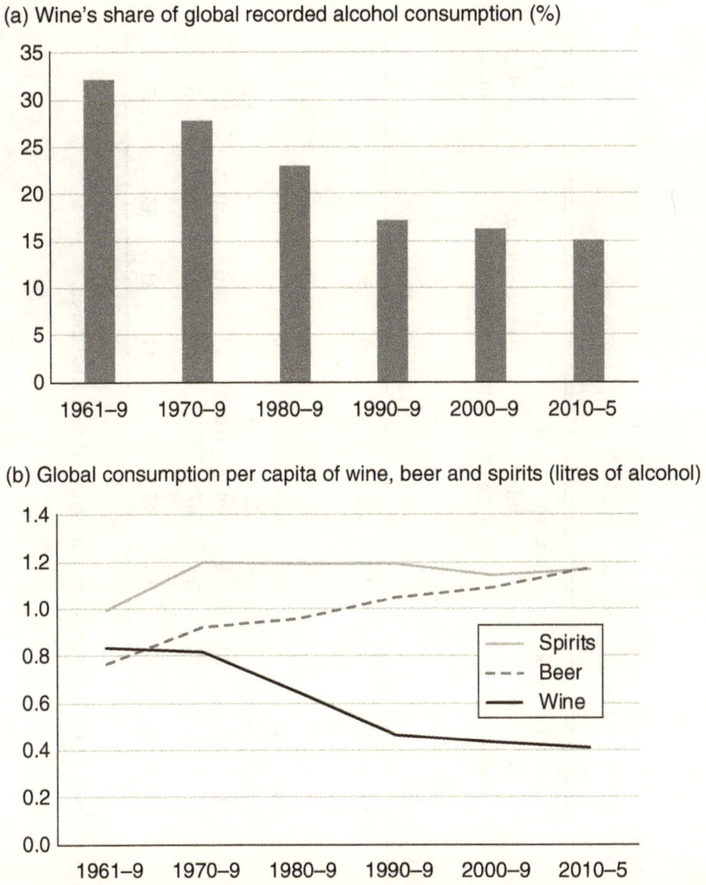

Figure 2.5 Wine's share of global recorded alcohol consumption, and average level of global consumption per capita of wine, beer and spirits, 1961 to 2015 (% and LAL).
Source: Compiled from author's revision of data in Anderson and Pinilla (2017).

There are three silver linings to this cloud for wine, though. First, wine's share of global retail expenditure on alcohol from 2010 to 2014 was well above its share of the volume of recorded alcohol consumption (21 percent compared to 15 percent). Second, beverage consumption mixes are converging across countries, so wine markets have been emerging in countries where beer or spirits previously dominated (Holmes and Anderson 2017). And third, alcohol consumption volumes and expenditures are still very low per capita in Asia and Sub-Saharan Africa, where incomes are growing fastest (Table 2.1). Wine's share of alcohol consumption is especially low in Asia, suggesting great potential for further growth in demand there

Table 2.1 *Alcohol per capita consumption volume and shares of beer, wine and spirits in alcohol consumption volume and expenditure, seven regions and the world, 1961–64 and 2010–14 (LAL and %)*

	Total alcohol consumption (LAL/capita)[a]		Share of alcohol volume, 1961–64 (%)[b]			Share of alcohol volume, 2010–14 (%)[b]			Share of alcohol expenditure, 2010–14 (%)			Alcohol's share of all expenditures, 2010–14 (%)
	1961–64	2010–14	Wine	Beer	Spirits	Wine	Beer	Spirits	Wine	Beer	Spirits	
Western Europe	12.3	8.4	**55**	29	16	**42**	38	20	40	34	26	3.9
Eastern Europe	1.9	7.2	22	22	**56**	14	42	**44**	46	20	34	5.9
North America	5.4	7.0	8	49	43	18	**49**	33	48	21	30	1.9
Latin America	6.5	5.1	**48**	34	18	11	**60**	29	64	10	26	4.2
Australia & NZ	6.5	7.1	10	**76**	14	39	**46**	15	53	28	19	3.5
Asia (incl. Pacific)	1.9	3.2	1	12	**87**	4	34	**62**	35	15	50	4.3
Africa & M East	1.0	1.7	27	**38**	35	14	**67**	19	60	15	25	2.5
WORLD	**2.5**	**2.7**	**34**	**29**	**37**	**15**	**43**	**42**	**44**	**21**	**35**	**3.5**

[a] These data are volume-based in LAL per year, five-year averages.
[b] The bold numbers indicate which beverage has the highest share in total alcohol consumption volume in the period shown.
Source: Holmes and Anderson (2017).

(see Chapters 17 and 18 of this volume). And while the *volume* of wine and other alcohol consumed peaks on average at about the per capita income level of western Europe in 1990 and then falls steadily thereafter, *expenditure* on wine peaks at a higher average income level as consumers raise the quality of their purchases, and it declines at a slower rate than does the volume consumed (Holmes and Anderson 2017).

With this overall perspective on global wine market developments, we turn now to examine contributions of key national economies to those developments, and then summarize effects they have had on national wine markets.

NATIONAL CONTRIBUTIONS TO GLOBAL WINE MARKET DEVELOPMENTS

More than three-quarters of global wine production in the middle half of the nineteenth century was due to just three countries: France, Italy and Spain. By the end of the first globalization wave, they, plus the nearby French colony of Algeria, were still as dominant, and with Austria and Hungary they accounted for all but one-tenth of the world's wine output in 1910–1913. Even fifty years later, the big four had a two-thirds share, and it took until 2006 before the share of France, Italy and Spain fell below 50 percent. The past quarter-century has seen numerous other countries expand, most notably the United States but also several temperate Southern Hemisphere countries and, most recently, China (Figure 2.6(a)).

France, Italy and Spain were also the largest consumers of wine in the 1860s, consistent with the fact that very little wine was internationally traded up to that time. Their share during the first globalization wave was three-quarters. Germany and Argentina accounted for another 2–3 percent each during 1860–1909 (Figure 2.6(b)). Data for other significant wine-consuming countries do not cover all those years, but if their average per capita consumption levels were the same for that period as for when their data start, then Romania, Hungary and Switzerland would account for another 4, 3 and 2 percent, respectively. In that case, all the rest of the world would have consumed no more than one-tenth of global wine throughout those five decades. This again suggests wine did not get brought along very much with the first globalization wave.

Nor did that change much in the subsequent six decades, as France, Italy and Spain plus Argentina accounted for nearly two-thirds still of global wine consumption during 1950–69. The share of France alone was 36 percent, helped by the fact that from 1931 the French government explicitly campaigned on behalf of its wine industry to encourage greater wine consumption in France (Phillips 2014, pp. 286–89) – despite the fact that

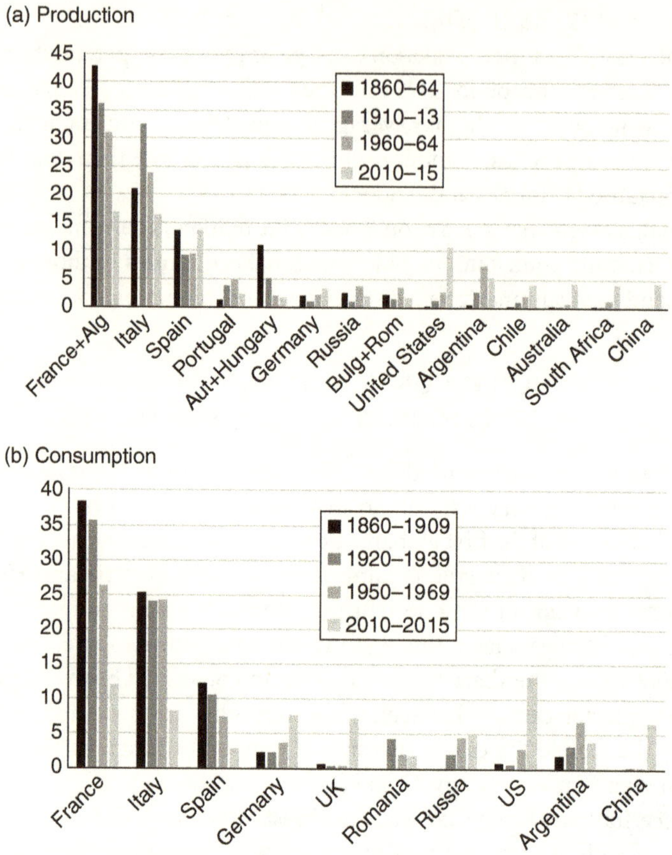

Figure 2.6 National shares of global wine production and consumption volumes, 1860 to 2015 (%).
Source: Compiled from data in Anderson and Pinilla (2017).

France already had at that time the highest per capita wine consumption in the world, at more than 150 litres per year. It is only since the 1980s that consumption in other countries has grown in importance, most notably in the United States and the United Kingdom, with China joining since the new millennium (Figure 2.6(b)). Note that while Britain was important for centuries as a consumer of premium wines from Bordeaux, it accounted for well under 1 percent of the volume of global wine sales prior to the early 1970s.

As we saw from Figure 2.3(a), less than 15 percent of global wine production was traded internationally before 1990, apart from a couple of years in the 1980s. Of that trade, the big four again dominated: France, Italy, Spain and Algeria contributed 80 to 90 percent of the world's wine exports for the 100 years to 1960, and to almost 70 percent in the next three decades. Even

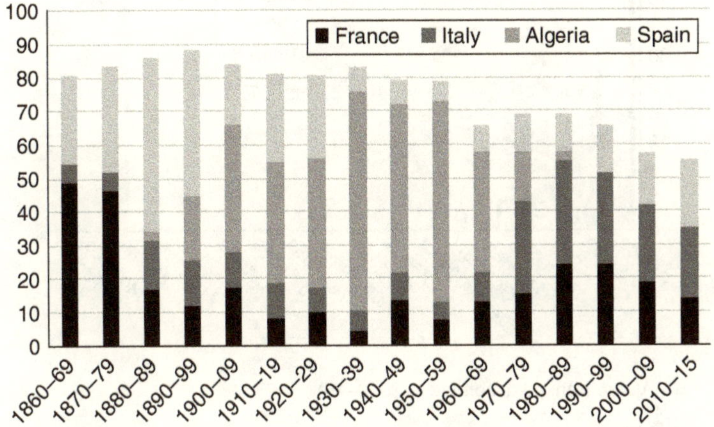

Figure 2.7 National shares of global wine export volume, France, Italy, Spain and Algeria, 1860 to 2015 (%).
Source: Compiled from data in Anderson and Pinilla (2017).

in the most-recent two decades, France and Italy accounted for two-fifths of that trade volume (Figure 2.7). But as Figure 2.8 reveals, a large number of countries had become contributors to the world's wine exports by the current decade, while North Africa had left the scene following their independence. The export takeoff by New World countries did not begin until the late 1980s, though, and then it accelerated in the 1990s and into the new century: having always accounted for less than 9 percent of the value of global wine exports before 1990, their share converged on the EU15's share by rising to 37 percent during the first decade of this century before plateauing (Figure 2.9). Australia took the lead, but was closely followed by several others (Figure 2.10).[8]

France became a wine importer from the latter 1850s because of crop losses due to mildew, but it was from the early 1870s, as phylloxera spread throughout the country, that it became the world's dominant importer of wine. Most of those imports came initially from Spain and to a lesser extent Italy. However, once massive investments in Algerian vineyards and wineries by French vignerons started yielding an exportable surplus,

[8] Australian wineries' international competitiveness over the past decade declined because of the real exchange rate appreciation associated with Australia's massive mining boom. That appreciation relative to the currencies of other wine-exporting countries enabled the latter to expand their sales in third countries at Australia's expense (Anderson and Wittwer 2013). This is a clear example of how, in a globalized world, one group's misfortune can be a boon to other groups.

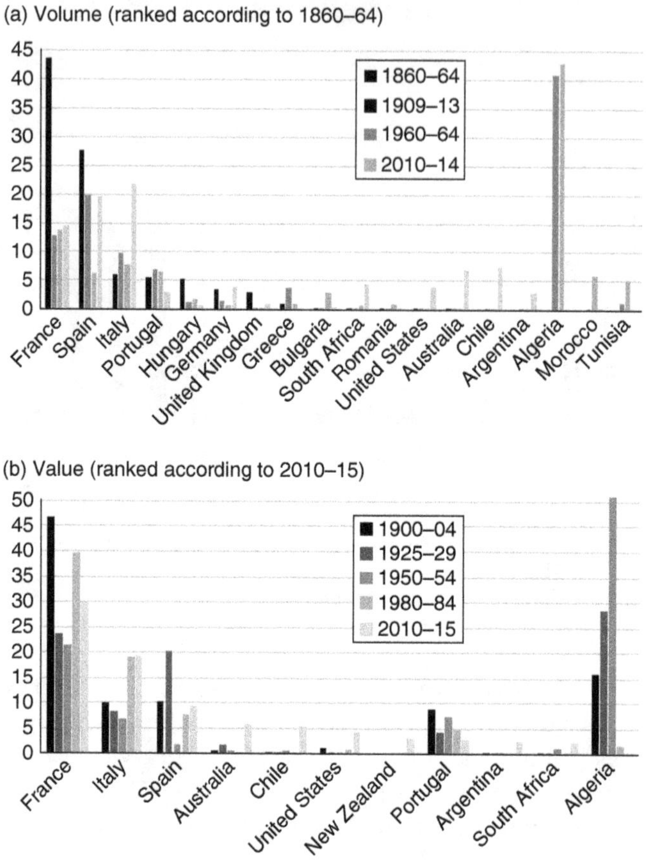

Figure 2.8 National shares of global wine export volume and value, 1860 to 2015 (%).
Source: Compiled from data in Anderson and Pinilla (2017).

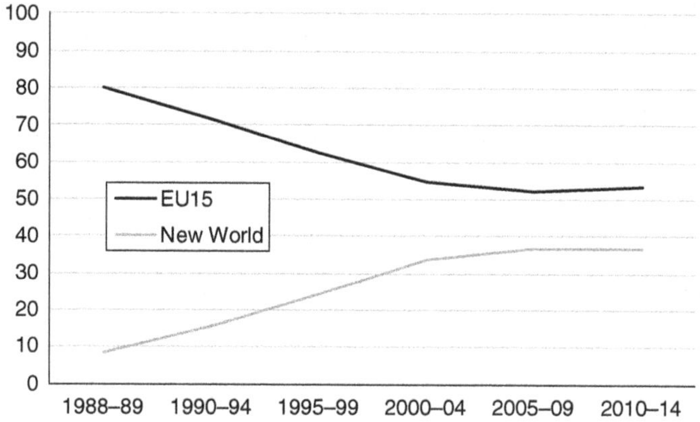

Figure 2.9 Shares of European Union 15 and New World[a] in value of global (excluding intra-EU15) wine exports, 1988 to 2014 (%).

[a] The 'New World' is defined here as Argentina, Australia, Canada, Chile, New Zealand, South Africa, the United States and Uruguay.

Source: Anderson, Nelgen and Pinilla (2017).

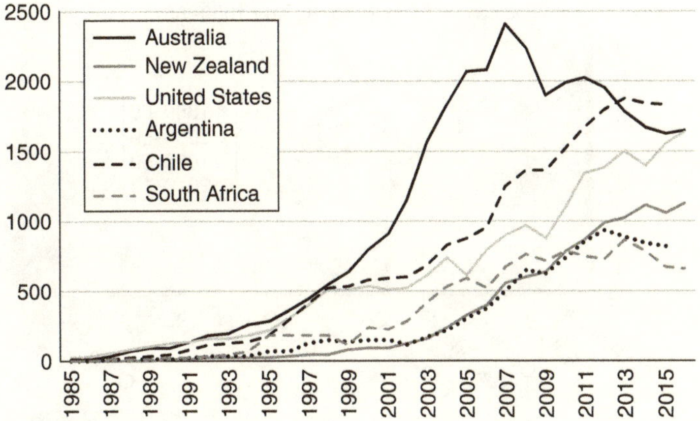

Figure 2.10 Value of wine exports, New World countries, 1985 to 2016 (current US$ million).
Source: Compiled from data in Anderson and Pinilla (2017).

barriers were erected to imports from all but Algeria (and later Morocco and Tunisia – see Chapter 16 in this volume). Germany, Russia, Switzerland and Britain were the only other significant wine importers prior to the 1970s. Only then did the United States, the United Kingdom, Belgium, Netherlands and others begin to increase their wine imports, with China and Hong Kong following after the turn of the century (Figure 2.11).

EFFECTS OF GLOBAL WINE MARKET DEVELOPMENTS ON NATIONAL MARKETS

How national wine markets are affected by global market developments is not easy to discern from the preceding figures because countries differ so much in size. To neutralize the effect of size, this section reports on intensive indicators such as per capita. These show that the vast differences between countries in their wine production, consumption and trade during the first globalization wave have shrunk hugely over the past three decades.

Convergence between Old World and New World countries in both wine production and consumption per capita is clear from Figure 2.12. France, Italy, Portugal and Argentina have all halved their production per capita since the 1950–90 period and are now comparable with Spain and Chile, in the 60 to 80 litre per year range. Australia and New Zealand are rapidly converging on that, exceeding 50 litres by 2010–15 (Figure 2.12(a)).

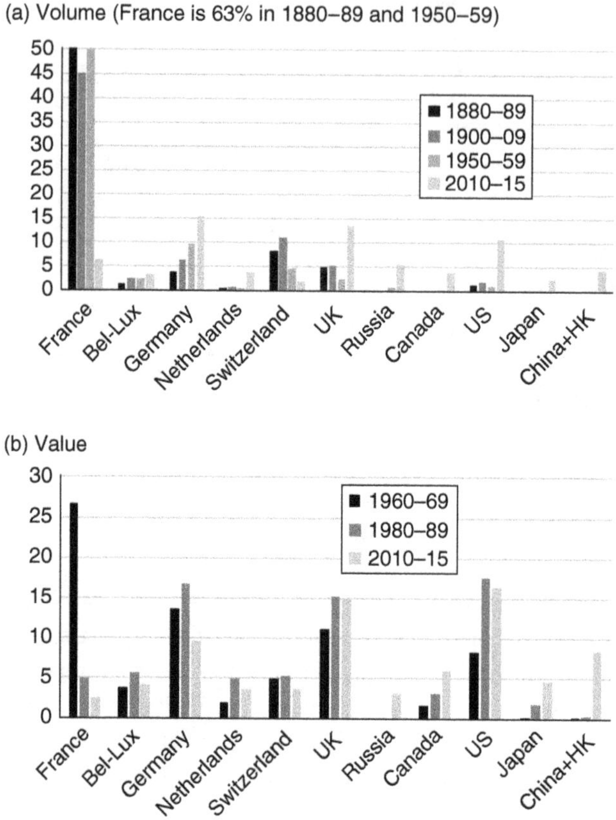

Figure 2.11 National shares of global wine import volume and value, 1860 to 2015 (%).
Source: Compiled from data in Anderson and Pinilla (2017).

It is helpful also to consider wine production per dollar of real GDP, since that gives a sense of the importance of the industry in the overall economy at any point in time. During the first globalization wave, at least six countries produced more than 10 litres of wine per real US$ '000 of GDP: Spain, Portugal, Italy, France, Algeria and Greece (Table 2.2). Those same six exceeded 25 litres also in the interwar years, when four others produced between 12 and 24 litres: Chile, Romania, Argentina and Bulgaria. Hungary was next with 8.5 litres; and probably Moldova and Georgia would have been above 10 litres had they then been separate countries. During 1960–1979, there were still no other countries in those ranges. Then by 2000–15, when real GDPs of all countries were much higher, the range had shrunk to no more than 5 litres, except for Moldova at 11 litres – another form of convergence across countries. But note that those same thirteen countries mentioned are still the highest ranked in 2000–15, together

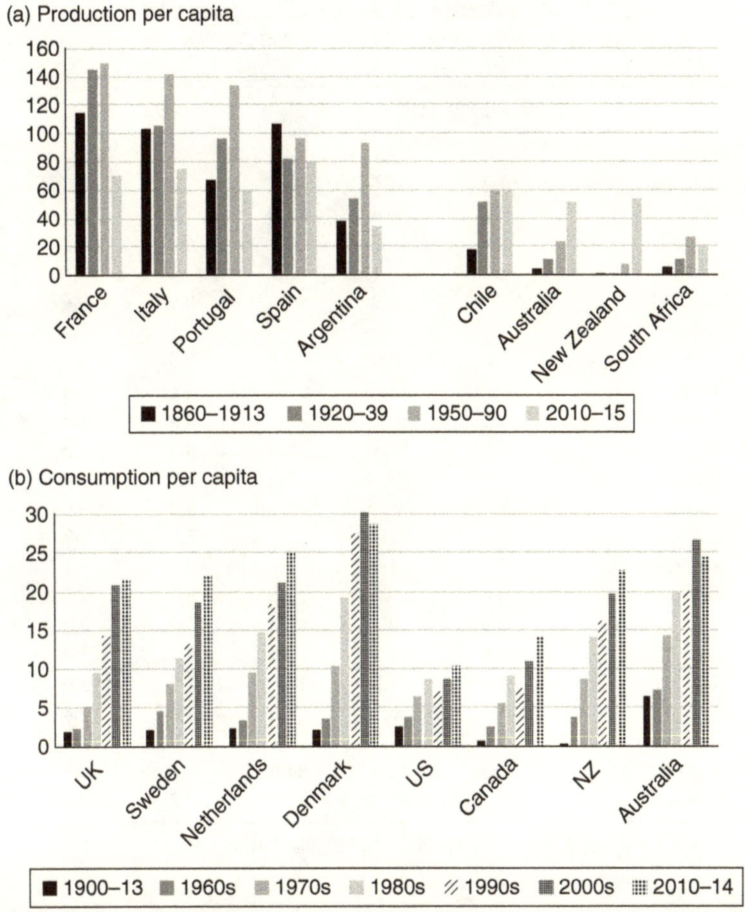

Figure 2.12 Wine production and consumption per capita, key Old World and New World countries, 1860 to 2015 (litres).
Source: Compiled from data in Anderson and Pinilla (2017).

with South Africa and Uruguay, covering the relatively narrow range of 2.4 to 5.2 litres per real US$ '000 of GDP.

Consumption per capita has more than halved from its peak in the interwar period of around 100 litres or more in each of France, Italy, Portugal and Spain, and from 60 or more litres in Argentina and Chile. By contrast, in other New World countries, as in Northwest Europe, consumption did not get above 10 litres per year before the 1960s, but has since risen to around 20 litres or more in many cases (Figure 2.12(b)). Changes in per capita wine consumption, and in wine's share of total alcohol consumption, between the last twenty-five years of the first globalization wave and the latest twenty-five years of the current globalization wave, are shown

Table 2.2 *Wine production volume per dollar of real GDP, various countries, 1860 to 2015 (litres per US$'000 of GDP at 1990 prices)*

	1860–1909	1920–39	1960–79	1980–99	2000–15
Spain	71.5	39.7	14.6	7.4	5.2
Portugal	61.1	62.6	24.5	8.1	4.3
Italy	54.4	36.8	14.0	7.6	4.2
France	50.9	35.3	12.1	6.4	3.5
Greece	26.5	25.1	8.3	4.2	2.4
Switzerland	7.0	1.9	1.0	0.9	0.6
Austria	6.9	3.6	3.0	2.1	1.2
Germany	1.8	0.9	0.9	0.8	0.5
Moldova				10.6	11.4
Romania		16.5	11.2	8.9	4.7
Bulgaria		12.4	10.6	6.7	2.6
Hungary		8.5	8.6	6.7	3.8
Georgia				4.0	3.6
Croatia				3.6	2.2
Australia	1.2	1.7	1.6	1.7	2.3
New Zealand	0.0	0.1	0.6	1.0	2.1
United States	0.3	0.2	0.3	0.3	0.3
Chile	6.8	16.7	10.9	4.7	3.9
Argentina	5.4	14.5	13.0	7.7	3.9
Uruguay	1.3	6.3	5.6	4.0	2.4
South Africa	4.9	4.8	5.4	5.9	4.3
Algeria	>50	>50	34.5	1.4	0.5
Morocco			7.2	0.7	0.3

Source: Compiled from data in Anderson and Pinilla (2017).

in Table 2.3. They reinforce the conclusion that consumption patterns are converging as globalization proceeds, with wine consumption having fallen mostly in those countries with relatively high per capita consumption prior to World War I, and rising elsewhere but mostly from very low bases.

Wine exports per capita changed in a less clear-cut pattern. Prior to the 1970s, that indicator was always below 10 litres per year in France and Italy, and also in Spain except during the last quarter of the nineteenth and first quarter of the twentieth century. Since then, it has more than doubled in France and Italy and increased fivefold in Spain. By contrast, exports from New World countries were miniscule in the first globalization wave and did not exceed 10 litres per capita until the 1990s, but then they too quadrupled in the subsequent twenty-five years, albeit from different bases. Spain and Chile now have the highest levels of exports per capita, exceeding the record levels achieved by Spain and Portugal when they responded

Table 2.3 *Wine per capita consumption and wine's share of alcohol consumption, selected countries, 1881–85, 1890–1914 and 1990–2014 (litres/year and %)*

	Per capita consumption (l)			% of alcohol consumption	
	1881–85	1890–1914	1990–2014	1890–1914	1990–2014
France	99	126	53	71	61
Portugal	39	67	53		62
Italy	90	100	45	91	71
Croatia		na	42		49
Switzerland	69	67	38	59	51
Argentina	30	46	34		63
Greece		37	31		48
Austria	12	31	30		34
Hungary	72	38	29		32
Denmark	2	1	28	2	37
Bel-Lux	3	4	26	4	32
Uruguay		na	25		60
Spain	87	80	25		32
Australia	4	5	23	11	35
Romania		na	23		37
Germany	4	4	22	5	25
United Kingdom	2	1	21	2	31
Georgia		na	20		59
Netherlands	2	2	20	4	31
Sweden		na	18		37
New Zealand	1	1	18	2	31
Bulgaria		19	17		24
Moldova		na	16		41
Chile	12	24	14		33
Ireland		na	13		17
Canada		1	10		19
Finland		na	10		19
United States	1	2	8	3	15
South Africa		5	8		21
Russia		1	6		8
Ukraine		na	4		9
Tunisia		8	2		35
Hong Kong		0	2		15
Brazil		na	2		5
Japan		0	2		4
Singapore		0	2		13
Morocco		2	1		43
Algeria	21	28	1		45

Source: Compiled from data in Anderson and Pinilla (2017).

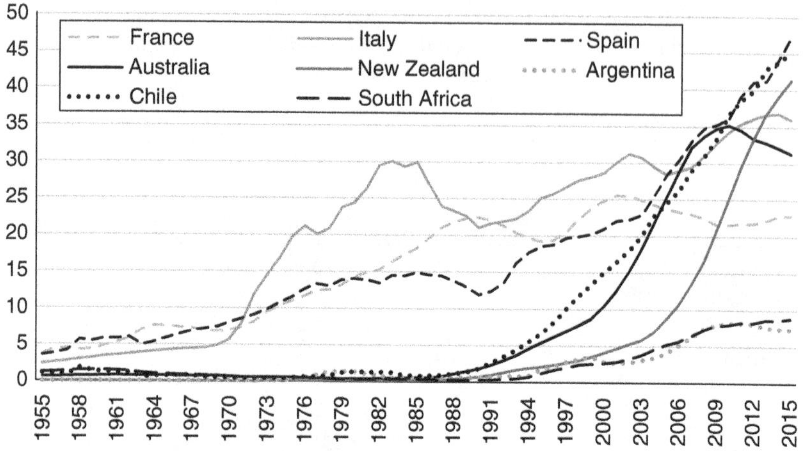

Figure 2.13 Volume of wine exports per capita, key Old World and New World countries, 1955 to 2015 (litres, five-year averages to the year shown).
Source: Compiled from data in Anderson and Pinilla (2017).

to France's need for imports in the 1880s. New Zealand exports, which took off only recently, are almost up to Chile on a per capita basis, while Australia has levelled out a little below Italy but about 50 percent above France. Argentina and South Africa also have expanded their exports dramatically, but on a per capita basis they are only about one-third France's level (Figure 2.13).

The takeoffs in exports in Australia, Chile and New Zealand were the result of deliberate strategies to grow their industries through exports, whereas in France, Italy and Spain the export expansions were more an indirect result of production not declining as fast as domestic demand for wine (Figure 2.14) – although export strategies were an explicit part of business plans in some regions of Europe too, notably Champagne and northern Italy. That meant the share of production exported grew more rapidly in Australia, Chile and New Zealand than in Europe, and to higher shares. Even South Africa is now back above France again, having been eclipsed in the 1860s when the British tariff preference for South African wines was removed (Figure 2.15).

Values of wine exports expanded at different rates to volumes in these various countries because of quality differences, and at different rates to the value of other exports in each country depending on changes in their respective economies' sectoral comparative advantages. One way to see the net effect of that on their international competitiveness in wine is to estimate an index of comparative advantage, defined as the share of wine in national merchandise exports divided by wine's share of global exports

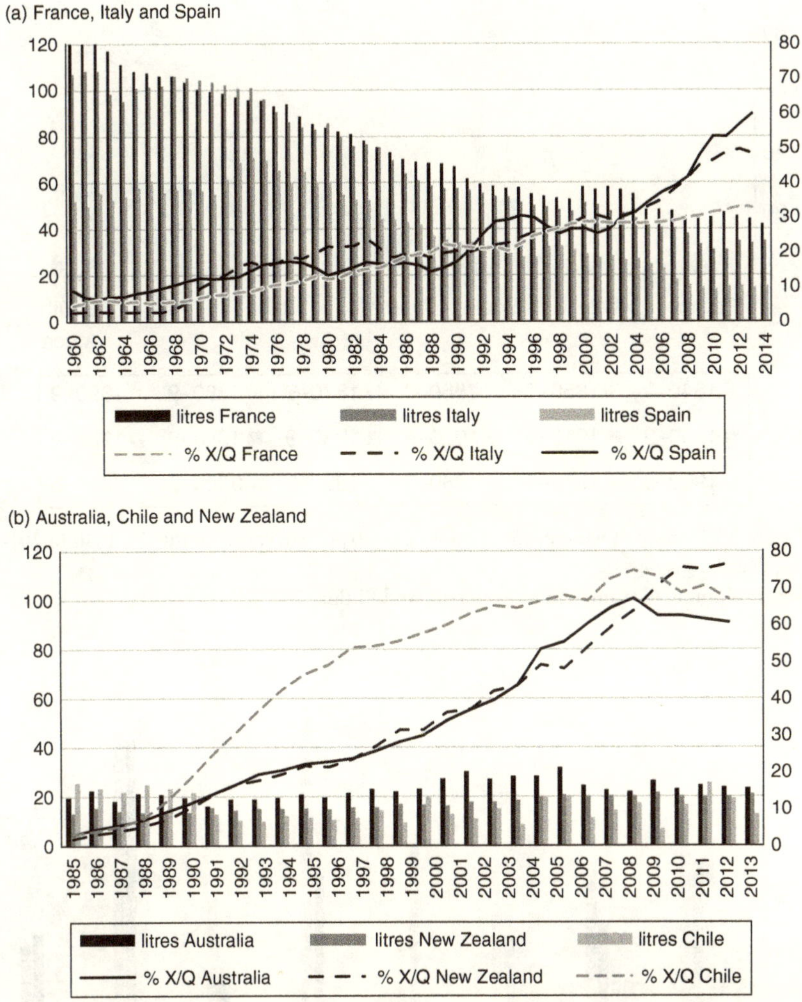

Figure 2.14 Per capita wine consumption and share of wine production exported, six countries, 1960 to 2014 (litres on left axis, % on right axis for five-year average to year shown).
Source: Compiled from data in Anderson and Pinilla (2017).

(Figure 2.16). That index reveals that France, Italy and Spain have been able to retain their strong comparative advantage in wine despite the dramatic strengthening of comparative advantage in key wine-exporting countries of the Southern Hemisphere.

The emergence of strong comparative advantages in wine in New World countries during the current globalization wave begs the question as to why

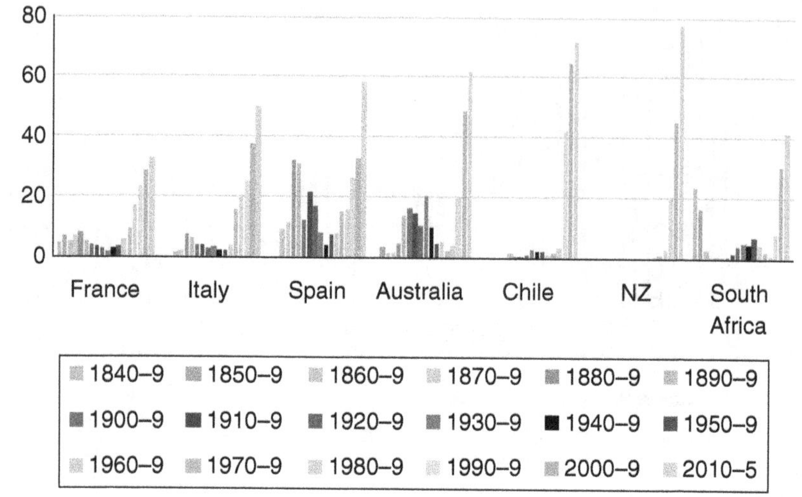

Figure 2.15 Share of wine production volume exported, seven countries, 1840 to 2014 (%, decadal averages).
Source: Compiled from data in Anderson and Pinilla (2017).

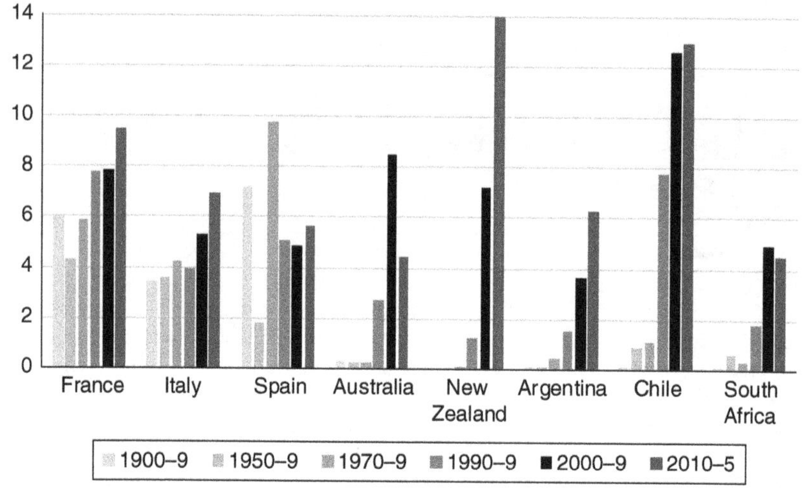

Figure 2.16 Index of 'revealed' comparative advantage (RCA) in wine,[a] eight countries, 1900 to 2015.
Note: The RCA is the share of wine in national merchandise exports divided by share in global exports. Countries with higher RCAs than those shown are Moldova and Georgia, whose RCAs in 2000–2015 averaged 64 and 28, respectively.
Source: Compiled from data in Anderson and Pinilla (2017).

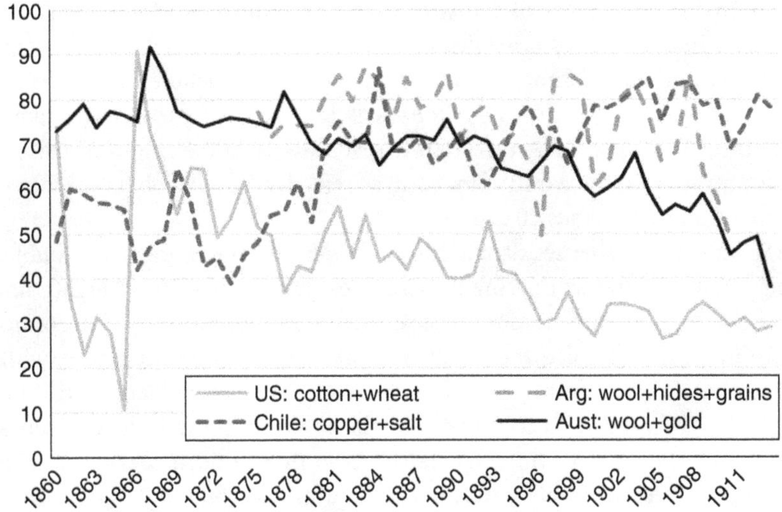

Figure 2.17 Share of top two goods in settler economies' exports, 1860 to 1913 (%).
Source: Anderson (2017a).

they did not emerge in the first globalization wave. Part of the answer, discussed in several chapters to follow, has to do with trade costs: in all those settler economies, only two products (both primary) accounted for the vast majority of their exports prior to 1914, both having high value-to-weight ratios sufficient to make them tradable (Figure 2.17). Evidently the perceived quality of those countries' wines was never high enough for them to attract prices that could cover production plus trade costs.

THE DIFFUSION OF WINEGRAPE VARIETIES

One way winegrowers compete for consumers' attention by trying to differentiate their product is to highlight their regional and varietal distinctiveness. The extent to which the choice of winegrape varieties alters over time is very slow in the premium regions within the European Union, because the industry has chosen to limit growers' choices by regulation. No such restrictions apply in the rest of the world, though, where changes are being made all the time as growers learn more about their terroir. A recent study developed a global database of vine bearing areas to see how the mix of varieties has changed between 1990 and 2010 (with less complete data also for 1980, 1970 and 1960). It examines more than 1,500 DNA-distinct winegrape varieties spanning over 640 regions in forty-eight countries that together account for 99 percent of the world's wine production (Anderson 2013, 2014a). That study was possible because of the seminal book by Robinson, Harding and Vouillamoz (2012), which provides a detailed guide to the world's commercially grown 'prime' varieties and their various synonyms, based on the latest DNA research. It reveals dramatic changes in varietal concentration in the world's vineyard, as reflected in the global rankings of varieties in 1990 versus 2010.

Specifically, Cabernet Sauvignon and Merlot have more than doubled their shares of the world vine bearing area, taking them from eighth and seventh to first and second places, and Tempranillo and Chardonnay have more than trebled their shares to take fourth and fifth places, while Syrah has jumped from thirty-fifth to sixth. Sauvignon Blanc and Pinot Noir are the other two to move into the top ten. These have all been at the expense of Airén, which has fallen from first to third, Garnacha from second to seventh, Trebbiano from fifth to ninth and Sultaniye (main synonyms: Thompson Seedless and Sultana) from third to more than thirty-fifth. As a consequence, the world's top thirty-five varieties as ranked in 1990 show a quite different mix and rank ordering to the comparable chart for 2010 (Figure 2.18). Evidently globalization has allowed many regions to alter their varietal mix in response to such forces as technological improvements, climate changes and evolving wine demand patterns.

WHERE TO FROM HERE?

The dramatic changes in national and global wine production, consumption and trade over the past 150-plus years, and particularly during the current globalization wave, raise lots of questions as to why patterns changed the way they did, and how they might change in coming decades. The rest of this book seeks to address such questions. Further comparisons will be helpful. For example, in contemplating possible future comparative advantages in wine, it is constructive to look at national vine bearing areas as a share of the total area under crop. Figure 2.19 reveals this share to be above 4 percent in the main wine-exporting countries of Europe, and 2 to 4 percent in numerous other European countries. Among the new exporters, by contrast, it is only Chile whose cropping has a high degree of vine intensity (and possibly New Zealand, for which there are no total crop area data). In Argentina, Australia and China, barely 0.5 percent of cropped land is under vine; in the United States, only 0.25 percent is; and that share is even smaller in emerging cool-climate areas such as Canada, southern England, elsewhere in Northwest Europe and Tasmania. Should the world's climate

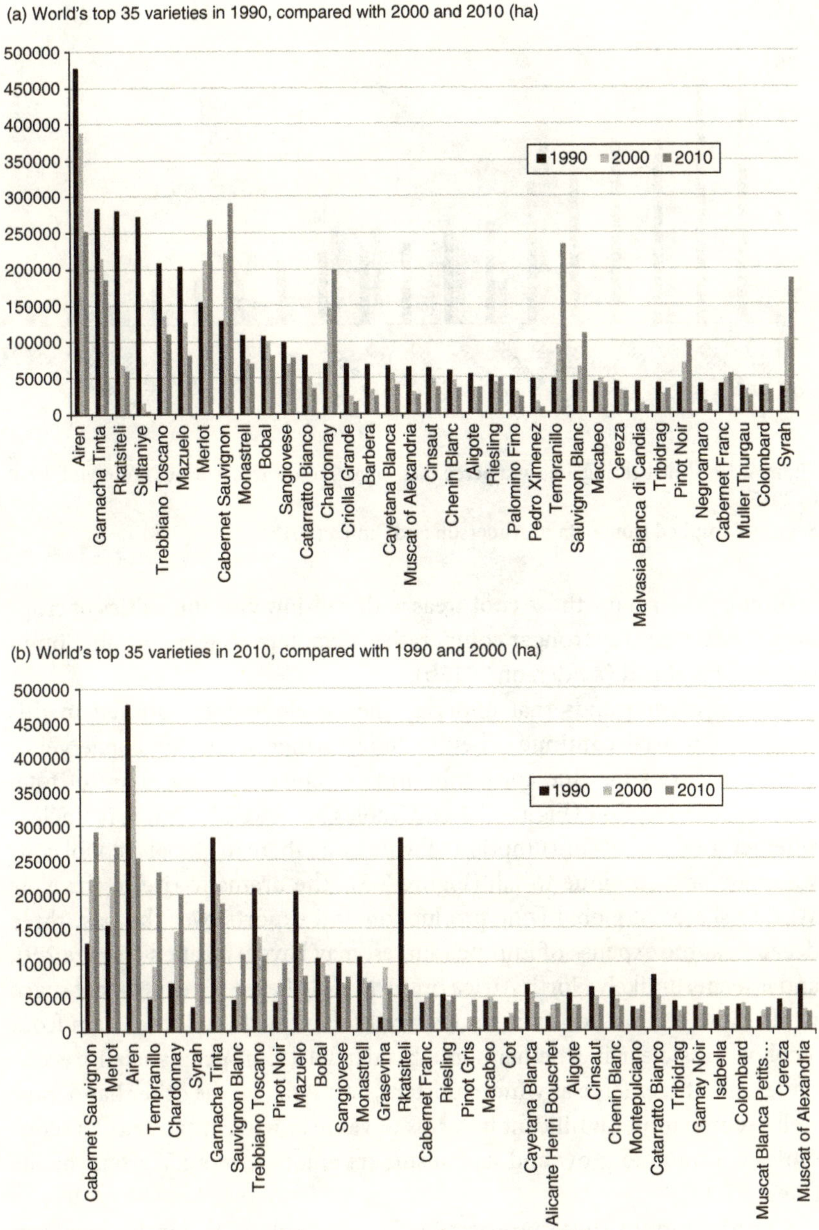

Figure 2.18 World's top thirty-five winegrape varieties in 1990, 2000 and 2010 (ha bearing area): (a) 1990, compared with 2000 and 2010; (b) 2010, compared with 1990 and 2000.

Source: Compiled from data in Anderson (2013).

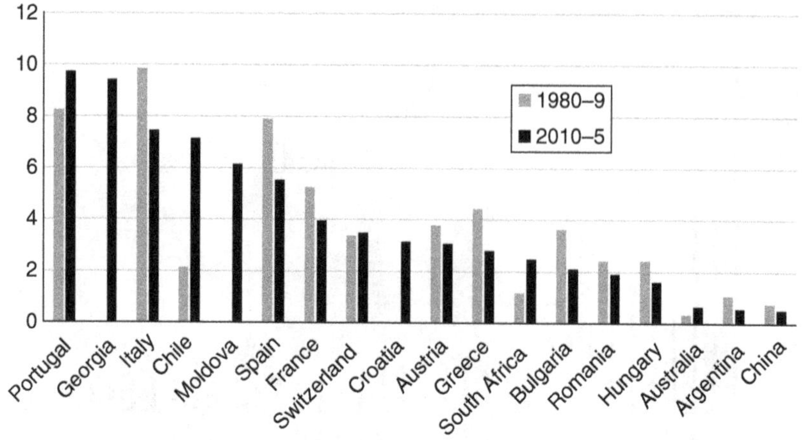

Figure 2.19 Vine bearing area as a percentage of total crop area, various countries, 1980 to 2015.
Source: Compiled from data in Anderson and Pinilla (2017).

continue to warm up, those cool areas with still-low vine intensities of cropping may develop a stronger comparative advantage in wine production in the decades ahead (Anderson 2017b).

Several other trends that underlay the developments outlined in this chapter may well continue. They include further scope for convergence across countries in wine consumption per capita and as a share of total alcohol consumption (Figure 2.4 and Tables 2.1 and 2.3), but it is unclear whether total global consumption of wine or its share in global alcohol consumption will continue to fall (Figure 2.5). The dramatic rise in the New World's shares of global wine production and exports over the past three decades, at the expense of Europe's shares, may have plateaued (Figure 2.9), and it seems unlikely North Africa or the Middle East will reenter that space while those regions continue to observe Mohammed's call to abstain from alcohol. Less clear is whether some former East European socialist economies might reemerge as wine exporters. East Asia, on the other hand, may well become more significant in terms of value of wine imports as its economies continue to grow and its consumers embrace more Western habits (Figure 2.11).

Contributors to these prospects will include various developments in institutions and policies affecting demands and supplies. On the demand side, will health lobbies succeed in their lobbying for higher taxes and other curbs on alcohol consumption? Will there be further deregulation of retailing liquor laws and supermarketing or online sales of wine at all hours?

Will consumers continue indefinitely to upgrade the quality of the wine they consume at the expense of quantity as their incomes grow? Will governments of wine-exporting countries lower barriers to imports so their consumers get access to a wider range of wines? With respect to wine supplies, will new technologies lower the cost of upgrading nonpremium and commercial grapes and wines to higher-quality products? Will those technological innovations help cooler-climate regions more than current regions? Will improvements in bulk shipping encourage even more wine to be exported in 20-foot shipping containers?[9] How will tightening immigration laws in various countries affect real wages and thereby international competitiveness? These are the types of questions addressed towards the end of each of the chapters in this volume.

REFERENCES

Anderson, K. (2010), 'Excise and Import Taxes on Wine vs Beer and Spirits: An International Comparison', *Economic Papers* 29(2): 215–28, June.

(with the assistance of N. R. Aryal) (2013), *Which Winegrape Varieties are Grown Where? A Global Empirical Picture*, Adelaide: University of Adelaide Press. Also freely available as an e-book at www.adelaide.edu.au/press/titles/winegrapes

(2014a), 'Evolving Varietal Distinctiveness of the World's Wine Regions: Evidence from a New Global Database', *Journal of Wine Economics* 9(3): 249–72.

(2014b), 'Excise Taxes on Wines, Beers and Spirits: An Updated International Comparison', *Wine and Viticulture Journal* 29(6): 66–71, November/December. Also available as Working Paper No. 170, American Association of Wine Economists, October.

(2017a), 'Sectoral Trends and Shocks in Australia's Economic Growth', *Australian Economic History Review* 57(1): 2–21, March.

(2017b), 'How Might Climate Changes and Preference Changes Affect the Competitiveness of the World's Wine Regions?', *Wine Economics and Policy* 6(2): 23–27, June.

Anderson, K. and H. G. Jensen (2016), 'How Much Does the European Union Assist Its Wine Producers?', *Journal of Wine Economics* 11(3): 289–305.

Anderson, K., S. Nelgen and V. Pinilla (2017), *Global Wine Markets, 1860 to 2016: A Statistical Compendium*, Adelaide: University of Adelaide Press. Freely available as an e-book at www.adelaide.edu.au/press/titles/

Anderson, K. and V. Pinilla (with the assistance of A. J. Holmes) (2017), *Annual Database of Global Wine Markets, 1835 to 2016*, freely available in Excel at the University of Adelaide's Wine Economics Research Centre, www.adelaide.edu.au/wine-econ/databases

[9] During 2002–14, the share of the world's wine exported in bulk rose from 31 percent to 40 percent in volume terms, and from 8 percent to 10 percent in value terms (Anderson, Nelgen and Pinilla 2017).

Anderson, K. and G. Wittwer (2013), 'Modeling Global Wine Markets to 2018: Exchange Rates, Taste Changes, and China's Import Growth', *Journal of Wine Economics* 8(2): 131–58.

Aparicio, G., V. Pinilla and R. Serrano (2009), 'Europe and the International Agricultural and Food Trade, 1870–2000', pp. 52–75 in *Agriculture and Economic Development in Europe since 1870*, edited by P. Lains and V. Pinilla, London: Routledge.

Bianco, A. D., V. L. Boatto, F. Caracciolo and F. G. Santeramo (2016), 'Tariffs and Non-tariff Frictions in the World Wine Trade', *European Review of Agricultural Economics* 43(1): 31–57, March.

Bordo, M. D., A. M. Taylor and J. G. Williamson (eds.) (2003), *Globalization in Historical Perspective*, Chicago: University of Chicago Press.

Campbell, C. (2004), *Phylloxera: How Wine Was Saved for the World*, London: HarperCollins.

Findlay, R. and K. H. O'Rourke (2007), *Power and Plenty: Trade, War, and the World Economy in the Second Millennium*, Princeton, NJ: Princeton University Press.

Flynn, D. O. and A. Giráldez (2004), 'Path Dependence, Time Lags and the Birth of Globalisation: A Critique of O'Rourke and Williamson', *European Review of Economic History* 8(1): 88–108.

Hatton, T., K. H. O'Rourke and J. C. Williamson (eds.) (2007), *The New Comparative Economic History*, Cambridge, MA: MIT Press.

Holmes, A. J. and K. Anderson (2017), 'Convergence in National Alcohol Consumption Patterns: New Global Indicators', *Journal of Wine Economics* 12(2): 117–48.

Johnson, H. (1989), *The Story of Wine*, London: Mitchell Beasley.

Lukacs, P. (2012), *Inventing Wine: A New History of One of the World's Most Ancient Pleasures*, New York: W. W. Norton.

O'Rourke, K. H. and J. C. Williamson (1999), *Globalization and History: The Evolution of a Nineteenth-Century Atlantic Economy*, Cambridge and New York: Cambridge University Press.

O'Rourke, K. H. and J. C. Williamson (2002), 'When Did Globalisation Begin?', *European Review of Economic History* 6(1): 23–50.

O'Rourke, K. H. and J. C. Williamson (2004), 'Once More: When Did Globalisation Begin?' *European Review of Economic History* 8(1): 109–17.

Phillips, R. (2014), *Alcohol: A History*, Chapel Hill: University of North Carolina Press.

Pomeranz, K. (2000), *The Great Divergence: Europe, China, and the Making of the Modern World Economy*, Princeton, NJ: Princeton University Press.

Robinson, J., J. Harding and J. Vouillamoz (2012), *Wine Grapes: A Complete Guide to 1,368 Vine Varieties, Including Their Origins and Flavours*, London: Allen Lane.

Swinnen, J. (ed.) (2011), *The Economics of Beer*, Oxford and New York: Oxford University Press.

Walmsley, T., A. Aguiar and B. Narayanan (2012), 'Introduction to the Global Trade Analysis Project and the GTAP Data Base', GTAP Working Paper No. 67, Purdue University.

PART II

TRADITIONAL MARKETS

3

France

Jean-Michel Chevet, Eva Fernández, Eric Giraud-Héraud
and Vicente Pinilla

Over the past 200 years, and also in preceding centuries, France has held a central position in the global wine market.[1] Over this period, it has always been among the world's three leading wine-producing and -exporting countries, and in some decades it has been a major importer. However, more important than its high volume of production, consumption or export is its absolute supremacy in the fine wine segment. This is no coincidence. From the mid-nineteenth century, and even before, France has been at the cutting edge in terms of the technology of wine production and of caring for vineyards and fighting vine diseases. Science, technology and modern marketing are the key elements of this evolution in which, particularly in the final decades of the twentieth century, France's position was challenged by producers in other countries, especially in the New World. That competition triggered France to intensify its efforts to sustain its primacy in the global wine industry.

However, French vineyards and wines are enormously heterogeneous. In addition to high-quality wines with very high prices, there has always been a spectrum of wines of varying quality, produced by both small and large farms in different regions of France. Talking about French wine is therefore almost as complex as talking about wines from a collection of countries such as in the New World: the wide diversity in terms of regions and types of wine has to be taken on board.

The economic development of wine in France has not traced a monotonic growth path of consecutive successes. On the contrary, the past two centuries have been spattered with shocks and difficulties, including vine plagues and diseases; the loss or closure of some foreign markets; and

[1] This study has received financial support from Spain's Ministry of Science and Innovation, project ECO2015-65582, and from the Government of Aragon through the Research Group 'Agri-food Economic History (Nineteenth and Twentieth Centuries)'.

overproduction, low prices and consequent social protests from winegrowers. This is why France has also been a pioneer in terms of public intervention in its wine market, introducing institutional innovations that have had long-lasting effects, such as the creation of the Appellations d'Origine or the limitation of cultivated areas.

In this chapter, we analyze the evolution of the French wine industry, examining its production, consumption and foreign trade. In doing so, we insert its developments in the context of the changes taking place over the past two centuries in the global economy, particularly the two waves of globalization. The chapter is divided into three parts. The first examines the period from the mid-nineteenth century to World War II. This is a key period, as changes were made and developed that have had important effects through to the present day. The second section analyzes the fifty years following World War II, and the final section examines the most-recent developments in the context of the profound globalization of the world's wine markets.

OVERVIEW: FRENCH WINE PRODUCTION AND TRADE, 1850–1938

Until World War II, France was undoubtedly the principal country in the world's wine markets. As well as being the number one wine producer and the largest wine consumer, it was also the main player in international trade. Its exports in terms of value were the highest in the world, and it was by far the world's leading importer. Algeria was a French colony, and its wine production was clearly controlled by the settlers of the metropole country. If we add the Algerian production to that of France, French hegemony was overwhelming.

The Expansion of Demand

From the mid-nineteenth century until 1938, the demand for wine in the French domestic market grew significantly, due to both population growth and increased per capita consumption. Another key factor was the French economy's transformation from mostly rural and based on the agricultural sector to one with an urban industrial predominance. During this period, the French population grew by six million, and per capita wine consumption doubled (Figure 3.1). The latter growth can be largely explained by the increase in per capita income in France due to its economic growth and industrialization,[2] since it has been estimated for this period that each

[2] The relaxation of domestic taxes in wine also boosted its consumption (Nourrison 1990).

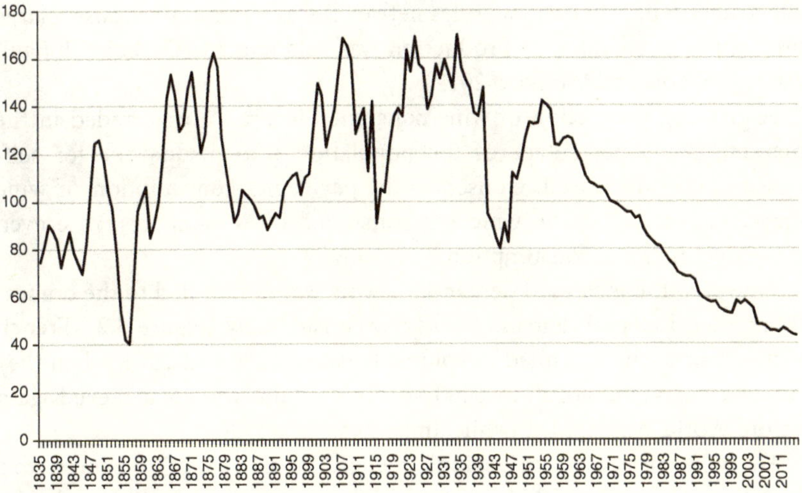

Figure 3.1 Volume of beverage wine consumption per capita, France, 1847 to 2014 (litres).
Source: Anderson and Pinilla (2017).

increase in income of 1 percent gave rise to a 0.9 percent increase in wine consumption (Pinilla and Ayuda 2008, pp. 591–92). In aggregate, wine consumption in France doubled. Urban development and social changes associated with the new lifestyles also had salient consequences. The social life of the towns was organized around cafés and restaurants, where high-quality wines such as champagne became the celebratory drinks of choice.

Accordingly, the success of the champagne trading houses was more than remarkable. At the end of the nineteenth century, their efforts had enabled this drink to become 'an "obligatory adjunt" to the social rituals of the emergent bourgeoisie of Europe' (Guy 2003, p. 11). This success was not accidental. The large champagne houses used extremely modern marketing techniques: the creation of brand-name identification, packaging, promotional trips and shows, advertising in the printed press and an intense consumer communication campaign, adapting the type of product to the tastes of each country. At the end of the nineteenth century, the champagne traders had successfully associated the consumption of this drink to public events (boat and plane christenings, sporting events, receptions of authorities, public banquets, royal coronations) and private celebrations (christenings, weddings, Christmas, parties in cabarets), where it became an 'obligatory' drink (Vizetelli 1882, p. 109; Desbois-Thibault 2003). This strategy required significant technological innovation. Furthermore, the construction of international sales networks was necessary because a large proportion of champagne production was sold abroad (Desbois-Thibault 2003; Wolikow and Wolikow 2012).

A growing proportion of wine consumed in France was traded in the market, as the percentage of the population who made wine for self-consumption decreased. Consequently, per capita consumption of wine marketed, excluding the wine self-consumed by winemakers, rose even more than national consumption.

However, the increased demand for wine was not limited to the domestic market. External demand also grew considerably (Figure 3.2). French wine exports almost tripled in volume between 1850 and 1874, when they reached a maximum of almost 400 ML. This volume was not achieved again before World War II. Meanwhile, imports were very low.

For wine producers in regions engaged in the export business, this period was one of great prosperity. The regions of Gironde (Bordeaux) and Champagne in particular benefitted with enormous increases in their exports.

Nevertheless, the problems that affected French production after this date due to the phylloxera plague and the resulting fall in output gave rise to a significant drop in the volume of exports, which continued to decline until World War II. However, the value of wine exports, deflated using a wholesale price index, more than quadrupled over the nineteenth century and remained at high levels until the beginning of World War I as their proportion of high-quality wines rose (Ayuda, Ferrer and Pinilla 2016).

Three main reasons explain the expansion of external demand. First, the mass emigration of Europeans to the Americas during the first wave of globalization meant that the population originating in countries where wine was a product of mass consumption (mainly Spain, Italy, Portugal) demanded wine, as this produce was integral to their diet and lifestyle. In countries where immigration from Mediterranean countries was significant, such as Argentina, Brazil, Chile, Uruguay and the United States, local winegrowers were initially incapable of satisfying the expanding demand, so France, which was the world's leading exporter in the mid-nineteenth century, was in an excellent position to supply those emerging markets.

Second, the colonial expansion of France gave rise to the deployment of soldiers, civil servants and settlers who continued to consume wine regularly when posted to a colony. The wine exported by France to its colonies accounted for 10 to 15 percent of its total wine exports during most of the period, and more than 25 percent in the 1930s (Table 3.1).

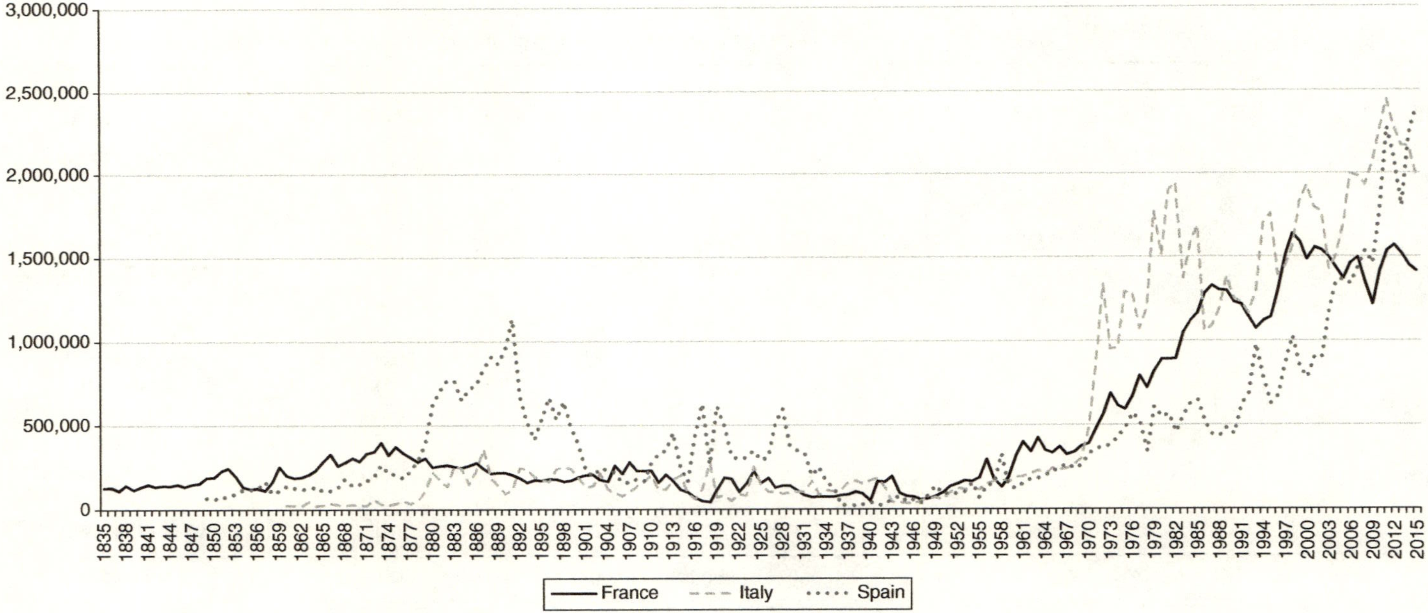

Figure 3.2 Volume of wine exports, France, Italy and Spain, 1835 to 2015 (KL).
Source: Anderson and Pinilla (2017).

Table 3.1 *Wine exports, France, 1847 to 1938 (p.a. at 1913 prices in million francs, and %)*

Exports to:	1847–59	1860–69	1870–79	1880–89	1890–99	1900–09	1910–19	1920–29	1930–38
United Kingdom	7	23	45	56	55	40	30	28	17
Germany	16	17	35	25	22	27	14	22	3
Belgium	10	14	23	27	29	43	23	36	13
Switzerland	8	19	35	18	10	21	8	14	9
Netherlands	5	5	8	7	7	7	5	7	3
Other Europe	26	22	15	11	8	13	11	9	5
United States	20	17	18	12	9	8	7	0	8
Canada	0	0	0	0	0	0	1	2	1
Argentina	3	14	25	25	10	9	8	3	1
Other Latin America	15	27	33	24	15	11	8	8	7
Africa	26	31	28	18	10	12	11	19	18
Asia	1	2	2	3	4	9	5	10	6
Oceania	0	1	1	1	2	2	1	1	0
Not assigned	3	9	12	17	16	21	14	16	8
World	**141**	**201**	**279**	**243**	**196**	**222**	**146**	**176**	**100**
% to French colonies	*18*	*14*	*10*	*9*	*9*	*11*	*12*	*16*	*29*

Source: Authors' calculations based on Tableau General du Commerce Exterieur de la France.

Third, during the second half of the nineteenth century, wine demand was increasing also in western European countries, where rapid industrialization was under way. Wines of a high quality and price in these countries became luxury products consumed at celebrations and parties and by the elite. Again France was in the best position to be the leading supplier of this privileged consumption, particularly with champagne, burgundy and fine Bordeaux clarets. The cuts in British tariffs after the bilateral agreement of 1860 had a clear impact on consumption in the United Kingdom by lowering the price of wines sold there (Simpson 2011, p. 88). The growth in demand led to only a slight increase in prices in France, though, as supplies responded quickly to the favourable economic situation abroad.

However, wine did not become a product of mass consumption in these countries. Contrary to France, their increase in incomes did not translate into a significant increase in per capita consumption. Citizens in these countries continued to prefer other alcoholic drinks such as beer or distilled spirits, dampening the market growth opportunities for French exports. For example, in Belgium, the Netherlands, Germany and the United Kingdom, wine represented between 1 percent and 10 percent of total alcohol consumption, as compared with 75 to 90 percent in the main producing countries of France, Italy or Spain (Pinilla and Ayuda 2007; Anderson and Pinilla 2017). The demand for French wine in global markets was limited also by the competition from wines of other countries.

In the nineteenth century, France's imports of foreign wines complemented national production, but imports did not compete with but rather supplemented domestic wines when there were shortages, due in particular to the spread of first oidium and later phylloxera. The oidium plague and its impact on French production between 1850 and 1857 gave rise to wine imports from 1854, particularly from Spain (Table 3.2). The impact of the phylloxera plague on production, from the beginning of the 1880s, was much greater. The fastest solution was to resort to imports again, mainly from Spain, in order to resolve two problems simultaneously: to guarantee supply of this staple product for French consumers, and to maintain wine export levels by mixing these imported wines with local product destined for export. By the 1890s, however, French winegrowers increasingly demanded protection against wines imported from Spain. The government's response was to significantly increase tariffs, which greatly limited the entry of foreign wines (Table 3.3).[3] Algeria, being a French colony and

[3] The elasticity of wines imported from abroad with respect to increases in duties was very high. It has been calculated that between 1874 and 1934, an increase of 1 percent in the tax

Table 3.2 *Volume of wine imports, France, 1850 to 1938 (ML p.a.)*

	Italy	Spain	Algeria	Other countries	All sources
1850–9	1	15	0	2	18
1860–9	1	15	0	3	19
1870–9	17	60	0	6	83
1880–9	148	629	47	48	938
1890–9	7	489	285	27	827
1900–9	4	63	475	9	562
1910–19	32	169	537	5	803
1920–9	15	162	609	18	895
1930–8	11	59	1,083	3	1,244

Source: Authors' calculations based on Tableau General du Commerce Exterieur de la France.

Table 3.3 *Wine import tariffs, France, 1850 to 1938 (% and constant Francs)*

	Duties as % of imports		Specific duties (constant Francs 1913 per hectolitre)	
	Foreign countries	French colonies	Foreign countries	French colonies
1850–9	0.52		0.27	
1860–9	1.07		0.26	
1870–9	9.53		3.14	
1880–9	5.81		2.62	
1890–9	23.74	0.02	8.05	0.01
1900–9	43.12	0.06	15.58	0.01
1910–19	24.99	0.05	7.29	0.01
1920–9	29.09	0.03	6.84	0.01
1930–8	64.45	0.04	16.65	0.01

Source: Authors' calculations based on Tableau General du Commerce Exterieur de la France.

having a tariff union with metropolitan France from 1884, was exempt from paying duties to the mother country, and so their imports increased rapidly. Thereafter, imports from Spain became highly irregular, supplementing local supplies only when production in mainland France and the colonies was insufficient.

The recovery of French production following the phylloxera plague did not eliminate the need to import wine (Figure 3.3). The vineyards destroyed by phylloxera were replaced often with hybrid direct-producer

on ordinary wine gave rise to a fall in the long term of 1.8 percent in imports' share of the French market (Pinilla and Ayuda 2002, pp. 71–5).

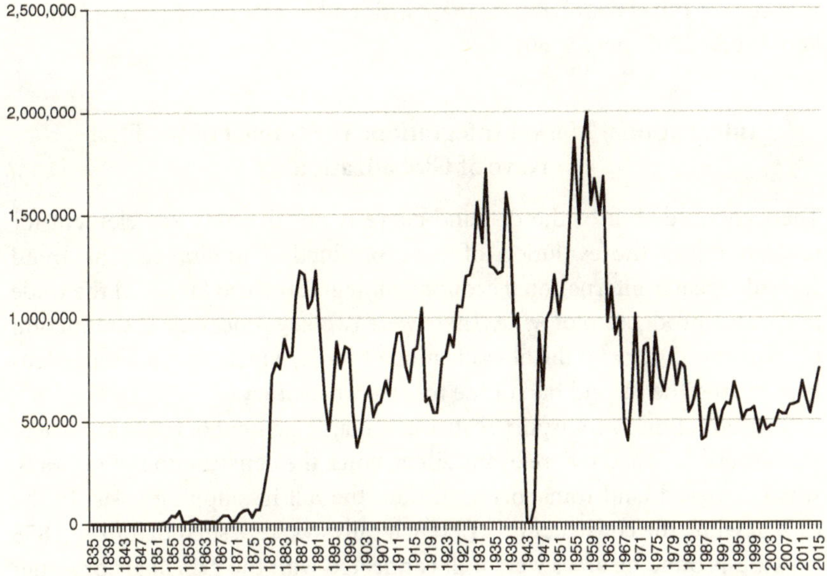

Figure 3.3 Volume of wine imports, France, 1835 to 2015 (KL).
Source: Anderson and Pinilla (2017).

vines, which produced lower-alcohol wines (around 6–7 degrees) with a paler colour, so it was felt necessary to mix them with wines with a higher alcohol content and deeper colour (such as Spanish or Algerian wines). While Spanish imports could be controlled by adjusting the level of the import tariff, Algerian wines continued to be freely imported. During the mid-1920s, they reached very high levels that competed directly with low-quality French wines (Meloni and Swinnen 2014, 2018), but colonial policy prevented restrictions on imports of these wines because winemaking was a key element of the economics of Europeans settling in Algeria (Isnard 1954; Pinilla and Ayuda 2002, pp. 61–7).

The demand for French wine abroad was affected by competition from other traditional producers in Spain and Italy, who took advantage of the French phylloxera crisis to gain a stronger foothold in some low-quality segments of foreign markets. They did so with some success in countries such as Switzerland, the United States and Argentina.

An additional new impact on the demand for French wine came from the increase in production of emerging producers in such countries as the United States, Argentina and Uruguay. Once these new producers reached a capacity to supply their domestic markets, tariffs were raised on wines imported from abroad. The American markets for wine exporters from

France and other countries shrank considerably as a consequence (Pinilla and Ayuda 2002, pp. 55–60).

International Market Integration: The Impact of the First Wave of Globalization

The rightward shift of the demand curve is not the only key element for understanding the evolution of wine production in France. The trend towards greater international economic integration also favoured the trade and hence production of wine. There were two key processes: the reduction of transport costs; and the liberalization of trade, which took place particularly during the second half of the nineteenth century.

The reduction in transport costs was a major element of the first wave of globalization. It had two relevant dimensions: the construction of railways, which lowered land transport costs; and the fall in shipping costs. In the case of wine, the construction of French railways were such that from 1858 all wine-producing areas were well connected with the principal consumer markets (mainly Paris and other large cities). The fall in transport costs was particularly beneficial for producers of the lowest-quality wines and those located farthest from large urban markets, such as those in the Midi region. Furthermore, the interconnection with new European railway networks facilitated exports to those neighbouring countries that produced little or no wine, such as Germany, Belgium, the Netherlands and Switzerland. The reduction in maritime transport costs particularly benefitted long-distance trade in high-quality bottled wine, transport costs for which became just a small proportion of the landed consumer price.

The liberalization of European trade involved the signing of bilateral treaties which had a most-favoured-nation clause. For France, the signing of the Cobden-Chevalier Treaty with Britain in 1860 boosted its exports to that country (Table 3.1) – they had been very sensitive until then to the high rates of tariff protection (Nye 2007). The climate of trade liberalization, which prevailed until the final decade of the century, contributed to the increase in exports. For wine, the early twentieth century constituted a less-favourable context due to the aforementioned tariff increases in American wine-producing countries. The situation became even worse after 1929, when the protectionist policies of the Great Depression reduced imports of higher-priced wines especially. As a result, France's share of the volume of global wine exports, which averaged 16 percent from 1900 to 1913 and 11 percent from 1920 to 1929, fell to just 4 percent from 1930 to 1938 (Anderson and Pinilla 2017).

From Golden Age to Phylloxera Crisis: 1850–1900

The third quarter of the nineteenth century was a golden age for French wine production and trade. The initial response to the expansion of demand was a moderate increase in the area under vines, which grew by approximately 10 percent from 1850 to 1870. However, in this period, the most relevant factor was the devastating transfer from the American continent to France of a series of fungal grapevine diseases, such as oidium, mildew and black rot, and the phylloxera insect. While the fungal diseases gave rise to a considerable drop in grape production, the impact of phylloxera was much more serious because it kills vines. The exchange of plants across the Atlantic therefore generated problems for which winegrowers had no solutions until science and technological innovation came to the rescue (Gale 2011). Scientific developments eventually found appropriate cures, but they increased production costs.

The first region in France where production was affected by phylloxera was the Midi, in the 1870s, from where it gradually spread throughout the country and culminated in the region of Champagne at the turn of the century. As a consequence, the fall in output did not occur simultaneously in all regions. Even so, in the 1880s and early 1890s, production averaged just 3,100 ML per year, compared with 5,700 ML during the boom of the 1870s. Such a sharp drop in production generated a substantial increase in the price of wine, which in real terms doubled.

Despite the efforts made by science to find a suitable solution to the phylloxera crisis, it was only from the mid-1880s that there was a consensus that the only solution was to replant with American vines. However, the adoption of American rootstocks was a difficult and complicated process. Direct-producer hybrids were planted first but were gradually abandoned due to the low quality of the wine obtained from their grapes. Finally, European varieties were grafted to American rootstocks, and even then significant effort was required to adapt them to the soils and climatic conditions of France (Paul 1996; Gale 2011). The replanting process began around 1880 and accelerated from 1890. It took until 1920 for the process to be completed.

The years of the phylloxera chaos were thus enormously complex. Domestic market demand fell much less than output despite higher prices (Figure 3.4).[4] Those winemakers who were faced with the task of replanting were unable to benefit from the higher prices, while those not affected

[4] Demand was highly inelastic with respect to price in the short term, but a low −0.33 percent in the long run (Pinilla and Ayuda 2008, p. 592).

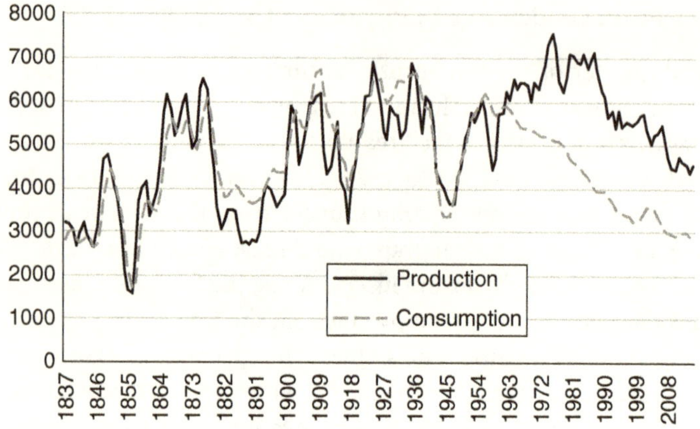

Figure 3.4 Volume of beverage wine production and consumption, France, 1835 to 2015 (ML, three-year averages to year shown).
Source: Anderson and Pinilla (2017).

until later on benefitted considerably from the higher prices. These high prices also encouraged the production of so-called artificial wines, by either hydrating imported raisins or adding hot water and sugar to fermentation tanks after draining off the good wine.[5]

The phylloxera plague not only represented an enormous cost due to the need to replant all of France's vineyards, but it also implied transcendental changes in production.[6] First, winegrowing became much more capital intensive and less land intensive. The high capital needs were not only related to the investment necessary for replanting, but also to a series of changes carried out in the growing process. The vines were planted less densely and in rows, with sufficient space left between them to work with ploughs. Wires were erected so that the vines could grow up them. The use of chemical products became a common and necessary practice.

[5] Lachiver (1988) estimates annual wine production using raisins in 1881–1896 at more than 200 ML and that obtained by adding water and sugar to pressed grapes at 150 ML per year in 1885–1899. Despite the importance that the reporting of fraud in artificial wine production had in the protests of the first decade of the twentieth century in the Midi region, these wines rarely accounted for more than 5 percent of national wine production (Pech 1975, p. 117; Meloni and Swinnen 2017, table 1). For more on this point, see Stanziani (2005).

[6] Gale (2011) estimates that the cost of buying the graft stocks necessary to replant French vineyards in 1880 would have been equivalent to 87 percent of the value of wine production that year. Based on Garrier (1989, p. 132), we estimate that the cost of reconstructing a hectare between 1885 and 1905 was equivalent to the value of wine production of between 4 and 6 has, depending on the method used.

As a result of the capital increase required and the strong initial investment, replanting occurred unequally in France. The overall trend was that only those regions or areas sufficiently specialized and with reasonable return expectations were replanted. Consequently, the more marginal vineyards disappeared, and the total area dedicated to growing vines decreased. Vineyards were also brought down from hills to lower ground. From 1910, the vineyards in France covered an area of around 1.5 million ha, 40 percent lower than the 2.5 million ha planted in 1875 (Figure 3.5). In terms of regional distribution, the changes were profound. The territorial relocation mostly favoured the Mediterranean Midi. Just four departments of this region accounted for more than 40 percent of wine production in the post-phylloxera era (Pech 1975). Meanwhile, the winegrowing area in the north and in the central-western regions (such as Charente) diminished considerably. However, the huge reduction in the area under vine was compensated for by a significant increase in yields, such that after 1900 production returned to prephylloxera levels (Figures 3.5 and 3.2).

This increase in yields also led to an increase in segmentation with respect to the qualities of wine produced. At the risk of oversimplifying, specialization increased in high-quality and bottled wines from those regions most specialized in exports, such as Champagne, Burgundy and Bordeaux, while production in the Midi was largely oriented towards bulk and ordinary wines for mass consumption in the domestic market, frequently reinforced by blending with wines with a higher alcohol content imported from Algeria or Spain. In the case of production destined for export, there was a clear trend towards exporting high-quality wines. Until the arrival of phylloxera, only 20 percent of the value of exported wine was bottled wine, but during the plague, that share increased significantly and remained high during the first third of the twentieth century, when it reached 50 percent. In the 1930s, bottled wine accounted for over 60 percent of the value of exported wine (Ayuda et al. 2016).

The situation also became complicated in foreign markets. The need to import wine to satisfy France's domestic demand and sustain its exports accelerated and consolidated the articulation of the global wine market with very long-term effects. First, an extraordinary and unique opportunity arose from these circumstances for those producers able to respond to the new French demand, particularly Spain, which was the country best positioned to do so (Pinilla and Serrano 2008). Second, producers in Spain and Italy who competed with France in the international market sought to take advantage of the difficulties encountered by France to expand their international market share, particularly in the low-quality segment. These

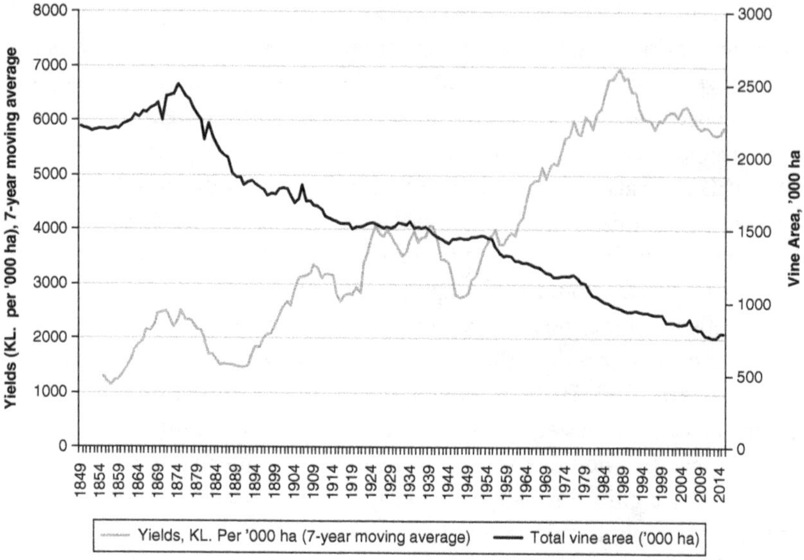

Figure 3.5 Total vine bearing area and yield, France, 1835 to 2015 (ha and KL per '000 ha).
Source: Anderson and Pinilla (2017).

attempts were fairly successful. Furthermore, emerging producers in the New World also used the French difficulties to increase their production, and in the final decade of the century they increased their tariff protection in order to reserve the home market for domestic producers (Table 3.3). Finally, Algerian wine producers, who were experiencing a boom thanks to the French colonial policy, found a golden opportunity to market their output produced in much larger vineyards than those in Metropolitan France, seeking to take advantage of their economies of scale.[7] Once colonial production had become able to supply the mainland market, Spanish wines were pushed out of France by a simple increase in tariff protection.

The situation also became complicated for exports, not only due to the growing competition emerging in some markets and the difficulties to maintain production oriented towards them, but also due to the weakening of demand in some key countries, particularly Britain, which was the centre of world imports of food and agricultural raw materials (Aparicio, Pinilla

[7] The scale of production was significantly higher in Algeria than in France. In Algeria, the 378 wine producers operating with more than 100 ha produced 38 percent of the wine in the 1930s, while their equivalents in France (just 127) produced only 3 percent (Cahill 1934).

and Serrano. 2009). According to Simpson (2011), the fall in demand could have been due to the expansion of exports during the golden years and fraudulent practices in exported wines, which destroyed the trust of consumers in products for which it was difficult to obtain sufficient information and which were prone to considerable variation in quality. The entrance of exports not only of fraudulent products sold as authentic wine, but also of lower-quality wines from key places such as the Bordeaux region, slowed the increase in consumption in these key markets and even caused a decline. Wine continued to be a luxury article reserved for the economic elite who were prepared to pay very high prices for exclusive products. The continued rise in the export of champagne, which at the end of the century was four times the figures of the mid-nineteenth century, contrasted with the strong fall in the rest of the wines.

From Crisis to Crisis and the Beginning of Public Intervention in the Industry: 1900–1938

The four first decades of the twentieth century were turbulent and problematic for French wine producers and exporters. The recovery in production became evident from the beginning of the century, reaching almost 7,000 ML in 1900. In addition to this high level of production, enormous volumes of wine were imported from abroad, particularly from Algeria. External demand was somewhat higher than that during the years of the phylloxera crisis, but still much lower than the maximum levels reached during the golden years. As a result, the prices of wine, which from the beginning of the 1890s had begun to fall as production recovered, continued their downward trend. In some years during the first decade of the century, they fell to levels that did not even cover production costs for low-quality wines. In the three following decades, producer prices remained relatively low and continued to fluctuate.[8] Excess supply was common during these four decades, and the disruption of World War I made the situation even more complex.

The structural situation of excess supply, which was worsened by the gradual increase in imports from Algeria, the external market situation and the new conditions for producing wine after vineyard reconstruction, generated a very difficult and complicated situation for most wine producers, depending on their region. Several developments during the first

[8] The high concentration of production in four departments of the Midi region meant that the annual variations in harvests due to weather had a large impact on the national harvest (Pech 1975).

third of the twentieth century, which extended those influences into the post–World War II era, are worth mentioning.

First, the excess supply, which was concentrated in the Midi region for low-quality wines, generated intense social conflict which culminated in revolts during the first decade of the century and an explosion in 1907. This open conflict between producers and the government led to mass resignations of local councils, tax strikes, public demonstrations of hundreds of thousands of people in many towns, insubordination of local reservists and violent repression of the protest movement by the authorities. The most important legacy of these actions was the building of capacity for collective action by winegrowers (Simpson 2011, p. 59). Their actions were twofold: a lobby was formed to pressure the authorities to favour their interests, and the emerging cooperative movement gained momentum to solve the problem for small producers of capturing the economies of scale needed for the new wine production conditions (Fernández and Simpson 2017).

Second, producers in high-quality wine regions, particularly Bordeaux, Burgundy or Champagne, who were concerned about the decline in external demand, concentrated their efforts on guaranteeing a product that was reliable for consumers and associated with luxury. To do this, they attempted to ensure that the wines made in their regions complied with minimum quality standards. They also avoided marketing wines from other regions under their brand names and origins; and they improved winemaking technologies in order to obtain better products.[9]

The concern for quality and the differentiation of their products from ordinary wine became a fundamental strategy for the wine industry in regions producing wines of high quality. The marketing techniques that had been successful for the champagne houses were not enough. It was necessary to assure consumers, particularly in foreign markets, that the high prices of these wines corresponded to their extraordinary quality. From the mid-nineteenth century, the champagne producers had built brands based on large investments in marketing and distribution networks, but they had also innovated technologically to ensure the quality of their products. In Bordeaux, where production was highly fragmented before the famous classification of 1855 was published, many other classifications were issued. The latter were based essentially on price, in order to inform consumers of the quality hierarchy of products (Phillips 2016, pp. 144–46).

[9] Louis Pasteur himself dedicated much effort to studying fermentation processes and the reasons that explained the deterioration of wines, such as yeasts and microbial processes (Loubère 1978, pp. 191–206).

That protected the reputation of the brands,[10] but technical innovation contributed to improve quality too (Roudié 1988).

Burgundy, which also had its own quality classification of wines from 1855, promoted the identification of the quality of each wine with its vintage (*millesime*) and its exact geographical location, stressing the characteristics of the land on which the wine was produced (*terroir*). This notion was later developed in the 1930s, whereby the concept of terroir included the history and culture of the producing area (Phillips 2016, pp. 235–36).

Third, the social conflict generated along the value chain, which was profoundly affected by the changes brought about by the phylloxera crisis, gave rise to increasing public intervention (Meloni and Swinnen 2013). The conflicts were varied and diverse. In the Midi region, there was a mass protest against fraud-induced low prices (Pech 1975). In Champagne, conflict arose first between those producers excluded from the new appellation of origin and the rest, and later between producers and traders. In Bordeaux, too, there were clashes between traders and small producers over the establishment of an appellation of origin (Guy 2003; Buvry 2005; Simpson 2011).

Initially, public intervention was carried out in the legislative field and was focused on seeking to combat fraud in production and limit production of so-called artificial wines. The increasing sale of fraudulent and adulterated wines and declining prices were major problems for quality wine producers from the late nineteenth century. The scarcity of wines caused by phylloxera had led merchants to adulterate wine with chemicals, and raise volume by adding water, sugar or industrial alcohol (Loubère 1990, pp. 104–6). Fraud concerning a wine's origin was another common practice by merchants who sold a blend of wines from different origins but sold it under a famous geographic name. By the early twentieth century, it was also frequent to find 'Burgundy' produced in Germany or Australia (Laurent 1958, p. 392).

Fraudulent practices continued after phylloxera, especially in regions where demand exceeded supply, as in Beaujolais (Simpson 2005). In response to falling demand caused by adulteration and counterfeiting, some wineries created their own brands and adopted strategies to ensure quality to consumers, such as forward integration into distribution. Producers of fine wines in Burgundy and Bordeaux also began to bottle wines at source and sell them under the name of the château (Loubère 1990,

10 The practice of adding 'chateau' to the wine brand or ownership increased from the mid-nineteenth century. There were fifty 'chateaux' in 1850, 700 in 1874, 1,000 in 1886, 1,800 in 1908, 2,000 in 1922 and 2,400 in 1949 (Garrier 2008, pp. 244–45).

pp. 109–10). Local producers believed that such fraudulent practices could explain the saturation of the market and falling prices in the early twentieth century, not least because they artificially increased the volume of production (Loubère 1990, pp. 113–14; Boulet and Bartoli 1995, p. 34; Simpson 2005). Producers in Champagne, Bordeaux and similar regions organized and lobbied the government for protection (Pijassou 1980; Roudié 1988; Simpson 2004 and 2005). In response, in 1905 France passed a law to prevent fraud, banning the sale of wines with an improper geographical name (Bréjoux and Blaquière 1948, p. 10; Pech 1975; Simpson 2004, p. 98; Stanziani 2005). Also, in 1907 an information system was created to disseminate facts about harvests and stock changes. Then during 1908–1911 a legislative framework was introduced to regulate the right to use geographic appellations of origin, which had the objective of guaranteeing the quality of wines from the areas included in them.

In 1908, the area of production of Champagne, and later Cognac, Armagnac, Banyuls, Clairette de Die and Bordeaux, began to be demarcated, so that only wines produced in the area could be sold under the geographical indication or appellation (Bréjoux and Blaquiére 1948, p. 11; Loubère 1990, pp. 113–14; Boulet and Bartoli 1995; Stanziani 2004; Simpson 2005). The first law with respect to the creation of the appellations was passed in 1919. This enabled interested parties to apply to the courts for their declaration and delimitation. It gave rise to a very complicated situation, with countless court proceedings and applications from a wide variety of different locations.

However, any local producer could take advantage of the higher prices and the advantages of the geographical name by extending their vine area or planting highly productive varieties. In fact, the share of wine with appellation in France's total wine production increased from 6 percent to 20 percent between 1920 to 1923 and 1932 to 1935 due to new plantings and higher yields (Bartoli and Boulet 1989, p. 43). Very abundant harvests of low-quality wines and low-alcohol content began to substantially reduce the value of the appellations created.

The cost of controlling demarcated wines was very high with existing traditional regulations such as statements of crops, the analysis of samples or the control of wine circulation. Furthermore, only wineries that had developed an image of quality through a single brand had incentives to market only quality wines under the regional name. To solve these free-rider problems, the Capus Act in 1927 established the obligation to strictly define the vine varieties, the production area and the methods of production, although it was only applied to Champagne. As the advantages of denominations increased, this encouraged production expansion and further eroded the advantages previously obtained (Berger 1978; Bréjoux and Blaquiére 1948; Boulet and Bartoli 1995).

In 1935, with the creation of the Appellations d' Origine Contrôlé, the provisions of the Capus Act were extended to the rest of the appellation wines. Under the control of an interprofessional organization, the Comité National des Appellations d' Origine, producers were forced to control themselves through strict regulations on varieties, yields and the alcohol content of wines (Hot 1938; Berger 1978; Lachiver 1988; Barthe 1989; Loubère 1990).

In the 1930s, public intervention went much further, seeking to regulate production, even anticipating the law commonly cited internationally as a starting point for these agricultural policies, namely the North American Agricultural Adjustment Act of 1933. The Statut de la Viticulture of 1931 sought to adjust supply to demand by establishing taxes on high yields, prohibiting the extension of vineyards (for all growers with more than 10 ha or who produced more than 50 KL), blocking excess production by producers, and obliging producers to distil part of the harvest to avoid surpluses. From 1934, grubbing-up premiums were introduced (compulsory from 1936 in some departments), sales were staggered to avoid falls in prices, and certain varieties of direct-producer hybrids were prohibited along with the marketing of the wine obtained from them. Finally, the law of 1935 created the controlled appellations of origin, establishing the geographical areas belonging to each appellation, the varieties permitted, the minimum alcohol contents and the permitted growing and winemaking procedures (Warner 1960; Lachiver 1988). The new *appellations* created under the law of 1935 added to those in force under the law of 1919. The new AOCs soon had an impact: in 1936, the year after their creation, their production represented 11 percent of the simple appellations, but by 1939 they represented 29 percent (Phillips 2016, p. 241).

Cooperatives were also seen as a solution to overproduction and falling prices, as an instrument of the state for implementing its regulatory policy (Loubère 1990; Fernández and Simpson 2017). Within the policy designed by the Statut of Viticulture, beginning in 1931 to 1935 with the blocking of surplus wines, France began granting short-term loans to cooperatives to store surplus production in an attempt to avoid sharp drops in prices. The government thereby attracted winegrowers to cooperation, while a part of production could remain in the cellars at least in the immediate months after harvest. Thus, between 1927 and 1939 the number of cooperatives increased from 353 to 827 (Fernández and Simpson 2017).

Obviously, external markets could not be controlled by French producers, traders or the government. Nor could the problems that arose internationally after World War I due to the Soviet revolution, the Austro-Hungarian Empire's collapse, Prohibition in the United States and intensifying protectionism in the southern cone of South America. Then the crash of 1929 and the subsequent Great Depression of the 1930s also led to a substantial fall in demand due to the fall in income.

FRANCE'S WINE INDUSTRY AFTER 1939

Crop shortages and high prices of wines during World War II and the immediate postwar years was followed by a series of overproduction crises, falling prices and increasing unrest in the wine sector in France.[11] In response to this, the French government introduced a highly interventionist policy. Previous measures of the *Statut de la Viticulture* aiming at eliminating poor quality surplus wines were reintroduced in 1953 (*Code du Vin*), which also aimed at increasing the average prices received by growers by focusing on quality (Bardissa 1976, pp. 42–3). The law of 1953 established a tax on high yields, the blocking and compulsory distillation of surplus production (10–16 percent of production), a subsidy for uprooting highly productive vines and the banning of new plantings. The Institut des Vins de Consommation Courante (IVCC) was created to develop this policy. Additionally, in 1959 the system of guaranteed and intervention prices that already existed for cereals, meat and milk was extended to wine (Branas 1957, pp. 84–5; Barthe 1975, pp. 8–11; Berger and Maurel 1980, p. 88; Spahni 1988, pp. 16–22; Barthe 1989, pp. 102–8; Gavignaud 2000, p. 146).

As a result of the subsidized uprooting and the banning of new plantings, a rapid decline in vine bearing area began in the mid-1950s at a rate of 200,000 ha every ten years (Figure 3.5). The vineyard area was especially reduced in the Midi, which was responsible for the production of most of the ordinary wines in France.[12] This process was accompanied by a decline in high-yield hybrid vines and common varieties such as Aramon, which were responsible for the production of very poor-quality wines. At the same time, the area planted with recommended higher-quality varieties increased,

[11] Harvests substantially declined in France in the 1940s as a result of the lack of labour, chemicals and draft animals and the destruction of vineyards during World War II (Lachiver 1988, p. 505).

[12] The vineyard area in the Midi decreased by almost one-third between 1950 and 1980 (authors' calculation from Lachiver 1988).

thanks to the Institut national de l'origine et de la qualité (INAO)[13] legislation that obliged growers to have a fixed proportion of 'noble' grape varieties (Lachiver 1988, pp. 509, 512).

This policy was complemented with increasing restrictions on imports. France has established the so-called qualitative complementarity within the colonial preferential system, based on the blending of metropolitan and Algerian wines. In the 1960s, 80 percent of French imports, an average of 1,000 ML, were red wines with high alcohol content. However, coinciding with the decreasing demand for ordinary wines in France, imports started to sharply decline in the mid-1960s (Figure 3.3). Following Algerian independence, imports from Algeria fell dramatically from 1965 to 1985, from over 800 ML to 30 ML (Bardissa 1976; Spahni 1988; Meloni and Swinnen 2014).

Besides import limitations and the regulation of the market for ordinary wines, efforts were made to improve the average quality of wines through the institution of appellations. The expansion of appellations continued after 1950, as observed in Table 3.4. The land under demarcated vines increased from 19 percent of the total from 1965 to 1969 to 52 percent in the early 1990s, and appellation wines constituted the majority of exports in the 1960s and 1970s (between 60 percent and 75 percent of total exports).

The expansion of appellation wines coincided with an important shift in the domestic consumption of wines in France. Before 1950, most western Europeans demanded cheap wines with a high alcohol content that was mainly acquired in bulk in traditional stores.[14] After the 1950s, however, the per capita quantity of wine started to decline in France (Figure 3.1), and preferences shifted from strong, cheap wines to lighter, higher-quality wines. This change in preferences occurred mainly as a consequence of rising per capita incomes and modernization of the retail distribution system.[15] Between 1960 and 1981 the consumption of appellation wines among the adult population increased from 13 to 24 litres per capita, while there was a decrease in consumption of ordinary wines from 115 to 73 litres. The weight of wines with appellation remained in the 1960s and 1970s around 10 to 12 percent of total consumption and amounted to 25 percent in the early 1980s, and 40 percent in 1990.[16]

[13] The INAO replaced the Comité National des Appelations d'Origine (CNAO) created in 1935.
[14] Nearly 80 percent of wines were sold in bulk in France before 1950 (Loubère 1990, p. 85).
[15] For changes in consumption and preferences, see Bettamio (1973, pp. 25–37); Garrier (2008); Boulet and Faillet (1973, pp. 45–52); Fernández (2012).
[16] Calculated from Loubère (1990, p. 168), ONIVINS (2001, p. 134) and Becker (1976, table 12).

Table 3.4 *Share of France's total vine area and wine export volume coming from regions of geographical indications (AOCs), 1965 to 1993 (%)*

	Share of vine area	Share of wine exports
1965–9	19	61
1970–4	21	74
1975–9	25	63
1980–4	31	45
1985–9	40	50
1990–3	46	52

Source: Authors' calculations from ONIVINS (1992, 2001).

Changes in consumption preferences shifted demand towards quality wines, but production of ordinary wines continued to increase. The area under vines declined, but yields rose from 4 to 6 KL per ha (Figure 3.5) as a consequence of the planting of highly productive varieties, the new methods of cultivation and new winemaking technologies (Branas 1957, pp. 67–8; Barthe 1975, pp. 4–6). Technological change in the wine industry accelerated after 1950, when the second phase of the 'wine revolution' started (Loubère 1990). The mechanization of viticulture, which had begun with the plow, was completed with the diffusion of tractors adapted to vineyards. New methods of pruning vineyards were introduced, and irrigation, fertilizer and other chemical use became widespread. Winemaking also was mechanized, with the introduction of continuous presses and other mechanical devices. Concrete tanks were replaced by steel containers for winemaking and wine preservation. Temperature control during fermentation was introduced, and conservation and aging in bottles were widely adopted. These new winemaking systems ensured freshness of wines could be retained longer. Consequently, the production of lighter wines, both in colour and body, increased alongside changes in demand in France and other major consuming countries (Loubère 1990, pp. 89–90).

However, these new methods of cultivation and winemaking also resulted in oversupply that accounted for an average of between 15 percent and 30 percent of total production in France from 1960 to 2000.[17] Permanent imbalance between supply and demand forced the government to impose mandatory distillation of wines. This policy was developed after the late 1960s by the Common Wine Policy of the European Economic

[17] Authors' calculation from OIV (1990–2000).

Community (EEC) which adopted France's highly interventionist policy (Meloni and Swinnen 2013). Plans to incentivize the uprooting of vines were also adopted by the EEC in an attempt to adjust supply to demand in the long term (Barceló 1991, p. 192).

Cooperatives were not only an instrument of the state for implementing its regulatory policy. The expansion of cooperatives during the first third of the twentieth century also contributed to the technical 'revolution' of the wine sector (Loubère 1990). The high cost of postphylloxera viticulture, which contrasted with the limited financial capacity of small growers, could be partially addressed with collective production. In addition, with cooperatives growers could devote themselves to cultivation and allow the cooperative to focus on improving the winemaking (Loubère 1990, pp. 97, 137). Cooperatives also facilitated increases in capital, knowledge and instruction. Decreasing production costs and higher industrial productivity ensued. Wine quality improved and market search expenses were reduced, increasing the marketability of wines and the prices obtained by winegrowers. Cooperatives had the cash flow to wait for the right time to sell, and could produce a more homogeneous wine of higher quality (Mandeville 1914, pp. 18–19, 35; Chevet 2009).

Cooperatives produced 35 percent of total output by 1957, and 52 percent by 2000 (Fernández and Simpson 2017). However, they mostly produced large volumes of ordinary wine and contributed little to the production of quality wines (Lachiver 1988, p. 541). The problem resulted, as highlighted by Fernández and Simpson (2017), from the fact that members were paid according to the weight and sugar content of grapes delivered. As a consequence, cooperative members had incentives to maximize their yields without worrying about quality (Gide 1926; Boulet and Laporte 1975, p. 25; Clavel and Baillaud 1985, pp. 101–3).

Distillation continued to be important in France between 1970 and 2000, although less wine was distilled in France as compared with Spain and Italy. This can be explained by the increasing production of quality wines in France that was stimulated by the increasing domestic demand for this type of wine and the producer incentives created through the institution of the Appellations d' Origine Contrôlé. Exports continued to increase through those three decades too (Figure 3.2).

The types of wines demanded abroad also changed from 1950. In Anglo-Saxon countries, wine consumption grew substantially. This expansion, which had to be met largely by imports, focused on light wines of higher quality than previously (Loubère 1990, p. 89; Fernández 2012). Changes in distribution, which included the increasing importance of supermarkets for wine selling and heavy investments in marketing and advertising (Spawton 1991, p. 287; Green, Ródriguez-Zúñiga and Seabra 2003; Fernández 2012), also influenced enormously this change in the international market for wine during the second half of the twentieth century. France took advantage of the increasing demand and was able to dominate the international market for quality wines by marketing bottled wines with geographical names (appellations),[18] especially in the expanding markets of the United Kingdom and the United States. Total exports rose at an annual rate of 5 percent from 1934 to 1973 (Fernández 2012). Despite appellation vineyards in France accounting for less than 30 percent of the national vine area before the 1970s, their wines accounted for the majority of France's export value, which caused their production to rise at an annual rate of 2.4 percent during the 1960s and 1970s, much more than total production (1 percent), as reflected in Table 3.5.[19] France specialized in the export of quality wines: the average prices of its wines sold in the international market were increasingly above those of other key wine-exporting countries (Figure 3.6). While it still imported wines, its average export price typically was about three times the average price of its imports (Anderson and Pinilla 2017).

From 1970, France continued its specialization in the export of fine wines, which allowed it to double its exports from 700 ML to almost 1400 ML. However, after the 1980s exports grew far faster for several New World countries (Anderson 2018, figure 12.7). *Appellation* wines dominated world export growth in the 1950s and 1960s, but changes in distribution and retailing after 1970 reduced the competitiveness of French appellations relative to that of large US and Australia wineries (Giraud-Héraud and Surry 2001; Anderson 2004). Both the United States and Australia were selling huge quantities of homogeneous wines under individual brands. During the 1990s especially, the strength of varietal wine from the New World grew in international markets. Wine production in Europe was highly fragmented, traditionally divided into small family farms, and unable to reach a high level of concentration in processing and distribution. Many producers offered a great variety of different wines with regional or local characteristics, marketed under geographical indication or chateaux names, whose quality and quantity differed each year. The fragmented production of

[18] This success was a key stimulus for its 'wine revolution', according to Loubère (1990, p. 165).

[19] This production growth was due to an increase in the area of protected vineyards and no growth in yield per hectare, as yields were strictly limited by law (Berger 1978).

Table 3.5 *Total and Appellations d'origine vine area by region, France, 2014–15 ('000 ha)*

	Total Area	%	Appellations d'origine area	%	% of Appellations d'origine in total area
Languedoc-Roussillon	222	29.6	69	15.7	31
Provence	85	11.4	64	14.5	75
Aquitaine	137	18.2	130	29.4	95
Corse	6	0.8	3	0.6	48
Midi-Pyrénées	34	4.5	10	2.3	30
Centre	21	2.8	19	4.2	88
Pays de la Loire	33	4.3	27	6.0	81
Rhône Alpes	48	6.4	36	8.1	75
Burgundy	31	4.2	31	7.0	99
Champagne	34	4.5	34	7.6	100
Alsace	16	2.1	16	3.5	99
Poitou	7	0.9	2	0.5	32
Poitou – Cognac	73	9.8	0	0.0	0
Others	5	0.6	2	0.5	44
Total	752	100.0	443	100.0	59

Source: Authors' calculations from FranceAgriMer (2016).

French and other European producers made it difficult for them to obtain economies of scale to cater to the new retailing establishments.[20]

RECENT DEVELOPMENTS

The French wine industry in recent years has been characterized by a decrease in national production, consumption and market shares. This situation has been exacerbated by the phenomena observed in Italy and Spain, which have similar production and consumption structures. French exports, however, are in a unique position compared to those neighbouring countries, as can be seen by distinguishing between the value and volume of exports. In terms of volume, there have been substantial declines between 1980 and 2016 in the market shares of France and Italy, as opposed to Spain. In terms of value, by contrast, France has significantly strengthened its position vis-à-vis its neighbours over that same period (Figure 3.6).

20 See Cavanagh and Clairmonte (1985) and Anderson (2004). Despite this growth, as the supply of each individual appellation was relatively small, price increases prompted some French wine producers to sell varietal wines in a similar way to California producers (Fernández 2012).

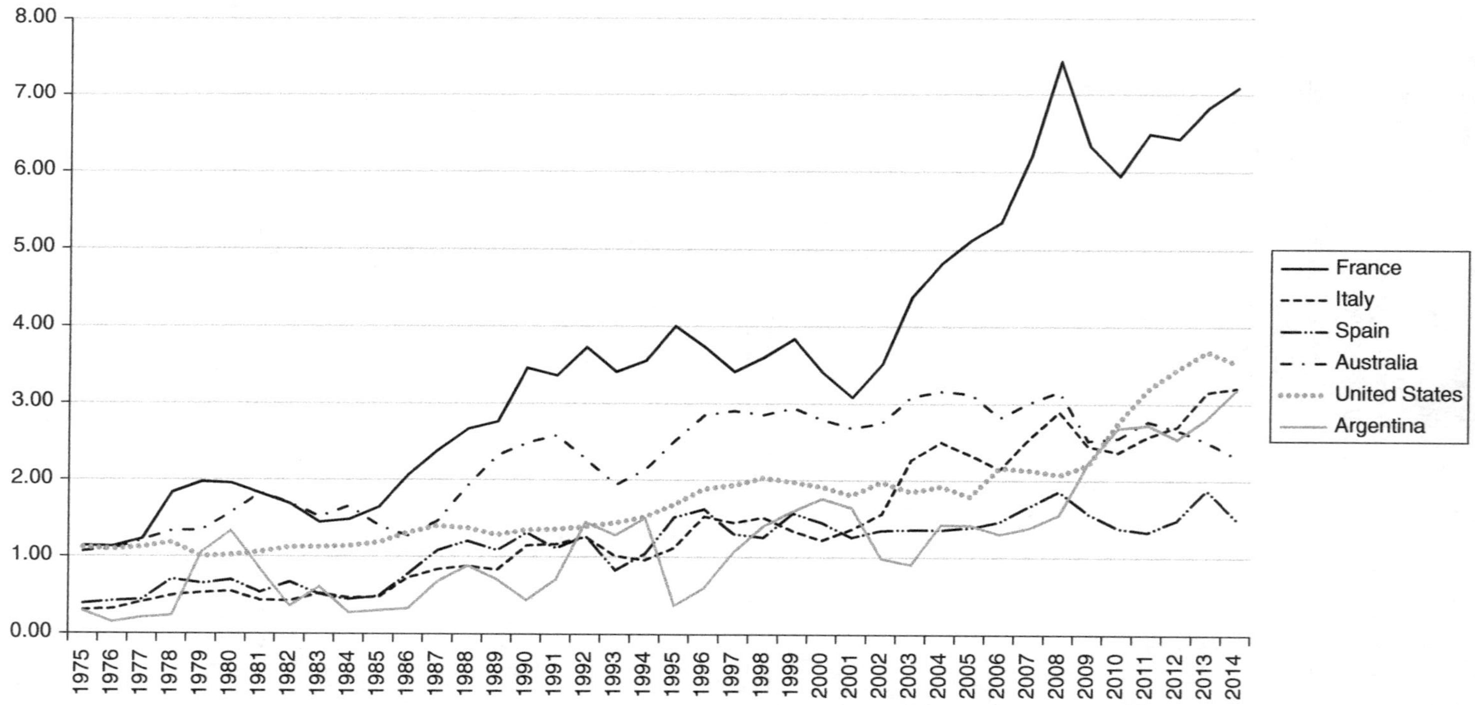

Figure 3.6 Unit value of wine exports, key exporting countries, 1975 to 2014 (current US$/litre).
Source: Anderson and Pinilla (2017).

Decline in Supply

Between 1980 and 2015, the French vineyard area declined by 295,000 ha (from 1.08 to 0.79 million ha), a loss of 27 percent. However, the decline appears to have stabilized since 2000. The other key European countries observed a similar or stronger downward trend: Italy lost 1.1 million ha over the same period (–61 percent) and Spain lost 0.7 million ha (–41 percent). By contrast, the global vineyard area increased by 2.5 million ha over the same period, an increase of 25 percent (Anderson and Pinilla 2017). As a result, France's share of world vineyard area declined from 13 percent to 11 percent between 1980 and 2015.[21]

At the same time, wine production decreased even more. Between the 1980–1984 and 2010–2014 periods, French wine production decreased from 6,802,200 KL to 4,558,324 KL, a decrease of 33 percent.[22] Italian production decreased by 43 percent, while Spanish production increased by 4 percent. World wine production decreased by about 20 percent and, in thirty-five years, France's share declined from 20 percent to 17 percent.

This decline in French production is due, in part, to the evolution of yields. Indeed, between 1986–1990 and 2009–2014, French yields dropped by 14 percent (while they stayed stable in Italy and increased in Spain by 67 percent, in Australia by 10 percent and in Chile by 23 percent). At the end of this period, Australian yields were one-third higher than French yields and about twice as high as Spanish yields, thanks to Australia's very efficient irrigation management.

However, the national French statistics hide large regional disparities, most notably between *appellations d'origine* vineyards and table wine vineyards. Yields of the former decreased by 11 to 23 percent, except in Champagne, where they dropped by only 4.5 percent. By contrast, the decrease in table wine yields was only about one-seventh in Languedoc, Provence and Vallée du Rhône.

Table 3.5 shows the geographical distribution of French vineyards. It can be seen that Languedoc-Roussillon accounts for close to one-third of the total French vineyard area, followed by Aquitaine and Provence. These

21 French statistics generally include data of Cognac production, an economically important spirit but with varying contribution to the French vineyard area. Thus, the Cognac vineyard area recorded 69,000 ha in 1960, 110,000 ha in 1975 and declined to 80,000 ha in 2015. The French vineyard area used for Cognac production, however, remained stable at 10–10.5 percent between 2009 and 2015.

22 Just 5.7 percent of the 6800 ML of wine produced at the beginning of the 1980s was used for Cognac distillation. Cognac production reached 15 percent of French wine production in the mid-1970s, remained stable until 1990 and then varied between 15 percent and 20 percent.

three regions combined account for close to 60 percent of France's vineyard area. However, Aquitaine ranks first in terms of *appellations d'origine* area.

Since the mid-1980s, Languedoc has lost 25 percent of both its total vineyard area and *appellations d'origine* area, compared with drops of only 13 percent in Provence and 4.5 percent in Aquitaine. It has, along with Poitou (Cognac production), the lowest proportion of *appellation* wines. Apart from these regions, Rhône-Alpes accounts for 6.4 percent of the French vineyard area, with the remaining French regions each representing less than 5 percent. The prestigious regions of Burgundy and Champagne account for 4.2 percent and 4.5 percent, respectively. In those two regions, nearly all vineyards are used for the production of *appellations d'origine* wines. Burgundy and Champagne also increased their total vineyard area by respectively 8.4 percent and 19.3 percent between 1985 and 2014. Loire vineyards, although accounting for a proportion similar to that of these two regions, has a much lower proportion of *appellations d'origine* area, and its total area decreased by one-fifth between 1985 and 2014. The Midi-Pyrénées wine region, which is as important as Burgundy and Champagne combined, declined by 19 percent over the same period. Alsace is a well-known but quite small wine region, representing 2.1 percent of French vineyard area and almost exclusively *appellations d'origine*. Its area increased by 9 percent between 1985 and 2014.

Structural Decline in Wine Consumption

Wine consumption in France has halved since the end of World War II, falling from 5700 ML in 1961–1964 to 2900 ML in 2015. In the early 1960s, wine consumption accounted for 94 percent of domestic production, with an average annual consumption per capita of 120 litres. This number dropped to 70 litres by the mid-1980s and to 45 litres in 2015, with domestic consumption accounting for only 60 percent of production around 1985 before slightly increasing to 65 percent in 2012–2014. Per capita wine consumption in France is getting closer to that of the other major European producers.

From the late 1980s to 2014, French alcohol consumption remained stable at about 29 ML. Together with Austria, Belgium and Germany, France has one of the highest consumption levels in the world. However, consumption is even higher in countries such as Bulgaria, Russia and Ukraine. Wine's share of all alcoholic beverage consumption in France has fallen, in terms of volume, from 65 percent in 1990 to 57 percent in 2014 (Anderson and Pinilla 2017).

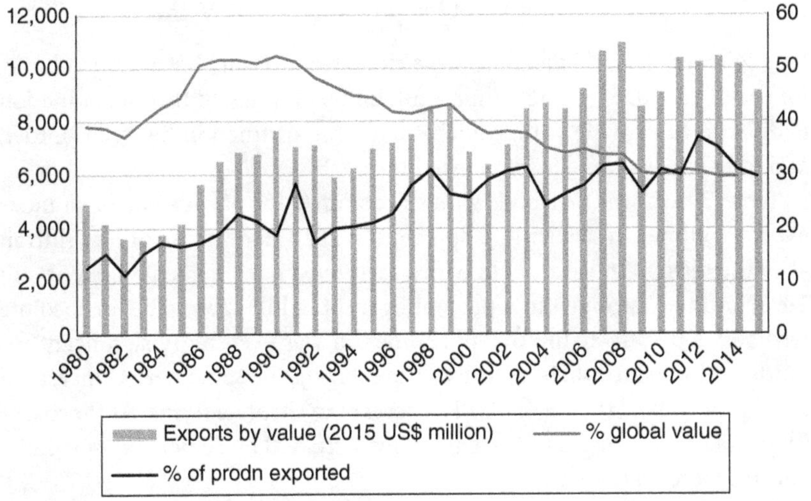

Figure 3.7 Value of wine exports, share of world wine export value, and share of domestic volume exported, France, 1980 to 2015 (2015 US$ million on left axis and % on right axis).
Source: Own calculations from Anderson and Pinilla (2017).

Compensatory Role for Exports and Increase in Quality

French exports for the 1980–2015 period exhibited moderate growth and accounted for a growing portion of French production (Figure 3.7).[23] However, this upward trend was not steady, and exports experienced a decline in the early 1980s and early 2000s. France's share of the value of global exports increased up to the mid-1980s, from around 40 percent to 50 percent, then slowly declined and stabilized around 2010 at 30 percent (Figure 3.7). In terms of volume of wine exports, though, the global market share of France, like that of Italy, has declined substantially, from just over 30 percent in the latter 1980s to less than 14 percent since 2013.

These numbers are consistent with the globalization of wine production. The evolution in value of exports of France, Italy and Spain show similar trends: substantial increases over the 1980–2015 period, with occasional crises intervening. Export values increased 6.5-fold in France, 9.5-fold in Italy and 12.7-fold in Spain between 1980–1984 and 2009–2014.

[23] In 2015, Cognac exports represented 97.5 percent of production and 27 percent of all spirits exports from France, with a relatively stable trade value (Bureau National Interprofessionnel du Cognac 2016).

Export Values and Proportion of Bulk Wine

France was the world's leading wine exporter in value, but not in volume, for the 1995–2015 period. While a full understanding of this phenomenon is difficult to provide with available data, the distinction between bottled and bulk wines provides some insights.

Table 3.6 shows that bulk wines accounted for 25 percent of France's export volumes in 1995 and 17 percent in 2014 (a decrease of one-fifth in absolute terms). In value, bulk wines accounted for 8 percent of exports in 1995, and that dropped to 4 percent by 2014, while their value in absolute terms rose by one-sixth. This phenomenon was even more significant for bottled wines since their export volume during the same period increased by 33 percent and their value by 170 percent in absolute terms. As for sparkling wines (including Champagne), they increased by 50 percent in volume and 192 percent in value.

These basic data show how premium positioning allowed France to remain the leading world exporter despite a strong reduction of its market share of export volume. This fact is also explained by the increasing international demand in the mid- to high-end segment of the quality range (consumers' willingness to pay in American and Asian markets).

Table 3.7 illustrates this through international comparisons between Australia and the other major exporting countries (France, Italy and Spain) for the 2000–2011 period. It should be noted that the four countries considered accounted for 82 percent of global exports in 2000 and still accounted for 70 percent in 2014. Here the distinction between bulk wines and bottled wines is striking. In 2000, Australia had the smallest share of bulk wine exports (representing only 14 percent of its total exports), while these represented a very high percentage in Italy (59 percent), in Spain (54 percent) and in global exports (42 percent). In 2011, bulk wine exports in Spain increased by about 195 percent, becoming the biggest wine exporter. Bulk wine exports in Australia also increased hugely (780 percent) and, as in Spain, since 2011 they have accounted for around half of Australia's total exports. By contrast, bulk wines remained stable in Italy, and France saw a 28 percent decrease in its bulk wine exports.

Table 3.8 shows bulk wine exports in terms of value. In that case, the share value of bulk wines in French exports is even smaller than in volume for the entire 2000–2011 period: in 2011 it was just 2.8 percent, representing a drop of 13 percent in eleven years. This share increased significantly in the other three countries. While Australian bulk wines accounted for only 7 percent of total exports in 2005, this number rose to 46 percent in 2011. Spanish bulk wines also saw a growth in value, but their share of total

Table 3.6 *Wine exports by product type, France, 1995 to 2014 (ML and '000 constant US$)*

	1995				2014				Variations in exports 1995–2014	
	Volume	%	Value	%	Volume	%	Value	%	Volume	Value
Bottle	778	66	1,846	61	1,037	72	4,984	62	33%	170%
Bulk	299	25	246	8	245	17	322	4	-18%	31%
Sparkling	106	9	937	31	158	11	2,733	34	50%	192%
Total	1,183	100	3,029	100	1,440	100	8,039	100	22%	166%

Source: Authors' calculations from FranceAgriMer (2015).

exports remained modest (20 percent) compared to Australia. Similarly, Italy saw an increase in value of bulk wine exports (by 70 percent in eleven years), but their share of national exports has declined.

These statistics demonstrate how the loss of market share and the decline in French exports over the recent period are in fact the consequences of changes in economic and production strategies. These strategies are supported by public policies promoting quality wines over production and export volumes.

Higher Imports than Other Main Wine-Exporting Countries

After a sharp decline post–World War II, French imports slowly decreased until 1980, then levelled off and started to increase again in 2000. While France accounted for about 16 percent of global imports around 1980, they now stand at only about 5 percent. French imports mostly come from Spain (about 60 percent), with Italy far behind. Spain accounted for 58 percent of the volume of French wine imports in 2010 and 75 percent in 2015. France's main wine imports consist of bulk wines without geographical denomination (68 percent from Spain and 5 percent from Italy). Over the past fifteen years, Spain took over Italy (which supplied 55 percent of that market in 2000) as the leading exporter to the French market. As for bottled wines, the market is held mostly by Spain and Portugal (especially Porto). Spain and Italy are small wine importers, with their imports representing no more than 2 percent of global imports.

In value, the trends are different, as Spain represents only 34 percent of French imports. Italy's value share remained steady over the past four years. Compared to 2000, Italy lost market shares in bulk wines and

Table 3.7 *Volume and share of wine exports shipped in bulk, France, Italy, Spain and Australia, 2000 to 2016 (ML and %)*

	2000			2008			2016			
	Volume	% Total	World export share (%)	Volume	% Total	World export share (%)	Volume	% Total	World export share (%)	% change 2000–16
France	39	12.5	2.0	173	25.0	4.4	315	38.7	10.3	971
Italy	398	51.5	18.0	1,624	65.7	41.4	1,267	56.8	31.4	218
Spain	365	24.6	16.5	264	19.3	6.7	214	14.9	5.3	–41
Australia	859	49.6	38.9	559	30.9	14.3	537	26.0	13.3	–37

Source: Anderson and Nelgen (2011) and Anderson, Nelgen and Pinilla (2017).

Table 3.8 *Value and share of wine exports shipped in bulk, France, Italy, Spain and Australia, 2000 to 2016 (US$m and %)*

	2000		2008		2016		
	Value	% from country	Value	% from country	Value	% from country	Variation 2000–16 (%)
France	37	4.1	188	8.9	313	18.4	747
Italy	206	17.8	521	18.0	550	18.5	167
Spain	303	6.0	406	4.0	314	3.4	4
Australia	320	14.3	488	9.0	426	6.8	33

Source: Anderson and Nelgen (2011) and Anderson, Nelgen and Pinilla (2012).

gained market shares in bottled wines (including sparkling wines), particularly in 2014 and 2015. Portugal, on the other hand, has experienced an erosion of its volume share in the last fifteen years; however, since 2005 it mainly exports bottled quality wines, which explains it high value share (15 percent in value against 5 percent in volume in 2015). Imports from other countries account for about 4 percent in volume and 20 percent in value. In the low-volume segment, imports are thus highly valued. There are therefore important differences between exporters such as the Maghreb or central/western European countries, where the wine prices are relatively low, and more atypical exporters where wine prices are high. French consumption habits based on specialty products (e.g., Porto) or wine origin criteria account for most of the discrepancy in import statistics between France and its neighbouring countries of Spain and Italy.

THE NEAR FUTURE

The decision to reduce French wine production (pulling out vines, improving varietal selection, creating protected geographical denominations), driven in part by public policy, allowed a sharp rise in added value. This higher added value comes from the packaging (bottles), the renowned *appellations d'origine* (Champagne, Bordeaux, Burgundy, etc.) and the qualitative repositioning of some wine regions (Languedoc-Roussillon). This is associated with important regional differences in France, with some regions experiencing growth in area, volume and value (Champagne, Alsace, Cognac) and others experiencing a decline in volume (Bordeaux, Vallée du Rhône, Languedoc-Roussillon). The French wine industry is divided into approximately ten production areas, each with its own identity, wine types, marketing schemes and size of production sites. Moreover, the presence of strong brands and powerful industrial groups in certain regions (e.g., Champagne, Cognac) often contrasts with the more isolated, fragmented production sites of other regions (Bordeaux, Burgundy).

Domestic consumption of wine is still declining, reaching less than 50 litres per capita per year (compared to 100 litres in 1975). This trend is strongly linked to changes in drinking habits (regular wine consumers in France now represent only 15 percent of the adult population) and is accompanied by the recent strong increase in Bag-in-Box consumption (which in 2015 accounted for 38 percent of market share in volume and 24 percent of still wines in value). The changes in the demand structure have also forced France to adjust to international market standards, meeting the requirements of the high-end segment markets in the United States and Asia and less-traditional consumption criteria, including new types of packaging, organic wines and health and environmental standards of emerging markets in Germany and Scandinavian countries.

REFERENCES

Anderson, K. (ed.) (2004), *The World's Wine Markets: Globalization at Work*, London: Edward Elgar.

(2018), 'Australia and New Zealand', ch. 12 in *Wine Globalization: A New Comparative History*, edited by K. Anderson and V. Pinilla, Cambridge and New York: Cambridge University Press.

Anderson, K. and S. Nelgen (2011), *Global Wine Markets, 1961 to 2009: A Statistical Compendium*, Adelaide: University of Adelaide Press. Also freely available as an ebook at www.adelaide.edu.au/ press/ titles/ global- wine and as Excel files at www .adelaide.edu.au/ wine- econ/ databases/ GWM

Anderson, K., S. Nelgen and V. Pinilla (2017), *Global Wine Markets, 1860 to 2016: A Statistical Compendium*, Adelaide: University of Adelaide Press. Also freely available as an ebook at www.adelaide.edu.au/press/

Anderson, K., D. Norman and G. Wittwer (2004), 'The Global Picture', pp. 14–58 in *The World's Wine Markets: Globalization at Work*, edited by K. Anderson, London: Edward Elgar.

Anderson, K. and V. Pinilla (with the assistance of A. J. Holmes) (2017), *Annual Database of Global Wine Markets, 1835 to 2015*, freely available in Excel at the University of Adelaide's Wine Economics Research Centre, www.adelaide.edu.au/wine-econ/databases

Aparicio, G., V. Pinilla and R. Serrano (2009), 'Europe and the International Trade in Agricultural and Food Products, 1870–2000', pp. 86–110 in *Agriculture and Economic Development in Europe Since 1870*, edited by P. Lains and V. Pinilla, London: Routledge.

Ayuda, M. I., H. Ferrer and V. Pinilla (2016), 'French Wine Exports, 1849–1938: A Gravity Model Approach', American Association of Wine Economists (AAWE) Conference paper, Bordeaux, June.

Barceló, L. V. (1991), *Liberalización, ajuste y reestructuración de la agricultura española*, Madrid: Instituto de Estudios Económicos.

Bardissa, J. (1976), *Cent ans de guerre du vin*, Paris: Tema éditions.

Barthe, R. (1975), *25 ans d'organisation communautaire du secteur vitivinicole (1950–75)*, Montpellier: École Nationale Supérieur Agronomique de Montpellier.

(1989), *L'Europe du vin. 25 ans d'organisation communautaire du secteur vitivinicole (1962–1987)*, Paris: Editions Cujas.

Bartoli, P. and D. Boulet (1989), *Dynamique et régulation de la sphère agro-alimentaire: l'exemple viticole*, Montpellier: INRA.

Becker, W. (1976), 'Importation et consommation du vin', in *Symposium international sur la consommation du vin dans le monde*, Avignon, 15–18 June: rapports et communications présentés par les conférenciers. [s.l.: s.n.].

Berger, A. (1978), *Le vin d'appellation d'origine contrôlée*, Paris: Institut National de la Recherche Agronomique, Economie et Sociologie Rurales.

Berger, A. and F. Maurel (1980), *La viticulture et l'économie du Languedoc du XVIIIe siècle à nos jours*, Montpellier: Les Editions du Faubourg.

Bettamio, G. (1973), *Il mercato comune del vino: aspetti e prospettive del settore vinicolo nella CEE*, Bologna: Edagricole.

Bureau National Interprofessionnel du Cognac (2016), www.cognac.fr, accessed 10 January 2017.

Boulet, D. and P. Bartoli (1995), *Fondements de l'économie des AOC et construction sociale de la qualité. L'exemple de la filière vitivinicole*, Montpellier: ENSA- INRA.

Boulet, D. and R. Faillet (1973), *Elements pour l'étude du système de production, transformation, distribution du vin*, Montpellier: INRA.

Boulet, D. and J. P. Laporte (1975), *Contributions a une analyse économique de l'organisation coopérative en agriculture. Études sur la coopération vinicole*, Montpellier: INRA.

Branas, J. (1957), *La production viticole de la zone franc en 1954: rapport au Conseil supérieur de l'agriculture (Section union française)*, Paris: Ministère de l'Agriculture.

Bréjoux, P. and J. Blaquiére (1948), *Précis de législation des appellations d'origine des vins et eaux-de-vie*, Montpellier: Causse, Graille, Castelnau.

Buvry, M. (2005), *Une histoire du champagne*, Saint-Cyr-sur-Loire: Editions Alan Sutton.

Cahill, R. (1934), *Economic Conditions in France*, London: Department of Overseas Trade.

Cavanagh, J. and F. F. Clairmonte (1985), *Alcoholic Beverages: Dimensions of Corporate Power*, London: Croom Helm.

Chevet, J. M. (2009), 'Cooperative Cellars and the Regrouping of the Supply in France in the Twentieth Century', pp. 253–280 in *Exploring the Food Chain: Food Production and Food Processing in Western Europe, 1850–1990*, edited by I. Segers, J. Bieleman and E. Buyst, Turnhout: Brepols.

Clavel, J. and R. Baillaud (1985), *Histoire et avenir des vins en Languedoc*, Toulouse: Privat.

Desbois-Thibault, C. (2003), *L'extraordinaire aventure du Champagne. Moët&Chandon. Una affaire de famille*, Paris: Presses Universitaires de France.

FranceAgriMer (2015), *Les synthèses de FranceAgriMer*, Montreuil: FranceAgriMer, 31 October.

(2016), *Données et bilan. Les chiffres de la filière viti-vinicole 2005/2015*, Montreuil: FranceAgriMer.
Fernández, E. (2012), 'Especialización en baja calidad: España y el mercado internacional del vino, 1950–1990', *Historia Agraria* 56: 41–76.
Fernández, E. and J. Simpson (2017), 'Product Quality or Market Regulation? Explaining the Slow Growth of Europe's Wine Cooperatives, 1880–1980', *Economic History Review* 70(1): 122–42.
Gale, G. (2011), *Dying on the Vine: How Phylloxera Transformed Wine*, Berkeley and Los Angeles: University of California Press.
Garrier, G. (1989), *Le phylloxéra: une guerre de trente ans 1870–1900*, París: Albin Michel.
(2008), *Histoire sociale et culturelle du vin; suivie de, Les mots de la vigne et du vin*, Paris: Larousse-Bordas.
Gavignaud, G. (2000), *Le Languedoc viticole, la Méditerranée et l'Europe au siècle dernier*, Montpellier: Publications de l'Université Paul Valéry.
Gide, C. (1926), *Les associations cooperatives agricoles*, Paris: Association pour l'enseignement de la cooperation.
Giraud-Héraud, E. and Y. Surry (2001), 'Les réponses de la recherche aux nouveaux enjeux de l'économie viti-vinicole', *Cahiers d'Economie et Sociologie Rurale* 60–1: 5–24.
Green, R., M. Ródriguez-Zúñiga and A. Seabra (2003), 'Las empresas de vino de los países del Mediterráneo, frente al mercado en transición', *Distribución y Consumo* 13(71): 77–93.
Guy, K. M. (2003), *When Champagne Became French. Wine and the Making of a National Identity*, Baltimore: Johns Hopkins University Press.
Hot, A. (1938), *Les appellations d'origine en France et a l'étranger*, Montpellier: Editions de La Journée vinicole.
Isnard, H. (1954), *La vigne en Algérie, étude géographique*, Gap: Ophrys.
Lachiver, M. (1988), *Vins, vignes et vignerons. Histoire du vignoble francais*, Lille: Fayard.
Laurent, R. (1958), *Les vignerons de la Côte d'Or au XIX siècle*, Paris: Société des Belles Lettres, Vol II.
Loubère, L. A. (1978), *The Red and the White: A History of Wine in France and Italy in the Nineteenth Century*, Albany: State University of New York Press.
(1990), *The Wine Revolution in France: The Twentieth Century*, Princeton, NJ: Princeton University Press.
Mandeville, L. (1914), *Étude sur les sociétés coopératives de vinification du midi de la France*, Toulouse: Impr. Douladoure-privat.
Meloni, G. and J. Swinnen (2013), 'The Political Economy of European Wine Regulations', *Journal of Wine Economics* 8(3): 244–84.
(2014), 'The Rise and Fall of the World's Largest Wine Exporter – and Its Institutional Legacy', *Journal of Wine Economics* 9(1): 3–33.
(2017), 'Standards, Tariffs and Trade: The Rise and Fall of the Raisin Trade Between Greece and France in the Late 19th Century and the Definition of Wine', AAWE Working Paper 208, January.
(2018), 'Algeria, Morocco and Tunisia', ch. 16 in *Wine' Globalization: A New Comparative History*, edited by K. Anderson and V. Pinilla, Cambridge and New York: Cambridge University Press.
Nourrison, D. (1990), *Le Buveur du XIXe siècle*, Paris: Albin Michel.
Nye, J. V. C. (2007), *War, Wine, and Taxes: The Political Economy of Anglo-French Trade, 1689–1900*, Princeton, NJ: Princeton University Press.

OIV (1990–2000), *Situations et statistiques du secteur vitivinicole mondial. Suplement to the Bulletin de L'Office International de la Vigne et du Vin*, Paris: OIV.

ONIVINS (1992), *Statistiques sur la filière viti-vinicole*, Paris: ONIVINS, Division Études et Marchés.

ONIVINS (2001), *Donnés chiffrées sur la filière viti-vinicole*, Paris: ONIVINS.

Paul, H. (1996), *Science, Vine and Wine in Modern France*, Cambridge and New York: Cambridge University Press.

Pech, R. (1975), *Enterprise viticole et capitalisme en Languedoc-Roussillon: du Phylloxera aux crises de mevente*, Toulouse: Publications de l'Université de Toulouse.

Phillips, R. (2016), *French Wine: A History*, Berkeley: University of California Press.

Pijassou, R. (1980), *Le Médoc: un grand vignoble de qualité*, Paris: J. Tallandier.

Pinilla, V. and M. I. Ayuda (2002), 'The Political Economy of the Wine Trade: Spanish Exports and the International Market, 1890–1935', *European Review of Economic History* 6: 51–85.

(2007), 'The International Wine Market, 1850–1938: An Opportunity for Export Growth in Southern Europe?' pp. 179–99 in *The Golden Grape: Wine, Society and Globalization, Multidisciplinary Perspectives on the Wine Industry*, edited by G. Campbell and N. Gibert, London: Palgrave Macmillan.

(2008), 'Market Dynamism and International Trade: A Case Study of Mediterranean Agricultural Products, 1850–1935', *Applied Economics* 40(5): 583–95.

Pinilla, V. and R. Serrano (2008), 'The Agricultural and Food Trade in the First Globalization: Spanish Table Wine Exports 1871 to 1935 – A Case Study', *Journal of Wine Economics* 3(2): 132–48.

Roudié, P. H. (1988), *Vignobles et vignerons du Bordelais: 1850–1980*, Paris: Éditions du Centre National de la Recherche Scientifique.

Simpson, J. (2004), 'Selling to Reluctant Drinkers: The British Wine Market, 1860–1914', *Economic History Review* 57(1): 80–108.

(2005), 'Cooperation and Conflicts: Institutional Innovation in France's Wine Markets, 1870–1911', *Business History Review* 79: 527–58.

(2011), *Creating Wine: The Emergence of a World Industry, 1840–1914*, Princeton, NJ: Princeton University Press.

Spahni, P. (1988), *The Common Wine Policy and Price Stabilization*, Avebury (Gower): Aldershot.

Spawton, A. L. (1991), 'Development in the Global Alcoholic Drinks Industry and Its Implications for the Future Marketing of Wine', pp. 275–88 in *Vine and Wine Economy: Proceedings of the International Symposium, Kecskemét, Hungary, 25–29 June 1990*, edited by E. P. Botos, Amsterdam: Elsevier.

Stanziani, A. (2004), 'La construction de la qualité du vin, 1880–1914', pp. 123–50 in *La qualité des produits en France, XVIIIe-XXe siècle*, edited by A. Stanziani, Belin: Paris.

(2005), *Histoire de la qualité alimentaire (XIXe-XXe siècle)*, Paris: Seuil.

Vizetelli, H. (1882), *A History of Champagne, with Notes on Other Sparkling Wines of France*, London: Henry Sotheran.

Warner, Ch. K. (1960), *The Winegrowers of France and the Government Since 1875*, New York: Columbia University Press.

Wolikow, C. and S. Wolikow (2012), *Champagne. Histoire inattendue*, Paris: Les editions de l'atelier.

4

Germany, Austria and Switzerland

Karl Storchmann

This chapter examines wine market developments in three contiguous countries sharing a common language, long histories of human settlement, including Roman influences two millennia ago, and a cool climate for growing winegrapes. Germany and Austria also share a history of changing national boundaries during the 180-year focus of the present study. This makes it difficult to assemble data (especially on international trade) for the communities that were within current national boundaries. Nonetheless, a serious effort has been made to compile wine production and consumption data to match the available real gross domestic product (GDP), population and total merchandise trade data that relate to the areas within the current borders of these countries.

Since the various turning points in the markets for wine in these countries are not the same, it is necessary to cover each country separately. We do so in order of their populations, beginning with Germany and ending with Switzerland.

GERMANY

Despite cultivating grapes since Roman times (Bassermann-Jordan 1907), Germany has never been a major wine-producing country. Its marginal climate restricts grape growing to the valleys of the Rhine River and its Ahr, Mosel, Nahe, Main, and Neckar tributaries in the southwest. In addition, some professional viticulture, although at a much smaller scale, can also be found in the valleys of the Saale-Unstrut and the Elbe River in the eastern part of present-day Germany.

However, Germany in its current borders has only existed since 1990, when West and East Germany reunified. At one time or another, a few other viticultural regions belonged to what was then called Germany (see also

Storchmann 2017). One was France's Alsace-Lorraine, which was part of the German Empire between 1871 and 1918; in some years it accounted for as much as one-third of German wine production. Similarly significant was the merger with Austria, which joined Nazi Germany in 1938 and became the province Reichsgau Ostmark until 1945. A few somewhat smaller wine-growing regions in Posen and Silesia (e.g., Zielona Góra, in German *Grünberg*), now in Poland, once belonged to Prussia and, in the century up to 1818, were virtually the only domestic wine suppliers within the kingdom. Since the present comparative analysis refers to areas within present-day national borders, the data for 'German wine production' exclude Alsace-Lorraine, the Polish regions and Austria by reaggregating regional production data available in official statistics.

Overview

The vineyard bearing area in present-day Germany from the mid-nineteenth century to the end of World War II is characterized by stepwise declines interrupted by short periods of stabilization. In 1947, the area was at a low of 49,500 ha before rapidly recovering to more than 100,000 ha by the end of the twentieth century. This is the highest level in Germany in almost 200 years (Figure 4.1).

Wine production in Germany follows the downward trend in vineyard area to the 1930s, and then grows faster than the vine area: between 1945 and 2015 the vine area doubled while wine production quintupled (Figure 4.1). Yield increases may be due to improved production technologies, more conducive climatic conditions or regional shifts in viticulture to more productive areas within Germany. Yields of Schloss Johannisberg in the Rheingau region, an estate that has farmed the same vineyards planted only with Riesling grapes for centuries, follow a very similar path since 1700 to those of Germany as a whole (Staab, Seelinger and Schleicher 2001; Storchmann 2005, 2017), which suggests changed production technologies or climatic conditions were key drivers. Aside from increasing average growing season temperatures, Storchmann (2017) mentions particularly the significant decline in the number of late spring frost days after 1900.

Up until 1930, France's wine yields averaged about 3 tonnes per hectare (t/ha), while Germany had about 2 t/ha and Spain and Italy only about one t/ha. However, beginning in the 1930s, Germany began to improve its vineyard productivity. At first, the rising yield trend was interrupted by World War II, but by the mid-1950s Germany reached the French vine productivity level of then about 4 t/ha. In the 1980s, German yields peaked

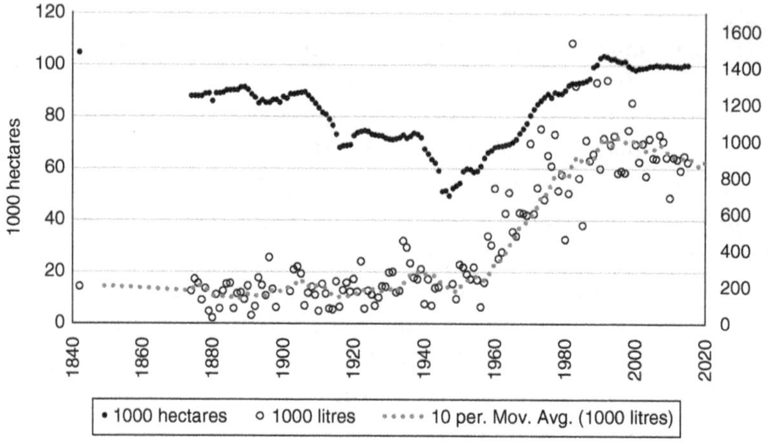

Figure 4.1 Vineyard bearing area (not including Alsace, Austria and Poland) and wine production, Germany, 1842 to 2015 ('000 ha and KL).
Source: Anderson and Pinilla (2017).

at 11 t/ha, well above French levels of 6 t/ha, before stabilizing at around 9 t/ha, or 50 percent above French and Italian yields and three times those of Spain.

Germany has always had one of the highest per capita alcohol consumption levels outside France and Italy, roughly comparable with the United Kingdom. During the second half of the nineteenth century, it was about 10 litres, compared to up to 25 litres in France. Except during the two World Wars, when France's alcohol consumption plummeted temporarily, this gap even widened over the first half of the twentieth century; but from the beginning of the economic recovery following World War II, Germany's per capita alcohol consumption steadily increased until the late 1970s, when it exceeded its previous peak consumption of 10.8 litres in 1900. However, since 1980 alcohol consumption has slowly declined in Germany as elsewhere, and is now just above the per capita alcohol consumption of France, the United Kingdom and the United States at slightly under 10 litres (Figure 4.2(a)). In Western Europe, only Belgians (11 litres) and Austrians (10.6 litres) consume more alcohol per capita than Germans (Anderson and Pinilla 2017).

In addition to changing aggregate levels, there have also been significant compositional changes in German alcohol consumption. In contrast to France and Italy, Germany's alcohol consumption has been dominated historically by beer. The beer share of total alcohol consumption has changed only a little over the past 150 years and has remained close to 50 percent.

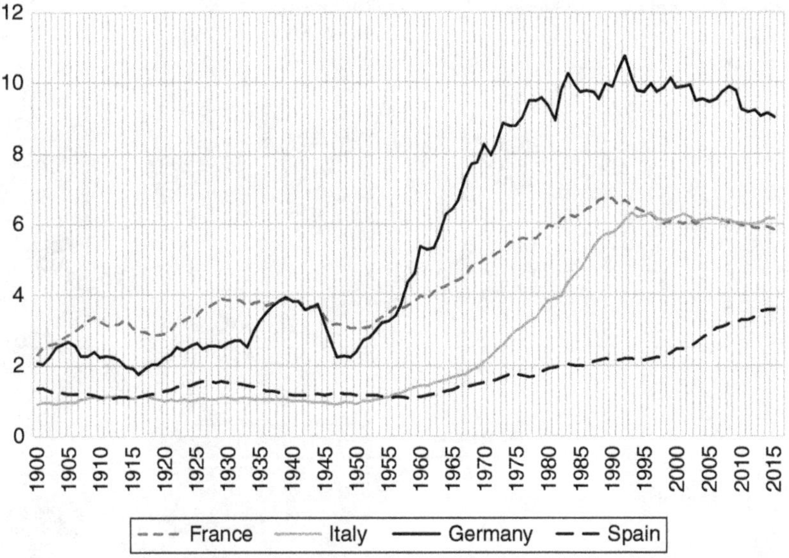

Figure 4.2 Wine yields in France, Germany, Italy and Spain, 1900 to 2015 (KL/ha, ten-year moving average).
Source: Anderson and Pinilla (2017).

However, wine has replaced much spirits consumption: the spirits' share was more than 40 percent in 1900, it fell to 24 percent by 1976 and now is just below 20 percent, while wine's share rose from 13 percent in 1900 to over 26 percent in 1976 to now about one-third (Figure 4.2(b)). There are also pronounced regional differences within Germany, though: the northern and eastern regions focus on beer and spirits while the southwestern regions, especially Baden-Württemberg, have the highest per capita wine consumption (Wiesgen-Pick 2016).

Although German viticulture has become more productive since the 1930s, domestic production has almost never been able to satisfy all domestic demands. Germany has been the world's largest wine importer by volume since 1976, and is ranked second or third for most of the previous ten decades behind France, Switzerland and occasionally the United Kingdom (Anderson and Pinilla 2017). Wine imports by Germany grew in the 1930s, and soared after post–World War II reconstruction, but wine exports also began growing from the 1970s. Such intraindustry trade made sense because Germany's competitiveness has been mostly in white wines, with reds being imported from warmer countries to its south. Since the 1960s, the share of imports in domestic wine consumption has risen from around 50 percent to more than 80 percent (Figure 4.3).

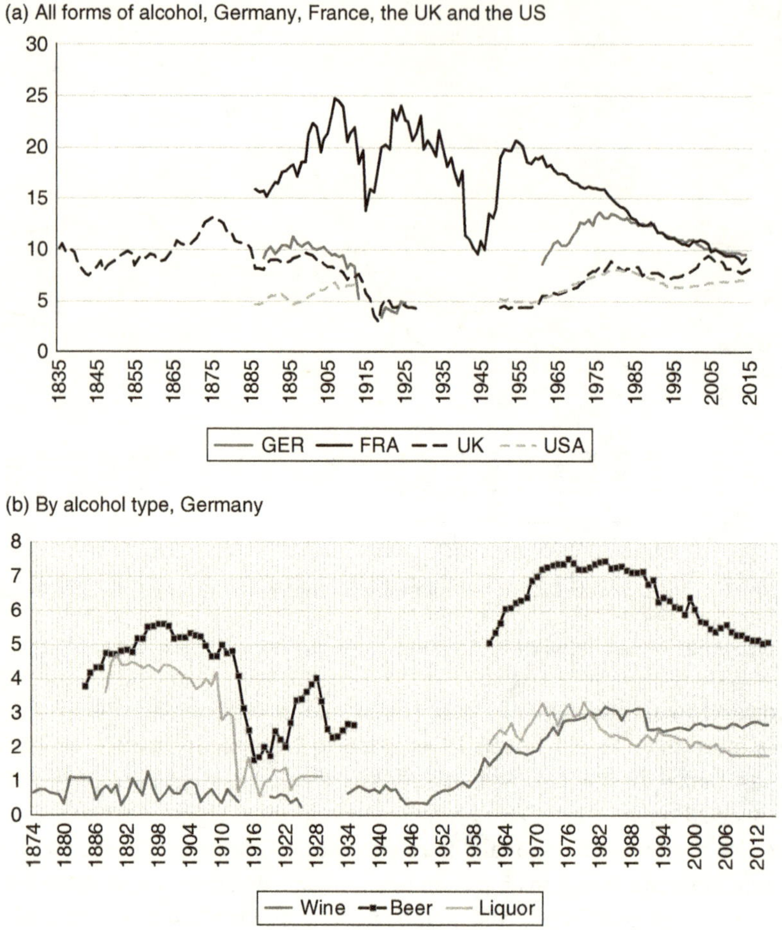

Figure 4.3 Per capita alcohol consumption in Germany, France, the United Kingdom and the United States, 1874 to 2015 (litres of alcohol).
Source: Anderson and Pinilla (2017).

To understand the forces behind these trends, the rest of this section is divided into five time periods.

From Napoleon to German Unification: 1794 to 1871

For most of its history, present-day Germany consisted of an extraordinary large number of small kingdoms, duchies and free cities, all sovereign economic zones with their own customs and tax regulations. This fragmentation was reduced somewhat during 1794 to 1815 when most of Germany was under French rule. In 1801, all German states west of the Rhine River, which included the wine regions Ahr, Mosel, Nahe, Rheinhessen and Pfalz, were incorporated into France. As a direct result, many of the old domestic customs and trade barriers ceased to exist. In addition, as in revolutionary France, the assets of the church and nobility were expropriated and put up for public auction (Storchmann 2006), leading to a substantial increase in the number of private, independent vintners. Along with the abolishment of the feudal upper class and the related constraints, the French authorities also introduced a vineyard classification system. As in Burgundy and other parts of France, prices of vineyard sites were assessed with the objective of introducing a 'fair tax' by levying land according to its profitability (Beck 1869; Ashenfelter and Storchmann 2010). In general, the institutional changes during the French period tended to be deregulatory and pro-business, and greatly benefitted viticulture (Meyer 1926; Winter-Tarvainen 1992).

However, the French period did not last long. After the Battle of Waterloo and Napoleon's final defeat, the Rhineland (which encompasses the viticultural regions of Mosel, Mittelrhein, Nahe and Ahr) fell to Prussia, while the Palatinate (Pfalz) fell to Bavaria. Hesse Darmstadt received what is now known as Rheinhessen (also the home of *Liebfraumilch*).

Being part of Prussia benefitted most vintners in the Rhine Province enormously. It meant all winemakers of the Mosel, Rhine, Nahe and Ahr regions had custom-free access to the vast Prussian markets in the east and the growing industrial clusters on the Ruhr. In addition, they enjoyed protection from non-Prussian competitors, including from southern German regions such as Baden, Württemberg, Palatinate (Pfalz) and Rheinhessen, due to high tariff barriers. As a result, within twenty years, the vineyard area in the Prussian Rhine Province grew by 57 percent between 1818 and 1837 (Robin 1845; Meitzen 1869).[1] However, the boom was to be followed by a 'wine crisis' involving tax reforms and customs unions, as well as detrimental weather conditions (Storchmann 2017).

The military defeat against Napoleon in 1806, the German Campaign of 1813–1814, which liberated the German states from French domination, and the final defeat of Napoleon in 1815 placed enormous burdens on the Prussian state. Prussia endured chronic annual budget deficits of up to 25 percent and was almost bankrupt in 1815 and again in 1818. Therefore, tax increases combined with tax harmonization between eastern and western provinces were needed (Winter-Tarvainen 1992).

1 Winter-Tarvainen (1992) provides detailed data for all Mosel and Saar counties from 1816 to 1832.

In 1819, Prussia introduced a so-called 'wine tax' in the form of a production tax. The tax was to be paid by vintners and was based on the French vineyard classification. Each vineyard's rank determined the specific tax rate to be applied, based on average prices of the outstanding 1818 and 1819 vintages. In addition, Prussia increased property tax rates and imposed a 'class tax' in 1820. The class tax was a precursor of modern income taxes, being levied on individuals or households according to their income and wealth. Overall, between 1818 and 1821, the per capita tax burden in the Prussian Rhine Province grew by 50 percent (Winter-Tarvainen 1992, p. 51).

In 1828, Prussia and Hesse Darmstadt (home of the wine region Rheinhessen) entered into customs agreements. This was followed in 1829 by an agreement between Prussia on the one hand, and Bavaria and Württemberg on the other. In the early 1830s, smaller states joined in, and on 1 January 1834 the *Zollverein*, or German Customs Union, formally came into being. The implications for vintners in the Prussian Rhine Province, which accounted for less than 15 percent of Germany's vine area, were sobering: they lost their monopoly position within Prussia and had to compete with winemakers from regions that were located in warmer and thus lower-cost climates, especially Württemberg and Baden, which were then by far the largest wine growing regions in Germany. In fact, before the implementation of the *Zollverein*, it was cheaper to ship wine almost tariff-free from Bordeaux to Hamburg than from the Rhine or Mosel to Berlin, which, in 1848, allegedly caused Chancellor Otto von Bismarck to state, 'Red wine from Bordeaux is the natural beverage of northern Germans' (Bassermann-Jordan 1907; Thiersch 2008).

After twenty below-average vintages, 1857 brought a bumper crop, with many more excellent vintages to follow. More importantly, the railway network within the *Zollverein* states grew from 2,000 kilometres in 1845 to almost 12,000 kilometres by 1860 (Winter-Tarvainen 1992). That opened markets far away from the Mosel and Rhine rivers.

In addition to better weather and improving transportation, the wine industry also benefitted from a new technology, so-called *gallization*. In contrast to *chaptalization*, where sugar is added to grape juice, gallization enhances wine by adding sugar water to the grape juice before fermentation. It dilutes and reduces the acidity of the finished wine, raises its alcoholic content and increases the volume of wine produced. It is named after the originator of the practice, Ludwig Gall, whose method was explicitly aimed at enabling vintners to make wine from unripe grapes (Gall 1854).

After the victory of Prussia over the Austrian Empire in 1866, Prussia became the undisputed leader among the German states. Otto von

Bismarck, the first German chancellor, saw the *Zollverein* as a vehicle towards German unity. What was a loose customs league of independent states, with a veto right for every member, became in 1867 a customs federation with majority decision-making. The late 1860s became the pinnacle of German free trade policy (Torp 2014). Each member state still maintained its own fiscal policy, though, and several states, such as Württemberg, Baden, and Hesse, imposed various taxes on wine consumption. Overall, the wine industry within the *Zollverein* flourished in the 1850s and 1860s and included a short period when wine exports even exceeded wine imports (Figure 4.3).

From German Unification to World War I: 1871 to 1918

After France's defeat in the Franco–Prussian War in 1871, all states of the *Zollverein* except Luxembourg unified as the German Empire under Prussian leadership. In addition, former French Alsace-Lorraine, a large wine-producing region, became part of the German Empire as well. But in Germany and elsewhere, trade policies became protectionist again. Wine tariffs increased by about 50 percent in 1879 (Bassemir 1930).

The high tariff phase lasted until 1890, when Leo von Caprivi succeeded Bismarck as German chancellor and was looking for markets for industrial products. In numerous bilateral treaties, Caprivi reduced Germany's import tariffs on grain and wine in exchange for lower tariffs abroad on German exports of industrial goods. Bilateral treaties with Italy in 1891 and with Spain in 1893 lowered the tariffs on their bulk wine exports to 20 Marks per 100 kilograms. In addition, a new category, 'blending wine' was introduced, and its imports were levied at only 10 Marks per 100 kilograms. Tariffs on must (grape juice) were reduced to 4 Marks per 100 kilograms (Bassemir 1930). Two attempts to introduce an empirewide excise tax on wine, in 1893 and in 1908, failed due to resistance in the German parliament (Thiersch 2008).

Despite the lowered protection level, German wine production was growing, and the continuing improvements in the railway network enhanced the competitiveness of domestic vintners against foreign wines that were imported via the sea route. But in the twenty-five years prior to World War I, as neighbouring countries recovered from phylloxera, wine prices were declining. As a result, the German vineyard area contracted from about 90,000 ha to 69,000 ha by the end of World War I (Figure 4.1).

In 1918, Germany introduced a very high import tariff of 600 Marks per KL on bulk wine. However, due to the war and the trade blockade, its relevance was minor since trade had come to a halt (Mueller 1913; Hassinger 1928; Bassemir 1930). Due to the absence of competing imports, the strong demand by the German army, and a series of four excellent vintages, the domestic wine industry survived World War I relatively well compared to other industries. Given the lucrative position of the wine industry and enormous postwar financing requirements, the German parliament finally introduced a wine excise tax (*Reichsweinsteuer*) on final consumption in July 1918, at 20 percent for still wine and 30 percent for sparkling wine. It was designed to expire or be renewed by July 1923.

Less attention was given to another turning point: average growing season temperatures began increasing and the number of damaging late-frost days after 15 April began to decrease significantly after the turn of the century (Storchmann 2005, 2017).

From World War I to Germany's Third Reich: 1918 to 1933

The economic situation after World War I was determined by the Treaty of Versailles of June 1919. It stipulated levels of German war reparation payments, principally to France, which put enormous burdens on the new German state. Industrial exports had come to an almost complete halt, the agricultural sector was incapable of producing enough food, imports were hampered by a lack of foreign currency and German inflation began in 1919. At that time, Germany's area under vines was the lowest it had been in 100 years.

German winemakers faced various pressures. The national wine excise tax (*Reichsweinsteuer*) was renewed and even augmented by a local tax on all local beverage consumption from 1923 to 1926 (Thiersch 2008). In conjunction with low incomes, it contributed to a halving in domestic wine consumption between 1910 and 1925 (Figure 4.2(a)) (Storchmann 2017).

Second, Germany's wine exports, which were between 20 and 25 ML before World War I, fell to virtually zero after the war (Figure 4.3), partly due to anti-German sentiments abroad but also due to reduced demand in the United Kingdom and Sweden and the loss of its largest export market, the United States, due to US prohibition (1919–1933).

Third, although German winemakers were protected by the high tariffs implemented in 1918, the Treaty of Versailles stipulated that France had the right to export a certain volume (the average level of its wine exports in 1911–1913) to Germany duty-free until 1925, and that the most-favoured-nation tariff rates apply to all allied nations and their associates. In addition, there was an abundance of French wine entering Germany duty-free through the French-occupied Saar region (Schnitzius 1964; Thiersch 2008). As well, a series of bilateral tariff agreements were signed with Spain (1923), Italy (1925) and France (1927). As a result, wine imports increased significantly and in 1927 and 1928, Germany was the world's second-largest wine importer by volume after France and ahead of Switzerland (Anderson and Pinilla 2017).

Germany's Third Reich: 1933 to 1945

When Hitler was appointed chancellor in 1933, his Nazi Party founded the *Reichsnährstand* (RNST), a government body responsible for all questions related to agrarian economy and politics. The Nazi Party did not trust markets and aimed at controlling production and prices for all agricultural goods, including wine. All former wine industry associations were dissolved or merged into the RNST (Herrmann 1980; Thiersch 2008; Deckers 2010; Keil and Zillien 2010).

The RNST instituted laws for new vineyard plantings and the regulation of all distribution channels (Thiersch 2008; Deckers 2010; Keil and Zillien 2010). One of the most important regulations was the introduction of a price floor in 1934, based on detailed cost estimates which distinguished several price classes. Winemakers initially welcomed the new regulation, since the price floor was perceived to be above the free market price. However, in 1936 the price floor was turned into a price ceiling which was not to be exceeded. RNST also regulated wine distribution by defining maximum margins. A maximum mark-up of 20 percent was stipulated initially, but later a flexible range was allowed (Thiersch 2008).

With the outbreak of World War II, these regulations were severely tightened to secure a large contingent of inexpensive wine for the German military. Wine brokers and retailers had to sell 40 percent of their lower qualities to the Wehrmacht at a set price of 1.40 Reichsmark per litre. This price was further lowered in 1943, leaving retailers, brokers and winemakers with little or no margin. In addition, to alleviate scarcities and avoid wine inventories, the entire wine production was to be registered and at least 80 percent was to be sold within eight months of its production (Herrmann 1980).

Given the complex system of agricultural price controls under the Nazi regime, unregulated imports had the potential to cause serious problems, since domestic prices were regularly above world market prices. Tariff barriers could only partially solve this problem. It was, therefore, planned to regulate wine imports similar to those regulating the corn (maize) market, where all imports pass through a state-owned monopoly that added a margin and then distributed imports to regional middlemen. Although a monopoly institution for wine was launched in 1936, it only dealt in oils, dairy and eggs; wine was exempt. The RNST decided that tariffs in conjunction with price controls and regulated trade margins were sufficient to protect domestic production.

The composition of German wine imports by country of origin changed considerably between 1897 and 1940. France had supplied well over half of Germany's wine imports before 1910, but that share fell to about 30 percent just before World War I, to 20 percent in the 1920s and then to 3 percent by 1940. The void was mainly filled by Italy, whose share of import volumes grew from 10 percent in 1930 to more than 40 percent in 1940. Imports from Spain were more erratic. While up to 45 percent of German wine imports came from Spain in the early 1930s, the Spanish Civil War brought this share down to 10 percent. Other significant importers in the 1930s were Greece, with import shares of 6 to 20 percent, and Hungary with shares of 4 to 14 percent.

During World War II, imports almost doubled compared to 1939 (Figure 4.3(a)). Most wines were imported from France, whose import share was 80 percent in 1944 (Herrmann 1980).

Compared to wine imports, German wine exports were minimal. In 1934, the Nazi regime established a state-run export agency (*Weinausfuhrstelle*) which controlled the quality and quantity of German wine exports (Thiersch 2008). During the 1930s, German wine exports hovered around 6 ML per year and never reached the pre–World War I levels of about 24 ML. With the outbreak of World War II, wine exports virtually ceased (Figure 4.3).

Post–World War II: Germany and the European Common Market

After World War II and the collapse and division of Germany, German viticulture was at its lowest point in history. The area under vines began falling even before World War II, but it declined further during and following the war. From a recorded vineyard area of 72,000 ha in 1939, only 49,500 ha were left in 1947, or less than half of the vineyard area 100 years earlier. However, not all of this decline can be attributed to the war, as some was due to the extremely harsh winter in 1939–1940 and again in 1941–1942 (Herrmann 1980).

Official foreign wine trade data for the period 1945–1949 do not exist. However, given the above average yields in 1946 and 1947, it is assumed that the Allied Forces confiscated some wine and exported it to the United States or the United Kingdom (Schnitzius 1964); and, as after the end of

World War I, the Saar region was occupied by French troops, and uncontrolled quantities of French wine were imported into Germany.

From Currency Reform to the Treaty of Rome: 1949 to 1958

The introduction of the Deutsche Mark (DM) in 1948 was a necessary condition for the revitalization of Germany's foreign trade. However, due to extremely low incomes, there was little demand for imported wine. In addition, trade needed to be approved by the agency of the occupying force.

The first wine imports were approved in February 1949 by the Joint Import-Export Agency (JIEA), a British-American regulatory agency for bizonal foreign trade located in Frankfurt/Main (Schnitzius 1964). Germany imported just 11 ML of wine worth 9.6 million DM that year. However, the demand for foreign wines increased rapidly, and in 1951 imports amounted to 119 ML.

Once again, the domestic wine industry deemed itself incapable of surviving on the world market without government support. From 1949 to 1958, Germany's wine imports were, therefore, regulated by a complex system of quotas and tariffs. The first pillar consisted of country-specific contingents for France, Italy, Spain, Greece, Yugoslavia and a few other smaller wine exporters. While the largest contingent in the early 1950s was reserved for Italy, France's share grew rapidly and, in 1956, it was about as large as the shares of Italy, Spain and Greece combined. The contingents were set in bilateral trade agreements and, in order to mitigate negative impacts on the domestic wine industry, which predominantly produced white wine, provided larger quotas for red wine (Thiersch 2008). In addition to these country-specific quotas, there was an 'open quota' to be filled by any country on a first-come-first-served basis, and a separate contingent for fermented grape juice (Weise 1958). The 1949 tariff, imposed in addition to the quota, doubled the average price level of imported wine (Schnitzius 1964; Thiersch 2008).

The government was reluctant to provide direct producer support, which remained small and was predominantly aimed at improving productivity. The main focus was put on supportive measures against recurring phylloxera infestations and on land consolidations in which small plots were merged into larger ones to exploit economies of scale. Further measures aimed at increasing wine quality, marketing, and the support of wine cooperatives (Thiersch 2008).

Parallelling the rapid growth in imports in the 1950s, wine exports increased as well, although at a much lower level; between 1950 and 1958, exports grew from 2.3 to 9.4 ML As before World War II, the main importers of German wine were the United Kingdom and the United States.

Preparations for the Common Market: 1958 to 1970

On 1 January 1958, the Treaty of Rome establishing the European Economic Community (EEC) provided a twelve-year transition phase before markets were fully open. The main implication for the German wine industry was to phase out its protective import quotas and tariffs over ten years. From 1970, no national protective measures were allowed. However, the federal government launched a stabilizing fund (*Stabilisierungsfonds*), financed jointly by the government and wine industry dues, to promote research, quality improvement and marketing. The fund also provided loans for surplus storage to control wine supplies and thereby the market price. The German government also declared that new vine plantings and replantings required permission, and plantings of certain varieties were prohibited.

Consumption and Trade

Per capita wine consumption growth by far exceeded income growth rates in the 1950s and reached its peak in 1990. Since then it has declined, from about 26 to 22 litres. From 1968 to 1975, Germany and France took turns in being the world's largest importer, but since 1976 Germany has been the world's largest wine importer by volume, accounting for more than one-fifth of global wine imports (Figure 4.4). Due to the high share of bulk wine in its imports, Germany is only the second- or third-largest wine importer by value: the United Kingdom has ranked ahead of Germany since 1985 (and the United States has exceeded the United Kingdom since 2010).

Between German reunification in 1990 and 2015, the volume of its wine imports grew 43 percent and their value increased by 70 percent in current US dollars. However, since 2005 the average price of imports has not risen anymore, because a rising share of those imports have been bulk wines. In 2000, bulk wine's share of German imports was 37 percent, its lowest point in recent history, but it had risen to 58 percent by 2015, making Germany by far the largest bulk wine importer in the world (accounting for 21 percent of the global total in 2015).

The composition of importing countries has changed as well. Italy has been reunified Germany's main wine supplier since 1991, during which time France's volume and value shares have nearly halved. Noteworthy is the rise of Spanish wine in the German wine market, from 5 percent of Germany's import volume in 1991 to 26 percent by 2015.

Rising Yields and Yield Restrictions

Most European countries have experienced significant increases in winegrape yields since the mid-1950s. Germany passed France in 1957 and since then has been the top-yielding wine country in Europe. Over the past

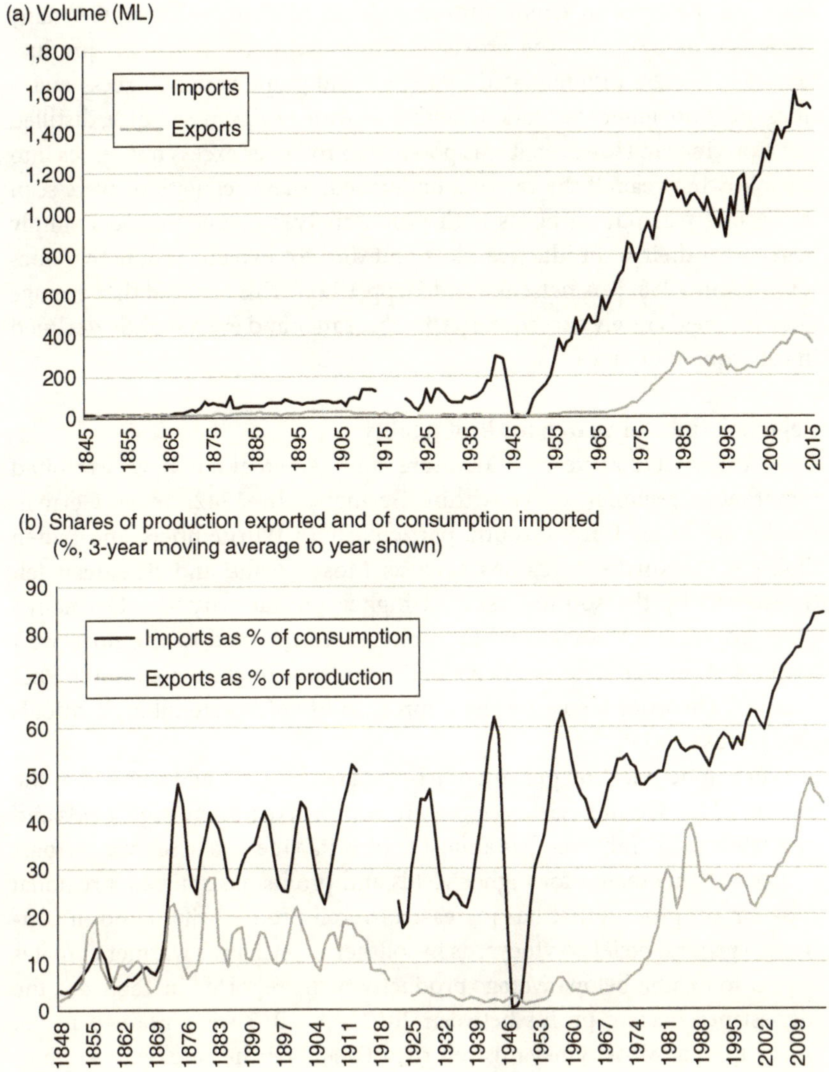

Figure 4.4 Volume of wine exports and imports and trade propensity, Germany, 1845 to 2015 (ML and %).
Source: Anderson and Pinilla (2017).

twenty years, German yields have constantly been in excess of 9 t/ha, about 50 percent above French and Italian yields.

Against the background of persistent wine oversupply (at minimum prices) in the European Union (EU) during the 1970s and 1980s, various yield regulations were instituted, mainly in France and Italy. Germany did not introduce maximum yield regulations until 1989. This regulation was based on a European Union provision from 1970 that obliged Germany to cap yields by 1990. The provision stipulated maximum wine productions per hectare differentiated by region and grape variety. Excess quantities must not enter the market, neither as wine nor as must, juice, distilled spirit or vinegar. However, it was possible to roll over excess quantities into the following years if the cap was underused. These regulations were seen in Germany as punishing its high productivity, so some vintners simply held on to their unproductive plots and did not expand productive ones (Hoffmann 1988; Kosmetschke and Hepp 1991). This ensured that average German yields rarely exceeded 10 t/ha thereafter and even slightly declined in subsequent decades.

Regional Shifts in Search for Profitability

Over the past 200 years, viticulture and winemaking have exhibited remarkable regional shifts within Germany. In 1842, most German vines were located in the south, particularly in Württemberg and Baden (Table 4.1). Northern regions such as Mosel, Nahe and Rheingau felt threatened by the south's assumed higher productivity. Yet Germany's vineyard area did not move south but instead shifted to the northwest because of serious yield problems in the south, as documented in the PhD thesis of Theordor Heuss on the unprofitability of Württemberg's viticulture (Heuss 1906).[2]

Württemberg lost 60 percent of its vine area by 1920 and was still at the bottom of the German yield ranking. In contrast, driven by high yields and profitability, Rheinhessen has almost tripled its vineyard area over the past 170 years. This search for higher yields and profits has spurred a regional substitution process that has increased overall productivity – and in contrast to general beliefs – vineyards in southern Germany's warmer climates appear to exhibit below-average productivity. As reported in Table 4.2, the highest per hectare profits between 2010 and 2015 were attained in the Mosel region. Mosel vineyards returned €6,300 per hectare, with a coefficient of variation of 12 percent. In contrast, Württemberg's vineyard land yielded only €2,600 with more than twice the variability.

Planting Rights

In 1976, the European Union introduced planting rights which forbids the planting of new vineyards unless the planter has permission (Deconinck

[2] In 1949, Heuss became the first president of the newly founded Federal Republic of Germany (West Germany).

Table 4.1 *Regional vineyard areas and yields, Germany, 1842, 1920 and 2015 (ha and t/ha)*

	1842		1920		2015	
	ha	t/ha	ha	t/ha	ha	t/ha
Württemberg	27053	0.8	10897	1.5	11118	9.7
Baden	20243	2.3	12675	3.0	15478	7.5
Franken	14887	1.8	3600	3.0	6013	6.9
Palatinate	13231	2.7	14968	4.8	22978	9.9
Rheinhessen	9996	3.6	13604	3.5	25753	9.7
Mosel-Saar	8763	2.2	8008	5.1	8488	8.9
Mittelrhein	4581	1.6	2014	2.5	439	6.4
Rheingau	4003	1.7	2314	2.2	3109	6.5
Nahe	2362	2.5	2671	2.2	4105	7.6
Ahr	1293	1.5	608	4.0	548	7.2

Sources: Robin (1845); Dieterici (1848); Statistisches Reichsamt (1922); Bundesministerium für Ernährung und Landwirtschaft (2016a).

Table 4.2 *Per hectare profits in winegrowing regions, Germany, 2010 to 2015 (current €/ha)*

	2010	2011	2012	2013	2014	2015	2010–15	Coeff. of variation (%)
Mosel	4,708	5,662	6,775	6,159	6,337	6,696	6,326	12
Rheinhessen	2,678	2,583	2,538	3,097	2,934	3,087	2,848	9
Palatinate	3,197	3,912	4,260	4,696	3,966	4,550	4,277	13
Württemberg	2,775	1,707	2,531	3,102	2,044	3,522	2,581	26
Franken	4,380	3,849	4,132	4,064	4,773	4,905	4,345	10
Total	**3,115**	**3,232**	**3,651**	**3,938**	**3,442**	**4,033**	**3,659**	**10**

Source: Bundesministerium für Ernährung und Landwirtschaft (2016a).

and Swinnen 2014). While the introduction of planting rights was aimed at limiting supply and stabilizing prices, several problems persist.

First, enforcement has been a major problem from the beginning as vintners in some wine-growing countries repeatedly ignore planting rights (Meloni and Swinnen 2016). For instance, in 2000, the EU found 120,500 ha of illegally planted vineyards, an area that exceeds the total vine area in Germany and Alsace combined. Most of the illegal plantings were found in Spain (55,088 ha), Italy (52,604 ha), and Greece (12,268 ha, i.e., one-sixth of all Greek vineyards were planted illegally). The EU retroactively legalized almost all of the irregular plantings (Commission of the European Communities 2007; Ashenfelter and Storchmann 2016).

Second, vineyard planting rights were allocated to the firms and countries with vineyards, thus granting monopoly rents to those vineyard owners. Cross-country trade in rights is not allowed. The European Commission recognizes this problem and planned to liberalize vineyard plantings by 2015, but due to lobbying pressure this deregulation did not occur. The current policy is a compromise and allows each country to expand its vineyard area by up to 1 percent of its 2015 area. This regulation, scheduled to stay in place until 2030, implies that, if the allowances are exhausted, the absolute largest vineyard expansion will take place in less-productive regions. In addition, to exacerbate the situation, and in response to lobbying pressure from the German wine industry, Germany chose to stay below the 1 percent allowance and voluntarily committed to only 0.3 percent. According to a letter of the German government to the European Commission, the reasoning for this unexpected move is that an increase in the supply of German wine would depress producer prices and, therefore, the incomes of German vintners (Bundesministerium für Ernährung und Landwirtschaft 2016b). Apparently, the German government does not regard imported wine as price-relevant for the German wine market. For 2016, the European Union permitted new plantings of 17,156 ha, only 308 of which were located in Germany (European Commission 2016; Wine-Inside 2016).[3] Thus regional shifts in vineyard area in the search for higher productivity will be difficult.

AUSTRIA

The borders of Austria have shifted over the past two centuries even more than Germany's. Austria's territorial losses occurred after World War I and were more significant than Germany's after 1945 (see, e.g., Storchmann 2017). Before World War I, Austria-Hungary comprised a territory of 676,600 km^2 and was Europe's second-largest country (after Russia) and its third most populous (after Germany and Russia). In 1918, Austria lost nearly 90 percent of its territory, and that loss becomes even more significant when looking just at viticultural areas. While Germany lost one-quarter of its vineyard area in 1918 (Alsace-Lorraine), Austria lost more than 95 percent of its area under vines after World War I.

We can broadly distinguish four different Austrian states, the Austrian Empire (1804–1867), Austria-Hungary (1867–1918), the First Republic

[3] Germany later even returned 45 ha of its allotment, and utilized only 263 ha.

(1918–1938) and the Second Republic (1955–present). During the interim period (1938–1955), Austria was annexed by Germany (1938–1945) and then occupied by Allied Forces (1945–1955).

Austrian Empire and Austria-Hungary: 1804 to 1918

The Austrian Empire (1804–1867) was a multinational state governed by the Austrian Emperor. The Austro-Hungarian Compromise (Ausgleich) of 1867 elevated the status of Hungary to become a separate entity from the empire, joining it in the dual monarchy of Austria-Hungary (1867–1918). The Cisleithanian (Austrian) and Transleithanian (Hungarian) regions of the empire were governed by separate parliaments and prime ministers.[4] Although Austria and Hungary shared a common currency, they were fiscally sovereign and independent entities. Present-day Austria is only partially identical with the Core-Austria of the nineteenth century, which comprised the states of Lower Austria (including Vienna), Styria, Carinthia, (North)-Tyrol, Vorarlberg, Upper Austria and Salzburg. Only the first four of these have professional vineyards. The Core-Austria of the nineteenth century is not fully identical with present-day Austria, for three reasons. First, Burgenland, a major wine state in current Austria, used to be a German-speaking part of Hungary and has never been part of Cisleithania (i.e., the Austrian part of the Austrian-Hungarian Empire). It was incorporated into Austria in 1922. Second, Styria, also a wine-producing state, which was formerly all Core-Austria, was divided after World War I, and about two-thirds of its territory went to Slovenia. Third, Tyrol was divided after World War I and South Tyrol, the wine-producing part of the state, went completely to Italy.

Production

Table 4.3 reports some trends in Austrian wine production from 1841 to 2015 by referring to the Cisleithanian states only. The top row displays all figures for Austria in its present-day borders, that is, Lower Austria, a small part of Styria, Carinthia, Vorarlberg, North Tyrol and Burgenland. Present-day Austria's vine area steadily declined from 54,000 ha in 1842 to less than 35,000 ha in 1950. The vineyard reached its all-time low at 25,000 ha directly after World War I (Anderson and Pinilla 2017). Most of

[4] The Latin names *Cisleithania* and *Transleithania* derive from the Leitha River, a tributary of the Danube forming the historical boundary between the Austrian empire with its capital Vienna and the Hungarian Kingdom with its capital Budapest.

Table 4.3 *Vineyard area and yields, Austria, 1842 to 2015 (ha and t/ha)*

	Ha under vines (bearing)						Yield (t/ha)		Red wine % of all prod'n	
	1842	1875	1890	1913	1950	2015	1890–1913	2000–2015	1890	2015
Austria (present-day borders)	53,987	50,566	48,741	42,430	34,682	43,611	2.1	5.4	2	35
Lower Austria (incl. Vienna)	46,215	39,911	39,713	35,053	23,802	26,876	2.2	5.4	2	25
Styria	31,446	32,668	34,056	26,660	2,616	4,546	1.7	5.1	9	24
Carinthia	n.a.	53	54	22	7[a]	167[a]	0.3	3.3	8[a]	40[a]
Vorarlberg	n.a.	249	244	63	n.a.	n.a.	1.2	n.a.	0	n.a.
North Tyrol	n.a.	267	262	0	n.a.	n.a.	1.8	n.a.	25	n.a.
Burgenland	n.a.	n.a.	n.a.	n.a.	8,518	11,585	n.a.	5.3	n.a.	58
South Tyrol	22,898	5,416	16,678	27,038			3.1		82	
Carniola	9,682	9,644	11,631	9,799			1.4		0	
Austrian Littoral	15,038	27,161	46,700	38,106			1.2		74	
of which: Goerz[b]		9,568	9,882	9,936			1.6		65	
Triest		1,027	1,087	582			1.1		61	
Istria		16,566	35,731	27,588			1.1		77	
Dalmatia	64,444	67,743	72,256	70,701			1.4		94	
Bohemia	2,573	771	861	495			1.2		42	
Moravia	29,805	15,474	12,134	10,644			1.4		13	

[a] Includes Vorarlberg and North Tyrol.

[b] Goerz and Gradisca. Grapes grown in the Bukovina region (between 30 and 70 ha) were not used for wine.

[c] Data are for 1854. In 1842, the Austrian Empire also included significant vineyard areas in Hungary (644,706 ha), Transylvania (58,676 ha) and Military Frontier (27,112 ha), all of which fell under Transleithanian rule, i.e., the Hungarian Crown, in 1867. In addition, until its independency in 1866, the Austrian Empire included the Kingdom of Lombardy-Venetia, with a 1842 vineyard area of 76,793 ha (Lombardy) and 96,881 ha (Venetia), respectively.

Source: Anderson and Pinilla (2017); K.K. Ackerbau-Ministerium (various years); K.K. Direction der administrativen Statistik ((1828–71); Wohlfahrt (n.a.); Statistik Austria (various years).

this development has been driven by Lower Austria, Austria's main wine-growing region.

Table 4.3 also reports yields. Compared to nineteenth century yields in the German Mosel Valley or Switzerland (Table 4.1 and Table 4.7 later in this chapter), Austrian yields are surprisingly low. In addition, there are substantial yield disparities among the various Austrian countries, which are only partially explained by the emergence of mildew and phylloxera.

Phylloxera appeared in Austria the first time in 1872 near Vienna and spread quickly. The Agricultural Ministry (*K.K. Ackerbauministerium*) began publishing phylloxera reports in 1874. The first publications were irregular, but from 1892 annual reports provide detailed accounts of infestations at the village level. According to the 1898–1899 report, the contamination rates vary greatly among Moravia (13 percent), Dalmatia (17 percent), Styria (45 percent), Goerz and Gradisca (47 percent), Lower Austria (56 percent), Istria (61 percent), Carniola (91 percent) and Triest (100 percent).

In addition, yield data from 1842, that is, before the occurrence of phylloxera and mildew in Europe, suggest that Dalmatia had always lagged. Official Statistics (K.K. Direction der administrativen Statistik 1842) report the following yields: Hungary 2.3 t/ha, Lower Austria 2.2 t/ha, Tyrol 2.0 t/ha, Military Frontier 1.8 t/ha, Lombardy 1.8 t/ha (1854), Bohemia 1.6 t/ha, Transylvania 1.5 t/ha, Moravia 1.4 t/ha, Venetia 1.4 t/ha (1854) and Dalmatia 1.0 t/ha. Therefore, with the exception of Triest, phylloxera is only a weak explanation for yield disparities among Austrian states; climatic and geographical variables may exhibit more explanatory power.

In addition to low yields, Dalmatia also received the lowest prices per tonne of wine. According to data provided by Mach (1899a, 1899b) and shown in Table 4.4, Dalmatian wine prices were the lowest in all Austrian countries, while wines from Moravia and Bohemia commanded the highest prices.

Consumption and Trade

Austria was not a unified, tariff-free market, and trade was sluggish. It took until 1850 to abolish border tariffs between Austria and Hungary, sixteen years after the launch of the German *Zollverein*. Dalmatia and Istria finally joined the tariff union in 1880 (Mach 1899b).

Table 4.5 reports income, consumption and trade figures for Austria from 1842 to 2015 together with comparable numbers for Germany. Note that while the population, income and consumption data refer to Austria in its present-day borders, the trade data for 1842 and 1890 refer to the Austrian customs union, which was much larger in 1890 than in 1842 and after 1918.

Table 4.4 *Prices of wine, Austria, 1840 to 1860 (gulden per KL)*

	1840	1850	1855	1860
Lower Austria	200	81	141	308
Styria	141	163	230	332
Carinthia and Carniola	156	177	226	403
Austrian Littoral	67	78	219	361
Tyrol	128	138	276	495
Bohemia	495	318	587	714
Moravia	135	213	226	484
Dalmatia	18	32	124	269

Source: Author's calculations based on Mach (1899b).

Table 4.5 *Wine production, consumption and trade, Germany and Austria, 1842 to 2015*

	1842	1890	1937	1950	1970	1990	2015
Austria							
Population (million)	4	5	7	7	8	7	9
Income per capita[a]	1515[b]	1624	1808	3706	9747	16895	24753
Wine prod'n (ML)	114	114	85	129	310	317	230
Wine consumption (litre/capita)		15[c]	21[d]	15	33	33	31
Beer consumption (litre/capita)		33[c]	33[d]	41	109	135	120
Wine exports (ML)	12	68	76	12	5.0	13	49
Wine imports (ML)	23	4	6	5	23	24.3	74
Germany							
Population (million)		48	68	69	78	80	82
Income per capita[a]		2430	4685	3880	10840	15930	22045
Wine prod'n (ML)	204	205	252	324	989	1017	887
Wine consumption (litre/capita)			5	6	16	26	22
Beer consumption (litre/capita)		105	60	na	155	158	113
Wine exports (ML)		19	8	4	35	278	369
Wine imports (ML)		74	107	86	688	1008	1540

[a] Per capita GDP in 1990 International Geary-Khamis dollars.
[b] 1840.
[c] Hoppe (1901).
[d] Statistisches Reichsamt (1938).
[e] Austrian Empire outside of the Austrian Customs Union (i.e., mainly Dalmatia, Austrian Littoral, Lombardy-Venetia and Hungary), data for 1861 (Mach, 1899b).

Sources: Anderson and Pinilla (2017); Wohlfahrt (n.a.).

In 1890, Austria's per capita wine consumption was about 15 litres, three times Germany's 5 litres (Hoppe 1901). However, wine consumption in Austria appears modest compared to France (92 litres) and Italy (90 litres). The same is true for beer when we compare Austria with beer-drinking nations such as the United Kingdom and Germany. In 1890, Austria's per capita beer consumption of 33 litres is small compared to the UK's 135 litres and Germany's 104 litres.

Table 4.5 suggests that, between 1842 and 1890, major changes have occurred in Austria's wine trade. In 1842, Austria was a net wine importer and imports were 23 ML – a volume that was not reached again until 1990. However, while imports fell substantially between 1842 and 1890, exports rose fivefold, to 68 ML. Since all trade data are for the area of the Austrian Customs Union, both effects are largely due to its expansion.[5] For instance, imports from Dalmatia were deemed domestic shipments from 1880 on, when Dalmatia joined the Customs Union, leading to a decline in recorded imports. At the same time, exports from Dalmatia to Russia or Turkey were deemed Austrian exports only from 1880 on, leading to increasing export figures. Aside from these technicalities, the wine trade was generally benefitting from the rapidly expanding rail network (Mach 1899a) and the free trade climate in all of Europe until the late 1870s. Austria could grow wine shipments to its main export market, the German *Zollverein*. Mach (1899b) reports that, even after the establishment of the Customs Union between Austria and Hungary in 1850, wine exports from Austria to Germany grew steadily from 24 ML in 1860 to almost 60 ML in 1869. The Austro–Prussian War of 1866 only briefly interrupted this development. However, Prussia's victory over Austria resulted in a shift in power within the German Confederation away from Austrian and toward Prussian hegemony. It also accelerated the economic integration and eventual unification of the German states, from which Austria was excluded.

Many contemporary authors still hoped that, although Austria-Hungary was not part of the newly established German Empire in 1871, it could join a German Customs Union (e.g., Hlubek 1864; Braumüller 1865). In fact, a Wine Commission appointed by the Austrian government recommended the reciprocal abolishment of all wine tariffs between Germany and Austria-Hungary (K.K. Ackerbau-Ministerium 1873). However, Austria's plan to join the German Customs Union did not materialize.

Austro-Hungarian wine exports peaked at 103 ML in 1889, a volume that has never been reached since. Only a few years later, its exports were just 20 ML and remained around that level. In 1892, Austro-Hungarian wine

[5] For details about the Austrian Customs Union, its development and economic effects, see also Komlos (1983).

imports began to rise dramatically, from 5ML in 1891 to 55 ML in 1892 and 154 ML in 1898. During that and the subsequent two decades, it accounted for one-tenth of global wine imports (Figure 4.4), and Austria turned from a net exporter to a net importer of wine. Since then, with the exceptions of 1950 and the periods 1978–85 and 2002–2005, Austria's wine imports (mostly from Italy) exceeded its exports.

First Austrian Republic and World War II: 1919 to 1945

After World War I, Austria became a republic and its territory was reduced to the core state of the present-day Austria. Compared to the Austria-Hungary of 1918, the new First Republic was now landlocked, and it lost to neighbouring countries all non-German-speaking provinces, as well as some German-speaking provinces, including South Tyrol. However, in 1922, Austria gained the mainly German-speaking Burgenland (except for its capital, Sopron), which, under the name Western Hungary, had been part of the Hungarian Kingdom. Burgenland has become one of Austria's large wine growing regions, and in 2015 accounted for one-quarter of Austria's vineyard area (Table 4.3).

After World War I, Austria's economy almost collapsed, as many neighbouring countries (Czechoslovakia, Hungary, Yugoslavia and Italy) imposed a trade blockade and refused to sell food and energy to Austria. Like Germany, although at a somewhat lower level, Austria experienced a rapid decline in the value of its currency in 1922, which severely affected imports. The wine trade came to an almost complete halt and did not recover until the mid-1950s (Figure 4.5). Meanwhile, wine consumption was highly taxed: in 1922, wine tax revenue amounted to 49 percent of all excise tax revenue and 14 percent of all tax revenue in Austria (Österreichisches Statistisches Zentralamt 1924).

The absence of trade was offset by an increasing domestic vineyard area. From 1922 to 1930, the Austrian vineyard grew from 25,000 ha to 35,000 ha (Anderson and Pinilla 2017). In addition, due to new technologies, particularly cold filtration, which enabled even small wineries to bottle their own wine, the share of bottled wine increased substantially in the 1920s. This development also furthered the production of quality wine (Postmann 2010). But even the expanding vineyard area and improving quality could not revive Austrian wine exports, which during the 1930s averaged only a tiny fraction of the volumes in the 1880s.

In March 1938, Austria was annexed by Germany and, in 1939, became the German province Ostmark. Between February 1940 and August 1945,

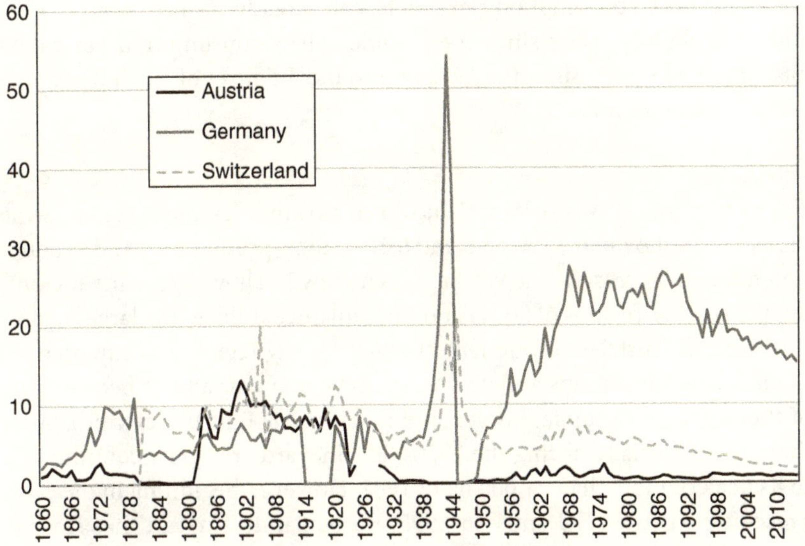

Figure 4.5 Share of world wine import volume, Germany, Austria and Switzerland, 1860 to 2014 (%).
Source: Anderson and Pinilla (2017).

German wine law applied to Austria and, as in Germany, the entire wine industry fell under the supervision of the *Reichsnährstand*, which set price ceilings and stipulated wine volumes to be set aside for military consumption, as discussed previously for Germany.

Post-World War II and the Second Austrian Republic: 1946 to the Present

After World War II, Austria was occupied by the allied powers and divided into four zones. The winegrowing regions of Lower Austria, Vienna and Burgenland were all located in the Soviet sector, while Styria was in the British sector. When Austria became independent in 1955, the Second Republic was proclaimed.

Incomes and Consumption

The decades that followed are characterized by moderate population growth (0.3 percent per annum) and a tenfold greater rate of growth in real per capita income (Table 4.5). As a result, per capita wine consumption more than doubled between 1950 and 2015, to 31 litres per capita. Meanwhile, per capita beer consumption almost tripled to 120 litres per capita. However, both wine and beer consumption per capita had already peaked around 1990 and have slightly fallen since then, while spirits consumption per capita has remained steady since the 1970s at around 1.5 litres of alcohol per year (Anderson and Pinilla 2017).

Production

The period since World War II has been positive for the Austrian wine industry. As shown in Tables 6.3 and 6.5, acreage, productivity and production have all increased. The vineyard area grew in all winegrowing regions, but the smaller regions of Styria and Burgenland exhibited the largest gains. Burgenland, Austria's second largest winegrowing region, has experienced the most significant ups and downs. In 1923, one year after it became part of the Austrian Republic, Burgenland had just 3,800 ha under vines. Since then, and especially during the 1970s, its vineyard area grew continuously to its peak of more than 21,000 ha in 1982. However, beginning in the years preceding Austria's EU entry in 1995, Burgenland's vineyard has steadily declined to 11,500 ha in 2015.

Average Austrian yields grew from 2.1 t/ha from 1890 to 1913 to 5.4 t/ha from 2000 to 2015, but productivity levels are still below those in Germany (9 t/ha) and France and Italy (6 t/ha). Austria has also seen a shift from white to red wine. Red wine's share, which was just 2 percent in 1890, is now more than one-third (Table 4.3).

Trade

The post–World War II period has also seen a strong rise in wine trade (Figure 4.6). Both exports and imports have grown to levels that even exceed pre–World War I levels, when Austria was much larger than now. However, the growth rates were far from constant.

First, wine imports grew rapidly, from virtually zero after World War II to 44 ML in 1960. However, from then until Austria's accession to the European Union in 1995, imports just fluctuated between 20 and 40 ML per year. After 1995, another growth period began, with wine imports trebling between 1994 and 1998 and rising even further in the new century.

Exports also rose from the late 1960s to the mid-1980s, but that rise was brought to a sudden halt by a wine glycol scandal in 1985, when several Austrian wineries were caught adulterating their wine with diethylene glycol,[6] which is a (harmless) substance used as an antifreezing agent. After

[6] Between 1978 and 1985, more than 340 tonnes of glycol were applied to adulterate at least 26 ML of wine. A total of 325 people were indicted and fifteen people received jail sentences of up to five years (Postmann 2010).

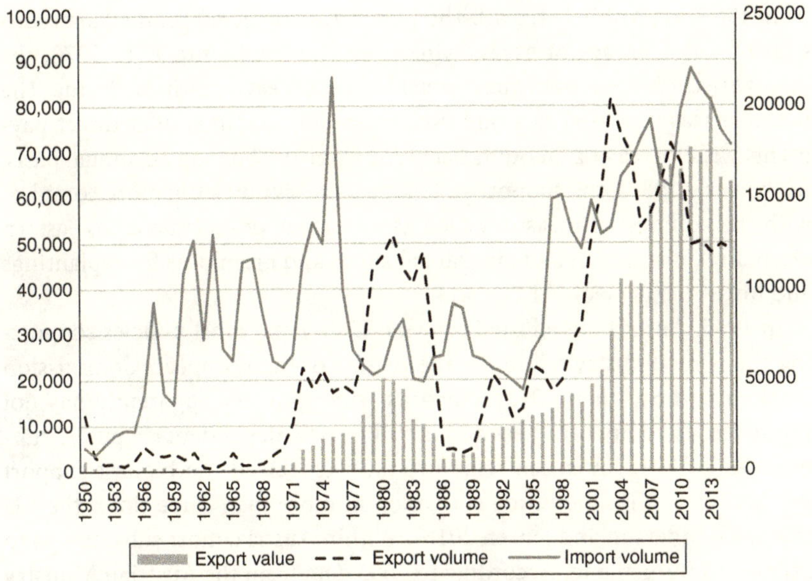

Figure 4.6 Volume of wine imports and exports, Austria, 1950 to 2015 (KL on left axis, current US$'000 on right axis).
Source: Anderson and Pinilla (2017).

Germany prohibited the sale of all Austrian wine on 9 July 1985, a global wave of prohibition followed (Brüders 1999; Postmann 2010). Austrian wine exports, which were above 48 ML in 1984, dropped by 90 percent in 1986 and even more in 1987 and 1988. The prescandal export levels were not reached again until the new century, sixteen years after the scandal. By then, the industry had raised the quality of its product and subsequently revamped its export promotion arm. As a consequence, from 1990 to 2015 the unit value of its exports has nearly trebled (Anderson and Pinilla 2017).

Public Support Policies

According to 2014 data from the Farm Accountancy Data Network of the European Commission (2017), Austrian vineyards are among the least profitable in Europe. That is despite the Austrian government supporting the wine industry in many ways. In 1965, planting limitations were imposed on wineries in Lower Austria and Burgenland. In 1966, the Austrian government established *Weinwirtschaftsfonds*, a government wine marketing agency. As elsewhere in the European Union, the Austrian Federal Ministry of Agriculture and Forestry began to intervene in the wine market and bought wine for storage, export and distillation purposes from 1969 on (Wohlfahrt, n.a.). The *Weinwirtschaftsfonds* granted loan subsidies for the storage of excess wine from the 1969 vintage. In 1970, the *Weinwirtschaftsfonds* paid direct subsidies for excess quantities of wine. The measure was first seen as a one-time intervention, but similar direct payments with increasing amounts occurred from 1977 on, on an annual basis. In the early 1980s, the support system became significantly more complex, with the addition of measures such as export supports (mainly to eastern Germany), distillation and vinegar subsidies and premiums for replantings and investments (Wohlfahrt n.a.).

In 1995, Austria joined the European Union and most policies supporting the wine industry fell under the regime of the European Commission (Meloni and Swinnen 2013). Austria's wine industry apparently has not improved its competitiveness and is still heavily dependent on public support. As of 2012, Austrian wine producers received the highest support per hectare within the European Union at more than three times the EU average (Anderson and Jensen 2016). Within Austria, most subsidies go to Styria and Burgenland. According to 2003 data from the Austrian Ministry of Finance, wine producers in Styria received the highest amounts per hectare (€382/ha), while those in Vienna (€74/ha) and Lower Austria (€161) receive the lowest supports (Homlong and Springler 2007). As has been the practice in all EU countries for decades, public supports have been used to sustain wine production in unprofitable regions and block structural changes and regional shifts.

SWITZERLAND

In contrast to Germany and Austria, Switzerland has enjoyed territorial integrity for centuries and has existed in its current borders since 1815. Currently, most Swiss wine is produced in the west and in the south of the country, in the French-speaking cantons of Geneva, Neuchâtel, Valais and Vaud, as well as in Italian-speaking Ticino. However, up to the late nineteenth century, most Swiss vineyards were located in the northern, German-speaking cantons, particularly in Zurich, Aargau and Thurgau (Table 4.6).

Today red varieties are planted on three-fifths of Switzerland's vineyard area, but the dominance of red varieties is relatively recent. Before the late 1990s, most varieties planted were white.

As in Germany, Swiss wine production experienced a significant boost after the French Revolution of 1789. The early industrialization in Switzerland and the resulting rising incomes led to domestic wine consumption growth.

Table 4.6 *Vineyard bearing area, Switzerland, 1877 to 2015 (ha)*

	1877	1910	1930	1960	2015
German-speaking of which:	13,545	7,818	2,279	1,533	2,620
Zurich	5,279	3,236	914	417	607
Aargau and Thurgau	4,286	2,213	475	363	642
French-speaking of which:	11,190	11,957	8,604	8,839	11,046
Vaud	6,570	6,003	3,645	3,410	3,771
Valais	1,140	2,897	3,160	3,615	4,906
Italian and Romansh-speaking	7,970	4,880	1,800	1,679	1,127
Switzerland, total	**32,705**	**24,655**	**12,683**	**12,051**	**14,793**

Sources: Brugger (1968); Schlegel (1973); Eidgenössisches Departement für Wirtschaft, Bildung und Forschung (2016).

Likewise, incomes were growing too in the bordering southern German states, especially Württemberg and Baden, which was particularly beneficial for exports from the northern Swiss cantons of Thurgau and Aargau. Only after the establishment of the South German Customs Union (*Süddeutscher Zollverein*) in 1828 did Swiss winemakers face increasing tariff barriers. That affected especially the exports of the canton of Thurgau. However, the rise in domestic demand more than offset these losses.

Between 1850 and 1880, Swiss viticulture enjoyed rapid growth and prosperity. Schauwecker (1913) reports that, from 1850 to 1870, wine prices soared. While the average prices per decade from 1790 to 1850 had been relatively stable, in the following twenty years prices increased by 50 percent in Schaffhausen and about 85 percent in Geneva. As a result, the area under vines expanded substantially, mostly at the expense of grazing land. Although reliable data for Switzerland in its entirety are only available from 1891, data for Zurich show that its vineyard area grew from 4,150 ha in 1851 to 5,590 ha in 1881, and similar increases are reported for Vaud, Geneva and Schaffhausen (Schauwecker 1913; Schlegel 1973). Around 1880, the overall vineyard area in Switzerland encompassed approximately 36,000 ha, a level that has never been reached again: it had gone down by one-quarter between 1877 and 1910, and had halved again by 1930 (Table 4.6). Only since the 1970s has the Swiss vineyard area begun a gradual recovery and has grown moderately to about 15,000 ha.

Associated with these overall changes, large parts of the vineyard area have moved west, especially into Valais (Table 4.6); all other regions experienced losses in their area under vines. For instance, Zurich's vineyard area shrank from 5,586 ha in 1881 to 417 ha in 1960. Most areas in eastern

Switzerland lost about 90 percent of their vines, but the vineyard area in the Italian and Romansh-speaking part fell as well. Even the vineyard area in Vaud, in western Switzerland, fell by half. In contrast, Valais has seen rapid growth in its area under vines, from 1,140 ha in 1877 to now almost 5,000 ha. Valais is the only canton with a thriving vineyard area, where one-third of all Swiss grapevines are now located.

The regional shift into the western cantons was induced by yields and, therefore, profitability. As reported in Table 4.7, vineyards in Valais and Vaud have almost always displayed significantly higher yields and revenue per hectare than those in Zurich and Ticino. During the early nineteenth century, the Valais vineyards earned revenue per hectare that was four times those in Zurich, and the difference between Valais and Zurich exceeded a factor of ten.

The main factors that contributed to the downfall of the Swiss wine industry at the end of the nineteenth century are falling yields, higher production costs than competitors and increasingly stiff competition from imported wines (Schauwecker 1913; Zaugg 1924; Welti 1940; Schlegel 1973).

First, after a series of excellent vintages in the 1870s, weather conditions were less conducive to grape growing and, as everywhere else in Europe, Swiss vineyards were affected by various diseases and pests, particularly downy mildew, in subsequent decades. As a result, per hectare yields fell by more than half (Storchmann 2017).

Second, in contrast to many neighbouring countries, Swiss vineyards are mostly small and family owned and managed. In addition, most vineyards are located on steep slopes, which require manual labour. The degree of mechanization that was achieved in other winegrowing countries could not be achieved in Switzerland (Schauwecker 1913; Zaugg 1924; Welti 1940; Schlegel 1973).

Third, falling yields were accompanied by falling prices, mainly due to rising wine imports that competed with domestic production. The importation of wine (and other goods) was facilitated by the rapid development of railways and tunnels in Switzerland.

And fourth, Switzerland had relatively low import tariffs. For instance, while Switzerland's wine import tariff in 1892 was CHF 3.00–3.50 per hectolitre of wine, neighbouring Germany charged CHF 24.70 (Schauwecker 1913; Welti 1940). The tariff barrier difference impaired Swiss wine exports to Germany and fostered German exports to Switzerland. It also made Switzerland a target of large wine-producing countries such as France, Italy, Spain and Austria (Dorner 1922). As a result, except for the periods 1930 to 1940 and 1948 to 1962, when France had slightly higher per capita imports

Table 4.7 *Volume and value of wine production and yield, Switzerland, 1900 to 2015*

	1900	1920	1950	1965	1980	2015
			Wine production (KL)			
Zurich	28,123	3,591	4,797	1,803	2,221	3,244
Vaud	77,032	17,090	26,421	25,349	19,857	21,803
Valais	24,573	18,960	11,453	41,727	37,397	32,784
Ticino	10,269	4,805	8,399	6,311	4,013	4,403
Switzerland	**210,325**	**60,554**	**72,030**	**96,559**	**84,196**	**85,045**
			Yield (KL/ha`)			
Zurich	5.86	2.09	6.92	4.62	4.74	5.35
Vaud	11.64	3.81	7.16	7.88	5.69	5.78
Valais	9.18	6.00	3.37	10.61	7.05	6.68
Ticino	1.29	0.98	4.68	5.46	4.85	4.01
Switzerland	**6.91**	**3.28**	**5.53**	**8.15**	**6.19**	**5.75**
			Value of production (1,000 SFr.)			
Zurich	6,368	5,298	5,055	3,328	8,681	.
Vaud	21,249	24,874	30,121	41,851	71,471	.
Valais	6,078	23,172	14,797	69,138	167,700	.
Ticino	1,457	2,973	7,007	8,944	14,189	.
Switzerland	**52,070**	**80,630**	**79,690**	**153,693**	**338,764**	.
			Value per ha (1,000 SFr/ha)			
Zurich	1.33	3.09	7.30	8.52	18.53	.
Vaud	3.21	5.55	8.16	13.01	20.47	.
Valais	2.27	7.33	4.35	17.58	31.63	.
Ticino	0.18	0.61	3.90	7.74	17.15	.
Switzerland	**1.71**	**4.37**	**6.11**	**12.97**	**24.90**	.

Source: Eidgenössisches Statistisches Amt (various volumes).

(mostly from Algeria), Switzerland has always exhibited the world's highest per capita wine imports by volume (Figure 4.7).

For much of the pre–World War I period, Switzerland imported as much wine as Germany and the United Kingdom combined, and was second only to France – even though in 1900 Switzerland's population was only 3.3 million compared with Germany's 54 million and the United Kingdom's 41 million. Only after World War II, when many trade barriers were lowered, did Germany and the United Kingdom move ahead of Switzerland to become the world's largest importers.

These developments in wine production, consumption and trade were facilitated by various policy changes. Similar to Germany, but in contrast

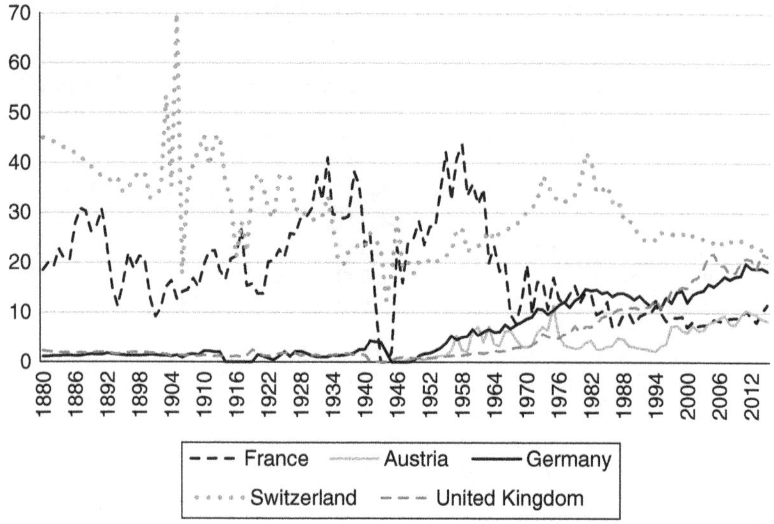

Figure 4.7 Per capita wine imports, Germany, Austria, Switzerland and comparator countries, 1880 to 2015 (litres).
Source: Anderson and Pinilla (2017).

to France and most other wine-producing countries, Switzerland did not impose a federal excise tax on wine until 1935 – and then it was revoked two years later. An attempt to reintroduce the wine excise tax was defeated in a 1966 referendum (Zurbrügg 2009).

In response to mounting tariff barriers in Germany and France in the late 1870s, the Swiss agricultural sector, including its wine industry, was calling for protection as well. However, due to conflicting interests between wine-growers, wine importers and consumers, the government resisted these demands for a long time. Only in the early twentieth century were wine tariffs eventually increased, from CHF 3.50/hl (set in 1872) to CHF 8.00/hl in 1906 (Schauwecker 1913; Welti 1940).

During and immediately after World War I, Swiss viticulture seemed to enjoy some renewed prosperity. Due to the limited availability of imported wine mainly from Italy, France and Spain during World War I, wine prices in Switzerland increased considerably and, for the first time, the government installed a quota system for Swiss wine exports between 1914 and 1917. In 1918, this quota system was replaced by a total prohibition of all wine exports (Dorner 1922). However, with increasing European wine production and the absence of war-induced transportation frictions in the early 1920s, wine imports rapidly increased to record highs. Wine prices fell and export quotas became obsolete.

In the 1920s, Switzerland began to follow the protectionist path of its neighbours and increased its wine tariff rates to CHF 24–33/hl in 1921 and further to CHF 30–50/hl in 1925. The rate depended on the wine's traits, with the upper bound charged for white wines with alcohol contents of above 13 percent (Welti 1940). Given the dominance of white varieties in Swiss viticulture at the time, higher rates for white wines are not surprising. The relative tariff burden reached its peak in 1936, when wine tariffs were 107 percent of the import value of all wines shipped into Switzerland (Welti 1940). Tariff revenue from wine imports had become a major budget item for the Swiss Federal government and would remain so for decades.

Switzerland provides substantial financial support to its agricultural sector, including to grapegrowers and winemakers. However, in contrast to growers of nonwine crops as well as to cattle and sheep farmers, the wine sector has benefitted little from direct payments such as supports for wine cultivation on steep slopes, conversion to ecological farming and the promotion of Swiss wine abroad. Rather, Switzerland relies on a complex system of import quotas and tariffs. While tariffs have existed for more than 120 years, a system of import quotas was added in the 1950s to augment protection of the domestic wine industry (Jörin 2000). Swiss wine import tariff rates are considerably above those of most other Organization for Economic Cooperation and Development (OECD) countries. For instance, while the United States levied 1 percent and most EU countries levied 4 percent on the value of a $9 premium bottle of wine in 1999, Switzerland's rate equalled 17 percent (Berger and Anderson 1999). The current quota system (as of January 2017) involves an annual wine import quota of 170 ML for still wine (red, rosé, and white), for which the low contingent tariff rate applies. The MFN rates per litre are CHF 0.91 for sparkling wine, CHF 0.50 for bottled white wine and red wine, CHF 0.34/0.42 for red bulk wine and CHF 0.34/0.46 for white bulk wine depending on alcohol content. The tax rates refer to the gross weight and include all packaging materials, including the transportation pallet. Once the import quota is exhausted, the tariff rates increase substantially and an out-of-quota rate applies. For instance, the rate for bottled still wine is between CHF 3.00 and CHF 5.10 (Schweizerische Eidgenossenschaft, Federal Customs Administration, 2017). However, to date the import quota has never been exhausted.

CONCLUSIONS

Germany, Austria and Switzerland share a long history of viticulture reaching back to Roman times, more than 2,000 years ago. They share a common language (with the exception of a significant share of French, Italian and Romansh speakers in Switzerland), are high-income countries and grow grapes in what are deemed 'cool' climates (with the exception of a few warm-climate regions, such as Dalmatia, that belonged to nineteenth century Austria). For most of their history, all three countries have been net wine importers. Germany and Switzerland currently rank number one worldwide for wine imports by volume and per capita, respectively. Due to their location in the middle of Europe, all three countries have been exposed to similar forces such as wars, business cycles, changes in the trade environment and climatic changes.

In spite of these commonalities, there are also profound differences among Germany, Austria and Switzerland. First, looking back 200 years, Germany has come into existence by unifying numerous small states in the nineteenth century (integration), while the Austrian Empire was decomposed into separate states after World War I (segregation). In contrast, Switzerland has enjoyed territorial integrity for centuries.

As a result, for the German states, the abolishment of customs barriers was a means to achieve unification. With the creation of a single free trade zone, the *Zollverein*, in 1834, the German states moved from economic integration to political integration in 1871. For the Austrian Empire (1804–1867) and later Austria-Hungary (1869–1918), free trade was a less pressing issue. In fact, free trade between Austria and Hungary, the two main parts of the empire, was possible only after 1850. Other far-flung states of the empire, such as Dalmatia, received free market access only after 1880. Switzerland did not have to integrate heterogeneous states on its territory and did not have any internal trade barriers. Until the 1920s, Switzerland also resisted following the protectionist moves of its neighbours that build up external trade barriers.

For almost 200 years, winegrowers in all three countries have asked for protectionist measures to shield them from wine imports from warmer-climate countries. During the 1830s, Mosel vintners feared the competition of southern German winemakers, Austrian winemakers were afraid of Dalmatian wines in 1870 and Swiss vintners were concerned about Italian wine imports in the 1920s. In general, grape growers in cool climates have always dreaded competition from warmer climates.

With the establishment of the European Common Market, German winegrowers, mostly unprotected, substantially improved their productivity and profitability. German vineyards exhibit the highest yields and, on average, the highest profitability per hectare within Europe. This was partially accomplished by intra-German substitutions. In search for profitability, the German vineyard moved northwest, from Württemberg and Baden toward Rheinhessen and Palatinate (Pfalz). In contrast, Austrian and Swiss viticulture still depends heavily on public protection (subsidies and tariffs, respectively).

It remains to be seen whether future challenges, such as climate change, can be mastered in a similar fashion. The European system of planting rights and maximum yield regulations may pose a major obstacle to successful adaptation. After all, the current system allots most increases in vineyard areas to incumbents. In 2016, the EU granted a combined 16,380 ha of new planting rights to Italy, Spain, France, Portugal and Greece, while Germany planted only 263 extra ha.

REFERENCES

Anderson, K. (2014), 'Excise Taxes on Wines, Beers and Spirits: An Updated International Comparison', AAWE Working Paper No. 170, American Association of Wine Economists, www.wine-economics.org

Anderson, K. and H. G. Jensen (2016), 'How Much Government Assistance Do European Wine Producers Receive?' *Journal of Wine Economics* 11(2): 289–305.

Anderson, K. and V. Pinilla (with the assistance of A.J. Holmes) (2017), *Annual Database of Global Wine Markets, 1835 to 2016*, freely available in Excel at the University of Adelaide's Wine Economics Research Centre, www.adelaide.edu.au/wine-econ/databases

Ashenfelter, O. and K. Storchmann (2010), 'Using Models of Solar Radiation and Weather to Assess the Economic Effect of Climate Change: The Case of Mosel Valley Vineyards', *Review of Economics and Statistics* 92(2): 333–49.

Ashenfelter, O. and K. Storchmann (2016), 'Climate Change and Wine: A Review of the Economic Implications', *Journal of Wine Economics* 11(1): 105–38.

Bassemir, E. (1930), *Subventionen und Zölle in ihrer Bedeutung für die Erhaltung des deutschen Weinbaues, dargestellt unter besonderer Berücksichtigung der preußischen Verhältnisse*, Doctoral Thesis, University of Cologne, Bonn: Ludwig.

Bassermann-Jordan, F. von (1907), *Geschichte des Weinbaus unter besonderer Berücksichtigung der bayerischen Rheinpfalz*, Frankfurt am Main: Keller.

Beck, O. (1869), *Der Weinbau an der Mosel und Saar nebst einer vom k. Katasterinspektor Steuerrath Clotten zu Trier angefertigten Steuerkarte*, Trier: Selbstverlag der königlichen Regierung zu Trier.

Berger, N. and K. Anderson (1999), 'Consumer and Import Taxes in the World Wine Market: Australia in International Perspective', *Australasian Agribusiness Review* 7(3), June, www.agrifood.info/review/1999/Berger.html

Braumüller, W. (1868), *Zur Frage des Oesterreichischen Weinexportes. Amtliche Consularberichte über die Verhältnisse des Weinhandels in den bedeutenderen Handelsplätzen*, Vienna: Österreichische Land-und Forstwirtschaftsgesellschaft in Wien.

Brüders, W. (1999), *Der Weinskandal*, Linz: Denkmayr.

Brugger, H. (1968), *Statistisches Handbuch der schweizerischen Landwirtschaft*, Bern: Komm. Verl. Verbandsdruckerei.

Bundesministerium für Ernährung und Landwirtschaft (BMEL) (2016a), *Ertragslage Garten- und Weinbau. Daten-Analysen 2016*, Berlin: BMEL.

Bundesministerium für Ernährung und Landwirtschaft (BMEL) (2016b), *Genehmigungssystem für Rebpflanzungen; Festlegung des Prozentsatzes*, Letter from BMEL to the European Commission. Online at www.ble.de/SharedDocs/Downloads/01_Markt/17_PflanzrechteWein/Genehmigung_Rebpflanzungen_Przentsatz.pdf;jsessionid=B6B6CA35143E5DDBF19C7E5A86DFE01D.1_cid335?__blob=publicationFile (accessed 30 January 2017).

Commission of the European Communities (2007), *Report from the Commission to the European Parliament and the Council on Management of Planting Rights Pursuant to Chapter I of Title II of Council Regulation (EC) No 1493/1999*, COM(2007) 370 final, Brussels: Commission of the European Communities.

Deckers, D. (2010), *Eine Geschichte des deutschen ein sim Zeichen des Traubenadlers*, Mainz: Verlag Philipp von Zabern.

Deconinck, K. and J. Swinnen (2014), 'The Economics of Planting Rights in Wine Production', *European Review of Agricultural Economics* 42(3): 419–40.

Dieterici, C. F. W. (1848), *Statistische übersicht der wichtigsten Gegenstände des Verkehrs und Verbrauchs im preußischen Staate und im deutschen Zollvereine*, Berlin and Posen: Verlag Ernst Siegfried Mittler.

Dorner, W. (1922), *Der Aussenhandel der Schweiz mit Wein während des Krieges 1914–1918, mit besonderer Berücksichtigung der Kontingentierung durch die S.S.S*, Bern: Akademische Buchhandlung Paul Haupt.

Eidgenössisches Departement für Wirtschaft, Bildung und Forschung (2016), *Das Weinjahr 2015*, Bern: Weinwirtschaftliche Statistik.

Eidgenössisches Statistisches Amt (various volumes, 1891–2016), *Statistisches Jahrbuch der Schweiz*, Basel: Druck und Verlag E. Birkhäuser & Cie.

European Commission (2016). Online at ec.europa.eu/agriculture/sites/agriculture/files/wine/statistics/scheme-authorisations_en.pdf (accessed 8 February 2017).

European Commission (2017), *Farm Accountancy Data Network*. Online at ec.europa.eu/agriculture/rica/ (accessed 6 February 2017).

Gall, L. (1854), *Praktische Anleitung, sehr gute Mittelweine selbst aus unreifen Trauben, und vortrefflichen Nachwein aus den Tresteren zu erzeugen, als Mittel, durch Vor- und Auslesen und Sortiren alljährlich auch werthvolle Desertwein zu gewinnen*, Trier: Verlag Gall.

Hassinger, J. (1928), *Die Entwicklung des deutschen Weinzolles seit der Schutzzollära unter besonderer Berücksichtigung der Handelsverträge nach dem Kriege*, PhD Thesis, University of Freiburg, Mainz: Druckerei Lehrlingshaus.

Herrmann, K. (1980), 'Die deutsche Weinwirtschaft während des Zweiten Weltkriegs', *Zeitschrift für Agrargeschichte und Agrarsoziologie* 28(2): 157–81.

Heuss, T. (1906), *Weinbau und Weingärtnerstand in Heilbronn am Neckar*, Dissertation, Munich, 1905. Reprinted 2005, Brackenheim: Carlesso Carlesso.

Hlubek, F. X. (1864), *Der Weinbau in Oesterreich*, Graz: Selbstverlag.

Hoffmann, D. (1988), 'Mengenregulierung: Planwirtschaftliches Torso?' *Weinwirtschaft Markt* 3(1988): 30–7.

Homlong, N. and E. Springler (2007), 'Regional Development in the European Union: Implications for Austria's Viticulture', pp. 243–60 in *The State of European Integration*, edited by Y. A. Stivachtis, Aldershot: Ashgate.

Hoppe, H. (1901), *Die Thatsachen über den Alkohol*, 2nd edition, Berlin: S. Calvary & Co.

Jörin, R. (2000), 'WTO-Projekt: Einzelmarktstudien: Die Regelung des Marktzutritts beim Wein', mimeo, ETH Zurich. Online at www.ethz.ch/content/dam/ethz/special-interest/usys/ied/agricultural-economics-dam/documents/Robert%20J/Projects/2000_BLW-Wein-Oct%202000.pdf (accessed 8 February 2017).

K.K. Ackerbau-Ministerium (1873), *Verhandlungen der Weinbau-Enquête in Wien, 1873*, Vienna: Faesy and Frick.

K.K. Ackerbau-Ministerium (1900), *Bericht über die Verbreitung der Reblaus (Phylloxera vastatrix) in Österreich in den Jahren 1898–1899, sowie über die Maßregeln, welche behufs Wiederherstellung des Weinbaues getroffen wurden und die Erfahrungen, die sich hierbei ergaben*, Vienna: Verlag des K.K. Ackerbauministeriums.

K.K. Ackerbau-Ministerium (various years), *Statistisches Jahrbuch des K.K. Ackerbau-Ministeriums, Erstes Heft. Production aus dem Pflanzenbau. Druck und Verlag der K.K. Hof- und Staatsdruckerei*, Vienna: Verlag des K.K. Ackerbauministeriums.

K.K. Direction der administrativen Statistik (1828–1871), *Tafeln zur Statistik der österreichischen Monarchie*, Vienna: K.K. Hof- und Staatsdruckerei.

K.K. Statistische Central-Commission (1901), *Österreichisches Statistisches Handbuch für die im Reichsrathe vertretenen Königreiche und Länder. 19. Jahrgang 1900*, Vienna: Verlag der K.K. Statistischen Central-Commission.

Keil, H. and F. Zillien (2010), *Der deutsche Wein 1930 bis 1945. Eine historische Betrachtung*, Dienheim am Rhein: Iatros Verlag.

Komlos, J. (1983), *The Habsburg Monarchy as a Customs Union: Economic Development in Austria-Hungary in the Nineteenth Century*, Princeton, NJ: Princeton University Press.

Kosmetschke, R. and R. Hepp (1991), *Strukturen und Tendenzen auf dem Weltweinmarkt*, Schriftenreihe des Bundesministers fuer Ernährung, Landwirtschaft und Forsten, Reihe A: Angewandte Wissenschaft, Heft 393. Münster: Landwirtschaftsverlag GmbH.

Mach, E. (1899a), *Der Weinbau Österreichs von 1848 bis 1898*, Vienna: Commissionsverlag Moritz Perles.

(1899b), 'Österreichs Weinbereitung und Weinverwertung', pp. 400–89 in *Austria: Comité zur Herausgabe der Geschichte der österreichischen Land- und Forstwirtschaft und ihrer Industrien 1848–1898*, Volume III, Vienna: Commissionsverlag Moritz Perles.

Meitzen, A. (1869), *Der Boden und die landwirtschaftlichen Verhältnisse des preußischen Staates nach dem Gebietsumfange vor 1866*, Berlin: Wiegandt and Hempel.

Meloni, G. and J. Swinnen (2013), 'The Political Economy of European Wine Regulations', *Journal of Wine Economics* 8(3): 244–84.

(2016), 'The Political and Economic History of Vineyard Planting Rights in Europe: From Montesquieu to the European Union', *Journal of Wine Economics* 11(3): 379–413.

Meyer, F. (1926), *Weinbau und Weinhandel an Mosel, Saar und Ruwer. Ein Rückblick auf die letzten 100 Jahre*, Koblenz: Görres-Druckerei Koblenz.

Mueller, R. (1913), *Die deutsche Weinkrisis unter besonderer Berücksichtigung der Verhältnisse im Moselweingebiet: Eine agrar- und handelspolitische Studie*, Stuttgart: Eigenverlag.

Österreichisches Statistisches Zentralamt (1924), *Statistisches Handbuch für die Republik Österreich 1924*, Vienna: Österreichisches Statistisches Zentralamt.

Postmann, K. P. (2010), *Wein österreich. Alles über Wein und seine Geschichte*, Vienna: Krenn.

Robin, J. (1845), *Die fremden und inländischen Weine in den deutschen Zollvereins-Staaten*, Berlin: Selbstverlag.

Schauwecker, C. (1913), *Der schweizerische Weinhandel unter dem Einflusse der gegenwärtigen Wirtschaftspolitik: Eine wirtschaftliche Studie*, Zurich and Leipzig: von Rascher and Co.

Schlegel, W. (1973), *Der Weinbau in der Schweiz*, Wiesbaden: Franz Steiner Verlag.

Schnitzius, D. (1964), *Deutschlands Wein-Außenhandel seit dem Ersten Weltkrieg*, PhD Thesis, University of Bonn, Bonn.

Schweizerische Eidgenossenschaft, Federal Customs Administration (2017), *Tares* Online at xtares.admin.ch/tares/login/loginFormFiller.do;jsessionid=4cwfYD7B0 17hQT4x1Dyn10krtzDWPq1N2QYqjM218c2ch4p228yN!-1493811114 (accessed 20 January 2017).

Staab, J., H. R. Seelinger and W. Schleicher (2001), *Nine Centuries of Wine and Culture on the Rhine*, Mainz: Woschek Verlag.

Statistik Austria (various years), *Ernteerhebung*, Vienna: Bundesministerium für Land- und Forstwirtschaft, Umwelt und Wasserwirtschaft. Available online at duz .bmlfuw.gv.at/Land/weinernte.html (accessed 8 February 2017).

Statistisches Reichsamt (1922), *Statistisches Jahrbuch für das Deutsche Reich 1921/22*, Berlin: Verlag für Politik und Wirtschaft.

Statistisches Reichsamt (1938), *Statistisches Jahrbuch für das Deutsche Reich 1937*, Berlin: Puttkammer and Mühlbrecht.

Storchmann, K. (2005), 'English Weather and Rhine Wine Quality: An Ordered Probit Model', *Journal of Wine Research* 16(2): 105–19.

(2006), 'Asymmetric Information and Markets in Transition: Vineyard Auctions in the Mosel Valley After the French Revolution', *Journal of European Economic History* 35(2): 395–424.

(2017), 'The Wine Industry in Germany, Austria and Switzerland 1835–2016', American Association of Wine Economists: AAWE Working Paper No. 214.

Thiersch, J. (2008), *Die Entwicklung der deutschen Weinwirtschaft nach dem Zweiten Weltkrieg, Staatliche Maßnahmen zu Organisation und Wiederaufbau der Weinwirtschaft*, Taunusstein: Verlag Driessen.

Torp, C. (2014), *The Challenges of Globalization: Economics, and Politics in Germany 1860–1914*, New York: Berghahn.

Türke, K. (1969), *Der Weinbau in Rheinhessen. Eine agrar- und sozialgeographische Untersuchung*, unpublished PhD Thesis, University of Bochum, Bochum.

United Nations (2017), Comtrade Database. Online at comtrade.un.org (accessed 8 February 2017).

Welti, F. (1940), *Probleme der schweizerischen Weinwirtschaft*, Zurich: Schulthess.

Weise, H. (1958), 'Der deutsche Wein im europäischen Markt', Kieler Studien Nr. 46, Kiel: Institut für Weltwirtschaft an der Universität Kiel.

Wiesgen-Pick, A. (2016), *Der Pro-Kopf-Verbrauch der verschiedenen alkoholhaltigen Getränke nach Bundesländern 2015*, Bonn: BSI Bundesverband der Deutschen Spirituosen-Industrie und -Importeure e.V. Online at www.spirituosen-verband .de/fileadmin/introduction/images/Daten_Fakten/BSI-Aufsatz_PKV_nach_BL_ 2015.pdf (accessed 20 January 2017).

Wine-Inside (2016), 'Neupflanzungen + Wiederbepflanzungen 2016 in 13 Weinbau treibenden L/ndern der EU'. Online at www.wein-inside.de/uploads/PFLANZUNGEN%20EU%202016%20Neupflanzungen%20und%20Wiederbepflanzungen%20mrwi.pdf (accessed 30 January 2017).

Winter-Tarvainen, A. (1992), *Weinbaukrise und preußischer Staat, Preußische Zoll- und Steuerpolitik in ihren Auswirkungen auf die soziale Situation der Moselwinzer im 19. Jahrhundert*, Trierer Historische Forschungen Vol. 18, Trier: Verlag Trierer Historische Forschungen.

Wohlfahrt, J. (n.a.), *Der österreichische Weinbau 1950–2010, Weinbau Dokumentation*, Rötzer-Druck: Eisenstadt.

Zaugg, F. (1924), *Erhebungen über Stand und Rentabilität des Rebbaus in der Schweiz*, Brugg: Verlag des Schweizerischen Bauernsekretariates.

Zurbrügg, C. (2009), *Die schweizerische Alkoholpolitik und Prävention im Wandel der Zeit. Unter besonderer Berücksichtigung der Rolle der Eidgenössischen Alkoholverwaltung*, Dossier for Eidgenössische Alkoholverwaltung, Bern: Federal Alcohol Agency.

5

Italy to 1938

Giovanni Federico and Pablo Martinelli

Wine has been essential for the Italian region's Mediterranean economy and life-style since the beginning of its civilization. Vines, unlike olive trees, can be cultivated almost everywhere on the peninsula, and wine was a basic item of everyday consumption and one of the most important products of the Italian economy. Yet Italy's wine industry in the nineteenth century was very different from the present-day one. It was fragmented into hundreds of thousands of small farms, each of them growing just a few vines, often scattered in the fields rather than in vineyards. Grapes were processed by producers with traditional equipment, and most wine was consumed by producers and the rest by dwellers of nearby cities. The quality of wine was poor by modern standards. Chianti was deemed by British experts the best Italian wine, and yet it was losing market share because it travelled very badly (Marescalchi and Dalmasso 1937; Biagioli 2000, pp. 331–34).

The conditions of Italian wine production improved slowly in the late nineteenth and early twentieth centuries. By 1938, the industry was still mostly traditional and backward, although one could find the first sprouts of postwar development. This chapter outlines this transformation from the outset of Italy's formation as a nation in 1861. In the next section, we show how important wine-growing was in the Italian economy pre–World War II, and we describe the main features of wine-growing. The main trends in production, consumption and prices from Unification to 1938 are then outlined. Improvements in quality are then discussed, combining anecdotal evidence with data for the late 1930s. Exports are then analysed before the chapter concludes.

WINE AND THE ITALIAN ECONOMY

The relevance of wine in the Italian economy over the six decades to 1951 is clear from Table 5.1.[1] The low figures for 1938 and 1951 are to some extent anomalous, as they reflect the collapse in the relative price of wine. In fact, when the shares of gross agricultural output are expressed in constant (1911) prices, they declined from 24.2 percent in 1891 and 23.1 percent in 1911 to 19.3 percent in 1938, with a modest rebound to 21.6 percent in 1951.

Wine was more important in Italy than in France and Spain, where it accounted for an average of about 10 percent of France's gross agricultural output (Toutain 1961, tables 76, 77), with a peak of 17 percent in the 1860s and 1870s, and for 11 to 16 percent of Spain's net agricultural output (Simpson 1994). Shares of GDP and of private consumption were correspondingly lower in France and Spain than in Italy.

Although wine was produced almost everywhere in Italy, its production was geographically fairly concentrated. Around 1930, only thirty out of 795 *zone agrarie* (agrarian zones), all in the mountains, did not produce any wine (Martinelli 2014). The agrarian zones were small, though, and thus none of them produced more than 2 percent of Italian wine. However, half of total wine was produced in 100 zones and a quarter in just thirty-five of them. The latter were rather scattered all over the peninsula, but the eleven most-productive ones, which accounted for 10 percent of total output, were concentrated in Southern Piedmont (four), Tuscany (four) and Sicily (three).

Italy stood apart in world wine-growing for the diffusion of *coltura promiscua* – the practice of growing vines intercropped together with other products *in the same plot*. In the words of an Austrian official surveying the countryside of Lombardy-Venetia for the cadaster:

> There is nothing more striking to the eye of a Northern traveler as those parallel rows of different trees that rise amid the wheat fields, and from the foot of which the vines rise, climb up to the beginning of the branches and are then stuck from tree to tree in the manner of garlands hanging in the air and full of fruit … Getting from the same field a crop of grain and wine, is something that can be had only in a climate as warm as is that of Italy. This method is ancient, as Cato and Varro already talked about it nineteen centuries ago, as a common practice in the country. If the climate were less hot, the shade of trees would damage far more the harvests of grains, and the grapes would be located so far from the ground to be not able to ripen … Most of the wine of the Regno Lombardo-Veneto is produced on

[1] The data on gross output in the four benchmark years are from a research project on Italian historical national accounts (Baffigi 2011). As discussed in this chapter, the series on wine output is currently being revised.

Table 5.1 *Wine's importance in the economy of Italy, 1891 to 1951 (% at current prices)*

	1891	1911	1938	1951
% of gross value of agric. output:				
Wine and by-products	***21.2***	***22.2***	***11.2***	***9.3***
Wheat	19.7	15.3	24.3	14.9
Other cereals and pulses	9.7	6.3	6.3	6.9
Other crops	9.6	11.8	12.1	12.6
Oil and by-products	5.2	4.4	2.8	6.1
Other tree crops	8.2	8.7	12.4	10.2
Livestock	14.3	20.0	21.3	28.5
Other animal products	12.1	11.3	9.6	11.4
All agriculture	100.0	100.0	100.0	100.0
Wine's share of total GDP (%)	8.6	7.7	2.9	2.0
Wine's share of total private consumption (%)	11.6	11.1	5.1	3.6

Sources: Authors' compilation from Federico (2000 table 1A and 1B) for gross output and expenditures on wine, Zamagni (1992, pp. 195–96) and Zamagni and Battilani (2000, p. 241) for mark-ups, and Baffigi (2011) for total gross domestic product (GDP) and consumption.

flatland … On flatland, vines are never cultivated otherwise than in the midst of cultivated fields … Vines are stuck to many kinds of trees, such as maple, poplar, willow, ash, cherry and even walnut … (Burger 1843, pp. 61–63).

Hanging vines to trees allowed them to grow much more and, as a consequence, to produce more than three times the quantity of grape per plant than the average specialized vine (ISTAT 1929). Although there was much discussion in the nineteenth century among agronomists about whether this method of cultivation gave grapes an undesirable taste (and about which trees were responsible for which effects on grapes), peasants paid little attention to these debates since the practice allowed saving on stakes and supplied additional quantities of wood.

According to the very careful data from the Catasto Agrario (ISTAT 1929), in the late 1920s, Italy had three times as many hectares intercropped as specialized (3 million ha against less than 1 million). Its output accounted for a little less than 50 percent of national production in the 1930s. Intercropping was not unknown in southern Europe, but it was much less diffused than in Italy (Table 5.2). Intercropping was clearly declining in France: it had accounted for 8.7 percent of output in 1882 (SAF 1897), but it was not even reported as a separate category in the 1929 Agrarian Census (SAF 1936). Ministerio de Economía Nacional (1931) does not report data

Table 5.2 *Intercropped winegrowing, Italy 1929, France 1892 and Spain 1930*

	Area (% of total vine area)	Output (% of total wine output)	Yield per ha (% of specialized)	Vines per ha (% of specialized)	Yield per vine (% of specialized)
Italy (1929)	76.2	44.1	24.7	7.2	322
France (1892)[a]	7.2	3.6	47.6	33.2	143
Spain (1930)	18.9	n.a.	n.a.	n.a.	n.a.

[a] The share of intercropped vines may be overvalued, as it excluded newly planted vines, which were 17 percent of the bearing area.

Source: France: SAF (1897, pp. 84–87); Spain: Ministerio de Economía Nacional (1930, pp. 104–5); Italy: ISTAT (1929), Tavola Riassuntiva.

on production of intercropped vines in Spain, but they could not have yielded more than one-tenth of total output.

Moreover, a nonspecialized, intercropped vineyard and a specialized one were very different in Italy than elsewhere. The former was made of much fewer vines (428) per hectare than the latter (5,838), or, for that matter, than intercropped vineyards in late nineteenth century France (2,786). The Catasto Agrario included in specialized vineyards also fields with olive trees or other tree crops, provided that grapes were the most important product (*superficie integrante a coltura mista prevalente*).[2] In contrast, if grapes were a secondary product, the acreage was defined as nonspecialized (*superficie ripetuta in altre colture legnose specializzate*). These cases, however, accounted for only 2.7 percent of Italy's nonspecialized area (a little more than 80,000 ha) and for less than 1 percent of all vines. The bulk of intercropped vines, therefore, was found scattered across arable land (*superficie ripetuta in coltura promiscua*).

It is important to stress that intercropping was not necessarily an inferior type of wine-growing. Specialized vineyards were an almost exclusive form of cultivation in most of southern Italy (with the exception of densely populated Campania). In the North, they were prevailing in Piedmont, in some hillside areas along the Po Valley and in some Alpine valleys, as well as in Istria. Intercropped vineyards were found almost everywhere else, but they were the prevailing form of cultivation in Venetia, Emilia and Central Italy. They produced some of the best Italian wine, including

2 Spanish statistics classified this pattern of cultivation as intercropping, and it accounted for most nonspecialized acreage (Ministerio de Economía Nacional (1930, p. 106). Therefore, the figures in Table 5.2 underestimate the difference between Spain and Italy.

the Chianti. In that area, vines were cultivated by sharecroppers in intercropped vines, but the quality was high thanks to the strict supervision of the owner and to the processing of grapes in large-scale wineries in each estate (*fattorie*).

Understanding the economic rationale for intercropping is a fascinating but not easy task. Intercropped vines were diffused where the density of rural population was very high (and thus labour-intensive crops like vines were more profitable) and where peasant dwellings were scattered in the countryside rather than concentrated in big villages (so called agro-towns) as in the South. This pattern of settlement reduced the costs for monitoring and caring for intercropped vines, increasing the appeal of intercropping as a risk-minimizing and land-intensive use of soil. Indeed, intercropping slowed the spread of the phylloxera in the country, since the intercropped vines were larger and had deeper and therefore more resistant roots than the specialized ones (Spagnoli 1948).

A CENTURY OF CHANGE

All Italian agricultural statistics after Unification but before the reorganization of the service in 1909 are rather unreliable (Federico 1982), but the data for wine are particularly problematic. Estimating wine output is impossible without data on acreage, that is, without a cadaster. Some pre-Unification states did have a cadaster and thus data on acreage, which in Table 5.3 we compare with the data from the Catasto Agrario (ISTAT 1929) for comparable territorial units.

The pre-Unification cadasters are not qualitatively comparable with the Catasto Agrario (the data for Piedmont in 1850 are surely underestimated), but they highlight how patterns of cultivation across Italy were well established before the twentieth century and, to a high degree, quite persistent. Indeed, they do not even report data for the pattern of cultivation which the Catasto shows to have been marginal in each area, such as specialized vineyards in Tuscany or intercropped vines in Sicily. This persistence is confirmed by the data for smaller territorial units. In the Papal States, specialized vines were mostly clustered in the Castelli Romani, the area east of Rome. In the Papal States and in the South (Kingdom of the Two Sicilies before 1861), both types of cultivation expanded in parallel, with a sharp increase in the specialized acreage in Apulia during the boom of the 1880s. Elsewhere, the growth of acreage under vines concentrated in the traditionally prevailing type, specialized vineyards in Piedmont and Sicily, intercropping in Tuscany and so on. Acreage declined only in minor producing areas, such as Sardinia and Milan.

Table 5.3 *Long-run changes in specialized and intercropped vine areas, Italy, 1550 to 1929 (ha)*

	1550 ca.	1750 ca.	1750 ca.	1810 ca.	1810 ca.	1840 ca.	1840 ca.	1929	1929
	Total	Spec.	Inter.	Spec.	Inter.	Spec.	Inter.	Spec.	Inter.
Piedmont		138,524	*170,632*	>153,900	n.a.	47,190?	n.a.	177,110	*49,532*
Liguria						20,360	n.a.	10,034	*34,667*
Sardinia						55,991	*5,787*	33,644	*14*
Milan	83,891							1,990	*18,668*
Venetia						1,139	*695,952*	29,016	*584,515*
Tuscany						0	*391,025*	24,563	*439,389*
South				337,008	*108,358*			360,400	*205,700*
Sicily						145,400	*0?*	193,243	*8,038*
Papal States						40,578	*718,026*	73,633	*1,090,548*

Sources: Piedmont 1750: Prato (1908, p. 62); Piedmont (without the departement of Stura and the arrondissement of Aoste) ca 1810: Almanach (1809); Liguria and Sardinia (1840): Aperçu Comparatif (1852); Milan (former Duchy of Milan) 1500: Pugliese (1924); Continental South 1810: Granata (1830); Papal States 1840: Galli (1840); Sicily 1840: Mortillaro (1854); Grand-Duchy of Tuscany 1840: Mazzini (1881); Venetia 1840: Scarpa (1963).

Unfortunately, after its Unification, Italy did not update these cadasters nor fill their gaps. Thus, the statistics before 1909 simply ignored the difference between specialized and nonspecialized vineyards, lumping them in a single figure for 'vineyards'. These data, and consequently the yields per hectare, are hardly comparable in time or space. The official statistics (*Notizie Periodiche di Statistica Agraria*, NPSA) started to distinguish acreage under *coltura specializzata* and *promiscua* after 1909, relying wherever possible on the preliminary work for the future cadaster and elsewhere on estimations. They show a modest decline in specialized vineyard data in the 1910s and 1920s, possibly related to the spread of phylloxera, but they are not wholly accurate. Indeed, the *Catasto Agrario* (1929), the first survey of the allocation of land in the whole country with modern and homogeneous criteria, reclassified massively the acreage from *promiscuo* to *specializzato*. The 1930s' data are fully reliable, and on the whole they show little change until World War II.

Without reliable acreage data, it is difficult to estimate accurately the production of wine. Indeed, before 1909 the output data are missing in several years, and the available ones are sometimes inconsistent. Thus, from 1862 to 1913, following Federico (2000, 2003), we reestimate production from the consumption side, using the new series of wages and prices, from ongoing research by Federico, Nuvolari and Vasta (2017), to obtain a proxy for income (assuming an income elasticity of 0.5 and a price elasticity of −0.3). We obtain a series of wine production within Italy's current borders (Figure 5.1) by multiplying consumption by population (ISTAT 1966) and adding net exports (Federico et al. 2012). The resulting (provisional) series fluctuates less than the true one because we do not take into account consumption smoothing via inventory changes. After 1914, we rely on official statistics (NPSA, *Bollettino Mensile di Statistica Agraria e Forestale* [BMSAF] and *Annuario Statistico dell'Agricoltura Italiana* [ASAI]), with some amendments before 1935.[3]

According to our estimate, wine consumption per capita remained stable at around 90 litres in the 1860s and 1870s, and then rose slowly from the 1880s to levels around 110–120 litres in the 1920s. Then consumption per capita declined down to 83 litres in 1933–1938. Overall, throughout the whole period Italian wine consumption per capita remained consistently lower than in France and higher than in Spain. The difference in total

3 We broadly follow the adjustment procedure suggested by Istituto Centrale di Statistica (ISTAT), that is, we adjust the level of production according to the old statistics by the gap between them and the Catasto in 1929. We use this procedure for all provinces before 1929, while from 1930 to 1935 we use it only for the provinces whose current statistics were not entirely based on the Cadastre.

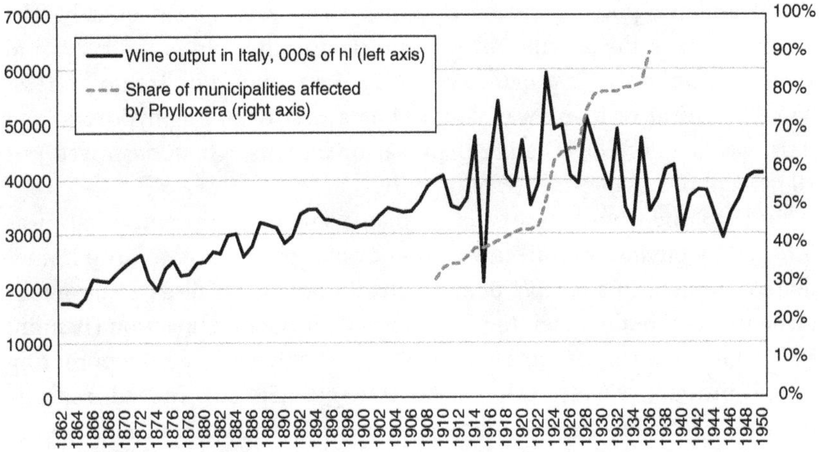

Figure 5.1 Wine production and the diffusion of phylloxera, Italy, 1862 to 1938 (kl and %).
Sources: Authors' compilation (see text) and, re. phylloxera, Spagnoli (1948).

alcoholic intake with France was even larger because Italians drank less spirits than the French and almost no beer (Anderson and Pinilla 2017).

The long-run growth in wine production (Figure 5.1) is consistent with the much more modest increase in acreage from Table 5.3 if there was a substantial increase in productivity or an intensification of cultivation. The long-run upward trend was brought to a halt by the Great Depression and also by the spread of phylloxera.

Phylloxera appeared in the early 1880s in three different locations: Valmadrera (north of Milan) in 1879, Sicily in 1880 and Sardinia in 1883. For about twenty years, the infection was limited to the islands, Calabria, Liguria (where it had spread from France) and the Lombard hillsides, but new infections were detected at the turn of the century in the provinces of Bari, Pisa and Udine (as well as in Alto Adige and Trentino). Yet initially diffusion was comparatively slow (Figure 5.1). On the eve of World War I, it affected only one-third of Italian municipalities (mostly in the South), about one-third of vineyards in Apulia (De Felice 1971, p. 266) but only one-tenth of the acreage in the province of Alessandria, which then included the area of Asti, one of the top wine-producing areas in Piedmont (Zannoni 1932).

The initial effect of phylloxera on production was very small and thus it did not lead to massive wine imports as was required in France (see Chevet et al. 2018; Meloni and Swinnen 2018). The lack of treatment during World

War I and the postwar years helped the disease to spread quickly. The infected area in the province of Alessandria grew fivefold in the 1920s and extended to the whole province by 1932. The province of Trento by 1928 had 43 percent of its prewar vineyard area destroyed by phylloxera, and thus was far more devastating than war operations, which destroyed just 10 percent of all vineyards (Rigotti 1931).

By 1935, the whole country, other than a small area in central Italy, was infected by phylloxera. Infection did not cause production to drop immediately, though: in a sample of eight Tuscan farms, the disease cut output by 60 percent, but only ten to fifteen years after the first infection (Bandini 1932). Growers from Apulia in the 1900s strongly opposed the uprooting of still-productive vines (De Felice 1971, pp. 258–62). Indeed, replanting was a very expensive option: its direct cost, without consideration of foregone output, equaled four to five times the value of yearly gross output of wine, according to an estimate for the whole northeast in 1942 by Montanari and Ceccarelli (1950, p. 140).[4] The cost and the low prices of the 1930s (as opposed to the high ones of the 1910s and 1920s) may have discouraged some farmers. By 1930, only 40 percent of the infected area had been replanted in Trentino (Rigotti 1931) and 56 percent in Alessandria (Zannoni 1932). On the other hand, there is evidence (although no hard data) that farmers in Chianti took the opportunity to replace traditional intercropped vines with intensive vineyards (Dalmasso 1932; Ministero dell'Agricoltura e delle Foreste 1932, pp. 104–9). But even a fast replanting could not avoid a decline in output, as newly vines need about ten years to resume full production. Spagnoli (1948) estimates that in the 1940s phylloxera reduced output by 10 percent and affected one-third of intercropped vineyards and one-tenth of specialized ones.

So far, we have considered wine as a homogeneous product, but we know this was not the case. On the one hand, there is some evidence of quality improvement at the top end on the market, which we review in the next section. On the other hand, peasants produced for domestic consumption the *vinello*, an inferior product that is excluded from output statistics, by pouring water (sometimes adding sugar) on the marc remaining after the first fermentation (Strucchi 1899; Ottavi and Strucchi 1912). The marc retained about one-fifth of the alcohol content of grapes (Dandolo 1820, vol. 2, p. 211; Tassinari 1945, p. 1157), which could be extracted by pressing the

[4] This order of magnitude is confirmed by Rigotti's estimate for the sole province of Trento in 1928 (Rigotti 1931, pp. 328–31), implying four years of output per hectare (Gross output data from Martinelli, 2014).

marc again (*vino torchiato*) or distilling them into grappa. Thus the actual production of wine and *vinello* depended on the allocation of marc between these three alternative uses. Peasants of the province of Treviso (Venetia) in the 1870s refused to have marc pressed, since this would have reduced the production of *vinello* (Vianello and Carpenè 1874). According to Dandolo (1820), in the Napoleonic Kingdom of Italy only half of the marc was pressed, thus about one-tenth of potential wine output was lost. About a century later, an official body (MAIC 1914) put forward a nationwide estimate of foregone potential output of 2.1 percent, which corresponds to a 13 to 14 percent loss for the former Kingdom of Italy (mostly in Emilia and Venetia). One might thus conclude that, in these areas, the practice of producing *vinello* had not significantly declined in the nineteenth century. It was possible to produce between two-thirds and as much *vinello* as wine: if all nonpressed marc had been used in the production of *vinello*, rather than distilled, on the eve of World War I, the output would have been equivalent to about one-tenth of the whole production of wine, that is, about 10 litres per capita.

It is likely that economic growth and urbanization reduced the consumption of *vinello*. It was surely an inferior product relative to wine for all consumers, and on top of this it could not sustain transportation and marketing costs and taxation for urban consumption. Indeed, the Milan tax statistics register a very small consumption of *vinello* in the 1910s (0.1–0.2 litres per capita), which disappeared in the 1930s (Città di Milano ad annum). We speculate that some of the increase in consumption of wine in the early decades of the twentieth century (most notably the postwar peak) reflected the substitution from *vinello*.

THE 'CREATION' OF ITALIAN WINE

Conventional wisdom (e.g., Pedrocco 1993) suggests that Italian wine in the nineteenth century was quite bad because most consumers were interested only in getting as much alcohol as possible at the lowest possible price. The rich drank the best wine from their estate and/or imported French wine. The only sector that was relatively modern produced so-called 'special' wines: marsala, vermouth and spumanti (sparkling wines).

Marsala, a fortified wine akin to Sherry, had been discovered and commercialized, according to possibly apocryphal record, by the Englishman Wodehouse in 1773. The recipe for vermouth (an infusion of herbs, including wormwood, in white wine) had been perfected in 1786 by Carpano in Turin. The first drinkable imitations of French champagne were produced almost contemporarily in 1865 by Gancia in Asti (Piedmont) and Carpene in Valdobbiadene (Veneto).

The available, sometimes apologetic, descriptions of the wineries stress their size and the modernity of their technology. According to the ministry for agriculture, on the eve of World War I, Italy produced 87,500 ML of 'special' wines, without any further distinction between types (MAIC 1914). Twenty-five years later, Italy produced 36,700 KL of marsala, 36,200 KL of vermouth, 5,300 KL of spumanti and 36,100 KL of other special wines, for a total of more than 100,000 KL (ISTAT 1940). Thus, special wines accounted for 2.4 to 2.9 percent of total output. They were essential for the economy of producing areas, but they aimed at specific niche markets in Italy and abroad.

The 'creation' of high-quality wines for table consumption was a much more difficult undertaking (Simpson 2011). Unlike the production of vermouth and perhaps marsala, it needed a radical overhaul of the whole production process, from the choice of grapes to the marketing of wine. By its nature, it has been a slow process, which affected literally millions of farms and thousands of wineries. Thus we know very little of it. The literature focuses on a few pioneers, who since the early nineteenth century tried to improve wine from their estates, imitating the parallel (and much more advanced) process in France. Dalmasso and Marescalchi (1937) hints to the key wake-up role of oidium, a disease of vines which spread in the 1840s and 1850s. The best-known among these pioneers is Ricasoli, who inherited the large estate of Brolio in the heart of Chianti in the 1830s (Biagioli 2000). He gave very detailed instructions to sharecroppers about the choice of varieties and the method of pruning and harvesting (the latter possibly to increase their sugar content), while he supervised personally the selection of grapes and the wine-making. He chose a mix of grapes which was later officially adopted as 'Chianti Classico', to be changed only a few years ago. Thus, in the 1860s the best Chianti from Brolio sold in Florence at a premium of about two-thirds over the price of common wine. Ricasoli also tried to find new outlets for his wine, opening a shop in Milan (on top of already existing ones in Firenze and Siena) and venturing into the American market. In the long run, his marketing strategy paid off, also thanks to the transfer of Italian capital to Florence (1866–1870), which let the Italian elites know about Chianti. Other landowners imitated him, so that at the beginning of the 1930s Dalmasso could praise wine-making in core areas of Tuscany as giving 'a reassuring impression of rational technicality, devoid of unnecessary and thus anti-economical exaggerations' (Dalmasso 1932, p. 110).

In areas of small-size peasant ownership, the cooperative wineries (*cantine sociali*) were a key agent of modernization. The idea had been broached as early as the 1870s, but their development was very slow. They do not appear as a distinct category in the first statistics of Italian cooperation in 1890 (Zangheri 1987, p. 186). An official publication (MAIC 1908) lists thirty-six cooperative wineries in 1906–1907, but most of them had been established in 1905 to apply for subsidies for purchasing equipment granted by a 1904 law. In 1927, the *cantine sociali* numbered just ninety-eight, producing 66,000 KL, about 1.6 percent of output (Fornasari and Zamagni 1997, p. 129). Ten years later, the number had risen to 176, producing about 100,000 KL or 2.6 percent of output (Ente Nazionale n.d, pp. 88–89). Most of them aimed at producing good wine for bulk sale rather than, as with Ricasoli, high-quality wine. Their contribution was to improve quality wine for mass consumption and to spread awareness of basic principles of modern cultivation and wine-making among farmers.

The role of the state as agent of transformation in the nineteenth century was limited to investment in professional education (see Banti 2004 for an overview). The Austrian government had established the first specialized schools for wine production in S. Michele all'Adige (Trentino) in 1874, and Italy imitated it by founding a school in Conegliano in 1876 (Lazzarini 2004) and later also in Avellino, Alba, Catania and Cagliari. These were worthy but tiny initiatives: in 1904–1909, the five schools graduated just 350 pupils.

The state intervention was more incisive in the twentieth century. As in other European countries, Italy had enacted regulations in 1888 to limit the transportation of wine saplings to prevent the spread of phylloxera (Royal decree no. 5252), but without much success.[5] When the situation became serious, it set up compulsory farmers' associations (*Consorzi anti-fillosserici*) to produce and distribute free saplings of American vines (1901 no. 355). The first *Consorzio* was established in Apulia in 1901, and they were extended to the whole country in 1907. In spite of controversies, and of some delay in response, the state initiative did help farmers to overcome the crisis in the long run (Montanari and Ceccarelli 1950 p. 138; De Felice 1971, pp. 260–67).

The key contribution of the state to the improvement of Italian wine industry was, however, the protection of 'typical wines' of higher quality against widespread fraud and abusive misnomers (Redazione IVA 1928; Dalmasso, Cosmo and Dell'Olio 1939). Italy started later than France, but

[5] The agricultural school of S. Michele was accused of spreading phylloxera in Trentino by importing infected vine saplings (Ruatti 1955).

a bit earlier than Spain. The initiative had been taken in the early twentieth century by Teobaldo Calissano, a member of parliament from Alba, a major wine-producing area in Piedmont, but with no success. A law was presented to the parliament in 1921, but it was saddled in the process until approved by royal decree on 7 March 1924 (no. 497). It was eventually converted into law in 1926 (18 March, no. 562) but the regulations, with the first official definition of 'typical wine', followed suit only in June 1927 (Royal Decree no. 1440). A (voluntary) association of producers, the Consorzio Chianti Classico, had been established three years before, but the implementation of the law proved so controversial that a new law was eventually prepared and passed in July 1930 (no. 1164), with regulations following shortly thereafter.

The 1930 law delimited for the first time the areas of typical wines and gave incentives for producers to join the Consorzi, which had to be officially recognized by Ministerial Decree. In subsequent years, such decrees were issued for Soave (23 October 1931), Castelli Romani (26 February 1932, with an additional decree for subvarieties and their production areas on 2 May 1933), Chianti and subareas (23 June 1932) and Barolo and Barbaresco (31 August 1933). Yet the law was not fully effective, as joining Consortia was not compulsory and fines for misnomers in domestic trade were absent. Hence, a third, more restrictive law was eventually passed (10 June 1937), incidentally absorbing producers' Consortia into the rising corporatist structure of the Italian Fascist state.

Documenting the change in the quality of Italian wine is rather difficult. There is fairly abundant anecdotal evidence, from agronomical journals, technical literature and reports to expositions (e.g., Florence in 1861), but very little hard data. The best proxies for quality are prices, and in the next section we use them to assess the relative quality of Italian exports. The available data on domestic prices are hardly useful as they all refer to common wine and thus there is no obvious yardstick to compare them in space and above all over time. Yet they highlight an important fact: the quality of wine varied a lot across the country, and these differences were permanent. The coefficient of variation of average prices for first-quality table wine was around 0.27 for about seventy markets in the 1880s and early 1890s (MAIC 1874–1896), and 0.24 for thirty markets in 1935–1938 (ISTAT 1935–1938). This dispersion must reflect differences in quality rather than transportation costs, as the coefficient for wheat, an even bulkier product, was around 0.06 in the 1880s.

The only available data on production of high-quality wines have been collected by the Industrial Census of the late 1930s (ISTAT 1940), which covered only wineries with a capacity over 50 Kl. It registered 7,932 such

Table 5.4 *Volume of production of quality wine, Italy, 1938 (KL)*

	Total output	Industrial output	Quality red	Quality white	Quality wine as % total output	Quality wine as % of industrial
Piedmont	351,387	100,814	23,354	na	6.6	23.2
Liguria	44,124	3,753	na	na	na	na
Lombardy	201,584	129,410	na	na	na	na
Trentino-A.A.	46,812	41,043	22,580	2,953	54.5	62.2
Veneto	227,216	86,142	21,475	10,193	13.9	36.8
Julian Venetia	46,516	45,056	na	na	na	na
Emilia	412,774	243,207	18,305	2,194	5.0	8.4
Tuscany	323,933	119,841	45,184	21	14.0	37.7
Marches	238,792	21,257	na	na	na	na
Umbria	142,958	15,582	na	1,621	1.1	10.4
Lazio	174,910	11,910	572	5,941	3.7	54.7
Abruzzi	157,595	2,899	na	na	na	na
Campania	294,341	10,438	157	247	0.1	3.9
Apulia	350,073	227,069	na	na	na	na
Basilicata	23,446	949	na	na	na	na
Calabria	46,505	5,280	na	na	na	na
Sicily	317,948	106,087	na	na	na	na
Sardinia	10,091	13,912	na	na	na	na
Italy	**3,411,005**	**1,184,647**	**131,627**	**23,170**	**4.5**	**13.1**

Source: ISTAT (1940), ASAI (1936–1938).

facilities with an average production of 140 KL, equivalent to about 200,000 bottles of 0.75 litres. Only seventy-two wineries – fourteen in Apulia, thirteen in Emilia and seven in the Trapani area (for marsala) produced more than 2000 KL of wine (2.7 million bottles), and only two of them might have exceeded 20 million bottles.[6] Table 5.4 compares the census data on industrial production, total and for quality wine only, to total wine output.

These figures are likely to be a lower bound. First, some very good wine was produced in areas which had not yet been officially recognized as such (note that there is no quality wine listed south of Naples). Second, in the listed areas, quality wine was also produced by peasants. Indeed, area-specific sources report substantially higher figures for the production of *vino tipico*

[6] The largest recorded winery in Bologna produced 8,650 KL, or 11.1 million bottles. We obtain the upper bound of size by assuming that all but one winery in each province produced 2,000 KL of wine and attributing the difference with total production to one single plant.

(although not all of it was up to the standards of the best wineries).[7] Even discounting some undervaluation, the shares of quality wine are strikingly low, with the exception of Trentino which, before 1918, belonged to Austria-Hungary and had a consolidated tradition of co-operation.

WINE EXPORTS

Before Unification in 1861, foreign trade in wine was very limited. In the 1850s, Tuscany (Parenti 1959) and the Papal States (Bonelli 1961) were net importers of wine, while Lombardy-Venetia (Glazier 1966) and the Duchies (Correnti and Maestri 1864, p. 430) were net exporters.[8] Piedmont (Romeo 1976) had been a net exporter of wine until the early 1850s, when oidium cut its production. However, traded quantities were small and in all likelihood only for local cross-border consumption (i.e., these flows would disappear if we considered post-Unification boundaries). The exception was Sicily, which exported substantial quantities of marsala – up to 30,000 KL in peak years – mostly to Britain (Battaglia 1983).

Exports of marsala continued after Unification, but total Italian exports remained small until the late 1870s, fluctuating around 20,000 Kl, equivalent to 5 percent of world exports. They accounted for only 1.5 percent of output and 2 percent of Italian exports (Figure 5.2).[9]

Italian exports boomed in the 1880s thanks to the phylloxera crisis in France, which absorbed four-fifths of them (Chevet et al. 2018). At their peak, Italian exports exceeded 200,000 KL, accounting for 6 to 8 percent of both Italian wine output and Italian merchandise exports and almost one-sixth of the volume of global wine exports.[10]

[7] Dalmasso et al. (1939) report a total output of 32,700 KL of quality wine (Soave, Valpolicella) for the Verona province vs 28000 KL from the Industrial Census (85 percent). The Ministero dell'Agricoltura e delle Foreste (1932, p. 363) estimates production of Chianti at 57,800 KL, out of a total of 166,500 KL in the provinces, versus 45,100 according to the Industrial Census. Garavini (1933) estimates between 2,800 (actually sold) and 3,800 KL (produced) of Orvieto wine, while the Industrial Census reports 1,600 KL. A detailed 1942 inquiry for all provinces in the Northeast (Montanari and Ceccarelli 1950) estimates as quality wine 80 percent of average wine production in the previous twelve years in Trentino–Alto Adige, 23 percent in Venetia and 40 percent in Venetia Giulia. Prosperi (1940) puts forward a figure of 40,000 KL in the Castelli Romani area versus 6,500 KL according to the Industrial Census.

[8] Graziani (1956–1957) does not quote wine among imports or exports of the Continental South – showing how irrelevant its trade was.

[9] All trade data, if not otherwise specified, are from the database underlying Federico et al. (2012).

[10] The peak in 1887 is spurious, as it reflects the expectation of an increase in French import duties.

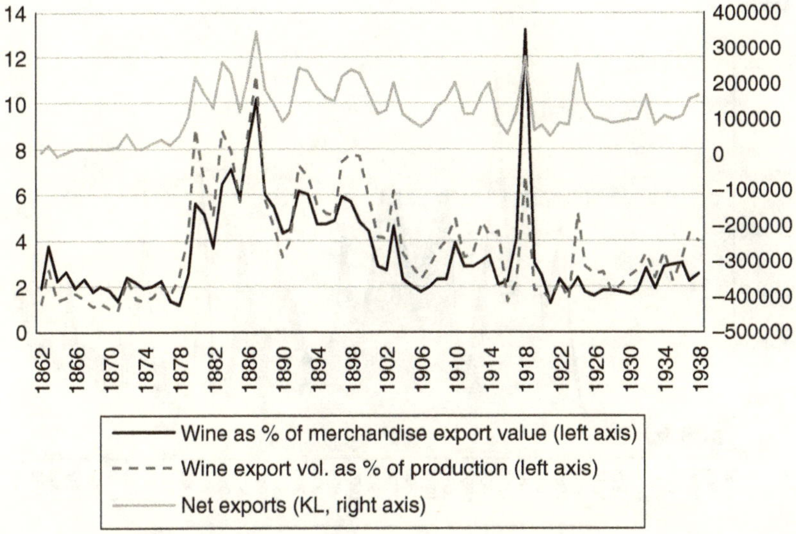

Figure 5.2 Wine export volume and share of production, and wine export value as share of merchandise exports, Italy, 1862 to 1938 (KL and %).
Sources: See text.

The boom created great expectations in the South and triggered massive investments in new plantations. The producers' hopes were dashed by the outbreak of a trade war with France that led to the imposition of very high duties on Italian wine in 1888. In the short term, the disaster was averted by negotiating a so-called wine clause with Austria-Hungary that led to a substantial cut in duties on their wine imports from Italy, effective from 1892. For about a decade, the Dual Monarchy was the main outlet (about 45 percent) for somewhat reduced Italian exports. The clause was not renewed in 1903, though, when Italian exports started to decline. They fluctuated between 100 and 200 ML, with the occasional peaks, until World War II. Wine remained a minor item in Italian exports, accounting for less than 5 percent of the total for all goods. The export destinations were more diversified than in the nineteenth century. Italy's main client was officially Switzerland (about one-third of exports), while Germany and above all the colonies became major markets in the late 1930s (Figure 5.3).

In the twentieth century, Italy was the fourth-largest exporter of wine in the world, well behind Algeria but also, barring exceptional years, behind Spain and France. Furthermore, its share of the volume of world exports declined from 14 percent in the early 1900s to about 10 percent on the eve of World War I and then to 6 to 7 percent after that war.

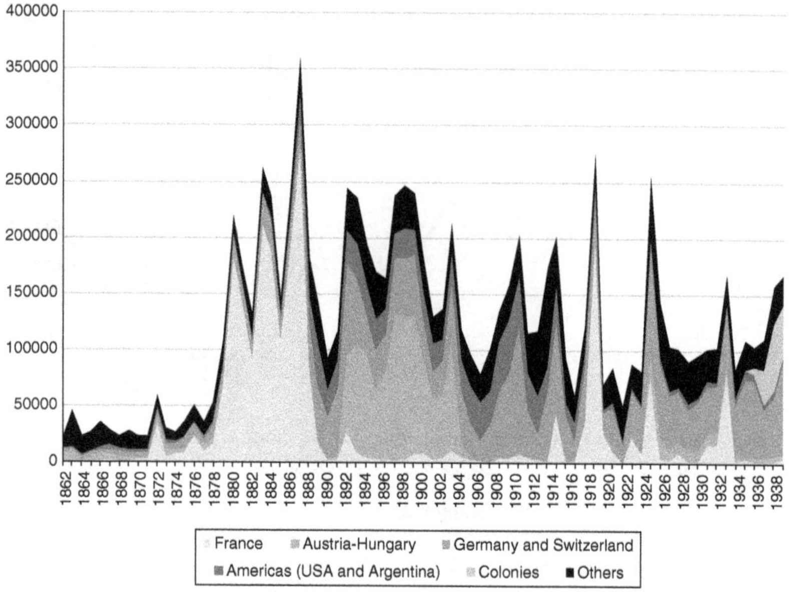

Figure 5.3 Exports of Italian wine, by destination, 1862 to 1938 (KL).
Source: Federico et al. (2012).

The Italian share of world exports was lower in the 1900s and higher afterwards if measured in value rather than in volume. This suggests an improvement in the relative quality of Italian wine, which we measure in Figure 5.4 with the ratios of the unit value of Italian exports to exports from France, the undisputed leader in the top end of the market, and from Spain and Algeria, Italy's main competitors in the mass market. Italian wine remained much cheaper than French wine throughout the whole period, with wide fluctuations but no clear upward trend in the ratio. The gap was very large in the 1860s, reduced in the 1870s, widened in the 1880s and 1890s, closed partially in the 1900s and in the 1920s and widened again in the 1930s. In contrast, Italian wine was somewhat better than Spanish wine (average ratio 1.28, or 1.12 excluding the wartime peak) and Algerian wine (ratio 1.45). Both ratios increased before World War I, albeit with huge fluctuations, suggesting some relative and, in all likelihood, absolute improvement.

Unfortunately, the Italian trade statistics until 1897 distinguish wine, both imports and exports, only according to the container (barrels or bottles). These latter accounted for about 3 to 4 percent of total exports (in volume) in the 1860s and 1870s and collapsed to less than 1 percent during

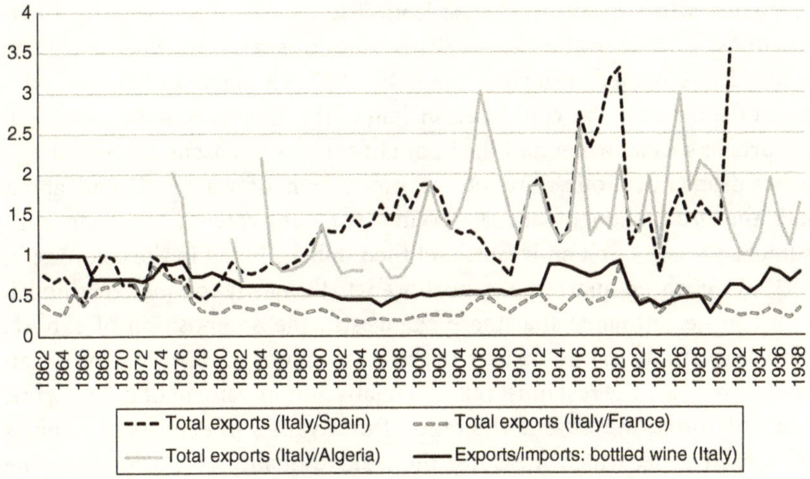

Figure 5.4 Relative quality of Italian wine exports,[a] 1862 to 1938.
[a] The average unit value of wine exports from Italy relative to that from other wine-exporting countries.
Sources: Federico et al. (2012), Anderson and Pinilla (2017).

the boom of the 1880s, remaining at such levels until 1898. These figures are lower-bound estimates of the share of quality wine on total exports: in all likelihood, bottles contained only quality wine, but some marsala and vermouths were exported in barrels as well.[11] The relative decline in average unit values of the 1880s and their increase in the 1890s reflect a change in destination of Italian wine. In the 1880s, Italy exported to France mostly *vino da taglio*, strong southern wine, which French used to mix with local wine in order to increase its alcohol content, while Austria-Hungary imported table wine.

Since 1898, trade statistics report separately exports of wine in *fiaschi*, a traditional container for Chianti wine (Ministero dell'Agricoltura e delle Foreste 1932, p. 281) and of vermouth (in barrels and bottles). They began to report separately exports of marsala (in barrels and bottles) in 1921 and exports and imports of 'spumante' (bottles only) in 1924. We thus can estimate total exports of 'quality wines' as the sum of wine in bottles and in fiaschi, spumante, marsala and vermouth. In this definition, the share

[11] Exports in barrels of marsala and vermouth accounted for three-quarters of total exports in 1898–1938, and for about 10 percent of total exports in barrels. Also, Chianti was exported in barrels rather than in bottles (Ministero del'Agricoltura e delle Foreste 1932, pp. 281–2).

of quality wine (by volume) rose from 2 to 3 percent in the early 1900s to almost a third in the late 1930s. Exports of sparkling wines and wine in bottles remained negligible (in 1936–1937, 95 percent of the production of spumante was consumed in Italy). The rise reflects the growth of exports of special wines and the boom of exports in fiaschi. In 1936–1937, exports absorbed one-third of the production of vermouth and about half the production of marsala. Wine in fiaschi catered to Italian consumers abroad – first emigrants and then Italians living in the colonies: in 1935–1938, three-quarters of exports went to the newly conquered Ethiopia.

It can be estimated that these changes in the composition of exports alone explain up to one-quarter of the rise in ratios of unit value of Italian wine exports.[12] The rest must reflect a relative improvement of Italian wine. The only proxy we have is the ratio of unit values of exports to imports of bottled wine, which measures the relative quality of top market wine (Figure 5.4).[13] It does not show a clear improvement, confirming the message of the stability of unit values relative to France. This implies also that in the twentieth century the improvement was concentrated in bulk exports, consistent with the upward trend in unit values relative to Spain and Algeria.

CONCLUSIONS

In the decades covered in this chapter, Italian wine-growing did not change much. It is possible to detect some early signs of what became the postwar transformation, though: the growth of production of special wines, the efforts to improve the quality of wines and the first attempts to give legal protection to area-specific labels, and so on. But even on the eve of World War II, the production of quality wine was limited and Italian wineries were small, and thus in all likelihood unable to exploit economies of scale in processing and above all marketing. Thus the big changes had to wait for the transformation of the whole Italian economy and society during the 'economic miracle' of the 1950s and 1960s. The rural exodus and the superfast growth of incomes (and, symmetrically, of the cost of labour) changed completely the patterns of consumption and the shape of Italian agriculture.

[12] We estimate a counterfactual series of unit values of Italian wine to 1938 assuming that common wine accounted for 99 percent of exports as in 1880.

[13] The relative export/import unit value of bottled spumanti, available only since 1924, is also stable around 0.4.

REFERENCES

Almanach (1809), *Almanach du Departement du Pô pour l'An 1809*, Turin: Chez Michel-Ange Morano.

Anderson, K. and V. Pinilla (with the assistance of A. J. Holmes) (2017), *Annual Database of Global Wine Markets, 1835 to 2016*, freely available in Excel at the University of Adelaide's Wine Economics Research Centre, www.adelaide.edu.au/wine-econ/databases.

Aperçu Comparatif (1852), 'Aperçu Comparatif des travaux enterpris por le cadastre des Etats Sardes. Rapport fait le 26 mai 1852 à la Commission du Cadastre nominée par la Chambre le 23 avril', pp. 607–59 in *Atti del Parlamento Subalpino, Sessione del 1852 (IV Legislatura) dal 4 marzo 1852 al 21 novembre 1853. Documenti. Vol. I*, Florence: Botta, 1867.

ASAI (1936–1938), ISTAT, *Annuario Statistico dell'Agricoltura Italiana*, ad annum.

Baffigi, A. (2011), 'Italian National Accounts, 1861–2011', Economic History Working Papers, Banca d'Italia, Rome.

Bandini, M. (1932), *Aspetti economici della Invasione Fillosserica in Toscana*, Studi e Monografie, n. 17, Milan and Rome: Istituto Nazionale di Economia Agraria.

Banti, A. M. (2004), 'Istruzione agraria, professioni tecniche e sviluppo agricolo', pp. 717–44 in *Agricoltura come manifattura*, edited by G. Biagioli and R. Pazzagli, Florence: Olschki.

Battaglia, R. (1983), *Sicilia e Gran Bretagna*, Milan: Giuffrè.

Biagioli, G. (2000), *Il modello del proprietario imprenditore nella Toscana dell'Ottocento: Bettino Ricasoli. Il patrimonio. Le fattorie*, Florence: Olschki.

BMSAF (ad annum), ISTAT *Bollettino Mensile di Statistica Agraria e Forestale*, ad annum, Rome.

Bonelli, F. (1961), 'Il commercio estero dello stato Pontificio nel secolo XIX', *Archivio Economico dell'Unificazione Italiana* serie I, vol. 9, Turin: ILTE.

Burger, G. (1843), *Agricoltura del Lombardo-Veneto*, Milan: Carrara.

Chevet, J.-M., E. Fernandez, E. Giraud-Héraud and V. Pinilla (2018), 'France', ch. 3 in *Wine' Globalization: A New Comparative History*, edited by K. Anderson and V. Pinilla, Cambridge and New York: Cambridge University Press.

Città di Milano (ad annum), *Bollettino Municipale Mensile* (1906–1926), later *Rivista mensile del comune di Milano*, Milan: Città di Milano.

Correnti, C. and P. Maestri (1864), *Annuario statistico italiano*, Turin: Tipografia Letteraria.

Dalmasso, G. (1932), 'Viticoltura ed enologia toscana', *Annuario della Stazione sperimentale di viticoltura ed enologia di Conegliano* 4: 7–281.

Dalmasso, G., I. Cosmo and G. Dell'Olio (1939), *I vini pregiati della provincia di Verona*, Rome: Tipografia Failli.

Dandolo, C. (1820), *Enologia. Ovvero l'arte di fare, conservare e far viaggiare i vini del regno*, 2nd edition, Milan: Sonzogno.

De Felice, F. (1971), *L'agricoltura in Terra di Bari dal 1880 al 1914*, Milan: Banca Commerciale Italiana.

Ente Nazionale (no date), *Dati statistici sulle organizzazioni cooperative*, Rome: Ente Nazionale fascista della Cooperazione.

Federico, G. (1982), 'Per una valutazione critica delle statistiche della produzione agricola italiana dopo l'Unità (1860–1913)', *Società e Storia* 15: 87–130.

(2000), 'Una stima del valore aggiunto dell'agricoltura italiana', pp. 5–112 in *I conti economici dell'Italia. 3.b. Il valore aggiunto per gli anni 1891, 1938 e 1951*, edited by G. M. Rey, Rome and Bari: Laterza.

(2003), 'Le nuove stime della produzione agricola italiana, 1860–1910: primi risultati ed implicazioni', *Rivista di Storia economica* 19(3): 359–81.

Federico, G., S. Natoli, G. Tattara and M. Vasta (2012), *Il commercio estero italiano 1861–1939*, Rome and Bari: Laterza.

Federico, G., Nuvolari, A. and Vasta, M. (2017), 'The origins of regional divide: evidence from real wages 1861-1913', CEPR DP 12358.

Fornasari, M. and V. Zamagni (1997), *Il movimento cooperativo in Italia*, Firenze: Vallecchi.

Galli, A. (1840), *Cenni Economico-Statistici sullo Stato Pontificio*, Rome: Tipografia Camerale.

Garavini, G. (1933), 'Delimitazione della zona di produzione del vino tipico di Orvieto. Relazione a S.E. IL ministro', *Nuovi annali dell'agricoltura* 13(3–4): 226–63.

Glazier, I. (1966), 'Il commercio estero del regno Lombardo Veneto dal 1815 al 1965', *Archivio Economico dell'Unificazione Italiana* 15(1): 1–143.

Granata, L. (1830), *Economia Rustica per lo Regno di Napoli*, Naples: Tip. Del Tasso.

Graziani, A. (1956–1957), 'Il commercio estero del regno delle Due Sicilie dal 1838 al 1858', *Atti dell'Accademia Pontaniana* 6: 200–17.

ISTAT (1929), *Catasto agrario del Regno d'Italia*, Rome: Istituto Centrale di statistica, ISTAT.

ISTAT (1935–1938), *'Bollettino dei prezzi', Supplement to the Gazzetta Ufficiale*, Rome: Istituto Centrale di statistica, ISTAT.

ISTAT (1940), *Censimento industriale e commerciale Volume I Industrie Alimentari 1937*, Rome: Istituto Centrale di statistica, ISTAT.

ISTAT (1966), *Lo sviluppo della popolazione italiana dal 1861 al 1961*, Annali di statistica serie VIII vol. 17, Rome: Istituto Centrale di statistica, ISTAT.

Lazzarini, A. (2004), 'Trasformazioni dell'agricoltura e istruzione agraria nel Veneto', pp. 359–409 in *Agricoltura come manifattura*, edited by G. Biagioli and R. Pazzagli, Firenze: Olschki.

Marescalchi, A. and G. Dalmasso (1937), *Storia della vite e del vino in Italia* I, Milan: Gualdoni.

Martinelli, P. (2014). 'Von Thünen South of the Alps: Access to Markets and Interwar Italian Agriculture', *European Review of Economic History* 18(2): 107–43.

Mazzini, C. M. (1881), 'La Toscana Agricola', in *Atti della Giunta per la Inchiesta Agraria e sulle condizioni della classe agricola. Vol. III Fasc. 1*, Rome: Tip Del Senato.

MAIC (1874–1896), *Bollettino settimanale dei prezzi dei prodotti agricoli e del pane*, Rome: Ministero di Agricoltura, industria e commercio, weekly.

MAIC (1908), 'Cantine Sociali ed associazioni di produttori di vino', in *Annali di Agricoltura*, Rome: Ministero di Agricoltura, industria e commercio.

MAIC (1914), *Il vino in Italia*, Rome: Ministero di Agricoltura, industria e commercio.

Meloni, G. and J. Swinnen (2018), 'Algeria, Morocco and Tunisia', ch. 16 in *Wine' Globalization: A New Comparative History*, edited by K. Anderson and V. Pinilla, Cambridge and New York: Cambridge University Press.

Ministerio de Economía Nacional (1931), *Anuario Estadístico de las Producciones Agrícolas 1930*, Madrid: Ministerio de Economía Nacional.

Ministero dell'Agricoltura e delle Foreste (1932), *Per la tutela del vino Chianti e degli altri vini tipici toscani. Relazione della commissione interministeriale per la delimitazione del territorio del vino Chianti*, Bologna: Ministero dell'Agricoltura e delle Foreste.

Montanari, V. and G. Ceccarelli (1950), *La viticoltura e l'enologia nelle Tre Venezie*, Treviso: Longo e Zoppelli.

Mortillaro, V. (1854), *Notizie Economico-statistiche ricavate sui catasti di Sicilia*, Palermo: Stamperia Pensante.

NPSA (ad annum), Ministero di Agricoltura, industria e commercio, *Notizie Periodiche di Statistica Agraria*, Rome: Ministero di Agricoltura, industria e commercio.

Ottavi, O. and A. Strucchi (1912), *Enologia*, Milan: Hoepli.

Parenti, G. (1959), 'Il commercio estero del Granducato di Toscana dal 1851 al 1859', pp. 1–15, in *Archivio Economico dell'Unificazione Italiana*, serie I, vol. VIII, fasc. 1, Turin: SELTE.

Pedrocco, G. (1993), 'Un caso ed un modello: viticoltura ed industria enologica', pp. 315–42 in *Studi sull'agricoltura italiana Annali Feltrinelli* XX, edited by P. P. D'Attorre and A. De Bernardi, Milan: Feltrinelli.

Prato, G. (1908), *La vita economica in Piemonte a mezzo il secolo XVIII*, Turin: Società Tipografico-Editrice Nazionale.

Prosperi, V. (1940), *I vini pregiati dei Castelli Romani*, Rome: REDA.

Pugliese, S. (1924), *Condizioni Economiche e Finanziarie della Lombardia nella prima metà del secolo XVIII*, Turin: Bocca.

Redazione IVA (1928), *Redazione dell'Italia Vinicola ed Agraria La legge sui vini tipici*, Casale Monferrato: Ottavi.

Rigotti, R. (1931), 'Rilievi Statistici e considerazioni sulla viticoltura trentina', *Esperienze e Ricerche dell'Istituto Agrario e Stazione Sperimentale di San Michele all'Adige*, Nuova serie, Volume Primo 1929–1930: 271–353.

Romeo, R. (1976), *Gli scambi degli stati sardi con l'estero nelle voci più importanti della bilancia commerciale (1819–1859)*, Turin: Biblioteca di 'Studi Peimontesi'.

Ruatti, G. (1955), *Lo sviluppo viticolo del Trentino*, Trento: Comitato Vitivinicolo della Provinica di Trento.

SAF (1897), Statistique Agricole de la France, *Résultats Généraux de l'Enquête Décennale de 1892 – Tableaux*, Paris: Imprimerie Nationale.

SAF (1936), Statistique Agricole de la France, *Résultats Généraux de l'Enquête de 1929*, Paris: Imprimerie Nationale.

Scarpa, G. (1963), *L'Agricoltura del Veneto nella prima metà del XIX secolo. L'utilizzazione del suolo*, Archivio Economico dell'Unificazione Italiana, Serie II, Volume VIII, Turin: ILTE.

Simpson, J. (1994), *The Long Siesta*, Cambridge and New York: Cambridge University Press.

(2011), *Creating Wine: The Emergence of a World Industry, 1840–1914*, Princeton: Princeton University Press.

Spagnoli, A. (1948), 'I danni della fillossera', *Bollettino di Statistica Agraria e Forestale* 9: 67–72, September.

Strucchi, A. (1899), *Il cantiniere*, 3rd edition, Milan: Hoepli.
Tassinari, G. (1945), *Manuale dell'Agronomo*, 2nd edition, Rome: REDA.
Toutain, J. C. (1961), 'Le Produit de l'Agriculture Française de 1700 a 1958' ['Histoire quantitative de l'economie française' (1) and (2)], *Cahiers de l'Institut de Science Economique Appliquee*, Serie AF 1 and 2, Paris: ISEA.
Vianello, A. and A. Carpenè (1874), *La vite ed il vino nella provincia di Treviso*, Rome, Turin and Florence: Loescher.
Zamagni, V. (1992), 'Il valore aggiunto del settore terziario in Italia nel 1911', pp. 191–239 in *I conti economici dell'Italia. 2 Il valore aggiunto per il 1911*, edited by G. M. Rey, Rome and Bari: Laterza.
Zamagni, V. and P. Battilani (2000), 'Stima del valore aggiunto dei servizi', pp. 241–371 in *I conti economici dell'Italia. 3.b. Il valore aggiunto per gli anni 1891, 1938 e 1951*, edited by G. M. Rey, Rome and Bari: Laterza.
Zangheri, R. (1987), 'Nascita e primi sviluppi', pp. 5–216 in *Storia del movimento cooperativo in Italia*, edited by R. Zangheri, G. Galasso and C. Valerio, Turin: Einaudi.
Zannoni, I. (1932), *Alessandria irrigua ed agraria*, Alessandria: Colombani.

6

Italy from 1939

Alessandro Corsi, Eugenio Pomarici and Roberta Sardone

Italy's wine industry was not hurt greatly by World War II. Damage to vineyards was redeemable, but wine production fell due to the reduction of labour in agriculture and the reorganization of food production in favour of war needs (Bonardi 2014). Given also the uncertainties of statistics during these years, the following analysis will consider the postwar period, when wine production returned quickly back to a level around that of the 1937–1939 prewar period of just under 4,000 million litres (ML). It was in the following decades that the Italian wine industry underwent deep and radical changes. They can be summarized as:

- Strong growth of the volume of wine production, which doubled between 1946 and the 1980s, followed by a rapid decrease
- A major change in wine sales destination, from a negligible share to about half of production being exported
- A sizeable shift from the production and consumption of basic and cheap wines to higher-quality wines
- A change in the organization of the wine value chain, with emerging players and an increasing vertical integration

This evolution happened in different phases, marked by different drivers and characteristics. Although somewhat arbitrary, we subdivide our discussion of the industry's postwar evolution into four periods, and in each section of the chapter we focus on grape growing, wine making, domestic consumption, exports and policies affecting the industry. Table 6.1 summarizes the main trends over those four periods, and Figures 6.1, 6.2 and 6.3 depict key indicators for all years from 1939. Additional relevant data, related to the four periods, are shown in Tables A6.1, A6.2, A6.3 and A6.4 (see Appendix).

Table 6.1 *Trends of key wine industry variables, Italy, 1946 to 2014*

	1946–70	1970–86	1986–2000	2000–14
Change in specialized (single-crop) grapevine area	+	-	–	–
Yield per ha variation (specialized area)	++++	++	+	-
Wine production volume variation	++++	+	–	–
Wine export volume	low but increasing	booming	increasing rapidly	increasing
Wine consumption variation	++++	–	–	–
Per capita wine consm. variation	+++	–	–	–
Real export price variation (national currency)	–	-	+++	+++
Exports as % of wine prod'n volume	+	++	+++	+++

Source: Authors' compilation from official sources and Anderson and Pinilla (2017).

1946–1970: STRUCTURAL CHANGE AND DOMESTIC CONSUMPTION-DRIVEN EXPANSION

The main aspects of the first twenty-five years of Italy's postwar development are growth in the volume of wine production driven by technical changes in vineyards on the supply side and by domestic consumption growth on the demand side. Exports had a negligible, though gradually increasing, role.

During 1946 to 1970, Italian wine production increased by 94 percent, which was very similar to the pace of wine output growth in the rest of the world, which expanded 97 percent. Growth was especially rapid during the first postwar decade. It was not due to any increase in vine area (although intercropped vines diminished dramatically while specialized vineyards expanded), but rather to large increases in yields, from an average of 0.9 to more than 3 KL of wine per hectare (Figures 6.1 and 6.2).

The main reason for this transformation was a dramatic change in specialization. In the later 1940s, three-quarters of the national area under vine involved intercropping, especially in the northeast and central regions (see Federico and Martinelli 2018). Between 1946 and 1970, the specialized vineyards area rose by one-eighth and the area of intercropping vineyards decreased by two-thirds (Figure 6.1, Table A6.1 and Corsi, Pomarici and Sardone 2004). This was part of the dramatic changes taking place in Italian agriculture during that period, as part of the overall industrial

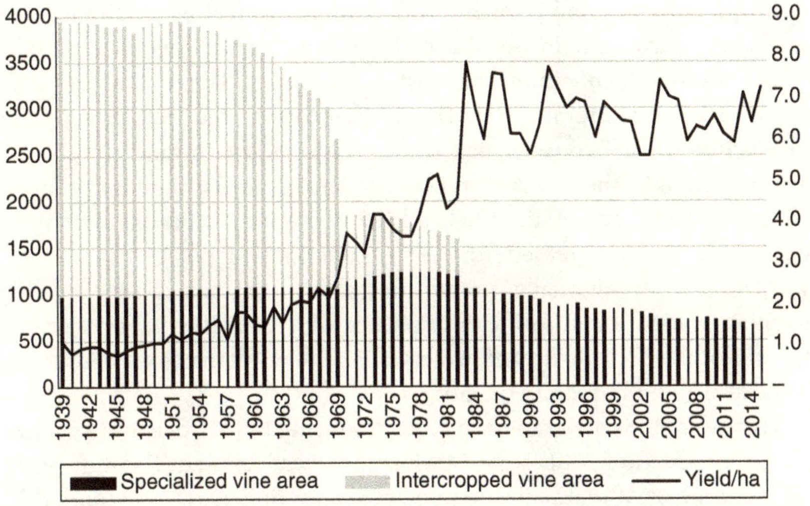

Figure 6.1 Winegrape bearing area and yield per hectare, Italy, 1939 to 2015 (ha and KL/ha).
Note: Figures about intercropped vine area show a sudden drop in 1970 and after 1982. In both cases, the drop is due to modifications in the statistical survey system. In 1970, data began to be extracted from the vineyard cadaster (*Catasto vinicolo*), which did not include surfaces with only scattered plants of grapevine. After 1982, the survey about intercropped vine area was interrupted, as it was at this point marginal.
Source: Anderson and Pinilla (2017).

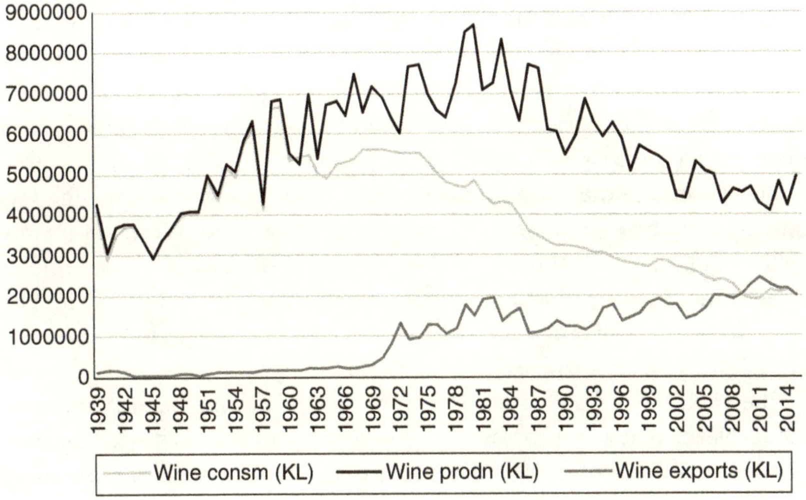

Figure 6.2 Volume of wine production, consumption[a] and exports, Italy, 1939 to 2015 (KL).

[a] Net of distillation.

Source: Anderson and Pinilla (2017).

development and rapid growth of the economy as real per capita income increased fourfold. It involved a huge exodus of rural labour, especially in the South, which eliminated most of the surplus labour that had long plagued the agricultural sector. That further pushed the sector away from production for self-consumption and towards a more commercial character. Accordingly, there was a dramatic reduction in the number of farms with vineyards: between the 1960 and 1970 agricultural censuses, the number of such farms decreased from 2.2 to 1.6 million (Table A6.1).

Wine was traditionally produced by farmers themselves, pressing together grapes of many different varieties. Less than 20 percent of grapes were processed in dedicated wineries, and few of them were oriented towards wines of premium quality.

There were 148 cooperatives in 1950, producing 140 ML of wine (3 percent of total production), only some of which were well reputed (Casalini 1953). Then a process of reorganization and concentration started, supported by a growing Italian equipment industry, as witnessed by the beginning of the international exposition SIMEI in 1963. The role of cooperatives grew and, in 1970, there were 690 of them, producing 1200 ML of wine (18 percent of total production). Among private companies, Credit Suisse financed the Winefood Company, pooling about ten wineries and creating an integrated firm.

The increase in wine production was driven mainly by growth in domestic demand, which rose by 72 percent over this period (Figure 6.2 and Table A6.1). This trend was due to the increase in both population (up 16 percent) and per capita consumption (up 47 percent). Those workers who moved out of agriculture kept their consumption habits initially, and their higher income allowed more consumption (Table A6.4). But that trend changed in the 1960s, signalling that basic (nonpremium) wine was moving from being a necessity to being an inferior good. Wine was mainly sold in bulk in small shops in the first postwar decade, when the role of supermarkets was very small: the first supermarket opened in 1957, and by 1970 there were still only 400 of them in Italy, accounting for just 17 percent of national grocery turnover (Tassinari 2015).

The traditional distribution structure did not favour quality improvement. Nevertheless, a process of repositioning started. In particular, two private wineries, Folonari and Ferrari, tried to develop a true branding strategy for commercial premium wines with intensive advertising. That modernization process was interrupted in 1968 by a case of adulteration, however, which discouraged consumers from trusting branded wines. Nevertheless, sales of traditional premium wines from Chianti, Barolo and

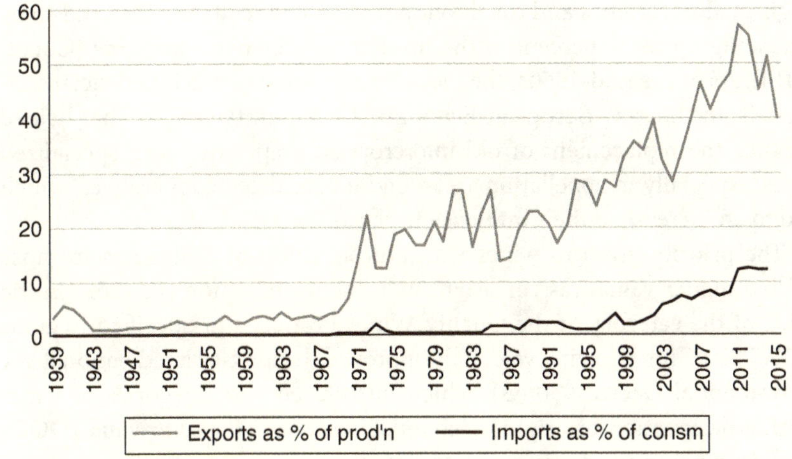

Figure 6.3 Wine exports as a share of production and imports as a share of consumption, Italy, 1939 to 2015 (%).
Source: Anderson and Pinilla (2017).

Barbaresco increased. As well, some new prestigious wines appeared, such as Amarone (proposed by Bertani in Veneto) and Sassicaia, which paved the way for what became known as the Super Tuscans. To help promote premium wines, the first wine show in Verona (*Giornate del vino italiano*) was organized in 1967, and forty-two wineries participated.

The role of international trade in wine was secondary for Italy in this postwar quarter-century, despite a rapid percentage increase in its exports. Wine imports were almost negligible, and increasingly composed of expensive wines (mostly French Champagne), as shown by a 143 percent increase in their real import unit value. The share of wine production exported grew from 1 percent to 8 percent (Figure 6.3 and Table A6.2).

Besides shipping cheap bulk wine, traditional Italian premium wineries increased their exports, while Cantine Riunite started shipping cheap bottled Lambrusco to Germany and the United States. Overall, the positioning of Italian export wines was in the low-priced segment, and only a little above the average price of the world's wine exports (Table A6.3).

The trends in grape and wine production in this first quarter-century were therefore mainly driven by the increasing domestic demand and by the technical changes in grape production. The latter was supported by two national intervention. The so-called *Piani Verdi* (Green Plans), which aimed at fostering the modernization of the Italian agriculture, supported the transition towards more specialized vineyards, the introduction of high-quality varieties and the development of cooperatives. They did so by financing up to 70 percent of the investments for new vineyards (Chiatti 2014). As of the mid-1960s, the industry also was assisted by financial support from the new European Economic Community (EEC). That helped finance the replacement of old intercropped grapevines with specialized ones, especially in appellation areas; and it subsidized cooperatives, which led to an increase in their influence in the sector.

The priority given to wines with a designation of origin and to those with a higher value was consistent with the introduction (in 1962) in the EEC of the category of the Quality Wines Produced in Specified Regions (QWPSR). The following year, Italy approved the long-awaited national law (Presidential Decree 930/63), which introduced two categories of wines with a designation of origin: *denominazione di origine controllata* (DOC) and *denominazione di origine controllata e garantita* (DOCG). The designation system developed quickly, from the first twelve designations approved in 1966, representing different territories from the Alps to Sicily, to seventy-six by 1970, nearly half of which are, anyway, in just three regions (Piedmont, Veneto and Tuscany). In terms of production too, wines with a designation of origin rapidly increased their share of total national production, from 1.5 percent in 1967 to nearly 5 percent in 1970 (Table A6.1).

1970–1985: ITALY IN THE EEC WINE SINGLE MARKET: CHEAP WINE EXPORTS AND OVERPRODUCTION

The second period is characterized by a transformation of the Italian system from one mainly directed to domestic consumption to one increasingly structurally oriented towards exports. This was mainly due to the implementation of the Common Market within the EEC, and to increased demand in foreign countries aided by movements in the Italian currency's exchange rate. This fifteen-year period ends with a peak in Italian exports, to be followed by a sharp drop due to the methanol scandal in 1986 that is a turning point in the evolution of the Italian wine sector.

In the 1970s, wine production continued to increase, reaching a peak in 1980 and then starting to decline, so that in 1986 it was about 11 percent less than in 1980 (Figure 6.2). Both the increase up to 1980 and the following decline were faster than the rest of the world's. The increase in production was initially ascribable to an increase in vineyard area, but from the mid-1970s the vine bearing area decreased. At the same time, yields increased sharply, from about 3–3.5 KL/ha at the beginning of the period to roughly 6–7 KL/ha by the mid-1980s (Figure 6.1).

The increase in production affected all wine categories, but DOCG wines were boosted by an EEC special regime that exempted them from a planting ban after 1977. The number of DOCGs more than doubled over the period, reaching 225 in 1985, when they represented over 10 percent of Italy's total wine production. DOCGs spread in almost all regions, but the production was concentrated in a few designations (D'Angelo 1974): fourteen designations accounted for two-thirds of national production, with Chianti alone producing nearly one-fifth. The increase in production of DOCGs wines was also sustained by cooperatives, which in 1985 produced half of the DOCG wine (Table A6.1).

Domestic sales started levelling off as per capita consumption began a long-term decline (Figure 6.2). The driving factor was the changes in lifestyles and workstyles. The reduction of physical effort in many work situations and the increase of white-collar jobs induced a reduction of basic wine consumption. Meanwhile, writers and journalists such as Soldati and Veronelli created a demand for hedonistic premium wines. That was assisted by the further growth of wine fairs, with Verona's wine fair becoming Vinitaly in 1971 and Vinitaly International in 1978. Besides DOCGs, new Super Tuscans in addition to Sassicaia, such as Tignanello and Ornellaia, had great success, while Galestro, an easy-to-drink, affordable Tuscan white wine, proved that the market was open to new wines in a modern style.

The domestic market in this period was still characterized by a minor role for supermarket chains (25 percent of grocery sales in 1980). Despite this, some cooperatives experimented with new containers and wine concepts to exploit opportunities developing in modern retail environment (Giacomini 2010; Williams 2014).

The decline in domestic consumption was partly accommodated by export growth, and partly by distilling an increasing share of nonpremium wine. Exports boomed over this period, moving from about 500 ML in 1970 to 1700 ML in 1985, or from 7 percent to 27 percent of production, with a peak of 1940 ML in 1982 (Figure 6.2 and Table A6.2).

The growth in exports involved several components. In 1970, wine in bulk represented the largest share of export, accounting for 82 percent in volume and 61 percent in value. Its success was mainly due to price competition, helped by exchange rate movements. The main destination in volume was France (accounting for 30 percent of Italy's wine exports in 1970 and 36 percent in 1985). Those wines substituted for France's imports of bulk wine from Algeria, following the implementation of the EEC's wine single market in 1970. Indeed, the increase in Italy's share of global wine exports mirrors the decline of Algeria's (see Chevet et al. 2018; Meloni and

Swinnen 2018). By 1982, Italy's share was 39 percent in volume and 20 percent in value terms – shares that have not been exceeded in the subsequent thirty-five years.

The increase in Italy's average export price was lower than for the rest of the world's, suggesting that Italy was mainly expanding exports of low-end wines over this period. Wine exports to France, mainly bulk high-alcohol wine destined to reinforce French wines, were favoured by the devaluation of the Italian Lira over the decade to 1985 (Tables A6.3 and A6.4). Exports to Germany suffered a smaller drop of price while US dollar prices of exports to the United States rose, despite greater devaluations of the Lira against their currencies.

Italy was increasing its shipments of bottled wine in this period, both still and sparkling, as Italian wine was enjoying an increasing reputation and a favourable price/quality ratio relative to French wines. Between 1980 and 1985, Cantine Riunite exported to the United States nearly 11 million cases of Lambrusco wine per year. The importer Villa Banfi (by John and Henry Mariani) reinvested part of profits in the Castello Banfi winery, which subsequently became one of the greatest producers of Brunello di Montalcino with a leading role in promoting the international success of this wine. The quality change is shown by the fact that in 1985, bottled wines, still and sparkling, represented 42 percent of Italy's export volume but 73 percent of its value.

Wine imports remained tiny over this period. They stagnated during the 1970s, as the macroeconomic situation and the devaluation of the Italian Lira discouraged Champagne consumption. However, they increased fourfold over the decade to 1986, thanks to the shift in relative prices. But that represented a rise only to 2 percent of the volume of wine consumption in Italy (Figure 6.3 and Table A6.2).

Another important driver of wine production trends in this period was the EEC's Common Agricultural Policy (CAP) (Scoppola and Zezza 1997; Munsie 2002). Market interventions (long- and short-term storage and distillation) were reserved for table wine and activated exceptionally in case of market disequilibria. Since production growth resulted in repeated years of surplus in both France and Italy, tension culminated and erupted as a "wine war" (1974–1981), when the vignerons of Languedoc-Roussillon repeatedly protested against 'unfair' imports from Italy, blocking the arrival of Italian ships.

As a reaction to frequent market imbalances, some measures for containing the production were implemented. They included a ban on establishing new vineyards for winegrapes except for vineyards located in areas with designation of origin (they were included in the ban only later, after the mid-1980s). Also, a voluntary program of (temporary or permanent) abandonment of winegrape growing was launched. In the second half of the 1970s that led to the grubbing up of at least 40,000 ha of Italian vineyards (50 percent of which were located in Puglia), which explains the one-third reduction in the national area under grapevines shown in Figure 6.1.

The attempt to contain production was strengthened in 1980 by some structural measures aimed at a tighter control on production, both in quantity and quality terms. Those measures included limiting the winegrape varieties allowed in each region, regulating replanting and the abandonment of lower-quality wines and restructuring vineyards within the framework of collective operations (Idda 1980).

Despite these attempts, at the beginning of the 1980s Italy, with over 7 million KL of wine produced, largely contributed to the peak of the EEC's production. It is in this period that the long season of distillations began (Table A6.1). The measures for voluntary and compulsory distillation granted to producers a minimum retirement price, which was nevertheless high enough to encourage production 'for distillation', especially in the southern regions of Italy, where high yields and high alcohol content were able to be produced at low cost. The result was the persistence of strong market imbalances and distillation of about 8 million KL of Italian wine (corresponding to 18 percent of national production) during the first half of the 1980s.

Overall, the preceding data suggest that the growth of production in this period, unlike the previous one, was driven by two main components. One was exports, mainly represented by very cheap basic wine but with an increasing share of higher-priced premium wines. The other was distillation, stimulated by the EEC's CAP measures that supported the production of low-quality wines from high-yielding vineyards.

1985–2000: SECTOR REORGANIZATION AND EXPORT BOOM

The final fifteen years of the century are characterized by a dramatic drop in production but a marked shift towards higher-quality wines and a strong increase in exports, stimulated by important EC interventions to clear the market and by a reorganization of the industry.

In 1986, Italy faced the greatest shock in its wine sector during the second half of the twentieth century: a methanol scandal. Some cases of wine adulteration were discovered when poisonous and cheap methanol was added to cheap wine to raise its alcoholic content. The scandal received worldwide media coverage and produced a large fall in both domestic consumption and exports of Italian wines. Thus it became a symbolic turning point for Italian wine production. Until then, even though production of high-quality wine was growing, most wines produced were low quality, many of them destined for distillation. Payments for grapes by both cooperatives and private processors were mostly based on volume rather than on quality parameters, and there was the possibility, due to an inadequate control system, to compensate for defects in wine must in the cellar by adopting legal and even illegal methods such as methyl alcohol or sucrose (Desana 1976; Fregoni 1986).

Following that scandal, a substantial improvement in food safety control in the whole Italian food sector occurred, and the Italian wine sector progressively got rid of those improper methods. Slowly but consistently, the quality of winemaking improved, allowing Italy to capture some of the increasing international demand for premium wines at higher average prices.

Wine production dropped so that in 2000 it was 23 percent lower than in 1985, a much larger decrease than in the rest of the world's 5 percent (Figure 6.2 and Table A6.1). The fall was in large part due to a decrease in vine area (20 percent, incentivized by the European Union (EU), as discussed later in this chapter), but also wine yields fell slightly (–4 percent). These are signs of the abandonment of marginal winegrape areas and of progressive limitations on yields in many areas to comply with appellation regulations. The number of grapegrowers also halved, to 790,000 in 2000, and the viticulture specialization process was essentially completed. The end result was a structure in which a minority of large commercial firms controlled over 85 percent of the vine area, though there were still 480,000 small firms (two-thirds of the total; see Table A6.1).

Several vertical integration moves accompanied this restructuring. As qualified wines fetched profitable prices, the most innovative grapegrowers extended their activity to processing and bottling. Historical private firms also started new investments in the most promising areas, integrating grape production or enlarging their existing vine area. This process benefitted from the structural supports from the CAP, and was also incentivized by the market appreciation of designation wines and by other supportive activities, such as wine guides and wine fairs.

The cooperative sector underwent a strong consolidation process in this period, to exploit economies of scale and improve the management of innovation. The number of wine cooperatives dropped from 1,000 in the first half of the 1980s to roughly 750 at the end of the century, while maintaining the same total production (40–50 percent of the national total), and their turnover increased because they were bottling a larger share of their wine. In 1986, some cooperatives bought Winefood from Credit Suisse, thereby establishing Gruppo Italiano Vini (GIV), which was destined to become the top Italian group in terms of turnover. Cooperatives were intensively engaged in production of premium wines, but also in modernizing basic wines, improving their organoleptic stability and price-quality ratio. Among basic wines, Tavernello, a wine in cartons produced by Caviro, was a big success, sustained by intensive television advertising. During the 1990s, its sales almost reached 100 ML per year, involving 30,000 winegrowers in more than three regions and five processing installations all delivering to a single packaging plant.

Despite the qualitative evolution of supply consistent with changing demand patterns, domestic consumption decreased (by 19 percent, net of distillation) (Figure 6.2 and Table A6.1). Indeed, this is the period of most rapid change in domestic wine consumption habits. Wine was no longer seen as a key component of the diet by providing energy. The strong decrease of basic wine consumption was thus not offset by an increase of premium wine. Meanwhile, there was an increase in beer consumption (by 23 percent), which was consistent with an international convergence in alcohol consumption patterns (see, e.g., Mitchell 2016).

The reorientation towards lower yields and the drastic reduction in the total vine area were not enough to deal with the decline in domestic consumption. Therefore, this period was characterized by both a wider use of distillation and rapid growth in exports (Figure 6.2 and Table A6.1). Exports fell to 14 percent of production in 1986–1987 due to the methanol scandal, down from 27 percent in 1981–1982. But in 2000 they were up to 34 percent of production (Figure 6.3), since they had grown by 84 percent in volume between the lowest level in 1986 and 2000, which was faster than in the rest of the world. The value of those exports almost trebled in US dollar terms, an outstanding achievement at a time of low inflation; and their unit value also rose faster than in the rest of the world (Tables A6.3 and A6.4).

That success of Italian exports was due to an upgrading of its products. The share of wine in bulk decreased over the period from 58 percent to 49 percent, while the share in bottled still wines rose from 36 percent in 1984–1986 to 46 percent by 2000 in volume terms and from 57 percent to 78 percent in value terms (Table A6.2).

The destination of exports changed accordingly. The French share dropped from 36 percent to 20 percent in volume and from 17 percent to 3 percent in value, a sign of the declining importance of exports of high-alcohol wine for blending. By contrast, the shares of Germany rose from 27 percent to 35 percent in volume and from 23 percent to 31 percent in value. Exports to the United States grew less rapidly and its share decreased to 10 percent in volume and 22 percent in value terms, but it remained the highest-priced market for Italian wines.

The reasons for these changing trends were different from the previous period. The role of the devaluation of the national currency in pushing exports was much weaker (Table A6.4); and the share of total exports with appellations or geographical indications grew substantially. This was supported by increasing marketing efforts of private companies and cooperatives. Large cooperatives invested substantially in advertising, and many entrepreneurs personally and intensively promoted their wines. The magazine *Decanter* awarded its *Decanter*'s Man of the Year to Piero Antinori in 1986 and Angelo Gaja in 1998. The interest in Italian wines led to multifacetted cooperation of the Californian company Mondavi with the Tuscan producer Frescobaldi (Super Tuscan Luce and popular premium Danzante), the acquisition by Mondavi of the Super Tuscan winery Ornellaia (later again of Italian ownership), the expansion of Italian activities of Castello Banfi (owned by US brothers Mariani) and Brown Forman's acquisition of Bolla.

Imports were highly volatile in this period, but their share of national availability (production less exports) generally remained well below 4 percent (Figure 6.3), and their unit value decreased (Table A6.3).

In this period, the CAP became even more crucial, with a more structured system of market measures (voluntary and mandatory distillations) combined with interventions for the containment of production potential. The huge quantities of distilled wine were a heavy burden for the EC budget and led to the introduction of stabilization mechanisms aimed at discouraging the production of low-quality wines in vineyards with very high yields (ISMEA 2000). Despite the ever-stricter constraints, during these years Italy distilled over 14,000 ML of wine (about one-sixth of the total volume of wine produced), although on a decreasing trend after mandatory distillation was no longer activated (1995). Italian distillation was concentrated in Puglia, Sicily and Emilia.

If distillation represented the short-term answer to surplus production, the long-run structural answer was the permanent abandonment of winegrape vineyards. A program of encouraging that entered into force in 1988–1989 and remained operative until 1997–1998. Italy participated actively in this program, and about 100,000 out of a total of 160,000 ha of vineyards were grubbed up under this program (ISMEA 1999). Most of the uprooting was in the south, mainly Puglia (about one-quarter), followed by Sicily and Sardinia.

The regulatory changes adopted within the CAP were of great importance to Italy (Pomarici and Sardone 2001). They allowed a more structured regulation of 'table wines with a geographical indication', whose importance was increasing in part as a response to the popular premium wines and the premium wines being exported from New World countries. A reform of the Italian legislation (Law 164/1992) introduced a new category of table wines (*indicazione geografica tipica*, or IGT) that had to comply with the same procedure as the wines with a designation. Furthermore, Law 164/92 allowed the overlapping of production areas recognized for wines of different categories: DOCG, DOC and IGT. As a result, a vineyard could be eligible for the production of wines belonging to all three categories, thus allowing winemakers to decide, year by year, the best category to choose.

However, the structural policy of the CAP also played a relevant role in the development of higher-quality production. It supported the restructuring of vineyards and the investments in processing and bottling, and it made possible the spread of better techniques such as the temperature control, the perfecting of oenological practices and the use of barriques, as well as the development of promotional activities.

2000–2014: ITALY AMONG THE LEADERS IN GLOBALIZED WINE MARKETS

The most recent period has seen the reinforcement of developments in the Italian wine industry as it competes successfully in international market, showing a capacity to keep up with the competition from New World producers. This has been possible because of further reorganization both of the grapegrowing sector and the winemaking industry, an evolution driven mostly by changes in (declining) domestic and (increasing) international demand.

At the beginning of the twenty-first century, wine production still tended to decrease, falling by one-fifth between 2000 and 2014. The drop was mainly due to a shrinking vine area while the wine yields remained almost stable (Figure 6.1). This trend was driven by market forces in the period 2000–2008, as in these years Italy did not implement CAP measures for subsidizing grubbing up of vines; but later the CAP measures gave again a drastic stimulus to reducing the area under vine. The decrease in production mainly concerned wines without origin, as by contrast DOCG and IGT supplies increased, their share of total output reaching 38 and 32 percent, respectively, by 2014 (Table A6.1).

The decrease in national vine area between 2000 and 2014 hides deep regional differences. There was a drastic drop in the southern and northwestern areas, a reduction similar to the national average in the central regions and in the islands, but a quite significant increase in three northeastern regions. The change in the distribution of vine areas was facilitated by the possibility of exchanging planting rights (until the end of 2015), which allowed a relocation of vineyards over the Italian peninsula, but it mainly reflects the differences among regions in effectively coping with the changes in global markets. Northeastern regions enjoyed great national and international success with two varieties, Pinot Grigio and Glera, the latter being the base of Prosecco sparkling wine.

The increase in production of DOCG and IGT wines did not change the concentration of supply in a few areas. Despite 405 designations (including seventy-three with a higher level of certification) and 119 indications recognized, Italy's production remains strongly based on a small number of well-known wines, which play a leading role in terms of both volume and value. The ten most relevant Protected Designation of Origin (PDO) wines represent 50 percent of the PDO global volume, while the weight of the top ten Protected Geographical Indication (PGI) wines accounts for 85 percent of the volumes produced (ISMEA 2014).

The reduction in wine production went along with a decrease in consumption until 2009, followed by a stabilization (Figure 6.2). Italy's per capita consumption at the end of the period was about 35 litres, although there are large differences in individual behavior: 48 percent of Italians of drinking age are not wine drinkers (42 percent in 2003), and the share of regular drinkers is just 21 percent, down from 30 percent in 2003 (ISTAT 2015).

This period is characterized by a remarkable evolution of the Italian wine industry, aimed at challenging a fully globalized wine market. Many Italian wine companies enlarged their supply in the higher-quality segments, but a relatively small group of large suppliers, some of them pure bottlers, successfully targeted the lower-priced commercial premium segment, exploiting economies of scale and effective quality control. The cooperatives experienced a further consolidation (in 2014, there were only 441, 40 percent less than in 2000), and seven of them are among the sixteen companies with a turnover larger than €100 million (Table A6.1). The largest one, Cantine Riunite & CIV, with a turnover of about €550 million, is one of the largest wine groups in the world.

The economic size of all types of Italian wine companies is increasing. In 2014, forty-two companies had an invested capital larger than €50 million, and thirty-four had capital between €25 and 50 million; in 2003, the numbers were, respectively, fourteen and sixteen (Mediobanca, various years). The increasing size of top wineries drove an enlargement of the area under vine held by large farms: vineyards larger than 20 ha in 2010 had a share of 33 percent, ten points more than in 2000. In this period, only a few Italian companies were acquired by foreign shareholder: Ruffino by Costellation Brands, Gancia by Russkij Standard and Mionetto by Henkell. Italian investments abroad were also few (Antinori, Zonin, Masi). Italian wine companies also kept away from the stock exchange, but the first two, Masi and Giordano (renamed Italian Wine Brands), are exceptions: they were listed in 2015.

Over this most recent period, the Italian wine industry's growth seems to have stabilized. It is characterized by the contemporaneous presence of integrated supply chains (private and cooperative) and of unintegrated supply chains with actors specialized in just one or two of the stages of production (grape growing, grape processing, bottling). A large part of Italy's production is now integrated: 41 percent of winegrapes (42 percent for PDO grapes, 47 percent for PGI grapes) are crushed by cooperatives and another 28 percent (37 percent for PDO grapes, 29 percent for PGI grapes) are crushed directly by winegrowers (Mazzarino and Corsi 2015). The remainder is either exchanged on the spot market or (especially for appellation wines) sold on a contractual basis. In terms of size, two groups compose the winemaking industry (2014): 136 companies with a turnover over €25 million (four over €200 million) generating 60 percent of Italy's wine turnover; and a galaxy of small quality-oriented integrated wineries, most of them exploiting the opportunities for wine tourism or challenging the international market (Mediobanca 2016). Such wineries, about 8,000 of them, boomed in the previous period and seem to have now stabilized (European Parliament 2012).

The progressive strengthening of the Italian wine industry allowed a continuous increase in exports, from over 1,800 ML in 2000 to a high of 2,400 ML in 2011, followed by a small decrease to 2,000 ML in 2015. In value terms, that growth was from 2.4 to 6 billion nominal US dollars. This is reflected in the unit value of exports, which rose from an average of $1.30 to $3 (Tables A6.2 and A6.3).

This favourable trend in Italian wine exports happened in a period of rapid change in the international wine market. In the first decade of the century, international wine trade increased markedly, but more so for bulk and sparkling wines than for bottled wines (Mariani, Pomarici and Boatto 2012). Italy decreased its share on world exports in volume, but increased slightly its share in value, thanks to different trends for various wine typologies. Its shares increased slightly for bottled wines; it also increased its share for sparkling wines and, contrary to the general tendency, at growing prices. Indeed, during recent years Italian dry sparkling wines have enjoyed remarkable success, particularly Prosecco, which has succeeded in building a good image and a market space completely independent of traditional sparkling wines, most notably Champagne. Only in the case of bulk wines is the share declining, but more so in volume than in value.

In short, everything suggests Italy became increasingly competitive in commercial and superpremium segments of the market rather than competing on price in the nonpremium segment. While expanding its share of traditional large and small importing countries, Italy has been particularly successful in its exports to eastern Europe (Mariani et al. 2012). By contrast, its share remains much lower relative to France and Australia in Asian markets (see Anderson 2018).

Some important trends also appear for imports, which quadrupled in volume over the period. The share of imports in domestic consumption rose from 2 percent in 2000 to 12 percent in 2014 (Figure 6.3). The growth in value terms was smaller, the difference being partly attributed to the devaluation of the dollar versus the Euro in this period (Tables A6.2, A6.3 and A6.4). But it is also due to the change in the import mix: not only expensive wines such as Champagne but also increasingly cheap bulk wine to satisfy the domestic demand for basic wine not fully satisfied by local production (following the decline in production in the South).

In this period, also the CAP had a significant impact on the evolution of the Italian winegrape growing sector, with the implementation of three different reforms (in 1999, 2008 and 2013). Overall, the main objective of the EU policy for wine changed from the simple control of the quantity of production to a greater emphasis on quality and on the improvement of competitiveness of EU wines in the global markets (European Parliament 2012). Despite the confirmation of a regime for the control of the production potential, some elements of flexibility were progressively introduced (e.g., new planting rights for QWPSR or table wines with a geographical indication, of which 13,000 ha were assigned to Italy).

The 2008 policy reform also established National Support Programs (NSPs), specific budgetary envelopes assigned to member states to finance actions from a given menu of eleven measures. In the selection of the measures, Italy decided to give greater importance to those with a potential impact on the competiveness of the national wine sector: restructuring of vineyards and promotion on third markets (Pomarici and Sardone 2009). A further triennial abandonment program (2009–2011) financed the grubbing up of about 28,500 ha of Italian vineyards (4 percent of the total area planted to vines).

Important changes also occurred because of the new EU norms about appellations and geographical indications, based on the concepts of PDO and PGI. The new framework led to a new national regulation (Legislative decree 61/2010) that resettled the traditional Italian categories of DOC and DOCG in the PDO scheme and the traditional category IGT in the PGI scheme, and it defined how to comply with the obligation for a systematic control by third parties.

In addition, the Legislative decree 61/2010 renewed the regulation of Consorzi di Tutela (Syndacat d'Appellation) to comply with the EU concept of interbranch organization, and it defined the rules and constraints in supply control. Most of the larger Consorzi utilized the possibility to control supply to stabilize prices.

The implementation of measures concerning restructuring and conversion allowed the quality improvements and the adjustment of production to changing market demands. They also facilitated the reduction of production costs as well as the modernization of agricultural practices (European Parliament 2012). Since 2000, over 220,000 ha of Italian vineyards, about one-third of the total area, were restructured thanks to the financial support of the NSP (Rete Rurale Nazionale 2012). The linkage between NSP measures and the increase of certified wines (DOCG and IGT) is not direct, but the role played by the measures of restructuring and conversion and also of promotion in this direction has been critical. The grants for restructuring and conversion were limited to vineyards destined for DOCGs and IGTs wines, and the support for promotion also required programs promoting DOCGs and IGTs or varietal wines.

FINAL REMARKS

Over the seven decades considered in this chapter, the Italian wine industry has changed dramatically, from a dispersed production system mainly oriented to self-consumption of supply and the local market with low-value wines, to a modern industry able to satisfy an increasingly demanding domestic supply and very competitive international markets with a wide range of wines. The current situation is the result of a long process driven by many factors, acting inside and outside the sector. National policies, interacting with the EU's CAP, have since1960 pushed the sector towards the production of premium wines and, after the methanol scandal, have stimulated the adoption of a new attitude towards quality in process management. A further and probably stronger stimulus in this direction came from the changing domestic and – more importantly – international demand, to which the Italian industry was able to react positively. In this context, different types of firms found room to thrive: wine producers deeply rooted in agriculture, mostly small- and medium-sized, but some quite big cooperatives and bottlers. All have been able to react successfully to the evolution of various markets, adapting their supply in terms of products and destinations. The wine industry is now the leader among national agribusinesses in Italy. Indeed, despite the wine industry being ranked third in turnover in Italy's agrofood sector, wine is the true food icon in the 'Made in Italy' campaign and the largest contributor to Italian agrofood exports. The share of wine in the value of all merchandise exported by Italy grew to a remarkable 1.3 percent, which is not much lower than in France (1.8 percent) and far higher than the 0.2 percent for the world as a whole in 2014 (Anderson and Pinilla 2017).

The progressive evolution of Italy's wine sector did not change uniformly across regions of course. Many excellent premium wines, mostly DOCG wines, are produced in all Italian regions, but it involved a much larger supply reduction in the relatively warm South, where a mix of factors intervened, including entrepreneurial vision and policy orientation towards nonpremium and commercial premium wines, ecophysiological conditions and logistic difficulties.

Over the four periods considered, the Italian wine sector kept its 'national character', as the Italian wine industry evolved without being really involved in the intensive internationalization processes of large companies – specializing in wine or not – that occurred in other countries (Green, Rodríguez Zúñiga and Seabra Pinto 2006). Reasons for this could be the high prices of Italian wineries located in attractive areas and an institutional environment considered uncomfortable by foreign investors (Mariani and Pomarici 2011).[1] The 'national character' was preserved also in terms of grape varieties grown. Despite an absolute and relative increase of some French (international) varieties, a rich array of Italian traditional grapes

[1] Recently (2016–2017), some new acquisitions of small- and medium-sized Italian wineries occurred, including the case of Biondi-Santi (Brunello di Montalcino), now controlled by French group EPI. However, at least at this point, this doesn't appear to be a change of tendency.

(most notably the red Sangiovese and the white Trebbiano) still characterize Italian wine supplies (Anderson 2013; D'Agata 2014).

The Italian wine industry has evolved to cover a wide product range, with success in both the basic segment with products mainly destined to the domestic market, and in the commercial premium and superpremium segments. In terms of the value of world production, Italy in 2009 had the largest shares of nonpremium and commercial premium wines, and in terms of the value of world exports Italy had the largest share of commercial premium wines (22 percent) and the second-largest, after France, of superpremium wines (17 percent), according to Anderson and Nelgen (2011). Italy is trying to challenge France also in the iconic segments of the wine market, searching for space in the most elitist distribution channels. In so doing, quite paradoxically, the Super Tuscan Masseto is distributed also by some Bordeaux negociants (Rosen 2008).

After World War II, the Italian wine sector evolved differently from other countries, modifying its profile in the world's wine markets. Italy's shares of world production and consumption have decreased since the 1970s, while its share of export value has increased steadily and its share of export volume increased to the end of the century, becoming ranked as the second in the world and close behind Spain (Table 6.2). The dramatic increase in exports of bulk wine from 1970 reduced the ratio of Italian to world average prices to near 0.5, and it took four decades to bring it back to near 1.0, thanks to a progressive upgrade of shipped wine (Figure 6.4). The dramatic decrease in per capita consumption drove the reduction in Italy's share of world wine consumption and also of the world alcohol consumption (which dropped from 10 percent in 1961 to below 2 percent since 2009 as wine was only partially substituted by beer and spirits). The change in the Italian pattern of alcohol assumption shows some similarities with the global one, as wine's share of global alcohol consumption has decreased and beer's share has increased (Anderson and Pinilla 2017).

Looking at the future, the Italian wine industry seems capable of responding to challenges as they come along in the market, at home and abroad, but it has to deal with some critical issues. On the production side, effective strategies to mitigate climate change and to achieve substantial progress in environmental sustainability are urgent. On the demand side, current consumption levels may fall further. At the industry level, there are problems of coordination among the different players along the value chain (winegrowers, winemakers, cooperatives, industrial bottlers) that cause inefficiencies to persist, which need to be resolved to compensate for the disadvantages of the still relative small average size of Italian wine companies.

Table 6.2 *Italy's shares of global wine markets, 1946 to 2014 (%, three-year averages centred on year shown)*

	1947[a]	1970	1985	2000	2014
Area under vine[b]	34.3	20.1	11.9	11.2	9.3
Wine production volume	22.1	24.2	22.9	19.6	16.0
Wine consumption volume	22.2	21.1	15.1	12.6	8.6
Wine export value	17.2	13.8	17.3	18.4	19.5
Wine export volume	9.4	16.6	29.6	29.2	21.0
Wine import value	0.04	1.9	1.0	1.4	1.2
Wine import volume	0.01	0.7	1.4	1.1	2.5
Alcohol consumption volume	n.a.	7.5	4.4	2.8	1.9
Beer consumption volume	n.a.	0.9	1.3	1.2	1.1
Spirit consumption volume	n.a.	2.2	1.2	0.6	0.5

[a] Refers to average for just 1946 and 1947.

[b] Figures for 1947 and 1970 include Italy's intercropped area, whereas in subsequent years only the specialized areas are included.

Source: Anderson and Pinilla (2017).

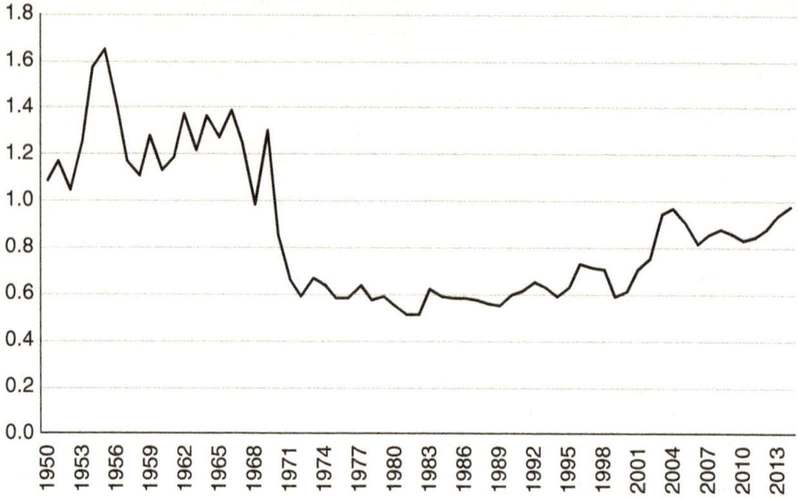

Figure 6.4 Average price of wine exports from Italy relative to world average, 1950 to 2014.

Source: Anderson and Pinilla (2017).

APPENDIX

Table A6.1 *Evolution of wine market structure, Italy, 1946 to 2014 (three-year averages centred on year shown)*

	1947[a]	1970	1985	2000	2014
Supply					
Grape area and yield					
Area under vine: single crop ('000 ha)	989	1,118	1,036	830	671
Area under vine: intercropped ('000 ha)	2,865	1,004	–	–	–
Grape yield: single crop (t/ha)	2.4	7.7	9.4	10.4	10.5
Grape yield: intercropped (t/ha)	1.0	1.5	–	–	–
Grapegrowers[b]					
Total ('000)	–	1,619	1,483	791	388
Professional ('000)	–	–	–	300	197
Wine production					
Total (ML)	3,510	6,825	7,033	5,402	4,652
DOC + DOCG (ML)	–	331	774	1,155	1,756
IGT (ML)	–	–	–	1,413	1,489
DOCG+DOC wines (number)	–	70	225	332	405
IGT wines (n.)	–	–	–	113	118
Wine yield (KL/ha)[c]	0.9	3.2	6.8	6.5	6.9
Cooperatives[b]					
Number	–	690	1,000	748	441
Members ('000)	–	–	380	338	170
Share of total production volume (%)	–	18	47	44	50
Share of PDO/PGI production (%)	–	–	45	–	49
Demand/use					
Apparent consumption (ML)[d]	3,469	5,979	3,898	3,152	2,727
Per capita consumption (litres/year)	76	104	69	50	34
Distillation (ML)	–	326	1,746	463	117
Export as % of total sales	1	8	20	34	45
Self sufficiency (%)	101	122	179	191	220

[a] Refers to average for just 1946 and 1947.

[b] Single year.

[c] Based on total area under vine.

[d] Net of distillation.

Sources: Official sources (ISTAT, INEA, CREA, ISMEA) and Anderson and Pinilla (2017).

Table A6.2 *Destination and composition of wine exports and imports, Italy, 1946 to 2014 (three-year averages centred on year shown)*

	Value (current US$ million)					Volume (ML)				
	1947[a]	1970	1985	2000	2014	1947[a]	1970	1985	2000	2014
Exports	0	126	765	2,419	6,570	0	544	1,437	1,852	2,105
Destinations (%)										
France	–	24	17	6	3	–	30	36	20	4
Germany	–	30	23	31	19	–	34	27	35	29
United Kindom	–	3	9	9	13	–	1	5	7	15
United States	–	14	34	22	22	–	4	17	10	15
Other countries		29	17	32	43		31	15	28	37
Composition (%)										
Bottled	24	32	57	78	75	11	16	36	46	61
Bulk	73	61	27	14	8	87	82	58	49	27
Sparkling	3	7	16	8	17	2	2	6	5	12
Imports	0	20	74	183	386	0	24	48	64	262
Composition (%)										
Bottled	–	–	–	22	18	–	–	–	22	8
Bulk	–	–	–	10	42	–	–	–	61	89
Sparkling	–	–	–	68	40	–	–	–	17	3

[a] Refers to average for just 1946 and 1947.

Source: Official sources (ISTAT) and Anderson and Pinilla (2017).

Table A6.3 *Unit value of wine exports and imports, Italy, 1946 to 2014 (current US$/litre, three-year averages centred on year shown)*

	1947[a]	1970	1985	2000	2014
Exports	0.31	0.23	0.53	1.31	2.57
Bottled	0.55	0.50	0.86	2.52	3.18
Bulk	0.22	0.18	0.25	0.50	0.76
Sparkling	0.71	0.80	1.45	2.61	3.56
Imports	0.31	0.84	1.54	2.84	1.18
Exports/imports	1.00	0.31	0.34	0.47	2.19

[a] Refers to average for just 1946 and 1947.

Source: Official sources (ISTAT) and Anderson and Pinilla (2017).

Table A6.4 *Basic economic statistics, Italy, 1947 to 2014 (three-year averages centred on year shown)*

	1947[a]	1970	1985	2000	2014
Real GDP (gk$ mill.)	124,434	520,981	799,981	1,077,572	1,078,175
Real GDP pc (gk$)	2,359	9,706	14,138	18,928	17,466
POP (x 1.000)	45,725	53,678	56,584	56,931	61,725
Nom. exch rate (€/US$)	0.13	0.32	0.89	1.05	0.80
CPI (2015=100)	1.9	5.7	40.1	76.3	100.0
All exp (mill. US$)	656 [b]	13,346	82,828	240,190	502,025
All imp (mill. US$)	1,429[b]	14,471	90,743	231,871	453,856

[a] Refers to average for just 1946 and 1947.

[b] Single year (1947)

Source: Anderson and Pinilla (2017).

REFERENCES

Anderson, K. (2013), *Which Winegrape Varieties Are Grown Where? A Global Empirical Picture*, Adelaide: University of Adelaide Press.

(2018), 'Asia and Other Emerging Regions', ch. 17 in *Wine Globalization: A New Comparative History*, edited by K. Anderson and V. Pinilla, Cambridge and New York: Cambridge University Press.

Anderson, K. and S. Nelgen (2011), *Global Wine Markets, 1961 to 2009*, Adelaide: University of Adelaide Press.

Anderson, K. and V. Pinilla (with the assistance of A. J. Holmes) (2017), *Annual Database of Global Wine Markets, 1835 to 2016*, freely available in Excel at the University of Adelaide's Wine Economics Research Centre, www.adelaide.edu.au/wine-econ/databases

Bonardi, L. (2014), 'Spazio e produzione vitivinicola in Italia dall'Unità a oggi. Tendenze e tappe principali', *Territori del vino in Italia* 5. Available at revuesshs.u-bourgogne.fr/territoiresduvin/document.php?id=1621

Casalini, M. (1953), *Le cantine sociali cooperative*, Rome: Centro tecnico per la cooperazione agricola.

Chevet, J.-M., E. Fernandez, E. Giraud-Héraud and V. Pinilla (2018), 'France', ch. 3 in *Wine Globalization: A New Comparative History*, edited by K. Anderson and V. Pinilla, Cambridge and New York: Cambridge University Press.

Chiatti, R. (2014), *L'agricoltura italiana tra sviluppo economico e fallimento ambientale. Il caso dell'Italia centrale. Toscana, Marche e Umbria dal secondo dopoguerra alla fine degli anni Ottanta*, Tesi di dottorato in 'Società, politica e culture dal tardo medioevo all'età contemporanea' (XXV ciclo), Facoltà di Lettere e Filosofia, Università degli Studi di Roma 'La Sapienza'.

Corsi, A., E. Pomarici and R. Sardone (2004), 'Italy', pp. 73–97 in *The World's Wine Markets: Globalization at Work*, edited by K. Anderson, London: Edward Elgar.

D'Agata, I. (2014), *Native Wine Grapes of Italy*, Berkeley: University of California Press.

D'Angelo, M. (1974), 'Il punto sulla situazione della D.O.C. attraverso interessanti tabelle di raffronto', *Politica ed economia vitivinicola* 9: 41–4.

Desana, P. (1976), 'Esigenze di coordinamento per porre in atto una valida politica vitivinicola', *VigneVini* 9(3): 5.

European Parliament (2012), *The Liberalisation of Planting Rights in the EU Wine Sector*, Study for the Directorate-General for Internal Policies, Policy Department Structural and Cohesion Policies, Brussels: European Parliament.

Federico, G. and P. Martinelli (2018), 'Italy to 1938', ch. 5 in *Wine Globalization: A New Comparative History*, edited by K. Anderson and V. Pinilla, Cambridge and New York: Cambridge University Press.

Fregoni, M. (1986), 'Alcol metilico: la punta di un iceberg', *VigneVini* 3: 17–18.

Giacomini, C. (2010), 'Tavernello" il vino più bevuto nelle famiglie italiane: un caso di successo', *Mercati e competitività* 2: 143–55.

Green, R., M. Rodríguez Zúñiga and A. Seabra Pinto (2006), 'Imprese del vino: un sistema in continua evoluzione', pp. 74–114 in *Il mercato del vino: tendenze strutturali e strategie dei concorrenti*, edited G. P. Cesaretti, R. Green, A. Mariani and E. Pomarici, Milan: Franco Angeli.

Idda, L. (1980), 'La Nuova strada indicata dalla CEE per il settore vitivinicolo', *Agricoltura informazioni* 3(14/15): 3–7.

INEA (various years), *Annuario dell'agricoltura italiana*, Rome: Istituto nazionale di economia agraria.

ISMEA (various years), *La filiera Vino*, Milan: Agrisole – Il Sole 24 Ore.

ISMEA (2014), *Vini a denominazione di origine. Struttura, produzione e mercato*, Report, Rome: ISMEA.

ISTAT (2015), *Aspetti della vita quotidiana 2013*, Rome: ISTAT.

Mariani, A. and E. Pomarici (2011), *Strategie per il vino italiano*, Naples: Edizioni Scientifiche Italiane.

Mariani, A., E. Pomarici and V. Boatto (2012), 'The International Wine Trade: Recent Trends and Critical Issues', *Wine Economics and Policy* 1(1): 24–40.

Mazzarino, S. and A. Corsi (2015), 'I flussi dell'uva verso la vinificazione: un'analisi comparata per regioni e macroaree', *Economia agro-alimentare* 20(1): 29–58.

Mediobanca (various years), *Indagine sul settore vincolo*, Milan: Ufficio studi – MBRES.

Meloni, G. and J. Swinnen (2018), 'Algeria, Morocco and Tunisia', ch. 16 in *Wine Globalization: A New Comparative History*, edited by K. Anderson and V. Pinilla, Cambridge and New York: Cambridge University Press.

Mitchell, L. (2016), 'Demand for Wine and Alcoholic Beverages in the European Union: A Monolithic Market?' *Journal of Wine Economics* 11(3): 414–35.

Munsie, J. A. (2002), *A Brief History of the International Regulation of Wine Production*, Third-Year Undergraduate Paper, available at nrs.harvard.edu/urn-3:HUL.InstRepos:8944668

Pomarici, E. and R. Sardone (eds.) (2001), *Il settore vitivinicolo in Italia. Strutture produttive, mercati e competitività alla luce della nuova Organizzazione Comune di Mercato*, Rome: Studi & Ricerche, INEA.

(eds.) (2009), *L'OCM vino. La difficile transizione verso una strategia di comparto*, Rome: Rapporto dell'Osservatorio sulle politiche agricole dell'UE, INEA.

Rete Rurale Nazionale (2012), *Il programma di sostegno del vino: bilancio del primo triennio di applicazione e prospettive future*, Rome: Piano strategico dello sviluppo rurale, MIPAAF.

Rosen, M. (2008), 'Ornellaia's Masseto: first Italian wine to be sold through the Place de Bordeaux', Decanter.com (accessed 18 November 2008). Available at www.decanter.com/wine-news/ornellaias-masseto-first-italian-wine-to-be-sold-through-the-place-de-bordeaux-76165/

Scoppola, M. and A. Zezza (eds.) (1997), *La riforma dell'Organizzazione Comune di Mercato e la vitivinicoltura italiana*, Rome: Studi & Ricerche, INEA.

Tassinari, V. (2015), *Noi, le Coop rosse, tra supermercati e riforme mancate*, Soveria Mannelli, CZ: Rubbettino

Williams, S. (2014), *Il caso Tavernello: Un successo del modello imprenditoriale cooperativo*, Faenza, RA: Homeless Book.

7

Portugal

Pedro Lains

Wine has been an important part of Portuguese agriculture for a very long period of time. The evolution of its output and exports is closely related to changes in domestic economic conditions as well as changes in the international markets. Vines were cultivated all over the territory, from the northern hills of Trás-os-Montes, to the Douro Valley, from the coastal region of Estremadura to the dry climates of southern Alentejo and farther to the islands of Madeira and the Azores. Until recently, wine was also an important source of calorie intake, together with grains, olive oil, fish and meat. The small size of the domestic economy, its geographical position at the southern periphery of Europe and the evolution of domestic economic policies and international treaties and tariffs are key elements for the understanding of the evolution of wine production and trade in Portugal. Portugal has lagged behind economic development elsewhere in Europe for a long time, and most of its industries reflect that backwardness and were seldom on the technological frontier. Yet the economic history of Portugal is also punctuated by instances where local innovation and technological advances were of great relevance, and winemaking provides examples of such positive developments.

Portugal's wine producers managed to develop a strong export sector from earlier periods in history. Indeed, David Ricardo's famous treatise on comparative advantage used as an example the exchange of wine for cloth between industrializing Britain and agrarian Portugal (Ricardo 1817). The country is ranked highly by a number of global wine market indicators.[1] For example, since the nineteenth century it has had around 10 percent of its total crop land under vine, which is one of the highest in the world and

[1] See Anderson and Pinilla (2017).

about twenty times the global average. True, the yields of those vineyards are lower than in neighbouring countries, so its wine production per capita is usually a little below the leaders, France and Italy, but often ahead of Spain. It is frequently ranked second or third in the world in terms of the value of wine exports per capita, after Spain during 1860–90 and Algeria from 1890 to 1960 (and briefly Tunisia post–World War II). The share of wine in its total exports was higher than for any country other than Algeria up to 1970. Only in the past quarter-century has it slipped in its ranking by that indicator. Moreover, Portugal has consumed as much wine per capita as its wealthier neighbours most of the past ten decades and is ranked first globally in terms of wine's share of national alcohol consumption.

In the eighteenth century, due to changes in international politics, port wine developed into a buoyant export industry with Great Britain as its most important market at the time. Yet port remained a relatively small part of total wine production in the country, and the sector evolved with little transformation from what it had been in earlier times. By the mid-nineteenth century, Portugal's vines, as those of other southern European producers, especially France and Spain, were affected by oidium and phylloxera that were imported from North America. The reaction to the those diseases involved a great transformation of the sector, leading to higher levels of productivity in wine production, lowering of the quality of that wine and a greater share of international trade. These adjustments continued to the end of the nineteenth century.

Thereafter, the sector continued to expand across the country, but it catered mainly to the domestic market and protected colonial markets and involved overproduction and a succession of crises. Then in the 1930s came the regulation which improved conditions of winegrowers and the quality of their wine, albeit only partially. According to a widely publicized official slogan of the time, 'to drink wine is to feed one million people in Portugal'. That was a major trait of the sector up to the end of the Estado Novo in 1974, and accession to the European Communities in 1986. In the last decades of the twentieth century, Portugal's wine industry followed at a distance the major transformations of the sector elsewhere in the world, including the increase in the share of quality wines catering for social consumption. As a result, wineries have increased in size and brands have become more important.

In this chapter, identify three waves of globalization of Portugal's wine since 1750 and provide a description and an understanding of the fundamental features of those waves. For that purpose, we deal with four traits of Portugal's wine sector in each wave, namely production, domestic consumption, exports and commercial policies. We start in the first section by providing a long-term overview of the weight of the industry in Portugal's agricultural sector. The following section deals with the emergence of the port wine industry and its relevance for the wine sector as a whole. The third section examines the transformations of output, productivity and foreign trade stemming from the phylloxera invasion. The focus then shifts to the regulations introduced in the 1930s, the rapid increase in production for domestic consumption up to the 1980s, and the export boom that occurred in the most recent decade, before drawing together the main conclusions of the chapter.

THE AGRARIAN BACKGROUND

Due to the efforts of a number of economic historians, particularly Reis (2016), it is now possible to depict the long-term trend of agricultural output and productivity in Portugal. The evolution of agricultural output in the eighteenth century is the outcome of different forces about which there is still uncertainty. In some cases, we found a close relationship between agricultural cycles and major political events at the domestic or international level, but in other cases the causes of the cycle relate to changes in climate conditions, demographic factors, innovations in crops and technological change, institutional bottlenecks and protectionist and other types of economic policies. The role of foreign markets has certainly had an impact as well, but not necessarily a dominant one throughout the centuries (Freire and Lains 2016).

The evolution of agricultural (and wine) output is shown in Figure 7.1, and Table 7.1 presents long-term trend rates of growth between peak years. There are clearly four main long-term trends since 1750 marked by the peak years of 1821, 1902, 1962 and 2015. The second half of the eighteenth century and first two decades of the nineteenth century was a period of almost no growth. It contrasts with the next period, to the end of the nineteenth century, when the trend growth rate was 0.36 percent per year. The first six decades of the twentieth century were marked by a higher trend growth rate of 1.52 percent per year, and it was followed by a slowdown to 0.60 percent per year for the period 1962 to 2015.

Portuguese agriculture went through a 'silent revolution' over the eighteenth century, driven by the development of markets and market integration and within an 'unchanged institutional and political context' (Serrão 2009, pp. 47–48). This was also a period of large inflows of gold from Brazil, which could have financed food imports, but instead domestic agricultural

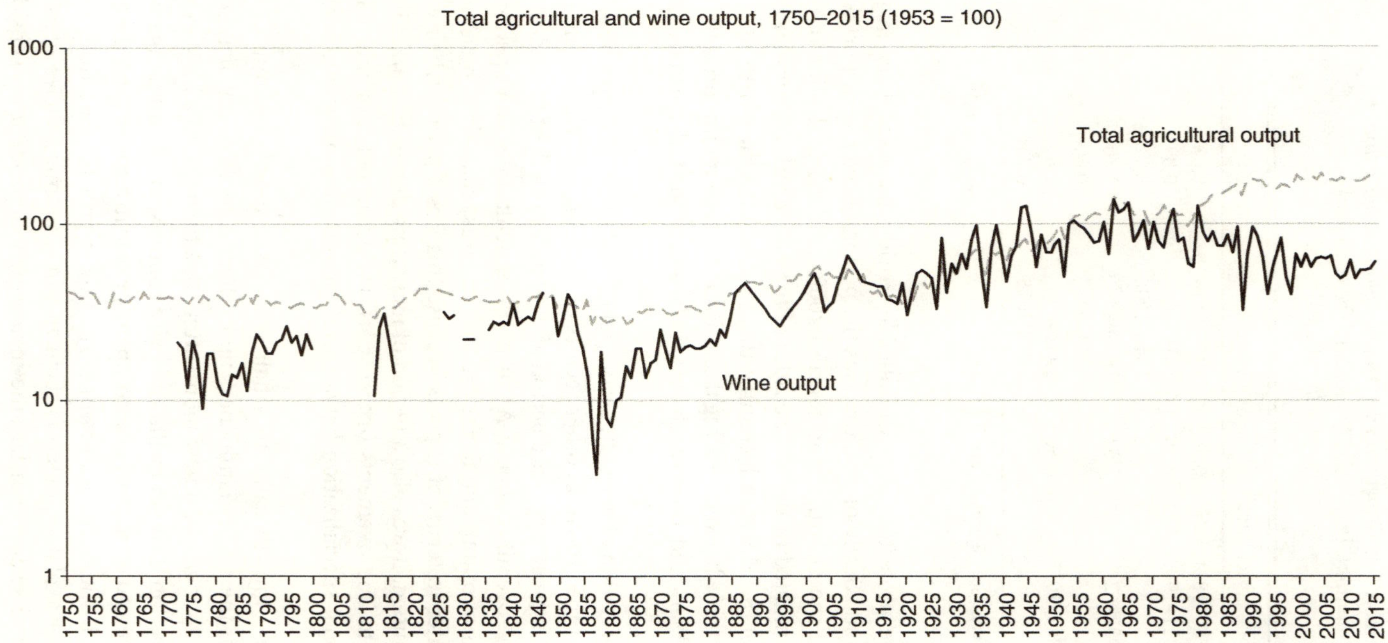

Figure 7.1 Volume of wine and total agricultural output, 1750 to 2015 (real values, semilogarithmic scale, 1953 = 100).

Sources: Total output: 1750–1848, Reis (2016); 1848–1997, Lains (2007); 1997–2015, Instituto Nacional de Estatística (2016). Wine output: 1772–1835, Martins (1998); 1835–2015, Anderson and Pinilla (2017).

Table 7.1 *Growth in wine volume and total agricultural output, Portugal, 1750 to 2015 (peak-to-peak yearly growth rates, %)*

Total agriculture		Wine	
1750–1821	0.08	1775–1814	0.88
1821–1902	0.36	1814–46	0.89
		1846–1908	0.77
1902–62	1.52	1908–43	1.80
		1943–62	0.60
1962–2015	0.60	1962–99	-1.89
		1999–2015	-0.73

Source: See Figures 7.1 and 7.2.

markets were protected from the outside world (discussed later in this chapter). Paradoxically or not, this was the period of the rise of port wine exports from the Douro region (Serrão 2009, 2016). The decline of output was accentuated in the last decades of the eighteenth century and the first decade of the nineteenth century, thanks to wars in the North Atlantic that affected trade between Portugal and Brazil and, more importantly, the Napoleonic Wars and the French invasions of continental Portugal from 1807 to 1811.

The interpretation of agricultural output growth after 1850 may be set in the context of the growth in other sectors of the economy. The second half of the nineteenth century was a period of moderate growth of the industrial sector and the overall economy. As such, the agricultural sector's performance in terms of output and factor productivity was relatively good. And it was even better in terms of exports because this was a period when wine exports expanded. It was also a period of increasing domestic market integration due to improvements in transport, including railways and roads, and to regional specialization between urban and rural areas and within rural areas.

Agricultural growth came to a halt after 1902, mostly because of the exhaustion of the positive influences up to then. After World War I, however, farm output gained a new momentum, this time due to a large extent to state protection through tariffs and price controls, public investments in infrastructure and education to accompany private investment and the bettering of the institutional framework. The slower-growth years from 1962 to 2015 may be explained in terms of changes in economic policies affecting the agricultural sector, as it became increasingly dependent on subsidies and regulations, but growth in the late 1980s was associated with Portugal's accession to the European Communities.[2]

Growth of output and productivity was accompanied by changes in the structure of the agricultural sector, which were largely due to changes in the structure of demand, particularly domestic demand, because the sector remained relatively closed to international competition. Changes in domestic demand were related to changes in national income, thus favouring sectors producing products with high-income elasticities of demand such as animal products, fruits and vegetables.

By 1850, Portugal was still largely a rural economy, with two-thirds of its active population employed in agriculture. That share declined only slowly, and did not fall below one-third until 1974. Industry expanded faster than agriculture up to 1930, and then there were two decades of even growth before industrialization regained momentum. Despite the relative decline of agriculture, and despite the sector's relative backwardness by European standards, Portugal's agricultural sector went through periods of growth of total factor productivity and associated structural changes in land use and product mix (Lains 2003). Total factor productivity increased by 0.75 in 1865–1902, by 0.4 percent, in 1902–27, and then peaked at 1.9 percent in 1927–63 before declining during 1962–73 (at -0.8 percent per year; see Lains (2009, p. 340).

Wine has had a large share of total agricultural output. In 1515, it was 15 percent (Reis 2016, p. 174), in 1850 it was 19 percent, during 1861–70 it averaged 22 percent and in 1900–09 it peaked at 23 percent. These are extremely high shares by international standards. True, it had declined to 13.5 percent in 1935–39, but it remained at that level for some time and even by 1970–73 it was 11 percent and was still 9 percent in 2013.[3] Figure 7.1 depicts the evolution of wine output volume from 1772 to 2015, expressed as an index to aid comparison with the evolution of total agricultural output. It shows that output increased faster for wine than for the rest of the agricultural sector from 1772 to a peak in 1846, and then it fell sharply due to the oidium disease that affected vines by the mid-nineteenth century. Then wine output expanded faster than agriculture again, to another peak in 1908, followed by a period where the two curves rose similarly through to the 1960s. Thereafter, wine expanded slower than other total agricultural output.

[2] See Lains (2003, 2009), Martins (2005), Soares (2005) and Amaral and Freire (2016).

[3] See Reis (2016, p. 174), Lains (2009, p. 343) and Instituto Nacional de Estatística (2016, pp. 145, 150).

Wine output evolved according to particular determinants, including changes in external demand, the spread of diseases, changes in the structure of output and the evolution of domestic demand. These are the focus of the following sections.

CONTRA RICARDO: PORT FOR EXPORT, 1750–1860

Early modern economies were not very open, as it was the case for Portugal and its wine output was mostly consumed in the domestic market and wine exports were relatively unimportant, as were food imports. The main import was grain, but it accounted for only 1.4 percent of food consumption by value in 1700. By 1800, the external food balance was slightly negative, and the value of wine exports was just below that of grain imports. Table 7.2 shows that olive oil contributed more to export earnings than wine in 1700, but since then the value of wine exports increased greatly while that of olive oil exports stagnated through to 1850. For most of the sixteenth and seventeenth century, Portugal's wine exports were insignificant before they increased rapidly from the late seventeenth century: wine exports doubled in real value from 1600 to 1650 and then increased 4.7 times during 1650–1700. Yet wine exports accounted for just 1 percent of the total value of national food consumption in 1700 and 1750, before they increased sixfold during 1750–1800. By the beginning of the nineteenth century, wine exports accounted for 3.8 percent of total food consumption, but they slipped back to 3.1 percent by 1850.[4]

Wine production for exports, despite being small in scale, was one of the most dynamic sectors of the economy, particularly exports of port wine through the City of Porto at the mouth of the River Douro. Those exports were fortified wines produced from vines cultivated in the steep slopes of the valley. They required considerable investment in the preparation of land, winemaking, manufacturing of casks and transportation including the improvement of the navigability of the Douro River, and of the roads and the ships required to export the wine.

Figure 7.2 depicts the evolution of port wine output and exports from 1772 to 1850. It shows output was overwhelmingly exported up to the end of the eighteenth century, and then both output and exports declined, although the latter at a faster pace. The first half of the nineteenth century was a period of decline for this particular segment of Portugal's wine sector.

[4] See Costa and Reis (2016). Serrão (2016, table 5.1) suggests that the share was 7 percent during 1778–95.

Table 7.2 *External food balances, Portugal, 1700 to 1850 (tonnes of silver equivalent and %)*

	Wine exports (1)	Olive oil exports (2)	Grain imports (3)	External food balance (1+2+3)	Total food consumption (5)	External food balance/ Total food consumption (4 as % of 5)	Wine exports/ total food consumption (1 as % of 5)
1700	18.2	21.4	14.4	25.2	1,858	1.4	1.0
1750	20.4	6.1	23.0	3.5	2,311	0.2	0.9
1800	128.5	8.3	151.6	−14.8	3,360	−0.4	3.8
1850	115.2	10.3	10.0	115.5	3,742	3.1	3.1

Source: Costa and Reis (2016, table 1).

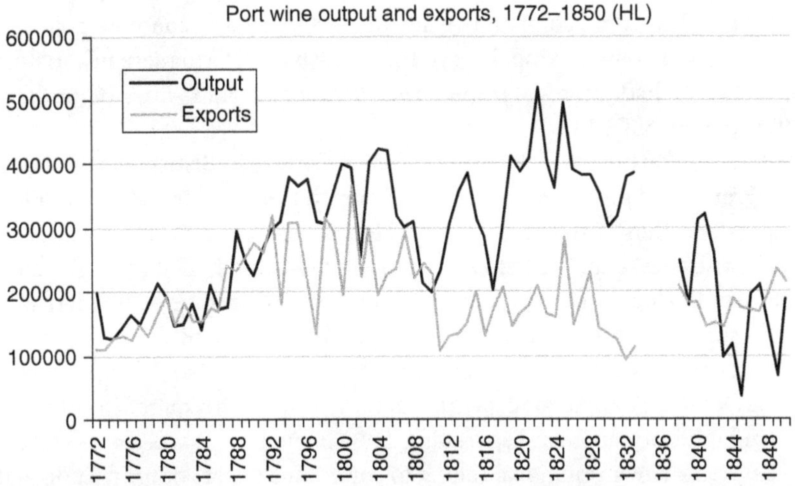

Figure 7.2 Volume of port wine production and exports, Portugal, 1772 to 1850 (HL). *Source*: Martins (1990, pp. 229–30).

Port wine exports were dependent on external factors, particularly trade agreements with Great Britain, the growth of international demand for fortified wines and the international situation in terms of war and peace. Port wine was one of the first sectors in Portugal to be subject to specific policy measures, including the demarcation of the region of production, but political intervention apparently did not affect the growth of output (Martins 1988, p. 393).

The emergence of port wine is closely link to international politics and in particular to the interest that England had in establishing an alliance with Portugal, at the time of French expansionism under Louis XIV which culminated in the Wars of Spanish Succession (1701–14). Portugal was a precious ally for England not only because of the strategic position of the port of Lisbon, but also because it was a source of Brazilian gold. The wine market in England was developing rapidly, and a replacement of French wines from Bordeaux was needed. Port wine was the ready answer, and it was the aim of the commercial and defence treaties signed between the two countries in 1703, which became known as the Methuen Treaty.

While port production and exports preceded the Anglo–French wars, the new international setting provided the right circumstances for its development and success in the English market (see Alexandre 2008, pp. 139–40, and Cardoso forthcoming). The Methuen Treaty favoured Portuguese wines to the detriment of French ones, and in return Portugal conceded to Britain special treatment for its exports of woollens. The port trade evolved not out of Ricardian comparative advantage but out of economic policy in part driven by rent seeking. In fact, the English and Portuguese negotiators of the treaty had interests, respectively, in woollens and wines (Grantham 1999; Anderson 2014).

By 1710, Portugal had a 50 percent market share in British wine imports and France had just 5 percent, having dropped from 70 percent in the 1680s (Palma and Reis 2016, pp. 33–34). Table 7.3 shows that Portugal's share in the British market peaked at 72 percent in the second half of the eighteenth century. Portugal's share fell over the nineteenth century but increased again slightly in the first decades of the twentieth century.

Port wine was not just a story of demand and protectionism. The wine sector of the Douro region had to adapt to the new market, which required investments in land transformation, transportation and winemaking. It was also necessary to develop a new institutional setting to control the quality of production and prices (Simpson 2011). The outcome was that port rose from insignificant in the 1680s to a peak in 1800, when it accounted for 40 percent of Portugal's wine production, implying a remarkable 3.7 percent annual growth over that period. In a relatively short time, port had become the country's second most important engine of preindustrial economic dynamism, along with maize.

Port wine production was one of the most advanced economic sectors in eighteenth century Portugal, even when compared to manufactures and services. It was an industry that was widely exposed to international market forces. It was also the first to be regulated in an extensive way, with the creation of the Companhia das Vinhas do Alto Douro in 1756, which defined the Douro wine region and regulated output, prices and commercialization (Martins 1988, p. 392). Although it was set up by the state, as a

Table 7.3 *Origin of volume of wine imports by the United Kingdom,[a] 1675 to 1939 (%)*

	Portugal	France	Spain	Other	Total
1675–99	24.2	23.2	43.6	9.0	100
1700–49	57.0	4.5	32.7	5.8	100
1750–99	72.0	5.4	19.9	2.7	100
1800–49	48.3	7.4	30.5	13.9	100
1850–99	19.7	24.9	29.8	25.6	100
1900–39	26.1	19.0	20.9	34.1	100

[a] England to 1785.
Source: Author's computation drawing on Anderson and Pinilla (2017).

majestic company it stemmed mostly from the want to auto-regulate from the producers and mostly from traders. This arrangement may have had advantages in the short term, but it also limited the growth of the sector and added to conflicts between growers and traders. It led to the merchants in Porto taking control of the sector, as: its board was composed almost totally of merchants from Porto and later also from London.[5] But the Douro producer and trade companies were 'remarkably hybrid in character', reflecting the regional and international complexity of the trade, which put together producers from remote rural regions in Portugal, to traders in Porto and in London (Duguid and Lopes 1999).

With the rise of liberalism from the 1820 revolution onwards, the role of the Douro Company was increasingly put into question. In 1834, its majestic powers were abolished and it was turned into a regular commercial company, thereby abolishing the monopoly of port wine exports through Porto. In 1852, it lost all of its powers regarding the production and trade of port wine, and in 1865 the sector was fully liberalized. The liberalization lasted nominally until 1907, but protection of the sector became mostly indirect (Alexandre 2008, pp. 146–47; Pereira 2008, pp. 179–80). As trade expanded, many Douro farmers stopped their wine production and instead sold their grapes to Porto export merchants. Later those merchants lost their trade to British merchants. This vertical integration of port wine, which led to the transfer of power from the producers to the merchants in Porto and then in London, was a consequence of the need to compete in an increasingly competitive market, where the control of quality was of paramount importance and merchants were better qualified to guarantee it than scattered producers (Duguid 2005, pp. 525–26).

[5] See Pereira (2008, pp. 176–77). See also Duguid (2005) and Alexandre (2008, p. 141).

From 1678 to 1987, four cycles have been identified for the port wine sector, in terms of production and trade (Martins 1988, pp. 394–403; 1991). The first cycle stretches from 1678 to 1810 involved the creation and consolidation of the sector in terms of both production and trade. Output increased rapidly at 3.5 percent per year and port exports became Portugal's top export item (apart from reexports of cotton and sugar imported from Brazil), accounting in 1800 for 15 percent of total exports. Port wine during these 132 years was virtually totally exported to a single market, namely England or Britain. By the end of the eighteenth century, port accounted for 60 percent of all English wine imports.

A period of instability and stagnation followed, a consequence of overall military activity and political instability in Europe and in Portugal, which lasted from 1810 to 1865. During 1811–13, exports to Britain halved, and that new lower level lasted for most of the rest of the nineteenth century. Total port exports declined by one-third between 1790–1809 and 1864, aggravated by the fact that in 1850–52 the Douro region was affected by oidium (Martins 1988, pp. 403–9). Britain remained by far the largest market, with about 90 percent of total exports from Portugal in 1850–52.

The negative trend was reversed in the 1860s due to the diversification of countries of destination for the exports. Britain's relative weight declined as new markets developed in Germany and other northern countries, as well as in France and Brazil. Export prices, however, declined and port wine became less important in Portugal's trade as the Portuguese economy diversified. Even so, by 1930–39 port still accounted for 20 percent of total exports from Portugal, down from 30 percent in the 1870–79.

New firms were founded, new international trade treaties were signed and new regulations were enacted to protect brands. But the government in Lisbon preferred to protect trade rather than production. From 1865 to 1907, production and trade were totally liberalized, following the general trend in Portugal then. This stimulated fast growth but did not improve quality. By 1907, new regulations were enacted but they proved highly ineffective.[6]

Things start to improve with the ascension of the Estado Novo, when the Casa do Douro, the Grémio dos Exportadores, and the Instituto do Vinho do Porto were founded. This provided a new institutional framework that would last for most of the twentieth century. Prior to the 1950s, port was divided into the modern classification of 'vintage' and 'tawny' and producers did their own blending (Duguid 2005, p. 524n). From the 1960s onwards, a new positive cycle was marked by growth and market diversification.

[6] As also for Spain and other countries. See Pan-Montojo (2009) and Simpson (2011).

By the decade of the 1980s, France had become the largest market for Portugal's port exports, with a 40 percent market share. Moreover, commercialization was also transformed as bottle wine exports increased their share to 80 percent of total wine exports in 1986. Also, the firm structure of the sector changed, with the number of export firms falling to forty-three in the 1980s (from 113 in 1934–1935). It was trade that conditioned production rather than the other way round, such that the state protected traders more than producers (Martins 1988) and producers had little influence on the market.

The dynamism of port wine production and exports was not matched by the rest of Portugal's wine sector, which was relatively backward like the rest of Portuguese agriculture as compared to agriculture in northern Europe.

PHYLLOXERA, THE EXPORT BOOM AND ITS BACKLASH, 1860–1930

Following two decades of recovery in response to the stabilization of the domestic and international markets, in 1852, Portugal's vines were affected by a mildew fungus (oidium) that originated in North America. The disease reached first the Douro region, due to its wider contacts with the outside world, and spread rapidly southwards and caused a sharp contraction in wine output (see Figure 7.1 above). From the peak in 1851 to the trough in 1857, total wine output fell by almost 90 percent. Exports contracted by one-third as stocks were depleted. Yet there was a fast recovery, as the cure by sulphite was readily available and was used comprehensively despite its relatively high cost. The rapid recovery demonstrates the dynamism and capacity to adjust of Portugal's wine sector. Government intervention was kept to a minimum, but it was also a turning point in that respect, as new policies were introduced (Martins 1996).

Soon after wineries recovered from oidium, they were affected by another disease also imported from North America, the phylloxera insect. That far more devastating disease arrived first in France in the early 1860s and it reached the Douro region in 1865. Historically, this is the region that has been affected first by various global factors, both positive and negative (Martins 1991, p. 653; Matias 2002; Freire 2010; Simpson 2011). By 1883, one-quarter of Portugal's vine area had been affected by phylloxera, of which 90 percent was in the Douro region. Ten years later, half of the national vine area had been attacked. In order to combat the insect, winegrowers resorted to carbon sulphide, and the substitution of American for

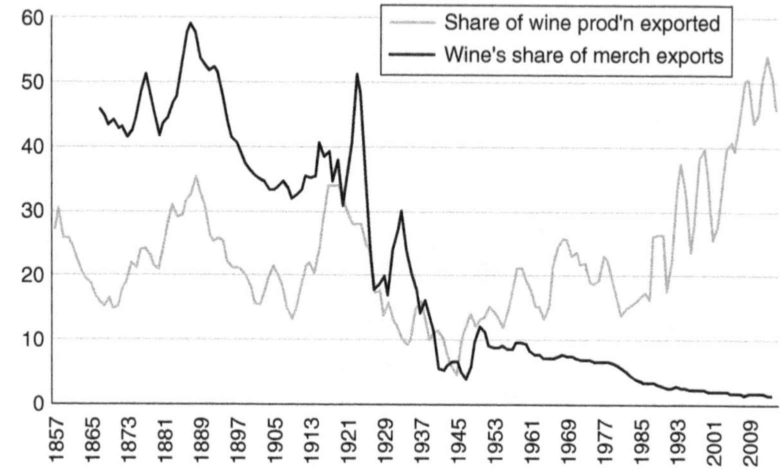

Figure 7.3 Share of wine production exported, and wine's share of all merchandise exports, Portugal, 1855 to 2015 (%, three-year moving average).
Source: Anderson and Pinilla (2017).

local vine rootstocks. The new rootstocks were considerably more productive, not only because they matured one or two years earlier than the local ones, but also because they produced on average one-third more grapes. In the process, the Douro region ceased to be the leader and the relevance of the south increased considerably (Martins 1991).

Policies also changed, as the Douro Company was closed in 1852, and in 1865 the Douro region ceased to have privileges. By the end of the nineteenth century, the area under vines was considerably larger than before phylloxera arrived in Portugal, and wine output expanded accordingly (Martins 2005, pp. 222, 232–33). The volume of wine output increased by 0.61 percent per year between the two peak years from 1846 and 1908. Then there was a sharp decline, which to a large extent was due to the rise of protectionist policies and then to the consequences of World War I, which contracted exports (Table 7.1).

Wineries spread across the country in many different ways and fashions, and they were cultivated with other crops such as olive and other fruit trees or vegetables, in both lowlands and up to 1,000 metres of altitude (Pereira 1983, p. 141). According to one estimate, half of Portugal's active population in 1900 was directly or indirectly involved in wine production (Freire 2010, p. 51). At an estimated 983 *reis* per hectare, the value of land occupied by vines was one of the highest in Portugal during 1900–09, after fruits and vegetables at 1,277 *reis* and rice at 1,000 *reis*, higher than that of potato and maize and well above that of wheat.[7] Wine production brought higher returns than that of grains, was not affected by import competition and the instability that it provoked, and it employed labour more regularly through the year (Martins 2005, pp. 235–36). Urbanization and the growth of transport infrastructure in Portugal were crucial contributors to that, as they increased domestic wine consumption (as also in Spain; see Fernández and Pinilla 2014, p. 69).

From the beginning of the twentieth century to the immediate aftermath of World War I, wine exports increased again and reached slightly above 30 percent of output in 1919. However, the growth of wine output in the interwar period was insufficient to stop the decline in the share of the sector in total agricultural output, which fell from 23 percent in 1900–09 to 13.5 percent in 1935–39. The share of wine in Portugal's total exports also declined, from close to half prior to the 1890s to one-third in 1910–13, one-sixth in 1935–38 and one-tenth in the 1950s (Figure 7.3). Clearly, the domestic sector was largely dominant as an outlet for Portugal's wine sector We have to explain its evolution looking to what happened within borders, in terms of the growth and changing patterns of consumption, but its large exposition to international trade also needs to be taken into account.

The increase in output after phylloxera was, however, mostly made out of wines with low quality standards which were sold in bulk in the domestic and the international markets, mainly to France, where they were to fortify and improve the quality of wines produced there. The increase in exports went along with an increase in the domestic consumption, which was related to changes in the structure of demand for agricultural products. Figure 7.3 shows the evolution of the wine export shares by volume. The share of exports increased to 40.5 percent in 1886, declining thereafter to 11.4 percent in 1908, to increase again reaching another peak during World War I and declined to World War II to increase again thereafter.[8]

Global wine trade was rather limited by the middle of the nineteenth century, mostly because of the high costs of conservation and transportation. Thus trade was overwhelmingly in liquor wines, such as port and sherry. During the rest of the century, the cost of shipping table wines was reduced and the methods of production improved so that wines lasted for longer. But the growth of trade was also an outcome of the liberalization of trade since the 1860s and most and foremost from the sharp increase in the

[7] Lains (2003, p. 60). One pound sterling was equivalent to 4,500 *reis*.

[8] There are no data for wine exports for some of the World War I years, so interpolations were used.

demand for imports in France due to the attack of its vineyards by phylloxera. Consumption across Europe and other continents was also increasing, as a consequence of rising incomes and industrialization. The wine export surge lasted, however, for only a few decades, as by 1892 France and other wine importers increased tariffs in order to protect domestic production or, in the case of France, production from the North African colonies, namely Algeria.[9]

By the mid-nineteenth century, port, Madeira and table wines were by far Portugal's single largest export items, amounting to 51.9 percent of total exports, and Britain the largest market, importing 75 percent of exports by volume, in 1850–54, then decreasing to 58 percent, in 1910–14. In the following decades, that overall picture changed considerably, particularly in the last decades of the nineteenth century, as Portugal's exports diversified both in terms of its composition and regional distribution.

Even if the Portuguese response to increases in international demand was not fully satisfactory, there were two instances in which wine exports were rather responsive. Firstly, in spite of the wine disease that affected the Douro port wine production area in 1867–68, wine producers of the region, taking advantage of the freedom to export all kinds of wines from Porto granted in 1865, managed to keep their exports up by mixing the genuine port wines with wines from the southern regions of Portugal not yet affected by phylloxera (Pereira 1983, p. 225; Lains 1986). The mixture of wines led to a decline in quality and complaints from British importers. Nevertheless, the volume and price of exports did not decline until after 1870, following a general fall in international prices. The maintenance of export levels contrasts with the drastic decrease in port wine production. According to official estimates, in 1880 output had decreased by 24 ML, and a further decrease of 54 ML was registered in 1888.

Exports went through the phylloxera crisis without drastic decline, as: by 1880, the export peak of 1875–77 had already been reached, and they increased further until 1886. Brazil accounted for most of this increase, which may reflect the decrease in quality of port wines after phylloxera (Pereira 1983, p. 130; Martins 1990, p. 229). There was a peak in the 1880s which was due to the increase of exports to France, whose vineyards had been severely affected by phylloxera. The main market for port wine was Britain, which by 1850–54 imported 75 percent of the volume exported by Portugal. This proportion decreased to 58 percent by 1910–14.

[9] Pinilla and Ayuda (2002, pp. 54–55). For the rise and fall of the Algerian wine sector, see Meloni and Swinnen (2014).

Wine exports could not continue to depend on port wine, however, given that its strong alcoholic content pleased neither the British consumer nor the custom officer. Furthermore, the 1892 Méline tariff discriminated against heavier wines; and from 1906, Germany discriminated in favour of Italian Marsala wine, which was a strong competitor for port and Madeira. The alternative would have been to export more table wine. Portuguese table wines were known to be strong, almost as strong as port wine. For the boom in the French market, this happened to be an advantage because France imported wine to distil and mix with its own wines. In 1880–84, 40 percent of total output was exported, and the share of exports in port wine output was 79 percent in 1860–64 and 105 percent in 1909–13.[10] In 1888, Portugal's share by volume of French wine imports was 8 percent, down from 15 percent in 1876. After 1889, wine sales to France were reduced, as French vineyards recovered and the imports from other sources, such as Algeria, increased (Lains 1986, p. 401).

In 1891, France increased its tariffs on foreign wine, thus protecting imports from Algeria. This led to a crisis in the Spanish wine sector, which up to then was France's main supplier (Pinilla and Ayuda 2002, pp. 52–53). In 1891, wine exports from Spain peaked at thirty-two times the level of 1850 and six times that of 1877, before suddenly falling to half that peak by the end of the 1890s. Between 1890 and 1938, imports of wine into France averaged 10 to 25 percent of domestic output, and the Spanish quota fell from the maximum of 80 percent of that market to a maximum of 26 percent by the 1930s. That decline was mostly all due to tariff protection (Pinilla and Serrano 2008, p. 136).

Meanwhile, the share of Portuguese wines sold on the British market decreased from 37 percent of total volume imports to 21 percent during 1891–1896. The main reason for this decline was a shift in taste in Britain away from consumption of high-alcohol wines. The structure of the British tariff schedule did not help either. Britain in 1860 imposed higher tariffs on heavier wines, port and sherry, discriminating in favour of lighter wines from France. In the abundant consular correspondence between Lisbon and London on this subject, the British government defended this discrimination as a tax on the alcoholic content of wine. However, it was diplomatically important for Britain to improve relations with France, and the 1860 Cobden–Chevalier Treaty led to discrimination in favour of French wines, which happened to have lower alcoholic content, and against those of Portugal (and Spain).

[10] Exports exceed production in some years because they draw from stocks of previous years' production.

Wine duties in Britain were subsequently reduced in 1876 and 1886. Nevertheless, Portuguese wines were still too alcoholic to benefit from the reductions in tariffs. Spanish exporters adapted better to the changes in the British market: 96 percent of Spanish wines exported to Britain in 1876 fell within the higher duty scale, but twenty-two years later this proportion had fallen to 25 percent. Spanish table wine exports increased from 1.4 ML to 15 ML over that period. The comparable trend for Portugal was 96 percent of heavy wines in 1876 and 94 percent in 1898. It is thus not surprising that Portuguese wine exports to Britain increased in the period only from 0.9 to 1.3 ML. The larger increase in Spanish exports of lighter wines was due to a treaty with Britain in 1886 which reduced the scale in their favour. However, the fact is that Spain produced such wines and Portugal did not. In 1886, Portugal already had most-favoured-nation treatment from Britain, and as such it was not barred from exporting the same kind of wines, if only they were produced at competitive prices (Lains 1986, p. 403). Market diversification was achieved by increasing sales to Germany and the United States, as well as Brazil and the African colonies.

By 1910–14, Scandinavia and Germany purchased 27 percent of Portugal's port wine export volume (Pereira 1983, pp. 217–32; Martins 1990, pp. 248–51). Exports of table wine were marked by a large increase in exports to France in the 1880s, before which Portugal's main markets were Britain and Brazil. After the temporary boom in exports to France, table wine export levels were maintained and eventually increased after 1900–04, while exports to France fell back to their earlier level. This was due to the favourable trend in exports to Brazil and to Portugal's African colonies, the latter protected after 1892 (Martins 1990, pp. 252–53; Lanero 2014, p. 88). Wine was already the single most important export to those colonies in 1870, but the amounts were very small. By the end of the nineteenth century, wine trade to the colonies had expanded considerably, but then they declined during World War I along with the local economy (Clarence-Smith 1985, pp. 68, 94, 120–22; Lains 1986).

Portugal had difficulty securing trade agreements with its major partners as protectionist measures were successively implemented across Europe. The commercial treaties between Portugal and France from 1866 and 1882 were not reconfirmed by France during the French tariff reforms of 1890–91. In 1892, France applied its general tariff on Portuguese wines whereas Spain was exporting wines to France at the lower minimum tariff. In 1894, France imposed its higher tariff on wines from Italy, Switzerland and Portugal; Germany did likewise on Spain and Portugal, as did Italy on France and Portugal. Wine was predominantly exported to neighbouring countries, or to countries to which nationals had immigrated. That was the case of wine imports into France, mainly from Spain and the French colony of Algeria, and into Germany, mainly from Italy through Austria or Switzerland, and from France (Martins 1990, p. 116).

Another reason that may explain Portugal's lack of commercial treaties after the mid-1880s is linked to the relative unimportance of this country. This is evident from the British reaction to Portugal discriminating against her products in retaliation to the preferential treatment that Britain had given to French wines under the Cobden–Chevalier Treaty of 1860. Despite the complaints from British merchants who were paying higher import duties in Portugal from 1866, Britain kept wine duties according to their alcoholic content, providing a de facto preferential treatment for French lighter wines. There was not much Portugal could do about it, after ten years of negotiations with Britain and after at least three years' discussion in parliament, Portugal finally gave most-favoured-nation status to Britain in 1876, without compensations in return (Lains 1986).

The share of Portugal in the volume and value of global wine exports peaked during the two decades of the world wars, at 9 percent, with rises before World War I and steady falls since World War II (Figure 7.4). Its share of global wine production increased through to the 1940s but catering mostly to the domestic market as export volumes, and the export ratio declined after World War I (Figures 7.3 and 7.4). Wine followed a general trend in Portuguese agriculture during the protectionist period that started with grains in the early 1890s and spread to the other sectors during World War I and its aftermath. With Spanish producers facing a shortfall in demand in South America and also in Europe, where wine consumption was still relatively small and growing only slowly, winegrower prices and profits were depressed up to at least the 1930 (Fernández and Pinilla 2014).

Growth of wine output and consumption during the second half of the nineteenth century was mostly concentrated in Europe. From the beginning of the twentieth century, Spain and Portugal suffered from the same negative factors, as France gave preference to wines from Algeria, as consumption in the more industrialized nations plateaued and protectionism increased, as abolition took hold in the United States and as expanded wine production in other parts of the world increased the level of competition (Pinilla and Ayuda 2007, pp. 180–81). There was also a redistribution of wine regions at the world level as output in the Americas expanded, as well as in the French colonies in North Africa, particularly Algeria. Between 1960 and 1900, France, Italy, Spain and Portugal accounted for 79 percent of world output, but by 1910–14 that share had

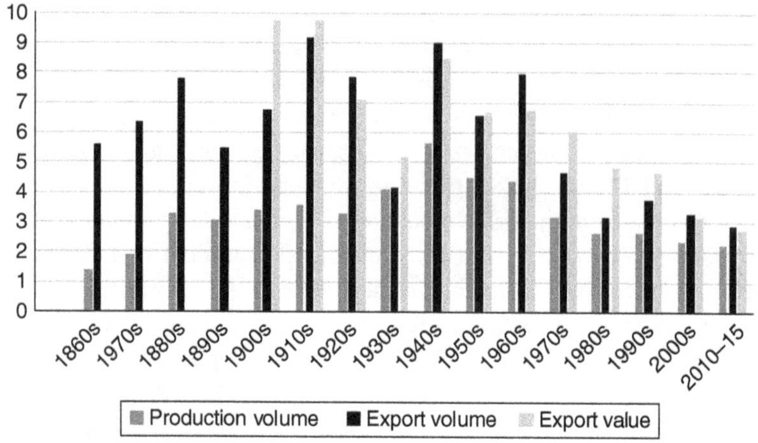

Figure 7.4 Portugal's shares of global wine production and exports, 1860 to 2015 (%).
Source: Anderson and Pinilla (2017).

fallen to 73 percent and by the 1930s to 68 percent, before it fell at a slower rate through to 1990 (averaging 62 percent over those six decades; see Anderson and Pinilla 2017).

The wine sector's political leverage in Portugal remained relatively small for most of the nineteenth century. By the turn of the twentieth century, however, as output increased and exports declined and wine ceased to be simply a local problem and became a national one, some proactive measures were taken by the Portuguese governments. Portugal was a pioneer in the creation of wine regions, with the Douro wine region founded in 1756, but little had been done since then, and port wine remained an exception for all that time. From 1907 to 1911, six new wine regions were set up by the Portuguese government, most in the region around Lisbon, namely, Carcavelos, Colares and Bucelas, as well as Setúbal, 30 kilometres to the south of Lisbon, Vinhos Verdes in the north and Madeira, added to the existent Douro wine region that was also reorganized (Martins 1991, p. 683; Freire 2010, p. 53).

The domestic and international turmoil of the interwar period impeded the consolidation of institutional changes that would promote a better equilibrium for the wine industry, which was severely affected by an increasing productive capacity that faced a thriving domestic and international demand. Domestic and international politics would however change soon, and paradoxically the new authoritarian regime and reinforced protectionism at the international level would assist relevant changes in the sector.

DOMESTIC CONSOLIDATION AND THE THIRD WAVE, 1930–2015

The Estado Novo led to an overhaul of the institutional framework of the Portuguese state, and the agricultural and wine sectors were naturally affected to a large extent. State intervention spread across many fields, including education, health and research, as well as roads and electrification and irrigation. Portugal remained one of the poorest western European economies, with low levels of instruction and capital per labour, but the dictatorship, looking for sources of political legitimization, was able to build a new set of infrastructures that impacted positively in the economy, at least in the short and medium term. The agricultural sector output kept growing for at least three more decades, whereas volatility of prices and incomes were to a large extent contained. The paradox of having protectionism accompanied by growth and structural change was not unlike what happened in a few other peripheral countries of Europe.[11] Wheat and wine were two of the most protected sectors from the 1930s onwards, while others hit by the crisis in the 1930s, namely producers of pork, beef, dairy, potato and wood, did not receive relevant protection from the state (Lanero 2014, pp. 90–91).

The new institutional setting increased the level of regulation of production and commercialization of the wine sector. The measures that were taken were mostly aimed at controlling the level of output and assuring better storage conditions and distribution in the domestic and colonial markets, then at increasing the quality of the wines produced for export to European markets. In 1937, the six wine regions created between 1907 and 1911 were consolidated and put under the supervision of the *Junta Nacional dos Vinhos*, one of the many institutions that characterized the corporatist state (Freire 2010, p. 53). After 1950, the concern with quality somehow increased and measures were implemented to improve the quality of grapes, providing technical assistance and fostering the creation of producer's cooperatives.

Yet the share of output from the demarcated wine regions changed very little in the years to come, from 62 percent of total wine output in 1939–49 to 58 percent in 1960–69. The production of table wines still accounted for 96 percent of total wine output in 1939–1949, and 95 percent in 1960–73. Contrarily, better-quality port wines accounted for only 2.5 percent and 3.5 percent of total output in the same two periods (Baptista 1993, pp. 209, 215). The number of wine cooperatives increased from just one in 1935 to nineteen in 1955 and fifty-seven in 1969, and in

[11] See Lains (2007), Lanero (2014) and references cited therein.

this latter year cooperatives accounted for 24 percent of total wine output (Baptista 1993, pp. 235–36; Lanero 2014, p. 91).

Other southern European winegrowers facing rising wages and lower wine prices also resorted to the creation of cooperatives in order to increase their ability to survive, and especially so in France, followed by Italy, Spain and Portugal. In France, winegrowers had easier access to capital, as the French government provided a large part of the capital needed at lower interest rates (Simpson 2000, p. 115). Cooperatives in Spain accounted for 40 percent of total wine production in 1964, when there numbered 600 (Martínez-Carrión and Medina-Albaladejo 2010, p. 88).

Wine output expanded considerably and increased its share of agriculture in the Portuguese economy, thanks to state assistance and price protection, but also to the shape of comparative advantages of the country. The increase in wine production was, however, accompanied by a fall in relative prices and thus the weight of the wine sector in total agricultural output, at current prices, declined from 23.3 percent in 1900–09 to 13.5 percent in 1935–1939, and it remained at that lower share through to the early 1970s (Lains 2009, p. 343). The vine area under production remained relatively stable, fluctuating between 300,000 and 400,000 ha from the late nineteenth century up to 1970 before declining gradually to around 200,000 ha. Wine productivity measured by output per hectare increased steeply in Portugal during the second half of the twentieth century (Freire 2010, pp. 40–41). Figure 7.5 shows the doubling in wine production per hectare between 1930 and 1980.

Trends in the wine sector in Portugal followed closely trends of the other three large Mediterranean producers, namely France, Italy and Spain, as the output share in that group of four countries fell from 63 percent of the world total, in 1960–64, to just 49 percent in 2010–14. Grape yields varied considerably in the same countries, from the maximum of 10.4 tonnes per hectare, in Italy in 2005–09, to a minimum of 2.5 tonnes per hectare in Spain in 1965–69. Portugal's yields declined from 6.0 tonnes in 1961–1964 to 3.0 tonnes in 1985–89, and increased from then to 4.5 tonnes in 2000–2004 and 4.0 tonnes in 2005–09 (Anderson and Nelgen 2011, table 97).

Price and revenue volatility increased as output exceeded demand. In the 1930s, overproduction and low prices in the domestic market were joined by economic depression in international markets. Wine production cannot rapidly adapt to changes in markets, as vines are a medium-term investment (Martins 1996, p. 415; Freire 2010, pp. 17–18). But port wines were not as affected as table wines. This was a major characteristic of the sector that put it in a different group from the rest of Portuguese agriculture. The fact that output could not adjust quickly to changes in demand implied that

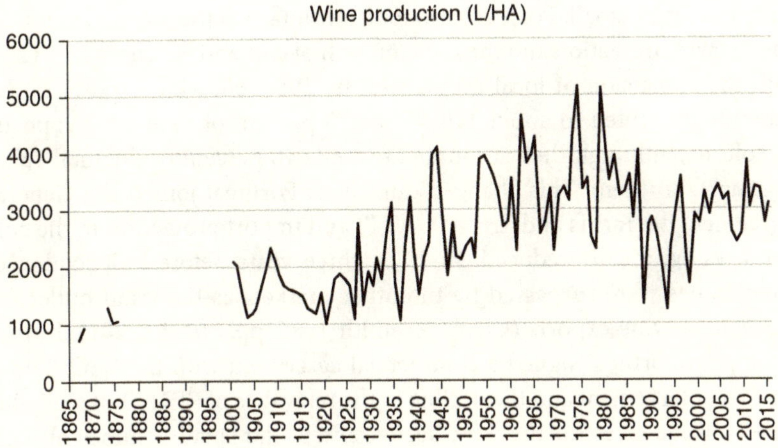

Figure 7.5 Wine production per hectare, Portugal, 1865 to 2015 (litres per hectare).
Source: Author's computation from data in Anderson and Pinilla (2017).

the sector was affected by successive crises, which translated to high levels of income volatility for winemaker and grapegrowers.

Per capita consumption of wine peaked in the mid-1950s in France, in the late 1950s in Italy, in the mid-1970s in Spain and in the latter 1960s in Portugal. Wine per capita consumption declined in the four Mediterranean countries during the second half of the twentieth century, and in 2010–14 consumption levels were similar in the cases of France, Italy and Portugal, at a little over 40 litres per capita, whereas Spain had fallen by then to around 15 litres.

For most of the twentieth century up to the 1980s, wine producers in Spain catered mostly for the domestic market, which was dominated by poor-quality wines sold in bulk (Simpson 2000, pp. 98–99). The domestic market expanded rather slowly and had not much potential for further growth. In fact, as incomes increased and preferences changed, the growth in demand was increasingly concentrated in higher-quality wines sold in bottles and under brands. Then the state intervened with the aim of contracting production by reducing the area under vines and promoting quality improvements in the wines produced (Fernández 2012, pp. 41–42). The international market also improved, which Spanish producers were able to capitalize on (Fernández and Pinilla 2014). The sustained increase in output was thus largely dependent on export markets, particularly for wines of higher quality.

As before, success in global markets was dependent in part on the capacity to secure international trade agreements. Portugal joined the European Free Trade Association (EFTA) as a developing economy and had preferential treatment for some of its agricultural exports, including wine, but the gains from trade were very small. Portugal also took advantage of the colonial markets, due to tariff protection and the rapid growth of demand for wine associated with the expansion of local economies. By 1956–60, wine exports to the colonies amounted to about 110 ML or 73 percent of total wine exports, by volume, although they accounted for only 10 percent of the total value of exports to them. This changed quickly as Portugal joined the General Agreement on Tariffs and Trade (GATT) and import protection in the colonies was gradually reduced. In 1972, three years before independence, the colonies were surpassed by the other markets as the main outlet for Portuguese wine exports (Clarence-Smith 1985, pp. 161–62, 201). In that same year, Portugal signed a commercial agreement with the EEC, before the first enlargement and the decline in the relevance of EFTA, but also with little consequences for the wine sector, except the small volumes of high quality that was exported (Amaro 1978).

The share of output exported thus rose consistently, after declining from 1930 onwards to a low close to 5 percent during World War II, reaching 30 percent again in the late 1960s. It was only by the end of the twentieth century that the wine export share reached a new peak at 50 percent. The increase in the share of exports was at least as fast in Portugal as in its three neighbouring countries, and in 2013–15 it was 46 percent, the same as Italy's, above France's 32 percent and close to Spain's 50 percent. Figure 7.6 shows the growth in wine output and exports, as well as in the unit value of exports. In the decades to the end of the period, export volume increased as did their unit value, whereas output declined. These trends were markedly different from what occurred in previous years. Yet the growth of Portugal's wine export volume after 1980 was lower than that of the other three key Mediterranean countries, contributing to its continuing decline in global exports (Figure 7.4). However, Portugal's unit values of wine exports were second only to those of France, as shown in Table 7.4.

From about 1980 onwards, world wine trade expanded rapidly, due to the increase in consumption of better-quality wines in the more developed economies, the trend being accompanied by improvements in trade practices, including the expansion of branding. Spain and even more so Portugal lagged behind in joining that positive trend. What happened since 1980 was coined 'a revolution in the vineyards and wines of Spain's' (Martínez-Carrión and Medina-Albaladejo 2010, p. 77). The response of European producers was different from that of other world regions, such as the United States and Australia that increasingly produced homogeneous quality wines on a large scale, whereas European countries continued producing in the traditional way, only increasing the level of output.

Table 7.4 *Unit value of wine exports, Portugal, France, Italy and Spain, 1850 to 2015 (annual averages, nominal US$/KL)*

	Portugal	France	Italy	Spain
1850–59	247	192	n.a.	118
1860–69	245	225	95	130
1870–79	217	150	89	134
1880–89	118	194	65	75
1890–99	119	246	53	38
1900–09	109	204	63	52
1910–19	103	292	129	64
1920–29	84	244	120	79
1930–39	106	327	95	57
1940–49	123	496	271	47
1950–59	166	468	194	28
1960–69	188	462	243	200
1970–79	724	1,177	334	432
1980–89	1,623	1,995	615	738
1990–99	2,427	3,604	1,335	1,176
2000–09	2,522	4,965	2,233	1,473
2010–15	3,020	6,539	2,896	1,469

Source: Anderson and Pinilla (2017).

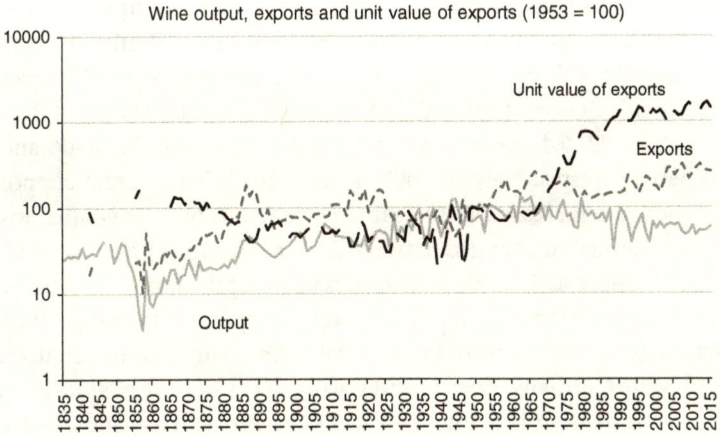

Figure 7.6 Volume of wine production and exports and unit value of wine exports, Portugal, 1835 to 2015 (real values, semilogarithmic scale, 1953 = 100).
Sources: See Figure 7.1.

Yet European producers still accounted for a large share of global wine trade throughout 1970–2000, which was still overwhelmingly sold in the European market (Fernández and Pinilla 2014, pp. 88–89). The growth of multinational firms operating in alcoholic beverages also helped exports, and their relevance increased in countries such as the United Kingdom, France and the Netherlands from the 1960s. But not so in Portugal (Lopes 2005). The main reason for Portugal's lag resided in the relatively small size of the firms operating there.

World trade in quality wine surged again after the turn of the century (Fernández and Pinilla 2014, pp. 91–92). In Spain, the consumption of quality wines increased from 14 percent in 1987 to 38 percent of total consumption in 2009. In per capita terms, table wines consumption declined from 36 to 8 litres per person in the same period of time, whereas quality wines remained at 6 litres. The change in the structure of wine consumption was also accompanied by a change of where it was consumed, which was increasingly more so outside the residence, that is socially. The Spanish 'wine revolution' also reached Spanish vineyards, as the area was reduced by one-third between 1980 and 2009 and the types of vines produced changed considerably too. Yields increased by 85 percent during 1994–2009 to 32 HL/litre in 2009, making Spain one of the highest yielding countries in the world (Martínez-Carrión and Medina-Albaladejo 2010).

Spanish and Portuguese wine producers have not been the most favoured within the European Common Market (Fernández and Pinilla 2014, p. 90). A nominal rate of direct protection to prices estimated by the Organization for Economic Cooperation and Development (OECD) stands at 8.6 percent in 1986–92, 6.4 percent in 1993–99, 1.7 percent in 2000–06 and 0.3 and 0 percent respectively in 2007–13 and 2014. Yet indirect support to wine producers increased in the same period, and on average the level of support remained unchanged between 2007 and 2012, with a 'nominal rate of total producer assistance', which measures total support as percentage of gross value of wine production, averaging 20 percent in that period. The largest recipients of aid were France, Italy and Spain, and in equal-fourth position were Germany, Austria and Portugal. Per hectare of vine, Portugal and Spain came slightly below the EU-27 average, whereas Italy, Germany and France came above the average. Producers in France received double the amount that producers in Portugal and Spain. Per litre of wine produced, Portugal was even with France, and both were above the EU-27 average, whereas Italy and Germany were slightly below (Anderson and Jensen 2016, p. 294).

EU subsidies are granted in a complex framework which can hardly be captured by any particular country or type of producer. Initially, in 1966, such regulations were mainly French and to a lesser extent Italian. The EU regulates quantities, prices and quality of wines. The first two are forms of direct protection to producers and distributors, and the third is only indirect as it is also consumer protection. Seven out of the eight European Common Market 1966 wine tariffs were copied from those of France, implying that all the other five EEC countries had to adjust, particularly in Germany, where a substantial reduction in tariffs for wines was required for containers below 2 litres (Meloni and Swinnen 2013, pp. 266–67).

In Portugal, in 2012 wine still had a large weight in the agricultural sector, representing in 2012 11 percent of value added and 8 percent of employment, thus with a labour productivity above the average. Its export performance was also positive, particularly in bottled wines, which increased at 4.6 percent per year during 2005–11. Apparently, the sector has been unable to fully exploit subsidies, which is probably due to difficulties in investment stemming either from low availability of funds from the financial sector or difficulties in securing markets. As a result, only about half of EU-approved support funds were spent (ViniPortugal n.d., p. 25).

In 1997, associations representing merchants, producers, wine cooperatives, distillers, farmers and wine regions founded the nonprofit association with the name ViniPortugal with the aim of marketing Portugal's wine in foreign markets.[12] The date of creation of the association is indicative of Portugal's delay. But the list of things to be done probably does not differ from lists of other associations in other countries or even from other times. What really matter are the reasons why the sound measures are not followed, which may have more to do with limits to investment, which may be the outcome of low profitability, low levels of starting capital to serve as collateral or lack of financial intermediates of capacity to influence economic policies and subsidies.[13]

CONCLUSION: A REVERSAL OF FORTUNES?

Wine is neither a homogeneous nor a diversified product. Instead the sector is composed by a scale of types, catering for differentiated markets. Following a long period of low levels of international trade, from 1870 to 1930, globalization and phylloxera transformed the wine sector, as production,

[12] www.viniportugal.pt/AboutUs.

[13] For Spain, see Martínez-Carrión and Medina-Albaladejo (2010).

productivity and international trade increased. From 1930 onwards, another transformation took place, as the outcome of state intervention, definition of wine regions and increasing regulation, catering mostly for protected domestic markets, but with some exports of higher-quality wines. Since 1980, a new transformation occurred as the domestic markets of southern European countries increasingly demanded higher-quality wines.

It is clear from this study that Portugal's wine producers were able to adjust with significant rapidity and efficiency to changes in both domestic and international market conditions. Presumably that stemmed from the large wine comparative advantage Portugal has enjoyed over the past 250 years. Despite the growth of the sector, it is only in recent decades that Portugal's wines have been competing well in international markets, due to the country exporting wines of better quality.

We have defined in this chapter three waves of globalization of Portugal's wines, each with very different traits. The first wave was that of port exported mainly to Britain, which increased rapidly in the eighteenth and the first decades of the nineteenth century, but then declined. The second wave occurred as a consequence of growth of demand for table wines in France because of phylloxera, and this wave came to a halt by the last decades of the nineteenth century. The third wave occurred at the end of the twentieth century and is still ongoing. This is occurring in a context of widespread international competition. A key question now regarding this third wave is whether/when it is going to end. Success in this third wave for Portugal is based on previous developments in its domestic market – in contrast to the second wave, when producers were simply taking advantage of changes in the international markets. Because the latest wave is to a large extent related to parallel changes in the domestic market, they provide a more solid base for such developments. This wave may thus lead to a reversal of fortune for Portugal's wines in international markets.

REFERENCES

Alexandre, V. (2008), 'A Real Companhia Velha no primeiro quartel do século XIX: o contexto internacional', *População e Sociedade* 16: 139–49.

Amaral, L. and D. Freire (2016), 'Agricultural Policy, Growth and Demise, 1930–2000', pp. 245–76 in *An Agrarian History of Portugal, 1000–2000: Economic Development on the European Frontier*, edited by D. Freire and P. Lains, Leiden: Brill.

Amaro, R. R. (1978), 'A agricultura portuguesa e a integração europeia: a experiência do passado (EFTA) e a perspectiva do futuro (CEE)', *Análise Social* 14(2): 279–310.

Anderson, K. and S. Nelgen (2011), *Global Wine Markets, 1961 to 2009: A Statistical Compendium*, Adelaide: University of Adelaide Press.

Anderson, K. and H. G. Jensen (2016), 'How Much Government Assistance Do European Wine Producers Receive?', *Journal of Wine Economics* 11(2): 289–305.

Anderson, K. and V. Pinilla (with the assistance of A. J. Holmes) (2017), *Annual Database of Global Wine Markets, 1835 to 2016*, Wine Economics Research Centre, University of Adelaide, to be posted at www.adelaide.edu.au/wine-econ/databases/global-wine-history

Anderson, R. W. (2014), 'Rent Seeking and the Treaty of Methuen', *Journal of Public Finance and Public Choice* 32(1–3): 19–29.

Baptista, F. O. (1993), *A Política Agrária do Estado Novo*, Porto: Afrontamento.

Cardoso, J. L. (2017), 'The Anglo-Portuguese Methuen Treaty of 1703: Opportunities and Constraints of Economic Development', pp. 105–124 in *The Politics of Commercial Treaties in the Eighteenth Century: Balance of Power, Balance of Trade*, edited by A. Alimento and K. Stapelbroek, London: Palgrave Macmillan. DOI: 10.1007/978-3-319-53574-6.

Clarence-Smith, G. (1985), *The Third Portuguese Empire, 1825–1975: A Study in Economic Imperialism*, Manchester: Manchester University Press.

Costa, L. F. and J. Reis (2016), 'The Chronic Food Deficit of Early Modern Portugal: Curse or Myth?' *Gabinete de História Económica e Social* Working Papers 58.

Duguid, P. (2005), 'Networks and Knowledge: The Beginning and End of the Port Commodity Chain, 1703–1860', *Business History Review* 79: 493–526, Autumn.

Duguid, P. and T. S. Lopes (1999), 'Ambiguous Company: Institutions and Organizations in the Port Wine Trade, 1814–1834', *Scandinavian Economic History Review* 48(1): 84–102.

Fernández, E. (2010), 'Unsuccessful Responses to Quality Uncertainty: Brands in Spain's Sherry Industry, 1920–1990', *Business History* 52(1): 100–19.

(2012), 'Especialización en baja calidad: España y el mercado internacional del vino, 1950–1990', *Historia Agraria* 56: 41–76, April.

Fernández, E. and V. Pinilla (2014), 'Historia económica del vino en España (1850–2000)', pp. 67–98 in *La Economía del Vino en España y en el Mundo*, edited by R. Compés López and J. S. Castillo Valero, Almería: Cajamar Caja Rural.

Freire, D. (2010), *Produzir e Beber: A Questão do Vinho no Estado Novo*, Lisbon: Âncora.

Grantham, G. (1999), 'Contra Ricardo: On the Macroeconomics of Pre-industrial Economies', *European Review of Economic History* 3(2): 199–232.

Instituto Nacional de Estatística (2016), *Estatísticas Agrícolas – 2015*, Lisbon: Instituto Nacional de Estatística.

Lains, P. (1986), 'Exportações portuguesas, 1850–1913: A tese da dependência revisitada', *Análise Social* 22(2): 381–419.

(2003), 'New Wine in Old Bottles: Output and Productivity Trends in Portuguese Agriculture, 1850–1950', *European Review of Economic History* 7(1): 43–72.

(2007), 'Growth in a Protected Environment: Portugal, 1850–1950', *Research in Economic History* 24: 121–63.

(2009), 'The Role of Agriculture in Portuguese Economic Development, 1870–1973', pp. 333–52 in *Agriculture and Economic Growth in Europe Since 1870*, edited by P. Lains and V. Pinilla, London: Routledge.

(2016), 'Agriculture and Economic Development on the European Frontier, 1000–2000', pp. 277–311 in *An Agrarian History of Portugal, 1000–2000: Economic Development on the European Frontier*, edited by D. Freire and P. Lains, Leiden: Brill.

Lains, P. and P. S. Sousa (1998), 'Estatística e produção agrícola em Portugal, 1848–1914', *Análise Social* 33(5): 935–68.

Lanero, D. (2014), 'The Portuguese Estado Novo: Programmes and Obstacles to the Modernization of Agriculture, 1933–1950', pp. 85–111 in *Agriculture in the Age of Fascism: Authoritarian Technocracy and Rural Modernization, 1922-194*, edited by L. Fernández Prieto, L. Pan Montojo and M. Cabo Villaverde, Turnhout: Brepols.

Lopes, T. S. (2005), 'Competing with Multinationals: Strategies of the Portuguese Alcohol Industry', *Business History Review* 79: 559–85, Autumn.

Martínez-Carrión, J. M. and F. J. Medina-Albaladejo (2010), 'Change and Development in the Spanish Wine Sector, 1950–2009', *Journal of Wine Research* 21(1): 77–95.

Martins, C. A. (1988), 'Os ciclos do vinho do Porto: ensaio de periodização', *Análise Social* 24(1): 391–429.

(1990), *Memória do Vinho do Porto*, Lisbon: Instituto de Ciências Sociais da Universidade de Lisboa.

(1991), 'A filoxera na viticultura nacional', *Análise Social* 26(3–4): 653–88.

(1996), 'A intervenção política dos vinhateiros no século XIX', *Análise Social* 31(2–3): 413–35.

(1998), *Vinha, Vinho e Política Vinícola Nacional. Do Pombalismo à Regeneração*, 3 Volumes, unpublished PhD Dissertation, Évora: Universidade de Évora.

(2005), 'A agricultura', pp. 219–58 in *História Económica de Portugal, 1700-2000*, edited by P. Lains and Á. Ferreira da Silva, Volume 2, Lisbon: Imprensa de Ciências Sociais.

Matias, M. G. (2002), *Vinho e Vinhas em Tempo de Crise: O Oídio e a Filoxera na Região Oeste, 1850–1890*, Caldas da Rainha: Património Histórico-Grupo de Estudos.

Meloni, G. and J. Swinnen (2013), 'The Political Economy of European Wine Regulations', *Journal of Wine Economics* 8(3): 244–84.

(2014), 'The Rise and Fall of the World's Largest Wine Exporter and Its Institutional Legacy', *Journal of Wine Economics* 9(1): 3–33.

Palma, N. and J. Reis (2016), 'From Convergence to Divergence: Portuguese Demography and Economic Growth', Groningen Growth and Development Centre Research Memorandum 161, University of Groningen, Groningen.

Pan-Montojo, J. (2009), 'Las vitivinicultura europeas: de la primera a la segunda globalización', *Mundo Agrario* 9(1): 1–29.

Pereira, G. M. (2008), 'Nos 250 anos da região demarcada do Douro: Da companhia pombalina à regulação interprofissiona', *População e Sociedade* 16: 175–85.

Pereira, M. H. (1983), *Livre-Câmbio e Desenvolvimento Económico*, Lisbon: Sá da Costa Editora.

Pinilla, V. and M. I. Ayuda (2002), 'The Political Economy of the Wine Trade: Spanish Exports and the International Market', *European Review of Economic History* 6(1): 51–85.

(2007), 'The International Wine Market, 1850–1938: An Opportunity for Export Growth in Southern Europe?', pp. 179–219 in *Wine Society and Globalization: Multidisciplinary Perspectives on the Wine Industry*, edited by G. Campbell and N. Gibert, New York: Palgrave Macmillan.

Pinilla, V. and R. Serrano (2008), 'The Agricultural and Food Trade in the First Globalization: Spanish Table Wine Exports 1871 to 1935, A Case Study', *Journal of Wine Economics* 3(2): 132–48.

Reis, J. (2016), 'Gross Agricultural Output: A Quantitative, Unified Perspective, 1500–1850', pp. 172–216 in *An Agrarian History of Portugal. Economic Development on the European Frontier, 1000–2000*, edited by D. Freire and P. Lains, Leiden: Brill.

Ricardo, D. (1817), *On The Principles of Political Economy and Taxation*, London: John Murray Albemarle-Street (third edition 1821).

Serrão, J. V. (2009), 'Land Management Responses to Market Changes: Portugal Seventeenth to Nineteenth Centuries', pp. 47–73 in *Markets and Agricultural Change in Europe from the Thirteenth to the Twentieth Centuries*, edited by V. Pinilla, Turnhout: Brepols.

(2016), 'Extensive Growth and Market Expansion, 1703–1820', pp. 132–71 in *An Agrarian History of Portugal, 1000–2000: Economic Development on the European Frontier*, edited by D. Freire and P. Lains, Leiden: Brill.

Simpson, J. (2000), 'Cooperation and Cooperatives in Southern European Wine Production: The Nature of a Successful Institutional Innovation, 1880–1950', pp. 95–126 in *New Frontiers in Agricultural History*, edited by K. D. Kauffman, Bradford: Emerald.

(2011), *Creating Wine: The Emergence of a World Industry, 1840–1914*, Princeton, NJ: Princeton University Press.

Soares, F. B. (2005), 'A agricultura', pp. 157–83 in *História Económica de Portugal, 1700–2000*, Volume 3, edited by P. Lains and Á. Ferreira da Silva, Lisbon: Imprensa de Ciências Sociais.

ViniPortugal (n.d.), *Plano Estratégico para a Internacionalização do Sector de Vinhos de Portugal*, Lisbon: ViniPortugal.

8

Spain

Eva Fernández and Vicente Pinilla

Spain played a crucial role in the growth of international trade in wine in the mid-nineteenth century, when its production and exports greatly increased after French vineyards were devastated by phylloxera and France sought deep-colored and high-alcohol wines beyond its borders.[1]

However, until recently, incentives to modernize Spain's wine industry and improve quality were scarce. Modernization efforts concentrated mostly on replanting after the phylloxera plague and expanding production thereafter. Although Sherry producers and some *bodegas* in la Rioja produced fine wines, most of the focus until the 1980s was on output of ordinary wines for the domestic market.

Spain's wine industry was also shaped by fluctuations in foreign demand that created cyclical problems of overproduction and falling prices. Exports historically depended on the size of harvests in France and Algeria, and suffered the consequences of various waves of protectionist policies in European wine-importing countries. The growth of Spanish wine exports was boosted when Spain gained full membership of the European Common Wine Market at the beginning of the 1990s. Although important technological changes were introduced in winemaking and the highest-quality Spanish wines are well regarded in export and domestic markets, Spain's exports continued to be mostly low-priced wines.

Cyclical episodes of falling prices created increasing unrest in the sector. Until the 1930s, the state responded to this discontent by controlling fraudulent practices and attempting to reduce the quantity of wines sold in markets. When the overproduction crisis became more severe in the 1950s, the government began intervening by guaranteeing minimum prices, removing

[1] This study has received financial support from Spain's Ministry of Science and Innovation, project ECO2015-65582, and project ECO2015-66196-P, and from the Government of Aragon, through the Research Group "Agri-food Economic History (19th and 20th Centuries)."

poor-quality wines, regulating the alcohol industry, and introducing legislation to encourage geographical indications. Growers responded by forming cooperatives for processing grapes, storing wines and creating various geographical indications. However, cooperatives expanded mainly for the storage of lower-quality wines, while Spain's appellations (contrary to those in France) imposed loose quality controls. Meanwhile, private brands were only important for Sherries and Riojas, as the wine industry in Spain (as elsewhere in Europe) has been characterized by a large number of small-scale winegrowers and *bodegas* producing a wide variety of wines.

Although exports have increased substantially in the past two decades, a significant share continues to be sold in bulk. Export opportunities in new markets are limited because of Spain's specialization in cheap table wines. Nevertheless, production restrictions and quality controls began to be gradually applied in Spain's appellations from the 1970s, in response to the severe decline in domestic consumption and the limited international demand for cheap wines.

In this chapter, we explore two factors explaining the slow modernization of Spain's wine sector and the low investment in quality wines: the regulation of markets by the state, which led to expand production of ordinary wines, and the greater barriers to entry into foreign markets for quality wines (which are dominated by French appellations) as distinct from cheap wines.

SPAIN'S GOLDEN ERA OF ORDINARY TABLE WINE EXPORTS IN THE SECOND HALF OF THE NINETEENTH CENTURY

In the 1850s, the Spanish agricultural sector began a period of expansion due to increasing domestic demand and the growing integration of Spain into the international economy in what became the first wave of globalization (Gallego and Pinilla 1986). As Spain slowly industrialized, it began specializing in the export of products characteristic of Mediterranean agriculture, mainly to more-developed European countries (Pinilla and Ayuda 2010). Wine was the most important of those products until the end of the nineteenth century.

Like other Mediterranean countries, Spain had a long winemaking tradition. Wine was usually produced in rural areas for self-consumption or to be sold in nearby towns. Its consumption was an integral part of local diets.[2]

[2] It even formed part of wages. Many agricultural workers, particularly those engaged in the reaping and harvesting of cereals, received payment in money plus a certain daily quantity of wine.

A few areas have long been engaged in exports (fortified wines from Jerez, grape spirit from the Catalonian coast), but they are exceptions.

In the second half of the nineteenth century, a series of changes in Spain's economy and society boosted and facilitated expansion of wine production and consumption. First, the liberal governments designed a market institutional framework within which the farmers could respond to demand stimuli. Second, the integration of the domestic market, which was deepened by the railway (Herranz 2016, pp. 321–28), gave rise to an increase in output in those areas most equipped to do so. Wine sales to cities or deficit areas grew as transportation costs fell. And third, urban development and the slow yet persistent increase in per capita income also favored the consumption of wine among the urban population. Similar to other European countries, Spain's highest-income groups demanded high-quality wines such as champagne, imitating the consumer patterns of France, a country that had a strong cultural influence on Spain in the nineteenth century.

However, the main driver of demand in this period was the external market, most of all France, although Britain and other countries in northern Europe and the American continent also absorbed a part of Spain's growing output (Table 8.1).

In 1850, Spanish wine exports were balanced between table wine and Sherry and other fortified wines. The principal market for table wines was the American continent, particularly Cuba, which was still a colony, and the River Plate region. In the case of fortified wines, approximately 80 percent of Sherry exports went to Britain. These wines already had a long export tradition, as they were easier to transport and preserve due to their high alcohol content, which reduced potential spoilage.

The fall in output in France, brought about by the oidium plague, generated the first major boost to exports to this country. Subsequently, wine exports increased moderately until the mid-1870s (Figure 8.1). The phylloxera plague, which had arrived in France in 1863, began to have serious effects on that country's wine production after 1875. Consequently, the French producers needed to import large volumes of wine in order to maintain export levels and to supply increasing domestic demand. This situation provided a golden opportunity for Spanish producers. The favorable tariff treatment offered by France in 1877 enabled nearby regions in Spain, such as Aragon, Navarre and La Rioja in the Ebro Valley, to supply France using the recently built railway. Spanish regions on the Mediterranean coast, such as Catalonia or Valencia, also exported wine to France but by sea. Encouraged by rising prices, Spain's exports rose substantially. The export

Table 8.1 *Volume of Spain's exports of table wine in casks, by destination, 1871 to 1935 (ML per year)*

	1871–5	1876–80	1881–5	1886–90	1891–95	1896-1900	1901–5	1906–10	1911–15	1916–20	1921–25	1926–30	1931–5
Canary I./Spanish N. Africa	81	39	24	205	823	960	1,878	2,795	5,778	5,477	11,926	13,387	8,208
France	30,663	179,315	547,854	697,966	502,521	391,835	94,650	42,783	141,765	275,716	156,165	278,928	95,354
United Kingdom	8,187	8,985	8,769	9,880	10,685	17,696	13,513	6,933	5,148	4,743	3,645	3,376	1,750
Rest of Europe	10,080	10,873	12,559	10,105	15,228	30,422	36,231	32,045	60,906	121,221	61,597	53,049	46,641
Latin America	100,329	93,578	101,321	97,477	97,730	79,805	57,669	53,236	47,930	22,751	16,396	13,412	3,966
North America	2,558	1,980	2,697	1,961	798	339	521	362	469	731	121	181	64
Asia	1,582	1,431	2,187	2,263	3,049	3,796	2,131	1,655	865	453	533	449	1,234
Africa	5,197	5,263	6,479	4,342	3,988	4,139	682	872	6,540	14,411	16,309	10,533	8,529
European colonies	518	748	801	1,362	1,550	1,397	1,179	272	236	54	82	1,047	2,426
Not classified	0	0	0	0	0	4,252	0	0	0	0	0	0	44
Total	159,195	302,213	682,690	825,561	636,373	534,640	208,454	140,952	269,637	445,557	266,773	374,360	168,217
Share (%) to:													
France	19	59	80	85	79	73	45	30	53	62	59	75	57
Other Europe	12	7	3	2	4	9	24	28	25	28	25	15	29
Latin America	63	31	15	12	15	15	28	38	18	5	6	4	2

Source: Authors' compilation from annual data in Dirección General de Aduanas (1871–1935).

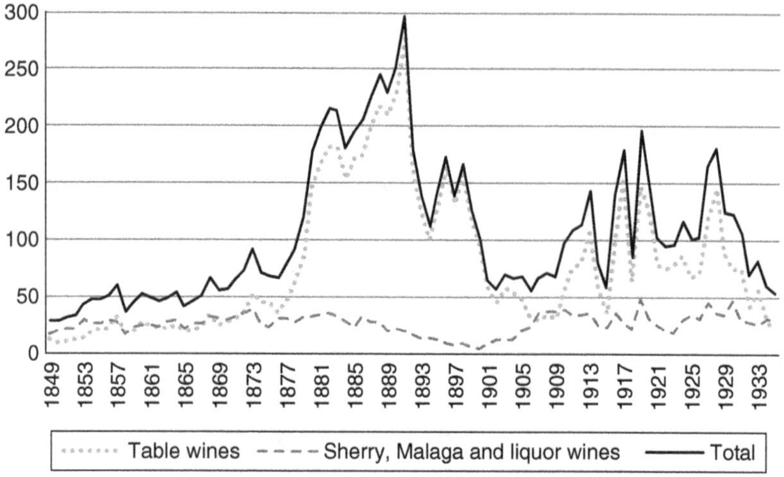

Figure 8.1 Volume of wine exports, Spain, 1849 to 1935 (million Spanish pesetas at 1913 prices).
Source: Own calculation from the annual data of Dirección General de Aduanas (1849–1935).

boom to France reached its peak at the beginning of the 1890s, when ordinary wine exports exceeded 1,000 million litres (ML).

Spanish exports to other European destinations and Latin America also benefited from France's problems at a time when demand in these countries' high-income groups and immigrants from Mediterranean Europe were expanding. Spain's strategy involved competing in the low-quality, low-price segment and achieved a significant increase in exports. At the same time, Sherry exports also maintained a good pace.

The immediate response of farmers to this upward trend in demand and strong price increase was to substantially increase their vineyard area. Although the data available for the mid-nineteenth century should be regarded with caution, we estimate that Spain's vineyard area increased by around 40 percent between 1860 and 1888. This growth was mostly concentrated in areas best connected with France, and in some regions was spectacular.[3] In some cases, this expansion was undertaken to the detriment of other crops, but in many cases it involved bringing into production marginal land that was not suitable for other uses (Pinilla 1995a).

[3] Between 1857 and 1889, in the province of Zaragoza in Aragon, which was well connected with France by rail, the area under vine grew from 46,838 to 88,544 hectares (Pinilla 1995a, p. 65).

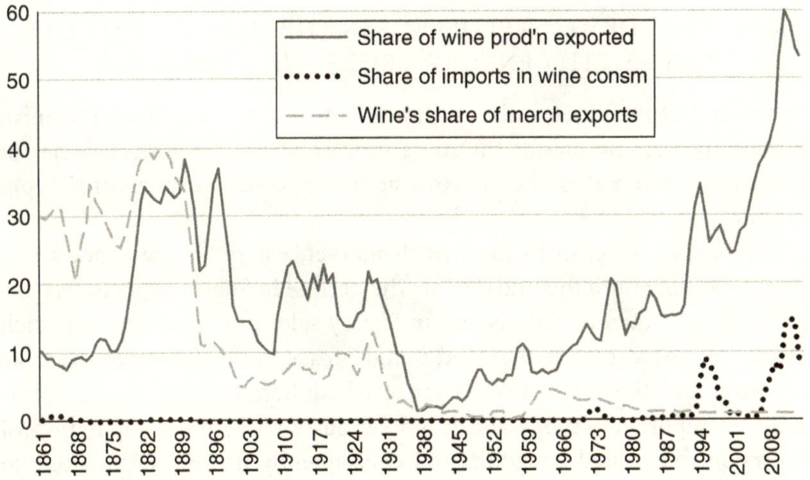

Figure 8.2 Shares of wine production exported, of wine consumption imported, and wine's share of exports of all goods, Spain, 1860 to 2015 (%, three-year moving averages around year shown).
Source: Anderson and Pinilla (2017).

The increasing exports boosted revenues for winemakers, but did not stimulate an improvement in the quality of their wines. The French demanded wines with a high alcohol content and deep color to mix with their own, and Spanish producers concentrated on supplying that type of product. Technological innovations did not play a significant role, although some improvements were made in the cultivation of vines, in the pressing process and in equipment used to make wine. Output increased to satisfy the intense external demand, and the share of Spain's production volume that was exported reached 47 percent in 1891, a share that was not exceeded until 2010 (Figure 8.2).

High demand for exports encouraged fraudulent practices in wine production, however. The most common frauds were the addition of gypsum, alcohol not distilled from grapes, and chemical products. This generated many problems in both domestic and external markets (Pan-Montojo 1994, pp. 160–73).

As a result of the export boom, wine increased its share of agricultural output to 15.6 percent by 1891 to become Spain's most important horticultural crop (Grupo de Estudios de Historia Rural 1983, p. 244). Moreover, wine became the main good exported by Spain. In the 1880s and 1890s, it accounted for more than 30 percent of the total value of Spanish exported goods (Figure 8.2).

EXTERNAL DEMAND PROBLEMS IN THE FIRST HALF OF THE TWENTIETH CENTURY: CRISES AND OVERSUPPLY

By the end of the nineteenth century, the most buoyant sector in Spanish agriculture became one of the most problematic. A prolonged series of problems in external markets led to a significant drop in exports of all types of wine.

The problems began in the British market, where Sherry exports had grown strongly until the mid-1870s. The decline in Sherry exports was initially compensated by an increase in Sherry sales in other countries, such as France. The strong demand led to a decrease in the quality of the wine exported and the widespread practice of adulteration. An intense campaign to report imitations and fraud seriously affected the reputation of Sherry in the United Kingdom and consequently its sales (Pan-Montojo 1994, pp. 110–15; Simpson 2004). The change in the demand pattern for Sherry was also related to a certain modification of tastes. Until the 1860s, there had been a preference for fortified wines, usually with added alcohol. However, British tastes shifted gradually toward so-called natural wines, of which the red wines from Bordeaux were clearly the leaders (Morilla 2002; Ludington 2013).

However, the most relevant problems were related to the enormous difficulties for Spanish exports seeking to penetrate the French market. The replanting of French vineyards, and the development of new vineyards in Algeria, led to a rapid recovery of output to prephylloxera levels. That in turn generated intense pressure from winemakers on the French government to increase protection against foreign wine. As a result, at the end of 1891 the favorable tariff treatment for Spanish imports ended, and in 1892 the new Méline tariff substantially increased duties on wine imported into France. Substantial volumes of Spanish wine were still imported into France in the 1890s, thanks to quotas being temporarily authorized in response to pressure applied by exporters in the Bordeaux region. Those imports were mixed with Bordeaux wine (up to 50 percent), much of which was subsequently exported. But the protectionist policy gradually strangled imports, as the *ad valorem* duties paid on imports rose from less than 7 percent in 1890 to 45 percent by 1901.

The difficulties for Spanish winegrowers did not end there. In the region that became the principal wine-producing area of France, the Midi, the replanting of vineyards after the phylloxera plague was completed with French-American hybrids. Being highly productive, those hybrids produced wines with little alcohol and a pale color. Hybrid French wine thus needed to be blended with wine with a higher alcohol content and deeper color. While Spanish wine had that property, so too did Algerian wine. Algeria was a French colony and, from 1871, enjoyed a customs union with metropolitan France. That meant Algerian wine imports were free from duties and therefore were much cheaper within France than wines from other origins and subject to high tariffs. This led to the substitution of Spanish wine with Algerian wine.

The impact of the wine tariff increase was lethal for Spanish exports. Each 1 percent increase in the French tariff represented a long-term fall of 1.8 percent in the share that imports from countries such as Spain on French wine consumption (Pinilla and Ayuda 2002, pp. 71–75). From the beginning of the century, Spanish exports to France dropped to very low levels compared to those in the second half of the nineteenth century, and they were extraordinarily irregular, increasing when the French-Algerian harvest was poor and decreasing dramatically when it was high.[4]

The decline in exports to France and Britain was not the only problem facing Spanish producers. Some of Spain's traditional clients, such as Argentina and Uruguay, introduced protectionist policies to favor their own domestic winegrowers. The expansion of wine production in the River Plate region was spectacular, more than trebling between 1900 and 1938. Consequently, with tariffs above 66 percent in *ad valorem* terms, their imports plummeted (Pinilla and Serrano 2008). Exports to the emerging North American market also waned when Californian producers demanded and obtained higher protection.[5]

Although Spanish exports enjoyed a certain degree of success when sales in northern European countries increased, this could not nearly compensate for the losses in the French and American markets. The principal problem was the stagnant demand for wine in the industrialized countries of Europe at the beginning of the twentieth century. Consumer patterns of alcoholic drinks in this region had traditionally relegated wine to a marginal position, and temperance movements meant consumption there did not grow much during this period despite income growth (Pinilla and Ayuda 2007, 2008). In contrast to wine-producing countries such as France, Spain and Italy, where wine consumption represented 70 to 95 percent of total alcohol

[4] In the short term, a fall in the French-Algerian harvest of 1 percent increased the share of Spanish exports in wine consumption in France by 1.9 percent (Pinilla and Ayuda 2002, p. 74).

[5] Before Prohibition, in 1919, the North American tariff stood at 85 percent *ad valorem*, and after Prohibition was abolished in 1933 the tariff exceeded 120 percent (Pinilla and Ayuda 2002, pp. 56–61).

consumption, in the countries of northwestern Europe (Britain, Denmark, the Netherlands, Belgium), it was lower than 5 percent (Anderson and Pinilla 2017). As a result, despite the competitiveness of Spanish ordinary wine in the low-quality segment, the scant increase in demand provided very limited opportunities for Spanish exporters (Pinilla and Ayuda 2002, pp. 76–79).

For all these reasons, the Spanish wine sector faced enormously irregular and weak demand for its surplus wine. During the first third of the twentieth century, its share of production exported oscillating between 10 percent and 20 percent (Figure 8.2). Wine's share of Spain's total exports of total agricultural goods fell from a maximum of 53 percent during 1870–1890 to only 12 percent in 1929–1935 (Pinilla 1995b, p. 161). Before 1891, wine accounted for one-third of total Spanish exports, compared to just one-tenth in France and Italy. However, from the beginning of the twentieth century, Spain's share fell to levels below 10 percent, although it was still higher than the French or Italian shares (Anderson and Pinilla 2017). The economic crisis beginning in 1929 reinforced protectionism even more, causing Spanish wine exports to fall back to the levels of the 1870s.

PROBLEMS FOR WINE PRODUCERS PROMPTS THE EXPANSION OF QUALITY WINES

The arrival of phylloxera in Spain caused serious damage to producers and severely affected production from the mid-1890s. It put many winemakers out of business, and migration out of winegrowing areas rose dramatically. In light of the previous French experience, it was clear that the only feasible alternative was the replanting of all vineyards with American vines that were immune to this disease. Such replanting required significant capital investment during a period of falling export earnings. The logical consequence was a reduction in the area under vines in Spain and a tendency to concentrate production in the hands of those with a long winemaking tradition and with sufficient capital to invest.

During the first third of the twentieth century, wine production in Spain fell dramatically, partly due to the effects of the plague and also due to the reduction in the area under vine. Output fell to its minimum level by 1915, when it stood at around one-third of the level reached in 1892. It gradually recovered but did not regain its previous peak until the 1960s. The area under vines increased in the 1930s until it reached levels similar to those of the end of the nineteenth century, which meant an oversupply and thus low prices and profitability for winegrowers. There had already been a decreasing trend in the relative price of wine and the profitability of vineyards up to World War I, but after 1920 the slump in wine prices was particularly acute, especially between 1920 and 1925 and between 1930 and 1935. The share of wine production in the value of total horticultural crops decreased significantly until it reached 7.8 percent in 1931, roughly half the weight that it had had forty years earlier (Grupo de Estudios de Historia Rural 1983, p. 244).

In contrast with this difficult and complicated situation for ordinary wine producers, from the end of the nineteenth century the production of high-quality Spanish bottled wine marketed under recognized brand names grew significantly. The earliest case that we can find in Spain of quality wine production is that of Sherry. These wines had been exported in small quantities to the British market from before the eighteenth century, which encouraged Sherry makers to attempt to shift their production from young musts to more homogeneous products, the quality of which did not depend on the annual harvest. The solera system, whereby wines from different years are mixed as they age, originated in the second half of the eighteenth century, although it became consolidated and widespread at the end of the 1830s. This change implied the development of a modern sector with meticulous production techniques adapted to British tastes and with a clear division of functions between winemakers, storage companies responsible for the aging process, and export companies (Maldonado 1999). Export companies sold the product to British agents who acted as wholesalers in the British market, where they sold the wine to local traders, who sometimes marketed it under their own brand name. Consequently, British-Spanish companies, which acted as both exporters and agents, began to emerge in the mid-nineteenth century, such as González Byass in 1855 (Montañés 2000).

Sherry prices paid to the producers rose from 1860 and, after the reduction of British tariffs during the same decade, exports increased strongly. Higher prices encouraged British importers to search for similar but cheaper wines, which they obtained not only from areas close to Jerez, such as Montilla, but also from other countries, such as South Africa and Australia. The most dangerous competitor was the "sherry" from Hamburg, made with alcohol distilled from beetroot or potato, which produced a poor-quality wine.

The imitation, adulterations, and sale of low-quality wines seriously affected the reputation of Sherry in the British market, and sales fell considerably. When British demand recovered, it shifted toward other types of wine, such as the clarets from Bordeaux or lower-quality fortified wines. Sherry from Jerez would never recover its exceptional position in the British wine market (Simpson 2011, pp. 171–90).

In order to provide a brand guarantee and fight against fraud, from 1896 the aging and exporting wineries (particularly Pedro Domecq and González Byass) began to bottle Sherry. This gave rise to an increase in exports to the British market beginning in the 1920s. Under the new legislative framework established by the Estatuto del Vino (Wine Statute) of 1932, the appellation of origin (*Denominación de Origen*) of Jerez was created in 1933. It established a series of measures to control the quality of wine produced, such as geographic boundaries of vineyards, the age and minimum alcohol content of wines, limitation of yields, and minimum export prices. However, the regulatory council operated for barely six years due to difficult circumstances caused by the Spanish Civil War and the World War II (Fernández 2008b).

The great export boom of the 1880s did not stimulate the development of the production of other quality wines in Spain, as this type of product was not demanded in the French market. In other external markets, France dominated quality wine exports. Even so, Spanish quality wines made a modest start at the end of the nineteenth century based on a few wineries founded in the 1860s that imitated French production methods. This was the case of La Rioja, where a series of new wineries specialized in the production of Bordeaux-style red wines, which emerged between 1858 and 1878 (Hernández Marco 2002; Gonzalez Inchaurraga 2006). Meanwhile, in the Catalonian town of San Sadurní, experiments in the production of sparkling, champagne-type wines began in the 1880s.

The end of the trade agreement with France in 1891 was decisive for the expansion of quality wines. An expanding consumption of Bordeaux-style reds and champagne in Spain by the upper classes began to be supplied by domestic producers. The high duties to which the French wines were subject in Spain (see Figure 8.3) provided opportunities for such producers. After the end of the golden age of exports to France, these producers found opportunities by improving the quality of their output and imitating French techniques.

In La Rioja, during the last decade of the nineteenth century, in addition to the existing wineries that used Bordeaux techniques, many more emerged and went on to become leading winemakers of this region for many years (González Inchaurraga 2006, pp. 131–36). While the Rioja region was by far the most successful imitator of the Bordeaux techniques to produce quality wines, other areas also adopted French techniques, including Valbuena de Duero (Valladolid), where the emblematic Vega Sicilia winery was established in 1865.

Many of these quality wineries depended on the assistance of technical personnel from France. That involved trips by winemakers to the Bordeaux region to learn the techniques, or sometimes the relocation of Bordeaux

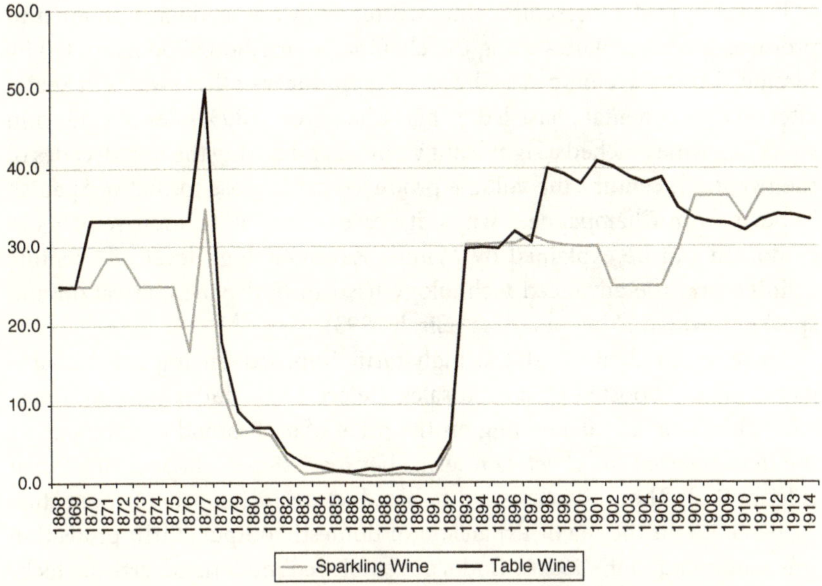

Figure 8.3 Wine duties as a percentage of wine imports, Spain, 1868 to 1914 (%).
Source: Authors' compilation from annual data in Dirección General de Aduanas (1868–1914).

winemakers to Spain who brought their techniques and grape varieties with them, as in the case of Bodegas Lalanne in Aragon, established in 1894 (Pinilla 2002).

The change in the production model toward quality wine production, usually with an aging process, required capital investments in high-quality varieties of grapes, facilities (wineries), and technical resources. A significant part of the capital necessary for setting up these new businesses was provided by traders and wholesalers who profited during the years of the export boom to France (Pan-Montojo 2003).

The development of this type of wine was facilitated by the end of the bilateral agreements that had been signed between Spain and France in 1877 and 1882 (Pan-Montojo 1994). These agreements reduced the tariffs that each of the two countries had to pay for their wines to enter the other to extremely low levels. In 1893, the end of these agreements meant that quality French wine was subject to high tariffs in Spain (Figure 8.3), giving Spanish producers in this market segment more sales opportunities.

In 1925, the first Rioja designation of origin was constituted, although the legislative changes of 1932 and the war meant that, in practice, it did not begin operating until the 1940s (Gómez Urdañez 2000).

From the mid-nineteenth century, attempts were made in Catalonia to produce sparkling wines using the champagne method. Codorniu, led by Manuel Raventós, emerged as the leading producer of these wines in Spain, after an experimental phase led by his father. From 1893, sales of Codorniu sparkling wine reached a significant volume, and during the first decades of the twentieth century the volume produced came close to that of Spanish imports from Champagne – which it exceeded in 1911. Improvements in Codorniu can be explained by Manuel Raventós' high level of scientific training and the advanced technology used in both vine cultivation and sparkling winemaking practices (Giralt 1993).

There is no doubt that the high tariff imposed on imported champagne greatly boosted Codorniu sales. Before 1891, duties were minimal. After this date, and depending on the price of each brand of champagne, the duties varied in *ad valorem* terms between 25 percent and 50 percent (Figure 8.3). These increases led to a reduction in imports of more than 50 percent and the major expansion of domestic output. Tariff protection was reinforced in the 1920s. Codorniu employed modern advertising techniques, aimed not just at stimulating consumption, but at increasing brand prestige (Valls 2003, pp. 153–57). The success of Codorniu led to the emergence of a production centre of sparkling wines in San Sadurní d'Anoia, which had become completely consolidated by the 1930s.

However, those development of higher-quality wines did not lead to these winemakers becoming dominant producers. Quality wine producers occupied a marginal position in total Spanish wine production, as consumers of quality wines constituted a very small part of the population. In the domestic market, the highest demand, in addition to the traditional consumption in rural areas, was in those urban areas that were growing most intensely during these years. Urban growth was closely linked to industrial development and domestic migration, which had increased significantly since 1910 (Silvestre 2005). Urban workers demanded cheap wine, while the demand for high-quality wines was low.

The predominance of a demand for mainly low-quality, low-priced wines with a high alcohol content both in the domestic market and abroad meant that Spain's winemaking techniques did not change significantly, with the exceptions of the aforementioned cases of newly emerging wineries that adopted modern French winemaking techniques in pursuit of high-quality wine consumers. The vast majority of winemakers opted to focus their efforts on replanting their vineyards that had been destroyed by phylloxera. Such replanting required large investments, leaving fewer resources to dedicate to improving winemaking techniques. As there was a low domestic demand for high-quality wines, most winemakers did not modify their production techniques and instead concentrated their investments on reconstructing their vineyards.

Two public policies emerged during the first third of the twentieth century to mitigate the serious problems in the sector. First, Spanish trade policy sought to improve the deteriorated position in the French market and to open new markets in other countries, although with little success (Pan-Montojo 2003; Serrano 1987). The second set of policies aimed to improve sales in the domestic market through a series of actions. They involved protecting from import competition the emerging Spanish producers of quality wines (such as the Rioja reds or the sparkling wines from Penedés), implementing regulatory policies to eliminate fraud and falsifications, reducing fiscal pressure on wine consumption, and eliminating or reducing competition with other alcoholic beverages by allowing distillation in years of abundant harvests (Pan-Montojo 1994, pp. 278–314; Pujol 1984). The desired results were not obtained in the external market, and the results varied in the domestic market. The minor success achieved in quality wines by restricting external competition through high tariffs did not assist producers of other wines.

SPAIN'S WINE INDUSTRY AFTER 1940

Between 1920 and 2014, wine production in Spain rose by more than 50 percent, reaching an annual output of about 3300 ML in 1986–1990 and 3,700 ML in 2010–2015. Part of this increase was due to the planting of some 400,000 extra hectares of vineyards through to the early 1980s, most of them in La Mancha, which expanded its vine area by 30 percent. Supply also increased due to increasing yields. After remaining relatively stagnant during the first three decades of the twentieth century, yields started to rise in the late 1950s, reaching 2,000 litres per hectare in the late 1980s and 3,500 litres in 2010–2014 (Figure 8.4). Despite this rise, throughout the twentieth century Spanish vineyard productivity remained very low compared to that of France and Italy (at 6,100 and 6,500 litres, respectively, in 1986–1990). Therefore, although Spain's vineyard area was the largest in the world with 1.5 million ha, it only ranked third in terms of productivity after France and Italy, which had less than a million hectares under vines (Fernández 2008b; Anderson and Pinilla 2017).

Between the late 1940s and 2013, the share of vines of the total agricultural crop area in Spain has declined from 8 percent to 5.3 percent. This situation was similar to that of France, where the share of vines fell from 7 percent to

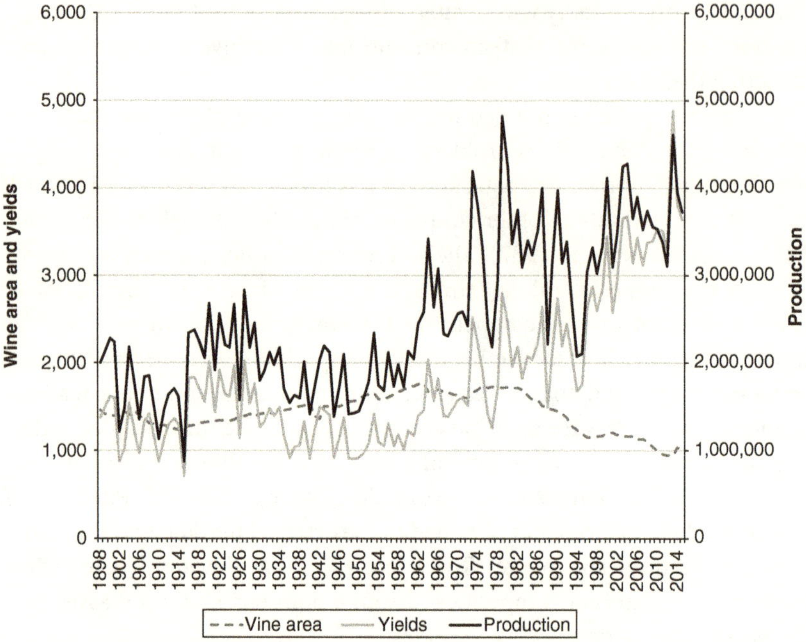

Figure 8.4 Total vine area, volume of wine production, and yields, Spain, 1898 to 2015 (‘000 ha, KL, and L/ha).
Source: Anderson and Pinilla (2017).

4 percent. However, the share of Spanish wines of total world wine production was the same in 1900 and in 2014 (12 percent and 13 percent, respectively), whereas the shares of French and Italian wines declined from 43 percent and 23 percent to 17 percent and 18 percent, respectively (Anderson and Pinilla 2017). This can be explained by their increasing yields (Figure 8.4).

The low productivity of Spain's vineyards was due to the characteristics of the soil and climate in winegrowing areas, which allowed for the planting of only 1,400 to 1,500 vines per hectare (compared to 5,000 to 6,000 in France's Languedoc region). These conditions produced deep-colored wines with a high alcohol content, suitable for blending with light wines (Hidalgo 1993). The “extreme” nature of most Spanish wine-producing regions was also due to the plantation policy of the Statute of Wine of 1932, which allowed vineyards only on dry-farm land with low fertility that was unsuitable for other uses. In addition, unlike in other countries, irrigation was prohibited in Spain until 1995 (Albisu 2004). The low yields are also explained by the high percentage of old vines and the limited changes introduced in cultivation (Hidalgo 1993, pp. 49–59; Fernandez 2008b).

The fact that Spain mostly produced ordinary wines with a high alcohol content and low value-added indicates that changes in winemaking occurred later than in France and Italy. The French advances of the "wine revolution" (new presses, steel containers, temperature control, and widespread bottling at source) began to be introduced in Spain only after the 1980s, three decades later than in France. In the case of the wine producing region of la Rioja, the modernization of the winemaking processes began a little earlier, thanks to the Jerez wineries and multinationals that invested in the region (especially Domecq, González Byass, Pepsi-Cola, Schenley, and Seagram). These companies introduced new production methods, including fermentation temperature control, new filtration systems, stainless steel containers, and aging in bottles rather than in oak barrels. With the introduction of these advances, the Rioja companies began to produce young, light, and fruity red and white wines, which had a higher demand in the new consuming countries (Fernández 2008b).

Incentives for innovations were limited because of the low demand for quality wines in the domestic market, where more than 80 percent of production was consumed. Until the 1990s, ordinary wines accounted for most of the domestic consumption and their volume increased by 40 percent between 1950 and 1970 (Fernández 2012). The domestic consumer preference for quality wines advanced very slowly in Spain, despite declining wine consumption, which fell from 69 litres per capita in 1975–1979 to 46 in 1985–1989 and 20 litres in 2011–2012. That is, the decline of per capita wine consumption, which in Italy and France was associated with a shift in preferences toward quality wines, occurred in Spain later than in those other countries, as shown in Figure 8.5. Quality wines, which represented only 1 percent of total consumption in Spain in the late 1950s, increased their share to 16 percent of wines in the late 1980s.[6]

The slow shift toward quality consumption until the 1980s can be explained by Spain's relatively low per capita income and the slow modernization of its distribution system. This, together with the higher excise taxes imposed on bottled wines, meant that most wines were sold in bulk in traditional stores (Fernández 2012).[7] More recently, the share of beer of total alcohol consumption has significantly increased to such an extent that it is currently higher than that of wine (Figure 8.6).

[6] For the pattern of wine consumption in Spain since the late 1980s, see Mtimet and Albisu (2006).

[7] In 1968, 60 percent of wine was acquired in bulk and more than 85 percent was purchased in traditional stores and warehouses. Even in urban areas, only 37 percent of consumers purchased bottled wine (Fernández 2012; Fernández and Pinilla 2014).

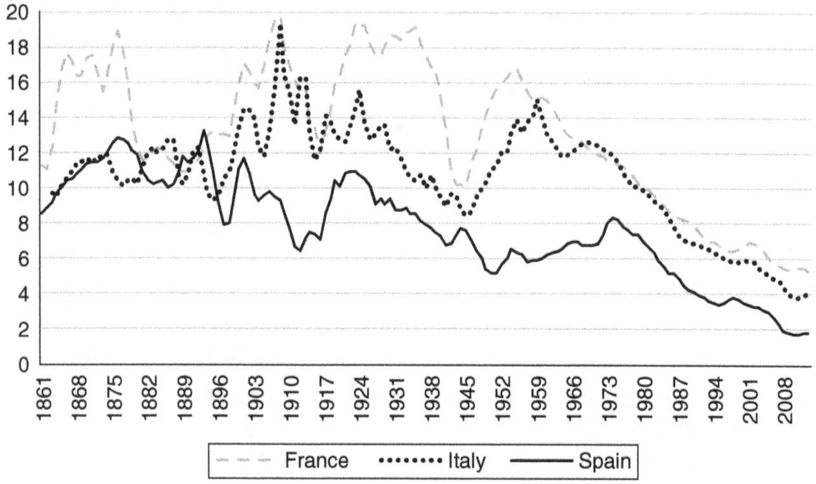

Figure 8.5 Volume of beverage wine consumption per capita, Spain, France, and Italy, 1862 to 2014 (litres of alcohol, three-year moving average around year shown).
Source: Anderson and Pinilla (2017).

Traditionally, most of the wine exported by Spain has been ordinary wine. Until 1980, Spain also held a strong position in the fortified wine market (Sherry), the sales of which accounted for more than 50 percent of the value of total exports in the period 1955–1970 (Fernández 2010). Total exports began to grow in volume in the 1950s. In the 1960s, the volume of exported wine almost doubled, reaching more than 300 ML (Figure 8.7). However, the annual growth rate of Spanish exports between 1934–1938 and the early 1970s was lower than that of France and Italy. The moderate growth of exports increased the availability of wines in the domestic market and contributed to lower wine prices. The percentage of production sold abroad (8–10 percent) remained much lower than during the 1910s and 1920s, when it accounted for around 20 percent of production (Figure 8.2).

In the United States and the United Kingdom, which were markets with growth potential, Spanish exports expanded but focused on the cheap wine segment. In most cases, Spanish wines were sold as cheap imitations of French wines. In these markets, where Spanish exporters developed a strategy of competing on price, Spanish wines had an image in the 1980s of inferior products and a low reputation among consumers, according to *Harpers* magazine (Fernández 2012).

Spanish exports grew slowly because they were mostly concentrated in western Europe (75 percent of the total), where the quantity demanded

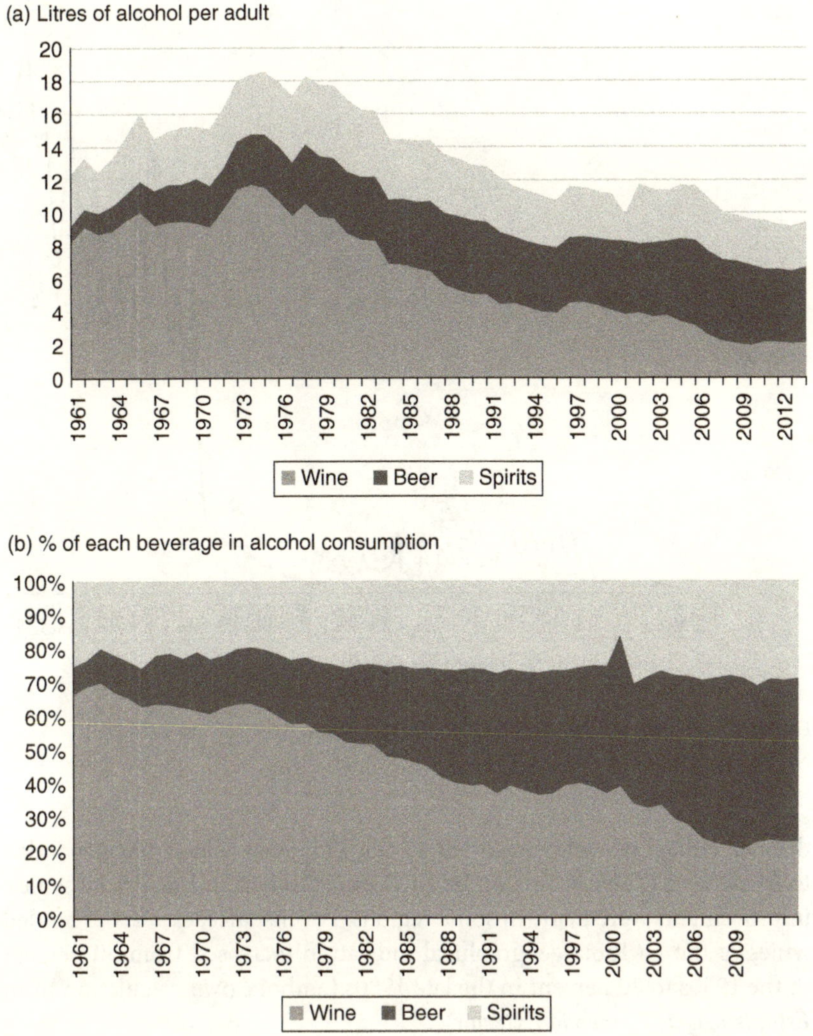

Figure 8.6 Volume of alcohol consumption per adult, by type, Spain, 1961 to 2014 (litres of alcohol and %).
Source: Anderson and Pinilla (2017).

only grew slowly.[8] The competition from Algerian wines and the abundant French and Italian production constituted important barriers to Spanish exports, especially those to the European Economic Community (EEC), which accounted for one-third of total Spanish exports. By 2009,

[8] The expansion of Spanish exports to the EEC rose at an annual rate of 0.7 percent and to the rest of western Europe at 2.3 percent, much lower than in Eastern Europe (10 percent) or the United States (5 percent). See Fernández (2012).

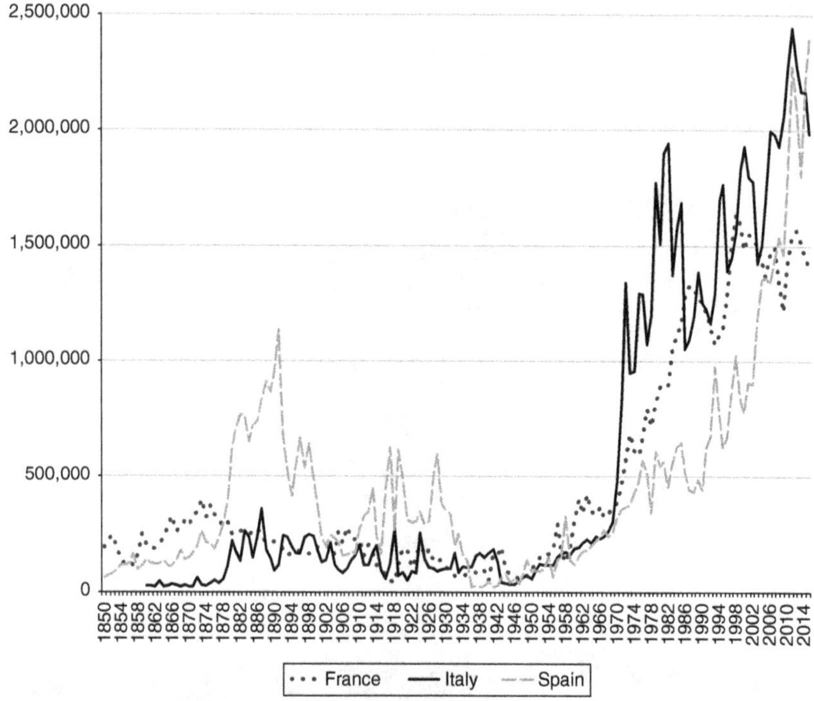

Figure 8.7 Volume of wine exports, Spain, France, and Italy, 1850 to 2015 (KL).
Source: Anderson and Pinilla (2017).

the percentage of wines exported to the European Union has expanded to 51 percent (Table 8.2). Despite this concentration in low-priced wines, improvements were made in some regions. For instance, exports of bottled wines of the La Rioja geographical indication increased from 50 percent in the 1950s to 80 percent in the late 1980s (authors' own calculation from *Estadísticas de Comercio Exterior*).

As a consequence of the decline of Algerian wine exports after 1970 (Meloni and Swinnen 2018), Spain's sales rose from 300 to almost 600 ML in the five years following 1970 (Figure 8.6). However, exports continued to grow slowly in the 1980s as a consequence of the structural surpluses in wine-producing areas of western Europe, with total Spanish exports stabilizing at around 600 ML per year until the mid-1980s.

Another factor contributing to this stagnation, following the loss of the British market by Sherry wines after 1980, was the poor adaptation of the Spanish wine industry to changes in the patterns of international consumption, and in particular an increasing preference for higher value-added

Table 8.2 *Volume of Spain's wine exports, by destination, 1955 to 2010 (%)*

	1955	1965	1970	1995	2010
EEC/EU	28	42	31	51	70
Germany	12	19	10	15	15
Belgium	11	11	4	4	3
France	0	3	6	17	19
Italy	3	1	2	1	5
United Kingdom	1	5	7	14	7
Switzerland	41	28	26	5	2
USA	0	2	3	9	3
Other	24	24	32	40	25
Total	100	100	100	100	100

Source: Fernández and Pinilla (2014) and Spanish Foreign Trade Statistics.

wines (wines with appellation and varietal wines) in the fastest-growing import markets of Germany, the United Kingdom and the United States. As a result, Spain, which had been the world's leading exporter in terms of volume until World War II, dropped to third place in the last third of the twentieth century, with a volume of foreign sales of 800 ML, half that of Italian exports and 60 percent of those from France.

The loss of the international markets had negative consequences for Spain. Together with the fall in domestic consumption, the decline in the growth rate of exports resulted in large surpluses after the 1980s, despite the decrease in the area under vines (Figure 8.4). The response to the increasing unrest in the sector caused by the falling prices and increasing oversupply was market regulation and indirect subsidies through the blockage and distilling of part of the harvest. This policy started in 1953 when, after a major overproduction crisis, a commission for purchasing surplus wines and the system of guaranteed prices were established (Fernández 2008b). This policy, as well as the rising demand for alcohol and wines in the Jerez region, led to an impressive expansion of La Mancha's low-quality wines (Fernández, 2008b). The government also incentivized the storage of surplus wines in cooperatives, which resulted in a rapid expansion of these associations, which grew in number from eighty-eight in 1921 to 407 in 1957 and 715 in 2000. The cooperatives produced 50 percent of total output by 1969 and 70 percent by 2000 (Fernández and Simpson 2017).

This scenario enables us to conclude that the institution created to improve the quality of wines, the geographical indications (Denominación de Origen), did not have the expected impact. The government established a legislative framework according to geographical indications in the 1930s as a response to the increasing unrest of producers of fine wines in la Rioja and Jerez. Demand for these regional wines was decreasing, and growers and merchants saw this institution as a way to raise the prestige of their wines abroad. The geographical indication of Sherry was created in 1933, and those of other wines with a certain degree of international recognition, such as Malaga, Montilla, Penedes, Jumilla, or Rioja, were established in the 1940s and 1950s.

Geographical indications were also created in regions producing ordinary wines such as Valencia, Utiel-Requena, Cheste, or Alicante. The large denomination of La Mancha, covering more than 200,000 ha of vines and producing wines of very different kinds, mostly for the domestic market, was also established in 1964. In regions where ordinary wines were produced, the main aim was to circumvent the measures limiting vineyard plantations, which were less restrictive in the case of appellations. This contrasts with France, where two types of appellations coexisted: controlled (subject to strict control of quality) and simple (VDQS, with more relaxed production and marketing standards) (Fernández 2008b).

As a result of the application of geographical indications to ordinary wines, denominated regions covered a high percentage of the vine area (55 percent in the late 1970s; Fernández, 2008b), contrary to the French appellations, which accounted for only 20 to 25 percent of the total area between 1965 and 1979 (Chevet et al. 2018). In the case of Sherry and Rioja, the denomination established the possibility of introducing wines from outside the region to guarantee a large quantity of wines and meet demand, favoring the interests of merchants (Fernández 2008a, b).

The changes occurring in the international wine market after the 1960s, mainly the declining demand for ordinary wines, resulted in a shift in the character of the Spanish appellations. The increase in demand intensified the frequency of fraudulent practices, which encouraged the Sherry and Rioja bodegas to impose greater controls, restrict production, and counter fraud. To prevent counterfeit wines, Jerez and Rioja geographical indications encouraged bottling at source. This obligation was implemented gradually because of the high costs of installing bottling plants and the opposition of merchants (Fernández 2008b).

However, despite the new policy and some reduction in the demarcated vineyard area, the general opinion by the mid-1980s was that the appellations of origin had barely begun to promote improvements in the varieties of vine and wine quality (Voss 1984, p. 41). In the early 1980s, and although most exported wines came from one of the geographical indications, Spain was not recognized in the international market as a producer of quality wines.[9]

RECENT DEVELOPMENTS

Important changes have occurred in the sector over the past two decades. On the one hand, it is essential to take the consequences of Spain joining the European Economic Community in 1986 into account; on the other hand, changes in the demand for and supply of wine have influenced the evolution of the sector.

Spain's accession to the European Economic Community (the current EU) had two main consequences. First, once the transition period ended in 1992, Spanish wine could freely enter the markets of the member states. Second, Spain's membership also implied that it had to adopt the Common Agricultural Policy (CAP). Therefore, the regulations of the union were applied, with the modulations that the policy authorized for each country, to the Spanish wine sector. Spain, in turn, participated in the shaping of these policies.

The impact of Spain's EU membership on its wine exports can only be described as spectacular. After 1990, Spain's exports experienced impressive growth, from about 600 ML in 1991 to 2,300 ML in 2014 (Figure 8.7). Exports of Spanish wines accounted for 15 percent of total production in 1975, 20 percent in 1985, 30 percent in 1995, 38 percent in 2005 and 65 percent in 2015 (Figure 8.2), which is a very high share in comparison with France (30 percent) and Italy (40 percent) in 2015 (Anderson and Pinilla 2017). At the same time, the wine trade volume specialization index has remained close to one from the 1950s until the present day (Anderson and Pinilla 2017). A large part of the export growth over the past few decades is a result of the increasing French demand for bulk wine (Martínez-Carrión and Medina-Albaladejo 2010), but foreign sales of bottled wines have also increased (Medina-Albaladejo and Martínez- Carrión 2013).

The experience of wine is not an isolated case, as the whole of Spain's agrifood sector has benefited from free access to the markets of EU member states (Clar, Serrano, and Pinilla 2015). However, the alcoholic drinks industry, of which wine is a key part, has only grown thanks to the boost derived from free access to the EU market, while many other agrifood industries have been more dynamic, with an increasing range of differentiated products, adapting to a highly segmented demand and taking

[9] *Wine and Spirit* (1980), no. 1267, p. 25.

advantage of economies of scale. In short, the boost in exports in most Spanish agrifood sectors has been due to a combination of the advantages of being able to access the enormous market of the EU and those of the so-called home-market effect, which has not occurred in the case of wine (Serrano et al. 2015).

This can be illustrated by breaking down Spanish wine exports into types of product. The foreign sales of all types of wine have grown substantially, but the volume of bulk wines has increased at a faster rate than that of bottled wine. In the first decade of the twenty-first century, bulk wine represented more than 50 percent of the total volume exported. If we compare wines with a geographical indication with table wines without one, during these years the former have represented only 20 percent of the total volume exported. When these comparisons are made in terms of value instead of volume, the scenario is very different: bottled wines represent around 60 percent of the total value exported, and wines with geographical indication always account for over 40 percent (Medina-Albadalejo and Martínez-Carrión 2013).

All of this illustrates that, although access to the EU market has substantially boosted exports of all types of Spanish wine, it has also enhanced the process of segmentation in the production and trade of wine. First, exports of better-quality wines (wine with geographical indications) have given rise to specialization in bottled wines, implying the introduction of modern production techniques with respect to both grapegrowing and the winemaking processes. Second, access to this market and the high demand for bulk wines in countries such as France and Italy have also given rise to growth in Spain's production and export of low-quality bulk wines.

Therefore, despite efforts to increase the quality of exported wine, the average price of Spain´s exports is much lower than that of France, and displays a downward trend over recent decades (authors' own calculation from Anderson and Pinilla, 2017). Moreover, the index of Spain's revealed comparative advantage in wine[10] has declined substantially, from 16 in 1965 to 6 in 2013, while those of France and Italy increased from 5 and 2 to 10 and 7 in the same period, respectively (Anderson and Pinilla 2017).

The low unit value of exported Spanish wine reflects the double specialization of wine production in Spain. It is important to note, however, that the two specializations share a common feature: the competitiveness of both types of Spanish wine is mainly derived from their excellent

[10] Wine's share of Spain's merchandise exports divided by wine's share of the value of global exports.

quality-price ratio. Cava (Spanish sparkling wine) is a good example of this. Its exports have shot up in recent decades and undoubtedly constitute a step forward for the Spanish wine sector. The foreign sales of this product have grown spectacularly due to the fact that cava constitutes a product with an acceptable quality given its low price, compared with French champagne (Compés, Montoro, and Simón 2014).

Wine production has also been conditioned by EU policies, namely the Common Organisation of Markets (COM) in Agricultural Products. Spain was first affected by the COM for wine passed in 1987, which subsidized the grubbing up of vineyards and the obligatory distillation to avoid surpluses. The COM of 1999 extended the prohibition on planting new vineyards and offered premiums for reconverting and restructuring vineyards, which in Spain implied a substantial increase in yields due to the introduction of irrigation in many vineyards, particularly in La Mancha, and the change to more-productive vines. The increase in production in this region, where a large share of Spain's vineyards were concentrated and which specialized in the low-quality segment, represented an increase in exports of Spanish bulk wine. Finally, the last COM, that of 2008, eliminated intervention measures such as subsidies for distillation and for the production of concentrated grape juice but maintained the premiums for restructuring, which enabled the continuation of the profound changes in varieties in order to adapt to the market, plus an increase in irrigated vineyards (Castillo, Compés, and García Alvarez-Coque 2014). All of this has led to higher yields and therefore increased production, particularly in regions such as La Mancha.[11] Furthermore, when the subsidies for distillation were discontinued, the wine that was formerly distilled was added to bulk wine exports.

Therefore, the effects of the successive COMs for wine are contradictory in Spain: while the grubbing up of vineyards to reduce production was subsidized, those that remained were supported to increase their yields. Similarly, the withdrawal of subsidies for distillation and grape juice production favored the export of bulk wines.[12]

[11] The area of irrigated vineyards in La Mancha has grown from 1.2 percent of 732,000 ha in 1986 to 43 percent of 465,000 ha today (Castillo et al. 2014, p. 281). In other words, the reduction in the cultivated area has been compensated for by the increase in yields, mostly due to the introduction of irrigation in vineyards.

[12] The case of wine is not exceptional in Spain's agricultural output. In general, the effect of adopting the CAP and the access to the single market gave rise to strong growth in production. This can be explained by the almost nonexistent national government support received by farmers before EU membership and the strong increase in this support after the adoption of the CAP (Clar et al. 2017). In the case of wine, Anderson and Jensen (2016) have highlighted that in the EU, the nominal rate of total producer assistance

From the demand perspective, the most important factor is the continued reduction in wine consumption, which has affected different types of wine in varying ways. Although domestic consumption has declined sharply since 1994 (per capita consumption fell at an annual rate of 2.3 percent between 1994 and 2009), consumption of quality wines with Spanish geographical indications increased (Albisu and Zeballos 2014). Since 2000, beer has had a higher share of the total consumption of alcoholic drinks than wine in Spain (Figure 8.6). Today, the consumption of beer is much higher than that of wine, and even the consumption of spirits is higher than that of wine. Beer consumption in Spain has grown spectacularly in recent decades and is now similar to that of traditional beer-consuming countries such as Austria or Germany. Beer consumption in Spain is twice that of France or Italy, while the consumption of wine in Spain is one-third lower than that of France or less than half Italian consumption (Anderson and Pinilla 2017). This change in the consumption of alcoholic drinks has had a profound effect on the demand for wine in the domestic market. The increased popularity of beer in Spain is related not just to the country's warm climate but to the fact that it has become a major summer tourist destination.

This fall in domestic consumption has forced producers to sell a higher percentage of their production in foreign markets. Foreign sales have increased from 20 percent of production in 1990–1992 to 60 percent after 2011 (Figure 8.2). The increase in production due to the higher yields has also incentivized this growing tendency to export, and foreign sales are now more than double those of the domestic market.

From the supply side, it is important to take into account the delay with which the technological revolution in the wine industry reached Spain, where its full development and application took place from the 1990s. Technological innovations, such as the control of fermentation temperatures, the systematic hiring of oenologists to oversee the processes, new storage tanks, or the change in varieties, have given rise to a clear improvement in quality. This has, on the one hand, enabled cheap bulk wines to have an acceptable quality for the uses for which they are required. On the other hand, in many denominations of origin, the efforts to improve quality have been remarkable: bulk wines have disappeared in domestic sales and all production is sold in bottles; both new and traditional varieties are

was 20 percent between 2007 and 2012, not almost zero as suggested by Organization of Economic Cooperation and Development (OECD) producer support calculations (OECD 2016).

used; the trends in the New World countries with respect to monovarietal wines are imitated; new market niches are being sought; and foreign sales have grown dramatically. Thus, the introduction of "controlled" geographical indications in Spain (Denominación de Origen Calificada) in the 1980s increased the average quality of wines in regions such as La Rioja. In La Rioja, production and sales almost tripled between 1983 and 2012 as a consequence of the increasing demand for this type of wine in both domestic and international markets. By 2012, most Rioja wines were exported to the United Kingdom (34 percent) and Germany (20 percent) (Barco and Navarro 2014). The demarcated vineyard area of La Mancha was also reduced after stricter quality controls were introduced in the legislation of geographical indication in the 1980s, and only 14 percent of all wines produced in La Mancha were controlled by a denomination by 2012 (Olmeda and Castillo 2014).

CONCLUSIONS

Wine has traditionally been an essential element of Spain's agricultural output. Wine exports, which were already significant in the eighteenth century, particularly in the case of Sherry, experienced a remarkable increase during the first wave of globalization. In the nineteenth and twentieth centuries, Spanish wine production represented a significant share of world production (around 10 percent).

A long-term analysis of the production and sale of wine in Spain suggests that foreign and domestic demand stimuli have given rise to a systematic specialization in the low-quality segment. Spain has played a major role in the global wine market since its formation in the mid-nineteenth century (more significant in the first wave of globalization than in the second). However, the type of wine exported, with the exception of Sherry, was of a low quality and largely used to mix with other wines. In the second half of the century, French demand generated little incentive to improve quality, as high-alcohol and deep-colored wines were sought. This demand coincided with the type of product demanded by the Spanish population

The end of the golden era for exports to France, the growing problems in other markets such as South America and the lowered consumption in more-developed countries generated problems for the Spanish winemaking sector. The industry encountered difficulties during the first third of the twentieth century, with problems of overproduction and highly irregular, falling prices. The most positive feature within these circumstances was the expansion of the production of high-quality wines, which until then were almost exclusively concentrated in Jerez, to other areas which used modern French techniques. However, the majority of the population continued to demand ordinary wines, which provided no incentive for a more far-reaching technical transformation.

Until the 1980s, wine consumption and exports in Spain hardly changed. Domestic demand was essentially based on low-quality wines sold in bulk while, until very recently, Spanish exports mainly constituted wines for coupages and ordinary wines. In fact, the international demand for these types of wine, with low value-added and a high alcohol content, increased until the 1970s, which enabled Spain to continue specializing in them without the need to introduce substantial changes in production or innovations to improve the quality of the wines. However, from the 1980s, this specialization began to create difficulties for Spanish producers when the demand for ordinary wines started to fall both in the domestic and external markets.

However, Spain's entry into the EU and import demand of some countries such as France and Italy gave rise to the spectacular growth in exports of low-quality bulk wines. The significant technical changes that have been made in wine production in Spain have improved the quality of many wines, particularly those from denominations of origin whose historical roots date back to the end of the nineteenth century. But even in the case of bottled table wines or the significant exports of sparkling wine, Spain mainly participates in a relatively low-price segment. It seems that, for some time, Spain has been stuck in a trap in which its competitiveness resides in exporting products with a good quality-price ratio, but with a low price per litre. Some bodegas have advanced in the premium wine segment and have received awards and international recognition, but their sales still represent only a very small fraction of Spain's total wine exports.

The phenomenon known as the "globalization of wine" has been spreading throughout the international market, but in order to benefit from it, substantial reforms have been necessary in the production and marketing of Spanish wines. For some, the small size of many wine-producing companies is a crucial problem. At present, the sales of 65 percent of exporters represent only 1 percent of total exports (Albisu et al. 2017). In the case of cooperatives, horizontal mergers between them or vertical mergers between production and marketing cooperatives could enable them to increase their size and improve their possibilities in foreign markets, as has been done in Italy. On the other hand, the high-quality wines produced in Spain must aspire to achieving a better position in the international market in order to access higher-price segments. This implies not only taking extreme care in ensuring the quality of the product but also reinforcing their brands, better orientating themselves to market and consumer tastes, and introducing greater product differentiation (Compés et al. 2014). The development of these strategies, which require creativity and innovation, is conditioned by the aforementioned small size of many exporting companies. If these firms do not grow in size, it will be difficult for all but the most iconic of them to succeed. Finally, exports are still too highly focused on European markets, which are very mature and in which Spanish companies have to compete with more-powerful producers. Exporters need to explore new markets and particularly capture a greater share of the Asian market, which has a high growth potential in the coming years (Anderson 2018).

REFERENCES

Albisu, L. M. (2004), 'Spain and Portugal', pp. 98–109 in *The World's Wine Markets. Globalization at Work*, edited by K. Anderson, Cheltenham: Edward Elgar.

Albisu, L. M., C. Escobar, R. del Rey and J. M. Gil (2017), 'Structural Features of the Spanish Wine Sector', unpublished mimeo.

Albisu, L. M. and M. G. Zeballos (2014), 'Consumo de vino en Espana: Tendencias y comportamiento del consumidor', pp. 99–140 in *La economía del vino en España y el mundo*, edited by J. S. Castillo and R. Compés, Almería: Cajamar Caja Rural.

Anderson, K. (2018), 'Asia and Other Emerging Regions', ch. 17 in *Wine Globalization: A New Comparative History*, edited by K. Anderson and V. Pinilla, Cambridge and New York: Cambridge University Press.

Anderson, K. and H. G. Jensen (2016), 'How Much Government Assistance Do European Wine Producers Receive?' *Journal of Wine Economics* 11(2): 289–305.

Anderson, K. and V. Pinilla (with the assistance of A. J. Holmes) (2017), *Annual Database of Global Wine Markets, 1835 to 2016*, Wine Economics Research Centre, University of Adelaide, posted at www.adelaide.edu.au/wine-econ/databases/global-wine-history

Barco, E. and M. C. Navarro (2014), 'Consumo de vino en Espana: Tendencias y comportamiento del consumidor', pp. 175–210 in *La economía del vino en España y el mundo*, edited by J. S. Castillo and R. Compés, Almería: Cajamar Caja Rural.

Castillo, J. S., Compés, R. and J. M. García Alvarez-Coque (2014), 'La regulación vitivinícola: Evolución en la UE y España y situación en el panorama internacional', pp. 271–310 in *La economía del vino en España y el mundo*, edited by J. S. Castillo and R. Compés, Almería: Cajamar Caja Rural.

Chevet, J. M., Fernández, E., Giraud-Héraud, E. and V. Pinilla (2018), 'France', ch. 3 in *Wine Globalization: A New Comparative History*, edited by K. Anderson and V. Pinilla, New York: Cambridge University Press.

Clar, E., Serrano, R. and V. Pinilla (2015), 'El comercio agroalimentario español en la segunda globalización, 1951–2011', *Historia Agraria* 65: 184–96.

Clar, E., M. Martín-Retortillo and V. Pinilla (forthcoming), 'The Spanish Path of Agrarian Change, 1950–2005: From Authoritarian to Export-oriented Productivism', *Journal of Agrarian Change* [Early view at DOI: 10.1111/joac.12220: 1-24].

Compés, R., C. Montoro and K. Simón (2014), 'Internacionalización, competitividad, diferenciación y estrategias de calidad', pp. 311–50 in *La economía del vino en España y el mundo*, edited by J. S. Castillo and R. Compés, Almería: Cajamar Caja Rural.

Dirección General de Aduanas (1849–1935), *Estadística del comercio exterior de España*, Madrid.

Fernández, E. (2008a), 'El fracaso del lobby viticultor en España frente al objetivo industrializador del estado, 1920–1936', *Historia Agraria* 45: 113–41.

(2008b), *Productores, comerciantes y el Estado: regulación y redistribución de rentas en el mercado del vino en España, 1890–1990*, PhD Thesis, Universidad Carlos III, Madrid.

(2010), 'Unsuccessful Responses to Quality Uncertainty: Brands in Spain's Sherry Industry, 1920–1990', *Business History* 52(1): 74–93.

(2012), 'Especialización en baja calidad: España y el mercado internacional del vino, 1950–1990', *Historia Agraria* 56: 41–76.

Fernández, E. and V. Pinilla (2014), 'Historia económica del vino en España 1850–2000', pp. 62–92 in *La economía del vino en España y el mundo*, edited by J. S. Castillo and R. Compés, Almería: Cajamar Caja Rural.

Fernández, E. and J. Simpson (2017), 'Product Quality or Market Regulation? Explaining the Slow Growth of Europe's Wine Cooperatives, 1880–1980', *Economic History Review* 70(1): 122–42.

Gallego, D. and V. Pinilla (1986), 'Del librecambio matizado al proteccionismo selectivo: el comercio exterior de productos agrarios y alimentos en España entre 1849–1935', *Revista de Historia Económica* 14(2): 371–420 and 14(3): 619–39.

Giralt, E. (1993), 'L'elaboriació de vins escumosos catalans abans de 1900', pp. 37–82 in *Vinyes i vins: mil anys d'historia*, edited by E. Giralt, Barcelona: Universitat de Barcelona, Vol. I.

Gómez Urdañez, J. L. (ed.) (2000), *El Rioja histórico. La Denominación de Origen y su Consejo Regulador*, Logroño: Consejo Regulador de la Denominación de Origen Calificada Rioja.

González Inchaurraga, J. (2006), *El marqués que reflotó el Rioja*, Madrid: Lid Editorial.

Grupo de Estudios de Historia Rural (1983), 'Notas sobre la producción agraria española, 1891–1931', *Revista de Historia Económica* 1(2): 185–252.

Hernández Marco, J. (2002), 'La búsqueda de vinos tipificados por las bodegas industriales: finanzas, organización y tecnología en las elaboraciones de la Compañía Vitícola del Norte de España S.A. (1882–1936)', pp. 153–86 in *Viñas, bodegas y mercados. El cambio técnico en la vitivinicultura española, 1850–1936*, edited by J. Carmona, J. Colomé, J. Pan-Montojo and J. Simpson, Zaragoza: Prensas Universitarias de Zaragoza.

Herranz, A. (2016), 'Una aproximación a la integración de los mercados españoles durante el siglo XIX', pp. 313–34 in *Estudios sobre el desarrollo económico español*, edited by D. Gallego, L. Germán, and V. Pinilla, Zaragoza: Prensas Universitarias de Zaragoza.

Hidalgo, L. (1993), *Tratado de viticultura general*, Madrid: Mundi-Prensa.

Ludington, C. C. (2013), *The Politics of Wine in Britain: A New Cultural History*, Basingstoke: Palgrave Macmillan.

Maldonado, J. (1999), *La formación del capitalismo en el marco de Jerez. De la vitivinicultura tradicional a la agroindustria vinatera moderna (siglos XVIII y XIX)*, Madrid: Huerga y Fierro.

Martínez-Carrión, J. M. and F. J. Medina-Albaladejo (2010), 'Change and Development in the Spanish Wine Sector, 1950–2009', *Journal of Wine Research* 21(1): 77–95.

Medina-Albaladejo, F. J. and J. M. Martínez-Carrión (2013), 'La competitividad de la industria vinícola española durante la globalización del vino', *Revista de Historia Industrial* 52: 139–74.

Meloni, G. and J. Swinnen (2018), 'North Africa', ch. 16 in *Wine Globalization: A New Comparative History*, edited by K. Anderson and V. Pinilla, Cambridge and New York: Cambridge University Press.

Montañés, E. (2000), *La empresa exportadora del Jerez. Historia económica de González Byass, 1833–1885*, Cádiz: Universidad de Cádiz /González Byass.

Morilla, J. (2002), 'Cambios en las preferencias de los consumidores de vino y respuestas de los productores en los dos últimos siglo', pp. 13–38 in *Viñas, bodegas y mercados. El cambio técnico en la vitivinicultura española, 1850–1936*, edited by J. Carmona, J. Colomé, J. Pan-Montojo and J. Simpson, Zaragoza: Prensas Universitarias de Zaragoza.

Mtimet, N. and Albisu, L. M. (2006). 'Spanish Wine Consumer Behavior: A Choice Experiment Approach', *Agribusiness* 22(3): 343–62.

OECD (2016), *Producer and Consumer Support Estimates* Database, www.oecd.org.

Olmeda, M. and J. S. Castillo, (2014), 'Los sistemas regionales de la vitivinicultura en España: el caso de Castilla-La Mancha', pp. 211–244 in *La economía del vino en España y el mundo*, edited by J. S. Castillo and R. Compés, Almería: Cajamar Caja Rural.

Pan-Montojo, J. (1994), *La bodega del mundo. La vid y el vino en España (1800–1936)*, Madrid: Alianza Editorial.

(2003), 'Las industrias vinícolas españolas: desarrollo y diversificación productiva entre el siglo XVIIIy 1960', pp. 313–334 in *Las industrias agroalimentarias en Italia y España durante los siglos XIX y XX*, edited by C. Barciela and A. Di Vittorio, Alicante: Publicaciones de la Universidad de Alicante.

Pinilla, V. (1995a), *Entre la inercia y el cambio. El sector agrario aragonés, 1850–1935*, Madrid: Ministerio de Agricultura, Pesca y Alimentación.

(1995b), 'Cambio agrario y comercio exterior en la España contemporánea', *Agricultura y Sociedad* 75: 153–79.

(2002), 'Cambio técnico en la vitivinicultura aragonesa, 1850–1936: una aproximación desde la teoría de la innovación inducida', pp. 89–113 in *Viñas, bodegas y mercados. El cambio técnico en la vitivinicultura española, 1850–1936*, edited by J. Carmona, J. Colomé, J. Pan-Montojo and J. Simpson, Zaragoza: Prensas Universitarias de Zaragoza.

Pinilla, V. and M. I. Ayuda (2002), 'The Political Economy of the Wine Trade: Spanish Exports and the International Market, 1890–1935', *European Review of Economic History* 6: 51–85.

(2007), 'The International Wine Market, 1850–1938: An Opportunity for Export Growth in Southern Europe?' pp. 179–199 in *The Golden Grape: Wine, Society and Globalization. Multidisciplinary Perspectives on the Wine Industry*, edited by G. Campbell and N. Gibert, London: Palgrave Macmillan.

(2008), 'Market Dynamism and International Trade: A Case Study of Mediterranean Agricultural Products, 1850–1935', *Applied Economics* 40(5): 583–95.

(2010), 'Taking Advantage of Globalization? Spain and the Building of the International Market in Mediterranean Horticultural Products, 1850–1935', *European Review of Economic History* 14(2): 239–74.

Pinilla, V. and R. Serrano (2008), 'The Agricultural and Food Trade in the First Globalization: Spanish Table Wine Exports 1871 to 1935 – A Case Study', *Journal of Wine Economics* 3(2): 132–48.

Pujol, J. (1984), 'Les crisis de malvenda del sector vitivinícola catalá el 1892 i el 1935', *Recerques* 15: 57–78.

Sánchez, J. L. (2014), 'El valor social y territorial del vino en España', pp. 31–66 in *La economía del vino en España y el mundo*, edited by J. S. Castillo and R. Compés, Almería: Cajamar Caja Rural.

Serrano, J. M. (1987), *El viraje proteccionista en la Restauación. La política comercial española, 1875–1895*, Madrid: Siglo XXI de España editores.

Serrano, R., N. García-Casarejos, S. Gil-Pareja, R. Llorca-Vivero and V. Pinilla (2015), 'The Internationalisation of the Spanish Food Industry: The Home Market Effect and European Market Integration', *Spanish Journal of Agricultural Research* 13(3): 1–13.

Silvestre, J. (2005), 'Internal Migrations in Spain, 1877–1930', *European Review of Economic History* 9(2): 233–65.

(2004), 'Selling to Reluctant Drinkers: The British Wine Market, 1860–1914', *Economic History Review* 57(1): 80–108.

(2011), *Creating Wine: The Emergence of a World Industry, 1840–1914*, Princeton, NJ: Princeton University Press.

Valls, F. (2003), 'La industria del cava. De la substitució d'importacions a la conquesta del mercat internacional', pp. 143–82 in *De l'Aiguardent al Cava. El procéss d'especialització vitivinicola a les comarques del Penedés-Garraf*, edited by J. Colomé, Barcelona: El 3 de vuit.

Voss, R. (1984), *The European Wine Industry: Production, Exports, Consumption and the EC Regime*, London: Economist Intelligence Unit.

9

United Kingdom

Charles C. Ludington

The British Isles produced some wine grapes in the high- and late-Medieval eras (up to c. 1500), and southern England has seen some new plantings in the past quarter-century, but the lands now known as the United Kingdom (UK) and Ireland have always been dependent on imports of wine.[1] Prior to 1880, the value of those imports surpassed those of any other country, and in more recent decades it has been one of the three largest importers of wine in the world. Moreover, since the late-seventeenth century Great Britain has been responsible for two significant wine-related phenomena. First, the demands and capital of wealthy English consumers helped to transform the Bordeaux region of France into a producer of luxury wines. Second, the demands of English middle-ranking consumers, along with Portuguese growers, spurred the invention of modern port wine, while wealthier British consumers helped to turn the very best port into a luxury product.

As those two phenomena indicate, wine in Britain has generally been the preserve of the elites and middle ranks. And while the boundaries of these groups are impossible to delineate precisely because of their porosity, we can say that most manual labourers, later to be called the working classes, rarely drank wine. Indeed, wine continues to be a relatively reliable class marker in Britain today – it remains a symbol of seeing oneself, or wanting to be seen, as middle class or above. So while economic and social historians love to speak of the 'growing middle classes' in every era since the late-middle ages (to the point that the working classes should have disappeared), it is helpful to measure social classes according to people's

[1] Research for this project has received funding from the European Union's Horizon 2020 research and innovation programme under the Marie Sklodowska-Curie grant agreement No 660618. I would also like to thank the School of History, University College Cork, and Kym Anderson and Vicente Pinilla for their help with the graphs.

self-perception. Drinking wine in Britain has been, and remains, one of the best ways to conduct this measurement.

This chapter argues that British wine consumption has been influenced by a complex interplay of taxation and war, price and marketing, national identity and social class, gender and political party and of course the perceived meanings of wine. Additionally, the availability, cost and perception of other beverages have greatly influenced British wine consumption. Thus, this chapter will focus on explaining historical shifts in taste for specific wines, but will also examine wine's place within a panoply of beverages, not all of which were alcoholic. Lastly, as this is a global comparative study, it will examine UK wine consumption and imports compared to those of other nations.

At the outset, it is important to say a word or two about the country being discussed. Britain is an island, often referred to as Great Britain, but it is neither a single nation nor a state. Britain consists of three nations, England, Wales and Scotland, and the state to which these nations belong, the United Kingdom, includes Northern Ireland. Great Britain became a state in 1707, when England (including Wales) was united with Scotland, while the United Kingdom, which united Great Britain and Ireland, was created as a state in 1801. Since 1921, however, the United Kingdom has included only Northern Ireland, roughly one-quarter of Ireland's land mass and population. With these distinctions in mind, this chapter will focus primarily on England, the largest constituent part of the both Britain and the United Kingdom, but it will also cite statistics and discuss trends that include all of Britain or the United Kingdom, and sometimes the constituent nations alone. However, when the term 'England' is used, it should be understood to include Wales, which has been united in government, law and religion with England since 1536.

WINE IN BRITAIN PRE-1700

Wine drinking in Britain preceded the arrival of the Romans in 43 A.D., increased after the Roman conquest, and continued in lesser amounts (because of diminished imports) after the collapse of Roman Britain in the early-fifth century. As Britain was re-Christianized by both Irish monks from the west and Continental missionaries from the south in the early medieval era, wine became affiliated with the Church through the ceremony of the Eucharist. But early English kings and their retinues, and political leaders in Wales, Scotland and Ireland, drank far more wine in secular settings. By the twelfth century in England, wine had become a widely consumed beverage and imports grew with the acquisition of Aquitaine in 1152. By the early-fourteenth century, those imports amounted to about 1 litre per capita

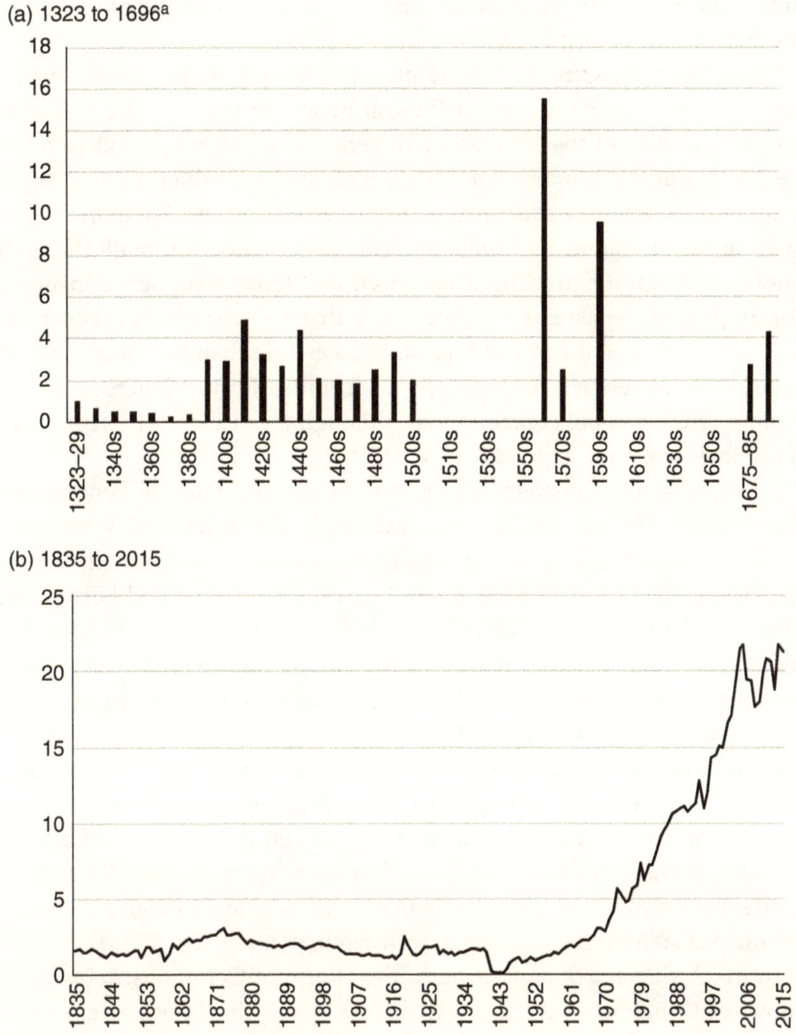

Figure 9.1 Volume of wine imports per capita, Britain, 1323 to 2015 (litres/year).[a]
[a] Decades with no bar showing mean data are unavailable, not zero imports.
Sources: James (1971) and Anderson and Pinilla (2017).

per annum, and to an average of about half that amount between 1323 and 1389 and twice that in the early-fifteenth century (Figure 9.1(a)).

In church ceremonies, wine survived the upheavals of the Reformation, even though most Protestants rejected the doctrine of transubstantiation. Having rebounded from both that calamity and the Black Death by 1550, the next ninety years once again saw England as one of the world's leading wine importers, importing anywhere from 15 to 50 megalitres (ML) per year between 1550 and 1640.

These figures suggest that wine played a more important role in foreign trade and the daily lives of English people in the period 1300–1640 than it would until the late-twentieth century. Yet in no period prior to the late-twentieth century did wine constitute more than a small share of total alcohol consumed in England. Beer was always far more popular in terms of volume and units of alcohol consumed, although the high amount of domestic brewing makes accurate statistics on beer consumption impossible to assemble. Wine was a drink of the court, aristocracy, gentry, members of the professions and successful urban merchants, but in the nineteenth century, for example, it accounted for just 2 percent of the volume of UK alcohol consumption (although a considerably larger share of tax-inclusive retail expenditure on alcohol).

In 1675, when complete import figures for the Port of London are first available, French wines (overwhelmingly claret, i.e., red wine from Bordeaux) accounted for 62 percent of all incoming wine, Spanish wines 33 percent, Rhenish (German) wines 4 percent and Italian and Portuguese wines less than 1 percent (JHC 1713, p. 363). While Charles II (1660–1685) and his courtiers were known to enjoy wine in abundance, what the king and his ministers appreciated as much as anything was the ability to tax wine and raise revenue. Indeed, wine duties were the single greatest source of royal revenue, and wine was the single most valuable import from France. Thus, wine was central to the vexing issue of the king's wealth, as well as to the question of how to keep as much specie (gold and silver coins) in England as possible, the latter issue being a prime concern of mercantilist theory. Consequently, wine was an instrument of both fiscal and foreign policy, and it remained so until the mid-nineteenth century (Ludington 2013).

By 1678, the court's opponents in the House of Commons, soon to be known as Whigs, wanted the king to declare openly that he was an enemy of France and an ally of the Netherlands. Charles was reluctant to do this as he was secretly receiving a pension from Louis XIV, who was both a friend and a cousin. Parliament responded by enacting a poll tax to raise money for war and prohibiting all trade with France. War never materialized, but Whigs in Parliament maintained the prohibition of trade with France on the grounds that French wine and clothing had a particularly pernicious effect on the English treasury and English manners (Pincus 1995, pp. 358–59). Because the king's supporters in Parliament, now known as Tories, objected to the embargo on French wine, claret became a symbol of the court's interest, and of the ruling political order, even if Whigs liked their claret too.

While the embargo of 1678–1685 against French wine was a nominal success, in reality it was a massive failure. According to London port records, fewer than four tuns of French wine were imported in 1679, fewer than two tuns in 1680 and only 65 gallons in 1683 – and these wines were taken as prizes of war. In 1681, 1682, 1684 and 1685, there were officially no French wine imports into London at all (JHC 1713, p. 363). Meanwhile, Portuguese wines, having only recently been imported into England in any substantial quantities, went from their official pre-embargo average of under 200 tuns annually to nearly 14,000 tuns in 1682 and almost 17,000 tuns in 1683. Official imports of Spanish, German and Italian wines in the period 1679–1685 also increased during the French wine embargo, but no wines gained as much ground on the London market as did Portuguese (Table 9.1).

The dramatic changes in English import figures from year to year were a result of the fact that English merchants circumvented the embargo by importing French wines (mostly claret) through whatever channels were available. The surreptitious nature of wine fraud makes it difficult to prove, especially three centuries later. However, what was once clandestine may be easily revealed by a comparison of export statistics from the city of Oporto in Portugal, with contemporaneous London import figures for Portuguese wines. According to the former, during the supposed bumper years for Portuguese wine exports to London in 1682, 1683 and 1685 – when the average annual amount was 14,272 tuns – the total number of tuns exported from Oporto to England averaged only 203 tuns per year (JHC 1713, p. 363). While some of this disparity can be explained by Portuguese wine exports from Lisbon and other Portuguese cities, Oporto was already the principal port of embarkation for Portuguese wines to England (National Archives 1692). In other words, during the embargo, most of what passed for Portuguese wine in England was not Portuguese at all. Instead, it was claret from Bordeaux.

When the Catholic Duke of York ascended to the throne in 1685 as James II, the embargo against French goods was duly removed by a new Tory Parliament, thus furthering the affiliation between Tories and claret. It is therefore no surprise that the taste for claret 'returned' with a vengeance in 1686. Once again legally imported, French wines averaged roughly 70 percent of total London wine imports during 1686–1689, and the English were once again, along with the Dutch, the greatest importers of Bordeaux wines in the world. (Francis 1972, p. 99).

While claret remained the 'common draught' or tavern wine of choice for Englishmen of all political stripes (the evidence is less clear for women), and for aristocrats and middling-sorts alike, it did not remain so for long.

Table 9.1 *Shares of wine import volumes by source, Britain, 1675 to 1940 (%, decadal)*

	France	Italy	Portugal	Spain	Germany	South Africa	Australia	Other counties	Total
1675–85	22	1	25	38	14	0	0	0	100
1686–96	28	1	22	45	5	0	0	0	100
1697–16	6	7	47	33	6	0	0	0	100
1717–26	6	1	52	39	2	0	0	0	100
1727–36	4	1	55	39	2	0	0	0	100
1737–46	2	1	75	20	2	0	0	0	100
1747–56	3	1	64	23	6	0	0	5	100
1757–66	2	0	52	16	15	0	0	15	100
1767–76	3	0	57	16	8	0	0	15	100
1777–86	3	0	63	14	1	0	0	19	100
1787–96	3	0	63	16	0	0	0	17	100
1797-1806	5	0	58	23	0	0	0	14	100
1807–16	12	0	45	20	0	1	0	22	100
1717–26	5	0	40	20	0	9	0	27	100
1827–36	4	0	32	30	0	7	0	26	100
1837–46	6	0	31	34	0	5	0	24	100
1847–52	6	0	30	36	0	3	0	24	100
1853–62	11	0	26	36	0	4	0	23	100
1863–9	19	0	18	39	0	0	0	24	100
1870–9	26	0	17	33	0	0	0	24	100
1880–9	33	0	18	25	0	0	1	24	100
1890–9	32	0	20	21	0	0	3	24	100
1900–9	27	0	21	21	0	0	5	26	100
1910–19	16	0	36	15	0	0	4	28	100
1920–9	17	0	39	17	0	1	8	19	100
1930–40	7	0	25	19	0	8	20	21	100

Source: Anderson and Pinilla (2017).

Prince William of Orange, military leader of the Netherlands and son-in-law to James II, arrived in England with a conquering army on 5 November 1688. By late December, James II was in exile in France. Parliament offered the crown to William and his English wife Mary on 13 February 1689, and not long after that implemented another embargo on French goods. As a result, no French wines were officially imported for the duration of the war, which lasted until 1697.

Port wine was the principal beneficiary of claret's decline. According to Thomas Cox, 'port-wines [came] into esteem in England since the beginning of the late war' (Cox 1701). Yet transforming national taste from claret to port was not without difficulty. As *The British Merchant* reminisced in

1713, the Portuguese wines 'being heavy and strong, did not at first please, and we hanker'd after the old claret of Bourdeaux [sic]; but in time the Quantities [of claret] wore off, and the Merchants found Ways and Means either to bring the Portuguese Wine to our Palates, or Custom brought our Palates to the Wine: So that we began to forget the French Wines, and like the others well enough' (King 1721, II: 277).

When the war ended in 1697, Parliament dropped the embargo against French goods. However, unlike at the end of the previous embargo, official French wine imports did not return to their pre-embargo levels. In fact, during the six-year period 1697–1702, the average amounts of wine imported into all of England and Wales show that Spanish wines predominated, with Portuguese wines placing second, and French wines a distant third, on par with Italian wines (Table 9.1).

Some of this Spanish and Portuguese wine was actually French, but it is significant that French wine did not return to its position atop the English market. This change in consumption habits reflected the effectiveness of the second embargo, which occurred during a time of war, and at a time when the power of the English state to regulate and tax trade was growing at a phenomenal rate (Brewer 1990). It also reflected a growing popular hatred of France as an existential threat to England. Finally, it reflected the price of French wines. Between 1692 and 1697, Parliament voted for three new tax increases on wine, thereby bringing the total import duty on French wine to roughly £51 per tun, while Portuguese wines (including madeira) paid only £21 per tun, Spanish (including canary) and Italian wines £22 and Rhenish and Hungarian wines £25 (Table 9.2). Therefore, regardless of quality, French wine was necessarily among the most expensive wines on the English market. One response to this situation by wealthy Bordeaux producers was to increase the quality and cost of their wine, so as to decrease the relative amount of tax paid on each bottle by English consumers. This was the primary impetus for producing a luxury wine instead of a traditional wine.

THE EMERGENCE OF LUXURY WINES CIRCA 1700

Luxury claret was different from the traditional claret that dominated the English market up to 1700. The latter was generically named, light in colour and body, and probably very little changed since the high middle ages. However, the claret that became popular among the English elite in the eighteenth century was carefully produced, discernibly superior in quality and expensive both because of high import tariffs in England and high

Table 9.2 *Taxes on British wine imports, by source, 1660 to 1862 (UK pounds per KL)*

	France	Germany	Spain	Portugal	South Africa
1660–65	7	9	8	8	
1666–84	7	9	8	8	
1685–91	14	20	19	18	
1692–95	22	20	19	18	
1696	47	20	19	18	
1697–1702	51	25	23	22	
1703	52	27	24	23	
1704–44	55	31	26	25	
1745–62	63	35	30	29	
1763–77	71	39	34	33	
1778	79	43	38	37	
1779	84	41	40	39	
1780–81	92	49	44	43	
1782–85	96	51	47	46	44
1786	65	51	37	37	37
1787–94	47	51	32	32	37
1795	78	64	51	51	57
1796–97	108	92	71	71	77
1798	111	96	73	73	79
1799–1801	107	92	71	71	77
1802	112	97	74	74	80
1803	131	109	87	87	87
1804	142	117	95	95	95
1805–24	144	119	96	96	96
1825–30	78	50	50	50	25
1831–59	58	58	58	58	29
1860	32	32	32	32	32
1861	16	21	21	21	21
1862	11	26	26	26	26

Source: Summarized from Ludington (2013, table A1).

production costs in France (Enjalbert 1953, p. 457). By necessity, the consumers of this new type of claret were wealthy. And because consumers ultimately give a commodity its various meanings, this new luxury claret was neither Tory nor Whig. Instead, it was 'polite', and in early-eighteenth-century England, politeness – the ability to afford, discuss and appreciate the finest material objects – was a form of political power (Klein 1994; Eagleton 1990).

Even another war with France that Whigs wanted, and another embargo against French goods that began in 1704, could not keep luxury clarets out of England. Export figures from Bordeaux during the war and embargo indicate that there was no direct trade to England (Huetz de Lemps 1975, pp. 148–50). However, English import figures for French wine tell a different story: throughout the war and embargo, they registered an annual average of over 800 tuns of French wine (JHC, 1713, p. 365). In other words, every year, despite the war and embargo, England continued to receive all of the luxury claret that a few wealthy Bordeaux vineyard owners could produce.

Proof that the English were purchasing luxury clarets during the War of the Spanish Succession, and that these wines were intended for no other customers, comes from advertisements in the *London Gazette*, the official voice of the English government. The advertisements were in fact notices of seized wines to be sold at government-sponsored auctions. Early in the war, seized claret was auctioned at £8, £40 and £60 per tun, indicating clear qualitative differences between the wines, although all the wine was simply called 'claret' (*London Gazette*, A). However, in 1704 the most expensive claret began to be referred to as 'New French Claret' (*London Gazette*, B). It is not stated in the notices what made these clarets 'new', although the careful use of the word by the auctioneer to describe the wine for sale was not merely an indication of age, as almost all claret – indeed, almost all wine – was new in that it was less than a year old when it was sold. Instead, the word 'new' was meant to describe a new type of claret (Pijassou 1980, I: 372–9).

In short, the language of luxury claret was beginning to catch up to its distinctive qualities. By May 1705, these new clarets were being referred to in the *London Gazette* by their vineyard name: 'choice new red Obrian [Haut Brion] and Pontack prize wines … to be had at Lloyd's' were once again being referred to by vineyard name (*London Gazette*, C). One month later, a wine called Margaux appeared in two different auctions, although typically the Court of Exchequer scribe found the French difficult and spelled it 'Margoose' (*London Gazette*, D). Within the year, claret named Latour and Lafite also appeared in England as captured wines. So determined were wealthy English consumers to drink this new type of claret that producers and purchasers were arranging for these luxury clarets to be 'captured' at sea.

SCOTLAND'S PREFERENCE FOR TRADITIONAL CLARET IN THE EIGHTEENTH CENTURY

While popular taste in England took an abrupt turn from French wine to Portuguese during the late Stuart and early Hanoverian era – and luxury claret became the fashionable wine for the elite – the same was not true in

Scotland. In North Britain, as Scotland was called in the wake of the Union of 1707, traditionally made claret was the predominant wine in aristocratic homes and rustic taverns, from the Highlands to the Lowlands, throughout much of the eighteenth century. This point is significant because one of the principal features of the Act of Union of 1707 was the equalization of duties at the English level for almost all goods, including wine. What allowed the Scots to continue drinking claret were high levels of fraud and smuggling, as well as complicit high-level officials (Ludington 2013, ch. 6).

Evidence abounds of wine fraud and smuggling in eighteenth-century Scotland. For example, Quarterly Customs Accounts for Leith (the port of Edinburgh) state that in the first quarter of 1745, there were nineteen wine cargoes landed at Leith, of which seventeen were Portuguese, one French and one Rhenish (Port of Leith 1745). At face value, then, this quarter was dominated by Portuguese wines. And yet, of the Portuguese wine cargoes, six arrived directly from Portugal in hogsheads (Bordeaux casks), even though Portuguese producers shipped their wines in pipes, which were twice as large as hogsheads. Another six shipments of alleged Portuguese wine arrived via Norway, but also in hogsheads. Merchants claiming to carry Portuguese or Spanish wine via Norway, usually Bergen or Christiansand, were essentially practicing a form of state-sanctioned deception to import French wine (Smout 1963, p. 158). Fake Norwegian documentation of the cargo made the declaration look genuine, thus absolving Scottish Customs officers from any involvement should the wine declaration be proven false. This practice also made the fraud more difficult to prosecute. Reassessing Leith imports for the first quarter of 1745, thirteen of nineteen shipments were French wine from Bordeaux.

THE SWITCH TO IBERIAN FORTIFIED WINES BY THE MIDDLE CLASSES, 1703–1750

If early- and mid-eighteenth-century Scots preferred traditional claret and the English elite preferred luxury claret, the English middle ranks relished port above all other wines. In 1718, members of the Ironmongers Company of London (a powerful livery company) celebrated the Lord Mayor's Day with 150 bottles of red port, ninety-six bottles of white port, thirty-six bottles of Canary and eighteen bottles of Rhenish wine. In other words, more than four-fifths of the wine they consumed that day was port, both red and white. Four years later, the Ironmongers' Lord Mayor's Day festivities show similar wine choices, while at their Quarterday Dinner in 1725, red port constituted fully 84 percent of the wine consumed.

Members of the Barber-Surgeons Company – who by the eighteenth century were mostly licensed medical doctors – exhibited a similar predilection for red port, on which they spent nearly three-quarters of their wine budget between the years 1720 and 1739. (Simon 1926, pp. 74–75). Because cost was not directly proportional to volume, and red port was usually the least expensive wine on the English market, it constituted more than three-quarters of the Barber-Surgeons' total wine consumption. Evidence from other middle-ranking professionals shows a similar predilection for port.

It makes economic sense that port would be the wine of the middle ranks. The Methuen Treaty of 1703 guaranteed that the tariff on Portuguese wines was at least one-third less than the tariff on French wines However, in 1745, 1763, 1778, 1779, 1780 and 1782 (all of them war years), the British government increased the duties on imported wine, so that by 1783 the duty on Portuguese wines stood at almost £46 per tun, or 84 percent over its 1714 level. The duty on other wines was even greater. French wines paid £96 per tun, Rhenish and Hungarian wines paid £51 and Spanish and Italian wines paid nearly £47.

While British fiscal policy helped to determine the cost of wines, the related domain of foreign policy helped to determine availability and reputation. Portuguese, Spanish and Italian wines should have been equally popular in Britain, as the duty on them was almost the same. However, Great Britain and Portugal remained steadfast allies during the early-eighteenth century, while Great Britain and Spain had a strained relationship. One result was that from the end of the War of the Spanish Succession in 1714 to the 1740s, Portuguese wines rose from 46 percent to over 70 percent of total wine imports into England (Table 9.1), and most of this wine was red port. Meanwhile, Italian wines, mostly from Tuscany, had high transport costs and were thought not to travel well in any case.

Port was popular with the English middle ranks because it was relatively cheap, but it was also popular because of its strength. After all, spirits of various types were becoming more fashionable in early-eighteenth-century England. However, port's strength was only partly a response to consumer demands. Another factor was nature itself, along with limited scientific understanding of the process of fermentation. Early versions of port wine were naturally strong in alcohol because the Douro Valley is relatively hot in the summer (compared to Bordeaux, for example) and as a result the ripened grapes contain high amounts of natural grape sugar. Added to that, the Portuguese method of slowing down (i.e., cooling) fermentation was to add a few gallons of brandy (distilled wine) into the fermentation vat. So, while unfortified port was already relatively strong, probably around

14 to 17 percent alcohol, port that had been fortified with brandy during the fermentation process and then again in preparation for shipping was stronger still. This strength appealed to middle-ranking English consumers, who believed they were getting better value for money with stronger, fuller-bodied wines, and who now found claret to be thin and weak – a drink for boys, not men, said Samuel Johnson (Ludington 2009).

Interestingly, port was originally intended by English merchants to be a substitute for traditional claret. But with different grapes, soil, climate and winemaking techniques in Portugal, port evolved into an altogether different type of wine. Nevertheless, by the middle decades of the eighteenth century, port was revered by middle-ranking Englishmen. For example, in 1766 the prominent London printer and bookseller, James Dodsley, published *The Cellar-Book: or, the Butler's Assistant, in Keeping a Regular Account of His Liquors*. That *Cellar-Book* was intended to be both prescriptive and descriptive of an aspiring gentleman's taste for wine (aristocrats would not have needed such guidance). In the introduction to the book, Dodsley included a sample page to instruct the butler or 'common servant' on how to use the book, and a list of what the 'gentleman's cellar' should contain (in bottles): 400 port, forty-eight claret, eighty-five white wine [unspecified], four sack, twenty-nine madeira, nineteen champagne, forty-eight burgundy, 235 ale, sixty cider, forty brandy, eighteen rum and thirty-four arrack (Dodsley 1766). In other words, a middle-ranking Englishman could expect to drink more than twice as much port as all other wines combined.

But again, we should not overstress the popularity of wine among the general English population in the eighteenth century. One estimate puts per capita beer consumption in England in 1700 at 5.5 pints per capita, per week, and this amount may have risen unevenly, along with real wages, in the first half of that century. Meanwhile, at the peak of the gin craze in the 1740s, Londoners over the age of fourteen averaged as much as 2.7 pints of gin per week. But just as most wine was consumed by the elites and middle ranks, most beer and gin was consumed by laborers. Moreover, when the government did intervene to curb gin production in 1751, some of the decline in gin consumption was made up for by increasing imports of rum and arrack, both used to make punch (Jennings 2016, p. 16). Lastly, first coffee and then (by 1720) tea became staple drinks of English society, quickly working their way from the elite to the working classes. By 1780, tea with sugar was a working-class necessity, and during the 1790s annual per capita consumption of tea and sugar in the United Kingdom stood at 2.1 pounds and 13 pounds, respectively (Burnett 1999, pp. 54–55). In terms of liquid volume, no alcohol came close.

THE ROLE OF PREFERENTIAL IMPORT TARIFFS AND WAR IN THE LATTER 1700S

In the second half of the eighteenth century, port began to be embraced by English elites as well. This was because the quality of the port improved due to Portuguese government regulations of production that began in 1756, and because port symbolized something that eighteenth-century English male aristocrats needed for their political legitimacy: unpretentious and virile masculinity. Moreover, the increased demand for port from the English elite coincided with – and helped to propel – a technological change that made port a markedly finer wine. That technological change was the development of the cylindrical bottle. Clearly, English consumers enjoyed port that was sweet, fiery and tannic, but they seemed to enjoy it even more when the wine had time to mellow. Stored on its side in cylindrical bottles, port could be aged for decades, and what could be a more obvious statement of wealth than the ability to let wine sit in one's cellar for years. Thus aged port, like luxury claret, became a symbol of the elite's good taste, but with an added dose of John Bull masculinity that luxury claret did not possess.

Another war in North America that began in 1785 meant more tax increases on wine, so by the end of 1782 import tariffs stood at £96 per tun on French wine, £51 for Rhenish wine, £46 for Spanish wine, £45 for Portuguese wine (Parliament of Great Britain 1897, pp. 131–57). As had been the case since the creation of Great Britain in 1707, French wines were taxed the most and Portuguese wines the least. Yet the result of these duty increases was not necessarily what the government hoped. Instead, as Adam Smith remarked in his *Inquiry into the Nature and Causes of the Wealth of Nations*, published two years prior to the tariff hike of 1778: 'The high duties which have been imposed upon the importation of many different sorts of foreign goods … have in many cases served only to encourage smuggling; and, in all cases have reduced the revenue of the customs beyond what moderate duties would have afforded' (Smith 1776, pp. 476–77).

Clearly, wine fraud and other forms of smuggling were problems for a government in desperate need of revenue, and this is what spurred the young Prime Minister William Pitt into action (Ashworth 2003; Mathias and O'Brian 1967). Pitt began by pushing through Parliament laws that enhanced the powers of revenue officers and made smuggling more difficult (Rose 1793, p. 24). The combined effect of these laws was an immediate increase in tax revenue. With momentum behind him, Pitt then succeeded in transferring part of the duty on wine and tobacco to the Excise Office.

This law simplified tax assessment and permitted Excise officers to interrogate wine merchants even after their wine had cleared Customs and been placed safely in their vaults.

While these changes in wine duties took place at home, Pitt's government was actively negotiating a commercial treaty with France. The French called for most-favoured-nation status on French wines; however, while reducing the duty on French wines would be a simple legislative change, giving them parity with the wines of Portugal would have violated the Methuen Treaty of 1703. Therefore, the British delegation under William Eden proposed a compromise, agreeing to import French wines at a rate no higher than those *now* paid by Portuguese wines, and then lowering the duty on Portuguese wine to one-third less than the revised duty on French wine. In fact, Pitt wanted to reduce the duty on all wines in the belief that it would undermine fraud and smuggling in the wine trade and thus increase revenue as much as £280,000 per year (Hansard 1815, p. 1433).

The Eden Treaty was concluded on 26 September 1786, whereupon Pitt consolidated all the remaining Customs duties on wine – thereby having one Customs duty and one Excise duty – and reduced the total duties to levels that complied with both the Eden Treaty with France and the Methuen Treaty with Portugal (Table 9.2). The rates resulting from this act, known as the Consolidation Act, cut the duty on French wine by approximately half of what it had been in 1785 (to £47 per tun) and on Portuguese and Spanish wines by roughly 30 percent (to £31 per tun), while the duty on Rhenish wines remained at £51 per tun.

The substantially reduced tariff rates of the Consolidation Act had an immediate impact on legal wine importation into Great Britain, especially Scotland. In the period 1787–1792, total legal wine imports in Scotland averaged 2,172 tuns per year, a jump of 128 percent from their 1764–1786 average. French wine imports increased most of all – 241 percent – while the amount of Spanish wine more than doubled and Portuguese wines nearly did so (Table 9.1). Nevertheless, during the entire period 1787–1792, French wine imports into Scotland averaged only 13 percent of the total annual amount, while Spanish wines accounted for 23 percent and Portuguese wines a full 60 percent (Customs 14, 1764–92).

In comparison, during the five-year period beginning in 1787, England imported an average of 25,400 tuns of wine per year, which was 56 percent greater than the post-1764 average. However, French wine remained a mere 4.3 percent of total, while Spanish wine comprised 17 percent and Portuguese wine 73 percent (Schumpeter 1960). In short, an overwhelming preference for Portuguese wines now bound all the British together.

In February 1793, revolutionary France declared war on Britain, and the British government reciprocated. All Eden Treaty agreements were annulled and trade between the warring nations declined precipitously. The prewar predominance of port throughout Britain was further enhanced by seven Customs and Excise duty increases between 1795 and 1805 that impacted French wines most of all (Tables 9.1 and 9.2). By 1806, the combined duty rate on French wines was roughly £144 pounds per tun, compared to £47 when the war began. At the other end of the scale, the duty on Portuguese and Spanish white wines was now at £96 per tun, and Spanish red wines at £107 per tun. Not surprisingly, Iberian wines continued to dominate the British market, and wine drinking was an increasingly elite affair. But for the diminishing number of people who could afford to drink wine, they may have done so in record-setting amounts.

THE RISE AND DEMISE OF DRUNKENNESS

The forty-year period of almost continuous war from 1775 until 1815 witnessed a dramatic increase, if not even a historical apex, in British elite and middling male drunkenness. Some of that drunkenness was due to the fact that fortified port was the most fashionable wine of the day. The annual legal wine imports into Great Britain more than doubled from the decade before the Eden Treaty of 1786 to the decade after, and throughout the Revolutionary and Napoleonic Wars, British imports as a whole remained far above their pre–Eden Treaty levels.

In some war years, as much as one-quarter of the wine imported into Great Britain was reexported, but even subtracting that amount from overall imports gives a net increase in wine retained for domestic consumption compared to the period before 1786. Consumption of spirits also increased during the 1780s and remained high throughout the wars despite the fact that it was heavily taxed (Wilson 1940, table 2). Conversely, per capita beer consumption declined during this forty-year period, although this had a greater impact on the labouring classes than upon the middling sorts and elite, for whom beer was rarely a recreational drink (Burnett 1999, pp. 115–20).

Even if statistical evidence of heavy drinking is ambiguous, anecdotal evidence is overwhelming. Stupefaction from alcohol was positively fashionable. 'Drunk as a Lord' was a socially charged phrase that emerged in late-seventeenth century England, and by the late-eighteenth-century the hard-drinking British aristocracy and gentry surpassed even their own formidable standards (Porter 1982, p. 34; Hendrickson 1997, p. 219). 'The Prince [of Wales], Mr. Pitt, Dundas, the Lord Chancellor Eldon, and many others, who gave the tone to society', wrote the aged Captain Gronow from the perspective of the 1860s, 'would, if they now appeared at an evening party, "as was their custom of an afternoon," be pronounced fit for nothing but bed. A three-bottle man [as in per diem consumption of wine] was not an unusual guest at a fashionable table; and the night was invariably spent in drinking bad port-wine to an enormous extent' (Gronow 1862, II: 75). Gronow was speaking about the first two decades of the eighteenth century.

But in the aftermath of war, a new generation of middle-ranking critics – now self-described 'middle class' – emerged to challenge the ruling order and the warrior masculinity that helped them to maintain their position at the top of the social pyramid. These new reformers championed a form of masculinity that valued hard work, moral rectitude, domesticity and relatively sober self-control. Tellingly, in an article written for the *Examiner* in December 1817, the American-born poet and essayist Leigh Hunt declared the 'Death of Merry England' (Wilson 2007, p. 332). This obituary was premature, but Hunt was on to something. Less sensitive observers might not have noticed a change in their country just yet, and in retrospect it is clear that Hunt spoke in the middle of a transitional period. Certainly 'Merry England' and its sottish Scottish equivalent did not die overnight, but British society, especially among the middle classes, was becoming more decorous, more serious and more sober. Wine imports retained for domestic consumption in the United Kingdom dropped from their wartime average of nearly 29,000 tuns per annum to just under 23,000 tuns for the period 1816–1825; spirit consumption in the United Kingdom declined in the decade after Waterloo; and per capita beer consumption in England, already waning, fell below 140 megalitres (ML) per year (Parliament of Great Britain 1897, pp. 150–51; Wilson 1940, table 2; Gourvish and Wilson 1994, table 2).

Some of the decline in alcohol consumption can be attributed to the postwar economic depression, because these downward trends reversed course by 1825, or 1830 in the case of beer; but British culture was also changing. The taverns and clubs that had once welcomed in so many British men as the evening began and spewed them out drunk onto the streets in the wee hours were either gone or changing. No longer bastions of intoxicated revelry, clubs in the 1820s and 1830s were transformed into learned societies where men might come to dine quietly, hear a lecture or discuss ways to 'improve' their towns, their cities or themselves (Tosh 1999, p. 125). 'Happily', wrote the prominent port shipper James Warre in 1823, 'inebriety is not the vice of the age' (Warre 1823, p. 36). One year later, the Scottish physician and wine historian Alexander Henderson wrote: 'A generation has scarcely passed away since it was no uncommon thing to see men of high intellectual acquirements, and of irreproachable character in other respects, protracting the nightly feast, till not only their cares, but their sense, were completely drowned in wine ... It was once the boast of many that they could indulge in these deep potations with impunity' (Henderson 1824, pp. 346–47).

Of course, taxation on wine also influenced consumption. At the time of the Treaty of Vienna in 1815, duties on wine stood at the unprecedentedly high levels of more than £144 per tun for French wine; £118 for Rhenish wine; and £96 per tun for Portuguese, Spanish and other European wines. Put another way, the duty on French wine was almost 3 shillings per quart bottle, while the duty on Portuguese and Spanish wines was just under 2 shillings. Wartime taxes on both domestic and imported alcohol remained in place after the war ended. And while all alcohol was relatively expensive in the midst of an economic depression, the tax on wine was especially high per unit of alcohol (Table 9.2).

Consequently, there was no increase in the wine trade despite the peace; instead, trade continued its wartime decline. Not surprisingly, wine merchants were distraught. James Warre published a lengthy pamphlet in 1823, arguing for an immediate reduction in the wine duties because the 'excess of duty is the principal cause of the diminished consumption' of wines. To prove his point, Warre focused on the wine trade statistics for the years 1787–1794, during which time Pitt's reduction of the wine duties had caused the volume of British wine imports to double. Likewise, the multiple wartime duty increases caused wine imports to revert to their pre-1787 level. 'The goose was killed,' said Warre, 'the golden egg was lost.' He gave no credence to the 'opinion entertained by some people, that wine is gone out of fashion, that our habits are changed, that soda water and ginger beer are now our only drinks.' Instead, he insisted, 'it is the price, not inclination, that compels abstinence' (Warre 1823, pp. 3, 24, 33–35). Price mattered, but so too did changes in taste, because in 1825 import duties on all wines were essentially cut in half, and, except for a brief spike in port imports in that same year, the main increase in imports came in Spanish wine, most of which was sherry.

THE RISE OF SHERRY

In the three decades from 1817 to 1846, Spanish wines retained for consumption in the United Kingdom increased from 22 percent to 33 percent, to 38 percent of the overall total. Meanwhile, Portuguese wines (excluding madeira) fell from 51 percent, to 44 percent, to 40 percent in the same three decades (Table 9.1; Parliament of Great Britain 1897, pp. 150–51). By 1840, port and sherry were consumed in roughly equal amounts, and by 1850 sherry was firmly in the lead.

Sherry's rise on the British market was dictated by middle-class consumers. As Warre wrote in 1823: 'It is not, however, those who indulge in an occasional debauch, nor your three-bottle men, that affect the general consumption of wine, for they are but few in number; it is the daily, though perhaps small consumption of the middling classes of society' (Warre 1823, p. 36). And as Henderson wrote in 1824, the middling classes of society were 'the drinkers of port and sherry' (Henderson 1824, p. 316). These were the preferred – and often only – wines in middle-class homes.

Historically, British consumers were quite familiar with sherry. It had been among the most fashionable of all wines in the Elizabethan and early-Stuart eras, when it was known as 'sack'. But to understand why sherry returned to popularity in the second quarter of the nineteenth century, one must look to the reputation of port, which was a decidedly masculine wine associated with the heavy drinking and warrior ethos of the revolutionary era. Sherry, however, was thought to be a feminine wine. Generally pale or brownish-yellow in color – although it can be dark brown – sherry was fortified but not French, feminine but not effeminizing. In the postwar era, it was a magical elixir. British elite and middle-class men turned to sherry to express their respectability, which, like politeness, required taming aggressive masculinity with a dose of feminine refinement.

But this did not mean that British men suddenly rejected port; instead, they saw sherry as a complement to port. As William Thackeray wrote in his 1855 novel, *The Newcomes: Memoirs of a Most Respectable Family*, a proper husband and father was 'respected for his kindness and famous for his port wine' (Thackeray 1855, p. 137). But equally true is the fact that the respectable men in Thackeray's novels drink port *and* sherry (and a small amount of claret as well). In other words, sherry gave respectable men the refinement they needed to prevent the descent into barbarism that so obviously plagued their Georgian-era forebears. Meanwhile, delicate (but surprisingly strong) sherry was the perfect expression of British middle-class womanhood. So much were port and sherry linked together as a pair that specially labeled decanters were sold in tandem, suggesting that these two wines, like man and woman, husband and wife, Victoria and Albert, were made for each other by a beneficent God (Ludington 2013, ch. 11).

CUTTING IMPORT DUTIES FROM 1825

The fiscal environment in which sherry gained popularity was one of decreasing taxes in the name of freer trade. In 1825, using the new 'Imperial' measurement system, Chancellor of the Exchequer Frederick Robinson simplified and reduced the duties on all wines. First, the excise duty on wine was removed and all wine duty collection was returned to the Customs Office. Second, the overall duty on Portuguese and Spanish wines was cut from 9s. 1d. to 4s. 9d. per imperial gallon, on Rhenish from 11s. 3d. to 4s. 9d. per imperial gallon, and on French wines from 13s. 9d. to 7s. 3d. per imperial gallon. Put in the terms that we have been using thus far, the duties on Portuguese and Spanish wines were cut from roughly £96 to £50 per tun, on Rhenish wines from £118 to £50 per tun and on French wines from £144 to £78 per tun. Portuguese wines still paid roughly 36 percent less duty than French wines, thereby maintaining the terms of the Methuen Treaty (Table 9.2). The duties on Cape wines from South Africa, which were considered British wines because of their colonial origin, were reduced from a mere 3 shillings to 2s. 5d. per imperial gallon (or £25 per tun). As appealingly low as that tax was, Cape wines were thought by most middle-class consumers to be fit only for the working classes, who drank very little wine of any sort. Consequently, Cape wines remained a small percentage of overall imports (Table 9.1).

In 1831, wine import taxes were cut yet again (Figure 9.2), in part to punish the Portuguese for maintaining the state-controlled Douro Company that determined what port wines could be shipped to the United Kingdom. As chancellor of the exchequer, and a Whig, John Spencer (Viscount Althorp and later third Earl Spencer) responded in 1831 with a slight increase in the duty on Portuguese, Spanish and Rhenish wines and a decrease in the duty on French wines, thereby equalizing the duty on *all* European wines at 5s. 6d. per imperial gallon, or just under £58 per tun. South African wines paid only half as much. After 127 years, the British unilaterally abrogated the Methuen Commercial Treaty in a single stroke and, unlike in 1713 when abrogation was considered within the broader framework of the Treaty of Utrecht, this time there were no major objections in Britain. In fact, the overwhelming response to the end of the Methuen Treaty in Britain was 'good riddance'.

The Whigs, having fully reversed their views on economic protectionism since the early-eighteenth century, had once again carried the day regarding a grand decision about British wine consumption. Yet the debate was not over, because another result of the end of the Methuen Treaty was that the first modern wine-writer in English, a journalist named Cyrus Redding,

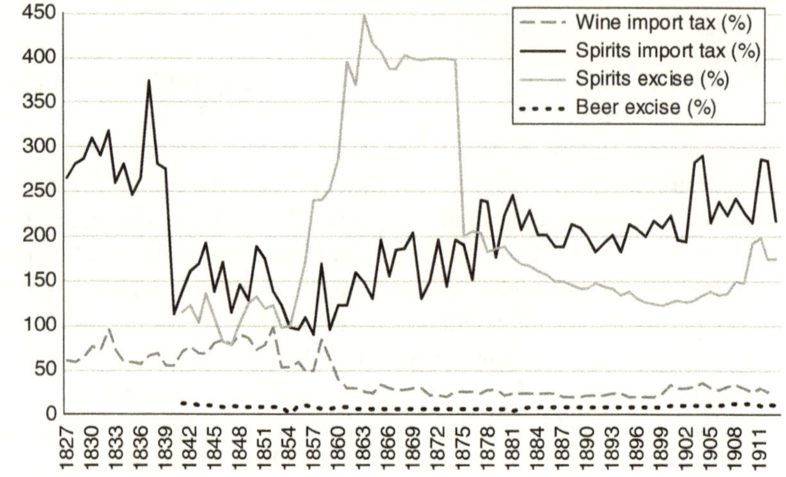

Figure 9.2 British wine and spirits import taxes and beer and spirits excise taxes, 1827 to 1913 (%, *ad valorem* equivalents).
Source: Tena (2006).

began openly to attack British preference for fortified wine (Redding 1833). This of course was a direct attack on the British preference for port and sherry, but it eventually resonated with the very middle classes it had intended to reform. Most importantly, William Gladstone, chancellor of the exchequer in Palmerston's second ministry (1859–1865), embraced the commercial, political, moral and civilizational dimensions of free trade in wine and constructed his policy accordingly (Briggs 1986, p. 34). First, he made a wine duty reduction central to the terms of the 1860 commercial treaty with France. Second, he set about selling the idea of a wine duty reduction to Parliament. The result was that Parliament passed the Act 23 Victoria, c. 22, on 29 February 1860, which immediately lowered the duty on all wines to 3 shillings per imperial gallon. Furthermore, on 1 January 1861, the new scale according to strength took effect, just as Gladstone had proposed.

Thus, beginning in 1861, all wine imported in bottles, regardless of strength, was taxed at 2 shillings per imperial gallon. However, the vast majority of wine imported into Britain still arrived in casks, and of this wine, anything over 15 percent alcohol by volume was also charged 2 shillings per imperial gallon, while wines below 15 percent but above 9 percent alcohol were taxed at 1s. 6d., and all wines below 9 percent alcohol at 1 shilling. At the other end of the spectrum, any wine above 26 percent alcohol (which included some ports and sherries) was to be taxed as brandy, at 8s. 2d. per imperial gallon.

But by 1862, the entire scale of duties on imported wines and brandies was deemed impractical because it required Customs officers to spend so much time gauging alcohol content. Consequently, in 1862, the wine duties were 'simplified' at 1 shilling per imperial gallon on all wines below 15 percent alcohol, and 2s. 6d. on all wines between 15 percent and 22 percent alcohol, and on all wines in bottle. Wines between 22 percent and 26 percent paid 2s. 9d. per imperial gallon, and anything above 26 percent was charged as brandy. In other words, nothing was really simplified. Instead, unfortified wines received a preferential rate.

Finally, along with lowering the duties in order to democratize the taste for wine, Gladstone sought to democratize the distribution of wines. Beginning in 1860, the Refreshment Houses Act made all restaurants and 'eating houses' eligible to purchase an annually renewable license to sell wine on premises. Moreover, in 1861, the Single Bottle Act enabled shopkeepers to purchase an annually renewable license to sell wine for consumption off premises, which was referred to as an 'off-license'. 'Gladstone's Claret', as inexpensive red Bordeaux wine was soon called, was now available in grocery stores and corner shops with 'off licenses', as well as the newly founded chain store Victoria Wines, that catered to a distinctly middle- and lower-middle-class clientele (Briggs 1986). In all of these ways, Gladstone hoped to link wine drinking with dining among all classes of society in Britain, and France was seen as the model.

One year into the changed fiscal regime, Gladstone was able to celebrate a smaller loss of revenue than anticipated due to a much larger increase in wine imports than expected: imports for the 1860–1861 fiscal year were up 36 percent from the previous year, and by far the greatest percentage increase came from French wines. (Gladstone 1863, p. 203). Between calendar year 1860 and 1861, French wine retained for home consumption in the United Kingdom jumped by 98 percent (Parliament of Great Britain 1897, p. 152). It mattered little to Gladstone that the import figures for Spanish wines increased most in absolute terms and that sherry and port still dominated the British market (Table 9.1). Clearly, he thought, a change was under way. Britons would soon be drinking light, French wines.

FREER TRADE AND AN EFFECTIVE REVERSAL OF PREFERENCES FROM 1860

In fact, a free(er) market in wine did not lead to a dramatic change in British taste. Moreover, the free market of economic liberal ideals was not (and never would be) free. Instead, the legislation of 1860–1862 reversed eighteenth-century fiscal policy by favouring light wines – which meant mostly French wines – over the stronger wines of Portugal and Spain. But there was some change. Sherry peaked on the UK market in 1873 at 43 ML, or 43 percent of total imports, and in the same year French wines constituted 29 percent of imports, while port stood at 19 percent. Sherry's decline after 1873 seems to have been brought about by the same cycle that hurt port in the mid-eighteenth century. Huge demand from the UK market led to shoddy and sometimes completely specious production at the lower end of the market, which hurt the wine's overall reputation (Simpson 2004). To combat the decline of sherry, Spanish diplomats successfully lobbied in 1888 to raise the cutoff level for light wines in the United Kingdom from 15 percent to 18 percent alcohol by volume, which allowed lighter sherries to pay the lower duty. But even with this change, the essence of UK fiscal policy was a return to the fiscal policies of the English and Scottish governments of the mid-seventeenth century: French wine held a privileged position, while wines from southern Europe paid more.

French wine imports into the United Kingdom surpassed those of Portugal in 1866, and those of Spain in 1876 (Parliament of Great Britain 1897, p. 152), but sherry and port together continued to account for more than half of all UK wine imports. Furthermore, French wine imports (mostly claret followed by champagne) began a steep decline after 1900. By 1913, on the eve of World War I, port was once again the most popular wine, accounting for 29 percent of UK imports, while sherry and French wines accounted for 25 percent each (Wilson 1940, pp. 361–63; Jennings 2016, p. 18). As a contributor to *Ridley's Wine and Spirit Trade Circular* drily noted in 1908, the change in duty 'may have brought the rich man's luxury within the poor man's reach, but not any nearer to his mouth, for neither then nor since has light claret become the beverage of those who earn by manual labour' (Wilson 1940, p. 39).

Wine's relative popularity among types of alcohol, even at a time when the United Kingdom was the world's leading importer, can be seen by looking at statistics from the mid-1870s, when all forms of alcohol reached their nineteenth-century apex (Figure 9.3). Per capita beer consumption peaked at 155 litres per head in 1875 (185 litres in England and Wales), spirit consumption peaked the same year at 5.9 litres, while wine peaked one year later and stood at a mere 2.5 litres per head. Both an economic recession and ever greater emphasis on working-class respectability caused all forms of alcohol to decline in the 1880s, but economic recovery from the mid-1890s did not witness a full return to previous levels of consumption. Per capita beer consumption in the United Kingdom fell to 121 litres in 1914, while spirit consumption fell to 3.1 litres. Wine consumption fell to 1.0 litres in 1914 (Burnett 1999, p. 182), but as always that figure alone does

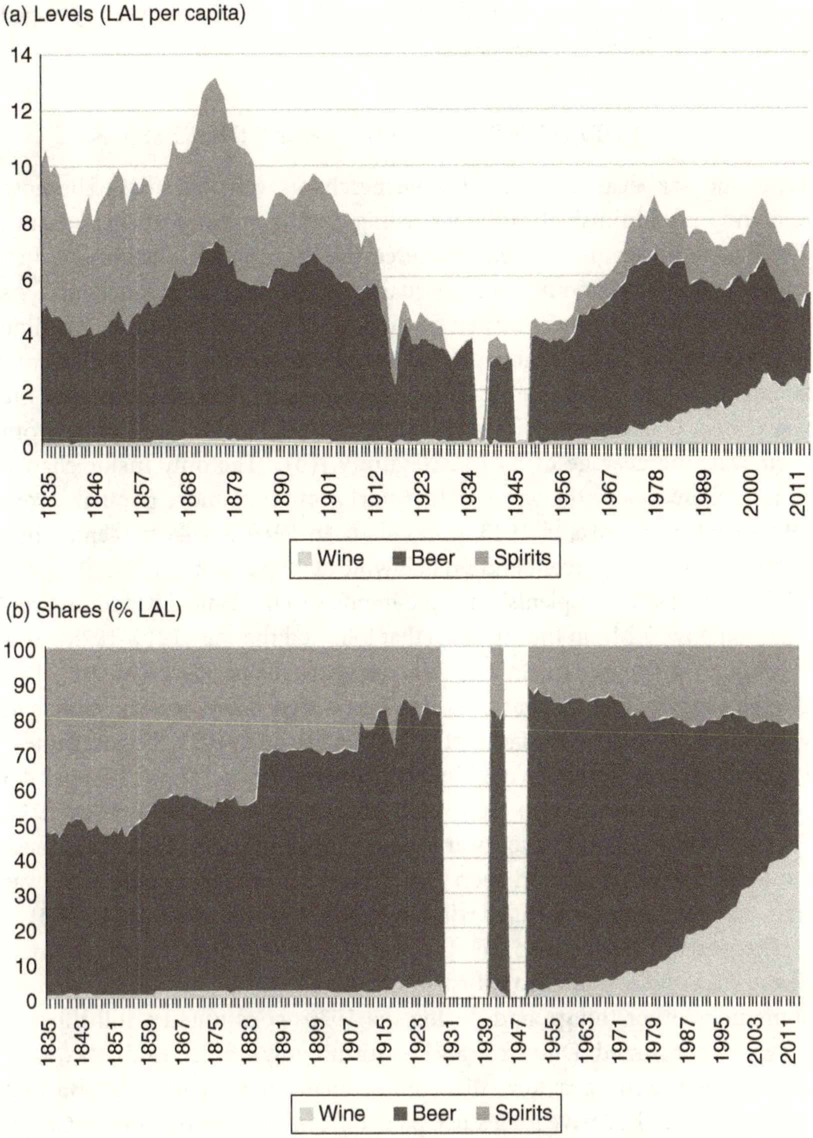

Figure 9.3 Levels and shares of wine, beer and spirits in the volume of alcohol consumption, Britain, 1835 to 2014 (LAL per capita and % LAL).
Source: Anderson and Pinilla (2017).

not reveal the class differences in wine consumption. The Colwyn Report to the British Parliament in 1926 showed emphatically that wine consumption rose with income. For instance, in 1913, per capita consumption of wine in families making between £50 and £100 per year was four (quart) bottles per year, while those with an annual income of £250 to £500 per year averaged thirty bottles (Burnett 1999, p. 153).

TWO WORLD WARS AND THE GREAT DEPRESSION

When the war began in July 1914, wine merchants were well stocked because demand had diminished in the preceding decade but imports held steady. The British government commandeered the brewing and distilling industries for the war economy, and the quality of beer and whisky declined. As a result, many consumers turned to wine, some for the first time. Wartime imports of wine were irregular, so the overall effect of the war was that consumers drank the available stock. Consequently, in 1919, the year after the war ended, UK wine imports skyrocketed to over 115 ML, well above from their wartime average of 54 ML (Figure 9.1(b)). The only major change in taste from before the war was that port grew even more popular. From 29 percent of imports in 1913, port's share in 1919 was 49 percent, while sherry stood at 21 percent and French wine at 20 percent.

Once stocks were replenished, wine imports to the United Kingdom averaged roughly 77 ML in the ten years that followed the war (1919–1928). This was significantly more than the 57 ML average of the period 1904–1913. This change suggests that the war itself had introduced many new consumers to wine, but it also reflects the fact that in 1919 and again in 1927, the government lowered taxes on 'Empire Wines'. In 1925, Australian wine imports topped 4.5 ML for the first time, and in 1933 South African wines did the same. By 1935, 'Empire Wines' accounted for over a quarter of all imports (Table 9.1). These wines were mostly 'port' and 'sherry', so while the provenance of the wines was new, the preference for fortified wines remained (Wilson 1940, pp. 45, 363).

The postwar period also saw the rise of 'British wines' to prominence. These wines were made from British or imported fruit, sometimes grapes, sometimes other things, and during the 1930s constituted a full third of all wines consumed. Duty-free and requiring only a small excise tax, they constituted the cheapest form of alcohol available to the consumer (Burnett 1999, p. 152). They have long since passed from fashion, but *Stone's Ginger Wine* remains a prominent example.

While the arrival of 'Empire Wines' sustained British import figures during the economic depression of the 1930s, wine was still disproportionately a drink of the wealthy, and many of those who drank wine did so in modest amounts and usually at family celebrations such as Christmas, birthdays or marriages. In 1935, the roughly 47 million people of the United Kingdom (now without the twenty-six counties of the Irish Free State) consumed

68 ML of wine, most of which was port and sherry. Compare that with the fact that this same population in 1935 consumed more than 50 ML of proof spirits. And further consider that this same population drank more than 3,860 ML of beer. That comes out to 82 litres of beer per person, or 144 pints per year for every man, woman and child (Wilson 1940, p. 335). When expressed in litres of alcohol, the share of wine in total alcohol consumption in the United Kingdom was very small, and remained so until the 1970s (Figure 9.3). Tea with milk and sugar, while not a substitute for alcohol except as a form of calories, was the most popular drink of all. Throughout the 1930s, per capita consumption was nearly 5 litres per year, or an average of five cups per day (Burnett 1999, p. 183).

On the eve of World War II, the United Kingdom was still an important wine market by value if not volume. The wealthiest Britons drank the very best claret, champagne and burgundy, as well as top-quality port and sherry, but less-affluent wine drinkers stuck to port and sherry alone, even if these wines did not always come from Portugal and Spain. As one would expect, World War II further diminished an already declining level of wine consumption in Britain. Total wine imports to the United Kingdom fell from 95 ML in 1940 to a mere 20 ML in 1945, or less than 0.5 litres per head. This downward trend was slowly reversed after the war ended, with wine consumption climbing to 0.9 litres per head by 1953 and doubling again to 1.8 litres by 1960 (Burnett 1999, p. 154). So change was already under way in the 1950s – but it was in the 1960s that the truly dramatic shift in British wine consumption began.

THE LATEST HALF-CENTURY: FROM BEER CONSUMING TO WINE CONSUMING

Since 1960, Britons have learned to drink once again. Between the late 1950s to the late 1970s, spirits consumption trebled, with Scottish whisky leading the way, and beer consumption nearly doubled. Beer consumption has since declined, while spirit consumption has held steady. But the really big story has been wine: its consumption rose more than fivefold over that two-decade period, and it has risen fivefold again since 1980 (Figure 9.3(a)).

Wine's phenomenal growth in the United Kingdom has also meant a huge change in patterns of alcohol consumption, as is clear from the right-hand side of Figure 9.3(b): beer's share of alcohol consumption has fallen from above 80 percent in the 1960s to less than 40 percent in the most recent decade, while wine's share has risen tenfold, from 4 percent to more than 40 percent. Finally, after 140 years, Gladstone's vision of a wine-drinking European nation has come to pass.

Table 9.3 *Shares of wine, beer and spirits in total alcohol consumption volume, United Kingdom and the world, 1835 to 2014 (% LAL)*

	1835–79	1880–1929	1950s	1960s	1970s	1980s	1990s	2000s	2010–14
Wine									
UK	2	3	3	4	7	14	22	35	41
World	na	na	na	32	28	23	17	16	15
Beer									
UK	51	70	83	81	75	65	57	44	37
World	na	na	na	30	31	34	39	41	43
Spirits									
UK	47	27	14	15	18	21	21	21	22
World	na	na	na	38	41	43	44	43	42

Source: Anderson and Pinilla (2017).

The UK's swing towards wine over the past half-century has been more dramatic than anywhere else in the world. Certainly there have been other countries in both northern Europe and East Asia that have become more wine-focused in their consumption (see Chapters 10 and 17 of this volume), but the UK's transformation is unprecedented. Moreover, it has happened at a time when wine's share of (recorded) alcohol consumption globally has more than halved, dropping from 32 percent in the 1960s to 15 percent in 2010–2014. The share of beer in UK alcohol consumption is now below the world average, having averaged 70 percent in the half-century prior to the Great Depression, and that of spirits is now only half the rest of the world's share, having been almost 50 percent in the middle half of the nineteenth century (Table 9.3).

Nor is it just European wines that Britons are now drinking. Most obviously, Australian wines rose on the British market, especially in the 1980s and 1990s, followed by other New World producers. The decline of European wines in the United Kingdom was not as steep in terms of value as it was in terms of volume shares, especially when sparkling wine is included. But having always enjoyed a market share of more than 90 percent up to the early 1990s, the drop since then to around 70 percent by value and 50 percent by volume (Table 9.4) was a severe blow.

In a typical pattern among new wine drinkers, the more they drank, the more discerning they became. As such, Australia's emphasis on inexpensive, mass-produced, and colourfully marketed wines, the very things that made them unintimidating to new consumers, eventually made them a turn-off to those looking for more challenging flavours or more social distinction,

Table 9.4 *Shares of wine import volumes and values by source, United Kingdom, 1990 to 2016 (%)*

	Europe	Australia and New Zealand	United States	South America	South Africa	World
Volume (%)						
1990–95	90	5	2	1	2	100
1996–2001	68	16	6	5	5	100
2002–07	55	21	9	7	8	100
2007–11	54	21	8	9	8	100
2012–16	53	22	8	10	7	100
1990–5	89	7	2	1	1	100
1996–2001	72	15	5	5	3	100
2002–07	65	19	6	5	5	100
2008–11	69	16	5	6	4	100
2012–16	71	13	6	7	3	100

Source: Anderson, Nelgen and Pinilla (2017).

or both. While their share is no longer growing, Australian wines are still prominent in the UK market, and they have served as a harbinger for more cosmopolitan British taste, which include large amounts of wine from New Zealand, the United States, South Africa, Argentina and Chile. European wines remain popular in the United Kingdom, but, among them, port and sherry are now a tiny minority (less than 5 percent of the total).

Such a dramatic shift in British beverage tastes begs the question of why. How could a downward trend beginning in the late 1870s, or in the longer term since the mid-1600s, have been so thoroughly reversed? Surprisingly, perhaps the least influential factor was taxation. It is true that Stafford Cripps lowered wine taxes in 1949, but this had little immediate effect on consumption. As we have seen, the real upward trend in alcohol consumption began after 1960. Wine duties were lowered in 1973 when the United Kingdom joined the European Community (EC), and again in 1984 after an EC directive that wine duties should be harmonized. These reductions may have helped increase wine consumption, but they are not the only factor given that the upward trend was already well under way. Moreover, the equalization of duties across Europe in 1984 did not prevent the UK government from increasing the tax by a few pence per bottle every year. By 1997, that tax was £1.80 per bottle, and in 2016 it was £2.08 per bottle, making British tax on wine among the highest in what is now the European Union. But so long as the British economy has been growing and real wages increasing, British consumers have endured the tiny tax increases on wine every year.

Thus, fiscal policy cannot explain the rise in UK wine consumption since 1960, but rising standards of living and the concomitant changes in cultural practices can (Jennings 2016, p. 25). Beginning in the 1960s, Britons began to eat out more at restaurants. Restaurants themselves signalled a special occasion, which in turn called for wine. Likewise, having invented the concept of holiday travel in the nineteenth century, postausterity Britons embraced the habit once again, and sunny southern Europe was the favourite destination. In France, Spain, Portugal, Italy and Greece, Britons learned to enjoy wine with their meals, and they brought the habit home with them. They realized too that the wine did not have to be expensive, aged and served in crystal decanters. Related to holidays spent on the European continent, Mediterranean-inspired food became all the rage in middle-class Britain under the tutelage of such authors as Elizabeth David and later Nigella Lawson and Jamie Oliver, all of whom emphasized the pleasure of wine with meals.

Retailers have responded to greater demand for wine by giving consumers a greater variety of choices and opportunities to purchase wine. The large supermarket Sainsbury's purchased an 'off-license' in 1962, and soon the other major retail grocers followed. When alcohol price maintenance rules were abolished by the government in 1966, price wars among supermarkets quickly followed, and consumers responded with enthusiasm. Likewise, wine bars emerged as an alternative to pubs and offered customers places to go specifically to drink wine. Wine bars were especially fashionable among women. This was in part because wine, and especially white wine, was considered feminine, while beer was still thought of as masculine. (Spirits could be either, depending on whether and how they were mixed.) More women in the workforce meant more financially independent women who drank more wine than beer or spirits.

As the demographics of British workplaces were changing to include more women, they were also changing from mining and manufacturing jobs to desk-based, service jobs. These jobs, almost regardless of salary, were considered 'middle class' because they did not entail hard, physical labour. Those who now had middle-class jobs naturally began to see themselves as middle class and thus to engage in middle-class habits such as drinking wine with meals. Indeed, wine's middle-class affiliation can be seen by the fact that the massive unemployment in Britain in the late 1970s and 1980s had little impact on the upward trend in wine consumption, because unemployment was overwhelmingly among unionized labourers.

As the standard of living in the United Kingdom increased for those who were not involved in mining and manufacturing, so too did the amenities of their middle-class homes. So alongside more eating out in restaurants, there was also more entertaining at home, and dinner parties often included wine. Related to this fact, as the English, Scottish and Northern Irish governments all cracked down on drinking and driving, drinking at home simply made more sense. And home drinking, precisely because it usually revolved around a meal, was often wine drinking. Moreover, pubs themselves have changed with the times in the last thirty years, increasing their food and wine options in order to broaden their appeal to women, to families, and to the middle classes who once saw pubs as dens of the working classes.

For all of these reasons, the United Kingdom has become not only a wine-drinking state but, since the 1990s it has routinely vied with the United States or Germany for first ranking among the world's leading importers of wines (Figure 9.4).

WHAT OF THE FUTURE?

Economic conditions and the price of wine will continue to matter for British consumers. For most people in Britain, drinking alcohol has long been associated with the good life. Rising real wages and improving living standards have almost always meant increased expenditure on alcohol, and especially so since 1960.

Because of its long-standing class and gender affiliations, wine has been a major beneficiary of Britain's post-1960 economic growth, with its transition to a service-based economy, the employment of women and London's return to global financial primacy. Wine has long been affiliated with wealth and middle-class or elite social and economic status in Britain, so it is unlikely that the United Kingdom will stop being an important market for expensive and highly coveted wines. However, as with so much else, the UK's pending exit from the European Union (Brexit) makes the long-term stability or growth in the British market for wines somewhat uncertain.

The falling pound in the wake of the Brexit vote already means that the costs of imported wines have increased, as have the cost of Britons' continental vacations, which may well become limited to those for whom wine needs no introduction. If real wages decline and the standard of living falls, Britons will drink less wine, for history shows that wine is not so culturally ingrained in the United Kingdom that it cannot be substituted with other beverages by the majority of consumers. If Britain is no longer in 'Europe', its citizens may begin to think of themselves as outside of wine-drinking European culture. In particular, if nativism prevails, beer and British-made spirits may be the drinks that a majority of Britons turn to in order

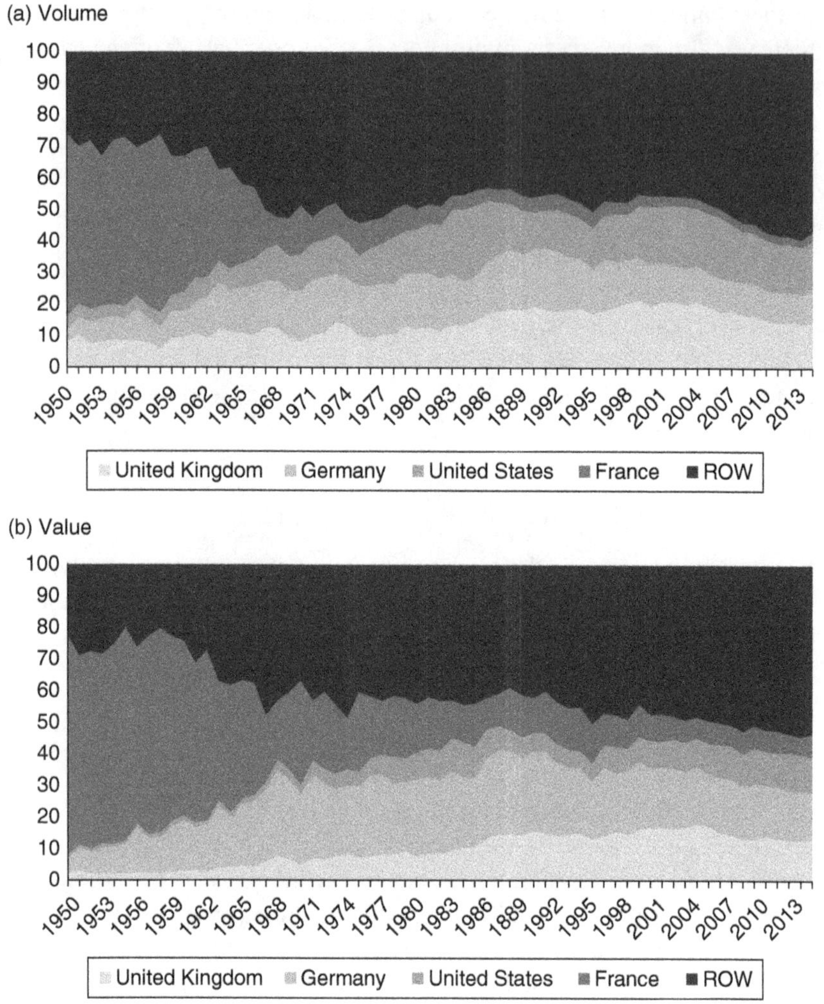

Figure 9.4 Shares of key importers in the volume and value of global wine imports, 1950 to 2014 (%).
Source: Anderson and Pinilla (2017).

to express their new identity – and tax changes may reinforce that shift in drinking patterns. New preferential trade agreements could also add to the decline in Europe's share of UK wine imports.

Meanwhile, Britain's fledgling domestic wine production, while growing along with global warming, is still in its infancy. It will probably benefit from Brexit (less competition at home, stronger competitiveness abroad because of the pound's devaluation), but it is unlikely to reduce very greatly the UK's dependence on imported wines, with the possible exception of sparkling wines, which have slowly increased in volume and quality. In fact, some champagne firms have been investing in English wineries in the past fifteen years, but whether they can help transform the United Kingdom into a major wine producer remains to be seen.

REFERENCES

Anderson, K. and V. Pinilla (with the assistance of A. J. Holmes) (2017), *Annual Database of Global Wine Markets, 1835 to 2016*, freely available in Excel at the University of Adelaide's Wine Economics Research Centre, www.adelaide.edu.au/wine-econ/databases

Anderson, K., S. Nelgen and V. Pinilla (2017), *Global Wine Markets, 1860 to 2016: A Statistical Compendium*, Adelaide: University of Adelaide Press.

Ashworth, W. J. (2003), *Customs and Excise: Trade, Production and Consumption in England, 1640–1845*, Oxford: Oxford University Press.

Brewer, J. (1990), *The Sinews of Power: War, Money and the English State, 1688–1783*, Cambridge, MA: Harvard University Press.

Briggs, A. (1986), *Wine for Sale: Victoria Wines and the Liquor Trade, 1860–1984*, Chicago: University of Chicago Press.

Burnett, J. (1999), *Liquid Pleasures: A Social History of Drink in Modern Britain*, London: Routledge.

Cox, T. (c. 1701), *An Account of the Kingdom of Portugal*, British Library, Add. Ms. 23736, f. 18.

Croft, J. (1787), *A Treatise on the Wines of Portugal, and What Can Be Gathered on the Subject and Nature of the Wines, Etc., Since the Establishment of the English Factory at Oporto*, York: J. Todd.

Customs 14 (1764–92), *Scottish Customs Records*, National Archives (Kew).

Dodsley, J. (1766), *The Cellar-Book: or, the Butler's Assistant, in Keeping a Regular Account of His Liquors*, London: J. Dodsley.

Eagleton, T. (1990), *The Ideology of the Aesthetic*, Cambridge, MA: Basil Blackwell.

Enjalbert, H (1953), 'Comment Naissent les Grands Crus: Bordeaux, Porto, Cognac', *Annales: Economies, Societés, Civilisations* 8(3): 315–28; and 8(3): 457–74.

Francis, A. D. (1972), *Wine Trade*, London: A. and C. Black.

Gladstone, W. E. (1863), *The Financial Statements of 1853, 1860–1863*, London: John Murray.

Gourvish, T. R. and R. G. Wilson (1994), *The British Brewing Industry, 1830–1980*, Cambridge and New York: Cambridge University Press.

Gronow, R. H. (1862), *The Reminiscences and Recollections of Captain Gronow: Being Anecdotes of the Camp, Court, Clubs, and Society, 1810–1860*, 2 volumes, London: Smith, Elder.

Hansard, T. C. (1815), *The Parliamentary History of England, from the Earliest Period to the Year 1803*, volume XXV, London: Longmans and Co.

Henderson, A. (1824), *The History of Ancient and Modern Wines*, London: Baldwin, Cradock and Joy.

Hendrickson, R. (ed.) (1997), *Encyclopedia of Word and Phrase Origins*, New York: Facts on File.

Huetz de Lemps, C. (1975), *Géographie du commerce de Bordeaux à la fin du règne de Louis XIV*, Paris: Ecole des Hautes Étudees en Sciences Sociales.

James, M. K. (1971), *Studies in the Medieval Wine Trade*, Oxford: Clarendon Press.

Jennings, P. (2016), *A History of Drink and the English, 1500–2000*, London: Routledge.

Johnson, H. (1989), *Vintage: The Story of Wine*, New York: Mitchell Beasley.

JHC (1713), *Journal of the House of Commons*, XVII, *An Account Shewing the Quantity of Wines Imported in to London and the Outports of England, in Sixteen Years and One Quarter, from Michaelmas 1696, to Christmas 1712* (report submitted by Charles Davenant, 21 May 1713).

King, C. (ed.) (1721), *The British Merchant, or, Commerce Preserv'd* (1713), 3 volumes, London: John Darby. Facsimile edition 1968, New York:

Klein, L. (1994), *Shaftesbury and the Culture of Politeness: Moral Discourse and Cultural Politics in Early-Eighteenth Century England*, Cambridge and New York: Cambridge University Press.

London Gazette, (A) no. 3963, 4 Nov. 1703; no. 4040, 31 July 1704; (B) no. 4055, 24 Sept. 1704; (C) no. 4123, 12 May 1705; (D) no. 4128, 4 June 1705; no. 4132, 18 June 1705.

Ludington, C. C. (2009), '"Claret Is the Liquor for Boys: Port for Men": How Port Became the Englishman's Wine, c. 1750–1800', *Journal of British Studies* 48(2): 364–90, April.

(2013), *The Politics of Wine in Britain: A New Cultural History*, Basingstoke: Palgrave Macmillan.

Mathias, P. and P. O'Brian (1967), 'Taxation in Britain and France, 1715–1810', *Journal of European Economic History* 5: 601–40.

National Archives (1692), 'Memorial of the Portugal Merchants of London, received by the Commissioners for Trade, 9 Aug. 1692', National Archives (Kew), C.O. 388/2, ff. 66–7.

Nye, J. V. C. (2010), 'Anglo-French Trade, 1689–1899: Agricultural Trade Policies, Alcohol Taxes, and War', ch. 5 in *The Political Economy of Agricultural Price Distortions*, edited by K. Anderson, Cambridge and New York: Cambridge University Press.

Parliament of Great Britain (1897), *Customs Tariffs of the United Kingdom, from 1800 to 1897, with Some Notes upon the History of More Important Branches of Receipt from 1660*, Parliamentary Report C.8706, London.

Pijassou, R. (1980), *Un Grand Vignoble de Qualité: le Médoc*, 2 volumes, Paris: Librairie Jules Tallandier.

Pincus, S. (1995), 'From Butterboxes to Wooden Shoes: The Shift in English Popular Sentiment from Anti-Dutch to Anti-French in the 1670s', *Historical Journal*, 38(2): 333–61, June.

Port of Leith (1745), *Collector's Quarterly Accounts*, 1 January 1745–31 March 1742, National Archives of Scotland, E504/22/1.

Porter, R. (1982), *English Society in the Eighteenth Century*, London: Allen Lane.

Redding, C. (1833), *A History and Description of Modern Wines*, London: Whitaker, Treacher, and Arnot.

Rose, G. (1793), *A Brief Examination into the Increase of the Revenue, Commerce and Navigation of Great Britain, Since the Conclusion of the Peace in 1783*, 4th edition, London: John Stockdale.

Schumpeter, E. B. (1960), *English Overseas Trade Statistics, 1697–1808*, Oxford: Clarendon Press.

Simon, A. L. (1926), *Bottlescrew Days: Wine Drinking in England During the Eighteenth Century*, London: Duckworth.

Simpson, J. (2004), 'Selling to Reluctant Drinkers: The British Wine Market, 1860–1914', *Economic History Review* 57(1): 80–108.

Smith, A. (1776), *The Wealth of Nations*, edited by A. Skinner, Harmondsworth: Penguin, 1999 edition.

Smout, T. C. (1963), *Scottish Trade on the Eve of Union, 1660–1707*, Edinburgh: Oliver and Boyd.

Tena, A. (2006), 'Assessing the Protectionist Intensity of Tariffs in Nineteenth-Century European Trade Policy', pp. 99–120 in *Classical Trade Protectionism, 1815–1914*, edited by J.-P. Dormois and P. Lains, London and New York: Routledge (cited in Nye 2010).

Thackeray, W. M. (1855), *The Newcomes: Memoirs of a Most Respectable Family*, New York: Harper and Sons.

Thomas, K. (2009), *The Ends of Life: Roads to Fulfillment in Early Modern England*, Oxford: Oxford University Press.

Tosh, J. (1999), *A Man's Place: Masculinity and the Middle-Class Home in Victorian England*, New Haven: Yale University Press.

Warre, J. (1823), *The Past, Present, and Probably the Future State of the Wine Trade: Proving that an Increase in Duty Caused a Decrease in Revenue; and a Decrease of Duty, an Increase of Revenue. Founded on Parliamentary and Other Authentic Documents. Most Respectfully Submitted to the Right Honourable the President of the Board of Trade*, London: J. Hatchard and Son and J. M. Richardson.

Wilson, B. (2007), *The Making of Victorian Values, Decency and Dissent in Britain, 1789-1837*, London and New York: Penguin.

Wilson, G. B. (1940), *Alcohol and the Nation*, London: Nicholson and Watson.

10

Other Europe, CIS and the Levant

Kym Anderson and Vicente Pinilla

Even though France and its western European neighbours have been the world's dominant wine players for centuries, the product did not originate there. Rather, it was at the same latitude as the south of France but roughly 3,000 kilometres to its east. Georgia, now an independent country wedged between the Black and Caspian seas, is reputably the cradle of wine, although its neighbouring countries make a similar claim (Unwin 1991; McGovern 2003, 2009). That part of the world has experienced perhaps 8,000 vintages, and Georgia alone is blessed with more than 500 indigenous *Vitis vinifera* winegrape varieties (Ketskhoveli, Ramishvili and Tabidze 2012). From that region, the cultivation of *vinífera* vines and the making of grape wine gradually spread west to the Levant,[1] Egypt and Greece by 2,500 BC. The Etruscans began vine cultivation in central Italy using native varieties in the 8th century BC, which is also when the Greek colonists began to take cuttings to southern Italy and Sicily. Viticulture was introduced to southern France by the Romans around 600 BC and was spread north in the second and first centuries BC. It took only until the fourth century AD for winegrapes to be well established in all those areas of Europe suited to its cultivation, and in North Africa.

While the drinking and hence production of wine in the Middle East went into decline following Mohammed's decree against alcohol in the seventh century AD. (Johnson 1989, pp. 98–101), elsewhere in eastern Mediterranean countries of the Levant – and in almost all countries from the Ural Mountains to the British Isles – wine was highly desired. However,

[1] The Levant includes Israel, Jordan, Lebanon, Palestine and Syria, and in times past has also included Cyprus, Egypt, Greece, Turkey and even Iraq. These countries, excluding Greece, produced just 0.2 percent of global wine output in 2012–14, of which half is due to Turkey. For the early history of wine in Israel, see, e.g., Walsh (2000). Israel's production revival is exemplified by the Golan Heights Winery (see www.golanwines.co.il/en).

in most of those countries where winegrapes could not be grown profitably (as in Britain; see the previous chapter), wine was consumed by only the wealthiest households. In these countries, wine was a luxury beverage chiefly connected to the ritual of entertainment and limited to special occasions (Imperial Economic Committee 1932). Indeed, it made up only a small fraction of such countries' alcohol consumption: countries tended to concentrate their consumption on those alcoholic beverages that could be produced at lowest cost locally, and excise and import tax differentials often reinforced that consumption bias.

International trade in wine itself was very limited until recent centuries. The transport of ordinary wine was not profitable, due to not only the high cost of such transportation but also problems in preserving wine during long-distance trips. Perhaps the first long-distance trade was down the Tigris and Euphrates rivers to Babylon and to the kings of Egypt, evidence of which stretches back to before 3100 BC (Phillips 2014, pp. 18–19). But as recently as 1300 AD, wine trade was still limited to relatively short distances within Europe (Francis 1972; Rose 2011). It travelled via three networks: the Mediterranean trade by sea and by land to Poland and the Baltic countries; the southern German trade via the Rhine River to northern Germany, Scandanavia and the Baltic countries; and western France's exports by sea to Britain and the low countries (Phillips 2000, p. 92). It was only after glass bottles were standardized and able to be stoppered – from the mid-nineteenth century – that fine wines could be shipped longer distances without risk of spoilage. The improvement in wine production techniques, especially in the fermentation process, also greatly helped to increase wine trade by raising the average quality of wine.

This chapter cannot hope to cover in detail all countries of Europe not covered in preceding countries plus those of the former Soviet Union and the Levant. Its much more modest purpose is simply to give a sense of the changing relative economic importance of such countries in the world's wine markets, and of wine in those countries' consumption of alcohol, over the past fifteen or so decades.[2]

As a group, these countries have accounted for less than one-eighth of global wine production since 1860; and during 1860–1960 they accounted in most years for less than one-sixth of global wine consumption. Why they are of contemporary interest to wine exporters, though, is because since 1960 their share of the world's wine consumption has doubled in volume

[2] Developments over a smaller number of decades are reported in Bentzen and Smith (2004) for Nordic countries and in Noev and Swinnen (2004) for Europe's transition economies.

terms (currently just under 30 percent), and their share of the value of global wine imports had trebled by the mid-1990s to one-quarter. That world import share has dropped little since then despite the growth of wine imports into North America, Asia and elsewhere over the past two decades. Meanwhile, these countries' share of the value of global wine exports has fallen from more than one-fifth in the 1970s to just one-twentieth in recent years.

This set of countries is quite eclectic, ranging from ones with a temperate climate that have been net exporters of wine in various periods (Bulgaria, Greece, Hungary, Romania and the former Yugoslavia) to others that have been too cold to have commercial wine production (Ireland plus the Nordic, Baltic and Low Countries and the Czech Republic), to the members of the Commonwealth of Independent States (CIS, the republics of the former Soviet Union), to the Levant countries east of the Mediterranean Sea.[3] A large minority of those countries are predominantly Moslem and so alcohol is not part of their diet, and the citizens of another substantial subset have been predominantly beer or spirits drinkers until quite recently.

The rest of this chapter elaborates on trends in wine production, wine and other alcohol consumption, and wine trade for these various subsets of countries. Particular attention is given to the convergence of their alcohol consumption patterns toward the rest of the world's and its consequences for the group's net imports of wine.

WINE PRODUCTION AND EXPORTS

This group of countries accounted for only 8 percent of global wine production in 2012–14, down from 13 percent in 1992–94 and from its peak since 1850 of 19 percent in 1982–84, before the antialcohol campaign led to major vine pulls in the Soviet Union. It accounted for even less of global wine exports, which peaked in value terms at 20 percent in the late 1960s but was barely one-quarter of that in 1992–94 and 2012–14 (columns 1 to 4 of Table 10.1) – similar to its share in the early-twentieth century (Figure 10.1). The Levant represents very small fractions of those two shares, in sharp contrast to the situation two millennia ago, when it

[3] Data for numerous countries in this set are not available for long periods because of changing national borders. Examples are the formation and then breakup of the Ottoman Empire (1299–1922), the Austro-Hungarian Empire (1867–1918), the Soviet Union (1922–1991), Yugoslavia (1918–1991) and Czechoslovakia (1918–1992). On the extent of border changes globally since 1816, see Griffiths and Butcher (2013).

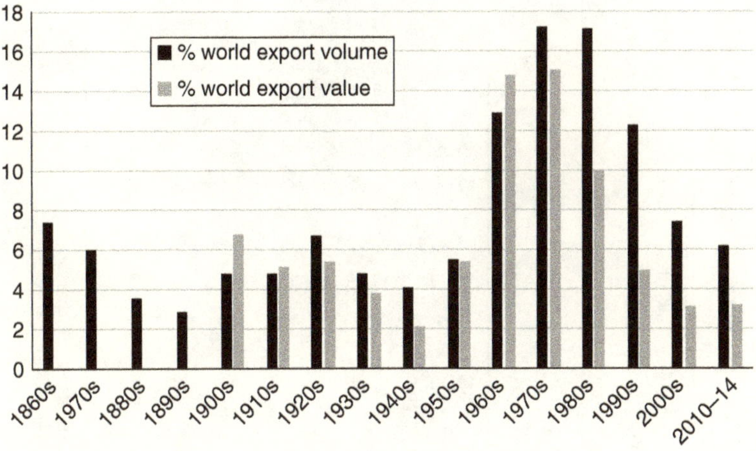

Figure 10.1 Shares of other European, CIS and Levant countries in world wine export volume and value, 1860 to 2014 (%).
Source: Anderson and Pinilla (2017).

was the world's main producer and exporter of grape wine (Unwin 1991; Phillips 2000, ch. 1).

Within this group of countries, only Greece, Romania and Hungary have been significant wine producers (in addition to the Soviet Union), and only one country (Ukraine) provided more than 1 percent of the world's wine exports in 2012–14 – and that has since shrunk following Russia's takeover in 2014 of Crimea. Hungary's most important 'export' markets in the imperial period were other parts of the Austro-Hungarian Empire and Germany, while countries of the former Soviet Union 'exported' mostly to Russia and other parts of the USSR, as did Bulgaria and Romania. In earlier decades, these countries' global export value and volume shares were similar, but since the early 1980s the value shares have been only about half the volume shares, indicating that the quality of those wines has not increased as rapidly as the quality of the rest of the world's exports (Figure 10.1).

Greece, however, was able to take advantage of the French phylloxera outbreak to expand its export. Instead of producing more wine, Greece specialized in the mid-nineteenth century in the production and export of raisins. Most Greek raisins were intended for direct consumption or pastry use. However, in France during the phylloxera years, large volumes of raisins were imported from Greece and Turkey and were used to produce wine from them (Meloni and Swinnen 2017; Chevet et al. 2018). Driven by French demand, Greek raisin production more than tripled between 1860

Table 10.1 *Wine production and export characteristics of other European, CIS and Levant countries, 1992–94 and 2012–14*

	% world wine prod'n volume		% world wine export value		% crop land in vines	Wine prod'n per capita (litres)		Wine export value per capita (US$)		% of wine prod'n volume exported		Wine comparative advantage index[a]	
	1992–94	2012–14	1992–94	2012–14	2012–14	1992–4	2012–14	1992–4	2012–14	1992–94	2012–14	1992–4	2012–14
	(1)	(2)	(3)	(4)	(5)	(6)	(7)	(8)	(9)	(10)	(11)	(12)	(13)
Bulgaria	0.7	0.5	0.9	0.2	2.2	22	18	9.3	8.2	58	37	9.9	1.1
Croatia	0.7	0.2	0.2	0.0	3.0	44	11	3.2	3.5	13	10	1.6	0.6
Georgia	0.6	0.4	0.0	0.4	9.5	32	25	0.7	29.3	2	32	21.5	24.7
Greece	1.3	1.1	0.7	0.2	2.8	33	28	6.2	7.4	16	9	3.3	1.3
Hungary	1.4	0.9	1.0	0.3	1.6	36	21	8.5	8.6	26	24	4.2	0.4
Macedonia	0.3	0.3	1.0	1.0	4.8	47	37	9.1	33.5	51	73	7.4	9.3
Moldova	1.6	0.5	0.6	0.4	6.1	98	38	11.5	36.5	34	84	46.3	32.4
Romania	2.0	1.0	0.2	0.0	1.9	24	14	0.7	0.7	5	4	1.4	0.2
Russia	1.4	1.8	0.0	0.0	0.0	3	3	0.0	0.7	1	0	0.0	0.0
Ukraine	0.7	0.5	0.6	1.7	0.2	3	3	0.9	1.2	41	43	2.6	0.5
Other[b]	2.7	1.3	1.2	1.2	n.a.	n.a.	n.a.	n.a.	n.a.	n.a.	n.a.	n.a.	n.a.
SUM OF ABOVE	**13.4**	**8.5**	**6.4**	**5.4**	n.a.	n.a.	n.a.	n.a.	n.a.	n.a.	n.a.	n.a.	n.a.

[a] Comparative advantage index = share of wine in national merchandise export value divided by share of wine in global merchandise export value.
[b] Other = Belgium, Denmark, Finland, Ireland, Luxembourg, Netherlands, Norway, Sweden, rest of eastern Europe and CIS plus Levant.
Source: Anderson and Pinilla (2017).

and 1890. Virtually all were destined for exports, which quadrupled over those three decades. Raisins already accounted for 50 percent of the value of Greece's exports in the 1850s, but that share rose to more than 70 percent in the decade to the mid-1880s and so became a fundamental activity in the Greek economy (Petmezas 1997). The fall in French demand for raisins following the requirement that raisin-based wine production be labelled as such from 1890 and the imposition of high tariffs on raisin imports (which increased during the 1890s) severely affected Greek production. Together with increasing competition from California in the international market for raisins, Greece faced a severe economic crisis (Morilla, Olmstead and Rhode 1999; Petmetzas 2009; Meloni and Swinnen 2017). After World War I, Greek raisin exports stagnated, while those in the United States almost tripled. In 1903–08, Greece accounted for three-quarters of the world's raisin exports, but by the 1920s its share had fallen to two-fifths (Pinilla and Ayuda 2009, p. 204).

Small shares of *global* wine production and exports do not necessarily mean the industry in this set of countries was a small contributor to *national* production or exports, of course. While most of the countries in this group have always produced less than 5 litres per capita per year, eight of them have relatively high shares of their total crop land under vines and are nontrivial wine producers. During 1900–1970, Greece produced per capita around 50 litres per year on average (one-third more than during 1860–1899) and Hungary produced 30–40 litres. Wine production in Bulgaria and Romania was much more variable, ranging from as little as 10 to as many as 60 litres per capita per year. Production per capita in all four countries has been falling over the past three decades, though, as it has in Croatia, Georgia, Macedonia and Moldova (columns 5 to 7 of Table 10.1).

The value of wine exports per capita and share of wine production exported have remained steady in five of these countries, but have grown dramatically for Georgia, Macedonia and Moldova (columns 8 to 11 of Table 10.1). Georgia and Moldova now have the strongest indexes of comparative advantage in wine[4] in the world, and Macedonia's index is just below those of New Zealand (14) and Chile (13) and equal to that of France (columns 12 and 13 of Table 10.1). The unit value of those exports varies greatly, though: in 2012–14, it ranged from less than US$1.20 per litre for Bulgaria, Moldova and Ukraine to $1.55 for Hungary, $2.90 for Greece and $3.60 for Croatia and Georgia. These average export prices compare

4 The Balassa index of 'revealed' comparative advantage is the share of wine in a country's merchandise exports divided by the share of wine in global merchandise trade.

with $1.60 for Spain, $2.30 for Chile, $2.50 for Australia, just over $3 for Italy and Portugal and $3.90 for Austria during 2012–14 (Anderson and Pinilla 2017). But recall that the countries under review in this chapter in total represent just 5 percent of global wine exports.

WINE CONSUMPTION AND IMPORTS

During the 100 years to 1960, this set of countries rarely accounted for more than one-sixth of the world's wine consumption, but by the mid-1980s their share had risen to one-fourth before falling back a little (columns 1 to 4 of Table 10.2). Their share of the value of global wine imports had trebled between the early 1960s and the mid-1990s, also to one-fourth, before dropping slightly because of the growth of wine imports into North America, Asia and elsewhere over the past two decades. Even so, the import shares were still 22 percent by value and 26 percent by volume in 2012–14. The biggest importers are Belgium and the Netherlands, but between them they reexport about one-sixth of their imports to neighbouring countries, making Russia the single biggest wine net importer among this set of countries in 2012–14 (columns 5 to 7 of Table 10.2). This is not unprecedented: in the 1840s, Russia was the world's largest importer of wine by value, slightly ahead of Britain (Figure 10.2).

In the second half of the nineteenth century, Russia imported mainly French champagne that was eagerly consumed by the aristocracy and the wealthiest social groups. The large producing houses of Champagne adapted their product to the tastes of their Russian consumers, who preferred a champagne sweeter than the driest demanded by the British. The main Champagne houses had permanent commercial agents in St Petersburg. But following the Russian Revolution and the move away from trade with the west by the USSR and the communist countries of eastern Europe, this set of countries' share of world wine imports slumped.

In northwestern Europe, wine consumption grew during 1860–1880, but from then to the 1920s consumption stayed almost constant. By 1925, only the largest wine producers in this group of countries, such as Greece, Bulgaria, Hungary and Romania, had significant shares of global wine consumption (with per capita consumption at about one-third that of France, Italy or Spain). In Scandinavia and the other countries in this set, average wine consumption remained very low until the 1980s. Hence, they plus the central and eastern European countries, the CIS and Levant had a combined share of global wine imports below 10 percent from the 1920s to the early 1960s (Figure 10.3).

Table 10.2 *Wine consumption and import characteristics of other European, CIS and Levant countries, 1925 to 2014*

	% world consumption volume				% world import value				Wine consm per capita (litres)		
	1925–29	1962–64	1982–84	2012–14	1962–64	1992–94	2012–14	1925–29	1962–64	1982–84	2012–14
	(1)	(2)	(3)	(4)	(5)	(6)	(7)	(8)	(9)	(10)	(11)
Belgium/ Luxembourg	0.3	0.4	0.8	1.4	3.4	7.6	4.0	6.5	9.0	21.5	29.1
Denmark	0.0	0.1	0.3	0.7	0.9	2.9	2.0	1.4	3.3	16.9	29.4
Finland	0.0	0.1	0.1	0.3	0.3	0.5	0.7	0.1	2.5	6.1	11.8
Greece	0.6	1.0	1.3	1.3	0.0	0.1	0.1	18.2	27.4	37.7	29.1
Ireland	0.0	0.0	0.0	0.3	0.4	0.6	0.9	1.0	2.2	3.3	18.3
Netherlands	0.1	0.1	0.9	1.4	1.5	5.9	3.6	1.9	2.5	16.7	21.1
Norway	0.0	0.0	0.1	0.4	0.3	0.6	1.3	n.a.	1.1	1.1	1.4
Sweden	0.0	0.1	0.3	1.0	1.6	2.4	2.2	0.8	3.7	10.0	24.9
Bulgaria	0.7	0.7	0.7	0.5	0.0	0.0	0.0	21.4	20.8	21.6	17.7
Croatia	0.0	n.a.	n.a.	0.7	n.a.	0.1	0.1	n.a.	n.a.	n.a.	41.9
Georgia	n.a.	n.a.	n.a.	0.4	n.a.	0.0	0.0	n.a.	n.a.	n.a.	21.5
Hungary	1.6	1.3	1.2	1.0	0.2	0.0	0.1	24.1	29.0	30.7	23.8
Moldova	n.a.	n.a.	n.a.	0.5	n.a.	0.0	0.0	n.a.	n.a.	n.a.	34.3
Romania	3.7	2.2	2.1	1.7	0.1	0.1	0.1	47.2	26.9	25.5	21.3
Russia	1.4	5.8	12.1	4.7	n.a.	2.4	3.0	1.5	5.9	12.3	8.0
Ukraine	n.a.	2.3	2.7	0.9	n.a.	0.2	0.3	n.a.	11.7	14.8	5.2
Other[a]	2.0	2.0	2.7	2.5	1.0	1.6	3.8	5.1	8.1	13.4	12.4
Sum of above	10.4	16.2	25.2	19.7	9.8	25.0	22.3	n.a.	n.a.	n.a.	n.a.

[a] Other = rest of eastern Europe and CIS plus Levant.

Source: Anderson and Pinilla (2017).

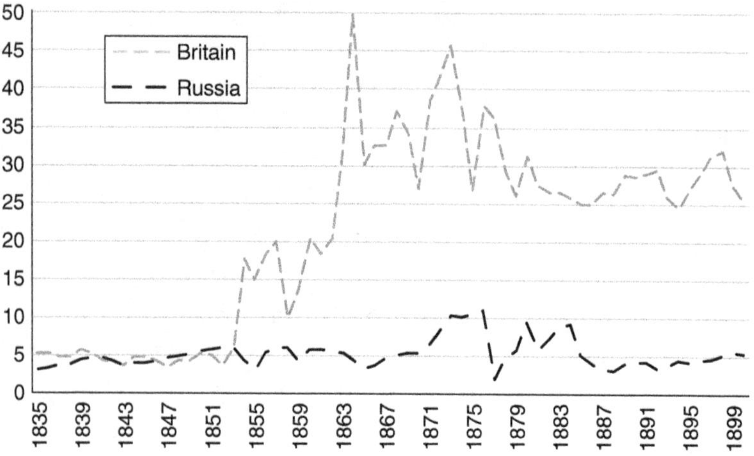

Figure 10.2 Value of wine imports, Russia and Britain, 1835 to 1900 (current US$ million).
Source: Anderson and Pinilla (2017).

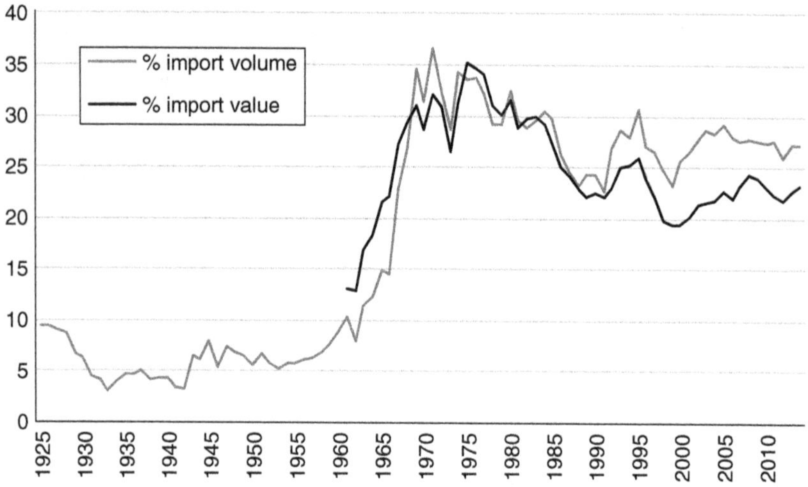

Figure 10.3 Shares of other European, CIS and Levant countries in world wine import volume and value, 1925 to 2014 (%).
Source: Anderson and Pinilla (2017).

The levels and changes in consumption of wine per capita still vary hugely across this group of countries.[5] The last four columns of Table 10.2 show per capita consumption rising rapidly from a low base over the past nine decades for Northwest European countries (Belgium/Luxembourg, Denmark, Finland, Ireland, Netherlands, Norway and Sweden), steady for some moderately high consuming countries (Greece, Bulgaria and Hungary), and falling in recent decades for Romania, Russia and Ukraine. To help understand those hugely differing levels of and changes in per capita consumption, it is helpful to examine them in the context of their overall alcohol consumption.

WINE RELATIVE TO OTHER ALCOHOL CONSUMPTION

With increasing globalization and interactions between cultures, countries are converging in their consumption patterns. The extent to which alcoholic beverage consumption patterns are converging across countries has been the subject of many previous studies. A new study by Holmes and Anderson (2017) updates earlier findings; covers all countries of the world since 1961 and key high-income countries since the 1880s; and distinguishes countries according to whether their alcoholic focus was on wine, beer or spirits in the early 1960s as well as their geographic region and their real per capita income.

If all products could be traded costlessly around the world, and there were no government interventions such as consumption or trade taxes or differences in value-added tax rates across jurisdictions, then the retail prices of each type of beverage would be identical throughout the world. According to Stigler and Becker (1977), the key reason then for major differences in consumption patterns would be differences in per capita incomes. If all beverages were normal goods, we might then expect convergence in the level and mix of alcoholic (or indeed all) beverages consumed as convergence across countries occurs in national average per capita incomes.

In reality, costs of trading beverages across national borders are not zero (even though they have declined greatly over the past 180 years), which means countries have tended in the past to concentrate their consumption on those alcoholic beverages that can be produced at the lowest cost locally.

[5] Not shown are various small countries, some of whose citizens are considerable wine consumers. The most notable is the Vatican (62 litres per capita per year in 2012–14). Others are Malta (32 litres in 2012–14), Cyprus (15 litres), Iceland (14 litres), Macedonia (10 litres) and the Czech Republic (9 litres).

Table 10.3 *VAT and ad valorem consumer tax equivalent of excise taxes on wines, beers and spirits,*[a] *other European, CIS and Levant countries, January 2012 (as % of the wholesale wholesale pretax prices per litre shown in column heads)*

	Ad valorem equivalent rates (%) at the quoted wholesale pretax price						
	Non premium wine	Commercial premium wine	Super premium wine	Sparkling wine	Beer	Spirits	VAT/GST (%)
	$2.50	$7.50	$20	$25	$2	$15	
Belgium	24	8	3	8	14	59	21
Czech Rep.	0	0	0	5	4	37	20
Denmark	72	24	9	10	27	68	25
Estonia	37	12	5	4	17	48	20
Finland	157	53	20	16	94	146	23
Greece	0	0	0	0	21	82	23
Hungary	0	0	0	2	15	31	27
Ireland	132	44	17	26	50	105	23
Israel	0	0	0	0	137	110	16
Luxembourg	0	0	0	0	6	35	15
Netherlands	36	12	5	12	17	51	19
Norway	343	114	43	34	179	292	25
Poland	18	6	2	2	14	37	23
Slovak Rep	0	0	0	4	11	36	20
Slovenia	0	0	0	0	32	34	20
Sweden	122	41	15	12	59	189	25
Turkey[b]	40	13	5	26	63	91	18
OECD unwted ave.	40	15	8	9	43	74	**18**

[a] Wine and beer degree alcohol contents are assumed to be 12 percent and 4.5 percent, respectively; the absolute alcohol content for spirits is assumed to be 40 percent.
[b] Turkey still wine data are for 2010.
Source: Anderson (2014).

Nor are excise taxes, import taxes, nontariff barriers and other regulations on beverages similar across countries, and they often also vary greatly across beverage types (Anderson 2010, 2014; Bianco et al. 2016); and value-added taxes vary across countries too (Table 10.3). Moreover, temperance movements have had different effects on the social acceptability of alcohol consumption at different times in various places. So too have concerns about human health: as per capita incomes rise, people can afford to spend more on alcohol consumption but also choose to limit its volume for health reasons; and some people are also substituting towards (especially still red)

Table 10.4 *Total alcohol per capita consumption volume and shares of beer, wine and spirits in that total,[a] selected countries and all regions of the world, 1961–64 and 2010–14 (LAL and %)*

	Consumption (LAL/capita)[a]		Share of consumption 1961–64 (%)[b]			Share of consumption 2010–14 (%)[b]		
	1961–4	2010–14	Wine	Beer	Spirits	Wine	Beer	Spirits
Belgium/Lux	8.5	9.6	13	**77**	11	35	**51**	14
Bulgaria	5.2	9.7	**48**	17	35	18	37	**44**
Croatia	Na	9.9	na	na	Na	**51**	39	11
Denmark	5.1	8.0	8	**77**	15	**47**	38	16
Finland	1.4	6.9	13	21	**66**	21	**53**	26
Georgia	Na	5.8	na	na	na	**49**	21	31
Greece	7.1	6.8	**46**	23	31	**53**	27	20
Hungary	7.1	9.5	**48**	28	24	30	**36**	34
Ireland	5.1	8.2	5	**76**	19	28	**52**	21
Moldova	Na	8.0	na	na	na	**43**	22	35
Netherlands	3.2	7.4	9	**47**	43	35	**48**	17
Norway	6.4	7.9	3	27	**69**	29	35	**36**
Romania	4.8	7.9	**64**	13	23	31	**53**	16
Russia	4.2	8.9	16	15	**69**	11	39	**49**
Sweden	4.8	6.1	9	39	**52**	**49**	37	15
Turkey	0.3	1.1	**39**	26	35	9	**58**	34
Ukraine	na	7.0	na	na	na	9	39	**52**
Wted averages								
W. Europe	12.3	8.4	**55**	29	16	**42**	38	20
E. Europe	Na	7.2	22	22	**56**	14	42	**44**
North America	5.4	7.0	8	49	43	18	**49**	33
Latin America	6.5	5.1	**48**	34	18	11	**60**	29
Australia+NZ	6.5	7.1	10	**76**	14	39	**46**	15
Asia (incl. Pacific)	1.9	3.2	1	12	**87**	4	34	**62**
Africa & M East	1.0	1.7	27	**38**	35	14	**67**	19
World	**2.5**	**2.7**	**34**	**29**	**37**	**15**	**43**	**42**

[a] These data are volume-based in litres of alcohol (LAL) per year, four- or five-year averages.
[b] The bold numbers indicate which beverage has the highest share in total alcohol consumption volume in the period shown.
Sources: Holmes and Anderson (2017).

wine because of its perceived positive influence on health when drunk in moderation.

Given all the preceding possible influences on beverage consumption patterns, it would not be surprising if there was an absence of convergence

Table 10.5 *Wine, beer and spirits consumption volume intensity indexes,[a] other European and CIS countries, 1962 to 2014*

	Wine			Beer			Spirits		
	1962–64	1992–94	2012–14	1962–64	1992–94	2012–14	1962–64	1992–94	2012–14
Belgium-Lux	0.36	1.52	2.22	2.57	1.53	1.19	0.31	0.29	0.34
Denmark	0.22	1.53	2.90	2.60	1.55	0.88	0.43	0.26	0.40
Finland	0.62	0.96	1.35	1.09	1.69	1.23	1.30	0.39	0.62
Germany	0.54	1.22	1.81	1.92	1.46	1.23	0.68	0.48	0.45
Greece	1.32	2.39	3.40	0.79	0.62	0.64	0.86	0.75	0.47
Ireland	0.15	0.39	1.77	2.56	1.89	1.19	0.53	0.44	0.51
Netherlands	0.26	1.42	2.21	1.60	1.30	1.12	1.21	0.54	0.42
Sweden	0.27	1.26	3.14	1.33	1.34	0.84	1.44	0.58	0.35
Bulgaria	1.32	1.68	1.34	0.60	0.88	0.86	1.00	0.82	1.02
Croatia	na	2.81	3.25	na	0.81	0.89	na	0.40	0.27
Georgia	na	4.45	2.97	na	0.03	0.48	na	0.42	0.80
Hungary	1.39	1.71	1.93	0.96	0.96	0.83	0.66	0.73	0.83
Moldova	na	na	3.08	na	na	0.48	na	na	0.76
Romania	1.85	2.20	2.00	0.42	0.81	1.27	0.66	0.66	0.34
Russia	0.47	0.39	0.71	0.49	0.37	0.94	1.94	1.84	1.17
Ukraine	na	0.39	0.57	na	0.61	0.90	na	1.62	1.27

[a] The intensity index is defined as the national relative to the global share of a beverage in total volume of alcohol consumed.

Source: Holmes and Anderson (2017).

in those patterns. Holmes and Anderson (2017) plot alcohol consumption per capita against real income per capita for fifty-three countries and residual regions spanning the world from 1961 to 2014 and find that the volume of consumption first tends to rise with per capita incomes but then falls. This is the case for each of wine, beer and spirits. These inverted U-shaped figures suggest that income convergence alone (the gradual catching up of developing countries and transition economies to the per capita incomes of high-income countries) would not necessarily lead to convergence in alcohol consumption patterns based on per capita volumes.

The volume of total alcohol consumption per capita and in shares of overall alcohol consumption volume due to wine, beer and spirits is shown in Table 10.4 for 1961–64 and 2010–14. Consumption-weighted averages for the regions of the world are reported at the bottom of that table, for easy comparison with the set of countries of concern in this chapter.

Total alcohol consumption per capita had been rising with per capita incomes until the 1980s, but then it began to fall in high-income countries, tracing out an inverted U-shaped trend over time. Even for the world as a whole, the weighted average was almost the same in 2010–14 as it was in

1961–64 (last row of Table 10.4) – having been higher than both of those period averages in each of the intervening decades. Among the countries listed in that table, the countries with higher consumption in the 1980s than in 2010–14 include Belgium, Denmark, Greece, Hungary and the Netherlands.

As for the mix of alcohols, Table 10.4 shows that it was very different across the countries listed, especially with respect to wine, which ranged from 3 percent to 64 percent of all national alcohol sales during 1961–64. But by 2010–14 the range had narrowed somewhat. Globally, wine's share of alcohol consumption more than halved over those five decades, from 34 percent to 15 percent, while beer's rose by more than one-third, from 29 percent to 42 percent (and spirits' rose but only a little, from 37 percent to 43 percent – see the final row of Table 10.4). Consistent with that global trend, of the seventeen individual countries listed in that table, wine was the main alcohol for eight of them in 1961–64 but only six in 2010–14, beer dominated for just four countries at the beginning but six by the end of that period, and spirits held the largest share for four countries at the end compared with five earlier (see the bold numbers in Table 10.4). Notice, though, that in 60 percent of the cases wine has a larger share of national alcohol consumption in 2012–14 than it had in 1962–64.

An additional way to examine the changing beverage mix of consumers is to calculate a beverage consumption intensity index. Holmes and Anderson (2017) define such an index as the national share of a beverage in the total volume of alcohol consumed divided by the global share that year. That is, it takes into account not just the change in a particular beverage share nationally but also what is happening to the popularity of that beverage in the rest of the world. Those indexes, reported in Table 10.5 for the half-century ending 2014, increase for wine for all sixteen countries shown and decrease for spirits for 70 percent of them, while being equally split for beer between rises and falls. That is, this set of countries has become more wine-focused over that period (or more accurately, moved away more from a low wine focus) than is true in the rest of the world.

SUMMARY AND PROSPECTS

This set of countries is very mixed. It includes the countries believed to be the first to make wine regularly perhaps as far back as 8,000 years ago, and the first to engage in international trade not only in vine cuttings and technologies but also in the finished product, beginning before the birth of Christ. It also includes two other groups: the vine-intensive countries of Eastern and Southeast Europe, and the wine-importing countries of Northeast Europe that have virtually no domestic wine production. The first of these subgroups, including the countries of the Levant, have been very minor global wine market participants over the past 180 years.

The second subgroup has been mainly focused on the quantity rather than quality of wines produced, especially under their socialist regimes. Wine is a traditional product in this region and so appeals less to the younger generation there, just as has happened in the key wine-exporting countries of Western Europe, where beer has become more popular. That could reverse if the domestic wine industry were to follow the lead of the New World countries (and Austria) since the late 1980s in raising the quality of the local product and focusing on export markets for growth, including in the commercial premium space dominated by supermarkets.[6]

Consumers in the third subgroup have been either beer- or spirits-focused until the latest wave of wine globalization. Their move to increasingly embrace wine has been driven by similar forces to those that have been operating in the United Kingdom. On the demand side, they include rising real wages and improving living standards that have boosted expenditure on alcohol and a desire for more variety in their consumption of beverages; and on the supply side, the forces at work include the increased availability of quaffable, consistent, easy-to-find imported wines free of technical faults and affordable. Climate change may make it possible for a domestic wine industry to emerge in some of these Northwest European countries, just as has happened in England, which will reinforce the tendency for consumers in those countries to become more wine-focused (Anderson 2017).

REFERENCES

Anderson, K. (2010), 'Excise and Import Taxes on Wine vs Beer and Spirits: An International Comparison', *Economic Papers* 29(2): 215–28.

(2013), 'Is Georgia the Next "New" Wine-Exporting Country?' *Journal of Wine Economics* 8(1): 1–28.

(2014), 'Excise Taxes on Wines, Beers and Spirits: An Updated International Comparison', Working Paper No. 170, American Association of Wine Economists, October.

(2017), 'How Might Climate Change and Preference Changes Affect the Competitiveness of the World's Wine Regions?' *Wine Economics and Policy* 6(2): 23–27, June.

[6] For an analysis of what that might involve for Georgia, see Anderson (2013).

Anderson, K. and V. Pinilla (with the assistance of A. J. Holmes) (2017), *Annual Database of Global Wine Markets, 1835 to 2016*, freely available in Excel at the University of Adelaide's Wine Economics Research Centre, www.adelaide.edu.au/wine-econ/databases

Bentzen, J. and V. Smith (2004), 'The Nordic Countries', ch. 8 (pp. 141–60) in *The World's Wine Markets: Globalization at Work*, edited by K. Anderson, Cheltenham, UK: Edward Elgar.

Bianco, A. D., V. L. Boatto, F. Caracciolo and F. G. Santeramo (2016), 'Tariffs and Non-tariff Frictions in the World Wine Trade', *European Review of Agricultural Economics* 43(1): 31–57, March.

Chevet, J. M., E. Fernández, E. Giraud-Héraud and V. Pinilla (2018), 'France', ch. 3 in *Wine Globalization: A New Comparative History*, edited by K. Anderson and V. Pinilla, Cambridge and New York: Cambridge University Press.

Francis, A. D. (1972), *The Wine Trade*, London: Adams and Charles Black.

Griffiths, R. D. and C. R. Butcher (2013), 'Introducing the International System(s) Dataset (ISD), 1816–2011', *International Interactions* 39(5): 748–68. Data Appendix is at www.ryan-griffiths.com/data/

Holmes, A. and K. Anderson (2017), 'Convergence in National Alcohol Consumption Patterns: New Global Indicators', *Journal of Wine Economics* 12(2): 117–48.

Imperial Economic Committee (1932), *Wine. Reports of the Imperial Economic Committee. Twenty-third Report*, London: Imperial Economic Committee.

Johnson, H. (1989), *The Story of Wine*, London: Mitchell Beasley.

Ketskhoveli, N., M. Ramishvili and D. Tabidze (2012), *Georgian Ampelography*, Tbilisi: Ministry of Culture and Monument Protection of Georgia. (First published in Georgian in 1960.)

McGovern, P. (2003), *Ancient Wine: The Search for the Origins of Viticulture*, Princeton, NJ: Princeton University Press.

(2009), *Uncorking the Past: The Quest for Wine, Beer, and Other Alcoholic Beverages*, Berkeley: University of California Press.

Meloni, G. and J. Swinnen (2017), 'Standards, Tariffs and Trade: The Rise and Fall of the Raisin Trade Between Greece and France in the Late 19th Century and the Definition of Wine', American Association of Wine Economists (AAWE) Working Paper 208, January.

Morilla, J., A. L. Olmstead and P. Rhode (1999), 'Horn of Plenty: The Globalization of Mediterranean Horticulture and the Economic Development of Southern Europe, 1880–1930', *Journal of Economic History* 59(2): 316–52.

Noev, N. and J. F. M. Swinnen (2004), 'Eastern Europe and the Former Soviet Union', ch. 9 (pp. 161–84) in *The World's Wine Markets: Globalization at Work*, edited by K. Anderson, Cheltenham, UK: Edward Elgar.

Petmezas, S. D. (1997), 'El comercio de la pasa de Corinto y su influencia sobre la economía griega del siglo XIX (1840–1914)', pp. 523–62 in *Impactos exteriores sobre el mundo rural mediterráneo*, edited by J. Morilla-Critz, J. Gómez-Pantoja and P. Cressier, Madrid: Ministerio de Agricultura, Pesca y Alimentación.

(2009), 'Agriculture and Economic Development in Greece, 1870–1973', pp. 353–74 in *Agriculture and Economic Development in Europe since 1870*, edited by P. Lains and V. Pinilla, London: Routledge.

Phillips, R. (2000), *A Short History of Wine*, London: Penguin. Revised edition published in 2015 as *9000 Years of Wine (A World History)*, Vancouver: Whitecap.
(2014), *Alcohol: A History*, Chapel Hill: University of North Carolina Press.
Pinilla, V. and M. I. Ayuda. (2009), 'Foreign Markets, Globalisation and Agricultural Change in Spain, 1850–1935', pp. 173–208 in *Markets and Agricultural Change in Europe from the 13th to the 20th Century*, edited by V. Pinilla, Turnhout: Brepols.
Rose, S. (2011), *The Wine Trade in Medieval Europe 1000–1500*, London and New York: Bloomsbury.
Stigler, G. J. and G. S. Becker (1977), 'De Gustibus non est Disputandum', *American Economic Review* 67(2): 76–90.
Unwin, T. (1991), *Wine and the Vine: An Historical Geography of Viticulture and the Wine Trade*, London and New York: Routledge.
Walsh, C. E. (2000), *The Fruit of the Vine: Viticulture in Ancient Israel*, Harvard Semitic Monographs, No. 60, Winona Lake, IN: Eisenbrauns.

PART III

NEWER MARKETS

11

Argentina

Steve Stein and Ana María Mateu

From the beginning of the twentieth century, Argentina has been one of the world's largest wine producers, moving between fifth and sixth place over the years. Beginning in the 1880s, what had been a handful of small, artisanal wineries focused on the limited regional markets of grape-growing areas – principally Mendoza and San Juan at the foot of the Andes – developed rapidly into a huge industry. The model established in the first thirty years of industry growth would last for a century after first emerging. Its form resulted from the interplay of the varied impacts of the globalization Argentina had been experiencing since the 1870s and official policies that worked to isolate the industry from the rest of the world.

For its part, globalization provided for Argentina a rapidly expanding immigrant population from southern Europe that included consumers who carried with them a Mediterranean culture extending from meanings of wine to types to the jugs that contained it; winemakers, owners, and workers, largely from Italy and Spain; and much of the machinery used for production. Simultaneously, to promote the fledgling industry, succeeding governments pursued policies that spanned high tariffs for protection from foreign competitors to generous subsidies designed to foster economic success. The result was near-total isolation from the rest of the wine world until the mid-1980s, when the worst crisis in its history forced the industry to look outward for the first time for survival.

Charting the interplay between globalization and isolation, this chapter focuses on three watershed periods of the country's wine history: the founding years from 1885 to 1915; the period of massive growth from 1950 that ended in profound crisis in 1980; and Argentina's wine revolution from the 1990s to the present.

THE FOUNDING YEARS, 1885 TO 1915

It is common to use the adjective "infant" when referring to the early development of any industry. For Argentina, adulthood came shockingly fast, whether measured by vineyard growth (from 1,500 ha in 1873 to 122,000 in 1910); number of wineries (334 in 1884 to 3,409 in 1914); or perhaps most revealing, production, which grew annually by 11 to 17 percent. Between 1901 and 1915 alone, it soared 90 percent, permitting Argentina to vault to the position of fifth largest producer in the world. In seeking the driving force for this expansion, globalization is a valuable concept (Fernandez 2004).

For Argentina, a key component of that globalization was the influx of an enormous wave of largely Mediterranean immigrants: between 1880 and 1910 alone, more than 3.2 million people arrived in Argentina, accounting for three-quarters of the country's population increase over those thirty years. As has been common with migrant flows, factors of attraction as well as expulsion were involved. On the "pull" side, the country's 1853 Constitution, from its preamble to several of its articles, boldly promoted European immigration by promising justice, peace, well-being, and liberty to anyone who wished to settle in Argentina, assuring potential arrivals that they could enter the country freely and enjoy all rights of citizenship. The same document was clear about the rationale for this policy: these immigrants would work the land, improve industries, and teach the population arts and sciences. Some twenty years later, the government sweetened the appeal to immigrants by offering no-cost temporary housing, help with finding a job, and free transportation to anywhere in the country the immigrants chose to live. These were attractive incentives to Europeans who felt "pushed out" of regions suffering from economic and political instability as the nineteenth century was drawing to a close.

Massive immigration had a transformative effect on all aspects of Argentina's emerging wine economy. Coming largely from Italy and Spain, countries with well-established wine traditions, the flood of people from southern Europe led to an enormous increase in consumption. Before the major influx that began in the 1870s, the annual average consumption of wine per capita was 23 litres. By 1910, consumption had risen to 62 litres, as foreigners grew to 29 percent of Argentina's population (Figure 11.1). This made wine the country's third most important consumer good after bread and meat, accounting for 8.7 percent of average family food and drink expenditures (Mateu 2002).

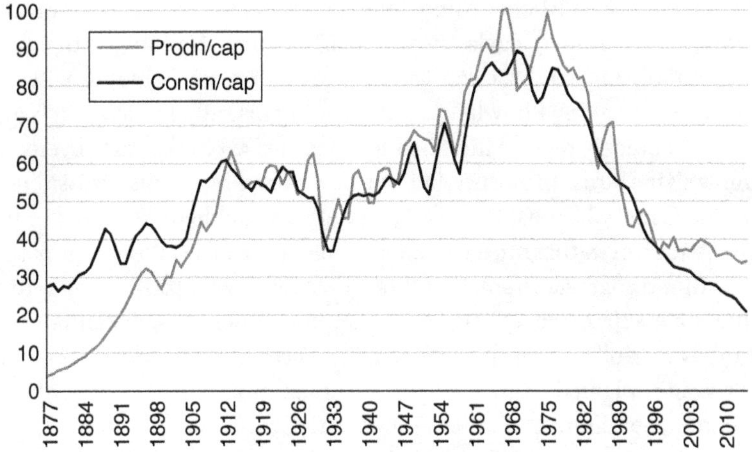

Figure 11.1 Volume of wine production and consumption per capita, Argentina, 1876 to 2014 (litres per year, three-year averages around year shown).
Source: Anderson and Pinilla (2017).

Despite the wish to have the new arrivals populate all of the country's "virgin lands," the largest number of them remained in Buenos Aires, making it the country's major population center and concomitantly its largest wine market. These immigrants were key to the capital's expansion from 177,000 to 1.2 million inhabitants between 1869 and 1910. Already by 1895, 40 percent of those inhabitants were foreign born, a proportion that rose to 50 percent by 1910. Initially, the city's thirsty immigrants were not drinking the local product. While wine had been produced at the foot of the Andes in Mendoza since the mid-sixteenth century, the one to two months of transporting to Buenos Aires on the backs of mules meant excessively high cost, and worse, most was ruined on the way. As a result, wines imported from Europe predominated, making Argentina the world's third largest wine importer through the 1880s after France and Switzerland (República Argentina 1898; Martìnez 1910; Anderson and Pinilla 2017).

Domestic transport costs were not the only barrier to the development of a domestic wine industry. An embarrassing episode years earlier of the illustrious Argentine politician, future president, and wine lover Domingo Faustino Sarmiento, when on a European trip, led to another constraint. "[A]t a weak moment the idea came to me of offering a bottle of San Juan wine. They acted as if I had tried to poison them, the best of our wines cutting such a poor figure alongside of those of Oporto, Bordeaux, Burgundy, etc." (Hanaway 2014, p. 5). An exasperated Sarmiento persuaded

French wine expert Michel Aimé Pouget to travel to Argentina from Chile to take charge of the Escuela Vitivinícola Nacional (National Viticultural/ Wine School) in Mendoza. Pouget crossed the Andes, bringing with him not only winemaking knowledge, but most importantly French grape stock that would quickly replace the existing vines of Uva Criolla that covered the country's vineyards. Introduced to the New World by Spanish missionaries from the Canary Islands, the Criolla variety was dubbed: "A high-yielding, very rustic crop … that produces an alcoholic wine of a yellowish pink color and with a disagreeable smell and taste" (Arata 1903, p. 122). As a result of the state-supported efforts of Pouget and others, a substantial number of Uva Criolla vines, that as late as 1885 still accounted for 99 percent of all grapes planted, were pulled up to make way for Malbec, Cabernet Sauvignon, Semilion, and other French varietals.

It was in the year 1885 that Mendoza's wine prospects changed radically: the railroad arrived to provide a connection between the country's most important wine production area and its primary consumer market. At the official opening of the new railroad, which would reduce shipping time to two or three days, President Julio Argentino Roca enthusiastically described Mendoza as a vast cornucopia of fruit suspended from the Andean peaks. Two years later, in less flowery but equally enthusiastic terms, prominent Mendoza politician and future governor Emilio Civit guaranteed his peers that "The future of Mendoza is assured to be brilliant and anyone who can save a single peso of his income or obtain a peso of credit with total confidence and faith in what is to come."[1] Mendocinos clearly heeded the call: within three decades of the arrival of the first train, 76 percent of all production in the region was wine-related (Bunge 1929; Martín 1992; Mateu 2003).

It was indeed the presence of those trains, products of globalization, that spurred the transformation of Argentine wine production from artisanal to industrial. They not only made shipment viable but also carried both the human and material resources to Mendoza that were vital to the industry's explosive growth.

Clearly, a *sine qua non* for that process was a labor force of sufficient size and with some experience in grape growing and winemaking. So with the railroad's arrival imminent, in 1884 Mendoza legislators passed a law that authorized payments to recruiting agents in Europe for each immigrant sent to the region. The qualities sought were morality and good health; experience in grape growing and winemaking; and preferably families who would share the tasks together. To southern European peasants living in unsure

[1] Civit (1887, p. 236). The Roca statement is found in Supplee (1988, p. 274).

political times and for those from wine regions who saw grand swaths of their vines drying up due to the severe phylloxera epidemic that that decimated vineyards throughout the Mediterranean, these recruiters held out the promise of rapid economic progress on large tracts of unexploited land.

Two decades earlier, Mendoza's immigrants were largely Chilean in origin and reached only 9 percent of the total population. With the growth of the wine industry, by 1913 that proportion rose to 37 percent, almost entirely people from Italy and Spain. The great majority dedicated themselves to the production of grapes and wine, and they quickly rose to a position of dominance throughout the industry. Particularly notable was the fact that by 1900 immigrants already represented 50 percent of owners, rising to 79 percent only three years later. With relatives and friends in Buenos Aires, they were able to build networks that spanned production and the consumer market (Barrio 2010).[2]

Just as the European presence in Argentina was the cornerstone of wine production and consumption, Mediterranean traditions that treated wine as a necessary part of the daily diet were key to the form it took. For the largely poor, male Italian and Spanish immigrants of peasant background, quality and taste were not fundamental to the "meanings" of wine. Rather the drink was seen principally as a source of calories or a healthy substitute for the nonpotable water in their rural homelands. Their "wine culture" quickly became a determining feature in the strategy of their adopted country's producers. Concretely, major wineries shared the view of Bodegas Arizu – the region's third largest – that Argentina's unsegmented consumer market "has no taste." As one contemporary critic remarked, the goal was "ordinary wines 'for the workers'... They think about hardy throats, not palates" (Mateu 2009, p. 158). And for those palates, typically a litre per day was considered indispensable. In this context, production was clearly driven by a simple calculus: lower price, more drunk, higher profits.

The descriptors of that massively and rapidly made beverage included "an elevated alcohol content," "thick," "cloudy," "inconsistent," "with no distinctiveness'" (Arata 1903, pages 202 and 254). While these wines certainly did not exhibit characteristics that would have pleased discriminating palates, their thickness, cloudiness, and deep color may very well have been appreciated by cost- and supply-conscious consumers and producers, as it made them perfect for the so-called process of "correction,"

[2] Similarly, from the beginning of the promotion of grape and wine production, Mendoza's provincial government recognized that irrigation was an absolute necessity, as the region is a virtual desert; hence the attraction of European experts to plan and build canals and set up distribution protocols.

"straightening out," "baptism" – in other words, their dilution with water, a process that habitually doubled the volume of wine produced. Producers, retailers, customers: all felt they were a winner with wines that could stand a greater injection of water than more refined products. As the rapidly growing domestic demand for strong cheap wines often outstripped supply, wineries realized that adding water to heavy, alcoholic products would enable them "to make lots of wine and above all quickly" (Arata 1903). For wholesale distributors and sale outlets, topping off the barrels received from Mendoza was a particularly effective strategy for increasing profits.

In this context, it is important to note that by the early twentieth century the same Malbec that has come to be Argentina's emblem of quality in the twenty-first century had become the country's most widely planted winegrape variety, accounting for 80 percent of all vines, precisely because of its strong color components that helped a watered-down beverage still appear as wine. And for the price-driven consumer whose wine experience defined the drink as a daily staple, the watered-down final product fit well into the family budget that typically devoted less than 3 percent to its purchase (Bottaro 1917; Galanti 1900, 1915).

Just as Mediterranean immigrants came to dominate Mendoza's industry and its principal markets of Buenos Aires and other large urban centers, so too did imported filters, manual pumps, and grape presses from Italy, France, and Spain became ubiquitous in the country's large wineries as early as the mid-1880s. In subsequent decades, the most prominent establishments added grape crushers, hydraulic presses, and pasteurizers from abroad to meet the exploding demand for wine. In the view of French traveler and wine expert Jules Huret, their impressive facilities more than rivaled some of Europe's best. In addition to ensuring rapid and massive production, the grandest establishments were able to show all that their "*sistemas modernísimas*" made them as up-to-date as any of their European counterparts (Huret and Gómez Carrillo 1913). For his part, prominent critic Pedro Arata deemed the considerable expenditure on imported equipment "an enormous waste," as it manufactured "the worst results of badly made wine." At the same time, he had to admit that "anyone who has visited the wineries of Mendoza will admire the luxury of the wine containers and sumptuousness of the buildings … Money, lots of money has been spent to store wine in these containers that cost like gold, that are gold in terms of their value" (Arata 1903, p. 202).

Whether for efficiency or for show, the National Winery Association in 1906 described the results of this process by boasting of the "great factories where enormous toneles (vats) sport their swollen bellies that release their precious juice, the dark juice from the vines that is poured out in a never-ending torrent of wealth and health ... this rich ocean of wine has a guaranteed destination; the coastal (Buenos Aires) markets are ours" (Anon. 1906, p. 565). The combination of up-to-date machinery and high demand led one of these factories, Bodega Tomba, to be dubbed the largest winery in the world. And Tomba's was apparently only one of several that on a single day produced as much wine as the most important winery of Spain made in a year. The contrast with Spain, and by extension with the rest of the Old World where small wineries were the norm, suggests that Argentina may indeed have been the originator of this class of wine factory (Richard-Jorba and Pérez Romagnoli 1994).

By the decade of the 1910s these establishments had ascended to near-total dominance of Argentina's wine scene. Largely immigrant-run wine factories had a key ally in creating a virtual production monopoly: the Argentine state at both the national and provincial levels. Emilio Civit, governor of Mendoza Province in 1909, summed up nicely the basic features of the government's relationship to the industry, using terms such as "protect," "defend," "stimulate," and "take care of" (Mateu 2002). That support included substantial tax incentives for the planting of vines and generous loans for winery equipment and construction.

Most important were laws promulgated at the national level that imposed high tariff barriers on imported wines to discourage foreign competition. Just as the Spanish Legate in Buenos Aires confidently predicted a year after the opening of rail communication that local wines would never challenge the dominance of the Mediterranean products (Fernandez 2008), Civit insisted that the government use import duties to "close domestic markets completely" to imports. Seconded by the industry, his suggestion was taken seriously; duties on imported wine increased from 40 percent to as high as 125 percent in the last quarter of the nineteenth century.

Recall that previously Argentina had been the world's third-largest importer of wines for the country's enormous and growing southern European immigrant population. Importers had benefited from the expanding consumer population and low international maritime freight rates that had declined precipitously over the nineteenth century (Pinilla and Ayuda 2002). Until the 1890s, wine was Argentina's single-largest imported product. Early on, France, Italy, and Spain were the major suppliers but, by the beginning of the 1880s, in part due to the effects of the phylloxera epidemic, Spain accounted for all but one-fifth of the trade. Nevertheless, with the tariff barrier in place, Figure 11.2 shows imports progressively diminished,

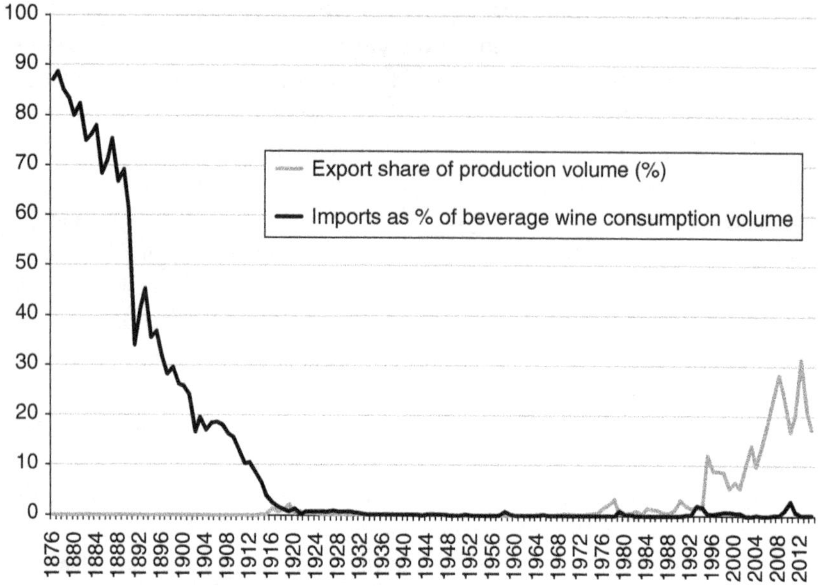

Figure 11.2 Share of wine consumption imported and of production exported, Argentina, 1876 to 2014 (%).
Source: Anderson and Pinilla (2017).

dropping from approximately 80 percent of wine consumed to just 1 percent by 1918 (Fernández 2004, 2008).

As Argentina's industry leaders increasingly saw themselves as "'dueños del mercado' (owners of the market) … confident of even greater protection in the future" (Civit 1887 p. 28), they established models of production that would last for a century. Contemporary expert A. N. Galante's summary of the early development of the industry succinctly summarized the situation: "given the form and goals of grape production, it was easy to have wine making established as a manufacturing activity and with almost assured success" (Galanti 1900, p. 94). While the uniformly poor quality of their wines precluded any pretensions of competing internationally, as long as Argentina's wine factories could manufacture at capacity for what was perceived as a continually expanding captive domestic market, they had no incentive to alter their practices or their standards.

THE CRISIS OF GROWTH, 1945 TO 1980

Increasing integration with Europe in the second half of the nineteenth century – demographically, culturally, technologically – had propelled wine in Argentina from meager artisanal production to the fifth largest in the world by 1915. Then ironically, it was the country's near-total isolation from the outside wine world, the result of the noncompetitive environment created by high tariffs that had virtually eliminated imports, that strongly influenced the path of winemaking in succeeding decades up to the waning years of the twentieth century. Yet while producers became largely inattentive to global wine developments, the country as a whole certainly was not. The Great Depression and World War II would have profound effects on Argentina, altering the content if not the pillars of its wine industry development model.

A decline in real income during the early years of the Depression led initially to a sharp drop in wine consumption, from 54 litres per capita in 1929 to 33 litres in 1932. Unable to sell to consumers suffering from the economic hardships of the times, wineries were left with large surpluses, generated in part by the 20,000 ha increase in vineyard lands during the 1920s. In reaction, the industry adopted several strategies to deal with the crisis. Growers began pulling up vines, and wineries cut back production, from 840 to 220 ML between 1929 and 1932. Later they went to the extreme of dumping "excess" wine into irrigation ditches.

These actions were supported by the Argentine state, continuing a practice of involvement in the wine economy that had begun in the 1880s with its protective tariffs. But this time limitation, not promotion, of production was the goal. Responding to the "collective desperation"[3] caused by a persistent reduction in demand, the government established the Junta Reguladora de Vinos in 1934. Its purpose was further elimination of vines and wines and regulation of prices. What had begun as the industry's response to market contraction became government policy.

By the end of the 1930s, these strategies appeared to have backfired. In the face of decreasing demand for exports and a reduced supply of imports, successive Argentine governments pursued policies of import-substituting industrialization. A major consequence was the substantial migration of rural Argentines to the country's growing industrial centers, particularly Buenos Aires, where they found employment and experienced growing incomes, part of which could be devoted to purchasing wine. So, as per capita consumption bounced back by the mid-1940s to 55 litres, surpassing pre-Depression levels, production lagged behind (Figure 11.3). The pressure on producers to satisfy a mounting demand for wine only increased after the election of populist politician Juan Domingo Perón in 1946. During

[3] The term "collective desperation" was published in *Los Andes*, 30 April 1945.

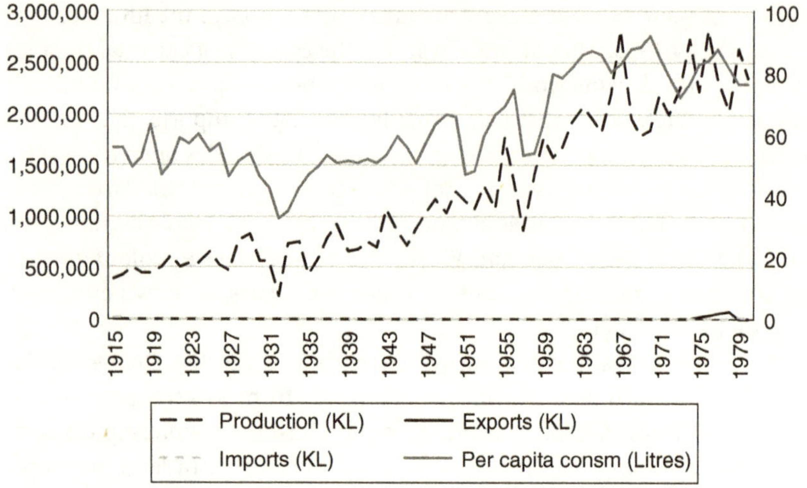

Figure 11.3 Volumes of wine production, exports and imports and per capita consumption, Argentina, 1915 to 1980 (KL [left axis] and litres per capita [right axis]).
Source: Anderson and Pinilla (2017).

the first two years of his presidency, with government policies supporting full employment and a significant redistribution of income that principally favored lower- and middle-class urban populations, workers' real wages rose nearly 70 percent.

Given the production slowdown years, aspiring drinkers ready to spend part of their added income on more wine were finding that often there was simply not enough to be had. It was then that Argentina's First Lady, Eva Perón, stepped in and promoted measures to ensure that all "her workers" had sufficient wine on the table. Reportedly exclaiming, "Caramba! What can we do? The only thing is to speak with the winery owners," the First Lady swiftly called a meeting with the heads of the country's largest firms; and she had a solution. Eva insisted that they add water. The result: the government promoted watering of the wine to increase supply. Concretely, wineries were required to add sufficient water to lower the alcohol content of their wines from the customary 13 percent down to 11 percent.[4]

Eva's watering fix was ultimately a short-term solution, as the demand for wine, measured by per capita consumption, continued to rise through most

4 The account of the meeting comes from one of the people present, Raúl De la Mota, and the industry's response was recounted by winery magnate Antonio Pulenta (interviews with the authors, August 2004).

the next two decades in Argentina. By 1949, it had grown to over 66 litres, a trend that overall continued to strengthen, reaching a historical highpoint of 92 litres in 1970 (Figure 11.3). During those years, succeeding Argentine governments, responding to pressures from their major political constituencies from the urban middle and lower classes, allied with producers and fostered a series of initiatives aimed at ensuring the availability of an ample supply of cheap wine. These were wines that, as leading producer Quinto Pulenta affirmed, even the poorest of Argentines could afford to "complement the daily diet in the great majority of our households" (Pulenta 1966, p. 9).

The first new measure to promote increases in production came in 1959; a law not only overturned a former prohibition of Criolla plantings, but encouraged their extensive use. Beginning in the 1960s, grape growers began pulling up those French vines that had helped launch the industry at the end of the nineteenth century, only to plant the very variety they had replaced a century earlier. While color, aromas, and taste were clearly not Criolla's strong points, the ability to grow on a variety of soils and its enormous output – producing three to four times more grapes per hectare than the prevailing Malbec – made it an arresting option. By the 1970s, Uva Criolla had once again became Argentina's dominant wine grape, greatly surpassing Malbec with fifteen times more vines. That some Malbec survived was only because the variety continued to exhibit its initial attraction: permitting heavily watered red wines to retain a recognizable level of color. As noted viticulturist Alberto Alcalde bitterly acknowledged, "Producers were desperately planting Criollas, and our excellent grapes were suffocated by those damned vines."[5]

In the following years, even more far-reaching laws provided massive tax incentives to encourage the expansion of wine production. Investors were able to deduct 100 percent of their total expenditures in new vineyards; agricultural machinery; delivery trucks; wells; irrigation equipment; fertilizers, fungicides and insecticides; winery buildings; and even houses for managers, workers, and their families. Added on was the 70 percent deducted from the amount of tax paid on profits. In some cases, these benefits reached 200 percent of total investments. Governments then further encouraged growth through the provision of credit at extremely low, fixed interest rates by state-run banks. Until the mid-1970s, large winemaking

[5] Alberto Alcalde (interview with the authors, August 2004). Industry leader Antonio Pulenta admitted that the only reason he kept a small number of Malbec vines was to ensure the acceptance of his inevitably watered red wines (interview with the authors, August 2004).

firms were the recipients of 80 to 90 percent of all loans made by government banks (Podestá 1982).[6]

An additional measure of state intervention in Argentina's wine economy was the government's acquisition of the country's largest winery, Bodegas y Viñedos Giol. Purchased originally in 1954, Giol's function was to regulate prices throughout the wine chain by purchasing and selling enormous volumes of grapes and wine. An important consequence of the Criolla and tax incentive legislation was the emergence of a large number of new firms that grew and purchased grapes, made wine, and then sold the product to large wineries for bottling and distribution. Most of Giol's purchases were from these "transfer wineries" (*bodegas trasladistas*). By the mid-1970s, the firm was processing 18 percent of all the wine in Mendoza, the country's largest production region, consequently building the largest wine storage facility in the world. While price control may have been its original purpose, Giol's activities largely served to stimulate further the expansion of wine supply (Olguin and Mellado 2010).

Together, these actions led the further massification of the Argentine wine industry. Grape land grew from 103,000 ha in 1943 to 250,000 thirty years later. Grape production expanded at an overall rate of 3.5 percent annually, and the amount of wine produced rose more than threefold in three decades (Figure 11.3). As a result, grapes per hectare yields became twice those of France and Italy, making Argentina the global leader in that category and vaulting the country to the position of the world's third-largest wine producer. Industry protagonists were filled with accolades for the region's Uva Criolla–driven record yields. Their official publication, *Vinos y viñas*, enthusiastically contrasted the "notable" achievement to the "comparatively inefficient European wine industry … unable to compete with Argentina's table wines." The Office of the Presidency of Argentina chimed in with praise for the wine sector that not only had been increasing the amount of vineyard land but moreover achieved much greater yields than European producers (Presidencia de la Nación 1970).

For wineries, speculation became the focus as they desperately planted more and more vineyards and produced more and more wine to reap

[6] The specific laws were 14.878, 11.682, 18.372, 18.905, 20.628, and 20.954. Why several governments fashioned these laws is a complex question. The supply shortages of the 1950s were behind an early industry push for the implementation of low-cost loans. But, by the mid-1960s and early 1970s, massive production had virtually overtaken demand, and even the industry itself was beginning to worry about a wine glut. Other possibilities included fomenting regional agricultural development or simply special interest politics and perhaps behind-the-scenes deals.

government benefits at the same time that sales increased. Profitability was clearly the order of the day, but the situation was not without snags. One was the inverse relationship between expanding production and declining profits per litre. Prices became depressed by an ever-growing supply and by government price controls designed to ensure the presence of abundant wine on everyone's table. A perennial complaint of industry leaders during the period was that they had made substantial investments – albeit most often tax-break induced – and these controls meant meager if any profits. So what did wine producers do to compensate? Generate ever-greater yields to reduce the per-litre cost. A vicious circle ensued as incentives abounded to produce ever more, ever lower-quality wine to increase sales and consequently profits.

A particularly revealing element of the wine panorama was the situation of so-called *vinos finos* that made up a paltry 3 percent of total volume. The near absence of those wines that would in later decades be at the apex of Argentina's prestigious international reputation resulted from a series of critical deterrents. Among these was the wine preferences of a market that had become used to the sweet, pink-colored Uva Criolla beverages, churned out by Argentina's mass producers to satisfy the so-called "*gusto argentino.*" Besides, the normal practice of adding ice and soda water ensured that all the underlying characteristics of the wine remained hidden. And in any case, the relative dryness and potential complexity of a fine Malbec or Cabernet Sauvignon simply did not meet the expectation of consumers who had been insulated for decades from the presence of any wines of similar style from abroad by Argentina's state-regulated, closed economy. As the owner of one of the country's largest wineries, Carlos Pulenta, explained, "All the big firms like ours (Peñaflor), as my father and his brothers did, grew with absolutely no competition from the outside."[7]

While wine isolation permitted the industry to sell their low-quality products within the country, it also closed off the opportunity for exports. From the early years of the late nineteenth century, international sales of Argentine wine were negligible at best, and in many years virtually nonexistent (Figure 11.3). Between 1900 and 1910, the latter was the case, as the highest export volume was 26 KL in 1904. Even in the years of highest production from the mid-1960s to the mid-1970s, exports never exceeded 11,000 KL, in most years topping out at under 3,000. The extraordinarily poor quality of the wine made for "the Argentine taste" clearly inhibited acceptance abroad. As industry magnate Quinto Pulenta pronounced,

[7] Interview with the authors, August 2003.

"We consider it utopian and almost infantile to expect to introduce fine wines abroad that could dislodge traditional European offerings" (Pulenta 1966, p. 10).

But there was another compelling factor that stopped the country's wineries for even seeking international sales: the confidence in a continually growing and thirsty domestic market. A 1966 editorial in the Wine Association's official publication, *Vinos, vinas y frutas*, directly related production increases to the expansion of demand, declaring that "the market is the synonym of the industry" (La hora de los mercados 1966, p. 281). And the numbers certainly seemed to support that view. In the mid-1940s, Argentina's per capita consumption stood at 55 litres; by 1970 it had reached its all-time high of 92. At 99 litres per capita, Buenos Aires roughly equaled Paris and Rome among the world's foremost wine drinking cities. This high level of consumption coincided with the recommendations of a member of the Argentine Wine Association's publication staff, who had laid out guidelines for daily drinking: for workers, between 0.75 and 1.5 litres; for employees and intellectuals, 0.75 litres; for all adults, at least 0.5 litres at each meal; and for children, according to their age, up to one glass of wine a day (Riveros 1954; Rodriguez 1973).

Banking on what appeared to be limitless expansion, Argentine winemakers had little incentive to attempt to sell poor-quality wines to a competitive external market. Rather, their perennial concern was to ensure that production kept pace with the growth of domestic consumption. The remarks of the head of the National Wine Institute's Economy and Development Department confidently supported the wine industry's nearly century-old inward-looking model. He boldly proclaimed in 1973 that Argentina continued to enjoy a uniform and limitless domestic market with "no indications that the post-war growth rate will change" (Rodriguez 1973, p. 39).

FROM CRISIS COMES REVOLUTION (FROM 1990)

Despite the optimism of industry and state actors, in word and deed, at the very the moment of this utterance, the country's century-old industry was about to enter into the greatest crisis of its history. Between the late 1940s and the early 1980s, what had incentivized expanding production had also disincentivized the making of good wine. While during its first century, quality had never been a serious priority of the industry, the effect of the government's promotion of *quantity* propelled a marked *quality decrease* during 1950–80. Additionally, the state's maintenance of tariff barriers continued to isolate consumers and producers alike from wines that could have threatened the model. But by the end of the 1970s, the overproduction of mediocre wine finally impelled people to question what they were drinking. The result was the most profound crisis in the industry's history, prompted most significantly by a two-thirds plunge in consumption over the next twenty years.

From the mid-1960s on, many observers inside and outside of the industry began to caution strenuously about an impending calamity, recognizing problems for the continuity of the supply/demand equilibrium. Citing transitory crises in 1962–63 and particularly in 1967–68, when a record-breaking harvest produced significantly more wine than consumers were ready to drink, they warned that the traditional model could not be sustained, as population and per capita income growth were notably lagging far behind rising wine production. The International Organization of Vine and Wine (OIV), the world's most influential of outside observers, shared their alarm, pronouncing in 1974 that the balance between production and consumption had been definitively shattered in Argentina (Martínez and Perone 1974). Concern was becoming commonplace even in the wine industry's official publication, where, by the late 1960s, numerous articles and editorials cautioned that "the providential equilibrium of our industry is now seriously endangered by overproduction" ("La hora de unirse," 1967, p. 477). These expressions of alarm were not exaggerated; before the end of the next decade, 75 to 80 percent of all wine made in Argentina remained unsold.

Why did wineries fail to heed the clear signs that the industry's traditional model was on the edge of a crash? For the answer, one only needs to remember the driving forces of the recent past: those tax breaks and credit incentives that made the making and selling wine largely peripheral to core business objectives of maximizing profits through government perks. Irrespective of those enticements, or indeed because of them, Argentina's wine economy entered a full-blown collapse in 1980. That collapse is clearly revealed by the precipitous decline in both domestic wine prices and consumption beginning in 1970. From that year through 1982, the nominal price shrunk nearly 75 percent, some 10 pesos per litre to 2.5 pesos. In the same period, consumption dropped 23 percent, from 92 to 71 litres per capita, a trend that would continue in successive years, reaching a low point of 20 litres in 2014 (Figures 11.4 and 11.5).

The fact that these phenomena occurred simultaneously may seem a contradiction. Yet a more detailed analysis of the situation explains this apparent incongruity. The explanation of the drop in wine price is quite straightforward. Winegrowers had continued for years to raise output in

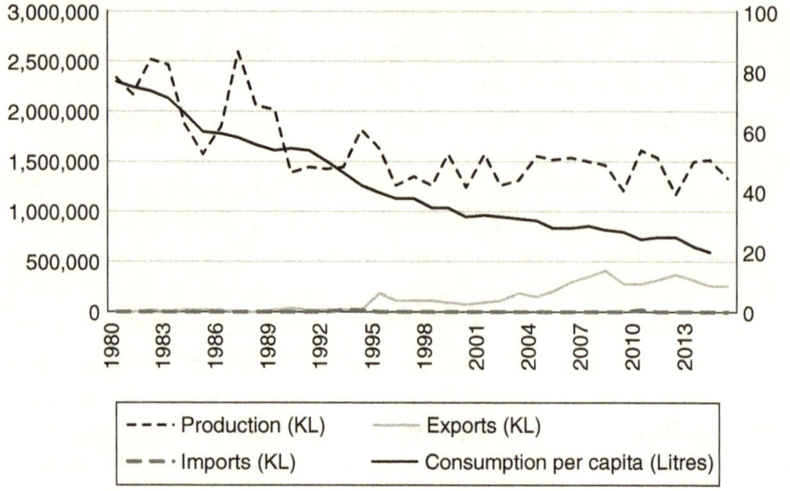

Figure 11.4 Volumes of wine production, exports and imports, and per capita consumption, Argentina, 1980 to 2015 (KL on left axis and litres per capita on right axis).
Source: Anderson and Pinilla (2017).

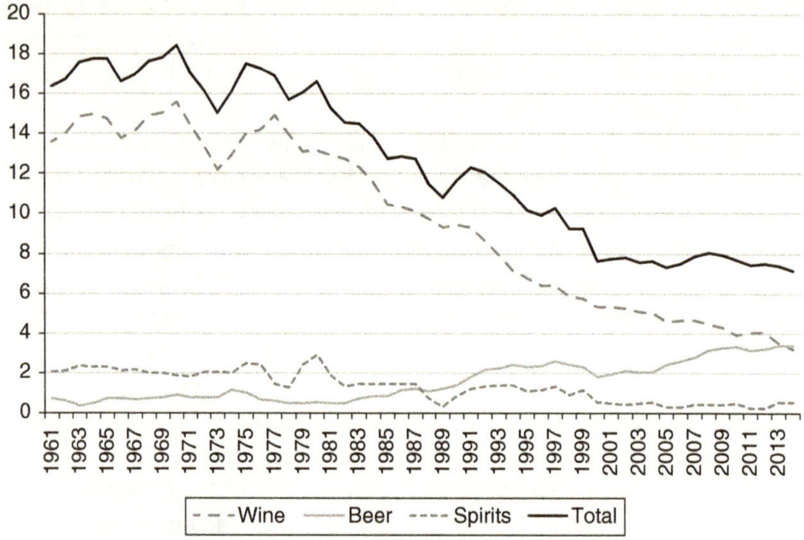

Figure 11.5 Per capita consumption of wine, beer, and spirits, Argentina, 1961 to 2014 (litres of alcohol).
Source: Anderson and Pinilla (2017).

the face of a stagnant market, and production excesses inevitably led to price decreases. But what about the fact that people were drinking less and less wine while prices were trending downward? Argentina's consumption decline paralleled in some ways that process in Europe's traditional wine-drinking countries, although it began a decade later and presented several distinctive features. Important early on was the reduction in real income during the military government (1976–83), particularly for working- and middle-class Argentines who traditionally bought the most wine. Then, in the following years, would-be consumers faced nearly world-record hyper-inflation, never knowing how much less their pesos would buy from one day to the next. Simultaneously, city dwellers' mealtime habits were undergoing an important change as the traditional early afternoon main repast at home – accompanied by abundant wine and followed by a siesta – was being displaced by the *horario corrido*, an eight-hour workday with a short lunch break. Raúl de la Mota neatly summarized the effects: "A meal disappeared, and with it came the disappearance of a major component of that family meal: wine. A person who works straight through could not drink wine, because wine put him to sleep."[8]

During the same period, alternative beverages progressively began to dislodge wine from the Argentine diet, at lunch and afterward, and low-alcohol content may very well have been a reason for their increasing popularity. The liberalizing of trade by the military and subsequent governments opened the door to soft drinks. Introduced with well-financed promotional campaigns, they rapidly grew in acceptance along with bottled water and lower-alcohol beer. By 1982, soda consumption matched that of wine, surpassing it in 1985 and thereafter. So alcohol content and public relations were certainly significant factors. As well, given the extremely low price of wine, another factor was almost certainly the precipitous decline in quality over the previous two decades. For many, reliable sodas, beers, and bottled waters may simply have been a better choice than the "insipid," "sickly sweet" liquid found in most wine glasses of the period.

As wine consumption began its sharp decline, the impact on vineyards and wineries was dramatic. While initially some upped their production as a means of survival, the biggest crisis in the industry's 100-year history quickly led to drastic cutbacks. As the decade of the 1980s progressed, over one-third of the establishments went bankrupt and were abandoned. Small and middle-sized wineries were particularly vulnerable during those years. Those that simply could not afford to update and upgrade for the

[8] Interview with the authors, August 2005.

most part closed their doors. It was the larger, better capitalized firms that survived. Simultaneously, vast acres of vineyards were eradicated to make room for other projects, particularly urban and suburban development. And not just the Uva Criolla vines that had boomed over the past two decades were removed: Malbec, the grape that would eventually become the emblem of Argentina's wine resurgence, was almost wiped out, declining from 50,000 ha in 1970 to only 10,000 in 1990. Still, Malbec fared better than other fine varietals. Cabernet Sauvignon was reduced to 3,500 ha, Merlot to 1,000, and Chardonnay to a mere 80 ha (Aspiazu and Basualdo 2003; Merino 2004).

At a moment when the very viability of the industry was threatened, a small number of forward-looking industry leaders warned that survival depended on achieving profound and fundamental changes. Led by Nicolás Catena Zapata, one of the few winery owners who survived the crisis with all his resources intact, producers began in the late 1980s a process that would become known as the "*reconversión*" of the Argentine wine industry. The three bedrocks of that process were (1) the pursuit of international consumers, given the contraction of local consumer demand; (2) the reorientation of production for wines that could attain sufficient quality to compete internationally; and (3) the introduction of sweeping upgrades of technology and know-how in the winery and in the vineyard, focused on quality improvement. In short, the goal of Argentina's wine revolution was quality improvement.[9] That goal was achieved by a thorough restructuring of winery and vineyard practices; and the incentive, as well as the blueprint, was the move toward exports.

During the 1990s, more and more industry leaders had been insisting that the guiding principle could no longer be quantity for a captive domestic market, but rather quality wines with international consumers as the target. The consensus that international markets constituted the salvation of the industry was reflected in the boldly presented title of a 1999 article in the Wine Association magazine: "Adapt the product TO THE TASTE OF THE INTERNATIONAL CONSUMER." What had become an industry cant was repeated once more in 2004 by Angel Vespa, the director of the Wine Industry Association: "The Argentine wine sector faces a great mission: to consolidate its position as a trusted supplier of wines to broad

[9] Upgrades in Argentina paralleled similar trends throughout the wine world, old and new, from the Super Tuscan movement in Italy to California's varietal focus. These phenomena have been an intrinsic element of agricultural development given modern globalization's stress on quality and distinctiveness.

international markets" (Bodegas & terruños 1999, pp. 18–19, emphasis in the original; Vespa, 2004, p. 11).

While it was only in the 1990s that the prospects of export growth gained precedence, Argentina was hardly starting from scratch. The country had a century-old wine industry with numerous established vineyards, a legion of wineries of all sizes and shapes, and an enormous amount of accumulated experience from laborers in the vineyards to high-level managers in the wineries. While in all these areas it was crucial to upgrade to achieve internationally competitive wines, the country's long tradition of wine production provided a valuable foundation on which to build. Also, conditioned by a perennial "culture of crisis," Argentines had learned throughout their history to maneuver in order to lose the least or to make the most of an uncertain environment. This led to the emergence of a parallel "culture of agility," clearly evident in the decision-making of major protagonists of the reconverted industry. Their strategies benefited from considerable flexibility of appropriate terroirs in a country with the largest extension of vineyard lands in the world, spanning over 1,700 kilometres from north to south that together offer a wealth of temperature variations and altitudes. Consequently, Argentines have had many more options than most of their Old World counterparts and even than their Chilean neighbors, whose vineyards are located in a much more Mediterranean-like region. And given the virtual absence of regulatory constraints for making their wines, Argentine producers have been free to grow their grapes and craft and sell their wines in accord with what they deem most important for types, quality, and market preferences.[10]

The decision to "reconvert" came at a moment as rare as it was lucky in Argentine history: economic stability coincided with the availability of substantial financial resources to accomplish the task. Just at the time when eventual export leaders were beginning to make the decision to upgrade, macroeconomic circumstances in Argentina favored an enormous influx of private investment. Beginning in the 1990s as part of its deregulation of the economy, the government of Carlos Menem (1989–99) eliminated rules limiting foreign investment, liberalized the currency exchange market, ended export duties, and eased restrictions on imports, specifically of those capital goods and services that were essential to the industry's upgrading ventures. Also, low inflation and a mandated dollar-peso parity exchange rate

[10] State regulations that do exist include dates for the end of harvest, a minimal time for the release of new wines, and the minimum percentage of alcohol for the product to be considered wine.

helped create a stable environment – with fixed domestic costs – attractive to potential investors. Under these conditions, foreign banks in particular were eager to lend and became quite aggressive at making low-interest, long-term loans to wine entrepreneurs.

The overvalued Argentine currency made the prices of imports of key equipment exceedingly attractive. Surprisingly, the strong peso did not prevent land and labor costs in the country from remaining cheap. Excellent vineyard land in Mendoza sold for half of what it would cost in Chile, one-third of the price of Australia, and one-tenth the value in Napa or France.

The investment in the Argentine industry during the heart of the *reconversión* was truly staggering. Between 1991 and 2001 alone, it totaled an estimated $1 billion from abroad and $500 million locally. The importance placed on building exports is clear: 70 percent of investments went to fund production for the international market (Aspiazu and Basualdo 2000; Wehring 2006; Merino 2007).

The industry used the strong peso to buy top-quality imported vine stock, cutting-edge winery equipment, and the world's most prestigious flying consultants. In addition to importing Quality A clones, largely from France and Italy, investments in local nurseries provided an accessible supply of vines adapted to local conditions. Vineyards also benefited, progressively changing over from flood to drip irrigation. For the wineries, technological innovations meant importing a broad variety of equipment that had previously been absent in the Argentine industry, including small oak barrels, stainless steel fermentation and storage tanks, bladder presses, destemmers, and bottling equipment.

One of the most significant technological innovations was the incorporation of modern cooling systems. Catena, for example, was the first to construct a large cold chamber for the low-temperature fermentation of white wines. By the end of the 1990s, forty to fifty Argentine wineries had upgraded nearly all their equipment, bringing their technology up to a level that matched their most advanced peers anywhere on the globe. As international wine consultant Sophie Jump pronounced in 2006, "Most of them have got facilities that the French would die for."[11]

With its new equipment, the industry had taken vital steps on the road to internationally competitive wines. Nevertheless, a major obstacle

[11] Sophie Jump quoted by Wehring (2006, p. 25). On the level and pace of the technological advance in general, see Aspiazu and Basualdo (2000, 2003). Also informative were interviews by the authors with Angel Mendoza (June 2005), Paul Hobbs (August 2004), Jeff Mausbach, Ceclia Razquin, Leandro Juárez, José Galante, Francisco Martinez, and Eduardo López (August 2003).

remained: the lack of enological know-how. This was overcome through genuine improvements in enologists' training. Within Argentina, the industry's increasing demand for trained experts produced the exponential growth of regional university programs and graduates. But the most visible development came from the outside. New investments in the industry underwrote travel abroad for local winemakers for learning trips to prominent wineries as well as for formal study programs. As well, prestigious wine professionals came to Argentina to guide innovation. Consulting was not limited to the production area; it extended also to marketing and branding.

By the end of the 1990s, those "recoverted" Argentine wineries that were ready to take up the export challenge nevertheless found themselves at a distinct disadvantage versus international rivals. The same overvalued currency that had subsidized the transformation of the industry made it difficult to compete on price against wines from other world regions. This situation changed radically in 2001 when the country suffered one of the worst economic crises in its modern history. Poverty reached unimaginable levels for many Argentines, cutting deeply into the middle and working classes. But an attendant effect of the crisis was the breaking of the peso-dollar parity system; at the end of 2001, the peso devalued by two-thirds from its one-to-one parity with the dollar. For the Argentine wine industry, the change in currency value could not have come at a better time. Having acquired state-of-the-art equipment and know-how with the strong peso, after 2002 industry leaders were able to take advantage of a vastly weaker currency and low and declining land and labor costs to place their wines among the world's leaders in terms of a price/quality ratio.

During the first decade of the twenty-first century, Argentina's exchange rates, three to four times more advantageous than those of major export competitors, including France, Italy, Spain, and Australia, made it the most competitive producer in the wine world. As Luis Steindl, the CEO of Mendoza's Bodega Norton, explained in 2007: "You can get the same quality (of wine) as other areas, and the direct cost of production is probably one-quarter of what it'd be in the United States and even less that what it would be in France." In the unvarnished verdict of wine entrepreneur Michael Evans, "You can make better wine here for less money than anywhere else in the world." Journalist David J. Lynch's conclusion is particularly telling, even if only part of the story: "It is not complex noses or poignant bouquets that explain Argentina's recent emergence in global wine markets, notably including the United States. It's basic economics" (Lynch 2007). Javier Merino of Area del Vino is even more emphatic, affirming that "without the advantage of a competitive exchange rate the "miracle" of Argentine wine would not have been possible" (Wasilevsky 2013b).

The significance of the currency advantage is clearly reflected in the take-off of Argentina's wine exports after 2001. While in 2001 they had totaled just over 88,000 KL, by 2007 they had risen to 414,000, growing at an annual 22 percent, four times the rate of growth of global wine exports for the same period and double that of Australia, Chile, and Spain. Their importance for the industry is clear, as international sales outpaced wine production, rising markedly in years when production was flat and even declining (Figure 11.4). In Argentina's foremost market, the United States, the extent of that rise is particularly striking: in 2002, imports of Argentine wine made up only 1.4 percent of total US imports while by 2009 that had expanded to 6.2 percent, vaulting them from ninth to fifth place in that category.

When considering the price/value ratio, value has been the more important component. That Argentine wineries were not principally driven to produce a low-priced product is clear when considering that between 2003 and 2010, the average price of their exported wines increased from 88 cents per litre to $2.67 (Merino and Estrella 2010; Merino 2015). The success of this strategy is particularly impressive when observing the evolution of the unit value of Argentine wines since the beginning of the country's wine revolution versus those of their most important competitors, New and Old World. Between 1995 and 2015, Argentina's unit value increased by 565 percent as compared to Chile's 21 percent rise and declines of 4 percent in Australia and 16 percent in Spain (Figure 11.6).

The low costs, relatively weak peso plus the quality leap that clearly facilitated the growth of exports became particularly significant in the years of the international financial downturn from 2008. As wine expert Jay Miller explained in 2009, "During economic crises people in the United States (Argentina's strongest export market) don't drink less, they drink more, but they drink cheaper, they buy less-expensive wines and that goes well for Argentinean wines …" (McIntyre 2009). Indeed, between 2008 and 2009, Argentina was the only winegrowing region in the world whose wine was being consumed more than in the previous year.

While their medium-priced wines may have been leaders in the price/quality ratio battles, the Argentines did not overlook the higher-level products. Aware of the impact of icon wines on the brand recognition of individual wineries and on the reputation of Brand Argentina as a whole, various winemakers dedicated considerable effort to producing bottlings that could both garner top awards at international wine competitions and the praise of influential critics from Robert Parker on down. Selling for up

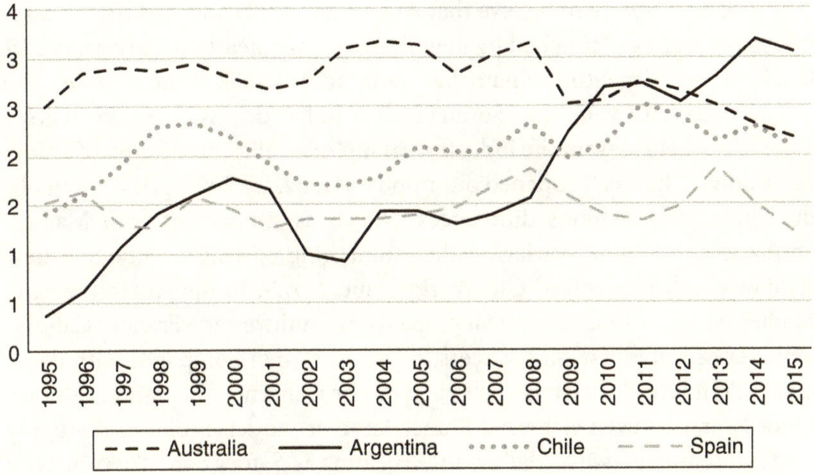

Figure 11.6 Unit value of wine exports, Argentina, Australia, Chile, and Spain, 1995 to 2015 (US$/litre).
Source: Anderson and Pinilla (2017).

to US$200, they embrace a variety of practices involving vineyard management and wine making, including planting at increasingly higher altitudes, relying on vines between forty and eighty years old in traditional vineyards, highly controlled pruning and canopy management, the selection of the best bunches at harvest, manual separation of the grapes on special sorting tables, the use of special yeasts for fermentation, and storage in new French oak barrels for extended periods. The results are reflected quantitatively in the increasingly high point scores garnered in prestigious publications such as *The Wine Advocate*, *The Wine Spectator*, and *The Wine Enthusiast*. Likewise, Argentina's top wines have enjoyed success at numerous award competitions. At the Brussels World Wine Championship in 2009, an Argentine bottling was declared the best red wine in the world. Two years later at the 2011 Decanter World Wine Awards in London, Argentina won more International Trophies than any other country since the beginning of the competition in 2004.[12]

[12] The ratings of Argentine wines jumped impressively over the course of the industry's *reconversion* and afterward. In 1993, for example, the maximum attained in *The Wine Spectator* was eighty-nine points; in 2006, it had risen to ninety-five points. For *The Wine Enthusiast*, the highest mark in 1996 was eighty-seven points; in 2007, it garnered ninety-four points. In subsequent years, top bottlings have consistently scored in the mid-nineties. Perhaps the crowning achievements came from Robert Parker's *Wine Advocate* that accorded ninety-nine ratings on two Malbecs, first in 2009 (Viña Cobos Malbec Marchiori Vineyard 2006), and then in 2011 (Achaval Ferrer Finca Altamira La Consulta 2009).

It is commonplace to believe that Argentina simply adopted the successful export strategy launched by neighboring Chile nearly twenty years earlier. However, Argentine winemakers point to Australia as their model. The highly successful wine duo Susana Balbo and Pedro Marchevsky echoed that widely held view in the industry, calling Australia's promotion of Shiraz "a paradigm that really opened our minds" (González 2004, p. 43). Actually, the Shiraz case exhibits differences as well as similarities with Malbec. Shiraz is not a "new" variety, rather something of a new name and new style of a well-recognized Old World grape, Syrah. In the Argentine case, Malbec was an almost unknown grape from southwestern France (Cahors) with very limited use and success, especially when compared with other major French red varietals such as Syrah or Cabernet Sauvignon, Merlot, Pinot Noir, and even Cabernet Franc. Another model similar and roughly contemporaneous with Malbec in Argentina is Sauvignon Blanc in New Zealand. But once again, it follows more closely the Australian case with the promotion of an already established and greatly successful variety in France that has seen somewhat less successful in other New World regions such as California.

That the emphasis on Malbec was a conscious strategy decision is best explained by leading winemaker Angel Mendoza. Seeing Australia's success with Shiraz in the early 2000s, he and his peers worked to establish Malbec as Argentina's signature grape, intent on making wine with similar characteristics. "We identified our challenge at all the wine fairs. We tasted Australian wine, and we said: 'We have to change. If we want to adopt that model, we have to change.' We winemakers would go from stand to stand tasting and we would say, 'Look at the fruit, look at the color, look, this is the expression of the way wine should be made.' "[13] Winery executive Sofía Pescarmona summed up the industry's faith in the variety: "No-one else has Malbec like us. As new as it is distinctive, Argentina's Malbec has successfully attracted that growing international market which seeks diverse wine experiences" (Meads 2004).

As Argentina's export leader, Malbec has accounted for over 50 percent of its international sales. Over the ten-year period between 2006 and 2015, international sales of the country's signature grape rose from 30 ML valued

[13] Angel Mendoza (interview with the authors, June 2005). Argentina may not have copied Chile's strategy, but the success of Malbec in the creation of Argentina's international identity has not been lost to its trans-Andean neighbor. Chile has tried to market Carmenere as its own unique contribution to wine consumers just as South Africa has attempted to establish an identity with Pinotage.

at $100 million to 134 ML at $500 million. In 2009 alone, those sales in the United States jumped 60 percent, making it the fastest-growing variety in Argentina's preeminent market (Blondel 2016). Not surprisingly, a major reason for its ascendance was that large numbers of consumers identified Malbec as their "top value choice," a clear indication of the industry's ability to price an attractive wine competitively. But price/quality ratio and distinctiveness are not the only elements of the variety's export success. The descriptors of Malbec, expressed in the wine press and by consumers, explain its popularity: "Malbec is popular in part because it offers a nice combination of fruit and structure without being overly challenging …," and "Malbec is soft and easy to drink, thanks to its approachable, juicy, fruit-driven profile, along with a multitude of bottlings for $15 or less." This wine merchant summed up nicely the various elements of the wine's particular appeal: "I can sell Malbec all day long. People just can't get enough of it. They just love the layers of ripe fruit and spice on the finish. And there's plenty of it, so most of it is pretty cheap" (Hobbs 2009; McIntyre 2009; Saieg 2010; Whitley 2010).

Notwithstanding these successes, Malbec's ascendance was neither always clear nor easy. As late as 2000, the variety continued to be considered by most winemakers as less promising than Cabernet Sauvignon, Syrah, and even the scarcely planted Pinot Noir. What was worse, still in 2000 Malbec vines were being pulled out to make way for new highways and housing developments. Despite continuing to be the most widely planted fine wine red grape, many resisted making it Argentina's emblematic wine. Even industry leader Nicolás Catena initially overlooked Malbec, instead choosing the most established French varieties for his first premium wines: Chardonnay and Cabernet Sauvignon. After all, he explained in 1995, "the international criteria of quality … are defined by the best French wines. The most expensive wines of Bordeaux and Burgundy have won that privilege" (Foster 1995).

Catena's reticence about Malbec did not last, as in succeeding years Malbec became the driving force for international success and has continued to grow in its proportion of vineyard land, rising from 10.5 percent in 2006 to 17 percent in 2015. Already in 2004, the variety received an enormous boost from influential critic Robert Parker's pronouncement that it had attained "startling heights in quality" and his accompanying prediction – among the twelve he made for the following decade – that Malbec would ascend "into the pantheon of noble wines." Soon the country's top wineries, including Catena, would begin to proudly stage expert tastings of their best Malbec bottlings at international wine shows including Bordeaux's prestigious Vinexpo (Parker 2004).

Ironically, a key element of the Argentina's wine revolution, particularly in the new millennium, has been the continued presence of a large, if diminished, number of local consumers. True, the high levels of consumption of 90+ litres per capita had long become a faint memory, and their precipitous fall was clearly a driving force behind the resolve to export. Yet even with the dip to 25 litres per capita, Argentina remained the world's fifth-largest wine-consuming country. Indeed, the emphasis on exports tends to cloud an important reality: in the midst of the export boom, domestic consumption continues to be consequential. The national market still drinks 77 percent of all wines produced. Additionally, of the approximately 1,300 wineries in Argentina, 20 percent are involved internationally, and of that number a mere twenty account for 60 percent of exports. In short, the domestic market has continued to occupy an important place in the calculations of the country's wine industry. Awareness of the sustained weight of the domestic market is shared by all major Argentine producers. The presence of this still large and even growing wine-drinking public within Argentina facilitates making tough decisions in terms of investment and restructuring for export growth. Paradoxically, it is the substantial number of domestic consumers that has permitted producers to take relatively large risks in the export area because they have a strong backup within their own country (INV 2016).

A distinct shift in the taste preferences of Argentine wine drinkers has paralleled export strategies. As lower-income groups shifted away from wine toward beer and soft drinks, wealthier and middle-class consumers, many of whom spent their country's strong national currency in the 1990s on international travel, began to insist on wines that tasted "as good as" those they found abroad. An overvalued peso also boosted, for the first time in nearly 100 years, the importation of European and California wines, some of which became taste setters. So, just as overall consumption was dropping in Argentina, the demand for locally produced, export-modeled premium wines was increasing; overall, the 10 percent annual decline in sales of lower-priced wines was matched by 10 percent increase for those very superpremium bottlings aimed at the international market. José Alberto Zuccardi, owner of Bodega Familia Zuccardi, one of the country's most successful export wineries, explains these important complementarities. "We started to export in 1991. At that moment we were aware that the greatest growth would happen abroad, but that didn't mean that we weren't going to take care of the internal market. On the contrary, we learned many things abroad that we applied here, as much about taste as about design and packaging" (Martinez 2006).

ARGENTINE WINE FUTURES

Beginning in the 1990s, the Argentine wine industry underwent a veritable revolution, from the thorough upgrading of vineyards and many wineries to a dramatic improvement in the quality of its products. A major influence on these developments was the decisive shift in emphasis from domestic consumers to export markets. For an entire century after its founding in the 1880s, the wine industry formulated its business plans based on the perception of an undifferentiated mass of local consumers. In contrast, recent years have witnessed the agile responses of the country's leading firms to the challenges of new markets, domestic as well as international, proving themselves sensitive to a multiplicity of consumer segments. But will the Argentine wine industry be able to confront the future challenges of an ever-changing panorama with the same agility? In answer, it is worth briefly outlining the major issues that will shape the future of Argentine wine and discovering what major industry actors are thinking. This concluding discussion focuses on three principal recent challenges for the sector: the impact of government macroeconomic policies, particularly in terms of inflation and currency value on industry profitability; the search for new international markets; and efforts to maintain if not increase the popularity of Argentina's wines by seeking diversity while continuing to boost quality.

After 2002, the highly favorable price/quality ratio of Argentine wine was certainly a crucial component of export success. But the hard-fought gains of competitively priced Argentine wines that helped make them so sought after during the recession years began, in 2011, to reverse direction. The devaluation of the peso at a rate of approximately 20 percent a year placed Argentina last among major wine-exporting countries with respect to currency expense. Also, devaluation was failing to keep pace with a growing inflation rate of 25 to 30 percent, making the maintenance of a highly competitive price/quality ratio increasingly difficult. The wine industry noticeably suffered as the costs of production – from labor to grapes to energy prices – roughly doubled between 2009 and 2013.

There are several indicators of the sector's pain: between 2011 and 2015, the level of competitiveness internationally and domestically for Argentine wines is estimated to have dropped 40 percent; at the same time, overall wine industry profits descended from 6.4 to 0.8 percent between 2011 and 2014; and for Argentina's emblematic Malbec, the level of profits per hectare of plantings declined from 52 percent in 2011 to just 4 percent in 2014. To stay above water, wineries found it necessary to increase prices. The result was that after a period of remarkable growth, in succeeding years the bottled wine export trend reversed direction, declining by 2,000 KL between 2010 and 2014 as consumers in the principal international markets continued to exhibit the very price sensitivity that had helped underpin earlier success (Aznar 2013; Veseth 2013; Merino 2015; INV 2016).

Despite strong lobbying efforts, the government's reticence to devalue in the face of persistent inflation kept Argentina's wine industry on the defensive. But with the election of a first executive more favorable to a free-market approach, a new resurgence appears to be on the horizon. Within a week of his inauguration in December 2015, President Mauricio Macri launched policies designed to stimulate export growth, specifically in agriculture. For the wine industry, a sharp peso devaluation has been the most significant measure that portends the recuperation of the profitability levels and international competitiveness that had evaded the industry during 2011–2015.

Even before the difficult post-2011 years, the most important internationally oriented wineries began to seek new markets beyond those they had established in North America and Europe, focusing particularly on Asia. As early as 2003, Nicolás Catena and others were researching the region as an important destination for exports. In 2011, for example, the country's most important winery association, Wines of Argentina, opened a China office in Beijing with the goal of attaining "a solid presence in the market within five years." General Manager Mario Giordano explained that the office would "assist, advise and help Argentine wineries to sell their wines in a market that cannot be compared to any other in terms of its complexity and cultural and logistical barriers" (Wines of Argentina 2011). To this end, the office organized Asian tours for Argentina's top wineries, with stops in Beijing, Guangzhou, Hong Kong, Taipei, Singapore, and Seoul. Measures of the success of this and similar endeavors include the following: the number of wineries exporting to China expanded from six in 2002 to seventy-two in 2013; between 2014 and 2015, shipments to China showed the greatest growth in value with a rise of 38 percent while in the same period Argentina's largest export market, the United States, rose only 1 percent; and Malbec became the first choice among China's new wine consumers (Wasilevsky 2013a, b; Observatorio Vitivinicula 2015).

The third element of the most recent evolution of wine in Argentina is the search for diversity with the development of new subregions, new approaches to terroir, and new winegrape varieties. When referring to the massive transformations of the sector beginning in the 1990s, the term "wine revolution" is an appropriate descriptor. But looking more closely at the process, indeed three revolutions have taken place. The first, which extended approximately from 1990–2000, was the upgrade of winery technology, enological, and viticultural know-how and the replacement of Uva Criolla with

French varieties. The second revolution from 2000 to 2012 saw the positioning of Malbec as Argentina's emblematic variety, as export leaders began to offer a broad range of diverse Malbecs at numerous price points, from entry level to iconic. Simultaneously, producers elected to cut yields by 30 percent or more and explore new vineyard locations in the quest to continue upgrading quality. Two of the most-favored directions in that search involved moving upward to higher elevations and moving outward from historic to newer grape-growing areas. The new-found popularity of the Uco Valley and surroundings in Mendoza and Cafayate in northern Salta are prime examples that combine both tendencies. Crucial to these endeavors was the introduction of drip irrigation, which permitted the exploration of areas where water was scarce and where sharp slopes limited the use of sprinklers in regions that had previously been considered problematical for winegrape growing.

Amid the down years of high inflation and an overvalued currency, a third wine revolution emerged as wineries, from large and established to boutique, began experimenting with specific microclimates for single-vineyard and even single-parcel plantings. As they investigated the effects of cooler, drier high elevations, some enologists and viticulturists began going further, analyzing the complexity of the soils. *New York Times* wine writer Eric Asimov describes one such single parcel area in the Uco Valley. Looking at so-called test pits, he explained that: "It revealed layers of pale beige limestone soil interspersed with large, smooth white rocks. Nearby was another pit, but the soil was completely different: chalky limestone infused with nothing larger than pebbles. Across the row was yet another pit, with no limestone, just loamy loess." Just as "the soils change radically from one row of vines to the next, sometimes over a matter of meters … wine produced from each of these soils are just as different" (Asimov 2016). The goal of this research is to attain a range of options for Malbec and at the same time introduce new varietals that express particularly well in these environments. Prime examples are the growing bottlings of distinctive Cabernet Francs and Bonardas in Mendoza, Pinot Noir in Patagonia, and Torrontés in Cafayate. As Argentine wine critic Giorgio Benedetti recently affirmed, "Finally terroir has triumphed" (Michellini 2014, p. 120).

REFERENCES

Anderson, K. and V. Pinilla (with the assistance of A. J. Holmes) (2017), *Annual Database of Global Wine Markets, 1835 to 2016*, freely available in Excel files at the University of Adelaide's Wine Economics Research Centre, www.adelaide.edu.au/wine-econ/databases

Anon. (1906), *Boletín del Centro Viti-Vinícola Nacional*, July.
Arata, P. (1903), *Investigación vinícola: Informes presentados al Ministro de Agricultura por la Comisión Nacional*, Buenos Aires: Talleres de Publicaciones de la Oficina Meteorológica Argentina.
Asimov, E. (2016), 'To Move Beyond Malbec, Look Below the Surface', available at: www.nytimes.com/2016/02/17/dining/malbec-mendoza-wine.html?emc=edit_tnt_20160211&nlid=60380288&tntemail0=y (accessed 17 February 2016).
Aspiazu, D. and E. Basualdo (2000), *El complejo vitivinícola argentino en los noventa: potencialidades y restricciones*, Buenos Aires: CEPAL.
(2003), *Estudios sectoriales. Componente: industria vitivinícola*, Buenos Aires: CEPAL-ONU.
Aznar, M. (2013), 'Exports of Wine in Bottle Surged by 5%', available at: www.winesur.com/top-news/export-turnover-surged-by-4-in-the-first-four-months-of-2013 (accessed 11 June 2015).
Barrio, P. (2010), *Hacer vino*, Rosario: Prohistoria Ediciones.
Blondel, G. (2016), 'El vino argentino', available at: www.cartafinanciera.com/pymes/el-vino-argentino?utm_source=newsletter (accessed 15 May 2016).
Bottaro, S. (1917), *La industria vitivinícola entre nosotros*, Buenos Aires: Universidad de Buenos Aires, Facultad de Ciencias Económicas.
Bunge, A. (1929), *Informe del Ing. Alejandro E. Bunge sobre el problema vitivinícola*, Buenos Aires: Cía. impresora argentina, s.a.
Civit, E. (1887), *Los viñedos de Francia y los de Mendoza*, Mendoza: Tip. Los Andes.
Fernández, A. (2004), *Un 'mercado étnico' en el Plata*, Madrid: Consejo Superior de Investigaciones Científicas.
(2008), 'Los importadores españoles, el comercio de vinos y las trasformaciones en el mercado entre 1880 y 1930', pp. 129–40 in *El vino y sus revoluciones: Una antología histórica sobre el desarrollo de la industria vitivinícola argentina*, 1st edition, edited by A. Mateu and S. Stein, Mendoza: EDIUNC.
Foster, D. (1995), *Revolución en el mundo de los vinos*, Buenos Aires: Ennio Ayosa Impresores.
Galanti, A. (1900), *La industria vitivinícola argentina*, Buenos Aires: Talleres S. Ostwald.
(1915), *Estudio crítico sobre la cuestión vitivinícola: Estudios y pronósticos de otros tiempos*, Buenos Aires: Talleres Gráficos de Juan Perrotti.
González, M. (2004), 'Bodega Dominio del Plata: Dos sueños, dos estilos, una familia', *Vinos y viñas*, April: 900.
Hanaway, N. (2014), 'Wine Country: The Vineyard as National Space in Nineteenth Century Argentina', pp. 89–103 in *Alcohol in Latin America: A Social and Cultural History*, 1st edition, edited by G. Pierce and A. Toxqui, Tucson: University of Arizona Press.
Hobbs, P. (2009), 'We Are Growing by Leaps and Bounds. We Cannot Compare Present-Day Argentina with the One From Ten Years Ago', available at: www.winesur.com/news/awards/%E2%80%9Cwe-are-growing-by-leaps-and-bounds-we-cannot-compare-present-day-argentina-with-the-one-from-ten-years-ago%E2%80%9 (accessed 6 August 2013).
Huret, J. and E. Gómez Carrillo (1913), *La Argentina*, Paris: E. Fasquelle.
INV, I. (2016), *Informes Anuales*, available at: www.inv.gov.ar/index.php/informes-anuales (accessed 15 September 2016).

'La hora de los mercados' (1966), *Vinos, vinas y frutas*, November: 281–82.

'La hora de unirse' (1967), *Vinos, viñas y frutas*, March: 477.

Lynch, D. J. (2007). 'Golden Days for Argentine Wine Could Turn Cloudy', *USA Today*, available at: www.usatoday.com/money/world/2007-11-15-argentina-wine_N.htm. Newspaper article

Martín, J. (1992), *Estado y empresas*, Mendoza: Editorial de la Universidad Nacional de Cuyo.

Martínez, A. (1910), *Censo general de población, edificación, comercio é industrias de la ciudad de Buenos Aires*, Buenos Aires: Compañía Sud-Americana de Billetes de Banco.

Martínez, M. and J. Perone (1974), 'Comentarios sobre la organización del mercado vitivinícola argentino,' *Cuadernos, Sección Economía (Universidad Nacional de Cuyo)* (144): 18.

Martínez, O. (2006), 'Vino argentino: exportar más para seguir creciendo', *Clarin* [online]. Available at: edant.clarin.com/suplementos/economico/2006/09/17/n-00701.htm (accessed 15 October 2009).

Mateu, A. (2002), 'De productores a comerciantes: Las estrategias de integración de una empresa vitivinícola', mineo, Jornadas de Productores y Comerciantes, Buenos Aires.

(2003). 'Mendoza, entre el orden y el progreso 1880–1918', pp. 200–31, in *Historia de Mendoza. Aspectos políticos, culturales y sociales*, 1st edition, edited by A. Roig and P. Lacoste, Mendoza: Editorial Cavier Bleu.

(2009), *Estudio y análisis de la modalidad empresarial vitivinícola de los Arizu en Mendoza*, Ph.D. thesis, Universidad Nacional de Cuyo.

McIntyre, D. (2009), 'Argentinian Wines, Especially Malbec, Are Highly Popular Among US Wine Drinkers', available at: www.winesur.com/news/awards/argentinian-wines-especially-malbec-are-highly-popular-among-us-wine-drinkers (accessed 4 April 2011).

Meads, S. (2004), 'More than Malbec', *Wine International Tasting*, May.

Merino, J. (2004), 'Reconversión agrícola: nuestros viñedos comienzan a parecerse a los del mundo', *Vinos y vinas*, pp. 1–14, April.

(2007), '¿Fincas baratas? – Los Andes Diario', available at: new.losandes.com.ar/article/fincas-224823 (accessed 5 February 2015).

(2015), 'Costs and Profitability: the Main Challenges of Argentina's Wine Industry', paper presented at the Annual Conference of the American Association of Wine Economists, Mendoza.

Merino, J. and J. Estrella (2010), 'Competitiveness of Argentinean Wineries', paperpresented at the Annual Conference of the American Association of Wine Economists, University of California, Davis.

Michellini, M. (2014), *Todo lo otro*, Buenos Aires: Master Driver.

Observatorio Vitivinícola Argentino (2015), 'China es el destino que más crece para los vinos argentinos', available at: observatoriova.com/2015/09/china-es-el-destino-que-mas-crece-para-los-vinos-argentinos/ (accessed 8 April 2016).

Olguín, P. and M. Mellado (2010), 'Fracaso empresario en la industria del vino. Los casos de Bodegas y Viñedos Giol y del Grupo Greco, Mendoza, 1974–1989', Anuario Instituto de Estudios Histórico-Sociales, Universidad del Centro, Tandil, pp. 463–78.

Parker, R. (2004), 'Parker Predicts the Future', available at: www.foodandwine.com/articles/parker-predicts-the-future (accessed 8 May 2005).
Pinilla, V. and M. Ayuda (2002), 'The Political Economy of the Wine Trade: Spanish Exports and the International Market, 1890–1935', *European Review of Economic History* 6(1): 51–85.
Podestá, R. A. (1982), 'La intervención del estado en la vitivinicultura', pp. 49–72 in *Crisis vitivinicola*, edited by Edgardo Diaz Araujo, G. Petra Rcabarren, Angel H. Medina, Carlos Magni Salmón, Ricardo A. Podestá, O. Molina Cabrera, Vicente Ramirez, A. Gonzalez Arroyo, Jorge Taccini, R. Reina Rutini, Jorge Perone, and Aldo Biondillo. Mendoza: Editorial Idearium.
Presidencia de la Nación, R. (1970), *Vitivinicultura*, Buenos Aires: Secretaria General.
Pulenta, Q. (1966), 'Exportación de vinos y lo que puede hacer la industria privada', *Vinos, vinas y frutas*, July: 9–12.
República Argentina (1898), *1895 – Segundo Censo de la República Argentina*, available at: www.santafe.gov.ar/archivos/estadisticas/censos/C1895-T2.pdf (accessed 10 March 2016).
Richard-Jorba, R. and E. Perez Romagnoli (1994), 'Una aproximación a la geografía del vino en Mendoza: Distribución y difusión de las bodegas en los comienzos de la etapa industrial, 1880–1910', *Revista de estudios regionales* 2: 151–73.
Riveros, J. (1954), 'El vino, sus propiedades y su consumo', *Vinos, vinas y frutas*, May: 531.
Rodríguez, M. (1973), 'El 'Gran Buenos Aires,' extraordinario consumidor de vino', *Anuario vitivinícola argentina*, 88–40.
Saieg, L. (2010), 'Malbec Consumption Triples', available at: www.winesur.com/top-news/malbec-consumption-triples (accessed 6 April 2012).
Supplee, J. (1988), *Provincial Elites and the Economic Transformation of Mendoza, Argentina, 1880–1914*, Ph.D. thesis, University of Texas, Austin.
Veseth, M. (2013), 'Stein's Law and the Coming Crisis in Argentinean Wine', available at: wineeconomist.com/2013/05/14/steins-law/ (accessed 11 June 2015).
Vespa, A. (2004), 'El desafío competitivo', *Vinos y viñas* 991: 11, August.
Wasilevsky, J. (2013a), 'Over 70 Argentine Wineries Export Wine to China', available at: www.winesur.com/news/over-70-argentine-wineries-export-wine-to-china (accessed 8 June 2015).
(2013b), 'Refuerzan su presencia en Singapur y Taiwán. Asia reemplaza una parte de las ventas a Europa', available at: www.areadelvino.com/articulo.php?num=25220 (accessed 8 June 2015).
(2016), 'El vino argentino en la era K: 10 años intensos y marcados a fuego por claros y oscuros', available at: www.iprofesional.com/notas/161442-El-vino-argentino-en-la-era-K-10-aos-intensos-y-marcados-a-fuego-por-claros-y-oscuros (accessed 5 March 2014).
Wehring, O. (2006), *Argentina Wine Industry Review*, Bromsgrove: n.a.
Whitley, R. (2010), 'The Long, Strange Trip of Argentine Malbec', available at: www.creators.com/lifestylefeatures/wine/wine-talk/the-long-strange-trip-of-argentine-malbec.html (accessed 8 March 2013).
Wines of Argentina (2011), 'Wines of Argentina Opens China Office', available at: www.winesofargentina.org/en/noticias/ver/2011/12/28/wines-of-argentina-pone-un-pie-en-china-para-promocionar-el-vino-nacional (accessed 13 March 2013).

12

Australia and New Zealand

Kym Anderson

The initial purpose of European settlement in Australia, which began in 1788, was as a prison for Britain following its defeat in the America War of Independence five years earlier.[1] For the next half-century, the continent's white population was dominated by poor adult males and youths from England and Ireland. They and the British officers in charge were heavy drinkers, predominantly of rum. That preference gradually shifted to beer over the next dozen decades, and wine continued to be a very minor part of beverage consumption in Australia until the last quarter of the twentieth century.

The lack of consumer interest in wine was mirrored on the supply side: Australia's annual wine production per capita took until the 1890s to reach 5 litres, and was still below 7 litres in 1920 and 15 litres just after World War II. In New Zealand (where British settlement formally began with the signing of the Treaty of Waitangi in 1840), it took to the mid-1950s for domestic wine consumption to reach 1 litre per capita, the late 1960s to exceed 5 litres, and the new millennium before regularly exceeding 15 litres. By contrast, average wine production per capita over the 1860–1890 period was often more than 100 litres in France, Italy and Spain.

Yet over just two decades from the mid-1980s, Australia's per capita consumption nearly trebled and New Zealand's doubled, wine production quadrupled in Australia and rose fivefold in New Zealand and the share of production exported rose from less than 2 percent to more than 60 percent in both countries – by which time Australia accounted for one-tenth of the value of global wine exports (and New Zealand's share from 2012 exceeded 3 percent).

[1] Thanks are due to Wine Australia for grants that financed travel and earlier research assistant support for this chapter and the book and subsequent papers on which it draws (Anderson 2015, 2017b, 2017c).

This chapter seeks to explain why it took so long for consumer interest and producer comparative advantage in wine to emerge in the Antipodes, and why the industry took off so spectacularly in both countries after the 1980s. It also seeks to shed light on the causes of another striking feature of Australia's wine industry: five very clear cycles around its long-term growth path, the most recent of which saw its spectacular recent growth reversed after the first few years of the new millennium while New Zealand continued to boom.

Such an explanation requires a comparative perspective, in two senses: intersectorally (since other industries were expanding also in these settler economies) and internationally. The latter is important to see the extent to which some of the drivers of Antipodean wine industry growth and cycles were shared with other countries (Hatton, O'Rourke and Taylor 2007), as well as to learn from the differences between these two Antipodean countries' experiences. New comparative data reveal that while Australian wineries led the way among New World wine exporters in the current globalization wave, they were hardly noticeable in the first globalization wave that ended just over 100 years ago – even though Europe's vineyards were devastated by phylloxera during that earlier wave.

The chapter draws on a simple economic framework for conceptualizing the drivers of wine industry growth and cycles and on two newly compiled databases of annual industry and macroeconomic data back to the mid-nineteenth century: a detailed Australian one with regional and varietal data (Anderson and Aryal 2015) and a global one with just national data (Anderson and Pinilla 2017).[2] It begins by reviewing briefly the evolving pattern of domestic alcohol consumption and imports before turning to more detailed analysis of the growth and cycles in wine production and exports in Australia and then of the recent boom in New Zealand.

DOMESTIC DEMAND FOR AND IMPORTS OF WINE

Australia does have native current bushes, but since they produce a sparse crop of very small berries, it is not surprising that there was no evidence of wine being consumed when European settlers arrived in 1788.[3] During

[2] Since this chapter draws so heavily on those two databases, for the sake of brevity they are not referred to when citing data from them.

[3] Australia's aboriginal population did produce a beerlike product from the nectar of native Banksia bushes and a ciderlike beverage from the sap of cider gum trees, but both had modest alcohol content (Brady 2008; Jiranek 2017). New Zealand's Maori people reputedly did not drink any alcohol prior to the arrival of Europeans.

their first fifty years, some settlers in New South Wales certainly experimented with imported vines and made wine to help satisfy their own demand (McIntyre 2012). They were helped by a grower's manual (Busby 1830) and a collection of several hundred cuttings covering scores of winegrape varieties that James Busby brought back from Europe at the end of 1831 (from which he in turn took cuttings to New Zealand in 1832). However, virtually no growers got to the stage of having a regular surplus of wine for commercial sale until the 1840s in Australia and the 1860s in New Zealand. Domestic alcohol consumption prior to that relied predominantly on imported wines along with imported spirits and beers, supplemented with only a small amount of domestic legal production of spirits and beers and a larger amount of homebrewed beer.

Precise consumption data are unavailable for the early decades of European settlement, but estimates have been generated. Butlin (1983) suggests the mix of wine, spirits and beer and the total volume of alcohol consumption per capita in New South Wales during 1800–1820 were probably similar to that in Britain at the time, at around 13 litres of alcohol per person. This is contrary to earlier claims by many commentators that New South Wales as a penal colony was far more alcoholic than European countries. In the 1830s, Australia's per capita consumption is estimated to have been 15 litres of alcohol, made up of 12 litres from spirits, 2 litres from wine and 1 litre from beer (Dingle 1980). New Zealand's in the latter 1850s was similar to Britain's, at around 7 litres, 80 percent of which was spirits and most of the rest beer (Ryan 2010).

Australia's consumption dropped substantially during the depression of the early 1840s, before rising hugely in the 1850s with the influx of male migrants and the boost in per capita incomes, thanks to that decade's gold mining boom in Victoria. As the dominance of adult males in the population subsequently fell, so too did per capita alcohol consumption – prodded by a temperance movement similar to that then operating in the United States and New Zealand. Consumption in both countries was down to 5 litres of alcohol per capita by the 1890s, to 4 litres by the late 1920s and below 3 litres during the Great Depression of the early 1930s. Thereafter, it rose steadily to a peak of 10 litres in the mid-1970s, mostly of beer, before falling back to around 8 litres in Australia and 6 in New Zealand (Figure 12.1).

Spirits dominated in the first 100 years of European settlement in the Antipodes partly because that was what the settlers' peers back in Britain and Ireland drank, and partly because it was the cheapest beverage to ship halfway around the world per unit of alcohol and was least likely to deteriorate on the trip. As well, beer was costly to produce domestically: for many

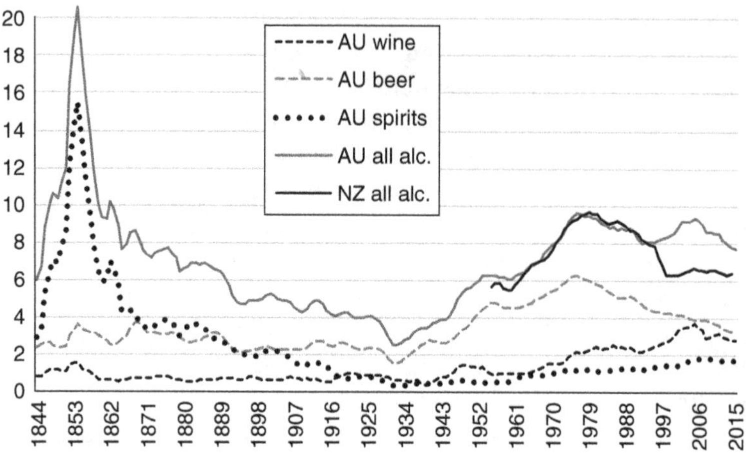

Figure 12.1 Per capita consumption of alcohol as wine, beer and spirits, Australia, 1843 to 2016, and New Zealand, 1955 to 2015 (litres of alcohol, three-year moving average).
Source: Anderson and Pinilla (2017).

decades, grains and flour were imported because cropping was not as profitable for local farmers as grazing. In the 1860s, there were still only two-thirds of a hectare of land being cropped per capita, of which about half in Australia was sown to wheat. Over the next four decades, that number rose to a little over 1 ha, but even so beer consumption per capita gradually fell until the easing of pressure from the temperance movement from the 1920s.

Meanwhile, wine was the preferred beverage of only a small fraction of the Antipodean population. Its per capita consumption rose during the 1850s' gold rush in Victoria, and during the two World Wars, when grain was kept for food rather than beer, but otherwise showed a flat trend until the 1960s (Figure 12.1). By then, after war-induced grain rationing to breweries and rations on beer and spirits consumption were removed, beer again comprised three-quarters of all alcohol consumption compared with less than one-eighth coming from wine (and most of that fortified).

Since the early 1960s, however, wine consumption per capita in both countries has trended upwards faster than per capita income, at the expense of beer as total alcohol consumption levelled off from the mid-1970s to the mid-1980s and then declined. Several factors contributed in addition to real income growth. One was brand advertising plus generic promotion domestically by Australia's Wine Bureau. Another was the influx of wine-preferring immigrants from southern Europe, who also influenced the per capita consumption of nonalcoholic beverages: tea-drinking shrunk by three-quarters, while coffee-drinking expanded sixfold in Australia in the second half of the twentieth century (Anderson 2017b, figure 2). Yet another factor was the fall in the real cost of air travel and of discounts for under-twenty-five-year-olds. That encouraged young people to travel to Europe, where they were exposed to cultures in which wine is integral. As well, Australia's Trade Practices Act of 1974 made retail price fixing illegal and stimulated the emergence and gradual spread of liquor chain stores and wine discounting throughout the country. By the mid-1970s, annual wine consumption per capita was twice its early 1960s average of 7 litres in Australia, and it reached three times that earlier level by the turn of this century. The rise was even steeper in New Zealand, from just 2 litres around 1960 to 20 litres by 2005. Both countries' per capita consumption levels are thus now above the much-diminished levels of Argentina, Chile, Uruguay and Spain, similar to Germany's, and more than half those of France and Italy.

Wine imports into Australia dominated its exports up to the 1890s, and again during 1976–1986, while New Zealand was a net importer of wine until the early 2000s. Australia's wine imports expanded considerably (and exports diminished) during the country's export-demand-driven mining booms from the mid-1970s to early 1980s and again from around 2005, when the country's real exchange rate temporarily strengthened greatly. About half of those imports from the mid-2000s came from New Zealand (mostly Sauvignon Blanc), during which time Australia absorbed between one-quarter and one-third of New Zealand's wine exports while supplying the vast majority of its (mostly red) wine imports. The share of imports in New Zealand's wine consumption grew in parallel with its share of production exported in the 1990s, but since then that share has declined as the industry's comparative advantage in wine strengthened and its domestic winegrape production diversified substantially in terms of varieties, styles and regions (Figure 12.2).

DOMESTIC PRODUCTION AND EXPORTS OF WINE

The Federation's first *Yearbook of Australia*, published in 1908, was very confident that the country's wine industry would rapidly expand its production and exports. In fact, sixteen years earlier it was claimed that 'many of the leading wine merchants of London and other important commercial centres admit that Australia promises to become a powerful rival in the world's markets with the old-established vineyards of Europe' (Irvine 1892, p. 6).[4] Meanwhile, in New Zealand, a report by Romeo

[4] Such an admission was not yet forthcoming from the French, however. At the international wine competition of the Vienna Exhibition of 1873, for example, the French judges, on hearing of the identity of the wines they had judged blind, are reported to have resigned when they learnt a prize-winning syrah was not French but from Bendigo, Victoria (Beeston 2001, p. 62).

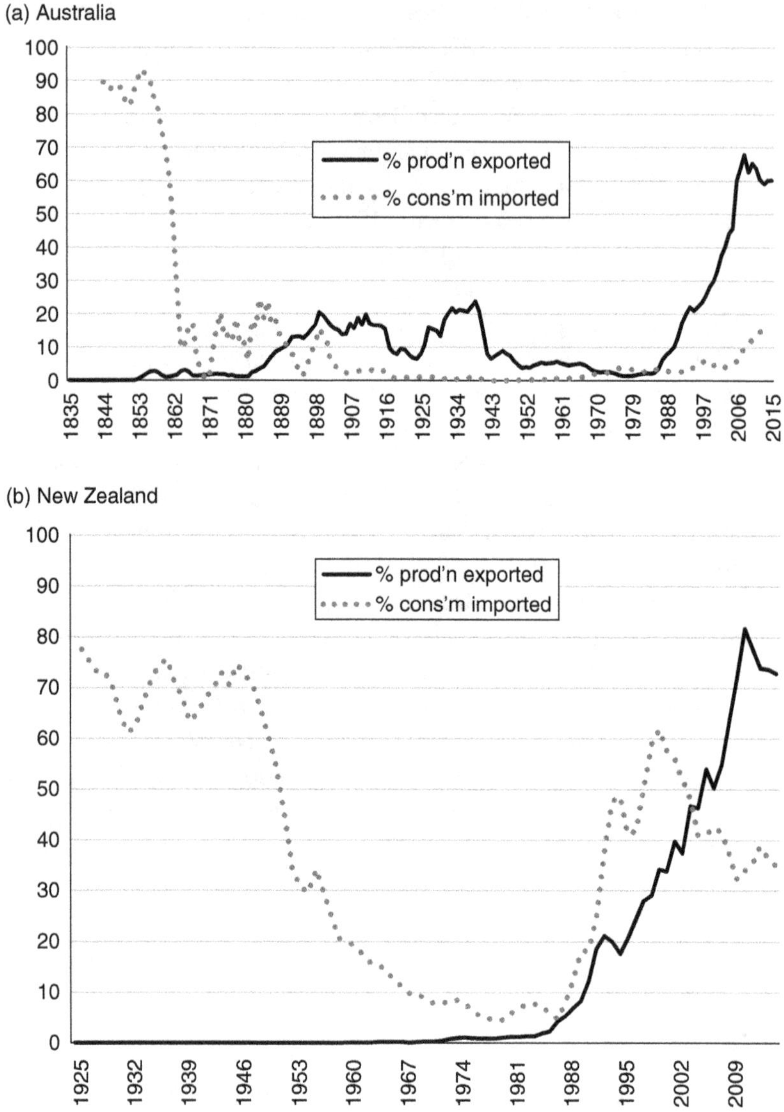

Figure 12.2 Exports as a percentage of wine production and imports as a percentage of wine consumption, Australia, 1835 to 2015, and New Zealand, 1925 to 2015 (three-year moving average around year shown).
Source: Anderson and Pinilla (2017).

Bragato (1895), following his visit from Victoria, was similarly effusive about prospects for producing high-yielding vines and high-quality wine in many parts of that country.

However, both the Australian and the New Zealand wine industries had very long gestation periods. Phylloxera appeared in both Victoria and

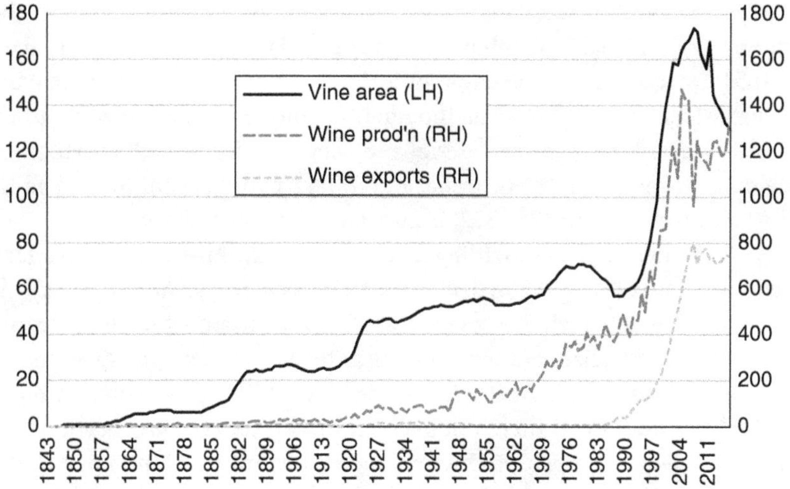

Figure 12.3 Vine area, wine production and wine exports, Australia, 1843 to 2016 ('000 ha and ML).
Source: Anderson and Pinilla (2017).

New Zealand at the end of the nineteenth century, and Australia's exports stayed around 20 percent of wine production for the next four decades and then shrunk to around 5 percent for the subsequent four decades while New Zealand's remained close to zero. It took until the late 1980s before their industries took off with an export-led boom (Figure 12.3). That is despite the fact that their winegrape production faces relatively few regulations and so – unlike in Europe – growers are free to choose their varieties of grapes, yields per hectare, how much to irrigate and so on. Wineries, too, face few regulations, so they can blend wines from various regions, blend whatever varieties they wish and advertise the varieties on their bottle label.

INDUSTRY GROWTH AND STRUCTURAL CHANGES IN AUSTRALIA SINCE 1788

There were four acres of vines in Parramatta in 1791, and a few more had been planted by Blaxland by 1816.[5] Macarthur had a further 20 acres at Camden by 1820, Blaxland exported a tiny sample in 1822 and Wyndham Estate was established in the Hunter Valley in 1828 and had two acres

[5] Very readable histories of the Australian wine industry can be found in Laffer (1949), Halliday (1994), Rankine (1996), Dunstan (1994), Beeston (2001), Faith (2003), McIntyre (2012) and Allen (2012). Aspects of the history of South Australia's industry during the

of vines by 1832. It was James Busby's planting of European vines in the Sydney Botanic Gardens following his trip to France and southern Spain in 1831 that accelerated the embryonic development of the Australian wine industry (McIntyre 2012). Even though his plantings in the Botanic Garden were neglected, he had the foresight to send duplicates to Macarthur, to Melbourne and to South Australia, and to take cuttings with him when he moved to New Zealand in 1832, from which their spread began.

As new migrants began settling in Victoria, South Australia and Western Australia from the late 1830s, demand for wine began to grow. Supply expansion was suspended when a severe recession hit Britain which temporarily starved the Australian colonies of finance for investment and spending in the early 1840s. South Australia probably would have contributed more in the latter 1840s had there not been an early discovery just north of the Barossa Valley of copper, production and exports of which boomed in the latter 1840s (the continent's first mining boom).

Annual wine production (including for distillation into brandy) was well under 100 KL prior to 1840. At that time, the colonies of Australia and New Zealand had less than 200 ha of grapevines, the majority of whose grapes were consumed fresh or as dried vine fruit.

Grape and wine production would have grown more had the demand for wool for Britain's booming textile mills not been so strong throughout the nineteenth century.[6] Wool's high price and relatively low transport cost per dollar of product meant wool (together with sheep meat from the 1880s) dominated exports of Australia and New Zealand in every decade up to the early 1960s, apart from short periods when gold dominated during and following the gold rushes of the 1850s in Victoria and the 1890s in Western Australia, and occasionally from the 1860s in New Zealand. Would-be Antipodean wine exporters therefore faced strong competition both internationally, from Old World wine producers exporting to British and other markets for wine, and intersectorally, from pastoralists and related agribusinesses in the domestic market for labour and capital as well

nineteenth century are recorded by Bell (1993, 1994) and Griffiths (1966). Unwin (1991) places Australia's history in global perspective in his seminal history of the world's wine industry stretching back well before Christ, as does Simpson (2011) in his in-depth history of the first globalization wave that ended at the start of World War I. The industry's entire period of development is analyzed with the help of annual data from 1843 by Anderson (2015). Histories of New Zealand's wine industry are documented in Cooper (1996), Stewart (2010) and Moran (2017).

6 Between the 1820s and the start of the twentieth century, about one-quarter of Britain's total imports were wool and cotton to feed its booming textile industry, and their share did not fall below one-tenth until the later 1950s (Anderson 1992, table 2.5).

as from gold mines. Nonetheless, Australia's vine area, wine production and wine exports trace out rising trends over most of the past two centuries (Figure 12.3). Their respective annual compound growth rates over the 170 years from 1843 to 2016 are 2.8 percent, 4.3 percent and 5.0 percent. By contrast, New Zealand's wine production did not reach 10 ML until half a century ago and 60 ML until the beginning of this century, but since then it has increased five-fold.

Around Australia's long-run growth path have been five multiyear cycles of various lengths (Table 12.1), in addition to annual fluctuations because of seasonal factors and changes in the relative profitability of directing multi-purpose grapes to wineries versus to the drying or fresh markets. The average cycle length has been almost thirty years, but ranging from nineteen to fifty-two years. The booms on average have been shorter than the following plateaus in which profits slump or become negative, which makes the most recent boom exceptional in that it has lasted nearly three times as long as the subsequent slump that has just finished.

Bearing in mind that rates of population and income growth also fluctuate, and that the overall area of land under crops in Australia has grown greatly over the past two centuries, it is helpful to examine not just extensive but also intensive growth indicators.

In the case of vine area, each rapid expansion phase has been followed by an often longer period of decline in the bearing area of vineyards per capita. Despite the near-trebling in vine area over the two decades straddling the new millennium, the per capita area did not quite reach the record level of 1924 before it began to decline again after 2007. Those sharp increases and slower subsequent declines are also evident when the vine area is shown relative to the total crop area (Figure 12.4). That indicator has fluctuated around a declining long-run trend since the end of the nineteenth century. Even so, wine production per capita and per dollar of real gross domestic product (GDP) have trended upwards, due to increasing yields per hectare as the share of vines being irrigated expanded or more grapes began to be used for wine rather than for drying or fresh consumption.[7]

Clearly the Australian wine industry's long-run growth path has not been as smooth as Figure 12.3 suggests. Exports boomed several times in the past, but in each case a plateau followed the boom and, because of an expanded

[7] The share of grapes used for winemaking was less than 30 percent during World War II and averaged around 40 percent for the next three decades and then 60 percent during 1975–1990 before rising over the 1990s to its current share of more than 90 percent (Anderson 2015, table 8).

Table 12.1 *Timing of booms and plateaus in the Australian wine industry's development, 1855 to 2015*

Vintages:	Boom/ plateau/cycle	Annual proportional increase (%/year) in:										Wine as % of all merch. exports
		No. of years	Vine area	Wine prod-uction	Wine export volume	Vine area per capita	Vines/ total crop area	Wine prod'n per capita	Wine prod'n per real $GDP	Wine exports per capita	% wine prod'n exported	
1855 to 1871	1st boom	16	13.9	17.3	16.7	9.9	5.8	13.4	12.6	12.7	1.9	n.a.
1871 to 1882	1st plateau	11	−1.2	−0.3	−5.0	−4.3	−9.4	−3.4	−5.4	−8.1	1.5	n.a.
1855 to 1882	**1st cycle**	**27**	**6.3**	**8.9**	**7.8**	**2.8**	**−0.4**	**5.4**	**3.9**	**4.3**	**1.7**	n.a.
1882 to 1896	2nd boom	14	11.2	7.9	19.7	8.4	9.4	5.6	6.9	17.3	9.5	n.a.
1896 to 1915	2nd plateau	19	−0.3	0.1	0.4	−1.8	−3.6	−1.2	−3.0	−1.5	17.1	0.20
1882 to 1915	**2nd cycle**	**33**	**3.6**	**3.0**	**7.0**	**1.7**	**0.4**	**1.2**	**0.9**	**5.1**	**13.9**	n.a.
1915 to 1925	3rd boom	10	7.3	10.6	5.2	5.8	7.0	8.3	7.0	2.6	8.4	0.16
1925 to 1967	3rd plateau	42	0.5	2.6	−1.7	−1.1	−0.6	0.9	−0.9	−3.4	10.6	0.33
1915 to 1967	**3rd cycle**	**52**	**1.1**	**3.1**	**1.0**	**−0.5**	**−0.1**	**1.6**	**0.0**	**−0.7**	**10.2**	**0.30**
1967 to 1975	4th boom	8	4.0	6.1	−1.4	0.0	5.1	4.2	1.9	−3.7	2.8	0.08
1975 to 1986	4th plateau	11	−1.0	1.5	7.8	−2.9	−4.4	0.1	−1.2	5.8	2.3	0.06
1967 to 1986	**4th cycle**	**19**	0.5	3.2	1.2	−1.3	−1.2	1.7	0.1	−0.4	**2.5**	**0.07**
1986 to 2007	5th boom	21	6.4	6.4	17.5	5.5	4.0	5.9	3.5	16.4	28.2	1.02
2007 to 2016	5th plateau	9	−3.1	−0.3	−0.7	−4.5	−3.4	−1.7	−3.4	−2.2	63.3	0.92
1986 to 2016	**5th cycle**	**30**	**2.7**	**4.0**	**15.7**	**1.2**	**2.2**	**2.5**	**0.7**	**14.1**	**37.4**	**0.99**
Average of first 4 booms		*12*	*9.1*	*10.5*	*10.1*	*6.0*	*6.8*	*7.9*	*7.1*	*7.2*	*8.3*	
Average of first 4 plateaus		*21*	*−0.5*	*1.0*	*0.4*	*−2.5*	*−4.5*	*−0.9*	*−2.6*	*−1.8*	*7.9*	
1843 to 2016		***173***	***2.8***	***4.3***	***5.0***[a]	***0.6***	***−0.1***	***2.2***	***0.8***[a]	***3.1***[a]	***12.9***[a]	

[a] 161 years from 1855 to 2016 inclusive.

Source: Anderson (2017b).

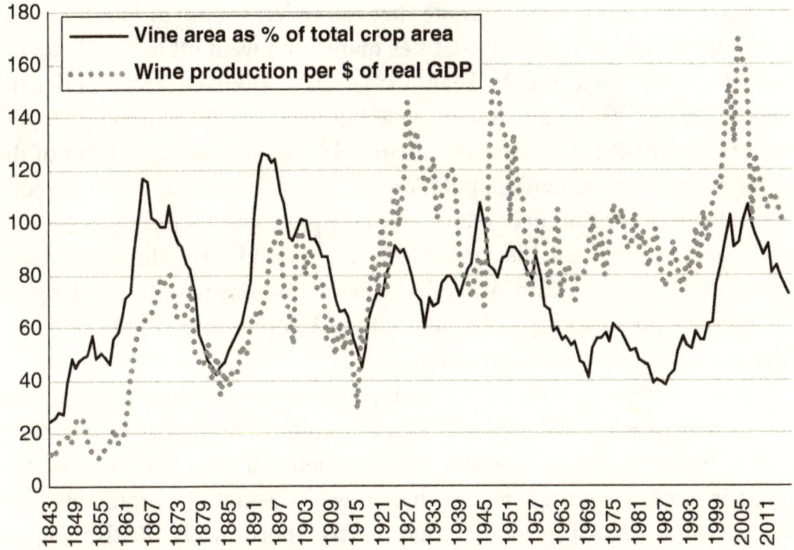

Figure 12.4 Vine area as a percentage of total crop area, and wine production per dollar of real GDP, Australia, 1843 to 2016 (2007 = 100).
Source: Updated from Anderson (2015).

acreage, grapegrowers went back to receiving low and at times negative returns.[8] Indeed, at the end of the 1976–1986 period, when exports were so low that Australia became a net importer of wine again, the Federal and South Australian governments introduced a vine-pull compensation scheme to encourage grapegrowers to move to alternative crops, so dire was the wine industry's view of its prospects at the time. Yet, like a phoenix, the industry rose again and grew with renewed vigour during the 1990s and early 2000s. The real value of both winegrape and wine production grew at more than 10 percent per year and the share of wine sales in export markets rose from just 2 to 3 percent in the mid-1980s to more than 60 percent (Figure 12.2).

Australia's First Cycle: Gold Rush and After, 1855 to 1882

The gold rush of the 1850s caused Australia's white population to almost treble that decade, raising substantially the domestic demand for alcoholic

[8] The export share of wine production for Australia exceeded that for the world only three times: in the lead-up to World War I, in the 1930s, and since the late 1990s. Apart from the 1930s and World War II, Australia's share of wine in total merchandise exports had always been below that for the world as a whole until the 1990s. That is, Australia had a comparative disadvantage in wine during almost all decades prior to the 1990s (Anderson 2017b).

beverages, including wine. Despite that expanded supply of labour, wages rose dramatically in the early 1850s as many men went off to the Victorian goldfields (Maddock and McLean 1984). That squeezed grape and wine production and profitability, with wine output in 1855 being only 70 percent of that in 1851. However, by the mid-1850s the dramatic extent of the increases in the continent's population and income was perceived correctly to lead to an expansion in demand for many products, including wine. As a result, the area of grapevines began to increase rapidly, trebling in the latter half of the 1850s in South Australia, where wine production quadrupled. By 1871, the area had expanded tenfold for Australia as a whole, and wine production had increased sixteenfold.

The consequent growth in wine supplies was so fast that it outstripped the growth in domestic demand in each colony, so export outlets were sought. Intercolonial trade within the continent was one option. However, transport costs were high, and each colony also sought to protect its local producers by imposing high import tariffs.[9] Fortunately, British import duties and ocean shipping costs began to fall in this period. Specifically, Britain in 1860 abolished the import tariff preference for South African wine (which had been taxed at half the rate of other countries' wines) and by 1862 had lowered the tariff on all wine with less than 26^0 proof spirit (equivalent to 14.9 percent alcohol) to one shilling instead of five shillings and nine pence per gallon. That made the dry wine duty only two-fifths that for the more alcoholic fortified wines from Portugal and Spain – having been nearly double the duty on fortifieds for most of the previous 160 years (Kelly 1867, p. 6; Ludington 2018). The cuts in dry wine tariffs, together with the creation of off-licence retailing (thanks to Gladstone's legislative changes in 1861), allowed Australia's exports to Britain to quadruple over the 1860s and double again by the mid-1870s. This, however, was from a very low level first established in the mid-1850s: throughout the 1860s and 1870s, Australia's modest wine exports amounted to less than 3 percent of its production (Figure 12.2).

Exports from Australia were inhibited not only because the wine it produced was generally of extremely low quality (mostly dry red, shipped bulk in hogsheads only weeks after the grapes had been crushed), but also because up until then very little had been invested in securing quality

[9] In 1858, the duties on wine coming into South Australia, Victoria and New South Wales were already quite high at 2.2, 4.4 and 6.6 cents per litre, respectively, but by 1876 they had been raised to nearly 9 cents per litre and by the early 1890s to the virtually prohibitive levels of 11 cents per litre for still wine and twice that for sparkling wine (Anderson 2015).

packaging, marketing and distribution arrangements in Britain (Irvine 1892; Bell 1994). Meanwhile, from the late 1860s producers suffered very low returns as a consequence of the rapid supply expansion outstripping demand growth. Kelly (1867, p. 1) opened his book by claiming that no industry in South Australia was as depressed as wine at that time. So poor were returns that the area of grapevines fell 10 percent nationally and almost 30 percent in South Australia during the 1870s.

The poor export performance to the late 1870s was not without some highlights, though. After the International Exhibition in Vienna in 1873, the official report to the Commissioners of Her Majesty's Customs praised Australia's wines, and similar accolades (along with some critical reports) flowed from the International Exhibition of 1882, which happened to be in Bordeaux. This recognition provided some hope for the future, especially as the phylloxera louse was spreading in Europe and so diminishing that continent's production.

Australia's Second Cycle: 1882 to 1915

The successes in international exhibitions, together with the prospect of forming an Australian Federation by the turn of the century which would see the removal of the high intercolonial trade restrictions, encouraged growers to expand the area under winegrapes substantially. True, there were phylloxera outbreaks in Geelong in the latter 1870s and gradually in other parts of Victoria (Pope 1971), and then in New Zealand before the end of the century. But the Victorian government responded with compensation for forced removal of diseased plants, and in 1890 offered subsidies of £2 per acre (A$10 per ha) to replant with resistant stocks over the subsequent three years. As a result, Victoria's vine area more than doubled between 1889 and 1894, from 5,200 to 12,300 ha. Unfortunately, that occurred just as the 1890s' depression hit and domestic alcohol sales were plummeting. The Rutherglen region of Victoria especially expanded, to compete with still red wines being imported from South Australia. That planting meant Australia's overall vineyard area and production of wine grew substantially during the 1880s and early 1890s, at about 11 percent and 8 percent per year, respectively (Table 12.1).

Australia's vineyard expansions were soon followed by expansions of winery capacity and improvements in winemaking technology. Given the heavy capital intensity of quality winemaking, this was associated with a concentration of winery ownership, which contributed to the industry's success in exporting as the new century approached. By the turn of the century, production was three times its 1880 level and one-sixth of the country's wine production was being exported (Figure 12.2) – notwithstanding the considerable difficulties still associated with exporting from Australia at that time (Irvine 1892). Australia's export success early in this cycle was helped partly by the reduced competition from France and other suppliers to Britain following the arrival and devastating spread of phylloxera in Europe in the 1870s and 1880s.

The buildup in exports during that first export boom, largely involving bulk full-bodied reds, was sustained for two more decades after the initial growth from 1885 to 1895, before being interrupted by World War I. While strong prejudices against New World wine remained in many quarters, a reputation for Australian dry wines had been established in Europe in the generic sense at least, even though varietal, regional and winery brand labelling was still absent (and would be until the 1950s).

However, by 1895, two-fifths of France's vine area had been transplanted onto American rootstocks, and yields per hectare rose rapidly with the demise of phylloxera. As well, French producers in the meantime had invested heavily in vineyards in North Africa, especially Algeria, and as soon as those vines were mature, their access to the French market was assisted by the raising of barriers to all other imports (Pinilla and Ayuda 2002; Meloni and Swinnen 2014, 2018; Chevet et al. 2018). This trade policy development depressed prices for wines in Europe and contributed to the cessation of acreage and production growth in Australia through to World War I.

In addition to the aforementioned two key domestic contributors to the industry's second expansion prior to that plateau (the anticipation of Federation and winery modernization and ownership concentration across Australia), there was another one: the imposition of tariff protection from imports of many manufactured products and some processed farm goods. Dried vine fruits were one of the first and most protected such goods, receiving tariff protection that doubled the local price when first introduced in 1904. That year also saw the formation of the Australia Dried Fruits Association, which by controlling over 90 percent of domestic production was able to raise the domestic price by diverting supplies to distilleries, or to the export market with the help of a government export subsidy (Sieper 1982). That raised the price of winegrapes as well, and hence the cost of producing wine. That cost was more or less offset by a tax also on wine imports, which has prevailed to the present (although the most-favoured-nation rate is only 5 percent currently).

Another international contributor to the export takeoff in this cycle was the lowering of intercontinental ocean transport costs. The development of the steamship played a crucial role in making intercontinental trade cheaper. Harley's (1988) index of British ocean freight rates remains relatively constant between 1740 and 1840, before dropping by about 70 percent between 1840 and 1910 – a dramatic decline that was mirrored on sea routes worldwide (Harley 1988; Mohammed and Williamson 2004; Findlay and O'Rourke 2007). Transport cost declines from around 1860 to World War I were especially large. On top of that, the increasing speed of ocean transport provided implied cost savings additional to those indicated by freight rate data, especially for perishable products. For distant Australia and New Zealand, transport costs were especially large in the early decades of European settlement. But for New Zealand, its wine production had still not reached 200 ML or 0.2 litres per capita on the eve of World War I, so there was still no prospect in sight of having a surplus for export.

Australia's Third Cycle: Export Supports Come and Go, 1915 to 1967

Towards the end of and following World War I there was a rapid vine area expansion in Australia (Table 12.1 and Figures 12.3 and 12.4). This was encouraged by the subsidized settlement on farms of ex-servicemen, particularly in the newly developed Murrumbidgee Irrigation Area of New South Wales and along the Murray River (Davidson 1969, ch. 4). Annual output of wine more than doubled in the decade to 1925, leading to a glut especially of Doradillo grapes whose price fell by two-thirds in 1924. Having been fuelled by assistance with land development and water infrastructure, the Australian government decided to further assist producers in the newly planted areas by offering an export bounty on wines with at least 34^{0} proof spirit (that is, fortified wines with more than 19 percent alcohol, for which the nonpremium Doradillo variety was relatively well suited).

The Wine Export Bounty Act, passed in 1924, provided the equivalent of 6 cents per litre plus excise duty drawback on the fortifying spirit, making a total of 8.8 cents per litre (Laffer 1949, pp. 78, 134). This came at a time when the average unit value of Australia's wine exports was less than 10 cents per litre. This generous export subsidy was intended to make Australia better able to compete with much-closer Portugal and Spain in the British market for sweet fortified wines.

Since an export subsidy is the equivalent of a production subsidy and a domestic consumption tax, this bounty dampened domestic fortified wine sales and table wine production, at the same time as boosting production and exports of fortified wines (and more so for lower-valued grapes and fortified wines, since the export bounty was a specific rather than an *ad valorem* duty). Australia's table wine production diminished substantially over the interwar period, reaching one-fifth of its 1923 level by the late 1930s. Production and consumption of beer rose rapidly in the 1930s, presumably as a cheaper substitute for domestic consumers in the wake of the diversion of grapes to the production of fortified wines for export.

The fortified wine export bounty was not all that assisted grapegrowers from the mid-1920s. In its June 1925 budget, the British government introduced, by way of thanks for war contributions, a tariff preference for wines from the British Empire. As a result, Australian table wines faced a British tariff of two shillings and its fortified wines four shillings per gallon, compared with double those rates for wines imported by Britain from Europe.

As well, the industry continued to be assisted by an import tariff on wine and brandy, a sales tax of 15 percent on imported but not domestically produced wine,[10] excise taxes on beer and spirits but not on wine and a lower excise tax on brandy than on other spirits. The import tax on wine was nontrivial, which helps explain both the low share of imported wine in domestic consumption and the relatively low overall level of wine consumption throughout this cycle (Figures 12.1 and 12.2). The extent to which those support measures raised the domestic prices of grapes and wine is indicated by estimated nominal rates of assistance (NRAs). The NRA for drying grapes averaged 25 percent in the interwar period and 10 percent in the two decades thereafter. Meanwhile, the NRA for wine from import tariffs averaged 24 percent over the 1950s and 1960s, which was slightly above the average for other manufactures and twice the average NRA for the agricultural sector (Anderson 2015, table A9).

Together these policies gave a considerable boost to Australia's depressed producers of low-valued winegrapes and fortified wines during the interwar years. They also encouraged wine importers in Britain to expand purchases ahead of sales when the Australian government in 1927 gave six months' notice that it was going to reduce the export subsidy by one-quarter: there was a big surge and then a temporary downturn in exports at the end of the 1920s (before they levelled out at an average of 16 ML per year for the 1930s).[11] Many of the wines shipped in 1927 were rushed in order to qualify

[10] Sales taxes were introduced in 1930, but with exemptions to domestic producers, so they had the same protective effect as an import tariff (Lloyd 1973, ch. 7).

[11] Together these changes meant Australia exported more wine to Britain in the 1926–40 period than did France (Laffer 1949, p. 125). Between the 1860s and the 1920s, France, Portugal and Spain each supplied more than 20 percent of British wine imports and together the combined import share of those three countries exceeded 80 percent each

for the high bounty before it was reduced, in the sense that they had not been given time to mature. That, together with poor storage treatment in Britain, ensured they were of low quality by the time they were sold there. This meant they not only fetched a low price but also secured a reputation for Australia as a new supplier of poor-quality fortified wine – replacing the relatively high reputation built up in previous decades for dry still red wine.[12]

In a further response, the Australian government established in 1929 the Wine Overseas Marketing Board (later known simply as the Australian Wine Board when its promotion mandate broadened to include the domestic market). Like many marketing boards at the time, it tried to set a minimum price for export wine during 1930–36, but had to abandon it, as the market price was barely half the set price.

With returns falling from the late 1920s, winemakers wanted to reduce by 25 percent the prices they paid growers for winegrapes. One response was that a South Australian Grapegrowers Cooperative was established as a competing winemaker, but that did little to stem the erosion in returns. In 1936, a vine-pull scheme sponsored by the South Australian government saw two-thirds of the Coonawarra region's vines uprooted. Meanwhile, in Victoria's Yarra Valley, farmers began turning to dairying, and in the Hunter Valley of New South Wales the acreage of vines was eventually halved. Not surprisingly, the total area of vines in Australia grew very little over this period; and it was five decades before the annual level of wine exports achieved in the late 1930s (artificially boosted to build stocks in Britain for the foreshadowed war) was again reached.

During World War II, domestic wine consumption rose. This was partly because beer and spirits sales were rationed, to boost foodgrain availability. Interstate trade in alcoholic beverages was banned during the war also, to conserve transport fuel. And the United Kingdom placed severe restrictions on wine imports from January 1941, providing only a small quota for Australia (Laffer 1949, pp. 87–94). That plus difficulties in obtaining space on ships meant Australia's annual wine exports to Britain during 1940–45 were only one-fifth those in the 1930s.

decade. Australia's share of British wine imports was just 5 percent in the first two decades of the twentieth century and 9 percent in the 1920s, but it rose to 24 percent in the 1930s (Anderson and Pinilla 2017, table 73). This is consistent with new evidence suggesting imperial preferences affected trade patterns nontrivially in the 1930s (de Bromhead et al. 2017).

12 Between 1920 and 1960, less than one-fifth of wine production became table wine, more than two-fifths was distilled and the remaining two-fifths was fortified (Anderson 2015, table 29).

Following World War II, consumers in the United Kingdom moved away from wine once their wartime rationing of grain used in beer production was lifted. Partly this was because of long-established consumer preferences, but two policy changes gave a helping hand. One was that Britain raised its tariff on fortified wines fivefold in 1947 and kept it very high until the end of the 1950s (when it was lowered but was still double the interwar rate). The other was that, in Australia, the wine export bounty was no longer provided after 1947–48.

As for supply, despite new irrigation schemes at Loxton in South Australia and Robinvale in Victoria, the area of vines and wine production grew only slowly from the mid-1940s to the mid-1960s (Figure 12.3). During that time, the Korean War–induced wool price boom and then subsidies to other farm products such as wheat, milk and tobacco appealed more to farmers. As well, tighter import restrictions on manufactured goods boosted the import-competing industrial sector, while the removal in the early 1960s of a ban on iron ore exports triggered a mining boom. Both of those trade policy changes indirectly dampened incentives in other tradables sectors, including wine (Anderson 2017a). As a consequence, wine production grew only 3 percent per year between 1946 and 1966, and wine exports remained flat (Table 12.1).

Australia's Fourth Cycle: Domestic Demand Changes, 1967 to 1986

Britain hiked its tariff on fortified wines again in the late 1960s and then in 1973 joined the European Economic Community (EEC), which provided duty-free access for wines from other EEC members. Meanwhile, the mining boom at home was reducing the competitiveness of Australia's non-mineral exporters. So for both demand and supply reasons, wine exports remained flat from the mid-1960s to mid-1980s, and exports to the United Kingdom shrunk by nine-tenths.[13] Grape and wine prices also remained low, particularly for reds. The low red prices attracted the attention of domestic consumers, and a taste swing ensued. In turn, numerous companies – many of them with no experience in making and marketing wines – perceived opportunities for taking over brands through corporate mergers or acquisitions. The surge in demand for domestic premium red wines from the late 1960s stimulated an expansion in their production. This was followed by an equally sudden surge in domestic consumer interest in premium white wines from the mid-1970s, which in turn was followed by a renewed interest

[13] Wine exports were so low in the mid-1960s that the Australian Wine Board closed its Wine Centre in London.

in reds in the following cycle. During these two cycles, the share of fortified wines in domestic sales shrank, from 53 percent to just 7 percent.

There were numerous takeovers of old family wineries by large corporations during this period (Anderson 2015, table 23(a)). In some cases, this added a sharper commercial edge to production, research and development (R&D) and marketing, not least because companies listed on the stock exchange had to regularly report their net returns to shareholders. One consequence was the commercial development of the 2- to 4-litre cask, or 'wine in a box', which added hugely to domestic demand at the low-quality end of the market. White wine eclipsed reds in the domestic market by 1976, and their sales continued to skyrocket: the volume of white wine sold in Australia in a plastic bag inside a box rose from 33 to 152 ML per year between 1978 and 1984, while bottled red and white wine sales declined from 73 to 55 ML. That was not enough to make the industry internationally competitive, however, particularly with the Australian dollar appreciating in the mid-1970s and again in the early 1980s thanks to rises in the international prices of some of Australia's primary export products (Anderson 2017a).

The move away from reds was partly triggered by a histamine health scare associated with red wine consumption (later shown to be a fiction). It was partly also because the reds produced to meet the domestic demand growth from the mid-1960s were of relatively low quality or not aged sufficiently when released for sale. One reason for the low quality is that Grenache grapes, whose demand had fallen away with the decline in sales of ports, were being used without great finesse in dry wine production. Meanwhile, new production techniques involving refrigeration and stainless steel pressure tanks brought out more fruit flavours and aromas in white wine, making it relatively more attractive particularly for newcomers to table wine consumption (notably women). A subsequent new technique for producing sparkling whites at low cost added to that in the 1980s, as did the fashion swing by wine consumers towards Chardonnay from the mid-1980s (a grape variety that played no part in the earlier swing to white wines – see Anderson 2016). Allowing the sale of wine in supermarkets added to that domestic consumer trend towards whites, since at that time women did most of the shopping for food and beverages in those stores and they preferred whites to heavier red wines.

Neither of the surges in production in the two decades to the mid-1980s, of first red and then white table wines, was export-driven. On the contrary, exports had remained of minor and declining importance over those two decades and the two preceding them. Hence most of production was adversely affected when the government introduced a 10 percent wholesale sales tax on wine in 1984 and raised it to 20 percent two years later. That plus the perceived oversupply situation especially in reds in the mid-1980s meant the prospects for grapegrowers and winemakers looked bleak – so much so that the South Australian and Federal governments financed a vine-pull scheme in 1985–86. By paying growers $3,250 per hectare to remove their vines, it contributed to the one-ninth net reduction in vineyard bearing area between 1985 and 1987. At the time, it seemed inconceivable to most observers that another boom was about to begin.

Australia's Fifth Cycle: Export Take-off from 1986

The latest boom began in 1986 not with a vine planting expansion, but rather with a steady increase in exports to take advantage of the historically low value of the Australian dollar. That export growth was possible partly because there was, in addition to no growth in the volume of domestic wine consumption per capita over the 1980s and early 1990s, a continuing decline in the proportion of wine production being diverted for distillation and a rapid increase from the early 1990s in the share of grape production going into wine. The slow growth in volume of domestic consumption occurred despite a considerable growth in disposable income in Australia. It was due partly to consumers moving away from quantity and towards higher-quality wines (that is, away from nonpremium [especially fortified and flagon] wines to premium still wines in bottles) and partly to the tax on domestic wine consumption that was introduced in 1984 and raised in 1986 and again in 1993.

The export boom was so large as to raise wine's share of Australia's total merchandise value above 1 percent for the first time in 1999. The previous peak had been just below 0.9 percent in 1932 when other exports were severely depressed. A new peak was reached in 2004 at 2.3 percent, just as mineral exports were taking off. Australia's wine export volume and value continued to grow until 2007.

Associated with these changes were hikes in the prices of Australian wines. The domestic consumer price and the export price of Australian wine both grew by around 50 percent over that period. Those price changes stimulated vine plantings, wine production and wine exports: the volumes of wine production and exports were, respectively, 25 percent and more than 1,000 percent greater in 1992–94 than 1984–86.

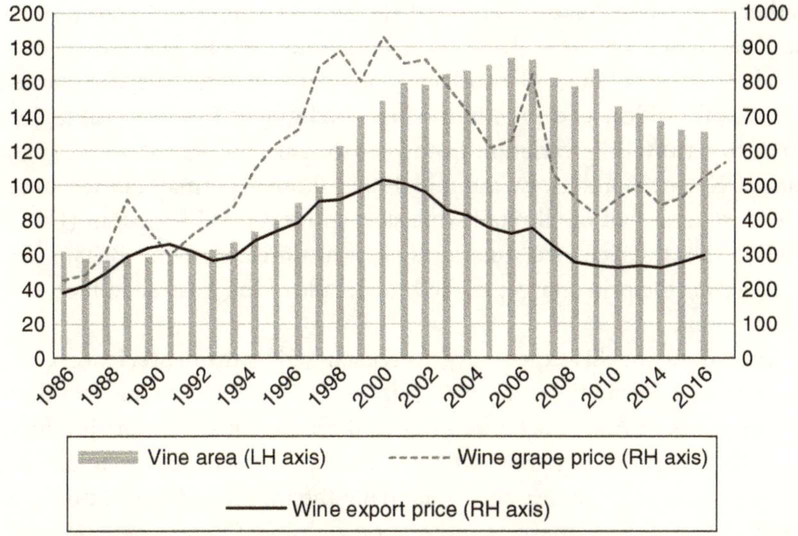

Figure 12.5 Vine area, and average price of winegrapes and of wine exports, Australia, 1985 to 2017 ('000 ha, A$ per tonne, and A$ per hectolitre).
Source: Anderson (2015).

Grapegrowers were major beneficiaries of the increase in Australian wine prices. The average price received for winegrapes was three times higher in 1999 than at the start of that decade, even though the export price rose only 60 percent (Figure 12.5).

An important contributor to this production and export growth relates to ownership concentration. There has been a huge increase in the number of Australian wine producers (peaking at 2,573 in 2014, compared with fewer than 200 in the early 1970s, 300 in the early 1980s and 530 in 1988). While most of the new wineries were very small, during this fifth boom, there were numerous mergers and takeovers by larger firms to form even larger conglomerates. The three biggest of those in terms of value of sales are Treasury Wine Estates, Accolade and Pernod Ricard, with Casella (maker of the Yellowtail brand) displacing Pernod Ricard in that list by volume of production or exports. The top three producers in 2014 accounted for more than 40 percent of the annual crush, of the number of bottles of wine sold and of the value of domestic sales. They also accounted for the majority of Australia's wine exports.

This ownership concentration provided the opportunity to reap large economies of scale not only in winemaking but also distribution and brand promotion, including through establishing their own sales offices abroad rather than relying on distributors.[14] The massive volumes of grapes grown and purchased by these firms from numerous regions enabled them to produce large volumes of consistent, popular wines for specific markets abroad. Those low-end premium wines used grapes from several regions so as to ensure little variation from year to year. This suited perfectly the large UK supermarkets. By the mid-1980s, those supermarkets accounted for more than half of all retail wine sales in the United Kingdom (Unwin 1991, p. 341). Given also Australia's close historical ties with Britain, that market was the prime target in the first decade of the Australian industry's latest boom.

The timing for this export surge was catalysed by the depreciation of the Australian dollar in the mid-1980s (Figure 12.6), which was due to a sharp fall in prices of Australia's coal, grain and other primary export products. That depreciation, together with low domestic prices for premium red grapes at the time, increased substantially the incentive for investment in developing overseas markets for Australian wine. Other factors expanding demand abroad for Australian wine at the time were food-safety scares associated with Chernobyl in April 1986 and scandals involving additives in Austrian and Italian wines (Rankine 1996). Also helpful in raising Australia's profile abroad was the win by an Australian sailing team of the America's Cup in 1983, the first visit to Australia by a group of Master of Wine graduates in 1984, and the release in 1986 of the popular comedy movie *Crocodile Dundee*. Meanwhile, competition from other New World countries was minimal: from South Africa because of anti-apartheid sentiment, from South America because of that region's macroeconomic and political instability and from the United States because the high value of its dollar ensured its exports were minimal. Generic marketing of Australian wine by the Australian Wine Export Council helped to build the country's international reputation for popular commercial premium-quality winegrape growing, winemaking and wine marketing.

This fifth boom was largely market-driven but was also influenced by changes in government interventions. The steady reduction in Australia's manufacturing protection and in assistance to some of its other agricultural industries, which began in 1972 and was accelerated through the 1980s and 1990s, parallelled and thus offset the price-reducing effect of reductions in

[14] The corporatization of firms helped in raising the enormous amounts of capital required for rapid expansion in the 1990s and beyond. The capital intensity of winegrape growing in the late 1990s was about 50 percent above that of other agriculture, and that of winemaking is more than one-fifth higher than that of other manufacturing.

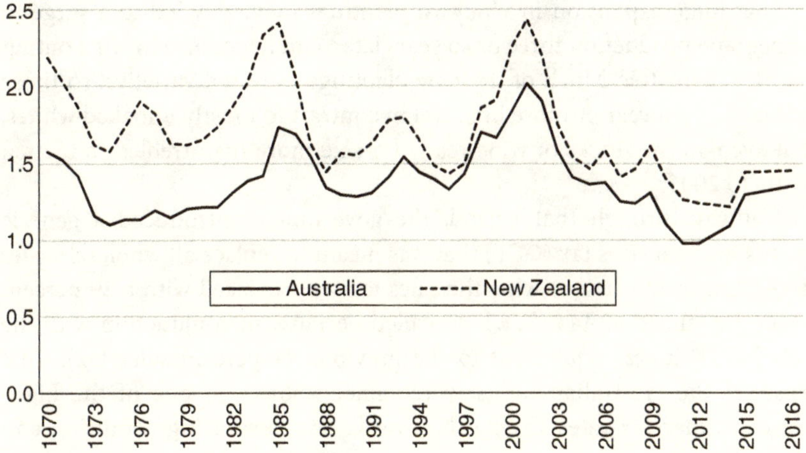

Figure 12.6 Real exchange rates,[a] Australia and New Zealand, 1970 to 2015.

[a] Local currency unit relative to the US$, adjusted for the difference between the country's consumer price index change and that of the United States.

Source: Anderson and Pinilla (2017).

nominal rates of assistance to grape and wine producers from 20 to 32 percent to below 5 percent over those two decades. The imposition from 1984 of the wholesale sales tax on wine dampened domestic sales and thereby encouraged exporting, while the government's vine-pull scheme in the mid-1980s led to the loss of some valuable old vines but the replacement of others with more profitable alternatives. By way of consolation for raising the wholesale sales tax again in 1993, the government assisted new plantings of vines by providing for accelerated depreciation of vineyard construction costs over just four years for tax purposes (even though the average life of the investments involved is closer to thirty years). That provision contributed nontrivially to the rapid acceleration in vineyard bearing area, which almost trebled during the boom (Table 12.1 and Figure 12.5).

In 1994–95, the wine industry developed and published a *Strategy 2025* document, laying out its targets for thirty years hence (AWF 1995). At the time, those targets were considered rather optimistic, since they involved a threefold increase in the real value of wine production, 55 percent of it for the export market. Getting halfway to those targets required having 80,000 ha of winegrapes bearing enough for a crush of 1,100 kt to produce 750 ML of wine at a wholesale pretax value of $3 billion ($4 per litre) in 1995–96 Australian dollars. By the turn of the century – that is, in just five vintages – the industry had reached that halfway point for achieving its targets thirty years out.

That huge expansion in vineyard plantings inevitably led to a surge in winegrape production three or so years later, and hence also in wine output shortly thereafter. Much of the new plantings were red varieties, so those wines spend a year or more in barrel in contrast to mostly unoaked whites, but even so the stocks of wine ready for sale more than trebled in the ten years to 2005.

Halfway through that period, the government introduced a generic goods-and-services tax (GST) that was meant to replace all wholesale sales taxes, but in the case of wine the sales tax was replaced with a 29 percent Wine Equalization Tax (WET, so-called because, in conjunction with the retail GST, it was equivalent to the previous 41 percent sales tax). That ensured the Australian industry remained subject to one of the highest consumer tax rates among the world's wine-exporting countries, and the only one to be subjected to an *ad valorem* rather than volumetric tax, which discriminates more against finer wines (Anderson 2010). In 2012, for example, that 29 percent wholesale tax on wine consumption in Australia compares with the equivalent of an 11 percent tax in New Zealand and an 8 percent tax average across all Organization for Economic Cooperation and Development (OECD) countries on a superpremium bottle of wine with a pretax price of $15 (or $20 per litre; see Table 12.2). Some relief has been provided to smaller wineries, though, in the form of a WET rebate up to a limit of A$500,000 per winery per year.

Meanwhile, several New World countries had begun to emulate the Australian export-led experience, leading to a growth spurt in their wine exports just a few years behind Australia's. Also, declining domestic consumption led several Old World suppliers plus Argentina and Chile to expand their exports. Thus Australian exporters began to face increasing competition just as the historically low value of the Australian dollar began its decade-long appreciation after 2001 (a fall in Figure 12.6). The latter contributed greatly to the decline from that time in the local-currency price of Australia's wine exports (Figure 12.5). The volume of those exports continued to expand each year until 2007, though, such was the need to dispose of rapidly growing stocks. Thereafter, when the volume of exports stabilized, their Australian dollars (AUD) value plummeted as the Australian dollar continued to rise in value in the wake of Australia's unprecedented improvement in its international terms of trade and the massive mining investment boom. The extent of that decline in the average wine export price from 2001 is as spectacular as its rise in the previous decade: by 2011, the average winegrape price had returned to the same nominal level as in 1989 (Figure 12.5).

Table 12.2 *Ad valorem equivalent of wholesale tax on domestic alcohol consumption at various price points, Australia and New Zealand, 2012 (%)*

	Non premium still wine ($2.50/litre)	Commercial premium still wine ($7.50/litre)	Super premium still wine ($20/litre)	Sparkling wine ($25/litre)	Beer ($2/ litre)	Spirits ($15/ litre)	GST/ VAT
Australia	29	29	29	29	107	184	10
New Zealand	86	29	11	9	52	352	15
All OECD countries (unweighted average)	40	15	8	9	43	74	18

Note: The prices shown refer to wholesale pretax prices per litre, so multiply by 0.75 to get per bottle prices and then add about 25 percent for retailer's margin plus the GST/VAT to get retail prices.
Source: Anderson (2014).

The resulting decline in AUD wine export prices saw a parallel decline in winegrape prices that was interrupted only by a short spike in 2008, following the drought-induced shortfall in production in the 2007 vintage. Domestic consumers have benefitted from this because the retail price index for wine has grown far less than the overall consumer price index every year for the decade from 2003.

The appreciating value of the Australian dollar also encouraged wine imports, which have grown dramatically since the turn of the century (Figure 12.2). New Zealand led the charge in supplying those imports, followed by France. Most of the wine from France has been relatively highly priced Champagne, while that from New Zealand has been mostly Sauvignon Blanc, which had a unit import value of around US$8 a litre during its first decade, compared with just US$5 for the wines being imported from Italy and Spain. Those import prices are well above Australia's export prices, which averaged just US$2.80 during 2000–10 and in 2011–13 were for the first time equalled by Chile and surpassed by the United States. New Zealand's Sauvignon Blanc has become the biggest-selling white wine in Australia, eclipsing Australian Chardonnay in the latter part of the first decade of this century, and has been a nontrivial contributor to the fall in the price of Australia's white wines and winegrapes. The surge in imports from New Zealand was particularly sharp from 2005, when the Australian government agreed that New Zealand wineries could receive the same rebate as Australian producers of the 29 percent tax on their wines sold in Australia (up to the ceiling of A$500,000 of sales per winery per year).

A direct consequence of the wine and grape price collapse was that both vineyard and winery asset prices plummeted after 2007, with some vineyards selling for no more than unimproved land value (as low as A$12,000 per hectare) even though the average cost of planting a vineyard was in the vicinity of A$30,000 per hectare. The collapse in value was partly because banks became disinterested in financing such purchases, and partly because listed corporations sought to shed their least-productive vineyard and winery assets to boost the rates of reported return on their remaining capital. The number of grapegrowing businesses fell by one-quarter between 2010 and 2015. The slump was in sharp contrast to the growth in industry asset prices in the United States and western Europe, which reached record levels in local currency terms at the start of the millennium's second decade, thanks to the weakening US dollar and Euro and the growth in demand for iconic wines and wineries by Chinese buyers.

NEW ZEALAND'S WINE BOOM

Not unlike in Australia, the wine industry in New Zealand has had many ups and downs in the two centuries since vines were first planted there in 1819 (by Samuel Marsden at the Bay of Islands). Cooper (1996) likens that history to a 'rollercoaster ride, soaring and plunging through successive periods of growth and optimism, decline and disillusionment'. Setbacks in the late nineteenth century included the assaults of powdery mildew and then phylloxera on the supply side and, on the demand side, the increasingly intense campaigning against alcohol consumption through to the 1920s that was almost as intense as in the United States.

Wine production expanded after the Labour government, which came to power in 1935, increased wine import tariffs and halved the volume of import licences – and required merchants to buy two litres of New Zealand wine for every litre they imported. It continued to grow through World War II (when American servicemen were hosted on leave) and in the subsequent two decades as government regulations eased on winery cellar door sales and on the licencing of retail outlets and of restaurants to sell wine with meals. Wine imports increased when wartime import restrictions were eased in the late 1940s, only to fall again when Labour returned to government in 1957 and tightened import restrictions once more in response to lobbying by the industry.[15]

[15] To progress its interests further, the industry formed a single united Wine Institute in 1975. Up until that time, most winemakers grew their own grapes, but gradually independent grapegrowers emerged and by the mid-1990s wineries produced only one-third of the grapes they crushed. Even so, those grapegrowers saw virtue in joining with winemakers in 2002 to form New Zealand Winegrowers.

A blow to producers came in 1984 when the government raised the excise tax on domestic sales of still wines by 83 percent and then opened the economy to foreign trade and investment. That trade policy move included removing barriers to wine imports and to direct foreign investment from Australia under the Australia–New Zealand Closer Economic Relations Trade Agreement (ANZCERTA). Together these policy changes caused local producer prices to fall and profits to vanish. In response, the government decided to subsidize a vine-pull scheme aimed at reducing the number of vines by one-quarter. Growers were paid NZ$6175 (=US$3,230) for every hectare of grapes they removed. The more astute ones pulled out their less desirable varieties (Müller-Thurgau was the most heavily culled) and used the subsidy to pay for replacing them with more marketable varieties, such as Sauvignon Blanc and Chardonnay, as there were no restrictions on new plantings.[16] So even though nearly 30 percent of the nation's vineyard area was removed, this was a catalyst to modernizing the industry.

An offsetting boost to the development of New Zealand's wine industry from the mid-1980s was that the country's real exchange rate then was even weaker than Australia's (Figure 12.6). That, together with flat domestic sales, made exporting suddenly appear attractive to producers in New Zealand, just as it was to Australian producers at that time. The takeoff from then was meteoric: over the next three decades, New Zealand increased about sixfold its vine area and wine production indicators. The number of wineries grew from 130 in 1990 (having been 100 as long ago as 1932) to 700 by 2012. Per capita consumption increased by only about 50 percent, however, so most of the output growth was destined for exports – which expanded from virtually zero to more than three-quarters of production by 2010–15 (Table 12.3), making it the world's most export-dependent wine-producing country. That happened despite a real appreciation in the NZ dollar similar

[16] From a clone of Sauvignon Blanc that was imported to New Zealand by Romeo Bragato in 1906 and retained in the Te Kauwhata Viticultural Research Centre, Ross Spence grafted some cuttings onto 1202 rootstock and from his nursery was able to plant 250 vines in his Matua Road vineyard in West Auckland in 1968. The crop suffered from leaf roll virus infection, but a sample of wine produced from the small crop was promising, and by 1974 Spence produced a commercial quantity from that block for his Matua Valley winery. That clone yielded less than 0.6 tonnes per hectare, so Spence sought a new virus-free clone. He found one (TK05196, later known as UCD1) in a Department of Agriculture trial block that had been planted in Corban's Kumeu vineyard in 1970 from material imported from the University of California, Davis. A source block of less than 3 ha was planted to this clone in 1978 at the Matua Waimauku Vineyard, from which plantings in Marborough blossomed from 1980 (Spence 2001). More recently, however, files of Pernot Ricard New Zealand, have revealed that firm to be the Sauvignon Blanc pioneer in Marborough, first planting 20 ha to UCD1 in its Brancott Estate vineyard in 1975 (Cooper 2008).

Table 12.3 *Varietal shares of bearing vineyard area, New Zealand, 1956 to 2016 (%)*

	1956	1966	1976	1986	1996	2006	2015
(a) Australia							
Syrah	13	12	19	14	14	27	29
Cabernet Sauvignon	0	1	6	9	13	19	18
Chardonnay	0	0	0	5	15	19	16
Merlot	0	0	0	0	2	7	6
Sauvignon Blanc	0	0	0	1	2	3	5
Pinot Noir	0	0	0	1	3	3	4
Semillon	3	7	5	7	6	4	3
Pinot Gris	0	0	0	00	0	1	3
Riesling	3	2	4	11	7	3	2
Muscat varieties	16	15	9	11	7	2	2
Garnacha	19	15	12	7	4	1	1
Doradillo	11	7	4	3	1	0	0
Pedro Ximenez	9	9	0	0	0	0	0
Sultana	5	4	21	7	11	0	0
Others	12	28	20	24	15	11	11
Total	100	100	100	100	100	100	100

	1986	1996	2006	2016
(b) New Zealand				
Sauvignon Blanc	7	17	39	58
Pinot Noir	3	7	18	15
Chardonnay	10	22	17	9
Merlot	1	5	6	4
Pinot Gris	0	1	3	7
Riesling	6	4	4	2
Müller-Thurgau	31	11	1	0
Cabernet Sauvignon	8	8	2	1
Syrah	0	0	1	1
Muscat varieties	6	3	1	0
Chenin Blanc	6	2	0	0
Others	22	20	8	3
Total	100	100	100	100

Sources: Anderson (2015) and New Zealand Winegrowers, *Annual Report*, various issues.

to Australia's during 2001–2014 thanks to a boom in the country's dairy exports. There was a slight fall in the US dollar value of New Zealand's wine exports in 2015, but that was true of all New World exporters because of the strengthening of the US dollar (Figure 2.9 of Chapter 2 of this book).

New Zealand has relatively little of its farm land under broadacre crops, so the share of vineyards in its total crop area is now ten times that of Australia, above France, Spain and Moldova, and almost as high as Italy, Portugal and Georgia (Anderson and Pinilla 2017, table 3).

In 2015, wine accounted for 3 percent of the value of all merchandise exports from New Zealand (Table 12.4), compared to just under 1 percent in Australia. That share divided by wine's share of all merchandise exports globally is known as the index of 'revealed' comparative advantage (RCA) in wine. New Zealand's RCA exceeded Australia's for the first time in 2007, and since then it has diverged ever further, and by 2014 was nearly four times the RCA for its bigger neighbour – and well above France and so exceeded only by Georgia and Moldova (Figure 12.7).

The majority of New Zealand's wine exports went to the United Kingdom and the United States, but, after 2005, between one-quarter and one-third of them were imported by Australia. That sales growth to Australia was stimulated not only by bilateral real exchange rate movements but also by the fact that wineries in New Zealand successfully lobbied Australia, under ANZCERTA, for a rebate of Australia's wine consumption tax up to a limit of A$500,000 of sales in Australia per winery per year. Almost all of those sales were white wines (mostly Sauvignon Blanc from the Marlborough region). Because China imports mostly red wines, it is not surprising that the share of exports going to Asia from New Zealand is less than the global average and far smaller than that from Australia during the past decade. The share of New Zealand's wine exports going to the United States has now caught up with Australia's (Table 12.5). Indeed, in 2016 the value of wine exports to the United States from New Zealand exceeded that from Australia for the first time (US$400 million versus $351 million). True, the volume of wine imported by the United States from Australia was more than twice the volume from New Zealand, but on average the latter was more than 2.5 times the price of Australian wine at the border in 2016.

Meanwhile, the majority of New Zealand's wine imports have been still reds, with two-thirds coming from Australia. As for many other products, the wine markets of Australia and New Zealand have become highly integrated and complementary, with the same large firms operating on both sides of the Tasman Sea. That integration has been facilitated by not just

Table 12.4 *New Zealand wine industry developments, 1960 to 2015*

	Vine area ('000 ha)	Wine production (ML)	Wine exports (ML)	Vine area per 10,000 people (ha)	Vines/ total crop area (%)	Wine prod'n per capita (L)	Wine exports per capita (L)	% wine prod'n exported	Wine cons'm per capita (L)	% wine cons'm imported	Wine's share of all merch. exports (%)
1960–64	1	5	0	2	0.1	2	0	0	2	18	0.0
1965–69	1	12	0	2	0.1	4	0	0	4	12	0.0
1970–74	2	26	0	5	0.4	9	0	0	8	8	0.0
1975–79	3	34	0	10	0.6	11	0	0	10	6	0.0
1980–84	5	48	1	16	1.0	15	0	1	13	7	0.0
1985–89	4	45	2	14	1.0	14	0	4	14	8	0.1
1990–94	6	44	7	17	1.2	12	2	17	14	30	0.2
1995–99	9	56	13	25	1.9	15	4	24	16	47	0.4
2000–04	14	75	31	35	2.8	19	8	43	18	61	0.9
2005–09	26	159	85	63	5.2	38	21	54	20	45	2.0
2010–14	35	237	174	78	5.9	54	39	75	21	39	2.5
2015	36	235	212	79	5.8	52	47	90	19	42	3.2

Source: Anderson and Pinilla (2017).

Table 12.5 *Direction of wine exports, by value, Australia and New Zealand, 1990 to 2015 (%)*

	Western Europe	North America	Asia	New Zealand	Other	Total
(a) Australia						
1990–95	60	23	8	9	1	100
1996-2001	58	29	7	5	1	100
2002–06	48	41	6	4	1	100
2007–12	41	37	17	4	2	100
2013–15	29	33	31	4	2	100
(b) New Zealand						
1990–95	79	6	6	9	0	100
1996-2001	64	17	5	14	0	100
2002–06	44	29	4	22	1	100
2007–12	34	27	6	31	1	100
2013–15	32	32	6	27	3	100

Source: Anderson, Nelgen and Pinilla (2017).

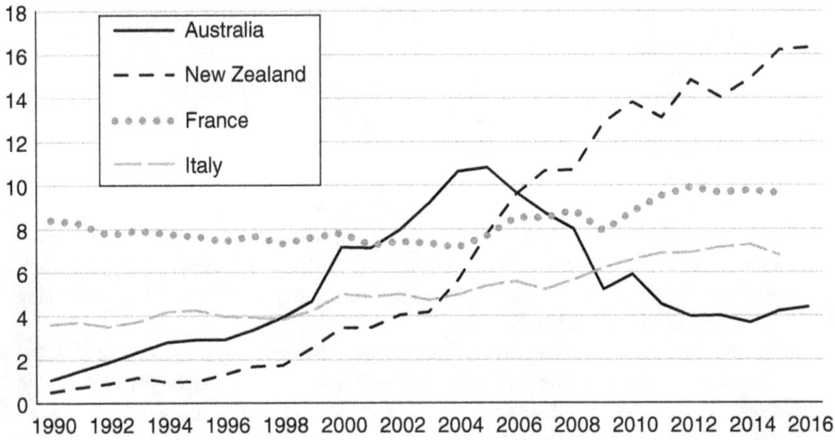

Figure 12.7 Index of 'revealed' comparative advantage in wine,[a] Australia, New Zealand, France and Italy, 1990 to 2016.

[a] Wine's share of a country's exports divided by wine's share of the global value of exports.
Source: Anderson and Pinilla (2017).

proximity but also the gradual deepening since 1983 of the Australia–New Zealand Closer Economic Relations Trade Agreement.

For some years now, New Zealand has had the world's highest average price of exported still wines and is second only to France for the unit value of exports of all wines (including sparking). During 2013–15, that average export price was more than twice the average price of Australian wine exports, but possibly similar to the average for wine exports from Australia's equally cool regions such as Tasmania and parts of southern Victoria and the Adelaide Hills. With lower costs of land and labour in New Zealand than in Australia during the previous two decades, it is not surprising that multinational wine companies were attracted to New Zealand. That in turn has reinforced the competitiveness of the country in international wine markets, as those firms brought with them the latest knowledge not only with respect to viticulture and oenology but also wine marketing and export market niche information. It has contributed to the fact that all but the smallest category of producers operated with healthy profits in all years during 2006–14, apart from a dip for some in 2010 (Deloitte and NZW 2014). That New Zealand situation was not unlike that in the United States, where during 2009–14 producers had relatively rosy financial results (Silicon Valley Bank 2016); but it contrasted markedly with that in Australia during 2012–15, where reportedly the vast majority of producers were not covering even their variable costs of production (WFA 2015).

REFERENCES

Allen, M. (2012), *The History of Australian Wine: Stories from the Vineyard to the Cellar Door*, Melbourne: Victory (Melbourne University Publishing Ltd).

Anderson, K. (ed.) (1992), *New Silk Roads: East Asia and World Textile Markets*, Cambridge and New York: Cambridge University Press.

(2010), 'Excise and Import Taxes on Wine vs Beer and Spirits: An International Comparison', *Economic Papers* 29(2): 215–28, June.

(2014), 'Excise Taxes on Wines, Beers and Spirits: An Updated International Comparison', *Wine and Viticulture Journal* 29(6): 66–71, November/December. Also available as Working Paper No. 170, American Association of Wine Economists, October 2014.

(with the assistance of N. R. Aryal) (2015), *Growth and Cycles in Australia's Wine Industry: A Statistical Compendium, 1843 to 2013*, Adelaide: University of Adelaide Press. Also freely available as an e-book at www.adelaide.edu.au/press/titles/austwine

(2016), 'Evolving Varietal and Quality Distinctiveness of Australia's Wine Regions', *Journal of Wine Research* 27(3): 173–92, September.

(2017a), 'Sectoral Trends and Shocks in Australia's Economic Growth', *Australian Economic History Review* 57(1): 2–21, March.

(2017b), 'Australia's Comparative Advantage in Wine: Why So Slow to Emerge?', Wine Economics Research Centre Working Paper 0317, University of Adelaide, November.

(2017c), 'Evolving from a Rum State: A Comparative History of Australia's Alcohol Consumption', Wine Economics Research Centre Working Paper 0617, University of Adelaide, December.

Anderson, K. and N. R. Aryal (2015), *Australian Grape and Wine Industry Database, 1843 to 2013*. Freely available at the Wine Economics Research Centre, University of Adelaide, Adelaide, at www.adelaide.edu.au/wine-econ/databases

Anderson, K., S. Nelgen and V. Pinilla (2017), *Global Wine Markets, 1860 to 2016: A Statistical Compendium*, Adelaide: University of Adelaide Press.

Anderson, K. and V. Pinilla (with the assistance of A. J. Holmes) (2017), *Annual Database of Global Wine Markets, 1835 to 2016.* Freely available in Excel files at the University of Adelaide's Wine Economics Research Centre, www.adelaide.edu.au/wine-econ/databases

AWF (Australian Wine Fund) (1995), *Strategy 2025: The Australian Wine Industry*, Adelaide: Winemakers' Federation of Australia (WFA) for the Australian Wine Foundation.

Beeston, J. (2001), *A Concise History of Australian Wine*, 3rd Edition, Sydney: Allen and Unwin.

Bell, G. (1993), 'The South Australian Wine Industry, 1858–1876', *Journal of Wine Research* 4(3): 147–63.

(1994), 'The London Market for Australian Wine, 1851–1901: A South Australian Perspective', *Journal of Wine Research* 5(1): 19–40.

Brady, M. (2008), *First Taste: How Indigenous Australians Learnt About Grog*, Canberra: Alcohol Education and Rehabilitation Foundation.

Bragato, R. (1895), *Report on the Prospects of Viticulture in New Zealand, and Instructions for Planting and Pruning*, Wellington: Government Printer.

Busby, J. (1830), *A Manual of Plain Directions for Planting and Cultivating Vineyards and for Making Wine in New South Wales*, Sydney: R. Mansfield.

Butlin, N. G. (1983), 'Yo, Ho, Ho and How Many Bottles of Rum?' *Australian Economic History Review* 23(1): 1–27, March.

Chevet, J.-M., E. Fernandez, E. Giraud-Héraud and V. Pinilla (2018), 'France', ch. 3 in *Wine' Globalization: A New Comparative History*, edited by K. Anderson and V. Pinilla, Cambridge and New York: Cambridge University Press.

Cooper, M. (1996), 'A Brief History of Wine in New Zealand', pp. 8–11 in *The Wines and Vineyards of New Zealand*, edited by M. Cooper, Auckland: Holder Moa Beckett. Updated and expanded in pp. 8–13 of his *Wine Atlas of New Zealand*, Auckland: Holder Moa, 2008.

(2008), 'Discovering the Roots of Sauvignon Blanc in New Zealand', *New Zealand Listener*, 1 March.

Davidson, B. R. (1969), *Australia Wet or Dry?* Melbourne: Melbourne University Press.

Dingle, A. E. (1980), '"The Truly Magnificent Thirst": An Historical Survey of Australian Drinking Habits', *Historical Studies* 19(75): 227–49.

de Bromhead, A., A. Fernihough, K. O'Rourke and M. Lampe (2017), 'When Britain Turned Inward: Protection and the Shift Towards Empire in Interwar Britain', NBER Working Paper 23164, Cambridge MA, February.

Deloitte and NZW (2014), *Vintage 2014 New Zealand Wine Industry Benchmarking Survey*, Auckland: New Zealand Winegrowers, December.

Dunstan, D. (1994), *Better Than Pommard! A History of Wine in Victoria*, Melbourne: Australian Scholarly Publishing and the Museum of Victoria.

Faith, N. (2003), *Australia's Liquid Gold*, London: Mitchell Beazley.

Findlay, R. and K. H. O'Rourke (2007), *Power and Plenty: Trade, War and the World Economy in the Second Millennium*, Princeton, NJ: Princeton University Press.

Griffiths, J. M. (1966), *The Wine Industry of South Australia 1880–1914*, unpublished B.A. Honours Thesis, Department of History, University of Adelaide, Adelaide.

Halliday, J. (1994), *A History of the Australian Wine Industry: 1949–1994*, Adelaide: Winetitles for the Australian Wine and Brandy Corporation.

Harley, C. K. (1988), 'Ocean Freight Rates and Productivity, 1740–1913: The Primacy of Mechanical Invention Reaffirmed', *Journal of Economic History* 48: 851–76, December.
Hatton, T. J., K. H. O'Rourke and J. G. Williamson (eds.) (2007), 'Introduction', pp. 1–14 in *The New Comparative Economic History: Essays in Honor of Jeffrey G. Williamson*, Cambridge, MA: MIT Press.
Irvine, H. W. H. (1892), *Report on the Australian Wine Trade*, Melbourne: R.S. Brain, Government Printer for the Victorian Minister of Agriculture.
Jiranek, V. (2017), Personal communication, 6 January.
Kelly, A. C. (1867), *Wine-growing in Australia*, Adelaide: E.S. Wigg.
Laffer, H. E. (1949), *The Wine Industry of Australia*, Adelaide: Australian Wine Board.
Lloyd, P. J. (1973), *Non-tariff Distortions of Australian Trade*, Canberra: Australian National University Press.
Ludington, C. (2018), 'United Kingdom', ch. 9 in *Wine Globalization: A New Comparative History*, edited by K. Anderson and V. Pinilla, Cambridge and New York: Cambridge University Press.
Maddock, R. and I. McLean (1984), 'Supply-Side Shocks: The Case of Australian Gold', *Journal of Economic History* 64(4): 1047–67, December.
McIntyre, J. (2012), *First Vintage: Wine in Colonial New South Wales*, Sydney: University of New South Wales Press.
Meloni, G. and J. Swinnen (2013), 'The Political Economy of European Wine Regulations', *Journal of Wine Economics* 8(3): 244–84, Winter.
(2014), 'The Rise and Fall of the World's Largest Wine Exporter — and Its Institutional Legacy', *Journal of Wine Economics* 9(1): 3–33, Spring.
(2018), 'Algeria, Morocco and Tunisia', ch. 16 in *Wine Globalization: A New Comparative History*, edited by K. Anderson and V. Pinilla, Cambridge and New York: Cambridge University Press.
Mohammed, S. I. and J. G. Williamson (2004), 'Freight Rates and Productivity Gains in British Tramp Shipping 1869–1950', *Explorations in Economic History* 41(2): 172–203.
Moran, W. (2017), *New Zealand Wine: The Land, the Vines, the People*, London and Melbourne: Hardie Grant.
Pinilla, V. and M. I. Ayuda (2002), 'The Political Economy of the Wine Trade: Spanish Exports and the International Market, 1890–1935', *European Review of Economic History* 6: 51–85.
Pope, D. (1971), 'Viticulture and Phylloxera in North-East Victoria', *Australian Economic History Review* 10(1).
Rankine, B. (1996), *Evolution of the Modern Australian Wine Industry: A Personal Appraisal*, Adelaide: Ryan Publications.
Ryan, G. (2010), 'Drink and the Historians: Sober Reflections on Alcohol in New Zealand 1840–1914', *New Zealand Journal of History* 44(1): 35–53, April.
Sieper, E. (1982), *Rationalizing Rustic Regulation*, Sydney: Centre for Independent Studies.
Silicon Valley Bank (2016), *State of the Wine Industry 2016*, Santa Clara, CA: Silicon Valley Bank.
Simpson, J. (2011), *Creating Wine: The Emergence of a World Industry, 1840–1914*, Princeton, NJ: Princeton University Press.

Spence, R. (2001), 'The History of Sauvignon Blanc', *New Zealand Winegrower*. Reprinted 16 June 2017 at www.ruralnewsgroup.co.nz/item/12075-the-history-of-sauvignon-blanc

Stewart, K. (2010), *Chancers and Visionaries: A History of New Zealand Wine*, Auckland: Godwit.

Unwin, T. (1991), *Wine and the Vine: An Historical Geography of Viticulture and the Wine Trade*, London and New York: Routledge.

WFA (2015), *Vintage Report 2015*, Adelaide: Winemakers Federation of Australia, July.

13

Chile

William Foster and Oscar Melo

The history of Chilean wine dates back to the arrival of Spanish conquistadors over 475 years ago.[1] While the country's Mediterranean climate and good soils meant early widespread plantings of vineyards, it was not until the latter half of nineteenth century that wine production and drinking habits began to evolve slowly from colonial traditions, based on the robust but unrefined País grape variety, to the industry's present-day global orientation and sophistication. This chapter begins with an overview of long-run trends in the wine sector's development and the cycles around those trends, and then turns to more detail regarding the modern industry and domestic wine consumption.

The slow introduction of French wine varieties and technologies initiated the evolution of the Chilean wine industry towards its present character. Yet this progress was punctuated by periods of fast growth and then stagnation due in major part to government regulations – motivated by both concerns regarding high rates of alcoholism and an industry wanting higher prices via production controls. With major economic policy reforms in the 1980s, the wine industry regained vitality and began looking outward to foreign markets for growth. We discuss the dramatic developments that have modernized and refocused the industry on foreign consumers, since transition to civilian government in 1990s. We then turn our attention from supply to demand to explore the evolution of domestic consumption patterns for wine and other alcoholic beverages, before summarizing and drawing some conclusions regarding the future for Chilean wine.

1 The authors are professors at the Department of Agricultural Economics at the Pontificia Universidad Católica de Chile. The authors would like to thank Viviana Rebufel for her assistance in data collection.

LONG-RUN WINE TRENDS, CYCLES AND TURNING POINTS

When distilling the history of Chilean wines, it is useful to emphasize four phases of development leading to the wine industry's final takeoff into international markets at the end of the last century. These phases are the colonial period prior to 1850, the period of French renovation from 1850 to 1880, an expansionary period from 1880 to the 1930s and the restrictive period beginning in the late 1930s that lasted until the mid-1970s.

Colonial Continuity: Prior to 1850

Soon after Pedro de Valdivia led in 1540 the first Spanish expedition southward from modern Peru to explore and conquer what would become the country of Chile, wine production began in the new settlement of La Serena on the Pacific coast.[2] By the mid-1550s, large vineyards planted around the small town of Santiago were growing the País grape variety, a variety deriving originally from Listán negro, or prieto, and related to Mission in California and Criolla in Argentina (Robinson, Harding and Vouillamoz. 2012). Soon thereafter, priests took vine cuttings eastward across the Andes to Santiago del Estero in present-day Argentina. The hardy, adaptable País variety, which likely originated in Spain and passed through Mexico and then Peru, was to become the most important variety for popular consumption in Chile for 400 years, and to this day it still occupies a significant fraction of land planted to wine grapes.

Expanding from around Santiago, wine production spread throughout Chile, from the semiarid north to the rainy, cooler coastal south around the colonial settlement of Concepción. Production reached perhaps as much as 1.6 ML by 1594. Even though that was only about one-tenth of the production in Peru at that time, it was respectable nevertheless considering the far smaller colonial population in Chile.

The success of wine production in South America, importantly in Peru, led to Spanish royal restrictions aimed at slowing new plantings and restraining intra-American wine trade so as to promote Spanish wine exports. By 1654, new vineyards required government authorization.

[2] The most complete synthesis of the early history of Chilean wine, from which this section draws heavily, is del Pozo (1998). Another source covering the period 1870 to 1930 is Fernandez Labbe (2010). A synthesis of the origin of Chilean wine with an emphasis on southern regions is found in Hernández and Moreno (2011). Other sources of pertinent information are Alvarado (2004), Cisterna (2013), Couyoumdjian (2006) and Hernandez (2000).

The government of Chile, by contrast, intervened in the domestic market for wine ostensibly on the side of consumers. Wine was considered so important that the authorities declared it an essential good (like bread, salt, potatoes and other staples) and sought to enforce fixed prices. Official price controls on wine lasted until the eighteenth century. The general population, influenced in part by indigenous culture, also emphasized other intoxicating beverages such as chicha and punches made with aguardiente. Hence domestic wine consumption may not have grown rapidly during the colonial period.

Domestic wine production did grow during that colonial period, despite Spain's effort to restrict it. Chilean wineries with surpluses could reach consumers in countries to the north, and there is some evidence that Chile began exports of wine very early. In 1578, Sir Francis Drake captured what could have been the colony's first wine exports (Johnson 1989, p. 174). Certainly Peru was importing some Chilean wine from the 1600s, although with some protectionist controls. The earliest reliable statistics regarding wine exports date from the last quarter of the 1700s. In 1795, for example, Chile's wine shipments to Lima represented about 5 percent of the value of all Chilean exports to Peru, which included most importantly wheat but also copper.

The French Renovation of the Wine Industry: From 1850 to 1880

An early, important milestone in the progress of Chile's modern wine industry is the establishment in 1830 near Santiago of the country's first agricultural experiment station by Claude Gay, a French botanist and naturalist. In a short period of time, the station had sixty varieties of wine grapes and 40,000 vines. But national wine production was not immediately influenced. Gay estimated that in 1850 there were approximately 30,000 ha in vineyards, of which half was near the city of Concepción in the cooler, rain-fed south, where today there is comparatively little wine production. Later, as the French influence on Chilean producers took hold and with the help of irrigation development, wine grape production shifted to around Santiago in the more arid north.

Beginning in the early 1850s, new wineries turned to European-style wines in earnest, when Silvestre Ochagavía Echazarreta, an important player in Chilean social and political life, began converting his vineyards to European varieties. Soon other extensive vineyards, owned by politicians, wealthy businesspeople and mining magnates, followed suit, planting Merlot, Cabernet Sauvignon, Malbec, Semillon, Riesling and other varieties. Thus began most of the large wineries that continue to the present, with such names as Concha y Toro, Errázuriz and Cousiño. With the employment of imported European experts and experience, wine quality improved, so much so that Chilean wine in the new style gained recognition in various international exhibitions, beginning with that in Vienna in 1873.

Even though new wineries closer to Santiago focused on European varieties, older vineyards maintained traditional patterns of production in terms of technology and the use of the País variety. Beginning with the first statistics available in 1861, and prior to the 1880s, annual wine production was on the order of 30 ML and showed no obvious trend, before volumes steadily increased thereafter (Figure 13.1(a)).

In addition to what is traditionally considered wine per se, during this period two grape-derived beverages, chicha and chacolí, were popularly consumed in large volumes. Chicha is a sweet drink made from partially fermented must – a ciderlike, usually low-alcohol beverage made usually from grapes, but also from other fruits, such as apples in the colder south. Chicha was consumed in two forms. The 'raw' form, taken from the still fermenting must, usually was consumed quickly after wine production began and was not stored for many months. The other form was a cooked version to stop fermentation, sanitize the product and condense it for extra sweetness. Chilean chacolí (not exactly similar but close to Basque/Spanish Txakoli) is a dry, low-alcohol and high-acidity wine drink. As the production (and demand) for standard wine increased in the last third of the nineteenth century, the absolute volumes of chicha and chacolí declined somewhat and their proportions declined significantly relative to wine. In the mid-1870s, chicha production in litres was about 90 percent of that of wine, and chacolí was about 80 percent that of wine. In the mid-1920s, chicha production was about 17 percent of that of wine and chacolí was 11 percent, and afterwards statistics on the two beverages are unavailable.[3]

Expansion: 1880 to 1938

Beginning in the early 1880s the volume of wine production grew rapidly, roughly tripling between 1885 and 1905 (Figure 13.1(a)). After a significant

[3] Before 1861, no data for chicha and chacolí are available. Similarly, there appear no data beyond the mid-1920s, when consumption of those beverages was declining. Today, chicha is still produced artisanally for rural families and local markets, and commercially in significant volumes for patriotic holidays due to symbolic appeal.

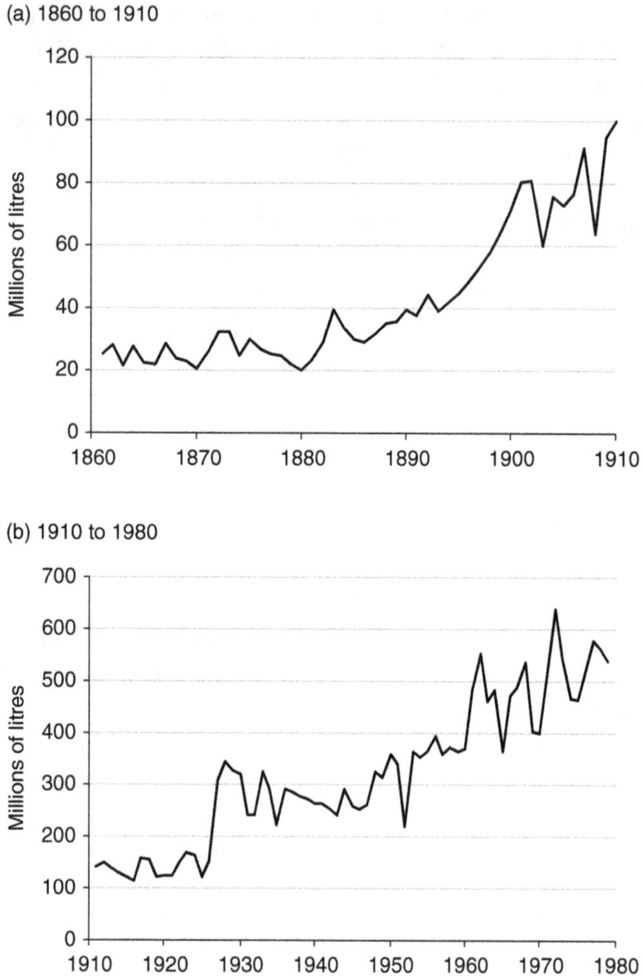

Figure 13.1 Chilean wine production, 1860 to 1980 (ML).
Source: Republic of Chile, *Anuario Estadístico de la República de Chile*, various years.

shock between 1905 and 1908 (volumes fell by 45 percent, perhaps influenced by the introduction in 1902 of new taxes on wine consumption), production returned to preshock levels but remained relatively stable until the late 1920s. As Figure 13.1(b) shows, production levels experienced another surge beginning in 1927, doubling volumes produced, but then remained relatively stable for two decades.

There were some exports of Chilean wine, beginning in 1877, and Chile did become South America's main wine exporter, shipping wine to its regional neighbours and intermittently to California. Nevertheless, export volumes remained very small relative to national production, usually around 1 percent. From the mid-1800s until the end of the 1970s, Chile's exports were overwhelmingly from the mining industry: copper, potash and other minerals. From 1880 for almost a century, the mining industry accounted for over 80 percent of total annual exports, pulling labour and materials from and raising production costs in other sectors. The tendency of the export success of one sector to undermine the international competitiveness and slow the export growth of other sectors, such as Chilean wine, was also seen in the cases of exports of Australian wool and gold and New Zealand wool and meat. Not until the late 1920s did Chilean wine export volumes reach beyond 2 percent of production. This increase was spurred in part by government export subsidies, a similar export policy to that implemented in Australia during the mid-1920s (Anderson and Pinilla 2017).

During the first fifty years of Chile's modern wine industry, exports were never an important outlet, and while per capita consumption did increase, there was a rapid rise in the quantity of wine produced, outpacing population growth significantly. In 1935, the population was 77 percent greater than in 1885, but wine production less exports had increased by 600 percent. Not only had Chile excellent growing conditions for wine grapes, but there was nothing stopping the import of winemakers, technology and know-how. Soon competition created what producers called a 'crisis of overproduction', which is to say wine prices were low and consumers were happy. Annual wine consumption per capita increased from below 20 litres prior to 1900 to 60 and more litres during the 1930s. This price-induced change in drinking habits dismayed legislators, fearful of what were perceived as the socially destructive consequences of their constituents' propensity to become intoxicated. Politicians chose to apply taxes to discourage wine consumption, which further depressed the industry.

Unsurprisingly, grape producers and winemakers, many of whom were from the country's influential aristocracy, sought government aid against the consequences of what they ominously insisted was excessive production. The various interests within the industry had begun to organize. Complaints both about surviving for decades with 'prices lower than costs' and about new discriminatory taxes were consolidated at the First National Congress of Wine in 1933. Soon thereafter appeared the 'bootlegger and Baptist' phenomenon of a political marriage between those with narrower commercial interests and those pursuing social reforms.[4]

[4] The original formulation of the idea is found in Yandle (1983). A more thorough treatment of the topic is in Smith and Yandle (2014).

Restrictions and Decadence: 1938 to 1973

The combination of politically prominent wine producers concerned about their bottom line and of interventionist politicians worried about *un veneno para el pueblo* – literally, a people's poison – came together in 1939 to prohibit new vineyards, regulate transplanting and otherwise limit production. The ostensible goal of the resulting government restrictions on wine production was to maintain domestic yearly consumption to 60 litres per capita. It was successful in reducing the number of vineyards by 10 percent and controlling the number of hectares under production. While remaining highly volatile year to year, average prices paid to producers did increase considerably, averaging 33 percent higher in the 1940s compared to the 1933–1939 period, and per capita consumption did fall. Nonetheless, the industry entered into decades of stagnation. Moreover, the same political atmosphere that made interventions in the wine industry possible also promoted an increase in economic protectionism more generally.

Looking back on this era of government restrictions, industry participants recognize that the 1940s 'began the decadence of the Chilean wine industry in comparison with the development of activities in the rest of the world. Our country's borders were closed to all imports except the essentials; among which obviously were not inputs for the wine industry' (Hernández 2000, p. 11, authors' translation). It would take another thirty-five years before Chile would reform its economic policies to allow economic activities generally – and the wine sector very dramatically – to take advantage of trade and liberalized markets.

THE MODERN INDUSTRY: FROM STAGNATION TO GROWTH AND INTERNATIONAL SUCCESS

The period between the 1940s and the mid-1970s was generally one of increasing government interventions in much of the economy. In broad brush strokes, the three main goals of agriculture-focused policies were to keep price inflation in check, avoid adding to budget deficits and improve foreign exchange earnings (Valdés and Foster 2006). So although there were some periods of moderated interventionism, the government tended to rely on price controls, by fixing nominal farm prices and marketing margins at the retail level for essential products (wage goods). An industrial policy of restricting imports – via tariffs, import licenses and other trade barriers – to stimulate domestic industries was in effect an implicit tax on potential exports. Wine and winegrowing areas, as was much of Chile's fruit and horticulture zone, were among those adversely affected.

Policies more directly relevant to grape producers and the wine industry were differentiated tariffs and prior deposits and other hindrances to imports of agricultural chemicals and machinery. Also, exchange rates were controlled to avoid currency overvaluation.

Given the import-substitution industrial strategy that motivated much of border and farm policies, the investment climate in the overall agricultural sector during the 1950s and 1960s was discouraging. The wine industry also suffered, even though it was less of a target for interventions due both to its not being considered an essential good and to its – albeit small – export revenue. Nevertheless, one indicator of the obstacles at the border and elsewhere to productivity-enhancing investments was that it took until the 1970s for the industry to import modern filtration and bottling machinery.

Uncertainty regarding the investment climate in agriculture increased notably in 1967 as a large-scale government agrarian reform program began to unfold. By converting large farms to cooperatives and collectives, this ambitious program aimed not just at land redistribution but also at the economic rationalization of what was considered an antique, inefficient system of conservative, laggard landowners and of low-skilled labour tied to estates. The land reform was based on expropriations, with partial compensation, of large farms (over 80 ha as measured by productive equivalents) and 'inefficient' operations (somewhat arbitrarily determined). The goal, at least in the short run, was to establish large, cooperative farms, operated, in part, for the benefit of farm labourers, guided by government experts.[5]

Representatives of the wine industry did manage to convince the then-governing coalition that applying the land reform expropriation rules without exception would threaten the survival of larger-scale, more integrated vineyard operations that had some export potential. Wine interests obtained an exception to farm size limits and also were permitted to use limited liability corporations to organize, something that was forbidden to other agricultural sectors. These exceptions helped maintain the coherent vertical integration of vineyards, winemaking, bottling and marketing until

[5] The proponents of the reforms in the late 1960s initiated under a Christian Democrat presidency did contend that, eventually, after training and experience under the government-assisted, large-scale cooperative model, capable farmers would receive smaller, individualized parcels. This plan, if ever firmly intended, was superseded by the following, more radically reform-minded government led by the Unidad Popular of Salvador Allende. For a thorough discussion of the Chilean agrarian reform experiment, see Valdés and Foster (2015).

the market-liberalizing reforms of the mid- and late 1970s, preserving an established industry base on which the wine sector would increase exports in the 1980s and then eventually break out rapidly into international markets with the transition to civilian government after 1988.

Transition and Restructuring: From the Mid-1970s to Early 1990s

In the early 1970s, the economic model grew even more interventionist, and the agricultural land expropriation program was intensified, reaching 40 to 50 percent of farm land (as measured by productive equivalents). Trade protectionism increased, and the government's import monopoly and export controls became stricter. Social order deteriorated and political events soon led to a military takeover and quickly thereafter to the beginning of a radical shift in economic policy.

The military government, beginning in late 1973, faced hyperinflation, large fiscal deficits and external debt, and much of the economy (including agriculture) was under state control. The government adopted a liberalized market model, reducing interventions in the economy, opening trade and strengthening property rights. A first phase of reform was instituted during the period 1973–83, introducing general macroeconomic reforms relatively quickly, but many sector-specific reforms took some time to implement. For agriculture, by 1978 large farm operations once under state control had been broken up into small 'family-size' parcels, and individual land titles were distributed to the earlier farmworker/beneficiaries of the previous land reform program. The government slowly reduced its involvement in the sector and moved, with several delays, to liberalize labour, input and product markets.

Although not of immediate significance, overall market liberalization in agriculture led the government in 1977 to repeal the thirty-eight-year-old law restricting the planting of new vineyards and requiring prior approval for replanting. More importantly for the wine sector and its potential for exports, there was an early and significant trade liberalization program: almost all nontariff barriers were eliminated and tariffs were reduced. Uniform tariffs were implemented, starting at 90 percent in 1975, and then falling eventually to 10 percent in 1979. But private investments in export agriculture were discouraged by exchange rate appreciation and reduced world commodity prices. During the decade, until another phase of further reforms beginning in the early 1980s, land in vineyards remained stable at slightly more than 100,000 ha, and wine volumes varied from year to year around an average of 550 ML. Wine exports fluctuated around 2 percent of production but began to increase. Per capita consumption had declined since 1960 by one-third, but had not yet begun the accelerated decline that was to come. More importantly, during the initial reform period the average value of exports per litre began to rise.

Following a financial crisis and severe recession in the early 1980s, further economic reforms were in place by 1984. The wine sector, along with other sectors, underwent significant changes in terms of the overall orientation of the industry towards export markets. Miguel Torres, a large Spanish producer, had begun operations in Chile in 1978, introducing up-to-date winery technology and management, and so had already set an example for innovations that were given added incentive soon thereafter.

The crisis led to significant devaluations of the Chilean currency, and during the period 1982–88 potential exporters saw a 90 percent depreciation in the real exchange rate, providing a positive jolt to the competitiveness of Chilean exports. With the effective decrease in real costs of reaching foreign consumers paying in US dollars, the wine sector began restructuring, reducing significantly the hectares and total production of the mass-market, cheap País variety and increasing the plantings and production of French varieties, notably Cabernet Sauvignon. Hectares in wine grapes fell approximately 6 percent annually during the 1980s, and per capita wine consumption fell on average 4.5 percent per year.

As detailed in Table 13.1, showing the evolution of sectoral performance since 1980, the wine industry began its transformation with a notable decline in hectares under production following the financial crisis of the early 1980s. Production reached a thirty-year low in 1992, a full 35 percent lower than production of only a decade before. Hectares bottomed out two years later and, from that point, began to rise very rapidly due to plantings of varieties with exports in mind. Exports, which had risen slightly prior to the return to civilian government in 1990, began to soar, going from 7 percent of production in 1989 to just under half of all production ten years later. During this period of radical transition, foreign investment in the sector also expanded.

Chilean Fruit and Wine Bursts into World Markets

In accordance with the Chilean Constitution approved by a referendum in 1980, a plebiscite was held in 1988 on the question of extending military-led government for another eight-year term. The electoral rejection that resulted was a vote for regularized presidential elections and a transition to civilian government. It was also a vote for a 'return to normalcy'

Table 13.1 *Evolution of the Chilean wine industry, 1980 to 2013*

	Wine grape area (1,000 ha)	Production (ML)	Apparent consumption litres/cap.	Export value (US$ millions)	Export volume ('000 litres)	Exports as % of volume of production	% of world export volume	Export price (US$/ litre)
1980	104	586	47	20	14	2.4	0.3	1.43
1985	68	320	36	11	11	3.4	0.2	0.98
1990	59	328	22	52	43	13.1	1.0	1.21
1995	54	291	10	182	129	44.3	2.3	1.41
1996	56	337	7	293	184	54.6	3.7	1.59
1997	64	382	8	412	216	56.7	5.3	1.91
1998	71	444	10	528	230	51.8	5.3	2.30
1999	85	371	14	537	230	61.9	5.5	2.34
2000	104	570	7	581	265	46.4	6.6	2.19
2001	107	504	17	595	309	61.3	7.4	1.93
2002	109	526	10	608	355	67.5	5.2	1.71
2003	110	641	8	678	403	62.9	5.5	1.68
2004	112	605	11	830	466	77.0	6.1	1.78
2005	114	736	12	872	416	56.5	5.2	2.10
2006	117	802	16	956	472	58.8	5.6	2.03
2007	118	792	12	1246	607	76.6	6.7	2.05
2008	105	825	12	1361	584	70.9	6.5	2.33
2009	112	982	8	1365	690	70.2	7.9	1.98
2010	117	841	15	1528	728	86.5	7.4	2.10
2011	126	947	11	1669	659	69.6	6.4	2.53
2012	129	1188	12	1767	743	62.6	7.6	2.38
2013	130	1211	18	1859	874	72.2	9.0	2.13

Source: Anderson and Pinilla (2017).

with respect to Chile's potential participation in international commerce. By 1990, with a new president in office, Chile's international standing was enhanced and the country began to attract greater attention from foreign investors and potential buyers of Chilean products. Thus began a period during the 1990s of a surge of Chilean fruit and wine onto world markets. Especially in the wine industry, foreign investments grew significantly and various alliances were formed with international firms.

Although there is not a conclusive and unequivocal set of drivers of the success of the Chilean wine industry, there was a confluence of factors that go far to explain how Chilean viticulture, which was formerly so oriented to the internal market, was able in a short space of time to secure a much more important role in world markets.

One factor was the shock of economic reforms, liberalization and macroeconomic stability, which began in the mid-1970s and solidified after the crisis in the early 1980s. That allowed investors to reap the rewards of successful new enterprises, and it reduced the political and macroeconomic uncertainty that had for decades inhibited private risk taking.

Second and simultaneously, a major currency devaluation in an environment open to trade effectively reduced internal real wages and boosted the competitiveness of all export industries, including wine, at a time when investor optimism was growing.

Third, while other potential, nonmining export sectors had to begin from a modest base (and sometimes from zero), the existing scale of the Chilean wine industry allowed a rapid shift of resources from serving domestic markets to seeking and catering to foreign buyers.

The fourth factor, which interacted with the third and is discussed in greater detail later in this chapter, was the swift change in consumer tastes towards other alcoholic beverages during the 1980s as incomes rose and the composition of the workforce shifted. Managers in the wine industry, anticipating declining internal demand, had an enhanced urgency to turn to exploring foreign markets.

The fifth factor is that, complementing the already existing capacity in the industry, foreign investors (most notably Miguel Torres) had begun in the late 1970s to introduce modern techniques and styles designed explicitly for European consumers. When economically advantageous, these techniques and styles were readily imitated. This form of knowledge spillover, in a fairly concentrated industry with few innovators, meant that the diffusion of ideas was immediate.

A sixth factor that came later was the policy commitment to trade agreements (discussed later in this chapter) that further reduced barriers to exports.

Developments in the overall productivity of the sector, in terms of improved winemaking capacity and new vineyard operations, were strikingly mirrored in the change in the composition of new plantings of nontraditional varieties. By 1994, the decline in total hectares of wine grapes had bottomed out and plantings began to expand. Six years later, by 2000, total hectares had almost doubled, returning to the level of 1980. The area planted to Cabernet Sauvignon had grown by over 220 percent, Merlot hectares had increased by over 440 percent, Chardonnay by 85 percent and Pinot Noir by over 1,000 percent. Varieties that were effectively nonexistent in 1994 began to flourish, especially Carmenère, Syrah and Cabernet Franc (Table 13.2). Hectares in the variety País, which in 1994 still represented

Table 13.2 *Area of wine grape vineyards, by variety, Chile, 1994 to 2014 (ha)*

Variety	1994	2000	2005	2010	2014
Cabernet Sauvignon	11,112	35,967	40,441	38,426	44,176
Merlot	2,353	12,824	13,142	10,640	12,480
Chardonnay	4,150	7,672	8,156	10,834	11,634
Sauvignon Blanc	5,981	6,790	8,379	13,278	15,142
Chenin Blanc	103	76	73	56	56
Pinot Noir	138	1,613	1,361	3,307	4,196
Riesling	307	286	305	400	420
Semillón	2,708	1,892	1,708	930	968
País	15,990	15,179	14,909	5,855	7,653
Carménère	-	4,719	6,849	9,502	11,319
Syrah	-	2,039	2,988	6,887	8,432
Cabernet Franc	-	689	1,099	1,345	1,661
Others	10,251	14,130	15,038	15,372	19,444
Total	53,093	103,876	114,448	116,831	137,582

Source: Oficina de Estudios y Políticas Agrarias, www.odepa.gob.cl.

30 percent of plantings, fell by over half during the next two decades, representing just 6 percent of the country's wine grape area by 2014.

During this same brief period, Chile began its long-run institutionalized commitment to international openness via negotiated trade agreements, signing accords with Canada, Mercosur (Argentina, Brazil, Paraguay and Uruguay), Mexico, Peru and Central America.

In the first decade of the new century, Chile continued adding agreements with the European Union, Korea, the United States, China, the so-called P4 (Chile, New Zealand, Singapore and Brunei), Japan, Australia and Turkey. (Appendix Table A13.1 lists the many free-trade agreements [FTAs] that Chile has signed over the last two decades.) Some of these agreements, notably the one with the United States, required a slow lowering over time of duties on Chilean wine, but they nevertheless signalled a credible commitment to accessible and lucrative markets in the future.[6]

Chilean winemakers began targeting higher-priced markets in Europe and North America, which reached 80 percent of total sales. Total export volumes and sales revenues have risen dramatically since the 1990s, reaching over US$1.8 billion for the most recent years. Figure 13.2 shows the

[6] Tariffs on wine trade between Chile and the United States fell over a twelve-year period and were finally eliminated at the beginning of 2016.

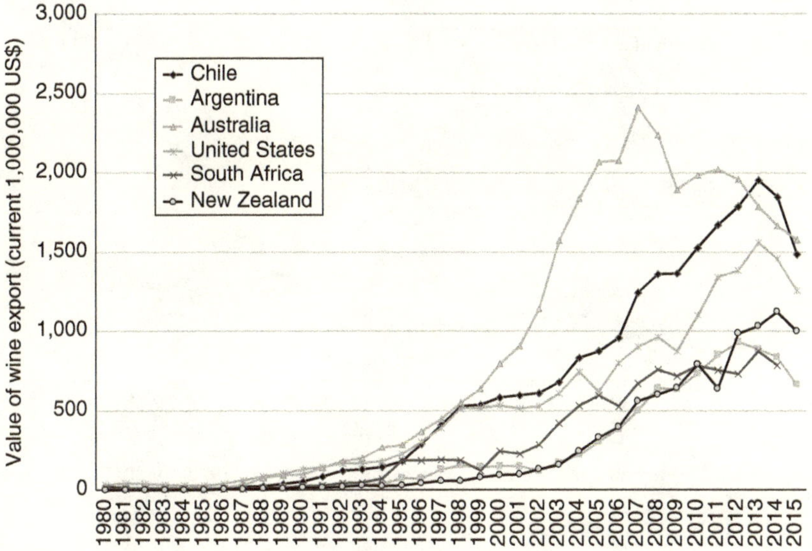

Figure 13.2 Value of wine exports, New World producers, 1980 to 2015 (US$1,000,000). *Source*: Anderson and Pinilla (2017).

evolution of export values of the largest New World wine exporters since 1980. Currently the leading New World wine exporters are Australia, Chile and the United States, all exporting more than US$1.5 billion annually, followed by New Zealand, Argentina and South Africa. By the late 1990s, Chile and Australia had overtaken the United States in terms of value of wine exports. Thereafter, Chilean exports rose slightly slower than those of Australia, the major New World competitor until 2007, when Australian exports slowed in volume and began declining in total value while Chilean exports continued increasing at close to their former rate. Chile became the largest New World exporter in 2012 in volume terms and a year later in terms of value as well.

Chilean wine export prices also rose rapidly during the breakout phase, increasing from slightly more than US$1 a litre in the 1980s to over US$2 at the end of the 1990s. This rise was due in large measure to the decline during this period in the proportion of wine exports in bulk and a concomitant rise in the export of higher-valued bottled products (Figure 13.3). Chilean prices were assisted by wine publications and other sources of tasting scores that indicated to the buying public the high quality of average Chilean wines compared to similarly priced wines of California and Australia. By the early 2000s, wines earning over US$30 per case

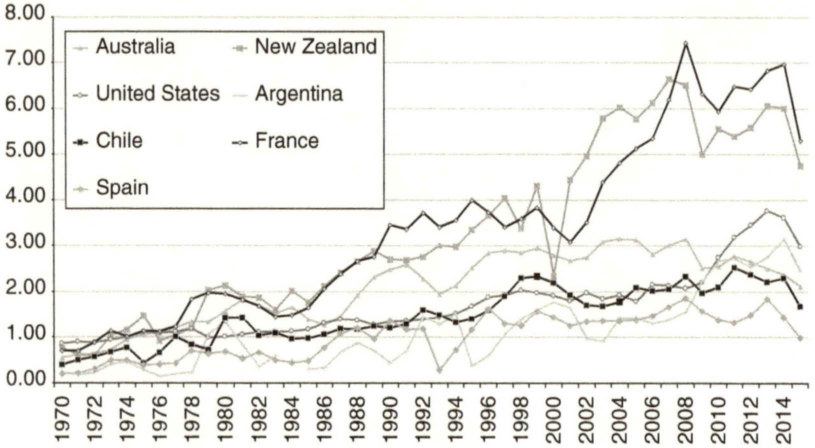

Figure 13.3 Wine export prices, key exporting countries, 1970 to 2015 (US$ per litre FOB).
Source: Anderson and Pinilla (2017).

($2.50 per 750 ML bottle) had reached about one-fifth of all exports. Over the past fifteen years, export unit values have fluctuated year to year between $1.60 and $2.50, with a general tendency to increase over time, and lately even while bulk exports expand. Nevertheless, Chilean export unit values remain significantly lower than those of its major competitors, while prices for New Zealand and French wines have risen significantly more rapidly than Chilean wines.

More recently, bulk sales have been increasing. While New Zealand and Chile appear to be devoting similar land resources to wine grapes, the two countries have differing compositions of exports, with New Zealand specializing in white wines and higher-price products and Chile focusing on reds with a significant proportion of its exports being lower-priced bottles and bulk wines. In 2015, bulk wine represented 47 percent of the volume of Chile's wine exports, compared with 34 percent for New Zealand's.

Figure 13.4 shows the evolution of Balassa's (1965) revealed comparative advantage indices for Chile and several comparable countries since the end of the Second World War. The contrast between the index for Chile prior to economic reforms and after is striking. The index for Chile exhibits a rapid increase beginning with the transition to democracy in 1988. It surpassed that of France, Spain, Argentina and Australia over the past two decades. The volatility of the index for Chile, in particular the significant decline between 2001 and 2006, is due to the impact of the high variability of the international price of copper (by far the country's principal export) on

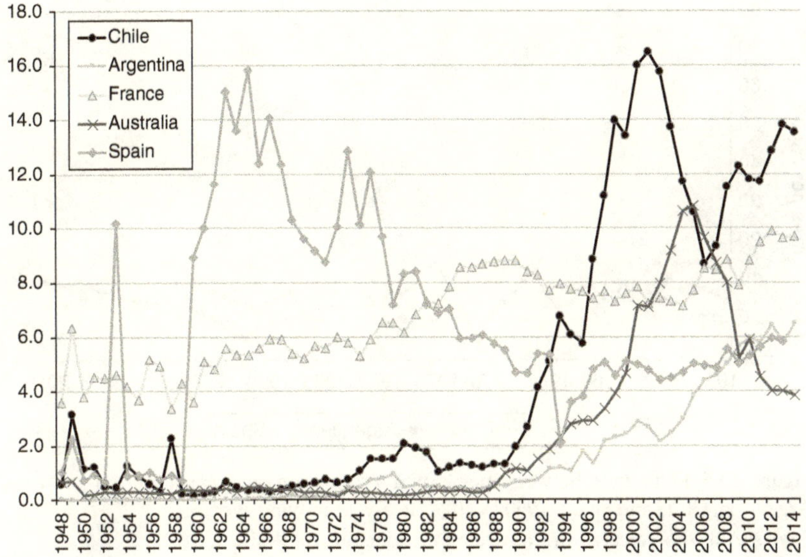

Figure 13.4 Wine 'revealed' comparative advantage index,[a] Chile and selected competitors, 1948 to 2014.

[a] The share of wine in national merchandise exports divided by its share in global exports.

Source: Anderson and Pinilla (2017).

the country's real exchange rate. Despite the volatility of the index, Chile's wine comparative advantage has increased faster than that of comparable wine exporters, and especially so during the past decade. The Chilean wine industry's contribution to the total value of national exports has been growing at a more rapid rate than the country's share of global wine exports.

To further illustrate the drastic change in industry focus from domestic to international markets between the mid-1980s and mid-1990s, Figure 13.5 shows the evolution of the difference between wine production and consumption per capita of Chile, Argentina and Spain. The notable collapse in consumption per capita in Chile beginning in the early 1980s (Figure 13.6) was matched by a drastic fall in production. Only in the early 1990s did production begin a rebound, but it was so rapid that production per capita recently has reach levels unseen since the 1960s. Meanwhile, per capita consumption stabilized and then began a slow drift upward. Spain and Argentina, having relatively high per capita consumption, also experienced a significant decline in domestic demand at approximately the same time as Chile. In contrast to Chile, Spain's increase in exports began in the mid-1970s, as shown in Figure 13.5 by a rise in the difference between per capita

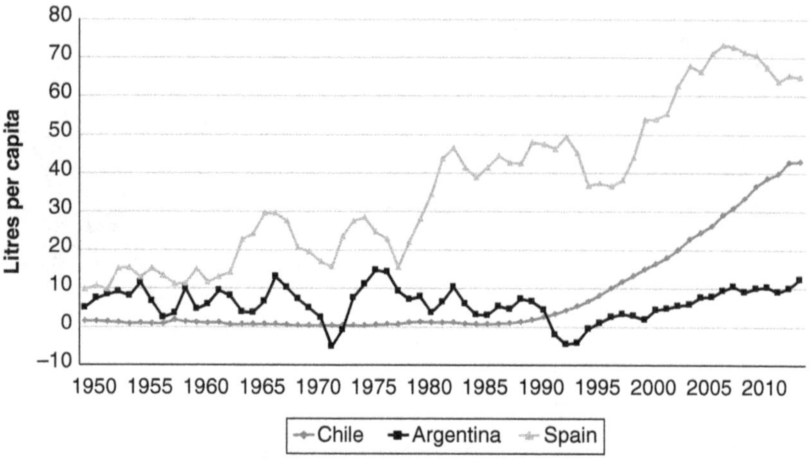

Figure 13.5 Difference between per capita production and consumption of wine, Argentina, Chile and Spain, 1950 to 2014 (five-year moving averages).
Source: Authors' calculation from data in Anderson and Pinilla (2017).

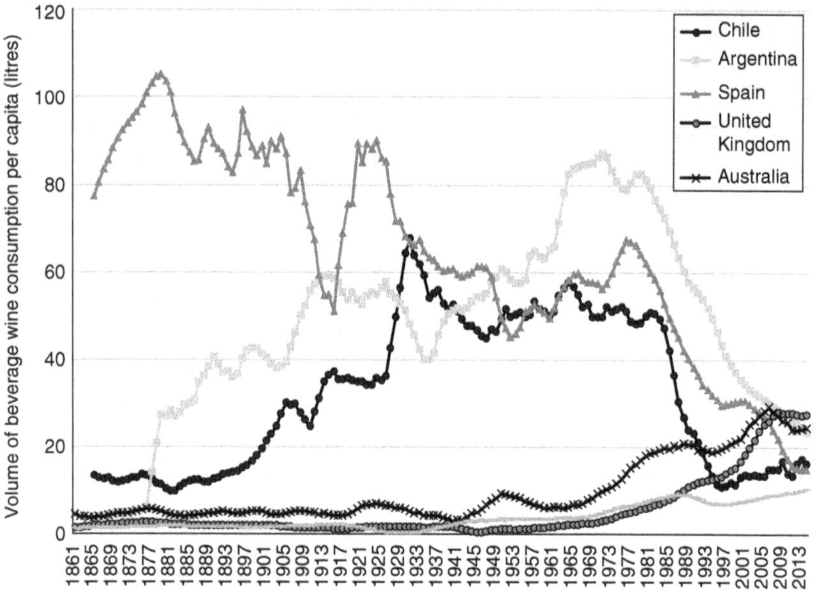

Figure 13.6 Wine consumption per capita, Chile and selected countries, 1861 to 2014 (litres, five-year moving average).
Source: Anderson and Pinilla (2017).

production and consumption. This increase, however, was in proportional terms much less rapid than that of Chile, which began from a much smaller base. The Argentine wine industry, however, did not begin its reorientation to exports until the late 1990s, and the increase in the difference between per capita production and consumption has risen at a considerably slower pace than that of Spain and Chile.

The industry leaders in the export boom were the very largest producers. The four largest wineries, which account for 80 percent of domestic sales, shipped over two-fifths of all Chilean wine exports, but they tend to focus exports on lower-priced wines in contrast to smaller operations. The four largest firms average about 60 percent of their exports in reserves and varietals. In contrast, small export wineries with production volumes in the order of only 10 ML, and with a relatively small domestic presence, typically never ship less than 90 percent in reserves and varietals.

Recent Years: Consolidation, Continued Growth

Industry growth has not slowed appreciably in recent years, despite concerns following the financial crisis of 2008–2009. Production volumes between 2008 and 2012 increased by about 45 percent, and wine exports in the near future are likely to surpass US$1.9 billion. Currently, exports make up approximately 75 percent of the value of total industry (foreign and domestic) sales. As a notable indicator of the wine sector's continued dynamism, recently Chile overtook Australia to become the fourth-largest exporter of wines, following France, Italy and Spain. It is now the leading exporter from the New World. Wine represents only 3 to 5 percent of the total value of all Chilean exports (which are dominated by copper and minerals), but nearly 15 percent of agroforestry and food sector exports.

The number of Chilean wine-exporting companies in 2016 was approximately 350, although not all export every year. Ten wine companies dominate exports, with over 50 percent of the total. Most exporters are characterized as small or medium-sized firms. Using a simple average across firms, approximately two-thirds of the average wine producer's revenue derives from international markets, with many firms depending even more heavily on foreign sales. Over time, national wine exports have diversified, and more recently volumes have increased faster than total value, suggesting that diversification has meant entering new or growing markets with lower-price products and bulk wine. Today, bulk wine makes up about 17 percent of Chile's total wine export value.

The list of principal countries to which Chile exports wine has changed notably over recent decades. Table 13.3 shows the value of exports by

Table 13.3 *Top twenty export destinations for Chilean denomination-of-origin wines, 2000, 2014 and 2015*

2000			2014			2015		
Country	Value exports ('000 US$)	% of total	Country	Value exports ('000 US$)	% of total	Country	Value exports ('000 US$)	% of total
UK	95,631	20	UK	177,486	11	China	163,099	10
US	76,091	16	US	148,892	9	UK	162,527	10
Japan	25,836	5	Japan	124,704	8	US	157,687	10
Canada	23,488	5	China	110,577	7	Japan	147,486	9
Germany	22,719	5	Brazil	109,207	7	Brazil	111,594	7
Denmark	19,514	4	Holland	98,637	6	Holland	82,720	5
Holland	18,274	4	Canada	65,713	4	Canada	62,938	4
Ireland	17,075	4	Denmark	44,695	3	Denmark	43,162	3
Sweden	14,896	3	Ireland	43,173	3	Ireland	39,374	2
Brazil	14,110	3	Germany	39,996	2	S. Korea	38,003	2
Mexico	12,207	3	Russia	38,709	2	México	35,708	2
Switzerland	9,085	2	S. Korea	37,055	2	Germany	34,698	2
Belgium	8,949	2	Mexico	32,438	2	Belgium	29,195	2
Finland	8,095	2	Belgium	29,219	2	Russia	21,486	1
Venezuela	7,113	1	Finland	23,627	1	Colombia	20,817	1
Norway	7,011	1	Sweden	21,864	1	France	19,649	1
France	5,640	1	Colombia	19,448	1	Finland	17,805	1
Colombia	5,113	1	Venezuela	18,057	1	Sweden	16,817	1
Others	43,816	9	Others	238,755	14	Others	223,756	14
Total	478,478		Total	1,661,004		Total	1,652,277	

Source: Oficina de Estudios y Políticas Agrarias, www.odepa.gob.cl based on the Chilean customs agency.

country of higher-quality wine (with a denomination of origin, or DO), which makes up about 75 percent of the value of total wine exports.[7] In 2000, the main export destinations were Europe (48 percent of the total) and North America (23 percent). Asia – almost all to Japan – had a 7 percent share, less than the 10 percent going to Latin American countries, excluding Mexico. The United Kingdom and the United States were, by far, the largest importers of Chilean wine, taking 22 percent and 18 percent of the total, respectively.

[7] Following recent regulatory changes, Chile now has fourteen official denominations of origin, stretching from the Elqui Valley in the arid north to the Malleco Valley in the cooler south. The largest DO, in terms of a count of wineries, is the Maipo Valley, south of Santiago in the middle of the country's wine-growing area.

Fifteen years later, although the value of exports to the United Kingdom has risen 70 percent and to the United States has doubled, the shares of Chile's total exports of wine to these two countries have each fallen to only 11 percent. The rise of Asia as an important export market is clear. Japan's share of Chilean wine exports in 2015 was 10 percent, China was 11 percent and South Korea was 3 percent. Summing over the various Asian export destinations shows that the Pacific market now makes up a quarter of Chile's exports of higher-quality wines. While Latin America's share has remained about 10 percent, exports to Brazil have risen almost eightfold over the past decade and a half, and now represent 8 percent of the value of DO wines exported from Chile.

Although Chilean firms are increasingly emphasizing exports to Asia and to China especially, they have not been as successful as their competitors, especially Australia. For several years, Chile ranked high among foreign suppliers to China, and became the third-ranked import source in 2015 in terms of value ($170 million) behind Australia ($440 million) and France ($863 million). Chile, however, has been losing its share of total Chinese imports to Australia, which has been increasing the value of its wine shipments to China at twice the rate of Chile. Moreover, per unit values for bottled wine imports from Chile in 2015 ($3.49) were less than half that of unit values from Australia ($7.76) and about two-thirds that of France ($5.19). More interestingly still is the fact that about two-thirds of the volume of Chile's wine exports to China are in bulk form, although with an average unit export value of just $0.55, which brings the unit export value of all wine exports to China down to slightly under $1.50.

A Note on Pisco

Before leaving the subject of wine production and exports, some remarks are warranted on another important alcoholic grape product, namely pisco. Aguardientes derived from wine have been produced in Chile since the earliest colonial times, and the specific product, pisco, has deep historical roots in Peru and the settlements in Chile's arid north. In fact, Chilean pisco has the oldest appellation of origin in South America, dating from 1931. By law, pisco refers only to distilled spirits produced from Muscat varieties of Vitis vinifera in the river valleys of the arid northern regions of Atacama and Coquimbo. The bulk of domestic pisco production has always been oriented to Chilean markets, but since 1990 exports of the aguardiente have grown by over 150 percent in volume and by over ten times in value, reaching in 2015 about $3.5 million. Despite the recent growth, pisco exports represent only about 1 percent of the country's total production of approximately 50 ML.

In terms of domestic consumption, pisco presently accounts for about 2.5 to 3 litres per capita. The pisco industry has attempted to develop and market higher-valued products and to increase foreign sales, as domestic per capita consumption has declined by about 50 percent from its high during the mid-1990s. Pisco, which is usually sold in greatest volume as a product for mixed drinks with 30 to 35 percent alcohol, competes with imports of whiskies and relatively much more inexpensive rum and other sugar-derived aguardientes. While whisky imports have risen about 250 percent since 2000 to reach 8.5 ML, the volume of rum and similar imports, such as cachaça, has risen over thirty times to about 50 ML, reaching the same level as the total volume of domestic pisco production. About 20 percent of the recent total value of Chilean pisco shipments is destined for Mercosur partners (mainly Argentina), and about 40 percent for the United States.

DOMESTIC CONSUMPTION OF WINE AND OTHER ALCOHOLIC BEVERAGES

Chilean wine consumption fell significantly over the past half-century, from a high of around 60 litres per capita annually in the early 1960s to a low of 15 to 17 litres in recent years. Alcohol consumption from wine fell by more than 75 percent, putting Chileans at a lower level than the British. This decline in consumption is similar to what happened in other Spanish-speaking, wine-drinking countries. As seen in Figure 13.6, there was a seeming convergence of consumer tastes in Spain, Argentina and Chile during the 1930s to the early 1960s, in the range of 50 litres per capita annual consumption. Thereafter, per capita consumption in the three countries began to converge to the tastes of the wealthier Anglosphere.

By the 2010s, the alcohol consumption profiles in the United States and Chile were converging, as US consumers gradually increased per capita wine consumption while Chilean consumers remained around 12 to 15 litres per capita. In 2014, apparent per capita consumption in Chile jumped slightly, reaching an apparent consumption level of about 17.5 litres, but much of the variation might be due to poor information regarding total inventories in the industry. While an apparent increase in domestic per capita consumption was good news for the wine industry, Chilean consumption still remains significantly below that of Chile's two Southern Cone neighbours of comparable income levels: Argentina has an annual per capita wine consumption of 23.5 litres and Uruguay of 29.2. Compared to other countries with similar high levels of consumption during the mid-twentieth century, a decline per se in Chilean wine consumption over time was not surprising. What is notable in the Chilean case was the rapidity and sharpness of the decline. In 1980, Chile ranked sixth in the list of heaviest wine drinkers. Today, the Wine Institute of California (2016) reports that Chile ranks as the forty-first heaviest consumer.

This decrease in per capita consumption can be linked directly to Chile's rapid economic development experienced since the mid-1970s and the associated change in the nature of employment and the rise in incomes of households. Development meant a rapid growth in demand for nonagricultural labour, especially in the service sector. Further, an overall shift from industrial protection of textiles and heavier manufacturing meant a decline in the blue-collar workforce. The change in labour demand, the rise of a more office-oriented, clerical workforce and the expansion of the middle class altered the nature of the workday for most Chileans. With the workforce shifting to jobs where punctuality and attentiveness were paid a premium, temperance, at least during the work week, became more important.

The privatization of the country's largest brewery during the economic reform phase also contributed: it led to higher-quality beer being available at attractive prices and to publicity campaigns aimed at consumers open to a lower-alcohol substitute to wine. Moreover, especially for those primarily interested in alcohol content, an expansion in the scale of production of the principal distilled spirit, pisco, led to a significant fall in its price relative to wine.

By the mid-2000s, beer consumption per capita doubled to about 30 litres per capita, from a low base in the early 1980s, although the relative price of beer to wine remained fairly constant. Beer consumption continued to rise, reaching more than 40 litres per capita annually in 2013. Currently, in terms of pure alcohol equivalents, Chileans over fifteen years of age have an average consumption of about 7.7 litres annually, of which about 31 percent is from wine, 36 percent from beer and 23 percent from pisco and other distilled spirits (Table 13.4).[8]

[8] The World Health Organization (WHO) published a brief synopsis of alcohol consumption in Chile with averages for 2008–10. The WHO asserted without supporting reference or citation that 'unrecorded' alcohol consumption amounted to an additional 2 litres annually of pure alcohol per capita (population older than fifteen years), which increased the total yearly consumption of pure alcohol to 9.6 litres per capita, a rate that would be the highest in Latin America. This addition to WHO statistics of 2 litres of pure alcohol per person older than fifteen years appears to the present authors as highly speculative and without much support.

Table 13.4 *Alcohol consumption, Chile, 2013*

	Volume (ML)	Percent alcohol	Pure alcohol (ML)	Percent of total pure alcohol	Litres pure alcohol per adult
Liquors and other distilled spirits	36	38.0	13.7	13.2	1.0
Piscos and pisco sour mixes	36	30.0	10.8	10.4	0.8
Beers	680	5.5	37.4	36.1	2.8
Wines	221	12.5	32.3	31.1	2.4
Others	90	10.0	9.0	9.1	0.7
Total			98.5	100.0	7.7

Note: The population fifteen and older is estimated at 13.5 million in 2013. The 'others' category is a simple estimate based on 10 percent of pure alcohol consumption of listed items.
Source: Authors' calculations based on data from Oficina de Estudios y Políticas Agrarias, www.odepa.gob.cl.

Recent concerns among policy makers regarding the health effects of alcohol consumption have led to higher taxes being imposed on alcoholic beverages. Ironically, by increasing all final prices of alcohol sources to consumers, the new alcohol tax regime has raised the price of beer and wine relative to distilled spirits. In addition to a value-added tax of 19 percent on all transactions, the alcohol tax increased from 15 percent to 20.5 percent of value for beers and wines and from 27 percent to 31.5 percent for distilled spirits. As yet, there is no clear evidence that this increase in taxes has led to an appreciable decline in alcoholic beverage consumption or a change in the mix of beverages.

CONCLUSIONS

After a significant expansion in the late 1800s, and a shift in consumer tastes from other alcoholic grape beverages to wine in the 1920s, the evolution of the Chilean wine industry during most of the last century, until the economic reforms of nearly forty years ago, was driven by developments in the domestic market. The wine sector, from grape production to marketing, was influenced directly by restrictions on land use in wine grapes, a regulation-prone state and taxes; and it was influenced indirectly by trade, exchange rate and industrial policies, all of which undermined competitiveness and discouraged risk-taking investments that might have otherwise stimulated greater industry dynamism.

Moreover, all potential export activities in Chile were overshadowed by the scale of the mining industry, which is almost exclusively oriented to exports and which tended to draw productive resources from other sectors, including agriculture and wine. Over the 1980s, while the importance of mining, in terms of absolute dollar export earnings, did not change appreciably, other aspects of the economic environment relevant to wine exports did. The wine industry, once concentrated on internal markets, refocused on the potential of international expansion, and did so rapidly after the political transition to civilian rule between 1988 and 1990.

The basis of economic growth more generally had been established by overall liberalization and macroeconomic stability, beginning in the mid-1970s. The potential international competitiveness of the wine industry had been enhanced by a currency devaluation which had effectively reduced internal real wages. As domestic per capita wine consumption began to fall rapidly in the 1980s, the wine industry quickly shifted its resources from domestic to international markets, first reducing the land originally devoted to the mass-consumption País variety and then expanding the production of varieties destined for foreign buyers. Moreover, the export potential of the industry was improved by foreign investors introducing modern techniques and styles, which were readily imitated. And so, in the early 1990s, as Chile unilaterally opened further its economy to trade and embarked on a series of bilateral trade agreements, the wine industry was prepared to compete and grow in international markets.

Growth over the past quarter-century has been steady, and Chile recently became the world's fourth-largest wine exporting country. The recent gains in overall nonmining Chilean exports have unfolded in the context of two broad, complementary processes: the learning-by-doing discovery of the country's comparative advantages following decades of an import-substituting industrial policy, and the unilateral and bilateral trade liberalization that facilitated the expansion of competitive industries into foreign markets in the developed world. But the export growth provoked by these changes has eventual limits, because the period of rapid discovery of comparative advantages has come to an end and there are only so many countries in the world with which Chile can sign free-trade agreements.

More recently, a third factor has been at work boosting and determining the direction of wine exports: the overall growth in incomes and evolving preferences in countries formerly not considered as offering large markets of potential wine drinkers. Markets in the Pacific, especially China, now absorb significant shares of both bottled and bulk wine exports from Chile. Income growth in China, India and other large Asian markets is likely to continue offering potential expansion of wine demand, but competitors, from France and Australia in particular, will remain a challenge to the realization of that potential for Chilean wineries.

Appendix Table A13.1 *Chile's Free-Trade Agreements, 1996 to 2015*

Agreement/partner(s)	Date of signature	Date of entry into force
Pacific Alliance	10 February 2014	20 July 2015
Thailand	4 October 2013	5 November 2015
Hong Kong, China	7 September 2012	29 November 2014
Vietnam	12 November 2011	4 February 2014
Malaysia	13 November 2010	18 April 2012
Turkey	14 July 2009	1 March 2011
Australia	30 July 2008	6 March 2009
Japan	27 March 2007	3 September 2007
Colombia	27 November 2006	8 May 2009
Peru	22 August 2006	1 March 2009
Panama	27 June 2006	7 March 2008
China	18 November 2005	1 October 2006
P4: New Zealand, Singapore, Brunei	18 July 2005	1 May 2006
European Free Trade Association (EFTA)	26 June 2003	1 December 2004
United States of America	6 June 2003	1 January 2004
Republic of Korea	15 February 2003	1 April 2004
European Union (UE)	18 November 2002	1 February 2003
Central America (Costa Rica, El Salvador, Guatemala, Honduras, Nicaragua)	18 October 1999	19 October 2012
Mexico	17 April 1998	1 August 1999
Canada	5 December 1996	5 July 1997
MERCOSUR	25 June 1996	1 October 1996

Source: Servicio de Información sobre Comercio Exterior. Organización de Estados Americanos. www.sice.oas.org/.

REFERENCES

Alvarado, D. P. (2004), 'De apetitos y de cañas: El consumo de alimentos y bebidas en Santiago a fines de Siglo XIX', *Historia-Santiago* 37(2): 391–417.

Anderson, K. and V. Pinilla (with the assistance of A. J. Holmes) (2017), *Annual Database of Global Wine Markets, 1835 to 2016*, freely available in Excel at the University of Adelaide's Wine Economics Research Centre, www.adelaide.edu.au/wine-econ/databases

Balassa, B. (1965), 'Trade Liberalisation and Revealed Comparative Advantage', *Manchester School* 33: 99–123.

Cisterna, N. S. (2013), 'Space and Terroir in the Chilean Wine Industry', ch. 3 (pp. 51–66) in *Wine and Culture: Vineyard to Glass*, edited by R. E. Black and R. C. Ulin, London and New York: Bloomsbury Academic.

Couyoumdjian, J. R. (2006), 'Vinos en Chile desde la independencia hasta el fin de la Belle Époque', *Historia-Santiago* 39(1): 23–64.

Del Pozo, J. (1998), *Historia del Vino Chileno desde 1850 hasta Hoy*, Santiago: Editorial Universitaria.

Fernandez Labbe, M. (2010), *Bebidas Alcohólicas en Chile*, Santiago: Ediciones Universidad Alberto Hurtado.

Foster, W. and A. Valdés (2006), 'Chilean Agriculture and Major Economic Reforms: Growth, Trade, Poverty and the Environment', *Région et Développement* 23: 187–214.

Hernández, A. (2000), *Introducción al Vino de Chile*, 2 ed., Santiago: Colección en Agricultura de la Facultad de Agronomía e Ingeniería Forestal, Pontificia Universidad de Chile.

Hernández, A. and Y. Moreno (2011), *The Origins of Chilean Wine: Curico, Maule, Itata and Bíobío*, Santiago: Origo Ediciones.

Johnson, H. (1989). *Story of Wine*, London: Mitchell Beasley.

Robinson, J., J. Harding and J. Vouillamoz (2012), *Wine Grapes: A Complete Guide to 1,368 Vine Varieties, Including Their Origins and Flavours*, London: Allen Lane.

Smith, A. and B. Yandle (2014), *Bootleggers and Baptists: How Economic Forces and Moral Persuasion Interact to Shape Regulatory Politics*, Washington, DC: Cato Institute.

Valdés, A. and W. Foster (2015), *La Reforma Agraria en Chile: Historia, Efectos y Lecciones*, Santiago: Ediciones Universidad Católica.

Wine Institute of California (2016), 'World Per Capita Wine Consumption, 2014', available at www.wineinstitute.org/resources/statistics

Yandle, B. (1983), 'Bootleggers and Baptists: The Education of a Regulatory Economist', *Regulation* 7(3): 12.

14

South Africa

Nick Vink, Willem H. Boshoff, Gavin Williams,
Johan Fourie and Lewis S. McLean

South Africa is the world's seventh-largest nation in terms of litres of wine produced and sixth-largest in terms of volume of wine exported.[1] This chapter explores the evolution of the wine industry in South Africa to this position over its more than 300-year history. As South Africa is one of the oldest of the New World wine regions, we highlight the deep origins of wine production at the southern tip of Africa. This narrative is supported by a new dataset on the country's wine production, trade and gross domestic product (GDP). We collate several existing but fragmented sources to provide missing production volumes for the Cape Colony from 1657 to 1909, and for South Africa from 1910 to 2015. This is the first such series that has been created for South Africa.

The analysis starts with a narrative description of the industry from its early beginnings, drawing on insights from the new data. This is followed by a comparison between South Africa and the other key southern hemisphere New World producers (Argentina, Australia, Chile and New Zealand). The final section concludes.

TRENDS IN SOUTH AFRICAN WINE PRODUCTION

The standard view of the South African wine industry is of a rich and cultured history of progress to the point where the industry is now able to take its rightful place in the global wine world. The reality, as always, is different, and the purpose in this section is to provide a more detailed and more

[1] In 2015, South Africa produced 1.2 billion litres of wine, and exported 415 ML to the value of US$786 million (Anderson and Pinilla 2017).

The authors would like to thank Mandy van der Merwe and Tom Keywood and for their research assistance, Christie Swanepoel for exchange rate data and Robert Ross for valuable advice on data sources.

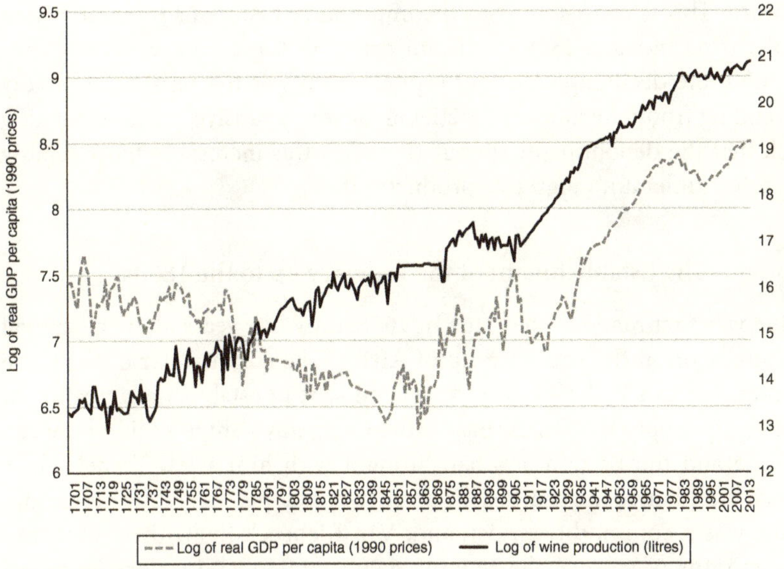

Figure 14.1 Volume of wine production and real GDP per capita, South Africa, 1700 to 2014 (in logs).
Source: Based on data in Anderson and Pinilla (2017).

nuanced narrative of the more important factors that resulted in the long-term trends in the industry described in Figure 14.1.

Less than a decade after European settlement in the mid-seventeenth century at the southern tip of Africa, the Cape produced wine from vines brought by the first governor, Jan van Riebeeck. This was part of the experimentation with fresh produce to find foods and beverages that would grow in the new settlement and that could keep sailors and passengers in good health during the long sea voyages from Europe to the East Indies. The volume of production was initially small, owing to the small number of European settlers, the large startup capital required and the priority placed on the production of foodstuffs to supply the passing ships. However, the conducive climate and terroir of the Cape soon made viticulture a thriving industry, augmented by the arrival from 1688 of wine-producing French Huguenots (Fourie and Von Fintel 2014).

One way to descriptively investigate the long-term trends in the physical volume of wine production over the ensuing centuries is to juxtapose production and GDP per capita (Figure 14.1). The graph suggests a negative correlation between the two series until the 1850s, when exports of merino wool and the first diamond boom in the 1870s propelled the economy forward. This is consistent with the importance historians have attributed to the wine industry as a significant driver of Cape prosperity, notwithstanding the declining GDP per capita, which was the result of a rapidly expanding frontier economy practicing mostly expansive, pastoral farming such that the denominator (population size) was increasing more rapidly than the numerator (aggregate production).

The Establishment of the Industry up to the 1800s

Wine was first made at the Cape in 1658, only five years after the arrival of Europeans at the southern tip of Africa. The commander of the Cape station, Jan van Riebeeck, who had been sent to establish a refreshment station to supply the Dutch East India Company's ships sailing between Europe and the East Indies, had brought with him a few French vines which he planted in the lush if windswept slopes of Table Mountain. Wine was a commodity in demand: Van Riebeeck knew that, after several months of voyage, the roughly 6,000 soldiers and sailors on board the ships anchoring in Table Bay[2] annually would be thirsty (Boshoff and Fourie 2010). He also found soon after settlement that alcohol could be a valuable commodity in trading with the indigenous stock farmer Khoe and hunter-gatherer San.

Yet despite the potential demand in these two markets, viticulture was slow to take off. The settlers that were released from Company service to encourage production focused almost entirely on cattle and wheat, two commodities that did not take long to earn a return on investment. Until early in the eighteenth century, viticulture was instead undertaken predominantly on the large estates set up by Company officials.

In 1685, Commander Simon van der Stel was granted land on the eastern slopes of Table Mountain, which became Constantia, and in 1700 his son, Willem Adriaan van der Stel, then the governor, was granted Vergelegen, 30,000 ha of land on the slopes of the Hottentots Holland Mountains. These two farms produced the bulk of Cape wine and earned exceptional returns for their owners, mostly because they could employ Company slaves and reserve the bulk of the produce for Company procurement.

This unfair advantage upset the increasing settler population, boosted by the arrival of several dozen French Huguenot families in 1688, many of

[2] The total settler and slave population of the Cape had not reached 1,000 by 1690, so the 'export' market on the ships constituted the largest part of the market for the farmers' produce, including wine.

whom were skilled in the art of making wine. The extravagance of Willem Adriaan van der Stel and his unilateral ability to determine who could participate in the monopoly of wine and meat at the Cape ultimately triggered a revolt amongst the settlers. In 1706, three farmers drew up a petition to the Lords XVII in Amsterdam, the shareholders of the Dutch East India Company (VOC), objecting to his behaviour. The petition was signed by sixty-three of the 550 or so settlers at the Cape. Although the petition was first rejected, the Lords XVII, fearing discontent in the Colony, finally recalled Willem Adriaan to the Netherlands. Three years after his departure, Vergelegen was split into four farms and sold to settler farmers. No VOC employees were subsequently allowed to own land at the Cape. Only then did wine production take off.

Wine production was affected also by the Cape's market institutions. At the end of August every year, the Company auctioned the rights to sell alcohol at the Cape. The seven franchises (or *pachts*) that were sold at these auctions, of which the most lucrative was the right to sell Cape wine in Cape Town, accounted for a significant part of total Company income. Throughout the century, settler farmers would complain to the shareholders of the Company about what they considered unfair institutions; prices were fixed and farmers would be forced to sell at low prices to the Company, only to see the Company (and the franchise owners) on-sell at significantly higher prices to the passing ships and their crew. It is for this reason that most historians considered the early Cape wine industry as inefficient and stagnant, producing poor-quality wine (given the weak incentives of fixed prices) and often prone to overproduction, as farmers tried to make up for low prices by boosting volume in the hope that higher future prices would protect their investments.

Van Duin and Ross (1987) challenged these notions of a poor-performing sector. They portrayed instead a sector that was expanding over the entire century, although in some periods more rapidly than in others. For example, over the half-century 1739–1743 to 1789–1793 (averages are taken to minimize outliers), the annual rate of growth in wine production was 3.1 percent, much faster than the GDP growth measured by Fourie and Van Zanden (2013). Although the rapid increase in the quantity of wine recorded after 1743 can be linked to the change in the basis on which statistics were collected, there were periods throughout the century of significant expansion (the late 1760s and early 1770s, and the late 1780s). Comparing growth in the quantity of wine produced to the number of vines planted, Van Duin and Ross (1987) argue that the downswings in the series were primarily the consequence of harvest failures, not of disinvestment.

One of the reasons for this improvement, Fourie and Von Fintel (2014) show, is the presence of skilled viticulturists in the group of Huguenot migrant families. Fourie and Von Fintel (2014) trace the region of origin of each of the Huguenot migrants and then measure their productivity at the Cape over several decades (based on *opgaafrol* microdata). They show that Huguenots who came from regions in France where viticulture was practiced were more likely to have been more productive winemakers at the Cape. These immigrants (and their descendants) could produce better quality wines – wines that could last upwards of six months and were therefore in greater demand by ship captains – and would become a wine elite, sometimes called the Cape gentry (Guelke and Shell 1983; Williams 2016), that would lead the industry for many generations.

This can also be seen in the regional divergence of wine production over the eighteenth century. Although wine was first made on the slopes of Table Mountain, the area west of the first mountain ranges, Stellenbosch and Drakenstein (modern-day Paarl and surroundings), became the wine barrel of the Cape Colony. This is also where most of the Huguenots settled. After 1760, wine production in the Cape district stagnated, but increased significantly in Stellenbosch and Drakenstein. By the end of the 1780s, Drakenstein produced 60 percent of all Cape wine.

The increase in wine production, as our results show, was not uniform across the century. Already at the end of the seventeenth century, soon after the arrival of Huguenots and because of the rapid expansion of estates such as Constantia and Vergelegen, wine production increased significantly. This boom in production was halted by the decision to prevent Company officials from owning estates, meaning that scale economies were lost as most of the largest estates were split up and sold to settler farmers. The smallpox epidemic of 1713 also decimated the Khoesan and the slave labour force that farmers relied on. Production picked up again in the 1720s and 1740s. Although the latter might be a consequence of the change in the rule to measure wine output as it entered Cape Town, it is probably also due to the Anglo–French War of 1744–1748, when the Company was forced to increase the fixed prices at which it purchased wine.

Stagnation and low prices were common for the 1750s, and this can be seen in the poor performance of the business cycle; but growth returned in the 1790s, despite a short recession, especially during the 1770s and 1780s, when demand for Cape wine increased significantly, both for consumption in Cape Town and for exports. This is confirmed when considering the increase in the value of the monopoly franchises over the period, a clear indication of a rise in the expected profit of wine sales.

By the end of the 1780s, the Colony had reached the peak of the business cycle. A financial crisis would hit the Colony in the 1790s (Havemann and Fourie 2015), reducing local demand. In addition, the Dutch East India Company was struggling to support the extensive trading network that it had built up over the previous two centuries. Fewer Dutch ships arrived in Table Bay, although its debilitating effect for the wine industry was somewhat mitigated by an increase in ships from other countries. However, when France occupied the Seven Provinces of the Netherlands in 1795, Britain decided to occupy the Cape in order to control the seas and the route to the East. Although the Cape was handed back to the Batavian Republic in 1803 at the Treaty of Amiens, Britain occupied the Cape again in 1806, and it formally became a British colony in 1814.

The Troubled 1800s and Early 1900s

The story of wine production in the Cape Colony in the nineteenth century can be broken into two halves. The two periods are separated both by the character and context of the industry and by the available sources. The first period begins with the Second British Occupation of the Cape in 1806 and ends with the Anglo–French Trade Treaty of 1860. The second period ends with the unification of the four colonies in 1910. The production of wine involved managing slaves and then free workers after the emancipation of slaves: finding a sufficient supply of reliable labour was a persistent problem. The quality of wine, with few exceptions, was low. This was partly because winegrape prices were uniform, so farmers sought to maximize yields. Trade treaties and tariffs were the most significant influence on export markets.

Wine production was not directly regulated as it had been by the Dutch East Indian Company, or would become under the Ko-operatieve Wijnbouwersvereeniging van Zuid-Afrika Beperkt (KWV, or Cooperative Wine Farmers' Association of South Africa, Limited), so that the cycles were more complex in the nineteenth century than in the preceding and subsequent centuries. These were the outcome of the intersections amongst numerous conditions, some of which are marked by the dates of events, others by cumulative changes. The list includes *inter alia* trade treaties and tariff agreements; laws regarding slavery; laws on the relations between masters and servants; the perpetual shortage of labour; nominal and 'real' wages of workers; the discovery of diamonds and of gold; the phylloxera epidemic; the South African War (1899–1902) and its consequences; and the Act of Union in 1910. These are discussed further in the following sections.

1806–1831: Abolition and Tariffs

The British governments of the Cape inherited a society and an economy founded on the labour of slaves. Wine was the most important source of tax revenues, and of export earnings. Green grape (*Semillon*) was ubiquitous in 1821. All of the other common varieties except Pontac (Hanepoot or Muscat d'Alexandrie, Muscadel, Steen or Chenin blanc, and probably Fransdruif or Palomino) had arrived in the Colony in the seventeenth century and were still amongst the seven most widely planted winegrapes in 1980. The wines sold in London were, in W.W. Bird's words, as 'notoriously bad' as in the Colony itself, and vinegar and brandy were 'a poor description' made from the 'refuse of the grape'. Its consumers were first concerned with the volume and strength of the liquor.

The demand for exports from the Cape rose from 1778 to 1815 during the Anglo–French and Napoleonic Wars between Britain and France, while the garrison at the Atlantic island of St Helena boosted the demand from 1815 to 1821. The sustained export-led and tariff preference–assisted expansion in wine production between 1815 and 1824 accelerated exports to Britain, raised prices and stimulated an expansion of production. Cape farmers continued to plant more vines and to press more grapes into wine to meet the rising demand from abroad and from within the Colony itself even after Cape Town wine prices had fallen by two-thirds between 1815 and 1821.

In 1813, the British government reduced the import tariffs on Cape wines by 38 percent. The Cape's tariff preferences were reversed and reduced in 1825 and again in 1830 to bring them into line with Portugal, the main exporter of fortified wine to Britain. Cape wine exports reached their height in 1829 when two-thirds of the 9,000 KL of wine pressed were exported. Exports stayed up between 2,500 KL and 4,700 KL during the decade of the 1830s.

The abolition of the slave trade in 1808 reduced the supply of slave men. Contrary to expectations, production expanded throughout the ensuing years until slaves were emancipated in 1838. Rayner (1986) tells us that the expansion of vine planting and winemaking was mainly carried out by aging slaves.

The Caledon Proclamation of 1809 (§1) (Elbourne 2003) combined conceptions of rights and of social order. It defined the status of the Khoi as "free men who should be subject to proper regularity in their places of abode and occupation but also find an encouragement for preferring entering the service of the inhabitants to leading an indolent life". Ordinance 50 of 1828 freed the Khoi from the restrictions of passes and punishments for 'vagrancy' without trial. Khoi chose daily or seasonal employment over monthly or annual contracts. They did not want to be tied to 'a contract for life'. Mission stations offered one alternative to residence on farms. Farmers and officials blamed the missions for 'draining off labour' – in fact, they provided 'reservoirs of occasional labour' (Marais 1968, p. 168).

Caledon's Proclamation established clearly in law the principle that wine could not be part of the workers' remuneration, a principle that was repeated in Ordinance 50 of 1828.

Emancipation and Freedom

Slaves were emancipated on 1 December 1838. None of the slaves shared the vision of Lord Glenelg, the Colonial Secretary, namely that their place was as 'free men who depend on employment for food and on character for employment.' (Ross 1983, p. 82). The first task for landowners was to get workers back on to their farms. What wine farmers wanted, and could not easily get, was farmworker households employed throughout the year with as little cash outlay as possible. Unsurprisingly, farmers protested after Emancipation when the slaves 'streamed to Cape Town where they followed an easy life' (*waar hulle 'n lui-lekker lewe gevoer het*) (*De Zuid Afrikaan*, quoted by Van Zyl 1975, p. 14). They saw freed slaves as itinerants (*loslopers*) who were beyond the moral and economic constraints of regular employment and a fixed place of abode.

The former slaves needed money and somewhere to live. Like Khoi before them, they preferred day labour (*loswerk*) over monthly incomes, and for their wives to stay at a distance from the farms. Those able to do so went to mission stations. Others went to Cape Town or Boland towns or found small plots from where they could find seasonal employment. Only when they had little choice did workers with families take residence on farms on monthly or annual contracts with low cash wages and 'garden plots'.

What were the economic consequences of the emancipation of slaves? Wine production followed close to the line of a rising trend during the period between 1830 and 1846 (Figure 14.1), and reached over 12,000 KL, the highest level hitherto recorded, in 1841. Wine exports, on the other hand, were reduced from some 4,265 KL in 1839 to half of that in 1842 and continued to fall further to under 1,000 KL in 1852. They recovered to some 4,200 KL in 1859, the year before the Anglo–French trade treaty cut off preferential access to the British market (Van Zyl 1993).

Production returns can be complemented by the series for wine prices. These increased from median prices of 75 shillings per leaguer[3] in the years

[3] This translates to $5.20 per KL in 1832 values, or $43 in 2014 values of the dollar (Officer and Williamson 2017)

from 1832–1838 to 93 shillings in 1840, and down to 48 shillings by 1852. During the same period, farmers had to raise the wages of day labourers, particularly at harvest, and to raise monthly wages in Stellenbosch and in Paarl from about 10 shillings to 15 shillings. Wine production increased by about 50 percent and prices doubled in the 1850s from 72 shillings in 1852 to reach 162 shillings (when 1 shilling = US$0.41). They benefitted from an expansion of demand due to the rise of wool exports from the eastern Cape, which exceeded the value of all vine products in 1853 (Williams 2016).

Masters and Servants

Throughout the nineteenth century and beyond, farmers continued to complain of shortages of labour. The Colonial Secretary rejected the Draft Vagrancy Act of 1834, but approved a Masters and Servants Ordinance in 1842. Between 1856 and 1909, the government and parliament of the Colony initiated commissions of inquiry, produced official reports and held select committees on labour supply (ten in all). They passed and amended the Masters and Servants Act and its twin, the Vagrancy Acts, thirteen times. These defined the terms of contracts of service and the penalties for breaching them, which were greater for servants than for masters. They subjected servants to their duties to and to the commands of their masters, to refrain from drunkenness, not 'to use abusive language to his master or his master's wife' and to permit masters to agree with one another on the terms of servants' employment.

Credit advances made it possible for farmers to recruit and tie workers to their own employment but not necessarily to enforce the debt. The main use for the Masters and Servants Act was to reclaim advances by workers who had deserted their employment. The lower or higher the price of wine, the fewer or more convictions under the two acts. The acts culminated in the unsuccessful 'Lash Bill' in 1888, whose purpose was to enable farmers to deliver offenders to the court and to return them the same day so that the master was not deprived of their labour.

The colonial government cast its net far and wide on and beyond the northern and eastern frontiers of the colony to find workers, where there was 'plenty of raw material for labour', as the chair of the 1879 Select Committee put it. Migrant labourers had no intention of working or remaining outside the season when their labour would be most required and their payments that much greater. The scarcity of labour was made worse for the wine farmers in 1890 when the railway was built through Worcester. At the same time, workers were required to deal with the elimination of the phylloxera louse from the vines. The imperfect solution that the farmers asked for and the government used was to employ convict labour, which was extended from public works and De Beers diamond mines to private employers. The increasing breadth of offences, the more stringent punishments and the extension of the search for sources of labour more widely is evidence of the limited effectiveness of the acts.

The *dop* system is the provision of cups of natural wine five or six times during the working day i.e., about a litre (Williams 2016). Male workers, and women, would then drink fortified wine at the weekend. Coloureds in the Western Districts of the Colony were the main consumers of wine, and formed most of the predominant residential and casual work force. Mr W. T. Hertzog explained to Select Committee 26/1879 that 'it is the custom of the country'. There were farmers who included wine in the rations of slaves by 1715. Some large-scale farmers certainly did so under British rule. After Emancipation, wine was provided as an incentive to freed slaves and became prevalent amongst resident as well as local day workers. It was common in the 1870s, and ubiquitous by the time of the Liquor Commission of 1893–1894. J. H. Hofmeyr succeeded in qualifying the commission's findings that custom enforces the practice of giving wine to workers from the start of the day and stimulates the craving for alcohol. Workers changed employers often but within the same district. As with credit advances, the system was an incentive to labourers to work for specific farmers. It may have reduced wages, but it was unlikely to increase the productivity of the workforce.

In short, during the six decades after the emancipation of slaves, a complex of interrelated institutions came into being. Some were formulated in laws; others were extralegal. They all indicate the scope for rural households to maintain within frames of constraints a degree of autonomy from the domination of landowners.

Diamonds and Gold

The Cape economy's prosperity from the 1840s to the 1860s depended on the export of wool, so its wine producers were affected by the collapse of prices in the United States in 1774. The only lengthy period when wine and brandy production in the Cape fell behind its long-term trend was between 1883 and 1909. The last quarter of the century was a period of investments in railways, technology, gold and immigration in the United States, and in South Africa. It was also a time when the terms of trade turned against agricultural producers, within countries and internationally.

The imposition of an excise tax in 1878 by the Cape government seems to have had little effect on production and prices. However, it had a far-reaching political consequence, namely the formation of the Afrikaner Bond under the leadership of J. H. Hofmeyr, with its political base amongst Dutch-speaking farmers.

In 1866, a diamond was discovered at Hopetown. The 'diamond rush' of 1870 and the annexation of the diamond fields by Britain realized very high export revenues for a short time (1870–1872). The economy of the Cape Colony benefitted directly from diamond exports and from spending by diggers and in time by De Beers. Not surprisingly, the demand for brandy production benefitted more than wine from the diggings. Production of 'ordinary' wine rose to over 20,000 KL and 'inferior' brandy to almost 5,000 KL in 1875, from 16,500 KL and 15,500 KL (and brandy from approximately 1,400 KL and 2,000 KL) in the 1856 and 1865 censuses, respectively.

The discovery of gold deposits on the Witwatersrand in 1886 potentially formed the biggest market that Cape wine producers had ever known. However, wine and brandy exports from the Cape to the Zuid-Afrikaansche Republiek (ZAR) were kept at bay by a trade treaty between the ZAR and Portugal (the colonizers of Mozambique) in 1875, which made it possible for Mozambican cane spirits and German potato spirits (relabelled as Portuguese) to be exported freely to the ZAR. In 1881, the new Volksraad (Parliament) of the ZAR granted 'a concession for the sole right to manufacture from grain, potato and other spirits and the right to sell in bulk and bottle free of licence such spirits', which was taken up by De Eerste Fabrieken of Sammy Marks in 1883. The distillery was protected from Cape brandies by a high tariff and able to harvest the profits opened up by the rapidly expanding number of miners on the Rand.

Production, Prices and Wages

How can we interpret the figures for production and prices for the period 1874 to the start of the South African War in 1899? If exports of wool can be credited for raising incomes in the Colony in the 1850s and 1860s, diamonds did so (and thereby expanded demand for wine) in the first four years of the 1870s and more modestly in the early 1880s (Figure 14.1). In 1887, wine production reached its highest level during the century at almost 36,000 KL. Wine production fell significantly thereafter to an average of 25,000 KL between 1888 and 1894.

Wine prices collapsed during the same decade. Wine and brandy prices reached their highest points in the century at US$99 and US$285 per KL in 1880–1881 and then fell all the way down to US$33 for wine and US$99 for brandy by 1886–1888. Wine exports first revived between 1884 and the discovery of gold on the Witwatersrand in 1886, but that discovery in the ZAR may be too early to account for the Cape's export increase.

Gold miners, black and white, preferred to drink spirits, and in the process protected grape farmers from the worst consequences of the depression. Brandy production stayed at much the same level as before but the price went up rapidly though not consistently from US$73 per KL in 1888 to US$245 two years later and US$344 in 1895 and 1896. Exports, primarily to the ZAR, responded to the diamond booms in 1871–1874 and in 1879 and the start in 1883 of gold mining in the eastern Transvaal. The effects of the Rand goldfields were much greater. The increased output, grade and value of gold from 1895 to 1899 expanded the market for 'ordinary' Cape wine and grape brandies, routed through Natal to avoid the ZAR tariffs. Available data (Table 14.1) show that the proportion of exports of wine from the Cape to the ZAR increased substantially after 1889, reaching above 10 percent in 1897, and above 25 percent during the war, despite the fact that total exports, which averaged 42 KL in the ten-year period 1894–1904, were 50 and 46 KL in 1900 and 1901 respectively.[4]

The changing balance between brandy and wine production opened the way to a shift in the geography of Cape viticulture. Wine and brandy production contracted in Paarl and in Stellenbosch, the largest wine-growing districts. Farmers across the mountains in Worcester and particularly in Robertson took advantage of the demand for brandy and their scope for extending their own production.

Scully (1990) sets out the relations between the annual prices of wine in Stellenbosch/Paarl and the average daily wages paid to farmworkers in the Colony. Those data suggest wages remained relatively stable during a period of falling and then rising winegrape prices until the 1890s, when they stayed fairly proportional to one another. In the previous decades of the depression, farmers had not been able to force wages down to compensate for the reduction in winegrape prices. This cannot be explained by the shortage of labour but would be consistent with Ricardo's 'iron law of wages'.

Vine Diseases

Cape vines were affected by three overlapping disease incidents in the nineteenth century. Anthracnose ('rust') reached epidemic levels between 1819 and 1821, while powdery mildew (oïdium), which arrived in 1859–1860,

[4] These calculations are based in the assumption that most wine from the Cape reached the ZAR via either Natal of Delagoa Bay rather than directly, because of the high tariffs levied on imports from the Cape.

Table 14.1 *Cape wine exports to the Zuid-Afrikaansche Republiek, 1878 to 1904*

	Total wine exports from the Cape Colony (KL)	Exports from Natal and Delagoa Bay (KL)	Total exports from the Cape, Natal & Delagoa Bay (KL)	% of total exports from Natal and Delagoa Bay
1878	83	1.8	85	2.1
1879	52	3.6	56	6.8
1880	56	2.0	58	3.6
1881	45	1.8	47	3.9
1882	47	1.0	48	2.1
1883	226	1.1	227	0.5
1884	289	1.2	290	0.4
1885	212	0.8	213	0.4
1886	311	3.5	315	1.1
1887	220	2.6	223	1.2
1888	170	1.5	172	0.9
1889	103	0.3	103	0.3
1890	64	5.0	69	7.8
1891	60	4.8	65	8.1
1892	73	3.8	77	5.2
1893	74	3.5	78	4.7
1894	56	3.8	60	6.8
1895	55	4.8	60	8.7
1896	45	5.4	50	12.0
1897	46	4.0	50	8.6
1898	29	4.3	33	15.0
1899	35	6.9	42	19.4
1900	50	13.4	63	26.7
1901	46	14.1	60	30.8
1902	39	11.0	50	28.3
1903	37	9.5	47	25.8
1904	34	7.7	42	22.9

Note: Most Cape exports were routed via Natal and Delagoa Bay to escape the high tariffs charged to direct exports from the Cape to the ZAR.
Source: Anderson and Pinilla (2017).

was brought under control in 1861 by following the French example of thrice-daily injecting of carbon bisulphide. These funguses changed the geography of vine planting. The 'rust' moved the sweet wine vines, muscadel and hanepoot, across the mountain (*over die berg*). In Paarl, which had the largest area of production, oïdium attacked steen and pontac grapes. Only green grape stood up well against both diseases.

The discovery of gold on the Witwatersrand was preceded by the most severe incident of them all, which started with the identification of phylloxera at Mowbray and Moddergat in January 1886. The phylloxera louse did not discriminate amongst varieties. The colony's government applied the measures then followed in France: submersion; uprooting and quarantine; injecting chemicals; and grafting, in that order. The first was marginal in its effect, as was planting vines in sand; the second infuriated farmers and may have contributed to the spread of the disease; carbon bisulphide was the preferred official solution, and grafting was regarded with suspicion. These remedies were all demanding of farm labourers, of whom there was a shortage. If free labour was not available, the government would have to command convicts or juvenile offenders to do the work. The government needed to find plant breeders, obtain rootstocks and distribute them amongst districts and farmers, and the farmer and workers then had to graft American rootstocks.

The aphid destroyed vineyards throughout the wine fields. It spread across the wine-producing districts in the last twenty years of the nineteenth century, and it was only after the South African War that American rootstocks had been planted and grafted to replace the diseased vines of the Cape. The planting of rootstocks near Cape Town and other vine-breeding stations compensated, if slowly and inefficiently in the view of the farmers, for the destruction of the vines by lice. However, there was no marked effect of the disease on the aggregate production of wine and brandy in the 1890s. The levels of production owed more to the effects of tariffs on demand than of 'rust' and powdery mildew on supply. It was only subsequent to the South African War that farmers were confronted with collapses in prices, which they shared with wine producers.

The Most Recent 100 Years: Segregation, Apartheid, Sanctions and Reform

The South African economy experienced a long post-Depression expansion that lasted for most of the twentieth century (see Figure 14.1), accompanied by an equally long expansion in agricultural production (see also Kirsten, Edwards and Vink 2009; Liebenberg 2012) and in wine production specifically (Figure 14.1). The story of the expansion in the wine industry is the story of the KWV: its establishment in 1918, the increasing extent of its control over all aspects of the industry in the ensuing decades and eventually its loss of statutory powers in 1997. The KWV was set up explicitly to deal with the surpluses of poor-quality wine that periodically confronted the industry. Even as late as 1990, only some 30 percent of the grape press in the industry was of a quality suitable for making wine: in earlier years, this proportion was far less (Estreicher 2013).

Government intentions to increase the excise duty on wine in 1916 coincided with falling prices for wine, which resulted in a congress of wine farmers with Charles W. H. Kohler, a leading figure in the industry, agitating for a cooperative of wine and brandy farmers. The aim of this institution was to act as a counter to the market power of 'the trade' (the 'producer wholesalers' in today's parlance, who bought grapes from individual grape farmers, grapes or wine from wine farmers or wine from farmer cooperatives). In order to achieve this, Kohler proposed the following:[5]

- KWV would set a minimum or floor price.
- Members would have to sell through the organization.
- An annual wine surplus would be declared and delivered to KWV free of charge.
- This surplus wine would be distilled for disposal at the discretion of KWV.
- No produce (wine or the distilled product) would be sold on the domestic market at lower than the minimum price.
- KWV's income from this scheme would be used to finance the purchase of distilleries, vats and buildings, while profits would be distributed to members on a *pro rata* basis.

This scheme was propagated amongst wine farmers at a series of meetings during 1917, and the constitution of the KWV was approved on 27 September, with the first organized meeting taking place on 2 November. KWV was then established on 15 December 1917 and formally registered under the Cape Companies Act No. 25 of 1892 on 8 January 1918. All but 5 percent of the wine farmers in the Cape signed the constitution by the end of 1917, with the exceptions including a few Stellenbosch farmers and most of the Constantia farmers who produced superior-quality wine.

The trade opposed the scheme from the outset. However, the industry, newly organized under the Western Province Wine Merchants and Distillers Association,[6] reached a 'gentlemen's agreement' with KWV whereby the former agreed to distil and store the surplus on behalf of KWV, and the producer-wholesalers agreed to purchase only from KWV. This was in exchange for an undertaking from KWV not to compete in the domestic market, and not to deal directly with their clients. These agreements were

[5] The rest of this subsection follows Van Zyl (1993).
[6] A neat example of the 'theory of countervailing power' (Galbraith 1952).

eventually taken up in the 1924 legislation, which also conferred a monopoly for imports and exports of 'surplus' wine to the KWV (the precursor to today's bulk wine). Further statutory powers were conferred in 1940, with regular amendments to the relevant legislation thereafter.

In 1922, plans were made to turn the surplus production into motor fuel. Despite this, a quarter of the production was destroyed between 1920 and 1923, with the surplus at 50 percent of production. KWV had all but lost the ability to stop its members from selling to the trade at lower than the minimum price, which lent impetus to the drive for statutory powers to curb what they regarded as free riding. These were granted over distilling wine in 1924 despite recognition that the cause of overproduction was the inferior quality of the produce. As expected, these moves were opposed by the producers of good-quality wine and by the trade. As a result, the Wine and Spirit Control Act of 1924 made important concessions to the trade and to producers of good wine, by excluding their produce from control; but that concession was withdrawn by legislation in 1940.

These measures brought stability, which allowed KWV to turn to export promotion measures, aided by an increase in imperial preference in 1924. Producers of good wine were able to increase exports, while KWV started exporting fortified wine on a substantial scale for the first time since 1861. Exports increased more rapidly than industry output from 1925 to the late 1930s despite the global Great Depression. Yet exports could not get rid of the whole surplus, resulting in a Commission of Inquiry (the Wine Commission) in 1935, which reported in 1937, leading to ever-tighter control by KWV. The aim in this case was to introduce controls over the level of production as well, achieved in the 1940 legislation via a quota system. This coincided with rising demand in the ensuing decades, leading to increases in production quotas, which, however, did not prevent a chronic shortage of wine during most of the 1960s and 1970s. KWV addressed this problem by assigning quotas to the irrigated Olifants and Orange River areas, where new distilleries were opened in 1977 and 1978. These resulted in an expansion of output far ahead of consumption.

The expansion of demand for urban labour during and after World War II and the restriction of African migration to the Western Cape until 1976 created a shortage of farm labour. One consequence was the expansion in the use of prison labour and the establishment of 'farm prisons' (Marcus 1989).

In 1966, the first sanctions were taken against South African wine exports, when a Finnish trade union refused to handle South African wines in Finnish harbours (Heino 1992). In the late 1970s, exports slumped again following Britain's accession to the European Economic Community (EEC) in 1973 and adoption of EEC tariffs in 1977. However, sanctions only really affected the industry in the mid- to late 1980s, with exports going from 7 percent of production in 1959–1961 to 1 percent in the late 1980s, by which time grape growers started to anticipate the forthcoming political changes.

The early 1970s saw the introduction of the 'wine of origin' certification, which came into force in 1973 under Act 25 of 1957. This regulated the description of the origin of wine, the cultivar and the vintage. It was accompanied almost two decades later by the Liquor Products Act of 1989, which set standards for liquor products and regulated the standards of imports and exports. The act also created a new Wine and Spirit Board to administer these regulations.

Between 1985 and 1991, the production quota system was amended a number of times, but there was general agreement that these amendments did not make the system flexible enough to react to market signals. Political change in South Africa, the development of the grape juice concentrate market and of diversified products such as flavoured wine and alcoholic fruit beverages ('ready-to-drinks', or RTDs) and increasing exports meant that production was not expanding as rapidly as demand; hence the quota system was suspended in 1992.

The South African economy went into decline in the early 1970s when inflation first reached double digits and per capita income growth turned negative for the period 1974–1994. Inflation remained in the double digits throughout this time, and was accompanied by a contraction in real per capita GDP until 1994 (Figure 14.1).

The contractionary period of the 1980s was followed by a boom in the wine industry that has lasted, with only a few interruptions, since the first democratic elections in 1994. The five-year contraction in output in 1990–1994 may surprise, as this was in the lead-up to the democratic elections, when South African wine found its way back to international markets. What happened during this period was a rapid replanting of vines. For example, in 1990 only 12 percent of vines were one of the six 'noble' (and relatively low-yielding) varieties, namely Cabernet Sauvignon, Shiraz, Pinotage, Merlot, Sauvignon Blanc and Chardonnay. That share had grown to more than half by 2000, and in Stellenbosch, the proportion increased from 30 percent to 83 percent. Farmers increased their incomes by moving to higher-value grapes to the extent that the total volume of wine production stagnated.

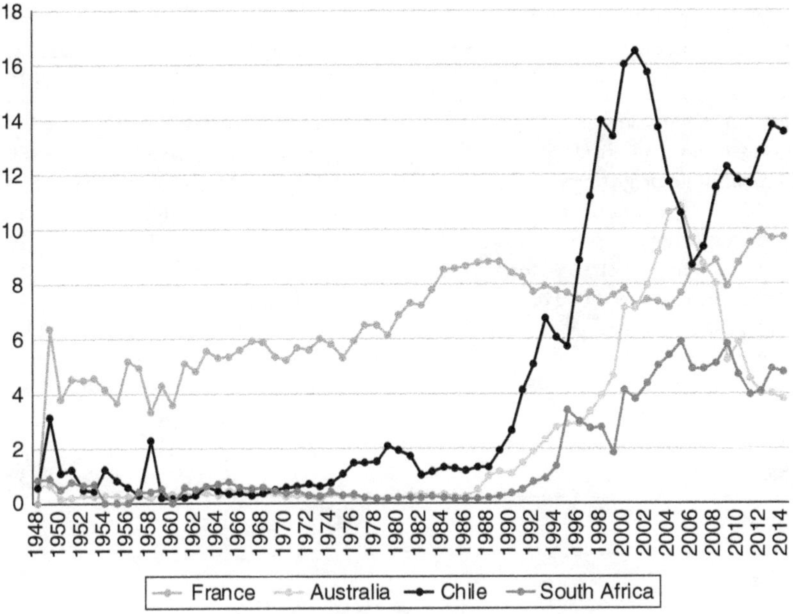

Figure 14.2 Revealed comparative advantage in wine,[a] South Africa and other countries, 1948 to 2014.

[a] Wine's share of national merchandise exports divided by its share of global exports.
Source: Anderson and Pinilla (2017).

Studies on the competitiveness of the industry since 1994 (e.g., Esterhuizen 2006; Van Rooyen, Esterhuizen and Stroebel 2011) generally support this analysis, as does the 'revealed' comparative advantage (RCA) index in Figure 14.2. The downswing in the RCA index in the 1990s was the result of strong performances by the Australian and Chilean wine industries during that period, combined with the relative strength of the Rand.

Table 14.2 tells the story in more detail. The number of wine farmers has declined by one-third, from 4,634 in 1995 to 3,314 in 2015. At the same time, the number of farms with their own cellars (producer cellars) increased from 183 in 1995 to 495 a decade later, and has more or less stabilized in the ensuing decade (which means there were 4,451 grape growers in 1995 and 2,829 in 2015, a decline of 37 percent). At the same time, the number of producer cellars, all originally cooperatives, declined from seventy-one to less than fifty, and is expected to decline further. While the new cellars were mostly small (with the proportion of cellars able to crush less than 100 tonnes of grapes growing from 30 percent to 51 percent of the total in the decade to 2005), the average size of the cellars increased thereafter. The first

Table 14.2 *Structural changes to the wine industry, South Africa, 1995 to 2015*

	1995	2000	2005	2010	2015
Number of wine farmers	4 634	4 501	4 360	3 596	3 314
Private cellars (number)	183	277	495	493	485[a]
Number of grape growers	4 451	4 224	3 865	3 103	2 829
Producer cellars (number)	71	69	65	54	49[a]
Producing wholesalers (number)	5	9	21	26	25[a]
% of cellars that crush <100 tonnes per annum		30	51	46	40[a]
Winegrape vine area ('000 ha)	84	94	102	101	99
Average farm size (ha)	18.1	20.8	23.3	28.1	29.8
Vines < 4 years as % of total		19.4	14.1	7.7	6.5
Good wine as % of total wine	62	65	69	79	81[a]
Domestic sales (ML)	371	389	345	346	383
Exports as a share of wine prod'n (%)	15	20	39	40	35
Share of crop that is red (%)	10	15	31	35	37[a]

[a] 2014.

Source: SAWIS (2015) and Anderson and Pinilla (2017).

rows of Table 14.2 therefore hint at some measure of consolidation of the industry, with fewer and larger farms, average cellar size increasing over the past decade and so on.

During this period, the area under winegrape vines increased from 84,000 ha to a little over 100,000, and has remained relatively stable since then. As a result, the average vineyard increased from 18 ha to almost 30 ha. The overall quality of the harvest has increased: a higher proportion of good wine is extracted from the total crush (increasing from 62 percent to 81 percent), exports have grown proportionally faster with around two-fifths of production being exported while the dependence on white wine grapes for distilling into brandy has declined (with the proportion of red wine increasing from 10 percent to 37 percent). However, there are troubling signs: domestic sales of wine have hardly moved over those twenty years, and farmers are not keeping up with the planting of new vineyards. Given a twenty-year replanting schedule, the expectation is that 20 percent of the vineyard should be less than four years old, but in South Africa, this has declined from close to 20 percent in 2000 to less than 7 percent by 2015.

However, the industry structure remains relatively fragmented, as is shown in Table 14.3, where the five southern hemisphere New World producers are arranged in descending order of total market share of the four largest companies. Although the largest firm in South Africa rivals that of

Table 14.3 *Shares of domestic still wine sales volume by the four largest firms, South Africa and other New World countries, 2014 (%)*

	Chile	Argentina	New Zealand	Australia	South Africa
Largest winery	31	27	23	16	31
2nd largest winery	30	14	11	9	3
3rd largest winery	29	12	10	9	2
4th largest winery	1	7	9	7	1
Combined share	91	60	53	41	36

Source: Anderson and Pinilla (2017).

Chile, where overall market share is the highest, South Africa still has the lowest concentration when the four largest firms are taken into account. No firm in South Africa dominates winegrape production, or export sales, unlike the extent of domination found in the United States (Howard et al. 2012) and Australia (Parliament of Australia 2016).

SOUTH AFRICA COMPARED WITH OTHER SOUTHERN HEMISPHERE WINE PRODUCERS

When the size of the economies and the wine industries of the southern hemisphere New World wine-producing countries are compared (Table 14.4), it is evident that New Zealand is an outlier. The wine industry is small, but has been successful in building a reputation for high-quality wine that is reflected in the high share of production exported as well as the high unit value of exports – the highest in the world for still wine, and second only to France when sparkling wine is included. Amongst those countries, South Africa has the highest yield when measured by litres of wine per bearing hectare.

The South American countries and South Africa share a low import propensity, in contrast to Australia and New Zealand, where intraindustry trade is considerable. Nominally, the duty on wines imported into South Africa is 25 percent, but under trade agreements with the European Union (EU), these duties have been removed. Even so, wine imports are tiny, which reflects the fact that South African wines sell on the domestic market at relatively low prices. Unlike the South American countries, which don't trade amongst themselves, Australia and New Zealand do, which partly explains their high import propensity. Australia, Chile and New Zealand export more than 60 percent of their production, compared with around 40 percent for South Africa (Table 14.4).

Table 14.4 *The South African wine industry in New World context, 2014*

	Australia	New Zealand	Argentina	Chile	South Africa
Area under vines ('000 ha)	137	36	226	138	124
Production (ML)	1186	320	1518	1214	1146
Average yield (KL/ha)	8.7	8.9	6.7	8.8	9.2
Consumption (ML)	553	94	861	226	428
Export as % of production	61	60	17	66	41
Imports as % of consumption	21	37	0.1	0.9	2.0
Unit value of exports (US$/l)	2.31	5.78	3.19	2.30	1.68
Total population (million)	2.6	4.5	43.0	17.8	54.0

Source: Anderson and Pinilla (2017).

Figure 14.3 shows the per capita recorded consumption of wine, beer and spirits in South Africa since 1962, where the volume of each product is weighted by its alcohol content. Therefore, for example, while the actual quantity of wine consumed in the country is around 8 litres per person, and beer over 50 litres per person, when adjusted for the alcohol content beer consumption is not much more than 3 litres per person, given its low alcohol content. The data show that per capita recorded consumption of beer has increased substantially over the period, from as low as 0.25 litre per person to over 3 litres, that is, more than twelvefold. On the other hand, the per capita consumption of spirits has actually decreased by almost half over this period, largely because of the steep decline in brandy consumption, which was sufficient to offset the increase in whisky consumption (SAWIS 2014).

Per capita wine consumption, though, has been stagnant over the whole period. There was a slight increase in the early 1970s, concomitant with the establishment of the first wine routes and the popularization of Estate wines, and again at the time of the democratization in the first part of the 1990s, but these are small movements along a rather flat trend in consumption.

These data should be interpreted with care. Per capita consumption of wine (measured in litres per person) in the southern hemisphere New World countries is shown in Figure 14.4. For Argentina and Chile, measured on the right-hand axis, consumption declined from above 90 litres per person in the case of Argentina and to almost 70 litres per person in Chile,[7] to levels similar to those of the other southern hemisphere countries shown. The exception is South Africa: per capital consumption has

[7] Per capita consumption in France, Italy, Portugal and Spain reached well above 100 litres per person in the past.

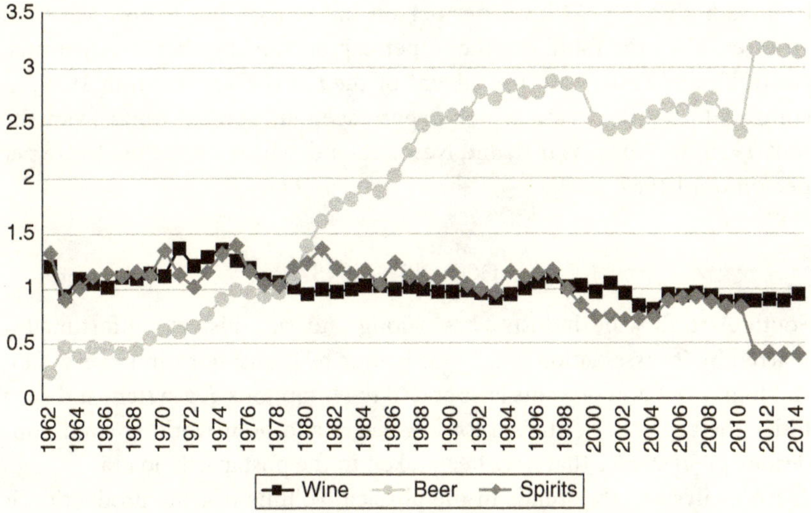

Figure 14.3 Per capita consumption of wine, beer and spirits, South Africa, 1961 to 2014 (litres of alcohol).
Source: Anderson and Pinilla (2017).

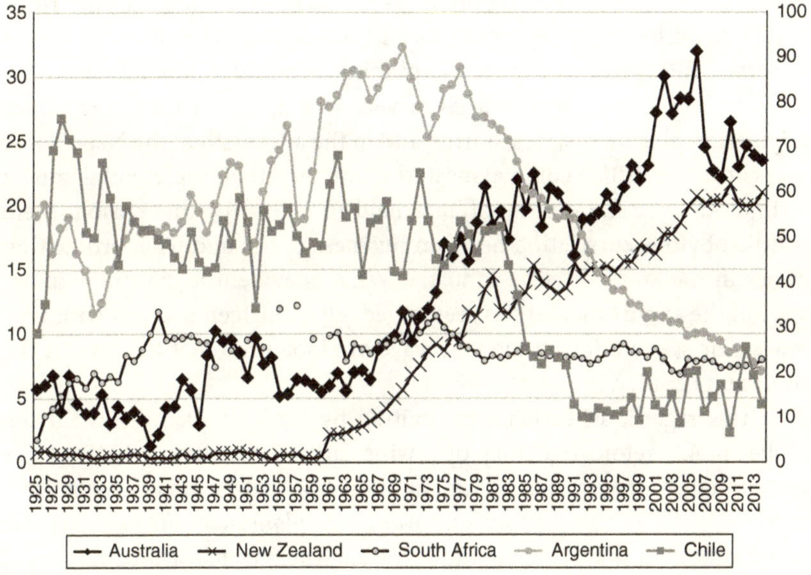

Figure 14.4 Per capita consumption of wine, southern hemisphere New World countries, 1925 to 2014 (litres).
Source: Anderson and Pinilla (2017).

been as high as 11–12 litres per person in the past, but is now less than 10 litres. Note the rapid decline in per capita consumption in Argentina, Australia and Chile with the advent of the Great Depression in 1929, in contrast to South Africa, which experienced an upward trend from the mid-1920s to World War II, and New Zealand, which was below 1 litre per person until 1962.

CONCLUSIONS

South Africa's wine industry has a long and rich history, unfortunately marred by its association with poor labour relations: born in slavery, subject to masters and servants laws and to the iniquitous *dop* system and even today the subject of criticism for low wages and poor working conditions despite great strides that have been taken in the postapartheid era.

An analysis of the trends in the physical volume of wine production is difficult in an industry that has been marred by overproduction of relatively poor-quality wine through most of its existence but that earns its profits mostly from selling product of higher quality that is pressed from lower-yielding grapes and marketed with a strong sense of place.

Nevertheless, it is clear that the industry as a whole has always been highly dependent on the export market, having experienced only three sustained periods of prosperity in its long history, all the result of increased exports. These were at the very beginning, when the population on the ships calling at the Cape in a given year was up to six times the settler population plus their slaves; during and in the aftermath of the Napoleonic Wars until the British colonial masters eliminated their preferential import tariff; and since the demise of apartheid in 1994. For this reason, there is little obvious correlation between business cycles and wine production cycles in the South African industry. What is evident is that the importance of the export market has reemerged, after thirteen decades with very few exports, even during the first wave of globalization at the turn of the twentieth century.

In this regard, an earlier contribution by Vink, Williams and Kirsten (2004, p. 42) retold the story of a wine farmer warning in 1918, at the beginning of a boom period for the industry, that he was '*...bang dat 't te lekker gaan. Die surplus sal kom want men plant agter die prys aan.*' He was 'frightened that it was going too well. The surplus will come [back] because farmers plant after the price.' Some surpluses, however, are better than others. Figure 14.5 shows the real price of the average litre of wine at the farmgate in South Africa from 1960 onwards. The real price of 'good

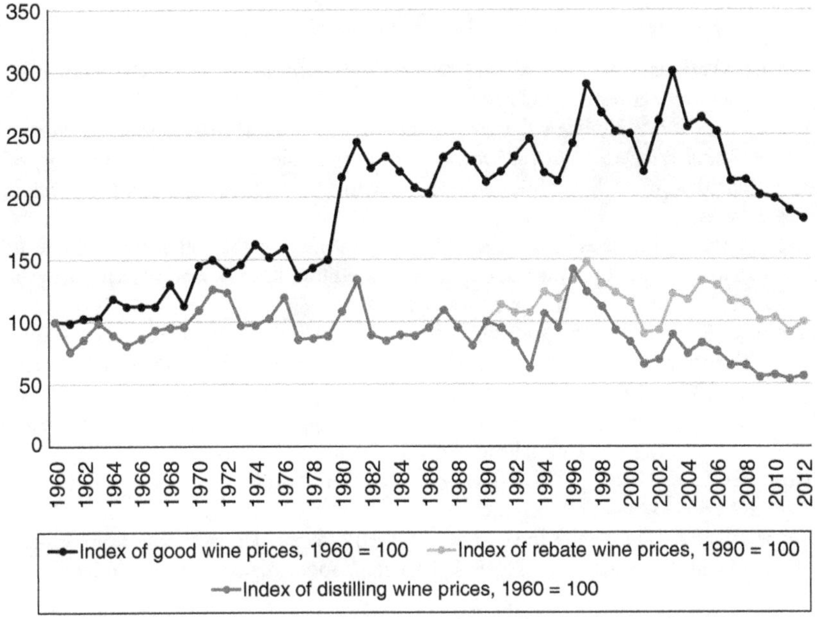

Figure 14.5 Index of the real farm-gate price of wine, South Africa, 1960 to 2012 (1962 = 100).
Source: Abstract (2012).

wine' increased steadily through the 1970s, then rose sharply between 1977 and 1981 relative to prices of distilling and rebate wines, encouraging quality wine production. This was followed by a period of stagnation during the era of boycotts and sanctions, then an increase in the aftermath of democratization. However, all of these prices have declined by up to one-third in real terms over the first decade of this century, and in 2012 were only 80 percent of their levels in 1983. On the other hand, prices in the superpremium and above segments have moved in the opposite direction. A bottle of Meerlust Rubicon 1980, arguably one of the earliest icon wines made and sold in South Africa and first released on the market in 1983 (Platter 1982), retailed for R4.86 (US$4.38), while in 2012 the retail price was an estimated R300 (US$36.58). In real terms, the price increased more than fourfold over this period. If the supply response is as predicted by our correspondent in 1918, the balance between volume and quality production may move further in favour of quality, given the price trends of the past few decades – even if this means many of these wines will become unaffordable for ordinary South Africans.

REFERENCES

Abstract (various years), *Abstract of Agricultural Statistics*, Pretoria: Department of Agriculture, Forestry and Fisheries.

Anderson, K. and V. Pinilla (with the assistance of A. J. Holmes) (2017), *Annual Database of Global Wine Markets, 1835 to 2016*, freely available in Excel at the University of Adelaide's Wine Economics Research Centre, www.adelaide.edu.au/wine-econ/databases

Boshoff, W. H. and J. Fourie (2010), 'The Significance of the Cape Trade Route to Economic Activity in the Cape Colony: A Medium-Term Business Cycle Analysis', *European Review of Economic History* 14(3): 469–503.

Elbourne, E. (2003), '"The Fact So Often Disputed by the Black Man": Khoekhoe Citizenship at the Cape in the Early to Mid-nineteenth Century', *Citizenship Studies* 7(4): 379–400.

Esterhuizen, D. (2006), *An Evaluation of the Competitiveness of the South African Agribusiness Sector*, Unpublished PhD, University of Pretoria, Pretoria.

Estreicher, S. K. (2013), 'A Brief History of Wine in South Africa', *European Review* 22(3): 504–37.

Fourie, J. and J.-L. Van Zanden (2013), 'GDP in the Dutch Cape Colony: The National Accounts of a Slave-Based Society', *South African Journal of Economics* 81(4): 467–90.

Fourie, J. and D. von Fintel (2014), 'Settler Skills and Colonial Development: The Huguenot Wine-Makers in Eighteenth-Century Dutch South Africa', *Economic History Review* 7(4): 932–63.

Galbraith, J. K. (1952), *American Capitalism: The Theory of Countervailing Power*, New Brunswick: Transaction Publishers (1993 Edition).

Guelke, L. and R. Shell (1989), 'An Early Colonial Landed Gentry: Land and Wealth in the Cape Colony, 1681-1732', *Journal of Historical Geography* 9(3): 265–86.

Havemann, R. and J. Fourie (2015), 'The Cape of Perfect Storms: Colonial Africa's First Financial Crash, 1788–1793', ERSA Working Paper, Economic Research Southern Africa, Cape Town.

Heino, T.-E. (1992), *Politics on Paper: Finland's South Africa Policy, 1945–1991*, Uppsala: Nordiska Afrikainstitutet.

Howard, P., T. Bogart, A. Grabowski, R. Mino, N. Molen and S. Schultze (2012), 'Concentration in the US Wine Industry', Michigan State University. Available at www.msu.edu/~howardp/wine.html (accessed 1 November 2013).

Kirsten, J., L. Edwards and N. Vink (2009), 'South Africa', pp. 147–74 in *Distortions to Agricultural Incentives in Africa*, edited by K. Anderson and W. A. Masters, Washington, DC: World Bank.

Liebenberg, F. (2012), *South African Agricultural Production, Productivity and Research Performance in the 20th Century*, Unpublished PhD thesis, University of Pretoria, Pretoria.

Marais, J. S. (1968), *The Cape Coloured People, 1652-1937*, London: Witwatersrand University Press.

Marcus, T. (1989), *Modernizing Super-exploitation: Restructuring South African Agriculture*, London: Zed Books.

Officer, L. H. and S. H. Williamson (2017), 'Computing "Real Value" over Time with a Conversion Between U.K. Pounds and U.S. Dollars, 1774 to Present', available at www.measuringworth.com/exchange (accessed 11 February 2017).

Parliament of Australia (2016), *Report of the Senate Standing Committees on Rural and Regional Affairs and Transport on the Australian Grape and Wine Industry*, Canberra: Parliament of Australia, 12 February. Available at www.aph.gov.au/Parliamentary_Business/Committees/Senate/Rural_and_Regional_Affairs_and_Transport/Australian_wine_industry/Report (accessed 19 October 2016).

Platter, J. (1982), *John Platter's Book of South African Wines*, Revised 1982 edition, Franschhoek: Johan Platter.

Rayner, M. I. (1986), *Wine and Slaves: The Failure of an Export Economy and the Ending of Slavery in the Cape Colony, South Africa, 1806–1834*, Unpublished PhD dissertation, Duke University, Durham, NC.

Ross, R. (1983), *Cape of Torments: Slavery and Resistance in South Africa*, London: Routledge.

SAWIS (various years), *SA Wine Industry Statistics*, available at www.sawis.co.za (accessed 7 May 2015).

Scully, P. (1990), *The Bouquet of Freedom: Social and Economic Relations in the Stellenbosch District, South Africa, c1870–1900*, Cape Town: Centre for African Studies, University of Cape Town.

Van Duin, P. and R. Ross (1987), *The Economy of the Cape Colony in the 18th Century*, Leiden: Centre for the Study of European Expansion.

Van Rooyen, J., D. Esterhuizen and L. Stroebel (2011), 'Analyzing the Competitive Performance of the South African Wine Industry', *International Food and Agribusiness Management Review* 14(4): 179–200.

Van Zyl, D. J. (1975), *Kaapse Wyn en Brandewyn*, 1795–1860, Cape Town: HAUM.

(1993), *KWV 75 Jare* [KWV 75 Years], Bound typescript, Africana Library, University of Stellenbosch, Stellebosch.

Vink, N., G. Williams and J. Kirsten (2004), 'South Africa', pp. 227–51 in *The World's Wine Markets: Globalization at Work*, edited by K. Anderson, London: Edward Elgar.

Williams, G. (2013), 'Who, Where, and When Were the Cape Gentry?' *Economic History of Developing Regions* 28(2): 83–111.

(2016), 'Slaves, Workers and Wine: the "Dop System" in the History of the Cape Wine Industry, 1658–1894', *Journal of Southern African Studies* 42(5): 893–909.

15

United States

Julian M. Alston, James T. Lapsley, Olena Sambucci
and Daniel A. Sumner

The wine industry in the United States is new by Old World standards but old by New World standards. In the colonial and postcolonial period up through the middle of the nineteenth century, it was a tiny industry with imports accounting for almost all of the still meager recorded US consumption of wine. US production developed gradually in the latter half of the nineteenth century, and began to develop significantly with the expansion of the California industry early in the twentieth century (Carosso 1951; Hutchinson 1969). The industry had to be recreated after the Prohibition era, 1920–1932, and parts of it were reborn again half a century ago with an aggressive move toward higher quality. The industry has continued to evolve in the decades since, in a context of increasingly interconnected and coevolving global and domestic markets, and changes in technology, climate, and government policy.

This chapter reviews and documents the history of the development of the wine and winegrape industry in the United States, with detailed statistical support where possible. We pay particular attention to the role of US government policy and broader changes in the US economy as they shaped the economic development of wine production and consumption, all in the context of the global market for wine, and technological and market innovation at home and abroad.

Despite some wine and winegrape production in most states in the United States, California accounts for the lion's share of the value and volume of production, and more detailed information on some aspects of the industry is available only for California. Consequently, much of the discussion of grape and wine production in this chapter focuses on California. The discussion of demand and policy issues, of course, takes a broader national perspective.

THE COLONIAL ERA, 1492 TO 1775

In 1524, when the Florentine explorer Giovanni da Verrazzano first navigated the eastern seaboard of what was eventually to become the United States, he would have seen a profusion of grapevines. Like many of the settlers to follow, he probably imagined great possibilities for a New World wine industry on those shores. It was not to be. Over the next three centuries and more, the history of winegrowing first on the east coast and subsequently across America is one of many optimistic beginnings followed by dashed hopes and despair.

Relative to other alcoholic beverages, wine consumption in the American colonies prior to the American Revolution was constrained by the inability of colonists to produce palatable wine for their own consumption or export, and British adherence to a mercantilist policy based on a belief that trade deficits weakened the empire. High import tariffs on European wines in Britain and its colonies (Nye 2007) raised the price of wine relative to other forms of alcohol that could be produced in the American colonies, such as apple cider, beer, and rum. With this incentive and other encouragement from colonial governments, colonists repeatedly experimented with wine production using native or imported grape varieties, but the result was always disappointing.

Grape varieties native to the eastern coast of North America produce small berries with little juice, high acidity, low sugar, and odd flavors when compared with European *Vitis vinifera* (Pinney 1989), while the European varieties found the environment challenging. Many settlers attempted to cultivate European varieties for wine many times up and down the Atlantic seaboard, and these attempts always ended badly. North America was not just home to many species of grapes, it was also home to numerous grape diseases such as powdery mildew; downy mildew; black rot; Pierce's disease; and the insect pest, phylloxera. Native grapes had coevolved with these diseases and pests and had acquired some degree of resistance to them. *V. vinifera* grapes were highly susceptible, and failed under disease and pest pressure combined with harsh winters and humid summers. Eventually, when an industry grew and first flourished in the United States in the late 1800s, it was on the opposite coast in places Verrazzano never saw, but which had much more in common with his native Tuscany.

Colonists mostly drank other alcoholic beverages, but turned to imports for wine consumption. Among imported wines, Madeira dominated, chiefly as a result of the 1663 Staple Act, which specifically exempted Madeira wines exported to British colonies from the duties on European wines (Hancock 2009). In his chapter on "Drawbacks" in *The Wealth of Nations*, first published in 1776, Adam Smith wrote, "Madeira wine, not being a European commodity, could be imported directly into America and the West Indies, countries which, in all their non-enumerated commodities, enjoyed a free trade to the island of Madeira" (Smith 1937, p. 469). Volumes of Madeira imported to British North America varied from year to year, ranging from 0.24 ML in 1715 to a high of 1.05 ML in 1730 (Hancock 2009).

Even without duties, Madeira was expensive relative to other alcoholic beverages. A 1770 bill of fare from a Virginia tavern gives a sense of costs. Madeira was offered at 4 shillings per quart (16 shillings per gallon), while a gallon of domestically produced rum (with much higher alcoholic content) sold for 10 shillings (Beechert 1949). Domestically produced small (low-alcohol) beer and, in the northern colonies, hard cider, were widely available. The aforementioned Virginia tavern sold quarts of cider at 5 pence, less than one-tenth of the cost of Madeira. One historian estimates that in 1770, on the eve of the Revolution, 57 litres of cider were consumed per capita, but only 0.38 litres of wine (Rorabaugh 1979). Less concentrated and twice as expensive as rum, and more alcoholic but an order of magnitude more expensive than cider, wine in the North American colonies was a luxury, generally reserved for the wealthy.

POSTCOLONIAL IMPORT DEPENDENCE: 1776 TO 1860

From Independence to the Civil War, wine remained an expensive imported beverage, eclipsed in volume by distilled spirits and beer. The vast majority of whiskey and beer was domestically produced and untaxed, while over 95 percent of wine, at least until the 1850s, was imported and subject to tariffs (United States Department of Treasury 1892). The federal government encouraged grape production (as other agriculture) through land grants and by disseminating information on grape varieties and winemaking through the aegis of the US Patent Office. Eventually, several natural hybrids between native species and *vinifera*, most notably Catawba and Isabella, were discovered and became the basis for a small wine industry clustered around the city of Cincinnati, Ohio, before the Civil War (Pinney 1989).

Fragmentary data document the small but growing share of domestic wine in US wine consumption, which in turn was a small part of all alcohol consumed. In 1840, 0.47 ML of domestic wine production accounted for just 2.6 percent of US wine consumption. A decade later, although having increased by 75 percent, US wine production of 0.84 ML still represented only 3.5 percent of US wine consumption. During the decade of the 1850s, American wine production grew eightfold to 6.8 ML, largely because of increased wine production in Cincinnati and the addition of California to the Union. But even in 1860, American wine production accounted for less than 17 percent of the 41.6 ML of wine consumed. In that year, Americans consumed 382 ML of beer and 341 ML of spirits, with wine accounting for 5 percent by volume of all alcohol consumed (United States Department of the Treasury 1892).[1]

Wine remained at a significant price disadvantage relative to distilled spirits, both because of the cost of transportation of wine from Europe and because domestic distilled spirits were untaxed. As America expanded westward, new lands were opened for grain and corn production. In a time of poor and expensive transportation, one economic method for bringing the crop to market was to distill it. Increased and geographically dispersed distillation of corn led to low prices for domestic whiskey until the Civil War. An 1865 study by the Department of the Treasury of retail New York prices by month from 1825 to 1863 shows that the price of domestic whiskey averaged about $0.07 per litre for the period. In contrast, the cheapest red wine averaged about $0.16 per litre for the period (United States Department of the Treasury 1863). Moreover, higher-alcohol specialty wines, such as Madeira or Port, were two to five times more expensive than the cheapest red wine.

Despite the price difference between whiskey and wine, a small market for wine in the United States continued, and volumes of imported wine increased from 4 ML in 1789 to 34 ML in 1860, roughly in proportion to population growth. Wine as an imported luxury good suffered in times of war and general economic distress. For example, during the Napoleonic Wars (1803–1815) and the war between the United States and Britain (1812–1815), US wine imports declined from an average of 18.5 ML per year in 1804–1808 to an average of 4.5 ML per year during the war years of 1809–1815. Similarly, the six years of economic distress that followed the "Panic of 1837" saw imported wine decline from 24 ML in 1836 to 3.8 ML in 1843. Wine imports also declined when tariffs rose. From 1830 until 1845, the wine tariff averaged about 22 percent of import value for the period. The tariff revision of 1846 switched from specific to *ad valorem* duties and

[1] With a few exceptions made for historical reference, quantities and values originally reported in other units have been converted to standard metric units throughout this chapter, to be consistent with the other data assembled for this book and reported in Anderson and Pinilla (2017).

reduced import duties for most goods. However, the new 40 percent *ad valorem* rate actually increased the tariff on red wine imports.

Commercial wine production in America became feasible with the discovery of "native" varieties such as the Alexander, which John Adlum used to produce a potable red wine in the early 1800s. Cincinnati became a center of this development. In 1850, Cincinnati had approximately 300 vineyards with 226 bearing hectares that produced 0.45 ML of wine. By 1853, over 320 ha were bearing, producing 1.2 ML of wine (Daacke 1967). But even during this boom, growers were plagued by disease, especially black rot and powdery mildew that often reduced harvests to uneconomic levels. With no understanding of the diseases or how to control them, growers suffered major crop losses every year.

Diseases, the Civil War, and the expansion of the city into vineyard land ended the Cincinnati wine boom (Pinney 1989). However, Cincinnati winemakers had shown that grapes could be grown commercially from native hybrids and that the resulting wine could be produced and sold. As the superintendent of the Census, Joseph Kennedy, put it in his 1864 conclusion to his discussion of grapes and wine in the Agricultural Census, "Vineyard culture in the United States may now be considered as fairly established. Wine is made in thirty of the thirty-four States of the Union, of different qualities of course, and with varied success. As to its future production in quantity, I should name, first, California ..." (Kennedy 1864, p. clx). We now turn to that state and how it came to dominate US wine production.

DEVELOPMENT OF AN INDUSTRY: 1861 TO 1919

The middle of the nineteenth century saw the beginnings of three great forces for the development and upheaval of the US wine industry. First, on the heels of the 1849 gold rush, the new state of California emerged as a major supplier of inexpensive wine based on *V. vinifera*. California grew from little production and almost no shipments east in 1860 to a position of national preeminence in wine production by 1880, a status it has held since. Second, this development of an industry built on *vinifera* varieties set the scene for a devastating collapse of production in the 1880s caused by phylloxera, a pest that had been helpful to the California industry in the previous decade by devastating French production. Third, precursors could be seen in state laws of what would become national Prohibition of commercial distribution of all alcohol a few decades later (Pinney 1989).

When California became a state in 1850, American wine producers could, for the first time, compete directly with Europeans. California did compete. By the mid-1880s, California supplied the majority of wine consumed in the United States and by 1900 California producers accounted for 96 percent of domestic wine production and 85 percent of all wine consumed (West 1935; Pinney 1989; Olmstead and Rhode 2009). During that period, California's production expanded sixfold, from 14 ML in 1870 to 89 ML in 1900 (Figure 15.1).

Vitis vinifera was introduced into southern California at San Diego by Franciscan missionaries (Brady 1984). The variety they imported, "Mission," is identical to Listan Prieto (Tapia et al. 2007) and produces a lightly colored, low-acid red wine. It was hardly ideal for the warm climate of southern California, but it grew and produced fruit that could be converted into crude wine. Before the population expansion with the gold rush and prior to statehood, winemaking was limited to home production for use on the local estancias or to be distilled into brandy. The European population was small, perhaps 14,000 people prior to statehood, and California's physical isolation made wine shipments to the East difficult. Still, southern California was the location of California's first *vinifera* plantings and wine made from its Mission vineyards dominated state production until the late 1860s (Pinney 1989). Wine production moved north with the influx of European prospectors, and grapes were planted in the Sierra foothills near the mines, and in the coastal counties surrounding San Francisco. New vineyards were still generally Mission, but even in the early 1850s, nurserymen were importing alternative varieties such as Cabernet Sauvignon and Sauvignon Blanc (Sullivan 1998).

California wine production increased from 0.22 ML in 1850 to 14.4 ML in 1870, with the bulk of the production consumed within California until the late 1860s. Olmstead and Rhode (1989) write that only about one-tenth of California's production in the mid-1860s was exported from California. The late 1860s and early 1870s saw a boom in grape prices and new vineyards (Carosso 1951). California wine producers shipped wine east, primarily to New York, where it competed with European cask wines. California wines received a mixed reception from Eastern wine dealers. More alcoholic and produced primarily from Mission grapes, California wines differed in taste and style from European wines, but California wines were untaxed and were price-competitive with European cask wine.

The first California wine boom ended abruptly with the Panic of 1873 and a five-year depression. Demand for wine fell and import volumes dropped by half to under 19 ML for the years 1876–1879. Californian production stagnated and averaged about 15 ML during the mid-1870s (West 1935), and Californian wine producers lobbied Congress to

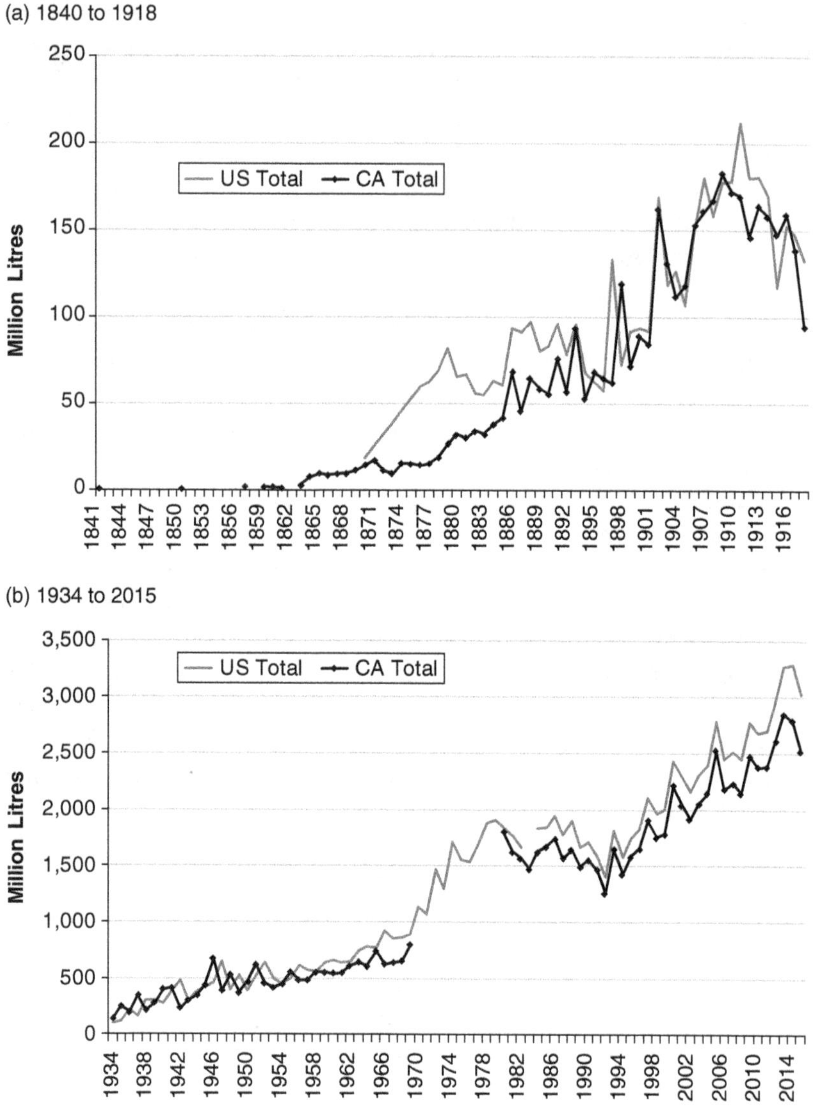

Figure 15.1 Wine production, California and the United States, 1840 to 2015 (ML).
Sources: Created by the authors using data from United States Department of the Treasury, Alcohol and Tobacco, Tax and Trade Bureau (TTB) (1984; 1984–2015) and Peninou (2000).

increase the tariff on foreign wines. In February of 1875, when tariffs were being reduced for most goods, Congress raised the tariff on imported cask wines from \$0.07 per litre to \$0.11 per litre (note that tariffs specified in dollars per gallon have been converted to metric equivalents here). In

March of 1883, the tariff was raised yet again, to $0.13 per litre, where it remained until 1894, when it was reduced to $0.08 per litre as a part of a broad reduction of US tariffs.

With the higher tariffs, landed prices in New York of the cheapest French red wine, the so-called Cargo Claret, went from under $0.16 per litre in the early 1870s to $0.24 per litre a decade later, increasing to $0.28 per litre in 1884, following the 1883 tariff increase. During the same period, California wine prices to New York averaged about $0.15 per litre. California cask wine shipments to New York expanded tenfold from the depression low of 1875 to 1898. This expansion accompanied rapidly declining rail freight rates. Increased shipments and lower transport costs allowed nominal wholesale prices in New York to decline from approximately $0.16 per litre in 1875–1876 to $0.10 per litre in 1897 and 1898.

The end of the depression in 1878 and new import tariffs sparked a winegrape planting boom in the first half of the 1880s. County assessor reports show that California's vineyard area of table, raisin and winegrapes almost quadrupled from 18,000 ha in 1880 to 69,000 ha in 1890 (Figure 15.2). Rhode (1995) details the broad shift in California from cereal crops to fruits and vegetables and documents that land in perennial crops expanded from 4 percent of planted area in 1879 to 20 percent in 1889. Expansion of grape area and winemaking were driven in part by the broader set of economic forces affecting other perennial crops, namely population growth, income growth, low interest rates, and lower rail transport costs (Rhode 1995).

Growers planted most of the new California vineyard area with imported *vinifera* varieties (California Board of State Viticultural Commissioners 1888). And, although winegrapes were planted throughout California, the major planting areas were located in the coastal counties of Sonoma, Napa, Alameda, and Santa Clara, around San Francisco Bay. Figure 15.1 shows production of wine in California in this period growing from 62 ML in 1877 to 97 ML in 1888.

Lower grape prices coupled with the expansion of phylloxera in California's northern coastal counties created a dilemma for grape growers in the 1880s. Phylloxera had been found in Sonoma vineyards as early as 1875, and was one reason for the establishment of the Board of Viticultural Commissioners. Prior to 1880, only a few vineyards had seemed to be affected and phylloxera was viewed as not being as aggressive in California as it was in France. However, with the planting boom of the early 1880s, phylloxera spread rapidly throughout the North Coast counties, infesting newly established vineyards. The individual grower with a phylloxera-infested vineyard had to decide whether to invest more money in replanting vineyards using resistant rootstocks at a time of low prices, or to simply

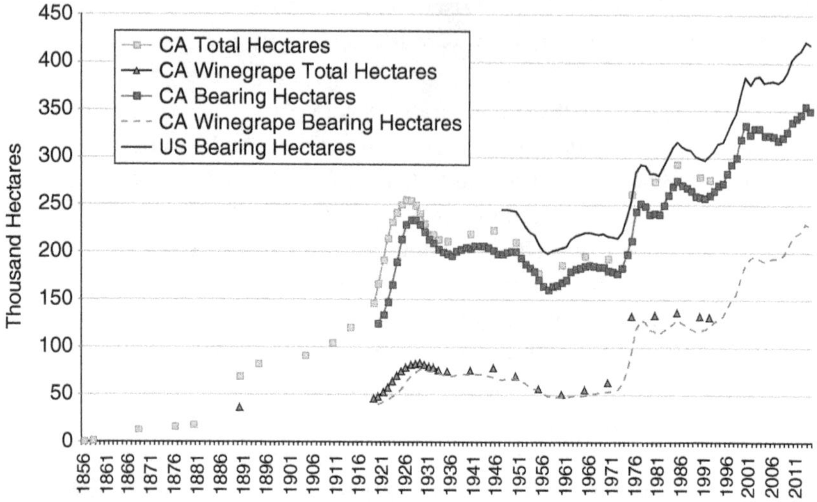

Figure 15.2 Grapevine area,[a] California and the United States, 1856 to 2014 ('000 ha).
[a] Area of "winegrapes" refers to area of specialized winegrape varieties and not the area of grapes used for winemaking. It does not include multipurpose grapes, of which significant volumes were used for winemaking at various times.
Sources: Created by the authors using data (in acres) from various sources, which were converted to hectares. Total grapevine area and total winegrape area for California are from Peninou (2000); bearing grapevine area and bearing winegrape area are from United States Department of Agriculture, National Agricultural Statistics Service (2015b); US bearing area of grapevines is from Johnson (1987) and United States Department of Agriculture, National Agricultural Statistics Service (2016).

let phylloxera take its toll, harvest a declining volume of grapes, and replant to some other crop when the vineyard finally died. Reports indicate that total California winegrape vineyard area fell from 61,000 ha, as estimated by Haraszthy (1888) in 1887, to 35,000 ha in 1891, as reported by the State Board of Viticultural Commissioners from its survey. Pinney (1989) reports that writers of the period estimated that in Napa County alone, 4,000 ha were lost to phylloxera in the four years 1889–1892.

Wine continued to be a small part of alcohol consumption in the United States with beer rising relative to spirits in the latter half of the nineteenth century (Figure 15.3). The total volume of wine consumed in the United States almost doubled from 59 ML in 1870 to 106 ML in 1900 which, while still tiny both per capita and compared with total alcohol consumption, did increase demand for grape production.

About this time, a change in alcohol tax law provided a further impetus for expansion of demand for winegrapes. Grape brandy used in the process of making domestic fortified wines was taxed at $0.90 per proof gallon, or

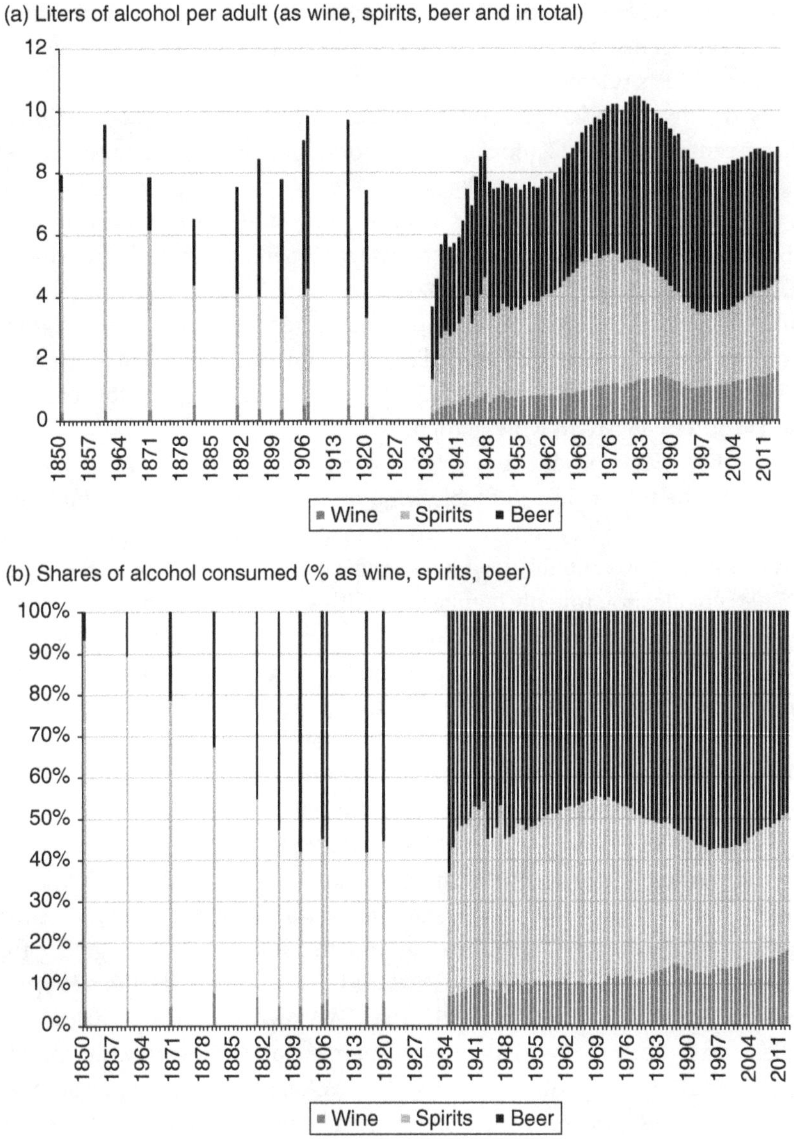

Figure 15.3 Consumption of alcohol per adult and shares consumed as wine, spirits and beer United States, 1850 to 2012 (LAL and %).
Note: Based on population aged above fourteen years prior to 1970 and above thirteen years thereafter.
Source: Created by the authors using data from LaVallee, Kim, and Yi (2014).

$0.24 per proof litre, the same rate as other distillates. In October 1890, a new US law allowed producers to fortify wines up to 24 percent alcohol, with grape brandy tax-free. The "Sweet Wine" bill, as it was called, disallowed fortification with spirits other than brandy, a common practice of eastern fortified wine producers. California wineries gained a competitive advantage against fortified wine producers in other states while reducing their own costs (Carosso 1951).

By the first decade of the twentieth century, fortified wines constituted 40 percent or more of California's total production. Fortified wines required significant volumes of grape brandy, which in turn required substantial amounts of wine. A litre of brandy of 50 percent alcohol concentration (a "proof" litre) required four litres of 12 to 13 percent alcohol dry wine as distillation stock. If a 12 percent base wine were fortified to the legal limit of 24 percent, each litre of base wine required just under half a litre of grape brandy, which would have been distilled from two litres of dry wine. In 1895, California produced about 23 ML of fortified wine, but this production required 46 ML of wine in total.

Fortified wine production helped stabilize California wine prices by reducing the total volume of table wine to be sold, while at the same time introducing a form of untaxed alcohol that competed with spirits. If 100 proof whiskey was cut in half with water in a glass, the drink contained about 25 percent alcohol, roughly comparable with a glass of fortified wine, which was innocuously referred to as "sweet" wine. Ironically, when faced with the coming of Prohibition, the California industry argued that table wine was a beverage of moderation and conveniently ignored the fact that over 40 percent of its production from 1900 to Prohibition was untaxed fortified wine.

Wholesale prices of wine shipped to New York recovered slightly following the passage of the Sweet Wine bill, but fell to $0.10 per litre following the onset of the Depression of 1893. In August of 1894, in an attempt to control falling wine prices, seven of the largest San Francisco wine merchants formed the California Wine Association (CWA). The CWA soon began buying other wineries throughout the state, ultimately giving the CWA a large share of both production and distribution of California wine. Pinney (1989) reports that by 1902, the CWA owned over fifty major wineries and produced approximately 70 percent of California wine. By the first decade of the twentieth century, the CWA had substantial power to set grape and wine prices for the California industry. Peninou and Unzelman (2000) estimate that the CWA accounted for 85 percent of California wine production and sales by 1919.

The period from 1900 to Prohibition was a generally prosperous time for the wine industry in California. US wine consumption more than doubled from just under 106 ML in 1900 to over 227 ML in 1911, before declining with the approach of Prohibition. The growth in wine consumption was a result of both an increase in per capita consumption of wine and population growth, primarily from the arrival of over six million immigrants from the wine-drinking regions of southern Europe, between 1901 and 1915 (Amerine and Singleton 1977).

In the early 1900s, the CWA increased production of fortified wines and moved its fortified wine production to California's San Joaquin Valley, where irrigated vineyards could produce yields two to three times larger than those of the nonirrigated coastal vineyards. From 1904 to 1914, California vineyard acreage increased by over 30,000 ha to a total of 121,000 ha (Figure 15.2). More than 60 percent of the increase in vineyard area, 25,000 ha, was located in the San Joaquin Valley (Peninou 2000). It was during this period that the San Joaquin Valley emerged as the largest regional producer of California wine by volume. In the cooler, coastal areas, grape acreage gradually declined, as landowners replanted vineyards to deciduous fruits such as apples in Sonoma County, prunes and walnuts in Napa County, and mixed stone fruits in Santa Clara County.

The national movement toward Prohibition was troubling to the CWA and to California grape growers, who banded together in 1908 to form the California Grape Growers' Association "to preach the gospel of the grape and the temperate use of wine" (Peninou and Unzelman 2000, pp. 117–18). That year, the CWA created a new division, Calwa Products Company, to manufacture and market unfermented grape juice, a venture that did not succeed. Following the national elections of 1916, which showed that national sentiment favored some form of prohibition of alcoholic beverages, the CWA announced to stockholders that it would liquidate its businesses and began selling vineyards and wineries.

THE PROHIBITION ERA AND ITS AFTERMATH: 1920 TO 1965

Prohibition became law on 17 January 1920, one year after ratification of the Eighteenth Amendment to the US Constitution, and was repealed fourteen years later after ratification of the Twenty-First Amendment. Importantly, Prohibition criminalized home brewing of beer and distillation for personal use but exempted home winemaking, giving rise to the expansion of vineyards as a source of grapes for home winemaking. During the Prohibition era, total California grape production increased from 1.2 million metric tons in 1920 to a peak of 2.2 million metric tons in 1927. When Prohibition was repealed, it was on the condition that individual states could define their own laws governing the production and sale of alcohol, an outcome that would leave as its legacy a byzantine and bizarre set of policies that continue to hamstring wine producers and marketers today.

The impact of national Prohibition on the US wine industry lasted much longer than did Prohibition itself. Upon Repeal, the wine industry faced many learning and other challenges to begin to revive wine production. In addition to losing fourteen years of operation, the industry had lost almost a generation of skills and experience, and much grape and wine research had been foregone. Prohibition cost the US wine industry perhaps a further decade during which the industry produced poor wines while new enterprises relearned the science and practice of wine production and marketing.

Two longer-term impacts of Prohibition affected the California wine industry for many more decades. One was the large area of poor-quality grape vines that were planted during Prohibition to satisfy the still legal home wine production, which resulted in low grape prices and poor-quality wine for decades to come. The second problem was the political compromise required to end Prohibition, which resulted in a constitutional amendment granting each state the right to control alcohol sales and distribution, even to the point of continuing Prohibition in its territory. Under the Twenty-First Amendment, rather than one uniform marketplace, the United States became in effect fifty-one different markets (fifty states plus the District of Columbia) – much like different countries – in terms of the regulation of alcohol production and sales.

Congress dealt with the actual complexities of funding and enforcing the Eighteenth Amendment through the National Prohibition Act that implemented Prohibition, generally referred to as the Volstead Act. The Volstead Act allowed the legal production of fruit juices from apples and grapes at home, so long as the "juice" was not removed from the premises (Pinney 2005). Grape growers, who had sold their grapes for $38 per metric ton in 1919, found that brokers offered prices as high as $100 per metric ton in the early 1920s. These brokers then shipped the grapes to buyers in the immigrant communities in the Midwest and East. The high prices in 1920 and 1921 led to a planting boom throughout California, with a (predictable) crash when the newly planted vineyards reached their full productive potential. California bearing winegrape acreage nearly doubled, from 39,900 ha in 1920 to 76,100 ha in 1930, while average winegrape prices dropped from $82 to $22 per metric ton at the depth of the Depression. During the decade of the 1920s, California's total bearing grape acreage, much of it composed of raisin and table grape varieties, expanded from 124,500 to 221,300 ha (United States Department of Agriculture, National Agricultural Statistics Service 2014c). Figure 15.4 shows bearing grape area by type from 1920 to 2010.

The near doubling of grape acreage during Prohibition drove down grape prices and caused low profitability for grape growers from 1924 onward.

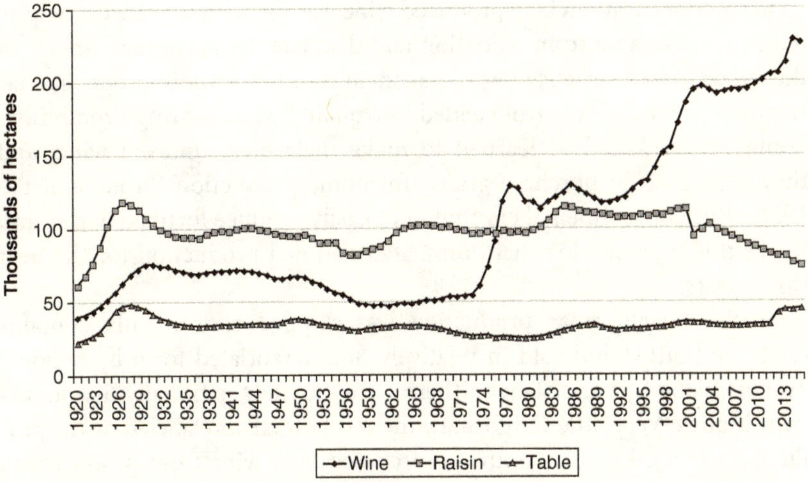

Figure 15.4 Bearing grape area by type of grape, California, 1920 to 2015 ('000 ha).
Sources: Created by the authors using data from United States Department of Agriculture, National Agricultural Statistics Service (2014b, 2014c, 2015b).

The planting boom also degraded the composition of California's vineyards. Prohibition-era grape brokers demanded grapes with thick skins that could be loaded in 23 kilogram wooden boxes and survive three to four days of transit in unrefrigerated rail cars to Eastern markets. Buyers, who often made "second" wines by adding water, sugar, and acid to grape pomace and refermenting the mixture, desired highly pigmented and tannic grapes that could stand dilution. Thick-skinned grapes high in color, such as Alicante Bouschet or Grand Noir, and grapes high in tannin, such as Petite Sirah, fetched the highest prices and dominated much of the new plantings. Growers also planted high-yielding varieties, such as Carignan, which could be sold for a profit at low prices. The result was that the plantings of Cabernet Sauvignon, Riesling, or Pinot Noir were forgotten, and wineries upon Repeal of Prohibition were faced with grapes ill-suited for high-quality table wine (Lapsley 1996).

Many obstacles faced the US wine industry upon Repeal of Prohibition. By 1936, 1,357 wineries were in operation (United States Department of the Treasury, Alcohol and Tobacco, Tax and Trade Bureau (TTB) 1984). But Repeal occurred at the depth of the Depression, when perhaps 25 percent of the labor force were unemployed and prices for all consumer goods were low. And, of course, substitutes such as beer and spirits were now also legal. Much, perhaps most, of the commercial wine production in the period following Repeal and up to World War II was of low quality. Approximately

75 percent of commercially produced wine was fortified sweet wine, whose major flavors came from oxidation and distillate. Inappropriate grapes in the hands of inexperienced winemakers in facilities without proper sanitation or temperature control yielded low-quality wine. During Prohibition, home winemakers had learned to make their own, untaxed wine, and they continued to purchase grapes for home production throughout the 1930s. But home winemakers could not easily produce fortified wines, and it was this type of wine that dominated national production for the next thirty years.

Much of California's production was shipped east in bulk containers to be bottled and sold in relatively undifferentiated form by regional bottlers using "generic" labels. There were very few nationally distributed wine brands. Very little California wine was bottled and labeled by the producing winery. Regional bottlers purchased bulk wine from producers in California and shipped it in rail tank cars to facilities where they bottled and distributed the wine in their region under their own labels. Such undifferentiated wine during a major depression led to low prices for grapes and wine, pushing wineries and vineyard owners toward bankruptcy.

As with many commodities, supply tightened and grape prices rose as World War II unfolded (Figure 15.5). In 1942, the United States government purchased at high prices all raisins for use in soldiers' meals. Raisin varieties had constituted over 50 percent of the grape harvest in the 1930s and early 1940s, and the elimination of raisins from the pool of grapes crushed for wine raised prices for winegrapes. The average price for winegrapes rose from $24 per metric ton in 1941 to $34 in 1942, and then jumped to $122 in 1944 before declining to $68 per metric ton in 1945 (United States Department of Agriculture, National Agricultural Statistics Service 2014c).

Federal policy also reduced the availability of wine substitutes. Barley was rationed, so brewers could not expand production to meet full demand, and distiller facilities were being used to produce industrial alcohol. Only wine produced from grapes with seeds was not needed for the war effort (Lapsley 1996). These forces and full employment increased the demand for wine and winegrapes at a time when wartime price controls limited the prices of the product – especially of bulk wine – but not the price of the raw materials (winegrapes) used to make them. One way around the resulting cost-price squeeze was for wine producers to bottle themselves wine that would previously have been sold in bulk, reinforcing the other influences encouraging producers to bottle wine in California.

In 1942, the four major US distillers – Schenley, National Distillers, Hiram Walker, and Seagram and Sons – all purchased significant California

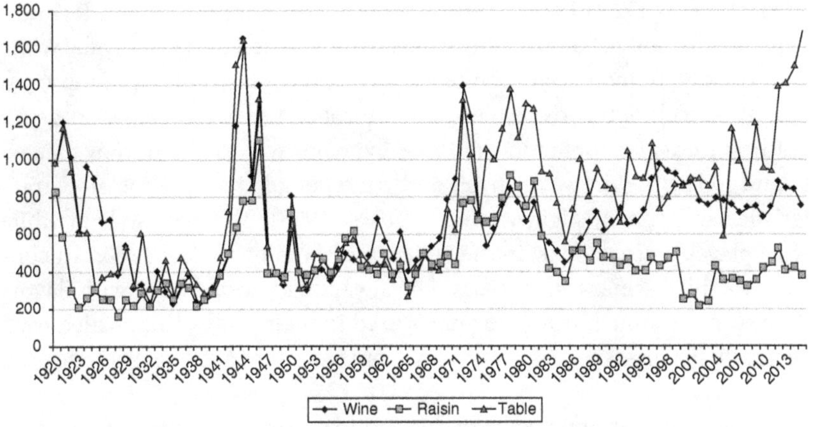

Figure 15.5 Real price of grapes, by type, California, 1920 to 2015 (2015 US$ per metric ton).
Sources: Created by the authors using data from United States Department of Agriculture, National Agricultural Statistics Service (2014a, 2014b, 2014c, 2015a, 2015b). Nominal values were deflated by the Consumer Price Index for all goods taken from United States Department of Labor/Bureau of Labor Statistics (2015).

wineries. For the first time since the CWA, California wine gained national distribution. Government requisition of tank cars for transport of war materials threatened the out-of-state bottlers' ability to move bulk wine from California to supply their regional brands. In response, they also purchased vineyards and wineries in California. By 1944, 40 percent of California's wineries had new owners, with almost all of them bottling their product in California (Lapsley 1996; Pinney 2005). Within five years, California had transitioned from producing a commodity that was bottled and branded outside California and not associated with the producer, to producing and bottling wine under the producer's brand name. This laid the foundation for a drawn-out (continuing) process of product differentiation and quality improvement in the wine industry.

At the end of the war, wine producers in California faced a difficult transition when other forms of alcohol were no longer constrained by government decrees. As whiskey once again became more readily available, wine sales slumped, from 530 ML in 1946 to 370 ML the following year. Some firms went bankrupt, the distillers exited the wine industry, and the remaining wine businesses took years to work their way back to profitability.

The dominant wine production trends from 1950 to 1965 were a gradual but general adoption of new technology, slow growth in per capita consumption, and industry consolidation as the number of wineries fell from

428 in 1950 to 232 in 1965 (Wine Institute 2016). Adoption of new technologies significantly changed table wine characteristics, particularly for white wines. Cold fermentation combined with pure yeast cultures, improved sanitation techniques, oxygen exclusion through use of inert gas, and sterile bottling were all adopted in the 1950s by major wineries, and they created a new style of white wine: fresh and fruity, emphasizing varietal characteristics, and, often, slightly sweet (Lapsley 1996). This new style of white wine played a crucial part in the table wine boom of the late 1960s. In contrast, fortified wines remained as they always had been: sweet, with flavors derived not so much from the grapes used in their production, which were generally flavorless to begin with, but from oxidation and the distillate used for fortification.

The most important change in this period was the beginning of a gradual shift from fortified wines to table wines that increasingly carried a varietal designation. Between 1950 and 1965, dessert wine consumption volume increased by only 12 percent, from 393 to 507 ML, which did not keep pace with population growth. During the same period, table wine consumption doubled, from 136 to 280 ML (Wine Institute 2016). Fortified wines still dominated and few observers predicted the dramatic growth, which has been called the "Table Wine Revolution," that was to follow.

FIFTY YEARS OF GROWTH AND CHANGE: 1965 TO 2015

The next fifty years saw a transformation of the industry to become much larger, more sophisticated, and more diversified. Improvements in quality reflected shifts in the location of production and an increased emphasis on premium specialized winegrape varieties used to produce generally higher-quality wine, a more differentiated product, and a continuation of the trend away from fortified wines; but they also reflected innovations in vineyards, in winemaking, and in marketing an evolving product range to an evolving consumer market. A picture of the large changes can be painted with reference to California's evolving pattern of winegrape production, for which we have comparatively detailed data.

The Table Wine Revolution

As Figure 15.4 shows, the total bearing acreage of grapes in California increased during the Prohibition era (1920–34) and then declined to a low around 1960. The bearing area of winegrapes began to creep up from around 50,000 ha throughout the 1960s and into the early

1970s. Winegrape acreage surged remarkably in the mid-1970s to almost 130,000 ha in 1978 – a 2.5-fold increase in about four years! California's total bearing acreage of all grapes also jumped – from about 190,000 ha through the 1960s and early 1970s to 250,000 ha in 1977. The area of specialized winegrapes grew, partly at the expense of raisin and table grape varieties, which also were used for making wine to some extent.

US production of wine increased from about 640 ML in 1960 to 1,060 ML in 1970 and 1,780 ML in 1980, an almost threefold increase – and greater than the increase in area of winegrapes. This was accomplished in part by small improvements in yields of winegrapes and in part by reductions in the share of the total used for distillation to fortify sweet wines (noting again that each litre of fortified wines uses two litres of table wine), which were declining in relative importance. Some of the increased demand for wine was satisfied by using multipurpose grapes for wine production when the raisin industry was in a downturn.

The boom in wine production and consumption was driven by demand from the "baby boom" cohort reaching adulthood. Consumption of wine per adult (aged twenty-one and older) increased from about 5.7 litres in 1960 to 8.1 litres in 1970, and then jumped to 12 litres by 1980, while the total adult population grew from 109 million in 1960 to 151 million in 1980.[2] White and blush wine consumption expanded, much of it made with lower-quality varietals (Alston, Anderson, and Sambucci 2015).

The improved quality of California wines was confirmed on May 24, 1976 when, at the so-called Judgment of Paris, French judges in blind tastings of top-quality red and white wines from France and California rated California wines best in each category (Stag's Leap Wine Cellars 1973 Napa Valley S.L.V. Cabernet Sauvignon and Chateau Montelena 1973 Napa Valley/Calistoga Chardonnay). This event made it undeniable that California was producing world-class wines (Taber 2005).

The No-Growth Decade of the 1980s

Winegrape acreage and wine production peaked in the late 1970s and did not begin growing again until the 1990s, perhaps because of overplanting in the 1970s during a general commodities boom. During the 1980s,

[2] This definition of adults excludes some people who were drinking wine, legally or illegally in some years. The legal drinking age has varied among states and over time. After repeal, the legal drinking age in some states was eighteen years. In the 1970s, the US government pressed states to adopt a legal drinking age of twenty-one years.

longer-term forces in the wine industry were still at work, masked by an end to rapid inflation, a recession, high interest rates, and changes in the global wine market. In the winegrape-growing industry, as in the broader farm economy, the boom of the 1970s was reversed by the slump of the 1980s, as prices collapsed in 1982, precipitating financial difficulties for many who had bet on the bubble. The investment in coastal vineyards (Monterey County in particular) in the 1970s led to a source of higher-quality but lower-priced grapes and varietal wines in the 1980s, when demand slowed.

In the 1980s, the bearing area of winegrapes remained flat, accompanied by a decline in production of wine. This decline in average yield reflected a continuing trend away from lower-quality and higher-yielding varieties such as Thompson Seedless and Colombard toward higher-quality specialized winegrape varieties such as Chardonnay and Cabernet Sauvignon grown in premium production regions. This trend has continued as demand has shifted from white to red and toward more premium varieties and premium regions (Alston et al. 2015).

While most consumers would have been more familiar with the semi-generic labels, such as California Burgundy, producers in the premium coastal valleys in California began to produce significant volumes of wines with varietal labels and geographic indications. Even so, of the total of 954 ML of wine shipped from California in 1985, only 15 percent sold for $4 or more per litre (in 1985 dollars). The total value of shipments in 1985 was $1.5 billion (Fredrikson 2016), or $3.3 billion when inflated to 2015 dollars.

Resurgence: 1990 to 2000

The 1990s saw a second expansion in bearing area of grapes in California, again driven by a surge in area of specialized winegrapes (Figure 15.4). Bearing area of winegrapes increased from 120,000 ha in 1992 to 190,000 ha in 2001 – a 60 percent increase. Red wine consumption tripled. A contributing factor to the shift to red wine was a public perception of health advantages, which some ascribe to a report by Morely Safer on "The French Paradox" aired on the news magazine show *60 Minutes* on November 17, 1991. This report noted the low incidence of cardiovascular disease among the French and suggested this might be linked to their high per capita consumption of red wine. Americans were open to such a convenient theory: sales of red wine in the United States increased by 39 percent in 1992 (Frank and Taylor 2016).

Some of this increased demand was met with imports. Imports had been important as a share of wine consumption from Colonial times and

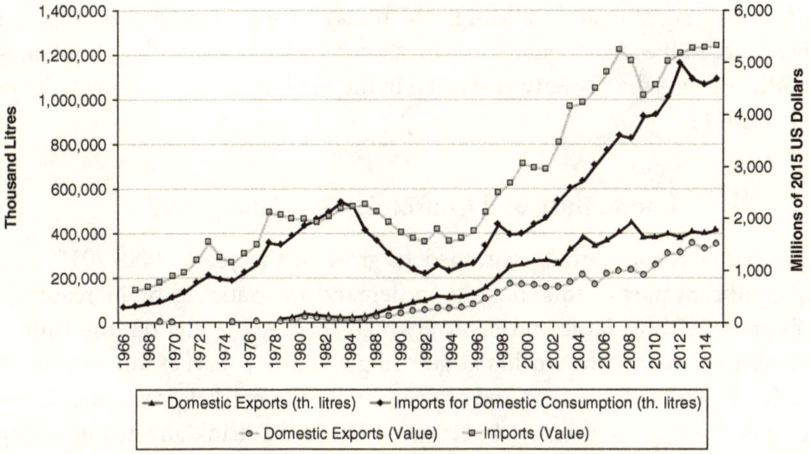

Figure 15.6 Real value and volume of wine imports and exports, United States, 1966 to 2015 (KL and 2015 US$ million).
Note: Nominal monetary values were deflated by the Consumer Price Index for all goods taken from United States Department of Labor/Bureau of Labor Statistics (2015).
Sources: Created by the authors using data from United States International Trade Commission (2016), Wine Institute (2016) and United States Department of Agriculture, Foreign Agricultural Service (2016).

through to the 1870s, when California's wine industry took off, after which imports (along with other areas of production in the United States) were comparatively unimportant until Prohibition, when they ceased altogether. Figure 15.6 shows import growth from the later 1960s. Imports grew rapidly through the early 1980s, from less than 348 ML in 1979 to almost 539 ML in 1984. This increase was followed by an even steeper decline in the late 1980s. More recently, imports grew from a little over 218 ML in 1991 to almost 534 ML in 2015, and now represent almost one-third of total consumption. US wine exports increased, too, from almost nothing in 1980 to a little over 414 ML in 2015. A contributing factor to the rise in imports and exports, especially for lower-priced bulk wine, has been the US duty drawback policy (Gabrielyan and Sumner 2016).

The 1990s was a time of prosperity in the industry, marred by a resurgence of phylloxera in the premium North Coast region, which had been planted widely to a susceptible rootstock (AxR1). As a consequence, much of the Napa Valley had to be replanted (Lapsley and Sumner 2014). When these vines were replanted, it was predominantly to premium wine varieties and mostly to reds – switching from Chardonnay to Cabernet Sauvignon in the premium regions. Grape growers also incorporated and used new ideas for irrigation and trellising, which may have contributed to observed increases in the sugar content of winegrapes, which increased by about one-tenth over less than twenty years, and in the alcohol content of wine (Alston et al. 2011).

Boom, Bust, and Consolidation: 2000 to 2015

Per capita consumption continued to grow in the years 2000–2015, and a significant part of this increase in demand was satisfied by increases in imports. With its large and relatively high-income population, the United States has become the world's largest single-country market for wine, both in total volume consumed and expenditures. The market growth occurred despite the facts that only 64 percent of US adults drink any alcohol; only 40 percent drink any wine; and, among the wine drinkers, only 13 percent drink wine as often as several times a week. So, after five centuries, the region that is now the United States remains a region of primarily beer drinkers and teetotalers (Franson 2015).

It is convenient to characterize current wine production and consumption in the United States as encompassing several segments. At one price extreme is a significant high-end wine industry, located mainly on the Central and North Coast of California, but also in Oregon and Washington State, producing highly differentiated wines identified by producer, variety, district, and other geographic indicators on the label. At the other price extreme is more affordable wine produced in the southern San Joaquin Valley, where grape yields are on the order of ten times higher and prices of winegrapes are commensurately very much lower. Much of the value and volume of wine produced and consumed comes from the segment between these extremes with grapes from the northern San Joaquin Valley, the central coast, or less favored regions of the North Coast and other areas of California and other states.

In 2015, California shipped 1,926 ML of wine with a total value of $11.8 billion. (Fredrikson 2016). Of this total, more than one-third of the value was in the category $18.67 per litre and higher and another more than one-third of the value was in the category $9.33 to $18.67 per litre. The total volume shipped from California more than doubled over the thirty-year period since 1985, and the real value increased by a factor of 3.6, reflecting the increase in average price and quality.

Since the turn of the twenty-first century, bearing area of winegrapes in California has grown considerably, increasing by 32 percent from 171,000 ha in 1999 to 226,000 ha in 2015, but unevenly, with virtually no growth between 2002 and 2013 when prices were generally down (Figure 15.4). More broadly, since the early 1990s there has been considerable growth in production of winegrapes and wine in the United States as a whole. Increases in national production reflect increases in area and production of winegrapes and wine in other states – especially Washington and Oregon – and to some extent reductions in use for distillation with the phasing out of fortified wines. The mix of varieties grown has changed, with an increased emphasis on premium red wine varieties.

Varietal Mix: Becoming Less Different

In 2014, the United States produced 4.5 million metric tons of grapes crushed for wine, with a farm value of $3.5 billion, which accounted for a little over 11 percent of the world's wine volume. Of the US total winegrape area of 247,000 ha in 2014, four states accounted for over 94 percent: California (CA), 81.2 percent; Washington (WA), 7.8 percent; Oregon (OR), 4.5 percent; and New York (NY), 1.4 percent. Of these, only New York is not on the West Coast and grows little *vinifera*. In 1990, California alone accounted for 88.1 percent of the total and New York accounted for 8.9 percent. In the twenty-five years since, while the total US winegrape area increased by about 50 percent, the winegrape area shrunk slightly in New York while growing rapidly in Oregon (fourfold) and Washington State (sixfold).

California contains several distinct wine production regions that differ in terms of their terrain, climate, soil types, mixture of varieties grown, and quality of grapes and wines produced. Alston et al. (2015) describe the US winegrape industry in terms of eight primary US wine-producing regions comprising five distinct regions of California plus the other significant wine-producing states (i.e., Washington, Oregon, and New York). They point to several distinct patterns. First, California dominates the total area, volume, and value of national wine production. Second, the regional shares differ significantly among measures of area, volume, and value of production. In particular, California's Southern Central Valley has a low total value of production relative to its much larger share of volume, while the North Coast region (mainly Napa and Sonoma Counties) has a high total value of production, although a much smaller share of volume. These patterns reflect the relatively high yield per hectare (and correspondingly low price per ton) of grapes from the Southern Central Valley and the conversely low yield and high price per ton in the North Coast. In 2015, in Napa County the average yield was 6.3 metric tons per hectare, and the average crush price was $4,780 per metric ton, almost ten times the average crush price in the Southern Central Valley, where the average yield was over 29 metric tons per hectare (United States Department of Agriculture, National Agricultural Statistics Service 2015a, b).

Alston et al. (2015) document and discuss the evolving patterns. Since 1980, the varietal mix has shifted toward red and away from white varieties and, for both red and white varieties, toward premium varieties – particularly Chardonnay, Cabernet Sauvignon, Merlot, Pinot Noir, and Syrah. In the most recent decade or so, in particular, the picture is dominated by increased plantings of popular premium red and white varieties, at the expense of less-favored varieties. The mix of varieties grown has become more like the mix grown in France and in the world as a whole, although with some variation in this aspect among US regions.

The distribution of grapes is linked to the distribution of wines shipped by price as reported by Fredrikson (2016). California shipped a total of 1,926 ML (including foreign bulk wines bottled in California, which accounted for 201 ML), of which 80 percent sold for more than $4 per litre and 48 percent sold for more than $9.33 per litre. Reflecting this general drift toward a greater share of higher-priced wine, the average unit value of the wines shipped from California in 2015 was $6.12 per litre, compared with $3.46 per litre (in 2015 dollar terms) in 1985.

Contemporary Perspectives

Annual US wine consumption per adult (twenty-one years and older) grew from 5.3 litres in 1950 to 8.1 litres in 1970, and peaked at 13.3 litres in 1985 before falling to remain less than 11 litres per adult over the decade of the 1990s (Figure 15.7). Over the two decades since its low of 9.3 litres per adult in 1993, however, wine consumption per adult has trended up monotonically to 14.8 litres in 2014. A significant part of this increase in demand has been satisfied by increases in imports (Figure 15.7). The United States has become the world's largest market for wine.

The United States is a physically and economically large and diverse geopolitical entity. Space matters. Most US wine is produced within 100 miles of the Pacific Ocean, mainly in California. Most Americans live far from there. This fact has been important in the long history of US wine production and consumption as well as now. In the United States, wine is consumed at higher rates per capita in the states where it is produced. Among the fifty states and the District of Columbia, people are ethnically and culturally diverse in ways that matter for wine. Partly for those reasons, policies affecting the marketing and consumption of wine vary systematically

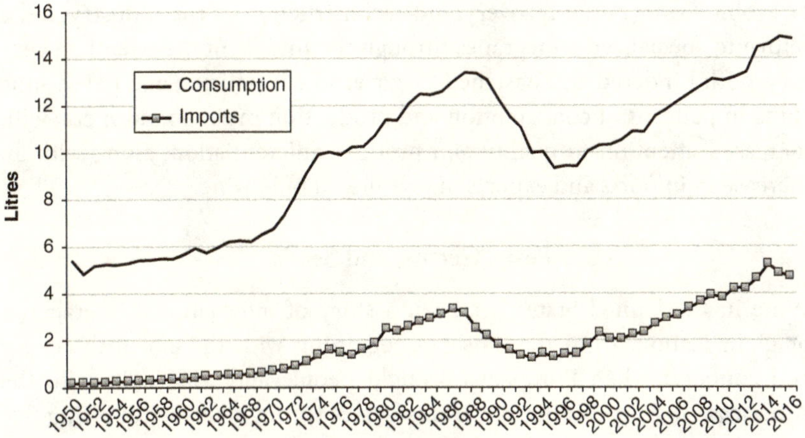

Figure 15.7 Wine consumption per adult, United States, 1950 to 2014 (litres).
Note: Adult population includes persons twenty-one years old or older.
Sources: Created by the authors using data from various sources. Total consumption data are from Wine Institute (2016), imports are from Wines & Vines (various years), population twenty-one and over is from Haines (2006) and the United States Census Bureau (2016).

among the states as a legacy of Prohibition and its Repeal. Much of the country – especially in the Midwest – was settled by northern Europeans, who are traditionally drinkers of beer or spirits, rather than wine; southern Europeans, who are more likely to be wine drinkers, are more predominant in the Northeast. Other significant ethnic groups – Hispanics, blacks, and Asians – are also more likely to be beer drinkers than wine drinkers. In some states, a large proportion of the population belong to religions that preach temperance or complete abstinence from consuming alcohol. Reflecting these various influences, total consumption of alcohol per adult and the share of wine versus beer and spirits have evolved over time and vary considerably among the states.

SYNTHESIS: EMERGING THEMES

This history of wine in America can be viewed in terms of several significant ongoing or recurrent influences. The main events in the history can be seen in terms of (a) the ongoing struggles against the biological barriers to development of an industry, eventually overcome about 150 years ago; (b) the subsequent destruction of the industry by government fiat, with consequences that lasted well beyond Repeal after fourteen years of Prohibition; (c) the recovery and reconstruction of the industry and a return to specialized winegrapes through the middle of the twentieth century, both hindered and hastened by government policies; and (d) seismic shifts in patterns of consumption and production in the modern era, with increased attention to quality and product differentiation, along with an increase in imports and exports of low-priced bulk wine.

Pests, Germs, and Seeds

Wine in the United States has been a story of international interaction, or globalization, from the outset – beginning with the era of discovery and conquest when Europeans brought people and wine culture to the Americas, and continuing in various guises throughout the following five centuries of international trade in wine and intercontinental movement of wine-consuming culture; winegrowing technology and ideas; planting materials; and, less happily, pests and diseases. The Columbian Exchange proved to be a double-edged sword, with pests and diseases, and partial solutions to them, traveling in both directions across the Atlantic.

Attempts to develop wine production during America's first four centuries of European settlement were heavily constrained and ultimately frustrated by the roles of native pests and diseases that ravaged the *V. vinifera* grapes introduced from Europe. While native American varieties flourished, they were generally not well suited to winemaking, but the *vinifera* vines were highly susceptible to native pests (in particular phylloxera) and diseases. Most of the continent was also not well suited climatically for growing high-quality winegrapes. The discovery of gold in California encouraged the development of an industry, which flourished briefly in the late nineteenth century before it, too, succumbed to phylloxera.

The phylloxera story highlights the role of international interconnectedness. The high international prices for wine resulting from the "Great French Wine Blight" in the late 1800s were helpful to the foundation of the California wine industry (notwithstanding the barriers France placed on foreign imports – see Chevet et al. 2018 and Meloni and Swinnen 2018). America also benefited from a demand for resistant rootstocks for the replanting of Europe. Other American pests and diseases exported to other countries – such as powdery mildew and downy mildew – were also no doubt helpful to the American wine industry by the same market mechanism. Americans also benefited from European investments in science and discovery to develop means to mitigate (though not eliminate) the damage wrought by these pests and diseases.

Roles of Government

Governments have actively influenced the production, marketing, and consumption of wine in America. From the time of first settlement, the British and various colonial governments actively encouraged the establishment of wine production along with other agricultural production and processing. This pattern continues today as federal and state governments fund the development of cold-tolerant or pest- or disease-resistant varieties (e.g., for Pierce's disease, among others) of grapes that will produce high-quality wines in states as diverse as Minnesota, Idaho, Virginia, and Texas, as well as in the current major producing regions.

Trade policy has been an important element. In the early years, wine in America was an imported luxury reserved mainly for the rich. Various trade policies were applied at different times to serve the interests of different groups such as British producers of Madeira early on and California producers in the late 1800s. Wine, like other alcohol, is a source of excise tax revenue for the government and was sometimes treated advantageously relative to other forms of alcohol. Nowadays, trade taxes are relatively minor impediments compared with other taxes and regulations on wine, many of which are part of the legacy of Prohibition. Recently, a wrinkle in federal import tariff and tax policy has encouraged both imports and exports of low-priced wine (Gabrielyan and Sumner 2016).

At the turn of the twentieth century, the California wine industry, spurred into production by the Gold Rush of the 1850s, was predominant in America. By 1900, California was producing quality table wine based on specialized winegrape varieties, encouraged to do so by the high (per unit) tariffs of the late 1800s combined with the high import prices caused by phylloxera in Europe. Twenty years later, in 1920 this industry was all but eliminated by government fiat. Among its many pernicious effects, Prohibition encouraged the replacement of premium winegrape varieties with other, higher-yielding varieties that would produce cheaper grapes better suited to shipping long distances for home winemaking, which remained legal.

After Repeal, in 1934, the industry continued to use these inferior varieties to produce undifferentiated bulk wine that was shipped east for bottling, and fortified wine. In the 1940s, wartime interventions in the markets for raisins, wine, and other alcohol caused a significant increase in demand for wine and winegrapes and led to a restructuring of the industry. By the end of the war, the foundations had been laid for the (re-)development of an industry producing wine bottled and branded in California. But it would take many years to complete that transition.

A more enduring legacy of Prohibition was its effects on the marketing channels for wine. As part of the price of Repeal, individual states set their state-specific policies and regulations on alcohol production and marketing, and these policies represent significant barriers to entry and impose considerable transaction costs on producers and consumers (Lapsley et al. 2016). The policies continue to evolve.

Quality Improvement

As noted, government policy has significantly influenced the incentives of American producers to produce quality table wine. American wine production differs from wine production in most other producing countries in two ways. First, America is home to many native varieties of grapes (and their pests and diseases), and part of the industry in America – away from the main producers on the Pacific Coast – is based on these varieties or hybrids, such as Norton or Concord. Second, significant quantities of grapes are grown in America for uses other than winemaking, to produce raisins, table grapes, or grape juice concentrate for use in food manufacturing and for juice, jams, and jellies. Some grapes, termed "multipurpose" for this reason, may be used for more than one purpose. This is true for Concord in particular but also for some *vinifera* varieties, in particular Thompson Seedless, which were at times significant as table grapes, winegrapes, and drying grapes.

The existence of multipurpose grapes makes deciphering some details of the history harder, because information on production of grapes does not always include details of utilization. And utilization could change quickly from one year to the next, especially in earlier times when hand labor was more important and vineyards were less dedicated to particular end-uses than nowadays. An increased emphasis on quality in wine (and in the table grape and raisin industries) along with changes in the technology of vineyards, such as dried-on-the-vine technology in raisins, have significantly reduced that flexibility over time, and much less wine is produced with multipurpose grapes now.

Over the most-recent fifty years, the American wine industry has evolved to produce a different product, in several segments. In particular, sweet fortified wine has essentially been replaced by dry table wine; and generic labels have been supplanted with varietal labels, in many instances accompanied by geographic indications and other quality signals. The transition has required a significant replanting of vineyards; a shifting emphasis to premium wine varieties; and, in the past twenty years, a greater emphasis on red wine varieties. Some of this was facilitated by an outbreak of phylloxera in the Napa and Sonoma valleys in the 1980s, which caused vineyards to be replanted much sooner than they would have been otherwise. The mix of varieties grown in California has become more like the mix grown in France or in the world as a whole (Alston et al. 2015). In addition to changes in the vineyards, there have been many changes in the winery to adopt innovations based in science, much of which has served to improve the quality of the final product.

The scale of the industry also has changed. The United States has become the world's largest market for wine. The US population is large and ethnically and culturally diverse. It is predominantly not a wine-drinking nation, though it is trending in that direction. Annual US wine consumption per adult almost trebled between 1950 and 2014, from 5.4 to 14.8 litres, and a significant part of this increase in demand was satisfied by increases in imports. The wine consumed in 1950 was primarily fortified wine or semisweet white wine, a far cry from the types of wine produced and consumed today. These changes in the mixture and extent of US wine production and consumption reflect a response to evolving consumer demand, as Americans have become more affluent and more interested in wine.

REFERENCES

Alston, J. M., K. Anderson and O. Sambucci (2015), 'Drifting Towards Bordeaux? The Evolving Varietal Emphasis of U.S. Wine Regions', *Journal of Wine Economics* 10(3): 349–78.

Alston, J. M., K. B. Fuller, J. T. Lapsley and G. Soleas (2011), 'Too Much of a Good Thing? Causes and Consequences of Increases in Sugar Content of California Wine Grapes', *Journal of Wine Economics* 6(2): 135–59.

Amerine, M. A. and S. V. L. Singleton (1977), *Wine: An Introduction*, Second Edition, Berkeley: University of California Press.

Anderson, K. and V. Pinilla (with the assistance of A. J. Holmes) (2017), *Annual Database of Global Wine Markets, 1835 to 2016*, freely available in Excel at the University of Adelaide's Wine Economics Research Centre, www.adelaide.edu.au/wine-econ/databases

Beechert, E. D. (1949), *The Wine Trade of the Thirteen Colonies*, Unpublished Master's Thesis, Graduate Division, University of California, Berkeley.

Brady, A. (1984), 'Alta California's First Vintage', in *Sotherby Book of California Wine*, edited by D. Muscadine, M. A. Amerine and B. Thompson, Berkeley: University of California Press.

California Board of State Viticultural Commissioners (1888), *Annual Report 1887*, Sacramento: State Printers.

(1891), *Directory of the Grape Growers, Wine Makers and Distillers of California and the Principal Grape Growers and Wine Makers of the Eastern States*, Sacramento: Johnson.

Carosso, V. P. (1951), *The California Wine Industry: A Study of the Formative Years*, Berkeley: University of California Press.

Chevet, J.-M., E. Fernandez, E. Giraud-Héraud and V. Pinilla (2018), 'France', ch. 3 in *Wine Globalization: A New Comparative History*, edited by K. Anderson and V. Pinilla, Cambridge and New York: Cambridge University Press.

Daacke, J. F. (1967), 'Grape-Growing and Wine-Making in Cincinnati, 1800–1870', *Cincinnati Historical Society Bulletin* 25(3): 196–212, July.

Frank, M. and R. Taylor (2016), 'Journalist Morley Safer, Who Highlighted Red Wine's Potential Health Benefits, Dies at 84', *Wine Spectator*, May 19. Available at www.winespectator.com/webfeature/show/id/Morley-Safer-Dies-at-84 (accessed May 22, 2016).

Franson, P. (2015), 'Sobering Data: Wine Market Council Looks at a Growing Taste for Other Beverages', *Napa Valley Register*, February 12. napavalleyregister.com/wine/sobering-data-wine-market-council-looks-at-a-growing-taste/article_80bfac3d-c0ec-5714-9f30-6885bbc6f208.html (accessed June 2, 2016).

Fredrikson, J. (2016), 'California Table Wine Shipments and Revenues by Price Segment 1980 to 2015', prepared by Gomberg, Fredrikson and Associates, personal communication.

Gabrielyan, G. T. and D. A. Sumner (2016), 'Wine Trade and the Economics of Import Duty and Excise Tax Drawbacks', American Association of Wine Economists 10th Annual Conference, Bordeaux, June 22.

Haines, M. R. (2006), 'Area and Population', pp. 26–39, Volume 1 – Population, *Historical Statistics of the United States – Millennial Edition*, edited by S. Carter, S. Gartner, M. Haines, A. L. Olmstead, R. Sutch, and G. Wright, Cambridge and New York: Cambridge University Press. Available at hsus.cambridge.org/HSUSWeb/toc/showTable.do?id=Aa1-109

Hancock, D. (2009), *Oceans of Wine: Madeira and the Emergence of American Trade and Taste*, New Haven, CT: Yale University Press.

Haraszthy, A. (1888), 'Report of the President', in *Annual Report for 1887*, edited by California Board of State Viticultural Commissioners, Sacramento: State Printers.

Hutchinson, R. B. (1969), *California Wine Industry*, Unpublished dissertation in Economics, University of California, Los Angeles.

Johnson, D. C. (1987), *Fruit and Nuts Bearing Acreage, 1947–83*, Statistical Bulletin No. 761, United States Department of Agriculture, National Agricultural Statistics Service, Washington, DC, December.

Kennedy, J. C. G. (1864), *Agriculture of the United States in 1860: Compiled from the Original Returns of the Eighth Census*, Washington, DC: United States Government Printing Office.

Lapsley, J. T. (1996), *Bottled Poetry: Napa Winemaking from Prohibition to the Modern Era*, Berkeley: University of California Press.

Lapsley, J. T., J. M. Alston and O. Sambucci (2016), 'Structural Features of the U.S. Wine Industry', mimeo, April, for inclusion in a a forthcoming book on *The Wine Industry Worldwide*, to be edited by A. Alonso Ugaglia et al., Davis: University of California.

Lapsley, J. T. and D. A. Sumner (2014), '"We Are Both Hosts": Napa, UC Davis, and the Search for Quality', in ch. 7 (pp. 180–212) *Public Universities and Regional Growth: Insights from the University of California*, edited by M. Kenney and D. C. Mowery, Stanford, CA: Stanford University Press.

LaVallee, R. A., T. Kim and H.-Y. Yi (2014), 'Apparent Per Capita Alcohol Consumption: National, State, and Regional Trends, 1977–2012', National Institutes of Health, National Institute on Alcohol Abuse and Alcoholism, Surveillance Report No. 98. Available at pubs.niaaa.nih.gov/publications/surveillance98/tab1_12.htm (accessed October 3, 2016).

Meloni, G. and J. Swinnen (2018), 'North Africa', ch. 16 in *Wine Globalization: A New Comparative History*, edited by K. Anderson and V. Pinilla, Cambridge and New York: Cambridge University Press.

Nye, J. V. C. (2007), *Wine War and Taxes: The Political Economy of the Anglo-French Trade, 1869–1900*, Princeton, NJ: Princeton University Press.

Olmstead, A. L. and P. W. Rhode (1989), 'Regional Perspectives on U.S. Agricultural Development Since 1880', Working Paper, Agricultural History Center, University of California, Davis.

(2009), 'Quantitative Indices on the Early Growth of the California Wine Industry', Robert Mondavi Institute Center for Wine Economics Working Paper 0901, May. vinecon.ucdavis.edu/publications/cwe0901.pdf (accessed May 3, 2016).

Peninou, E. (2000), *A Statistical History of Wine Grape Acreage in California, 1856–1992*, Unpublished Manuscript. Available at www.waywardtendrils.com/downloadvithistories.html (accessed May 25, 2016).

Peninou, E. and G. Unzelman (2000), *The California Wine Association and Its Member Wineries*, Santa Rosa, CA: Nomis Press.

Pinney, T. (1989), *A History of Wine in America: From Beginning to Prohibition*, Volume 1, Berkeley: University of California Press.

(2005), *A History of Wine in America: From Prohibition to the Present*, Volume 2, Berkeley: University of California Press.

Rhode, P. W. (1995), 'Learning, Capital Accumulation and the Transformation of California Agriculture', *Journal of Economic History* 55(4): 773–800, December.

Rorabaugh, W. J. (1979), *The Alcoholic Republic: An American Tradition*, New York: Oxford University Press.

Smith, A. (1937), *An Inquiry into the Nature and Causes of the Wealth of Nations*, 1776, New York: Random House.

Sullivan, C. (1998), *A Companion to California Wine*, Berkeley: University of California Press.

Taber, G. M. (2005), *Judgment of Paris*, New York: Scribner.

Tapia. A. M., et al. (2007), 'Determining the Spanish Origin of Representative Ancient American Grapevine Varieties', *American Journal of Enology and Viticulture* 58: 242–51.

United States Census Bureau (2016), *Population Estimates, Historical Data*, available at www.census.gov/popest/data/historical/index.html (accessed 15 October 2016).

United States Department of Agriculture, Foreign Agricultural Service (2016), *Export Sales Reporting Database*, available at www.fas.usda.gov/data (accessed October 15, 2016).

United States Department of Agriculture, National Agricultural Statistics Service (2014a), *California Grape Crush Reports for Years 2011–2014*, available at www.nass.usda.gov/Statistics_by_State/California/Publications/Grape_Crush/Reports/ (accessed October 15, 2016).

United States Department of Agriculture, National Agricultural Statistics Service (2014b), *California Grape Acreage Reports for Years 2011–2014*, available at www.nass.usda.gov/Statistics_by_State/California/Publications/Grape_Acreage/Reports/ (accessed October 15, 2016).

United States Department of Agriculture, National Agricultural Statistics Service (2014c), *California Grapes, 1920–2010*, revised, February.

United States Department of Agriculture, National Agricultural Statistics Service (2015a), *California Grape Crush Report*, available at www.nass.usda.gov/Statistics_by_State/California/Publications/Grape_Crush/Final/2015/201503gcbtb00.pdf (accessed October 15, 2016).

(2016), *Noncitrus Fruits and Nuts Summary* for years 1989–2016, available at http://usda.mannlib.cornell.edu/MannUsda/viewDocumentInfo.do?documentID=1113 (accessed October 15, 2016).

United States Department of Agriculture, National Agricultural Statistics Service (2015b), *California Grape Acreage Report*, available at www.nass.usda.gov/Statistics_by_State/California/Publications/Grape_Acreage/2016/201604gabtb10.pdf (accessed October 15, 2016).

United States Department of Labor/Bureau of Labor Statistics (2015), *Consumer Price Index Detailed Report*, December, available at www.bls.gov/cpi/cpid1512.pdf (accessed October 15, 2016).

United States Department of the Treasury (1863), Statement No. 27: 'The Range of Prices of Staple Articles in the New York Markets at the Beginning of Each Month by Year, 1825–1863.' *Report of the Secretary of the Treasury of the State of the Finances, for the Year Ending June 30, 1863*, Washington, DC: United States Government Printing Office.

United States Department of the Treasury (1892), *Quarterly Reports of the Chief of the Bureau of Statistic Showing the Imports and Exports of the United States for the Four Quarters of the Year Ending June 30, 1892*, Washington, DC: United States Government Printing Office.

United States Department of the Treasury, Alcohol and Tobacco, Tax and Trade Bureau (TTB) (1984), *Alcohol, Tobacco and Firearms Summary Statistics*, www.ttb.gov/statistics/production-figures1934-1982.pdf (accessed May 31, 2016).

United States Department of the Treasury, Alcohol and Tobacco, Tax and Trade Bureau (TTB) (1984–2015), *Alcohol, Tobacco and Firearms Summary Statistics, Yearly Wine Statistics*, available at www.ttb.gov/wine/wine-stats.shtml (accessed May 31, 2016).

United States International Trade Commission (2016), *Trade Database*, available at dataweb.usitc.gov/ (accessed October 15, 2016).

West, C. (circa 1935), *Economic Aspects of the Wine Industry in the United States*, Undated manuscript written for the Farm Credit Administration.

Wine Institute (1930–1960), *Annual Wine Industry Statistical Surveys*, Annual Issues, San Francisco, CA: Wine Institute.

Wine Institute (2016), *Statistics*, available at www.wineinstitute.org/resources/statistics (accessed June 2, 2016).

Wines & Vines (various years), available at www.winesandvines.com/ (accessed September 1, 2017).

16

Algeria, Morocco, and Tunisia

Giulia Meloni and Johan Swinnen

It is difficult to imagine today, but in 1960 Algeria was the largest exporter of wine in the world. It exported twice as much wine as the other three major exporters (France, Italy, and Spain) combined, and was the fourth-largest producer of wine in the world. This started with the collapse of phylloxera-ridden vineyards in France, which triggered massive vineyard investments in Algeria in the 1880s. In the fifty-year period between 1880 and 1930, Algerian wine production and exports grew dramatically, turning the industry from nonexistent into the world's largest exporter of wine (Meloni and Swinnen 2014).

The success of Algeria in wine trade also triggered vineyard investments in Tunisia and Morocco, two countries colonized by France later on.[1] While the impact was similar (a strong growth in vineyards and wine production, mostly for exports to France), both countries never reached the importance of the Algerian wine industry, in terms of area planted, production, or trade. The total vine area reached a maximum of 50,000 ha in Tunisia in the 1930s and 78,000 ha in Morocco in the 1960s. Algeria, by contrast, had almost 400,000 ha in the 1930s and produced more than two billion litres of wine, or ten times the maximum produced by Tunisia and Morocco. Moreover, the share of wine in the value of Algeria's merchandise exports reached almost 50 percent in the early twentieth century and again around 1960, but was always below 15 percent for Tunisia and Morocco (Table 16.1). Their

[1] Algeria was a French colony from 1830 to 1962; Tunisia was a French protectorate from 1881 to 1956; and Morocco was a French protectorate from 1912 to 1956. Algeria was a "true" colony that was considered part of France and divided into several departments, with total assimilation of culture, politics, regulations, and trade (direct control of the French administration). The protectorates of Tunisia and Morocco retained some sovereignty in that the indigenous rulers continued to govern at home under the influence of the French administration, which had indirect control through a French resident-general and a military presence (Wesseling 2004).

Table 16.1 *Wine's share of the value of all merchandise exports, France and North Africa, 1875 to 2013 (%)*

	France	Algeria	Tunisia	Morocco
1875–84	6.8	0.4	0.0	0.0
1885–94	6.9	29.5	4.0	0.0
1895–1904	5.7	48.9	3.7	0.4
1905–14	3.6	35.6	1.6	0.3
1915–24	2.4	31.5	5.6	0.1
1925–34	2.1	47.5	10.9	0.2
1935–44	6.3	24.7	14.8	0.6
1945–54	3.5	26.8	3.1	0.7
1955–64	1.8	45.5	13.8	4.0
1965–74	1.6	10.6	4.0	2.0
1975–84	1.5	1.1	0.7	0.4
1985–94	1.9	0.2	0.2	0.1
1995–2004	1.6	0.0	0.1	0.1
2005–13	1.6	0.0	0.0	0.1

Source: Anderson and Pinilla (2017).

production and exports were lower because both countries were colonized later and had less preferential access than Algeria to the French market.

This chapter documents the rise and the fall of wine production and exports in Algeria, Morocco, and Tunisia. The first section analyzes the growth of the wine industry in North Africa from the 1880s until the 1930s. Next, we analyze the brief halt in expansion in the 1930s and explain how it was caused by a combination of factors, including trade agreements and regulations. The third section examines the revival of the North African wine industry following the end of World War II (1939–1945), while the final section explains the collapse of the North African wine industry during the 1960s and 1970s.

THE GROWTH OF THE WINE INDUSTRY IN NORTH AFRICA, 1880 TO 1930

When France annexed Algeria in 1830, Tunisia in 1881, and Morocco in 1912, no one would have predicted that Algeria would become the world's largest exporter of wine and North Africa would account for almost two-thirds of the world's wine exports.[2] In these three countries, viticulture was

2 See Meloni and Swinnen (2014) for a detailed analysis of the rise and the fall of the Algerian wine industry.

not encouraged, as the Koran forbade alcohol consumption.[3] It was only after France began to colonize the region that North African viticulture developed. The French colonists and settlers consumed wine because it was considered the safest drink and it was part of their Mediterranean diet (Birebent 2007; Leroy-Beaulieu 1887). Developments differed in the three countries, though, so we consider them in turn.

Algeria

Three main factors contributed to the Algerian wine industry's development in the late nineteenth century (Meloni and Swinnen 2014). The first was the devastation by phylloxera of French vineyards. This induced an inflow of skills in winegrowing through the migration of many bankrupt French growers, which also increased the demand for Algerian wine.[4]

The second factor was technological progress in wine production. Prior to the 1860s, winegrowers did not have the technology to produce drinkable wines in a hot climate. However, by the late nineteenth century, advances in refrigeration allowed new systems to be introduced to control temperatures in the tank during wine fermentation.

The third contributor was the fact that trade with France was free: Algerian wine imports were not taxed.[5] That stimulated the growth of Algerian exports when high import tariffs were reimposed by France on wine imports from Spain and Italy in the late nineteenth century (Isnard 1947; Isnard and Labadie 1959; Blanc 1967; Meloni and Swinnen 2016). That increase in import tariffs reduced total wine imports and caused a substitution of wine imports from Spain and Italy[6] to imports from Algeria. Figure 16.1 shows that France's imports fell from more than 1 billion litres

3 Although wild grapevines have been present in North Africa since the first millennium BCE, when the Phoenicians and Carthaginians traded huge quantities of wine (and transplanted grapevines), the cultivation of vines never took off. Later, the Romans used this region as a granary for their empire (Lequément 1980; McGovern 2009).

4 The arrival of French winegrowers in Algeria was caused not only by phylloxera. There was conscious colonization by France involving the seizure of many lands from native populations (Pinilla and Ayuda 2002).

5 Algeria's external trade was entirely dependent on France. Initially (after annexation in 1830), there were tariffs on both French and Algerian products in the bilateral trade. In 1835, tariffs were removed from French products entering Algeria, but not vice versa. Algerian products were still considered "foreign" imports by France. In 1851, however, a new law permitted certain Algerian products, such as fruits, vegetables, cotton, and tobacco, to enter France duty-free. Wine was not initially included, but tariffs were lifted in 1867 (Isnard 1954, p. 30; Leroy-Beaulieu 1887, p. 176).

6 Tariff increases and tighter standards also caused the collapse of raisin imports by France from Greece (Meloni and Swinnen 2017).

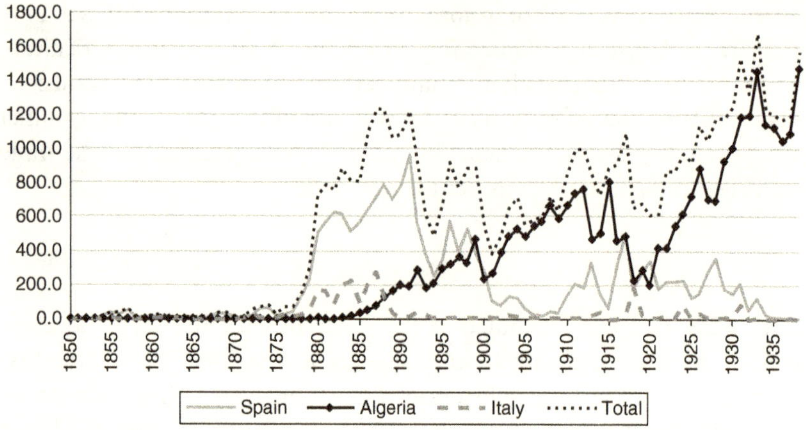

Figure 16.1 Volume of imports of bulk wines by France from major source countries, 1850 to 1938 (ML).
Source: Anderson and Pinilla (2017).

in the late 1880s to 500 ML in the early 1900s, mostly as a consequence of the decline in Spanish imports. Over this period, the importation of Algerian wine more than tripled, partially offsetting the reduced imports from Spain and Italy (and raisins from Greece). French wine imports roughly equaled the volume of Algerian production during the first two decades of the twentieth century (Figure 16.2).

Beginning in 1880, Algeria's vine plantations expanded massively. The area under vines increased from 20,000 to 150,000 ha between 1880 and 1900, and wine production followed quickly thereafter, rising from 2.5 ML in 1854 to 20 ML in 1872 and 40 ML in 1880. By the 1890s, French settlers did not need to import wine from France anymore but instead consumed Algerian wine (Figure 16.3). By 1900, Algerian production had reached 500 ML per year, and by 1915 it had doubled yet again to 1 billion litres as the vine area continued to expand (Figures 16.4, 16.5 and Table 16.2). The extent of the expansion generated some tension in France, but World War I (1914–1918) and the spread of Phylloxera in Algeria brought some relief to that Franco–Algerian wine conflict (Chevet et al. 2018). That was short-lived, though, as Algerian wine production and exports increased rapidly again in the 1920s and the early 1930s. Part of the reason for the increased production was the higher yields of replanted postphylloxera vineyards: yields in Algeria were 30 to 40 percent higher than in France over this period (Figure 16.6). Another reason for the competitiveness of Algeria was the economies of scale achieved by Algeria's large vineyards

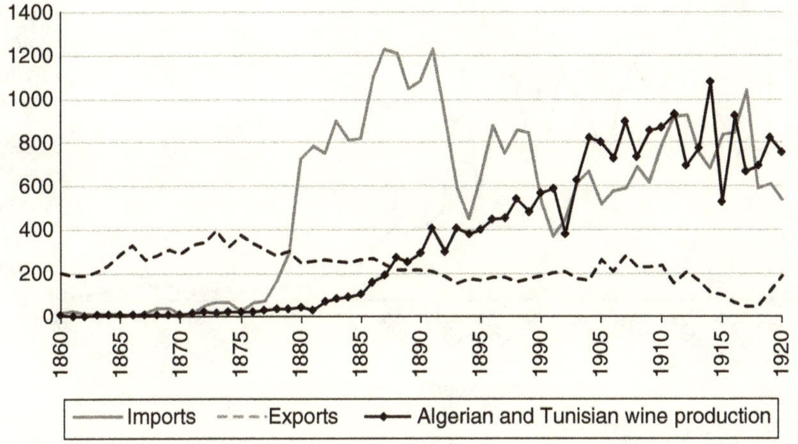

Figure 16.2 Volume of wine imports and exports of France and wine production of Algeria and Tunisia, 1860 to 1920 (ML).
Source: Meloni and Swinnen (2014).

(Cahill 1934; Pinilla and Ayuda 2002).[7] An even more important reason was the strong growth in vineyard area. Based on borrowings,[8] the cultivated vine area in Algeria increased from 175,000 ha in 1925 to 400,000 ha by 1935. As a result, production recovered, growing from 500 ML in 1922 to 2 billion litres by 1935.

Tunisia

The successful experience in Algeria encouraged other French settlers to replicate the experiment in Tunisia from 1881 (and in Morocco from 1912). Wine production in and exports from Tunisia were closely linked to French policies. Before the arrival of the French in 1881, less than 2,000 ha of grape vines were cultivated, partly for kosher wine for the Jewish community, but following the creation of the French protectorate, Tunisia's wine industry grew rapidly. As in Algeria, the French administration stimulated

[7] According to Cahill, 1934 (cited in Pinilla and Ayuda 2002): "Of the 10,000 wine producers in Algeria, 3.8% of them operated with more than 100 hectares of land. In France, of the million and a half wine producers, only 127 operated with more than this area. Those with more than 100 hectares in Algeria produced 38% of the wine, whilst their equivalents in France produced only 3%." See Table 16.2).

[8] In 1925, a law allowed agricultural credit banks to provide medium- and long-term loans (Isnard 1949).

Figure 16.3 Volume of wine imports and exports, Algeria, 1860 to 1920 (ML).
Note: The left vertical axis refers to Algerian wine imports, the right one to Algerian wine exports.
Source: Anderson and Pinilla (2017).

the extension of the vineyards by providing, among other things, loans for vineyard investment.

From 1881 to 1892, vineyard expansion was stimulated by the arrival of two different types of colonizers. The first wave of immigrants were French wealthy landowners and capitalists seeking new (cheap) land. The second wave of immigrants was triggered by the phylloxera crisis that had bankrupted Italian winegrowers (mainly from Sicily and Pantelleria, close to the Tunisian coast) who sought a new place to farm (Riban 1894, p. 57; Poncet 1962, p. 141).[9] These settlers brought new technologies, viticultural know-how, and capital to plant vines on a large scale. The new large wine estates combined capital to invest in modern technologies (e.g., mechanical wine presses),[10] the Algerian experience to produce wine in a hot climate, and a labor force experienced in winegrowers (Poncet 1962, p. 159).

Tunisian wine production and exports to France also benefited from a regime of preferential trade tariffs. A new law in 1890 changed the trade regime between France and Tunisia and permitted Tunisian wines to enter

9 The French and Italian settlers had very different-sized holdings. In 1892, a total of 331 French estates were owning 236,000 ha of land, with more than a third of them having an average size of more than 400 ha. By contrast, the average size of the estates owned by Italian immigrants was below 30 ha (Poncet 1962, p. 143).

10 European settlers borrowed substantial amounts of capital: a total of 1,500,000 francs were granted to invest in vineyards (Poncet 1962, p. 197). At the beginning of the twentieth century, French investments policy changed somewhat to support smaller vineyards.

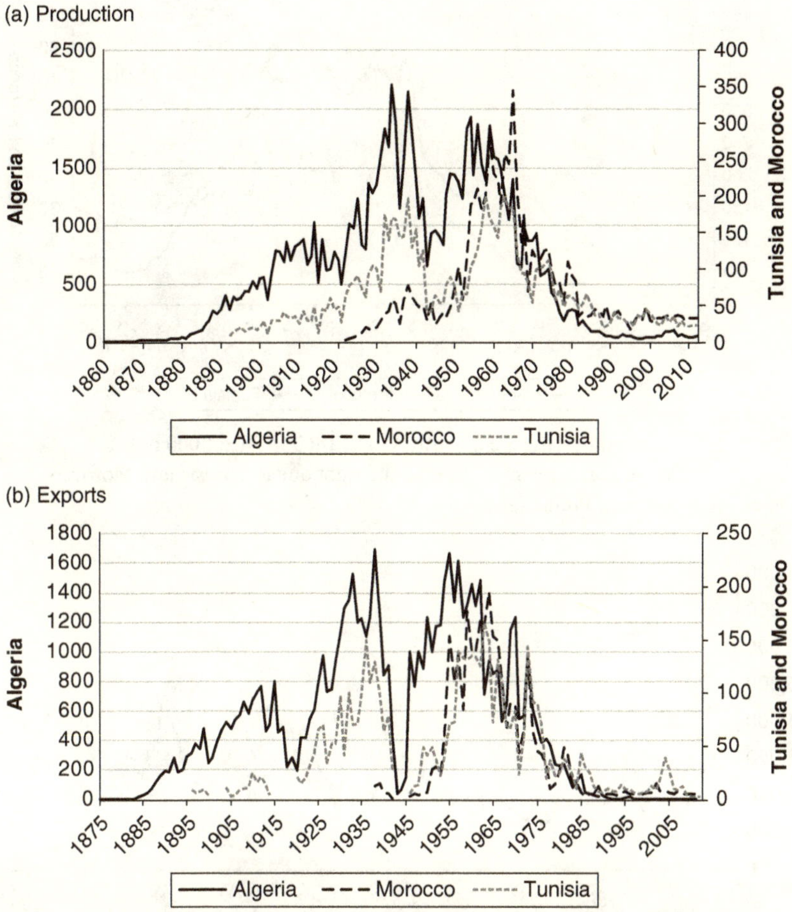

Figure 16.4 Volume of wine production and exports, North Africa, 1860 to 2012 (ML).
Note: The left vertical axis refers to Algeria, the right one to Tunisia and Morocco.
Source: Anderson and Pinilla (2017).

France duty-free, provided they had less than 11 percent alcohol (Nogaro and Moye 1910, p. 221; Poncet 1962, p. 488).

Vine planting (and consequently wine production) expanded massively. In 1892, around 6,000 ha were planted and production was 9.5 ML (Figures 16.4 and 16.5). World War I temporarily interrupted the expansion but it accelerated again in the 1920s (Znaien 2015). Tunisian wine production doubled from 50 ML in 1920 to almost 100 ML in 1925 and exports tripled from 20 to 60 ML over the same period (Figure 16.4). The spectacular growth was driven both by higher yields (from 2,000 litres per hectare in 1920 to 3,500 litres per

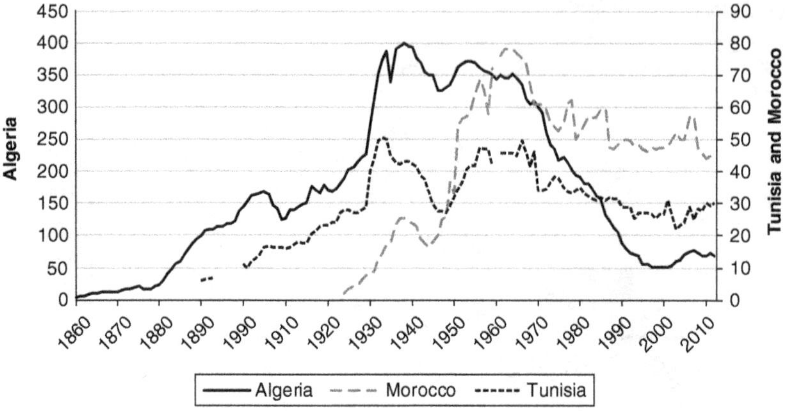

Figure 16.5 Vineyard bearing area, North Africa, 1860 to 2012 ('000 ha).
Note: The left vertical axis refers to Algeria, the right one to Tunisia and Morocco.
Source: Anderson and Pinilla (2017).

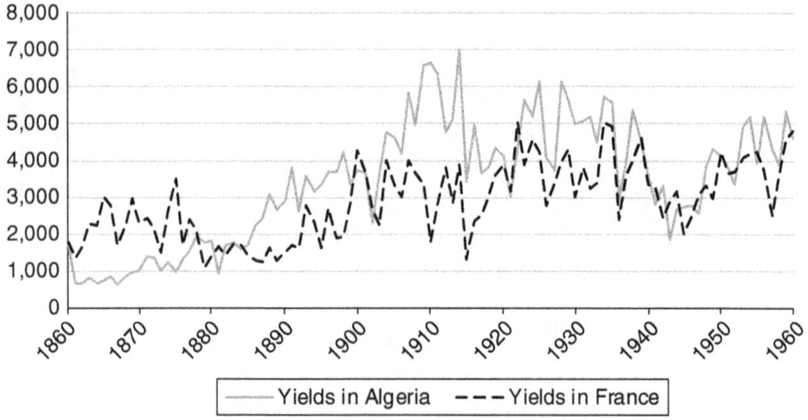

Figure 16.6 Vineyard yields, France and Algeria, 1860 to 1960 (litres of wine per ha).
Sources: Birebent (2007), Statistique Générale de la France (1878, 1901).

hectare in 1925) and by the expansion of vineyards from 18,000 ha in 1915 to 28,000 ha by 1925 (Tiengou des Royeries 1959, p. 77).[11]

[11] After World War I, more ruined Italian immigrants arrived. Their establishment was encouraged by the Protectorate buying large domains and selling land and vineyards to small (mainly Italian) settlers. The result was a shift in vineyards ownership. In 1913, French settlers owned 9,186 ha of vineyards and Italian settlers 6,448 ha. By 1920, Italians winegrowers had 10,112 ha, while the French stabilized their vineyard holdings at 9,436 ha. In 1938, half of the vineyards in Tunisia (about 24,000 ha out of a total of 43,000 ha)

Table 16.2 *Vine area and wine production, France and Algeria, 1900 to 1961*

	Vine area (million ha)	Production (ML)	Yield (KL/ha)	Winegrowers (thousand)	Vine area per winegrower (ha)
France					
1900–09	1.69	5,580	3.3	1,780	0.96
1910–19	1.55	4,320	2.8	1,540	1.01
1920–29	1.52	5,990	3.9	1,480	1.03
1930–39	1.53	5,880	3.8	1,510	1.02
1940–49	1.44	4,220	2.9	1,490	0.97
1950–61	1.35	5,290	3.9	1,500	
Algeria					
1900–09	0.15	670	4.4	12	12.3
1910–19	0.15	760	4.9	n.a.	n.a.
1920–29	0.19	950	4.9	10	18.7
1930–39	0.36	1,720	4.8	20	18.1
1940–49	0.35	1,070	3.0	27	12.8
1950–61	0.36	1,580	4.4	32	11.1

Sources: Anderson and Pinilla (2017) and authors' calculations based on Statistique Générale de la France (1878, 1901) and Birebent (2007, p. 222).

Morocco

When Morocco became France's third North African possession in 1912, it was divided in two protectorates: the southern part of the country was occupied by France, while the northern part was occupied by Spain. The number of European settlers increased from 65,000 in 1911 to 207,000 in 1936 (Tiengou des Royeries 1959, p. 89; Wesseling 2004). In 1912, around 2,000 ha were planted with vines, mainly for producing fresh grapes. The European settlers' demand for wine initially exceeded local production, such that Morocco imported about 18 ML of wine. However, by the end of the 1920s, government loans for agricultural investment had triggered a vineyard planting fever. Settlers borrowed substantial amounts of capital, which led to a tenfold increase of the area planted with vines by 1938, resulting in wine production increasing from 6 to 70 ML and wine imports decreasing from 26 ML in 1922 to 5.5 ML in 1933.

However, by the time wine production exceeded internal demand and Morocco was ready to export in the 1930s, the export market was already

were cultivated by 1,845 Italian winegrowers, who then represented two-thirds of all European winegrowers (Poncet 1962, p. 248; Huetz de Lemps 2001, p. 323).

flooded with Algerian (and Tunisian) wine, and French wine production had recovered.[12]

A PROTECTORATE IS NOT A COLONY: TARIFFS ON NORTH AFRICAN WINE IMPORTS

Wine imports by France from North Africa were initially not subject to tariffs, so they substituted for wines from Spain and Italy. Being a "true" colony, Algeria was part of a French custom union with zero internal tariffs, but Tunisia and Morocco, being French protectorates, had different trade relationships: they faced preferential tariffs and a system of duty-free quotas (Meloni and Swinnen 2016). As previously explained, Tunisia benefited from the 1890 law that permitted Tunisian wines to enter France duty-free. However, as French production recovered and Algerian imports continued to grow, there was strong pressure on the French government to constrain imports from Tunisia and Morocco. A first restrictive trade measure was introduced in 1928, when a new law imposed an annual quota of 55 ML on Tunisian wine which could enter France free of duty. Beyond that quota, wine imports were taxed at a minimum tariff rates (JORF 1930). Not surprisingly, Tunisia objected vehemently. Tunisia was producing 120 ML and exporting around 70 ML of wine (Figure 16.4).[13] Tunisian winegrowers therefore strongly lobbied the French government for a larger duty-free quota (Marseille 1984). After seven years of lobbying, a 1935 law increased the duty-free import quota to 75 ML of wines, and an extra 50 ML could be imported at a lower-than-normal tariff of 3,000 francs per litre (Chaudier 1898; Haight 1941, p. 244; Poncet 1962, p. 488; Marseille 1984).

Morocco, however, never benefited from preferential access to French wine markets. By the time it produced an export surplus in the mid-1930s, France was a saturated market and the French government was under strong political pressure from domestic wine producers to protect them. France therefore imposed high tariffs on Moroccan wines (Tiengou des Royeries 1959, p. 92).

The only "country" that escaped the protectionist wine trade regime change in France was Algeria. As a colony, it continued to export wine to France, and with its competitors blocked it continued to increase its exports

12 Morocco also exported wine to Belgium, Switzerland, and West Africa, but these markets were able to absorb only a small fraction of Morocco's excess production (Huetz de Lemps 2001).

13 Domestic consumption never exceeded 35 ML in Tunisia (Tiengou des Royeries 1959, p. 80).

until the middle of the twentieth century. Only a significant change in its political status with France would change this – and dramatically so, as explained in the following section.

NONTARIFF MEASURES RESTRICT NORTH AFRICAN EXPORTS

By the 1930s, France effectively had a ban on wine imports from Spain and Italy through tariffs and other regulations, and it limited its imports from Morocco and Tunisia through tariff quotas. However, the pressure on the French wine market continued. At first, the wines coming from the colonies served as *vin de coupage* for French wineries: they were blended with French wines to increase alcohol content.[14] However, from the end of the 1920s, they started to compete directly with French wines. With expanding internal production, growing imports from Algeria, and the fall in demand because of the 1929 Great Depression, prices kept falling. Between 1927 and 1935, real wine prices declined by 50 percent in France (Meloni and Swinnen 2014).

Import restrictions grew further as the wine crisis stimulated more protests from winegrowers in France (Chevet et al. 2018). France tried to stop wine imports from North Africa by means other than tariffs: it prohibited the blending of French wines with those of other countries, and it introduced laws aimed at reducing the vineyard area and banned new planting of vines.

The 1930 French law that prohibited the blending of foreign wines with national wines affected Moroccan and Tunisian wine exports, but not Algeria's.[15] As Algeria was formally part of France, Algerian wines were not considered "foreign wines" and therefore were not affected by the 1930 law (JORF 1930, article 4; Isnard 1966).[16]

The other major action taken by France, namely reducing the vine area and banning new planting of vines in North Africa,[17] was a response to

[14] French demand for higher-alcohol wines increased after the phylloxera outbreak. Hybrid vines (one of the solutions to phylloxera) produced wines with lower alcohol levels (between 8 and 10 percent). In order to increase the alcohol content, French wine producers had to either add sugar or blend their wines with North African wines that had a much higher alcohol levels of between 13 and 16 percent (Gautier 1930).

[15] The 1930 law established that: "Imported wines will be able to circulate for sale, be offered for sale or sold, if the indication of the country of origin and their alcohol content is clearly marked on the containers, invoices and other official documents …" Translation by the authors of Article 4 of JORF (1930).

[16] This regulation was eased for Tunisia in 1933: a new law considered Tunisian wines as "French wines," allowing their use in blending (Tiengou des Royeries 1959, p. 79).

[17] French winegrowers at first tried to lobby the government to impose import tariffs and quotas to protect them against Algerian wines. However, the French government was not

winegrowers from the south of France lobbying the government to halt the expansion of North African production (Meynier 1981, p. 129). Because almost all North African production was exported to France, a limit on vineyard expansion was equivalent to constraining imports. Between 1931 and 1935, various laws (*Statut Viticole*)[18] aimed at controlling the wine supply were introduced and applied to producers in both France and Algeria.[19] However, the policy hit (large) Algerian producers much harder than French producers. For instance, new planting of vines was forbidden for ten years for producers who owned vineyards of more than 10 ha or who produced more than 50,000 litres of wine. During the 1930–1935 period, the average vineyard for French winegrowers was just 1 ha, whereas in Algeria it was 22 ha. Furthermore, the average yield in France was 3,800 litres per hectare, whereas in Algeria it was almost 5,000 litres per hectare (Figure 16.6). Moreover, due to the hot climate, the obligation to store part of the excess production was more difficult for Algerian wine producers (Isnard 1947; Meloni and Swinnen 2014).

These laws did not immediately reduce total wine production but they stopped its growth and immediately halted the increase in vineyard area (Figure 16.5). The total vineyard area in Algeria never expanded beyond the level reached in the mid-1930s (400,000 ha).

Tunisia and Morocco were hit by similar regulations. In Tunisia, a 1932 law prohibited the expansion of vineyards above 10 ha. It was followed, a year later, by the total ban of new planting and replanting of vines. In 1934, grubbing-up premiums were provided to winegrowers who permanently (and voluntarily) abandoned vineyards.[20] In Tunisia, the total area planted with vines decreased from 51,000 ha in 1933 to 42,000 ha in 1937. Similarly, three laws were introduced in Morocco to halt the expansion of its vineyards. In 1935, an edict prohibited the planting of new vines and, in 1937, another edict provided restrictions not only on new plantings but also on the replanting of vines (Tiengou des Royeries 1959, pp. 80, 93; Poncet 1976).

willing to impose tariffs on Algerian wines, as it would have hurt the interests of French citizens overseas and because it was inconsistent with the integration of Algeria as French territory (Isnard and Labadie 1959; Barrows 1982).

[18] The *Statut Viticole* included the following measures: an obligation to store part of the excess production (*blocage*), obligatory distillation of surpluses, the establishment of a levy on large crops and yields, a ban on planting new vines, and premiums for grubbing up of "overproductive" vines (Loubère 1990).

[19] Article 17 of the 1931 law and article 54 of the 1935 law stated that the regulations were applicable to Algeria (Meloni and Swinnen 2014).

[20] Winegrowers committed to reducing their planted area by 10 percent, a percentage that was raised to 15 percent in 1935 (Tiengou des Royeries 1959, p. 80).

A Decade of Destruction

In the decade between 1935 and 1945, North African wine exports were (further) reduced by two external factors: the arrival in the region of phylloxera, and the destructions caused by World War I. The vine area declined by one-third with the arrival of phylloxera in Morocco (1935) and Tunisia (1936): vineyards in Tunisia decreased from 42,000 ha in 1937 to 30,000 in 1945, while vineyards in Morocco decreased from 26,000 ha to 18,000 ha over the same period (Figure 16.5).

Starting in 1939, Algerian wine exports were paralyzed because fighting in World War II (1939–1945) seriously affected maritime trade. It also caused destruction or abandonment of many vineyards in France and Algeria, leading to a sharp fall in wine production. The German occupation of Tunisia and severe droughts during 1941–1945 reduced its production and exports. World War II also stimulated wine demand in Morocco and Algeria, where local consumption increased after the landing of allied troops in 1942. In fact, demand increased so much that 25 ML of wine had to be imported in 1944. That war also affected French regulations: in the wake of falling North African production and exports, the Statut Viticole was repealed and planting restrictions were liberalized in 1942 (Chevet et al. 2018).

Postwar Recovery

After the war, wine production recovered as vineyards were replanted, with production in Algeria doubling from 900 ML in 1945 to 1.8 billion litres in 1953 and the Moroccan and Tunisian wine industries also witnessing an increase in wine production and exports (Figure 16.4(a)). In 1946, special loans were granted by the Tunisian government to winemakers eager to replant their vineyards (Isnard 1949).

As well, French wine and trade policies played a crucial role. France needed more wine than it could produce in the 1940s, so a new trade agreement between France and Morocco was reached in 1948: a total of 100 ML of Moroccan wines could enter France duty-free.[21] Moreover, the restrictive vine planting regulations were eased: in 1943, the Sultan Mohammed V allowed the planting of 10,000 ha of new vines and, from 1953 onward, allowed the planting of an additional 3,000 ha per year. Morocco's vine area

[21] The 100 million liter quota was provided for 30 ML of wines with less than 12 percent alcohol and 70 ML for wines above 12 percent (Tiengou des Royeries 1959, p. 95).

increased fourfold (from 20,000 ha in 1946 to about 70,000 ha in 1956) and its wine production increased sixfold (from 30 ML to 200 ML) over the same period (Figures 16.4 and 16.5).

A new customs agreement with Tunisia (1955) raised its duty-free quota to 125 ML (up from 75 ML). As a result, Tunisian wine production doubled during 1954–1958 to 200 ML and wine exports tripled, from 40 to 130 ML (Figures 16.4 and 16.5).

DECOLONIZATION AND THE COLLAPSE OF NORTH AFRICA'S WINE INDUSTRY

In 1961, North Africa still accounted, in volume terms, for almost two-thirds of the world's wine exports, and Algeria was still the world's largest exporter of wine (Figure 16.7 and Table 16.3). Moreover, Algeria's index of revealed comparative advantage was the highest of any country pre-1960 (Table 16.4). This lasted until the late 1950s and early 1960s, when independence was achieved for Morocco (1956), Tunisia (1956), and Algeria (1962). Thereafter, France imposed high tariffs on North African wine imports. The combination of high French import tariffs, a drop in domestic North African consumption, a loss in wine production skills, and mismanagement of the vineyards caused the collapse of the North African wine industry, and most dramatically in Algeria.

French Import Constraints After Independence

Until 1962, Algeria was not only a part of France but also, therefore, of the European Economic Community (EEC) from its inception in 1957. After independence, Algeria no longer enjoyed the same trade status with France or with the EEC. Algerian wine was no longer a "French product" and therefore was subject to tariffs. In 1964, a five-year agreement was reached between France and Algeria in which France committed to purchasing 3.9 billion litres of Algerian wine – decreasing from 900 million to 700 ML per year over the next five years. The negotiated import volumes were considerably lower than imports before independence (e.g., in 1961 Algeria exported 1.5 billion litres to France). Actual French imports were even lower since the French government did not fill the agreed quota. Consequently, Algerian wine exports to France fell by two-thirds in only a few years (Figure 16.4(b)).

After the independence of Tunisia and Morocco, France eliminated their preferential wine tariffs and did not allow any duty-free wine imports.

Table 16.3 *Share of world wine export volume, key countries, 1860 to 1970 (%)*

	1860	1875	1885	1900	1925	1950	1970
France	40.0	49.2	18.7	16	9.4	5.7	11.0
Italy	4.9	4.8	10.6	15.4	8.7	3.3	13.6
Portugal	4.1	6.7	9.3	6.9	6.2	5.9	5.8
Spain	27.8	27.3	51.5	32.5	17.5	5.1	9.2
Algeria	0.0	0.1	2.3	20.6	47.1	71.3	34.8
Tunisia	0.0	0.1	0.1	0.3	3.9	2.4	2.4
Morocco	0.0	0.0	0.0	0.0	0.0	0.4	2.5
Rest of the world	22.1	11.1	6.3	6.8	7.4	7.6	22.3

Source: Anderson and Pinilla (2017).

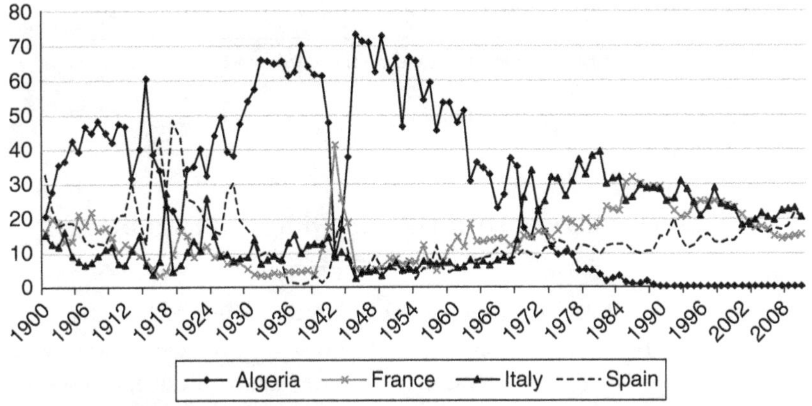

Figure 16.7 Shares of world wine export volume, key countries, 1900 to 2012 (%). *Source*: Anderson and Pinilla (2017).

Ironically, in 1955 (on the eve of its independence from France), Tunisia formed a customs union with France. This would change with independence. In 1959, a new bilateral trade agreement was reached, with Tunisian exports still enjoying some preferences in the French market. However, in 1964 the Tunisian government decided to nationalize vineyards belonging to European settlers. France retaliated by canceling the Franco–Tunisian trade agreement and stopping wine imports from Tunisia (Angles 1996; Valay 1966).

For Morocco as well, France decided in 1967 to eliminate the duty-free quota of 100 ML of wine imports. As a result, Morocco's exports decreased sharply, from 170 ML in 1959 to 70 ML in 1968, while Tunisia's fell from 130 ML to 60 ML (Figure 16.4(b)).

Table 16.4 *Index of revealed comparative advantage in wine,*[a] *key countries, 1900 to 2013*

	France	Algeria	Tunisia	Morocco	Georgia	Moldova
1900–09	6.0	43.2	2.5	0.5	–	–
1910–19	4.3	54.7	5.6	0.3	–	–
1920–29	3.8	58.2	12.3	0.2	–	–
1930–39	3.1	61.1	17.2	0.5	–	–
1940–49	5.0	76.1	9.1	0.2	–	–
1950–59	4.3	108.0	18.4	6.4	–	–
1960–69	4.9	54.5	2.5	0.4	–	–
1970–79	5.9	16.1	7.3	3.2	–	–
1980–89	8.1	1.8	1.3	0.9	–	–
1990–99	7.8	0.4	0.6	0.5	28.4	69.7
2000–09	7.9	0.1	0.4	0.4	32.6	81.4
2010–13	9.5	0.0	0.2	0.2	20.2	36.0

[a] Wine's share of national merchandise exports divided by wine's share of global merchandise exports.

Source: Anderson and Pinilla (2017).

Loss of Skills and Local Demand with the Departure of European Settlers

The departure of the French army and a large number of European settlers resulted in the loss of skilled labor and in a sharp decrease in wine consumption in North Africa countries. The departure of European settlers – owners of large estates or winegrowers with viticultural skills and knowledge – caused a disruption to production during the transition process, as well as a sharp fall in wine consumption. In Tunisia, about one hundred thousand Europeans left the country in 1956–1957, leading to a 30 percent drop in domestic wine consumption in one year, while in Morocco domestic consumption decreased by 70 percent after independence. In Algeria, the situation was even more dramatic, as 900,000 European-Algerians (*pieds-noirs*) emigrated to France between 1962 and 1975. Algeria's domestic wine consumption declined by about 90 percent between 1960 and 1975 (Stone 1997, p. 218; Huetz de Lemps 2001, pp. 317, 323, 328).

Nationalization and Poor Management

The collapse of North African wine exports was reinforced by reduced management skills, the nationalization of vineyards, and the inability to redirect exports to non-French markets. In 1969, Algeria signed a seven-year contract with the Soviet Union, which agreed to buy 500 ML of Algerian wine every year at a fixed price. The Soviet Union became Algeria's principal wine export market, which led to a brief surge in exports: in 1969 and 1970, wine exports increased to around 1.2 billion litres. But the recovery did not last. Exports to France continued to decline, and exports to the Soviet Union were not successful in that the prices set by the Soviet government were lower than world market prices for wine and unprofitable for Algeria (Sutton 1988).

Morocco and Tunisia also tried to redirect their wine exports. Morocco found other (minor) markets in Germany (10 ML in 1969) and in West Africa (Ivory Coast and Senegal), but at prices below production costs (Huetz de Lemps 2001, p. 328). Tunisia also (unsuccessfully) tried to export to other countries, such as the United States, Germany, and West Africa. However, already in 1965, the just-elected president of Tunisia, Habib Bourguiba, advised winegrowers to stop planting and to progressively replace vines with more profitable crops such as flowers and asparagus (Isnard 1966).

Moreover, after independence, vineyards were run by state organizations and governed by local politicians without much agricultural knowledge or winemaking skills. In Algeria, the ruling political party (the National Liberation Front) nationalized agricultural land in 1962, including vineyards and the entire wine sector. In 1968, the Office National de Commercialisation des Produits Vitivinicoles (the National Marketing Office for Viticulture Products, or ONCV) was created to manage the wine industry. In Morocco, too, vineyards were gradually taken over and owned by the Société de Développement Agricole (the Agricultural Development Corporation, or SODEA), which was established in 1972 to manage agricultural areas (Huetz de Lemps 2001, p. 328; Birebent 2007).

In summary, the combination of low domestic consumption, poor domestic management of the wine sector after its nationalization, and French import constraints caused a dramatic reduction in North African exports. The state-managed system was unable to respond effectively to the changed international market situation and could not find alternative outlets or reposition North African wines for a growing global market. In response, the government of Algeria decided to uproot 20 percent (71,300 ha) of the country's vineyards during 1971–1973 (Sutton 1988). The fall continued through the rest of the twentieth century. The largest impact was on Algerian wine production, which, by the early 1990s, was back to the negligible level it had been 120 years earlier.

THE FUTURE OF NORTH AFRICA'S WINE INDUSTRY

"Today, wine production along the North African coast is plummeting as the influence of Islam increases, but Morocco still makes some interesting wines and has the potential to produce more" (Robinson 2016, p. 1). Despite some attempts to stimulate wine production and exports, the only country that is taking advantage of both French private investments and national policy responses is Morocco. However, climate change probably represents the biggest challenge that this country (and the region's wine production) will face in the future.

New Investments in Morocco and Tunisia

Private investments have been made in the wine industry in Tunisia and Morocco since the late twentieth century. The main investments were by Italians, Swiss, Germans, and Austrians in Tunisia and by the French in Morocco. This led to an increase in wine quality, as these foreign investors brought superior winemaking and viticultural know-how.

In the early 1990s, on the initiative of King Hassan II, ex-law student in Bordeaux and friend of the mayor of Bordeaux (Chaban-Delmas), Morocco started attracting private investors by guaranteeing support for the banks and by granting land to grow vines.[22] Several companies started investing in Morocco, including Castel, William Pitters, and the Taillan group.[23] With the return of the French investors and oenologists, vineyards were renovated and new grape varieties and technology were introduced. This led to exports of some Moroccan wine to France, its only export market, as its links with Bordeaux persist (Géné 2010; Euromonitor 2016a; Lindsey 2016). Also, land was (partially) granted by King Hassan II to private Moroccan investors and winegrowers. This allowed some Moroccan winegrowers to

[22] The state-managed SODEA, which owned the majority of the vineyards, had to provide land to private investors. A legal partnership framework was established and corporations were created that were owned 40 percent by SODEA and the Moroccan Crédit Agricole and 60 percent by private investors. As land could not be purchased by foreigners, it was rented for thirty years under certain conditions relating to the export of production, renovating and replanting vineyards, and so on (Institut Français de la Vigne et du Vin 2001).

[23] More-recent investments involve the creation of Les Deux Domaines (established in 2000 by the actor Gérard Depardieu), Domaine de la Zouina (established in 2002 by Frenchmen Gérard Gribelin of Château de Fieuzal and Philippe Gervoson of Château Larrivet Haut-Brion), and La Ferme Rouge (established in 2008 by the French oenologist Jacques Poulain) (Casamayor 2012).

acquire the cellars left by French settlers. The most successful winegrower was Brahim Zniber, known as the "the lord of the barrels" (Géné 2010).[24]

In 2000, SODEA was still holding about 60 percent of the national vineyard area and accounted for 51 percent of the production of bulk wines (SODEA 2016). Recently, the ruling parties reduced their control of Morocco's wine industry. As a result, the total vine area dropped by 20 percent in six years (from 57,000 ha in 2007 to 46,000 ha in 2013), as many vine areas were converted to pasture. In 2008, the Moroccan Ministry of Agriculture and Fisheries decided to launch a public–private partnership and rent the land owned by SODEA to private winegrowers (Ministère de l'Agriculture Maroc 2000).[25] As the state monopoly no longer dominates the wine market, large commercial wine producers have substantially enlarged their shares. In 2014, the Brahim Zniber's group Diana Holding – with more than 2,500 ha of vineyards and controlling almost 60 percent of Moroccan wine production – was the main actor in Moroccan viticulture, followed by the French group Castel, representing slightly more than 20 percent of the country's wine production (Jaidani 2015).

In Tunisia also, the wine industry has been helped by private foreign investments (Italians, Swiss, Germans, and Austrians) since the late twentieth century. More recently, public investments have targeted specialized cooperatives and trained engineers.[26] However, three factors continue to negatively impact Tunisia's wine sector: vineyards and wineries are still nationalized (as the Ministry of Agriculture still controls the quantities of grapes and wine produced), the sector is discouraged by high taxes (e.g., wine consumption taxes and exceptional taxes on sparkling wines), and a total ban on the advertising of wine brands inhibits marketing efforts (Euromonitor 2016b).

In Algeria, there has been some renovation and modernization efforts,[27] but the ruling party is not facilitating foreign private investments

[24] After having granted facilities to the Bordeaux investors, the king told Brahim Zniber: "I forgot you, Brahim, I will give you 1,100 ha of vineyards and you will not have to associate yourself with the public companies" (Géné 2010, p. 1).

[25] The Agence pour le Développement Agricole (Agricultural Development Agency, or ADA) launched four tenders for agricultural land owned by the state for long-term leasing, including forty years for vineyards (Jaidani 2015).

[26] Les Vignerons De Carthage (UCCV), established in 1948, is a union of nine cooperative wineries owing 9,000 ha of vineyards and accounting for two-thirds of Tunisian wine production. Under the leadership of Belgacem D'Khili, an oenologist engineer of the Agro de Montpellier in southern France, the UCCV invested in restructuring of vineyards and introduced modern methods and high-performance equipment (Casamayor 2014).

[27] Since the introduction of National Agricultural Development Plan (Plan National de Développement Agricole, or PNDA) in 2000 and the ten-year National Agricultural

(Wallis 2005; Oxford Business Group 2008, 2010). Thus, many problems remain: winemaking methods date from the French colonization period; there is a scarcity of international vine varieties, and cellars are in poor condition (some machinery and equipment date from the early twentieth century). Another key obstacle to the development of the sector is the ONCV. Today it owns about 5,000 ha and 132 wineries, thereby controlling 95 percent of Algeria's wine production (Ilbert 2005; ONCV 2016).[28]

The Arab Spring

A major political shock (the Arab Spring) took place in 2010–2012, when Tunisia witnessed massive protests and riots that overturned its government.[29] In contrast, Algeria and Morocco managed to maintain political stability.[30] Through public spending programs and the redistribution of oil revenues,[31] Algeria eased public discontent due to high (youth) unemployment and food price inflation. With high oil prices, the Algerian government used its oil export revenues to create new public sector jobs, increase wages for civil servants, and decrease prices of basic foods. In Morocco as well, King Mohammed VI introduced constitutional reforms[32] without destabilizing the polity of the country nor its monarchy (Chikhi and Parent 2011; Lewis 2011; Achy 2012, 2013).

In Algeria, it is unlikely that the Arab Spring will lead to the privatization of vineyards and wineries or a major policy shift, as the established political parties are still ruling. In Tunisia, the new democracy, weakened by political divisions in the ruling coalition, risks undermining substantial economic

and Rural Development Plan (Plan National de Développement Agricole et Rurale, or PNDAR) launched in 2004, increased attention has been put on the wine industry. Public funds have been allocated for the modernization of wine production and wine cellars, for the replanting of vineyards and for the planting of more "noble" grapevines such as Cabernet Sauvignon, Pinot Noir, and Merlot (Oxford Business Group 2008, 2010).

28 Only three private companies operate in Algeria's wine sector (Ministère de la PME et de l'Artisanat 2005).

29 The 2010 uprising in Tunisia was the only one that resulted in a relatively "peaceful" political transition (to constitutional democracy), achieving free elections and a new constitution (Bennett-Jones 2014).

30 During the 2012 Algerian parliamentary election, as opposed to neighboring countries, Islamist parties did not manage to win against the established political parties, the National Liberation Front (FLN) and the National Rally for Democracy (RND) (Achy 2012).

31 Public spending in Algeria doubled in the 2011–2012 period, with its energy sector representing more than one-third of the gross domestic product (GDP), two-thirds of government revenue, and 98 percent of exports (Achy 2012).

32 Major constitutional reforms gave more power to the prime minister (and parliament) and established Berber as an official language, together with Arabic (Lewis 2011).

reforms. The state-managed wine system is likely to remain in place there as well. In Morocco, even if the land is still owned by the state, the rental process already started in 2008 (two years before the Arab Spring) is likely to continue, although it still limits the amount of vine area that winegrowers can rent.

Climate Change

With climate change, winegrowers will have to adapt either to new technologies (and new grapes) or to new grape-growing locations (for instance, by moving their vineyards to higher elevations). Climate change could possibly allow North Africa's wine industries to reposition themselves in the global market for more hot-region winegrapes given that the hot regions of California and Australia are struggling as well (Alston et al. 2018; Anderson 2018). In order to do so, all three North African countries would have to adopt technologies needed to produce drinkable wines in an even hotter climate. This will be a huge challenge. For Algeria, the scarcity of vine varieties and the outdated wineries and cellars are major obstacles to counter climate change. For Morocco and Tunisia, the situation may be more positive as foreign investors bring superior viticultural knowledge. However, another key obstacle remains: the state monopoly exercised in both Algeria and Tunisia does not promote the development of new technologies nor the search for premium winegrape varieties. In Morocco, the situation is more nuanced as the land is now rented to private investors who could potentially invest in new technologies. However, the rental of state land might be insufficient to allow large winegrowers to freely expand, as they could do by buying land in other more profitable places (e.g., at higher altitudes in order to cope with global warming).

North Africa Wine Futures

The future of the North African wine industry does not look promising. In Algeria and Tunisia, many problems remain despite the efforts at renovation and modernization. In Algeria, vineyards and wineries are still nationalized, the methods of winemaking date from the French colonial period, and the wineries and cellars are in poor conditions. In Tunisia, despite foreign private investments that have been made in the wine industry since the late twentieth century, the wine sector is also discouraged by the state-managed wine system, high consumer taxes, and the total ban on the advertising of wine brands. In both countries, it is unlikely that the Arab Spring will lead to the privatization of vineyards and wineries. The only country that might take advantage of both French private investments and national policy responses is Morocco. The ruling parties have reduced their control of the wine industry, and French oenologists and wine producers continue investing in the country, bringing their technology and wine knowledge. However, climate change probably represents the biggest challenge that the wine industry of this country (and the region) will face in the foreseeable future.

REFERENCES

Achy, L. (2012), 'Algeria Avoids the Arab Spring?' Carnegie Middle East Center, Carnegie Endowment for International Peace, May 31. Available at carnegieendowment.org/2012/05/31/algeria-avoids-arab-spring/b0xu/ (accessed September 26, 2016).

(2013), 'The Price of Stability in Algeria', Carnegie Middle East Center, Carnegie Middle East Center, April 25. Available at carnegie-mec.org/2013/04/25/price-ofstability-in-algeria/g1cs/ (accessed September 24, 2016).

Alston, J. M., J. Lapsley, L. Sambucci and D. Sumner (2018), 'The United States', ch. 15 in *Wine Globalization: A New Comparative History*, edited by K. Anderson and V. Pinilla, Cambridge: Cambridge University Press.

Anderson, K. (2018), 'Australia', ch. 12 in *Wine Globalization: A New Comparative History*, edited by K. Anderson and V. Pinilla, Cambridge: Cambridge University Press.

Anderson, K. and V. Pinilla (with the assistance of A. J. Holmes) (2017), *Annual Database of Global Wine Markets, 1835 to 2016*, freely available in Excel at the University of Adelaide's Wine Economics Research Centre, www.adelaide.edu.au/wine-econ/databases

Angles, S. (1996), 'Les Aspects Récents de la Viticulture Tunisienne', pp. 567–74 in *Des vignobles et des vins à travers le monde: Hommage à Alain Huetz de Lemps*, edited by C. Le Gars and P. Roudié, Cervin: Presses Universitaires de Bordeaux.

Barrows, S. (1982), 'Alcohol, France and Algeria: A Case Study in the International Liquor Trade', *Contemporary Drug Problem* 11: 525–43.

Bennett-Jones, O. (2014), 'Is Tunisia a Role Model for the Arab World?' *BBC News*, December 2. Available at www.bbc.com/news/world-africa-30273807/ (accessed September 22, 2016).

Birebent, P. (2007), *Hommes, vignes et vins de l'Algérie Française: 1830–1962*, Nice: Editions Jacques Gandini.

Blanc, G. (1967). *La vigne dans l'économie algérienne. Essai d'analyse des phénomènes de domination et des problèmes posés par l'accession à l'indépendance économiques dans le secteur agricole*, Thèse présentée et publiquement soutenue devant la Faculté de Droit et des Sciences Economiques de Montpellier pour l'obtention du grade de Docteur en Sciences Economiques.

Cahill, R. (1934), *Economic Conditions in France*, London: Department of Overseas Trade.

Casamayor, P. (2012), 'Terroirs Marocains: Ils font du Vin en Terre d'Islam', *La Revue du vin de France* 566: 38–46.

(2014), 'Vins de Tunisie: La Renaissance d'un Vignoble Antique', *La Revue du vin de France* 583: 78–80.

Chaudier, J. (1898), *Le régime douanier de la Tunisie: La loi française du 19 juillet 1890, le décret beylical du 2 mai 1898*, Montpellier: Imprimerie de Serre et Roumégous. Available at gallica.bnf.fr/ark:/12148/bpt6k57728089.

Chevet, J.-M., E. Fernandez, E. Giraud-Héraud and V. Pinilla (2018), 'France', ch. 4 in K. Anderson and V. Pinilla (eds.), *Wine Globalization: A New Comparative History*, Cambridge: Cambridge University Press.

Chikhi, L. and V. Parent (2011), 'Algeria Steps Up Grain Imports, Eyes Tunisia Virus', Reuters, January 26. Available at www.reuters.com/article/us-grains-algeria-idUSTRE70P3PY20110126/ (accessed May 3, 2016).

Euromonitor (2016a), 'Wine in Morocco', Euromonitor International. Available at www.euromonitor.com/wine-in-morocco/report/ (accessed October 23, 2016).

(2016b), 'Wine in Tunisia', Euromonitor International. Available at www.euromonitor.com/wine-in-tunisia/report/ (accessed October 22, 2016).

Gautier, M. E. F. (1930), 'L'évolution de l'Algérie de 1830 à 1930', in *Les 12 cahiers du Centenaire de l'Algérie* (Vol 3), edited by Comité National Métropolitain du Centenaire de l'Algérie, Orléans: A. Pigelet & Cie.

Géné, J. P. (2010), 'Sur la route du vin marocain', *Le Monde*, September 26. Available at www.lemonde.fr/vous/article/2010/09/26/sur-la-route-du-vin-marocain_1415238_3238.html (accessed September 26, 2016).

Haight, F. A. (1941), *A History of French Commercial Policies*. New York: Macmillan. Available at catalog.hathitrust.org/Record/001153650 (accessed November 6, 2016).

Huetz de Lemps, A. (2001), *Boissons et civilisations en Afrique*, Pessac: Presses Universitaires de Bordeaux.

Ilbert, H. (ed.) (2005), *Produits du terroir méditerranéen: conditions d'emergence, d'efficacité et modes de gouvernance, Rapport Final*, Montpellier: CIHEAM – IAMM. FEMISE Research Programme 2004–05.

Institut Français de la Vigne et du Vin (2001), 'Le Maroc Viticole', Institut Français de la Vigne et du Vin (IFV). Available at www.vignevin-sudouest.com/publications/voyage-etude/voyage-etude-maroc.php/ (accessed October 10, 2016).

Isnard, H. (1947), 'Vigne et colonisation en Algérie (1880–1947)', *Annales. Économies, Sociétés, Civilisations* 2(3): 288–300.

(1949), 'Le vignoble européen de Tunisie au lendemain de la guerre', *L'information géographique* 13(4): 159–61.

(1954), *La vigne en Algérie, étude géographique, Book II*, Ophrys: Gap.

(1966), 'La viticulture Nord-Africaine', pp. 37–48 in *Annuaire de l'Afrique du Nord-1965* (Vol. 4). Paris: Editions du CNRS.

Isnard, H. and J. H. Labadie (1959), 'Vineyards and Social Structure in Algeria', *Diogenes* 7: 63–81.

Jaidani, C. (2015), 'Viticulture: Le Maroc peut mieux faire', *FinanceNews*, September 7. Available at www.financenews.press.ma/site/economie/focus/12958-viticulture-le-maroc-peut-mieux-faire/ (accessed November 20, 2016).

JORF (1930), 'Loi du 1er Janvier 1930 sur les vins', *Journal Officiel de la République Française*, January 12, p. 394.

Lequément R. (1980), 'Le vin africain à l'époque impériale', *Antiquités Africaines* 16: 185–93.

Leroy-Beaulieu, P. (1887), *L'Algérie et la Tunisie*, Paris: Librairie Guillaumin.

Lewis, A. (2011), 'Why Has Morocco's King Survived the Arab Spring?' *BBC News*, November 24. Available at www.bbc.com/news/world-middle-east-15856989/ (accessed October 10, 2016).

Lindsey, U. (2016), 'Morocco's Atlas Mountains Seek Place on Winemaking Map', *Financial Times*, March 23, 2016. Available at www.ft.com/content/0daacbf4-ca66e967dd44/ (accessed April 22, 2016).

Loubère, L. A. (1990), *The Wine Revolution in France: The Twentieth Century*, Princeton, NJ: Princeton University Press.

Marseille, J. (1984), *Empire colonial et capitalisme français. Histoire d'un divorce*, Paris: Albin Michel.

McGovern, P. E. (2009), *Uncorking the Past: The Quest for Wine, Beer and Other Alcoholic Beverages*, Berkeley: University of California Press.

Meloni, G., and J. Swinnen (2014), 'The Rise and Fall of the World's Largest Wine Exporter – and Its Institutional Legacy', *Journal of Wine Economics* 9(1): 3–33.

(2016), 'Bugs, Tariffs and Colonies: The Political Economy of the Wine Trade 1860–1970', LICOS Discussion Paper 384/2016, KU Leuven, December. Available at feb.kuleuven.be/drc/licos/publications/dp/dp384/ (accessed December 3, 2016).

(2017), 'Standards, Tariffs and Trade: The Rise and Fall of the Raisin Trade Between Greece and France in the Late 19th Century and the Definition of Wine', LICOS Discussion Paper 386/2017, KU Leuven, January. Available at feb.kuleuven.be/drc/licos/publications/dp/dp386 (accessed January 10, 2017).

Meynier, G. (1981), *L'Algérie révélée: La guerre de 1914–1918 et le premier quart du XXe siècle*, Geneva and Paris: Librairie Droz.

Ministère de la PME et de l'Artisanat (2005), *Analyse de la filière boisson en Algérie: Rapport principal*, Algiers: Euro Développement Programme.

Ministère de l'Agriculture Maroc (2000), 'Investir en Agriculture', Ministère de l'Agriculture. Available at agrimaroc.net/invest_12.pdf/ (accessed October 10, 2016).

Nogaro, B. and M. Moye. (1910), *Les Régimes Douaniers. Législation Douanière et Traités de Commerce*. Paris: Colin. Available at archive.org/details/lesrgimesdouan00moyeuoft (accessed April 6, 2016).

ONCV (2016), 'Présentation de l'ONCV', National Marketing Office for Viticulture Products (ONCV). Available at www.oncv-groupe.com/Vins_Algerie/Presentation/Presentation_Fr.html/ (accessed October 10, 2016).

Oxford Business Group (2008), *The Report: Algeria 2008*, Oxford: Oxford Business Group.

(2010), *The Report: Algeria 2010*, Oxford: Oxford Business Group.

Pinilla, V. (2014), 'Wine Historical Statistics: A Quantitative Approach to its Consumption, Production and Trade, 1840–1938', American Association of Wine Economists (AAWE) Working Paper No. 167.

Pinilla, V. and M.-I. Ayuda (2002), 'The Political Economy of the Wine Trade: Spanish Exports and the International Market, 1890–1935', *European Review of Economic History* 6: 51–85.

Poncet, J. (1962), *La colonisation et l'agriculture européenne en Tunisie depuis 1881: Étude de géographie historique et économique*, Paris–La Haye: Mouton & Co.

(1976), 'La Crise des années 30 et ses répercussions sur la colonisation française en Tunisie', pp. 622–27 in *Revue française d'histoire d'outre-mer* 63(232–3), 3e et 4e trimestres 1976. L'Afrique et la crise de 1930 (1924–1938) sous la direction de Catherine Coquery-Vidrovitch.

Riban, C. (1894), *Causeries sur la Tunisie agricole*, Tunis: Imprimerie Rapide.

Robinson, J. (2016), 'Morocco', Jancis Robinson. Available at www.jancisrobinson.com/learn/wine-regions/morocco/ (accessed November 28, 2016).

SODEA (2016), 'Nos domaines d'activités', Société de Développement Agricole (SODEA). Available at www.sodea.com/activite/centre.htm/ (accessed December 1, 2016).

Statistique Générale de la France (1878), *Annuaire Statistique de la France. Ministère de l'agriculture et du commerce, Service de la statistique générale de France. 1878–1899.* Paris: Imprimerie Nationale. Available at gallica.bnf.fr/ark:/12148/cb343503965/date.

(1901), *Annuaire Statistique de la France. Ministère de l'agriculture et du commerce, Service de la statistique générale de France. 1901–1952.* Paris: Imprimerie Nationale. Available at gallica.bnf.fr/ark:/12148/cb34350395t/date

Stone, M. (1997), *The Agony of Algeria*, London: Hurst & Co.

Sutton, K. (1988), 'Algeria's Vineyards: A Problem of Decolonisation', *Méditerranée* 65(65): 55–66.

Tiengou des Royeries, Y. (1959), *La Production Viticole hors de France*, Paris: Librairies Techniques.

Valay, G. (1966), 'La Communauté Economique Européenne et les pays du Maghreb', *Revue de l'Occident musulman et de la Méditerranée* 2(1): 199–225.

Wallis, W. (2005), 'Wine Returns to the Menu for Algeria as Production Flows Again', *Financial Times*, October 10. Available at www.ft.com/cms/s/0/8a8c5c98-392a-11da-900a-00000e2511c8.html?ft_site=falcon&desktop=true/ (accessed October 2, 2016).

Wesseling, H. L. (2004), *The European Colonial Empires: 1815–1919*, Harlow: Pearson Education Limited.

Znaien, N. (2015), 'Le vin et la viticulture en Tunisie coloniale (1881–1956): Entre synapse et apartheid', *French Cultural Studies* 26(2): 140–51.

17

Asia and Other Emerging Regions

Kym Anderson

Five decades ago, Asia was barely noticeable in the global wine marketplace, and all other developing countries, apart from those examined in preceding chapters, also were very minor players. Since the 1990s, however, several East Asian economies have rapidly become significant importers of wine and, in China's case, also a significant producer of wine. This chapter therefore focuses mostly on developments in Asia, but finishes with a brief section on other developing country regions.

Rice wine is common in the rice-consuming parts of Asia, but wine made from grapes has had a very minor role traditionally.[1] Prior to this century, grape wine was consumed only by Asia's elite and produced only in tiny quantities and mostly in just Japan and – from the late 1980s – China.[2] However, income growth and a preference swing toward this traditional European product has changed the consumption situation dramatically. China is also expanding its area of vineyards and is now

[1] The exception is West Asia and the Caucasus region, which is where grape wine production began more than 8,000 years ago (McGovern 2003). However, most of Central and West Asia has adopted Islam and made alcohol consumption illegal. South Asia also has been a tiny actor in global wine markets. Although wine importation by India and Sri Lanka is beginning to grow, it is doing so from a very small base (and Bangladesh and Pakistan are Islamic), so the Asian focus in what follows is mostly East Asia. The Levant (eastern Mediterranean) countries are covered in Chapter 10 of this volume.

[2] "China" in this chapter, as elsewhere in this volume, refers to the mainland. Since Hong Kong, Taiwan, and Macao are separate customs territories, they are treated here as separate economies. Wine production from *Vitis vinifera* grapes began in China more than two millennia ago, having been introduced from Central Asia before 200 BC. But wine would have been only for the ruling elite's pleasure (Huang 2000, pp. 240–46; McGovern 2003, 2009). There have been commercial wineries in China since the end of the nineteenth century (Li 2015), but significant production got under way only in the 1990s. It took until June 2004 before a regulation was introduced in China to define wine as being made

the world's fifth-largest producer of grape wine (hereafter called just wine), up from fifteenth as recently as 2001.[3] Winegrape vineyards in a few other Asian countries are beginning to be developed too, making this one of the last frontiers for wine globalization. But because that supply expansion has not been able to keep up with growth in domestic demand, wine imports into Asia have surged this century. As a result, the region has become a major focus for all wine-exporting countries seeking new markets.

Asia has attracted the attention of wine exporters not only because of the volume growth in sales but also because – unusually for middle-income countries – those sales include high-quality wines. The average current US dollar price of Asia's wine imports grew at 7 percent per year between 2000 and 2009, compared with only 5.5 percent in the rest of the world. By 2014, Asia's average import price was nearly double the world average, and more than four times higher in the case of Hong Kong and Singapore. Even the unit values of imports of both still bottled and sparkling wines by China were above the global average in 2009 (Anderson and Nelgen 2011). Meanwhile, shortly after removing its tariff on wine imports in February 2008, Hong Kong became the world's most important market for ultrapremium and iconic wines.

This chapter reviews developments in Asia's wine production, consumption, and trade over the past half-century, before which its share of global wine imports was less than 1 percent. It also speculates on prospective developments in Asia over the next decade. It then briefly reviews the wine markets of other wine-importing developing countries before concluding that China is set to continue to be by far the most dominant player in Asia, and to change global markets for wines dramatically, just as it has been doing and will continue to do for so many other products.

only from fresh grapes or grape juice. For developments in East Asian wine markets in the 1990s, see Findlay et al. (2004).

3 China is also the world's largest producer of table grapes. Its total vineyard area surpassed that of France in 2014, at 799,000 ha compared with France's 792,000, making it second only to Spain's 1.02 million ha (OIV 2015). Care is needed with wine production data for China, not least because much of the "domestic" wine sold is a blend of Chinese and imported bulk wine and so overstates the production from Chinese grapes (Anderson and Harada 2017). That is why the Chinese production data in Anderson and Pinilla (2017) are somewhat lower than the Food and Agriculture Organization (FAO) and International Office of Vine and Wine (OIV) data, particularly in decades prior to the present one.

ASIA'S GRAPE AND WINE PRODUCTION

There are plenty of reasons for not expecting much winegrape production in most Asian countries.[4] They include the fact that there is almost no tradition of wine consumption domestically; most people's incomes until very recently have been too low for wine to be a priority; there are very few regions with suitable terroir, especially where it is not hot and/or humid; and in most of the many Islamic Asian communities, their religion frowns on alcohol.[5] It is thus not surprising that the only Asian countries with a significant area of grapevines (of which only a small fraction is used in winemaking) are in parts of Northeast Asia. About 1 percent of South Korea's small total area under crops has been devoted to vines over the past two decades, and no more than 0.5 percent of Japan's and Taiwan's since the 1970s, with little change over those periods and even smaller areas in earlier periods. Nor is it surprising that Asia's share of world winegrape and wine production had almost always been below 1 percent prior to 2000.

However, the share of total crop area under bearing vines in China has been growing rapidly since the turn of the century. By 2014, it was 0.6 percent, five times the share in the 1990s, and it may rise higher later this decade as new plantings come into production. That vine share in China's total crop area will soon be twice as high as Japan's and Taiwan's, and approaching South Korea's 1 percent. The only other Asian country with significant plantings of grapes is India, but there the share of cropland under vines (including for table grapes) has always been less than 0.1 percent. Even so, since these shares of total crop area are very low, they suggest there is scope for substantially more winegrape vineyard expansion in Asia without encroaching very much on land used for food production – bearing in mind also that quality winegrapes grow better on poor slopes than on the fertile flat land most desired for broadacre food crops.[6]

China has been open to foreign direct investment in vineyards and wineries since the economy's opening up after 1978, and has also welcomed flying vignerons as consultants. It even seems to have found ways to provide

4 The data in the next sections draw directly from Anderson and Nelgen (2011) and Anderson and Pinilla (2017).

5 Islamic Asian countries include Afghanistan, Azerbaijan, Bangladesh, Indonesia, Kazakhstan, Kyrgyzstan, Malaysia, Pakistan, Tajikistan, Turkmenistan, and Uzbekistan.

6 Australia has had only 0.7 percent of its crop area under vines in recent years. By contrast, shares in 2013 are as high as 4 percent in France, 5 to 6 percent in Spain and New Zealand, 8 percent in Italy, and 10 to 12 percent in Portugal.

adequate property rights for vineyard investors, notwithstanding the fact that farm land cannot be privately owned in China.

China's winegrape vineyards – which comprise only a small share of its total vineyard area –are heavily focusing on red varieties (considered by Chinese people to be best for their health), especially ones originating in France. In 2010, 96 percent of China's winegrape bearing area was planted to red varieties, of which 76 percent was accounted for by Cabernet Sauvignon, 12 percent Merlot, and 5 percent Carmenere, while Chardonnay dominates the area of white winegrapes (Anderson 2013, table 32).

Shandong is the province in China that markets the largest volume of wine, followed by neighboring Jilin, Henan, Hebei, and Tianjin provinces. Together those five provinces produce four-fifths of China's wine (Li and Bardají 2016). However, much of that wine is based on concentrated grape juice or bulk wine from Xinjiang or foreign countries, supplementing local fruit.[7] The coastal provinces of Shandong, Hebei, and Tianjin, in the latitude range 36°-40° North, benefit from sea breezes that moderate humidity levels. Their average temperatures range from lows of –5°C in the winter in the north to highs of 26°C in the summer in the south of this region. Summer and autumn can be humid, though, and monsoons, typhoons, hail, and floods cause occasional havoc. Vineyards tended to be established on flat fertile land to encourage high yields, resulting in poor-quality fruit (Li 2015).

Also well known in international wine circles are the provinces of Xinjiang in the far west (where there is so little rainfall that irrigation from snowmelt is necessary but vine pests and diseases are minimal) and Ningxia in the central north (where temperatures are between those of Xinjiang and the coast but it is still so cold in winter that vines need to be buried shortly after harvest). Other provinces that are expanding their wine production rapidly include Heilongjiang in the far northeast, Shaanxi in the center, and

[7] Domestic wine produced in one region of China is sometimes blended with wine produced in and packaged for final sale from another region, but the first region's production is double-counted because both regions report it as part of their region's and hence national wine output. Unfortunately, there are no data available to ascertain the extent to which this exaggerates the country's wine production statistics. Following Anderson and Harada (2017), imported bulk wine is assumed by Anderson and Pinilla (2017) to be blended with wine from local grapes and recorded as national wine production and so is subtracted from the official output statistics. This also avoids overstating the volume of apparent wine consumption in China which is estimated as domestic production plus net imports. It lowers official annual production (and apparent consumption) by between zero and 18 (13) percent, and on average by 10.2 (7.8) percent, over the period 1995 to 2016.

Yunnan in the south (where premium winegrapes are being produced by Louis Vuitton Moët Hennessy (LVMH) at altitudes between 2200 and 2600 meters so as to be cool enough in that subtropical latitude).

Apart from Ningxia and Yunnan, the vineyard areas of China's wineries are each often many hundreds of hectares. Even though there are more than 100 wineries in China, the top five account for more than 60 percent of China's wine production – not unlike in the wine-exporting countries of the Southern Hemisphere.

China's bearing area of vines is now five times that of the rest of Asia combined, having been roughly the same as the rest of Asia's in the mid-1980s. But because a large share of grape production (around four-fifths) is for fresh consumption in China, the global share of wine production has grown less rapidly and is much lower than China's global vine area share (Figure 17.1(a)). Wine production in China peaked in 2012 before being discouraged by government austerity measures, such that during 2013–16 it averaged no more than in 2011 and was one-sixth below the record 2012 year. In the rest of Asia, the global share of wine production is tiny: almost none of its grapes are used for wine production (Figure 17.1(b)).

ASIA'S WINE IMPORTS

Asia's share of global wine imports almost never exceeded 1 percent in either volume or value terms prior to 1970, and those shares were barely 2 percent by 1980 (Figure 17.1). For China, the import volume and value shares grew steadily over the decade to 2006, catalyzed by Premier Li Peng affirming in 1997 the health virtues of red wine. But then those shares accelerated once China began importing more ultrapremium wines for gift giving and banqueting. A love affair with Bordeaux wines in particular led to a documentary film (*Red Obsession*, directed by Warwick Ross) and a spate of books on the phenomenon (e.g., Mustacich 2015). However, at the end of 2012 the government imposed austerity and anticorruption measures that caused the import shares to decline a little, before returning to growth thereafter.

Meanwhile, for the rest of Asia, the share of the value of global wine imports has been more than twice the global import volume share (Figure 17.1(b)). This reflects the fact that throughout the past half-century, Asia's wine imports have been relatively high quality. The average price of Japan's wine imports was around twice the global average from the 1970s to the first decade of this century, and in recent years it has been even higher.

For China the average price of its wine imports was more than twice the global average until the mid-1990s. It then fell to half the global average until 2006, when it began rising again to slightly above the global average by 2011.

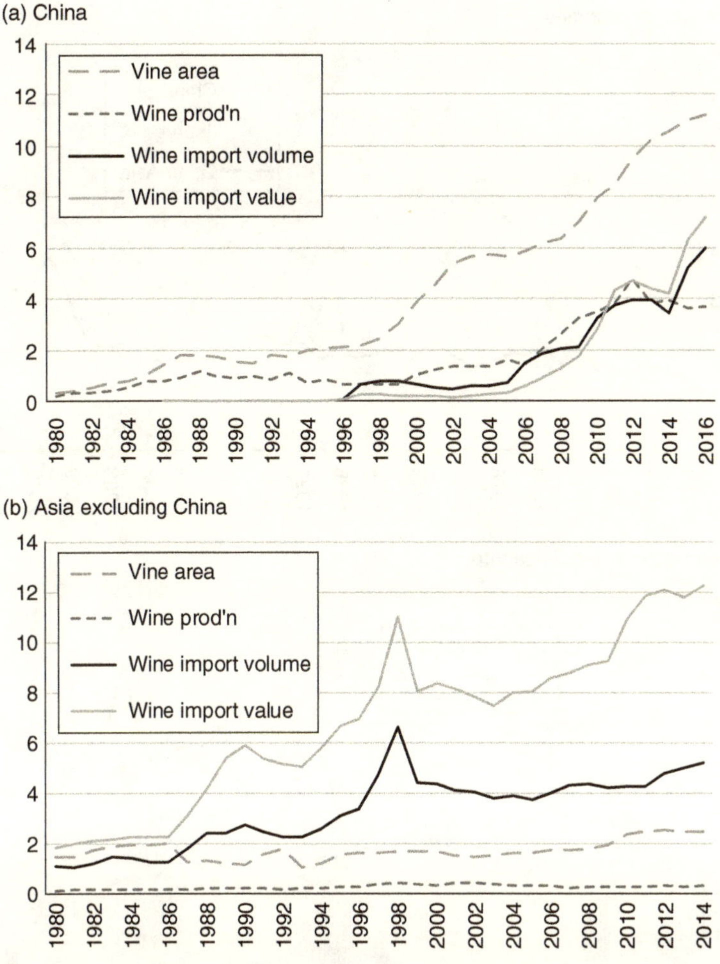

Figure 17.1 Shares of China and other Asian countries in global vine bearing area, wine production volume, and the volume and value of wine imports, 1980 to 2016 (%).
Source: Anderson and Pinilla (2017).

As for other Asian countries, their average import price also hovered around twice the world average from the 1960s until a decade ago, and then it shot up (Figure 17.2(a)). The latter rise coincides with the removal of wine import tariffs in Hong Kong, which suddenly made it one of the fine-wine capitals of the world. The quality of wine imports of equally affluent Singapore rose two decades earlier (Figure 17.2(b)).

Since the 1990s, China has imported a lot of low-priced wine in bulk (whereas most imports by the rest of Asia are in bottle), which it would

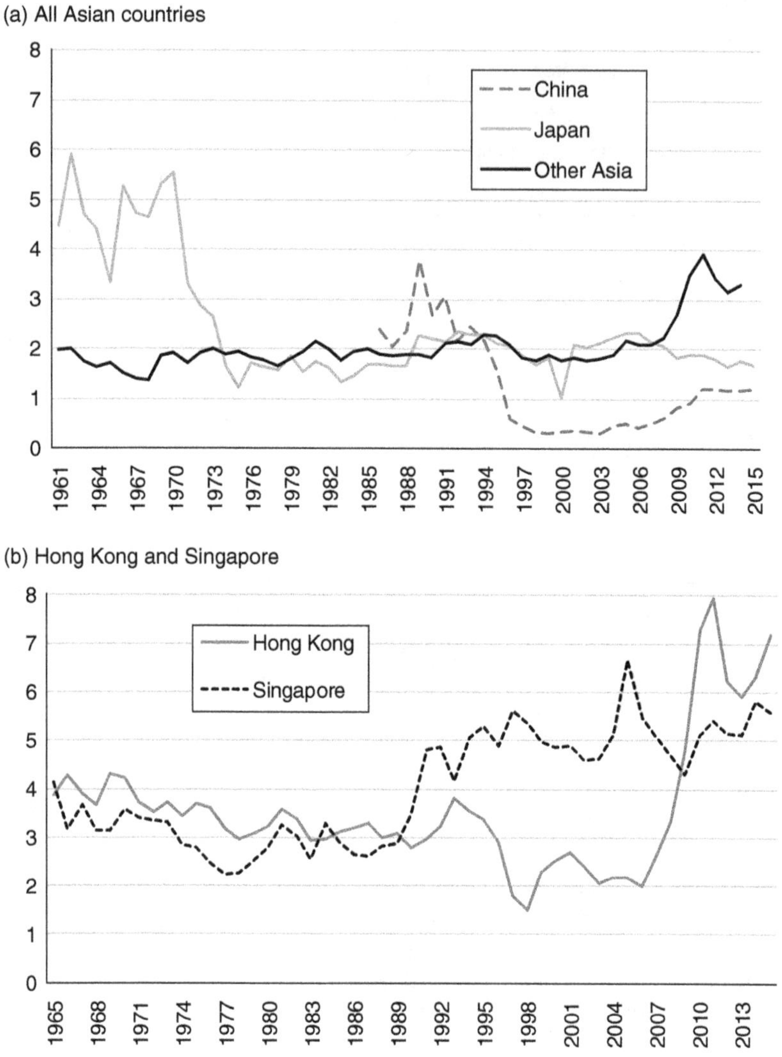

Figure 17.2 Average price of wine imports in Asia relative to the global average price, 1961 to 2015 (world = 1).
Source: Anderson and Pinilla (2017).

often blend with wine made from Chinese grapes. This was legally possible because national labeling laws, at least up until new regulations came into effect in 2005, were such that a bottle marked "Product of China" was not required to be all local content.[8]

[8] Japan has a similar practice, with bulk wine accounting for one-fifth if its total wine import volume over the past three decades. Japan in addition imports grape juice concentrate

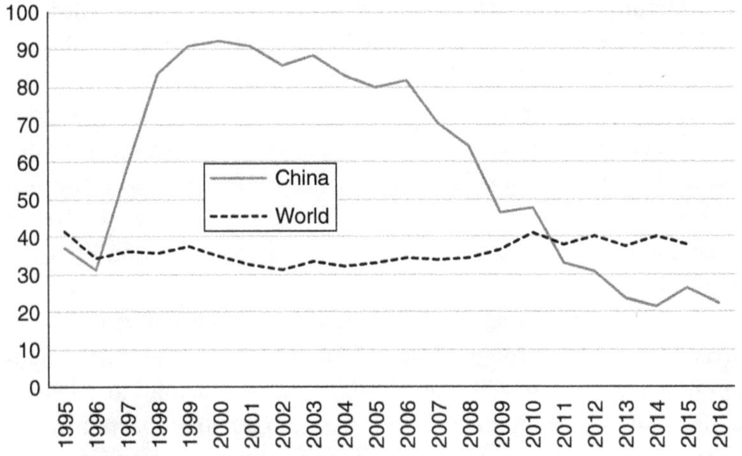

Figure 17.3 Share of bulk wine in the volume of wine imports of China and the world, 1995 to 2016 (%).
Source: Author's derivation from UN COMTRADE data.

Prior to 2008, the average price of China's bulk imports was between 60 and 70 US cents per litre. Low as that price is, the quality of those imports may still have been above that of the local product with which it was being blended. However, between then and 2012 the bulk wine import unit value doubled, as the quality of their locally produced wine rose and domestic wineries sought to raise the quality of their (blended) product. Meanwhile, the proportion of total wine imports by China arriving in bulk containers has fallen from more than 84 percent in the decade to 2006 to less than 25 percent in recent years. That contrasts greatly with the trend elsewhere in the world, where bulk wine accounted for less than 20 percent of wine import volumes between 1995 and 2005 but then grew to 40 percent (Figure 17.3). However, the annual *volume* of China's bulk wine imports remained roughly the same between 2006 and 2014, at a little over 90 ML; but then in 2015 and 2016 it was over 140 ML. China's total wine imports grew by more than one-third in 2015 and by a further one-sixth in 2016, in both volume and value terms.

(equal to between 5 and 10 percent of the value of wine imports by Japan), from which wines are produced by adding sugar and yeast. They may then be blended with domestically produced wine without having to declare on the bottle's front label that the product is of mixed origin. Thus Japan's self-sufficiency in wine (official production divided by that plus net imports of wine) overstates considerably the extent to which the country satisfies domestic wine demand with product made from local grapes (Anderson and Harada 2017).

The volatility in the quality of wine imported by China is reflected also in rapidly changing shares of various countries in China's volume and value of wine imports. Nonetheless, just six wine-exporting countries have dominated that trade over the past decade. France has been ranked first in both value and volume terms, Australia is second in value terms but equal third with Spain in volume terms, and Chile is ranked third in value terms but second in volume terms. The other two exporting countries, Italy and the United States, have considerably smaller shares than the top four (Table 17.1(a)).

The importance of each of those wine-exporting countries in global exports also varies through time, which contributes to their changing shares in China's imports. To net out that effect, it is helpful to calculate the trade intensity index, defined as the share of China's imports from wine-exporting country i divided by country i's share of global wine exports. Those ratios, reported in Table 17.1(b), reveal that while France has had an above-average intensity of trade with China (index > 1), the most intense relationship in value terms is with Australia and in volume terms is with Chile. The United States' index is close to 1, Spain's is between one-half and three-quarters, but Italy (and the rest-of-the-world group) have trade intensity indexes well below one-half.

ASIA'S WINE CONSUMPTION

It took until the mid-1980s before Asia's share of global wine consumption exceeded 1 percent. In fact, there are only five Asian countries plus Hong Kong and Taiwan where per capita grape wine consumption has exceeded 0.1 litres per year.[9] In each of those seven economies, the level in 2016 was well above that of 2000, and for Asia as a whole it more than trebled over those seventeen years, to 0.6 litres (Figure 17.4).

China overwhelmingly dominates Asia's increase in aggregate wine consumption (Figure 17.5). China accounted for barely half of Asia's wine consumption in 2000, but by 2016 it accounted for three-quarters. Equally populous India, by contrast, had a wine market that is less than one-sixtieth

[9] Hong Kong's apparent wine consumption volume, estimated as simply imports minus exports, is exaggerated to the extent that some of its imports are smuggled into China. If such unrecorded re-exports to the mainland are assumed to be 50 percent of Hong Kong's total recorded re-exports of wine, it would make little difference to estimated consumption in China but would lower estimated wine consumption per capita in Hong Kong from 4.7 to 2.9 litres during 2014 to 2016 (Anderson and Harada 2017).

Table 17.1 *Sources of China's wine imports and index of trade intensity,*[a] *by value and volume, 2008 to 2015*[b]

	Value			Volume		
	2008–10	2011–13	2015	2008–10	2011–13	2015
(a) China import shares (%)						
France	43	49	46	23	36	31
Australia	18	15	23	17	11	13
Chile	12	9	11	27	17	28
Spain	5	7	6	10	17	14
Italy	6	6	5	6	8	5
United States	5	5	3	5	4	2
Others	10	9	7	12	8	7
Total	100	100	100	100	100	100
(b) Index of trade intensity						
France	1.45	1.61	1.55	1.20	2.40	2.29
Australia	3.05	2.56	3.59	2.09	1.62	1.79
Chile	2.16	1.69	1.91	3.64	2.26	3.31
Spain	0.67	0.73	0.65	0.58	0.74	0.59
Italy	0.25	0.53	0.25	0.28	0.37	0.26
United States	0.72	1.05	0.51	1.11	1.02	0.54
Others	0.28	0.28	0.28	0.56	0.34	0.29
Total	1.00	1.00	1.00	1.00	1.00	1.00

[a] The intensity of trade index is defined as the share of China's imports from country i divided by country i's share of global exports.

[b] 2015 data refer to the twelve months to March 2016.

Source: Author's calculations based on data from Euromonitor International (2015) and Wine Australia (2016).

the size of China's in 2015, notwithstanding its double-digit growth during the past decade. China's share of global wine consumption has risen from less than 2 percent prior to the 2005 to 7 percent since 2013. As of 2015, it was ranked fifth in the world and only a percentage point behind fourth-ranked Germany.

During the first decade of this century, wine doubled its share of Asia's recorded consumption of alcohol, but that brought it to just 3 percent, or only one-fifth of wine's global share of recorded alcohol consumption. Only in seven Asian economies is wine's share of total alcohol consumption above the Asian average (Figure 17.6). Meanwhile, the share of wine in *global* alcohol consumption halved between 1970 and 2014. These two opposite trends together mean Asia is converging on the global average alcohol mix (as are

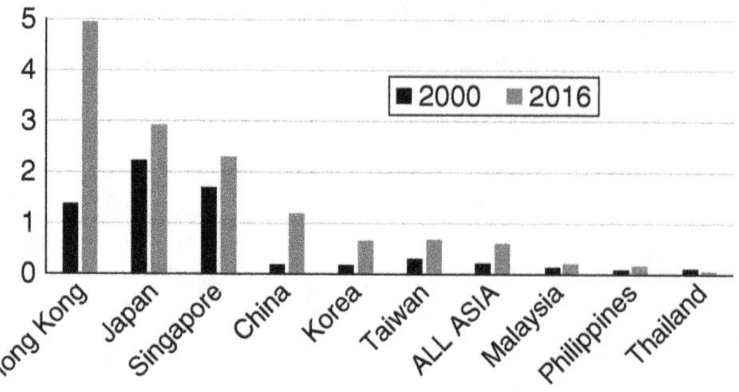

Figure 17.4 Per capita consumption of grape wine in Asia,[a] 2000 and 2016 (litres).
[a] Each of the other Asian countries consumes less than 0.15 litres per capita per year.
Source: Anderson and Pinilla (2017).

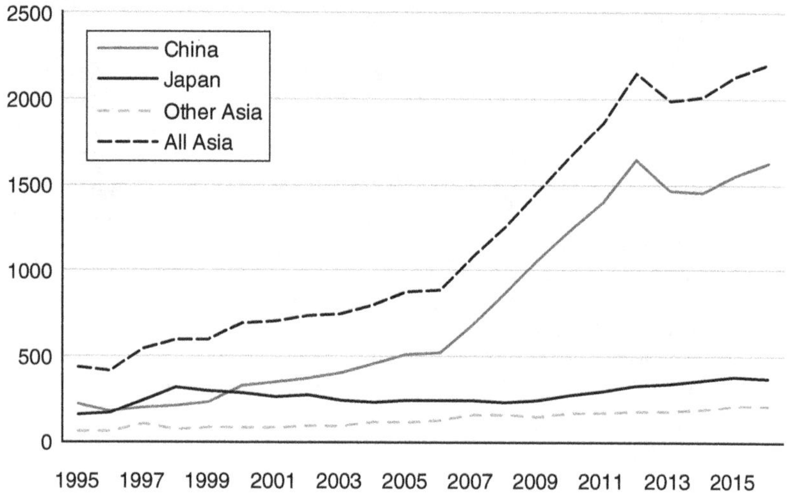

Figure 17.5 Total consumption of grape wine in Asia, 1995 to 2016 (ML).
Source: Anderson and Pinilla (2017).

numerous other regions – see Aizenman and Brooks 2008; Holmes and Anderson 2017). However, the region's consumers are still mainly focused on spirits, except in Malaysia and Singapore, where beer is the main focus (Table 17.2).[10] Only Hong Kong has wine as its strongest preference, reflecting that economy's zero tax on wine imports and high per capita income.

[10] The spirits category includes rice "wine," which is made in many Asian countries but each under a different name (sake in Japan, mijiu in China, cheongju in Korea, etc.). Even

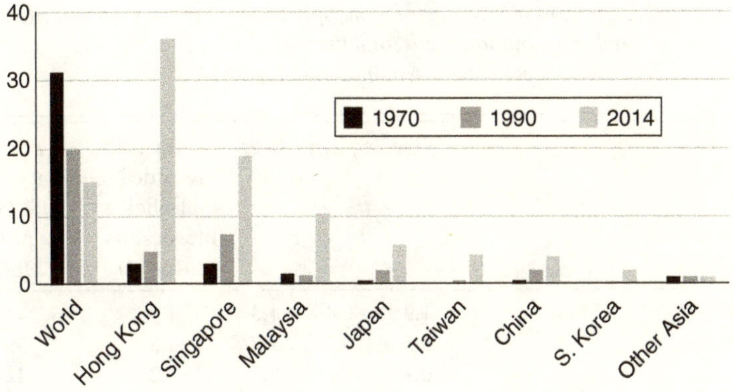

Figure 17.6 Wine's share of national alcohol consumption, selected Asian economies[a] and the world, 1970, 1990, and 2014 (%).

[a] For all countries in "Other Asia," wine's share of alcohol consumption is less than 3 percent.

Source: Anderson and Pinilla (2017).

This means that, despite the recent rapid growth in wine consumption in Asia, the potential for further expansion in sales there remains enormous, given the current very low level of per capita consumption and low share of wine in total alcohol purchases. The rapid aging, educating, and international traveling of the populations in Asia's emerging economies also lend themselves to a continuing expansion of demand for wine there.[11]

Since no Asian country has yet produced grape wine for export in noticeable quantities, its self-sufficiency in wine is reflected in the share of imports in its consumption. In 2014–15, that varied from around 30 percent in China (or as much as 50 percent according to Anderson and Harada 2017) to around 80 percent in Japan, more than 95 percent in South Korea, and virtually 100 percent in all other Asian countries. Given China's

though rice wine is fermented, it is brewed differently than beer, it looks like a clear spirit, and it is typically at least 15 percent alcohol compared with less than 5 percent for beer and 12 to 13 percent for grape wine. In Japan, during 2010–14, consumers got about twice as much of their alcohol from sake as from (grape) wine. The average retail price of sake in Japan in 2010 was US$22 per litre, compared with an average of $6 for rice wine in China, although some sell as cheaply as $1 a litre for use in Chinese cooking.

[11] True, the Chinese government's austerity and anticorruption drive in 2013–16 discouraged consumption of expensive wines and other luxuries, but that influence has been much less on lower-quality wines, which in China are by far the most voluminous. Fluctuating tolerance for excessive alcohol consumption is an abiding theme in China's history (Sterckx 2015).

Table 17.2 *Indexes of intensity of wine, spirits, and beer in total recorded alcohol consumption,[a] and total litres of alcohol consumption per capita, Asian economies, 2014*

	Wine	Spirits	Beer	Total recorded alcohol (litres/capita, 2010–14)	Per capita income (US$'000, Atlas method, 2014)
Hong Kong	1.9	0.4	1.3	1.9	40
Singapore	0.9	0.3	1.7	1.5	55
Japan	0.4	1.7	0.5	5.2	42
China	0.3	1.1	1.1	3.1	7
Malaysia	0.3	0.5	1.7	0.4	11
Korea	0.2	2.3	0.1	2.9	27
Taiwan	0.2	1.3	1.0	2.1	30
India	0.0	2.1	0.3	0.9	2
Thailand	0.0	1.8	0.6	5.1	6
Philippines	0.0	1.8	0.6	3.2	4
Other Asia	0.2	2.0	0.3	0.2	na
All Asia	***0.2***	***1.4***	***0.9***	***1.8***	***6***
World	**1.0**	**1.0**	**1.0**	**2.6**	**11**
Memo (% of all alcohol consm)					
All Asia	4	60	36		
World	16	43	41		

[a] This index of intensity is defined as the share of a particular beverage in overall alcohol consumption of an economy relative to that share for the world. Alcohol content varies across countries and over time, but their averages are 12 percent for wine, 40 percent for spirits, and 4.5 percent for beer.

Source: Holmes and Anderson (2017) and World Bank (2016).

dominance in Asian imports (Figure 17.7), that share has averaged around two-fifths for Asia as a whole since the turn of the century.

Notwithstanding China's dominance as an Asian wine importer, exporters are careful not to diminish the significance of some other Asian countries as importers of high-quality wine. As seen in Figure 17.2, and reflected in Figure 17.7 showing the shares of those countries in the *value* of world imports now far exceeding their *volume* shares, the average prices of other East Asian wine imports are well above that of most other countries. For producers of superpremium wine exports, these other East Asian markets are therefore important and potentially very profitable.

Asian wine imports would be considerably larger if import tariffs and excise taxes on wine were less. In numerous Asian countries, they exceed

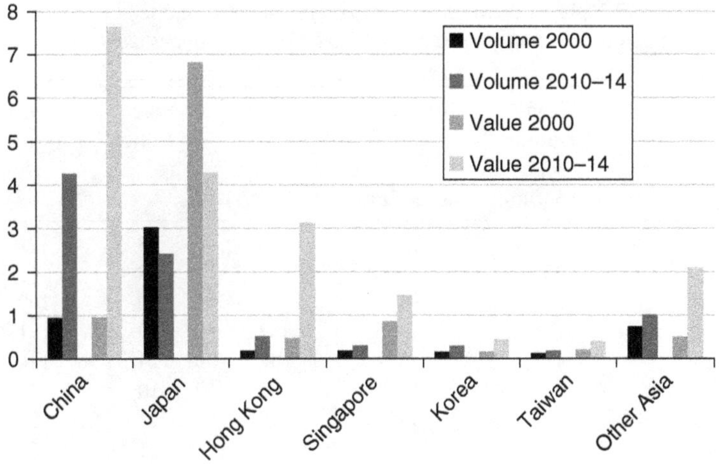

Figure 17.7 Shares in the volume and value of global wine imports, Asia, 2000 and 2010–14 (%).
Source: Anderson and Pinilla (2017).

those for beer and spirits on a per-litre-of-alcohol basis (Table 17.3). China's reduction in its wine import tariffs when it joined the World Trade Organization at the end of 2001, from 65 percent to 20 percent for bulk wine and to 14 percent for bottled wines, contributed to its surge in imports over the past dozen years (Figure 17.1(a)). The decision by Hong Kong to eliminate its tariff on wine imports in early 2008 is partly why its imports in Figure 17.2(b) are so much higher by the end than the beginning of the previous decade. And the recent implementation of bilateral free-trade agreements between Japan, South Korea, and China on the one hand, and Australia, Chile, and New Zealand on the other, is bringing tariffs on Northeast Asia's wine imports from those three wine-exporting countries down to zero.

SUMMARY OF ASIAN WINE MARKET DEVELOPMENTS SINCE THE 1960S

The long-run trends in the preceding features of Asian wine (and other alcohol) markets are summarized in Table 17.4. From the left half of that table, it is clear that Asia was a very minor player in global wine markets prior to the 1990s; and it is equally clear from the right half of the table that its importance has grown dramatically over the past quarter-century. Asia has also grown its shares of global beer and spirits consumption, albeit at

Table 17.3 *Ad valorem consumer tax equivalent[a] of excise plus import taxes on alcoholic beverages, selected Asian economies, 2008 (%)*

	Non premium wine ($2.50/litre)	Commercial premium wine ($7.50/litre)	Super premium wine ($20/litre)	Beer ($2/litre)	Spirits ($15/litre)
China	32	25	25	18	21
Japan	32	11	4	0	12
Hong Kong	0	0	0	0	100
India	165	155	152	100	151
Korea	46	46	46	124	114
Philippines	22	12	9	10	35
Taiwan	23	14	12	2	23
Thailand	232	117	81	51	52
Vietnam	88	88	88	96	115

[a] At the prices shown in the column headings (expressed in US dollars), excluding value-added taxes (VAT)/goods and services taxes (GST). Vietnam rates refer to 2012.

Source: Anderson (2010), expanded to include China and Vietnam.

Table 17.4 *Summary of Asian wine market developments since the 1960s*

Annual average of:	1960s	1970s	1980s	1990s	2000s	2010–14
Wine consumption (ML)	41	81	302	500	941	2034
% of global wine consumption	0.2	0.3	1.2	2.3	4.0	8.3
% of global beer consumption	5	6	10	19	25	32
% of global spirits consumption	22	28	39	43	46	54
Per capita wine consumption (L)	0.0	0.0	0.1	0.2	0.3	0.6
Alc. consumption per cap. (LAL)[a]	0.5	0.7	1.0	1.2	1.4	1.8
Asian/world alc. consumption/cap	0.2	0.3	0.4	0.5	0.6	0.7
Wine % total alcohol consumption	0.7	0.7	1.3	1.5	2.2	3.5
Beer % total alcohol consumption	16	16	18	28	35	37
Spirit % total alcohol consumption	83	83	80	70	63	60
Wine imports (ML)	12	33	71	190	380	840
% world wine import volume	0.5	0.8	1.6	3.7	5.2	8.4
Wine imports (US$m)	6	40	164	791	1943	5317
% world wine import value	0.9	1.5	2.8	7.2	9.2	16.1
Price of wine imports (US$/L)	0.49	1.20	2.31	4.16	5.12	6.33
Asian/world wine import price	1.9	2.0	1.9	2.0	1.8	1.9

[a] Recorded litres of alcohol consumption/capita (LAL, excluding home-brewed or -distilled alcohol.).

Source: Anderson and Pinilla (2017).

a slower pace than wine but from a much larger base: it now accounts for one-third of global sales of beer (up from one-twentieth in the 1960s) and half the world's spirits sales (up from one-fifth in the 1960s).

How much the region's importance in wine consumption might rise, and how much China's wine production might expand to satisfy at least some of the demand increase, is not easy to predict. Wine production in Asia outside China is expected to remain very small, but in China there is scope to divert to wineries some of the current four-fifths of grapes sold fresh or dried, and to convert other cropland to vineyards.

As for consumption, it is insightful to compare changes in Asian economies with changes in wine consumption per capita since 1960 in non–wine-producing countries of Northwest Europe as their real incomes rose. Figure 17.8 reveals that while both regions exhibit a positive relationship between real GDP and wine consumption, the slope of the trend is much steeper in Europe than Asia and the levels are now far greater. That suggests there is a great deal of scope yet for belated wine consumption growth in Asia.

Figure 17.9 also is instructive. It shows that while all types of alcohol have increased in China, since the 1980s recorded per capita consumption of beer has increased 1,000 percent but wine has risen "only" 600 percent. China's share of its alcohol consumption from beer has converged upward from well below to one-tenth above the global average, and that from spirits has converged downward from nearly three times to just one-seventh above the global average share. However, the share of China's alcohol consumption from wine has converged from almost zero but to only one-third of the global average share. This adds support to the suggestion that the scope for further growth in sales of wine in China is still enormous.

One way to encapsulate that convergence in Asia's alcohol mix toward the global average is to adapt an index developed by Anderson (2014) to capture the varietal similarity of various winegrape regions in the world. When so adapted, the index of similarity of a nation's alcoholic beverage mix ranges between zero and one, and is closer to one the more similar is a country's beverage mix to the mix (which is changing over time) in the world as a whole.[12] Those indexes for key Asian countries, reported in

[12] Define the index of similarity of a nation's alcoholic beverage mix as:

$$(1) \quad \omega_{ij} = \frac{\sum_{m=1}^{M} f_{im} f_{jm}}{\left(\sum_{m=1}^{M} f_{im}^2\right)^{1/2} \left(\sum_{m=1}^{M} f_{jm}^2\right)^{1/2}},$$

where f_{im} is the share of beverage m as a proportion of the total alcohol consumption in country i such that these proportions fall between zero and one and sum to one (i.e., there is

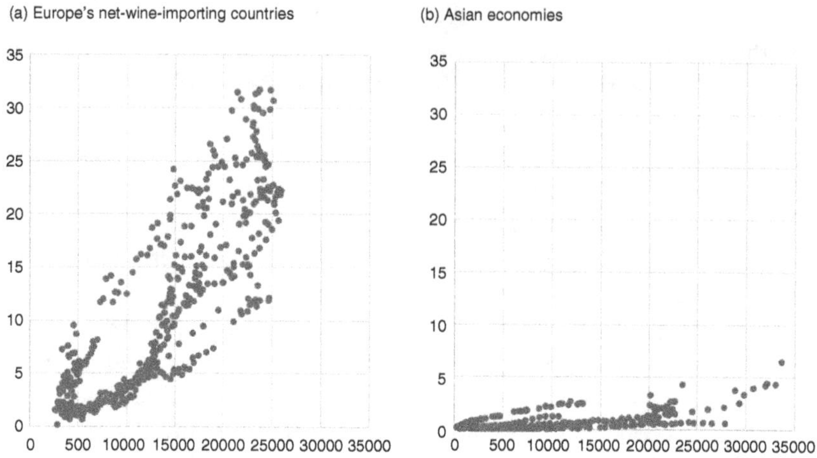

Figure 17.8 Relationship between real GDP per capita (horizontal axis in 1990 US dollars) and wine consumption per capita (vertical axis in litres), 1961 to 2014.
Source: Derived from data in Anderson and Pinilla (2017).

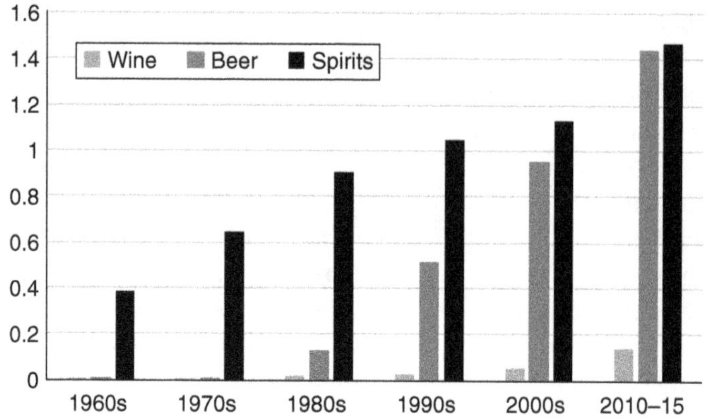

Figure 17.9 Per capita (recorded) consumption of alcohol by type, China, 1960 to 2015 (litres of alcohol per year).
Source: Anderson and Pinilla (2017).

a total of $M = 3$ different beverages, and $0 \leq f_{im} \leq 1$ and $\Sigma_m f_{im} = 1$), and j is the average shares of those beverages in world alcohol consumption. The numerator of equation (1) will be larger the more similar is country *i*'s beverage mix to that of the world as a whole. The denominator normalizes the measure to be unity when the national and global mixes are identical. That is, ω_{ij} will be one for a country with an identical mix to the world average.

Table 17.5 *Indexes of similarity of alcohol consumption mix,[a] Asian economies relative to the world average, 1960 to 2014*

	1960s	1970s	1980s	1990s	2000s	2010–14
China	0.64	0.68	0.77	0.91	0.96	0.98
Hong Kong	0.82	0.88	0.85	0.93	0.96	0.88
India	0.64	0.68	0.70	0.71	0.75	0.78
Japan	0.81	0.87	0.92	0.96	0.93	0.87
Korea	0.77	0.77	0.76	0.76	0.73	0.70
Malaysia	0.76	0.77	0.79	0.79	0.82	0.87
Philippines	0.80	0.85	0.87	0.85	0.88	0.86
Singapore	0.75	0.86	0.92	0.90	0.85	0.85
Taiwan	0.68	0.82	0.91	0.95	0.97	0.97
Thailand	0.66	0.69	0.71	0.78	0.87	0.86
Other Asia	0.67	0.71	0.73	0.77	0.78	0.77

[a] See footnote 12 for definition of index of similarity.

Source: Holmes and Anderson (2017), based on data in Anderson and Pinilla (2017).

Table 17.5, suggest that China has changed most and converged closest to the global beverage mix, and Japan and Korea (where rice "wine" and other spirits are dominant) have converged least over the past half-century.

Why is wine's consumption still so relatively low in China and elsewhere in Asia other than Hong Kong, both in absolute terms and as a share of total alcohol consumption? The taxes shown in Table 17.3 may be part of the explanation. The large reduction in China's wine import tariffs in 2002 and the removal of such tariffs in Hong Kong in 2008 certainly would have boosted China's wine consumption. In Japan and South Korea, rice "wine" matches their food well, so there is less desire to switch to grape wine. Another explanation is per capita income. Although there is no obvious association across the economies listed in Table 17.2 between income per capita and *total* alcohol consumption in 2010–14, income is reasonably positively associated with wine's share of total alcohol consumption. More strikingly, when looking over time, the middle rows of Table 17.4 show that, for Asia as a whole, recorded alcohol consumption per capita has increased substantially since the 1960s (from 0.5 to 1.8 litres, and from 0.2 to 0.7 times the global average).[13] Once consumer price indexes and expenditure data

[13] Part of that growth may have been a replacement of unrecorded alcohol consumption (home-brewed or -distilled products). Even during 2000–2010, the World Health Organization (WHO) estimates suggest that recorded alcohol consumption may be only two-thirds of total (recorded plus estimated unrecorded) consumption of alcohol in China (Holmes and Anderson 2017).

become available for each beverage type for Asian countries, it will be possible to test the importance of these hypotheses, as Holmes and Anderson (2017) have done for more advanced economies.

WINE MARKETS OF NON-ASIAN WINE-IMPORTING DEVELOPING COUNTRIES

Over the past 150 years, the wine markets in wine-importing countries of Latin America, Africa, and the Middle East (that is, all those developing countries not examined in this chapter or in earlier chapters in this volume) have been minor, and they have been growing only slowly during the past half-century. Certainly a few of them (e.g., Turkey) have a sizable area of vineyards, but their grapes are used mainly for eating rather than for wine. In aggregate, this set of countries – which is home to 25 percent of the world's population – accounted in 1961–64 for just 1 percent of the world's wine production and 2 percent of its consumption (and 5 percent of total recorded alcohol consumption); and by 2010–14, those shares had barely doubled (Table 17.6). They did have a larger share of global wine imports (5 percent in 1961–64), but that had fallen by about one-third by 2010–14 as past colonial influences faded.

WHAT LIES AHEAD?

This question was addressed by Anderson and Wittwer (2015), drawing on their model of global wine markets that was calibrated initially to 2009, based on the comprehensive volume and value data and trade and excise tax data provided in Anderson and Nelgen (2011, sections V– VII). They assume there would be a considerable swing toward consumption of all wine types in China, as the number of middle class in China (currently more than 250 million) is growing at perhaps 10 million per year (Kharas 2010; Barton, Chen, and Jin 2013; Lin, Wan, and Morgan 2016). With grape wine still accounting for less than 4 percent of alcohol consumption by China's 1.1 billion adults, Anderson and Wittwer (2015) argue it is not unreasonable to expect large increases in volumes of wine demanded. As for the rest of the world, they assume the long trend preference swing away from nonpremium to premium wines will continue. That study also assumes China's grape and wine industry capital and total factor productivity will grow faster in China than elsewhere, but not enough to prevent wine imports from continuing to grow rapidly. Almost half of that projected increase in imports is expected to come from France, much of it sparkling from Champagne.

Table 17.6 *Shares of wine-importing countries of Latin America, Africa, and the Middle East in global wine markets, 1961–64 and 2010–14 (%)*

	Vine area	Wine production	Wine import volume	Wine import value	Volume of wine consumption	Volume of alcohol consumption
Brazil						
1961–64	0.6	0.5	0.0	0.1	0.7	1.1
2010–14	1.2	1.1	0.8	0.9	1.7	5.7
Other Latin America[a]						
1961–64	0.3	0.4	0.2	0.9	0.5	2.3
2010–14	0.5	0.5	1.4	1.2	1.1	2.6
Turkey						
1961–64	6.8	0.1	0.0	0.0	0.1	0.1
2010–14	6.7	0.1	0.0	0.0	0.2	0.4
Other Africa & Middle East[b]						
1961–64	7.2	0.1	6.7	5.8	0.7	1.4
2010–14	7.5	0.1	3.2	2.3	1.0	2.0
Total of Above						
1961–64	**14.9**	**1.1**	**6.9**	**6.8**	**2.0**	**4.9**
2010–14	**16.2**	**1.7**	**5.4**	**4.4**	**4.0**	**10.7**
Asia						
1961–64	0.3	0.2	0.5	0.9	0.2	12.1
2010–14	12.0	4.7	8.4	16.1	8.3	38.5

[a] Includes all of the Caribbean, Mexico, Central America, and South America other than Argentina and Chile.

[b] Excludes South Africa, Algeria, Morocco, and Tunisia.

Source: Holmes and Anderson (2017).

The next chapter reports an updated set of projections of the world's wine markets by those same authors, for the period to 2025. It assumes more modest growth in real incomes in China than did Anderson and Wittwer (2015). Nonetheless, it notes that even if China's growth in GDP, industrialization, and infrastructure spending were to slow down more, Chinese households nonetheless are being encouraged to lower their extraordinarily high savings rates and consume more of their income. In addition, grape wine is encouraged as an alternative to China's dominant alcoholic beverages of (barley-based) beer and (rice- or sorghum-based) spirits because of its perceived health benefits and because it does not undermine food security by diminishing domestic foodgrain supplies. The roles that China's recently signed bilateral free-trade agreements might play in expanding the country's wine consumption via imports also are examined in the next chapter.

Two pertinent features of wine marketing where China is leading the world are in online shopping and in fine wine packaging. Online shopping is rife in China for consumer goods in general, and it is applying increasingly as well to wine sales – more so than in any other country. Social media also impacts on young consumers' preferences for wine styles and brands. The information and communication technology revolution is thus likely to have a more profound effect on wine consumption in China than elsewhere in coming years. How well wine-exporting countries are able to compete in that space, either directly or via importers/distributors, and how much other countries follow China's lead in online wine shopping and in elaborate packaging of finer wines, remains to be seen.

CONCLUSIONS

China has already become by far the most important wine-consuming country in Asia, and may well become an even more dominant market for wine exporters. Certainly the recent austerity drive and growth slowdown dampened the growth in superpremium and iconic wine sales in China, but because those quality wines are still only a small share of the total sales volume, the austerity drive's impact on China's aggregate wine consumption and import expansion may yet prove to be only minor.

While the recent and projected rates of increase in per capita wine consumption in China may be no faster than what occurred in several northwestern European countries in earlier decades, it is the sheer size of China's adult population of 1.1 billion – and the fact that grape wine still accounts for less than 4 percent of Chinese alcohol consumption – that makes this import growth opportunity unprecedented. It would be somewhat less if China's own winegrape production increases faster, but that is unlikely to be able to reduce the growth in China's wine imports very much this decade, especially at the superpremium end of the spectrum. Indeed, China's production of wine in 2014–16 averaged no higher than 2011 and was one-fifth below the record 2012 level.

Of course, projections are not predictions. Where exchange rates move, and how fast various countries' wine producers take advantage of the projected market growth opportunities in Asia, will be additional key determinants of the actual changes in market shares over the coming years. It remains to be seen whether France can hold onto its dominant position in

China. On the one hand, generic and brand promotion efforts in Asia by other wine-exporting countries are expanding, especially by firms in the New World. Should the European Union (EU) sign a free-trade agreement (FTA) with China, on the other hand, Europe's dominance in the Chinese market may increase even more than projected in the next chapter, possibly at the expense of New World suppliers (as happened to Australia when Chile and New Zealand managed to sign FTAs with China several years earlier).

Not all segments of the global wine industry are projected to benefit from market developments in China, with nonpremium producers in both the Old World and the New World facing falling prices if demand for their product continues to dwindle as expected. But those exporting firms willing to invest sufficiently in building relationships with their Chinese importer/distributor – or in grapegrowing, winemaking, or online retailing as joint venturers within China – may well enjoy long-term benefits from such investments, just as others have been doing and will continue to do in China for so many other products besides wine.

Meanwhile, the superpremium wine market in several other East Asian economies will remain an important and growing area of profitable sales for wine exporters. The three largest Islamic countries in Asia (Bangladesh, Indonesia, and Pakistan), by contrast, are far more remote possibilities. India potentially could be more important sooner, but internal and external trade restrictions and high import and excise taxes on wine have to date confined the growth in sales in that populous country. More likely is growth in wine imports by the fastest-growing economies in other developing country regions that do not frown on or prohibit alcohol consumption.

REFERENCES

Aizenman, J. and B. Brooks (2008), 'Globalization and Taste Convergence: The Cases of Wine and Beer', *Review of International Economics* 16(2): 217–33.

Anderson, K. (2010), 'Excise and Import Taxes on Wine vs Beer and Spirits: An International Comparison', *Economic Papers* 29(2): 215–28, June.

(2013), *Which Winegrape Varieties Are Grown Where? A Global Empirical Picture*, Adelaide: University of Adelaide Press.

(2014), 'Changing Varietal Distinctiveness of the World's Wine Regions: Evidence from a New Global Database', *Journal of Wine Economics* 9(3): 249–72.

Anderson, K. and K. Harada (2017), 'How Much Wine Is *Really* Produced and Consumed in China, Hong Kong and Japan?' Wine Economics Research Centre Working Paper 0517, University of Adelaide, November.

Anderson, K. and S. Nelgen (2011), *Global Wine Markets, 1961 to 2009: A Statistical Compendium*, Adelaide: University of Adelaide Press. Freely accessible as an e-book at www.adelaide.edu.au/press/titles/global-wine and as Excel files at www.adelaide.edu.au/wine-econ/databases/GWM

Anderson, K. and V. Pinilla (with the assistance of A. J. Holmes) (2017), *Annual Database of Global Wine Markets, 1835 to 2016*, Wine Economics Research Centre, University of Adelaide, at www.adelaide.edu.au/wine-econ/databases/global-wine-history

Anderson, K. and A. Strutt (2012), 'The Changing Geography of World Trade: Projections to 2030', *Journal of Asian Economics* 23(4): 303–23, August.

Anderson, K. and G. Wittwer (2015), 'Asia's Evolving Role in Global Wine Markets', *China Economic Review* 35: 1–14, September.

(2018), 'Projecting Global Wine Markets to 2025', ch. 18 in *Wine Globalization: A New Comparative History*, edited by K. Anderson and V. Pinilla, Cambridge and New York: Cambridge University Press.

Barro, R. J. (2016), 'Economic Growth and Convergence, Applied to China', *China and the World* 24(5): 5–19, September–October.

Barton, D., Y. Chen and A. Jin (2013), 'Mapping China's Middle Class', *McKinsey Quarterly*, June. www.mckinsey.com/insights/consumer_and_retail/mapping_chinas_middle_class

Euromonitor International (2015), *Passport: Wine in China*, London: Euromonitor International, May.

Findlay, C. F., R. Farrell, C. Chen and D. Wang (2004), 'East Asia', ch. 15 (pp. 307–26) in *The World's Wine Markets: Globalization at Work*, edited by K. Anderson, Cheltenham UK: Edward Elgar.

Holmes, A. J. and K. Anderson (2017), 'Convergence in National Alcohol Consumption Patterns: New Global Indicators', *Journal of Wine Economics* 12(2): 117–48.

Huang, H. T. (2000), *Biology and Biological Technology, Part 5: Fermentations and Food Science*, Volume 6 in the series of books on Science and Civilization in China, Cambridge and New York: Cambridge University Press.

Kharas, H. (2010), 'The Emerging Middle Class in Developing Countries', Working Paper 285, Organisation for Economic Cooperation and Development (OECD) Development Centre, Paris, January.

Li, D. (2015), 'China', pp. 173–76 in *The Oxford Companion to Wine*, edited by J. Robinson, London and New York: Oxford University Press.

Li, Y and I. Bardají (2016), 'A New Wine Superpower? An Analysis of the Chinese Wine Industry', American Association of Wine Economics (AAWE) Working Paper No. 198, June. www.wine-economics.org/aawe/wp-content/uploads/2016/06/AAWE_WP198.pdf

Lin, J. Y., G. Wan and P. J. Morgan (2016), 'Factors Affecting the Outlook for Medium-Term and Long-Term Growth in China', *China and the World* 24(5): 20–41, September–October.

McGovern, P. (2003), *Ancient Wine: The Search for the Origins of Viticulture*, Princeton, NJ: Princeton University Press.

(2009), *Uncorking the Past: The Quest for Wine, Beer, and Other Alcoholic Beverages*, Berkeley: University of California Press.

Mustacich, S. (2015), *Thirsty Dragon: China's Lust for Bordeaux and the Threat to the World's Best Wines*, New York: Henry Bolt and Co.

OIV (2015), *Le Vignoble Mondial*, Paris: Organisation Internationale de la Vigne et du Vin, May.

Sterckx, R. (2015), 'Alcohol and Historiography in Early China', *Global Food History* 1(1): 13–32.

Wine Australia (2016), *Export Market Guide: China*, Adelaide: Wine Australia, May.

World Bank (2016), *World Development Indicators*, Washington, DC: World Bank.

PART IV

WHAT'S AHEAD

18

Projecting Global Wine Markets to 2025

Kym Anderson and Glyn Wittwer

It is clear from the preceding chapters in this volume that national wine markets throughout the world are no longer independent, thanks to globalization. On the contrary, exposure to other countries' consumption patterns have led to consumer tastes converging to a considerable extent; and falling trade costs and trade policy reforms have enabled producers with a comparative advantage in wine production to become more export-focused, thus putting pressure on less-competitive producers elsewhere. Those developments have contributed to the share of global wine production that is exported (or global wine consumption that is imported) rising from less than 15 percent prior to the 1990s to above 40 percent today. That means both producers and consumers of wine are now much more affected by movements in real exchange rates (RERs), as well as by changes in wine import demands and export supplies that accompany each nation's and global economic growth and business cycles. As noted in the preceding chapter, rapid income growth and a burgeoning middle class in emerging Asian economies, particularly China, are causing Asia's demand for wine to surge. While that in turn has stimulated vineyard expansion and rapid growth in China's own wine production, local output growth has been unable to match domestic demand growth to date. (In fact, China's wine production was one-sixth lower in 2013–2016 than in its record 2012 year.)

In the wake of these rapid developments, anticipating where the world's various wine markets are headed over the next decade or so is difficult. However, a formal model of economic behaviour in those markets can assist in analysing prospective changes in an internally consistent way under various explicit assumptions.

The purpose of this chapter is to use a model of the world's wine markets to project those markets to 2025. We assume there is a continuation of the gradual trend towards premium wine consumption and away from nonpremium wines in high-income countries. Since real exchange rates have played a dominant role in the fortunes of some countries' wine markets in recent years, we consider three alternative paths over the 2014–2025 period for real exchange rates. Since growth in China's imports dominates the change in the trade picture over the next decade, two alternative sets of China economic growth assumptions also are considered, to provide a range of possibilities. And with the United Kingdom planning to exit the European Union (Brexit), we include one possible scenario of its impact on global wine markets.

The chapter begins by outlining our revised model of the world's wine markets (first developed by Wittwer, Berger and Anderson in 2003) and the way in which the model can be shocked to examine effects of changes in real exchange rates and other variables. The model's simulation results of prospective changes to grape and wine markets by 2025 for a baseline case are then summarised, followed by results for our alternative paths for real exchange rates, for Chinese growth over the next decade, and for the United Kingdom following Brexit. The final section draws out implications of the findings for wine markets and their participants in the years ahead.

REVISED MODEL OF THE WORLD'S WINE MARKETS AND ITS DATABASE

A model of the world's wine markets that was first published by Wittwer et al. (2003) has since been revised, updated and expanded by Anderson and Wittwer (2013). The enhancements to that original model include disaggregating wine markets into five types, namely nonpremium, commercial-premium, superpremium and iconic still wines and sparkling wine.[1] There are two types of grapes, premium and nonpremium. Nonpremium wine uses nonpremium grapes exclusively, superpremium and iconic wines use premium grapes exclusively and commercial-premium and sparkling wines use both types of grapes. The world is divided into forty-four individual nations and seven composite regions that capture all other countries.

The model's database is calibrated to 2014, based on the comprehensive wine market volume and value data and trade and excise tax data provided

[1] Commercial-premium still wines are defined by Anderson and Nelgen (2011) and Anderson, Nelgen and Pinilla (2017) to be those between US$2.50 and $7.50 per litre pretax at a country's border or wholesale. Since iconic still wines are a small subset of superpremium wines (they are assumed to have an average wholesale pretax price of $80 per litre and to account for just 0.45 percent of global wine production and consumption), for simplicity's sake they are not separately reported here.

in Anderson and Pinilla (2017) and Anderson et al. (2017). It is projected forward assuming aggregate national consumption, population and real exchange rate changes between 2014 and 2025 to the extent shown in Appendix Table 18.1.[2] Three alternatives to that baseline also are projected to 2025. One involves the real exchange rates of all countries being 10 percent lower against the US dollar than in the baseline in 2025 (as optimists suggested might happen under policies promised during 2016 US electioneering by now-President Trump); another involves slower economic growth in China; and a third alternative scenario looks at one possible outcome from Brexit.

Concerning preferences, there is assumed to continue to be a considerable swing towards all wine types in China and a swing away from nonpremium wines in all other countries. However, if China's aggregate consumption were to grow slower than the rate assumed in the baseline scenario, it would cause China's RER to depreciate against other currencies, thereby slowing China's growth in net imports of wine. It would also reduce aggregate consumption in Africa, which had been booming because of substantial Chinese investment in and trade with that continent.

In our baseline scenario, both grape and wine industry total factor productivity is assumed to grow at 1 percent per year everywhere, while grape and wine industry capital is assumed to grow net of depreciation at 1.5 percent per year in China but zero elsewhere (consistent with the zero growth in global wine production and consumption over the past two decades). An alternative scenario is included in which the US dollar appreciates by 10 percent relative to all other currencies in response to the stimulus provided by Donald Trump's move to the White House in January 2017. In another alternative scenario involving slower growth for China, it is assumed the reduced competition from imports because of the RER depreciation encourages China's domestic wine industry capital to grow at 3 percent instead of 1.5 percent per year. The third alternative scenario assumes that following the UK's exit from the European Union (EU), the UK pound depreciates by 10 percent in real terms, that the rate of UK economic growth halves for the period to 2025 and that the United Kingdom applies the EU's external tariff on wine to imports from EU member countries and also from Chile and South Africa. (The latter countries currently have free-trade agreements (FTAs) with the EU, but we assume the United

[2] The real exchange rate changes over the projection period are the changes expected in the nominal value of country i's currency relative to the US dollar times the expected ratio of the gross domestic product (GDP) deflator for the United States versus that for country i.

Kingdom does not have enough time by 2025 to negotiate and implement a new FTA with each of those two countries.)

This global model has supply-and-demand equations and hence quantities and prices for each of the grape and wine products and for a single composite of all other products in each country. Grapes are assumed to be not traded internationally, but other products are both exported and imported. Each market is assumed to have cleared before any shock, and to find a new market-clearing outcome following any exogenously introduced shock. All prices are expressed in real (2014 US dollar) terms. Detailed equations for the model are provided in the Appendix to Anderson and Wittwer (2013).

PROJECTING GLOBAL WINE MARKETS TO 2025

Global wine production and exports as projected in the baseline to 2025 are shown in Table 18.1, along with the 2014 actual data. Consistent with past trends, the model's volume of production (and consumption) rises little over that eleven-year period (9 percent), made up of a 6 percent decline in nonpremium wine and a one-sixth rise in commercial and fine wine. In value terms, though, wine output and consumption increases by about 50 percent in total and 60 percent in the two premium categories in real (2014 US dollar) terms. The international trade projections are similar, although a little larger, with the share of global production exported (= share of global consumption imported) rising two percentage points between 2014 and 2025.

The baseline projection does not alter greatly the 2014 shares of various countries in global wine production, apart from China, because it is assumed vineyard expansion there is faster than elsewhere.[3] In value terms, that means China moves from fifth to fourth by 2025 behind France, the United States and Italy, and Spain remains barely ahead of Australia and then Germany, which take the next three places (Figure 18.1(a)). In total wine production volume terms, China moves from sixth to fifth place, and Argentina drops from fifth to eighth (and from eighth to ninth in volume terms – see Appendix Table A18.2).

When subdivided into fine wine (still plus sparking), commercial premium wine and nonpremium wine, France and the United States retain the highest two places on the global ladder for fine wine production, and Spain

[3] This was to err on the conservative side. In fact, China's wine production fell steadily between 2012 and 2016, by a total of one-fifth, so China's wine imports may grow faster than in this baseline projection.

Table 18.1 *Volume and value of global wine production and exports, 2014 and projected 2025 (ML and 2014 US$ billion)*

	Production volume ('000 ML)			Production value (US$b)		
	2014	2025	*% change*	2014	2025	*% change*
Nonpremium wine	9.4	8.8	*−6*	10.1	9.6	*−5*
Commercial premium	9.9	11.8	*19*	26.2	42.3	*62*
Fine wine	5.6	6.6	*18*	39.2	62.3	*59*
Total wine	24.9	27.3	*9*	75.6	114.3	*51*
	Export volume ('000 ML)			Export value (US$b)		
Nonpremium wine	4.2	4.0	*−3*	4.4	4.5	*3*
Commercial premium	4.6	5.6	*23*	11.6	18.8	*63*
Fine wine	2.4	3.0	*24*	17.2	28.8	*68*
Total wine	11.1	12.6	*13*	33.1	52.1	*57*

Source: Authors' model results (see Appendix Tables A18.2 to A18.5 for national details).

and Italy retain the top two places for nonpremium wine. As for commercial premium wine (defined to be those between $2.50 and $7.50 per litre pretax at a country's wholesale level or national border), Italy retains the top ranking over our projections period, but at least in terms of value, China challenges France for second place, as it is assumed to raise the proportion of its nonpremium to commercial premium output faster than other countries.

The country rankings by projected value of total wine consumption change somewhat more than those for production by 2025, with China taking second place after the United States ahead of France and Germany, and then the UK slightly overtaking Italy to slip into fifth place (Figure 18.1(b)). The United States, France and Germany retain the top three rankings for consuming fine wine, but Canada slightly overtakes Italy for fourth place, in terms of value at least. As for commercial wine, China strengthens its number one position ahead of the United States, and the United Kingdom does likewise vis-à-vis Germany for third place (Appendix Table A18.3).

The projected changes in consumption volumes are shown in Figure 18.2, where it is clear that China is projected to dominate the increase in aggregate, although the United States is projected to lead the increase in consumption of fine wine. In western Europe and the Southern Hemisphere's New World countries, fine wines are projected to substitute for commercial wines (defined as the sum of commercial premium and nonpremium wines)

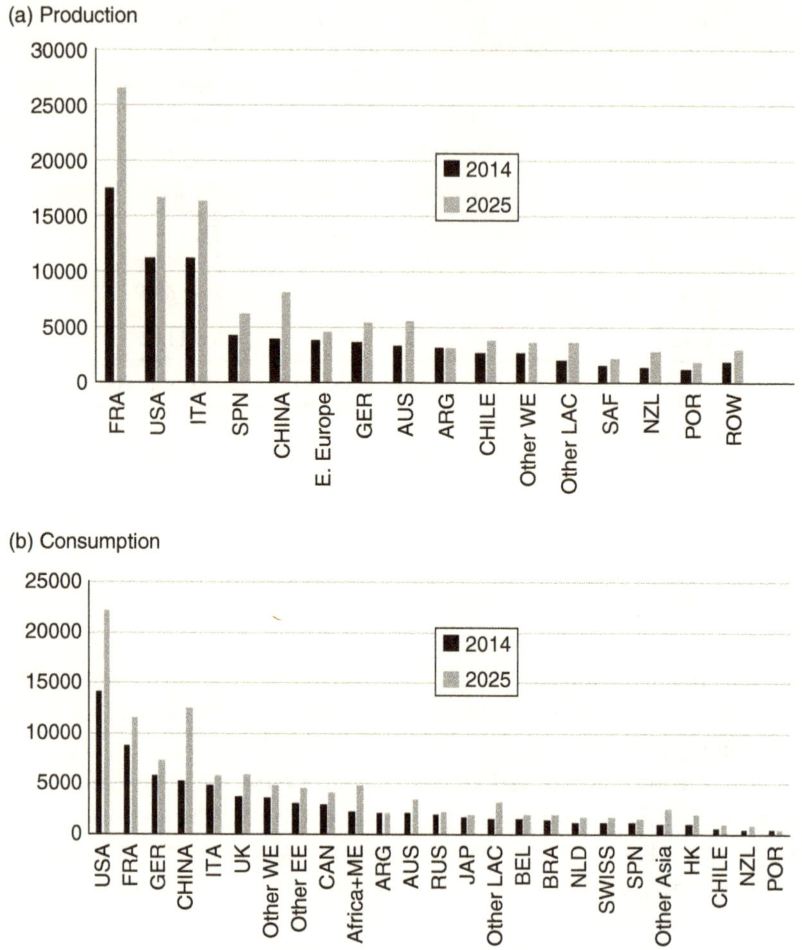

Figure 18.1 Value of wine production and consumption in key countries, 2014 and 2025 (2014 US$ million).
Source: Authors' model results.

with almost no change in total wine consumption. Sub-Saharan Africa is the next region that is projected to take off, with its growth accounting for more than one-third of the rest of the world's increase in volumes consumed.

Those differences in production versus consumption rankings are of course reflected in international trade. Figure 18.3 shows that France, Italy and Spain remain the three dominant exporters of wine in aggregate value, but that the rankings of the next few change to Australia being slightly ahead of Chile, and then the United States, Germany and New Zealand being almost equal in sixth place in value terms. France and then Italy are even more dominant in fine wine exports, and remain so by 2025, while

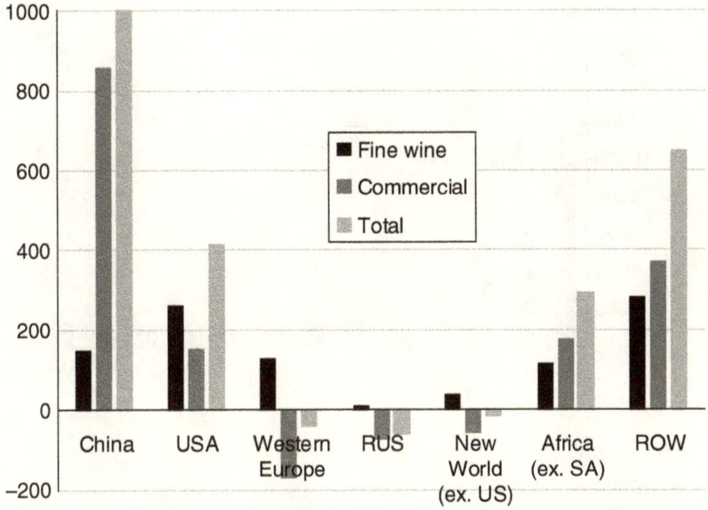

Figure 18.2 Change in volume of wine consumption, main regions, 2014 to 2025 (ML).[a]
[a] Fine wine is defined as superpremium and iconic still wines plus sparkling wines, the rest being commercial premium plus nonpremium still wines.
Source: Authors' model results.

Italy outranks France in the commercial premium export category and Spain outranks Italy, Australia and then Chile in the nonpremium export class (Appendix Table A18.4).

Among the importers, the United States and the United Kingdom are projected to continue to hold the first two places in 2025 in value terms, but China moves into third place slightly ahead of Germany, followed well behind by Canada, Hong Kong, Belgium-Luxembourg, Netherlands and Japan. Again, note that Sub-Saharan Africa is projected to experience the largest increase in imports of all the other regions, followed by Other Asia. Those developments are reflected also in the level and change in the shares of various countries and residual regions in the value of global wine imports (Figure 18.4). From Appendix Table A18.5, it is clear that the United States is the outstanding importer of fine wine in both 2014 and 2025, but the next rankings in value terms change from Canada, Germany and the United Kingdom to the United Kingdom, Canada and Germany. In the commercial premium category, where the United Kingdom is the dominant importer, there is a similar reshuffle of value rankings from Germany, the United States and China to China, the United States and Germany. As for nonpremium wine imports, in 2014 Germany was first ranked followed in second place by France in volume terms and the United Kingdom in value terms. By 2025,

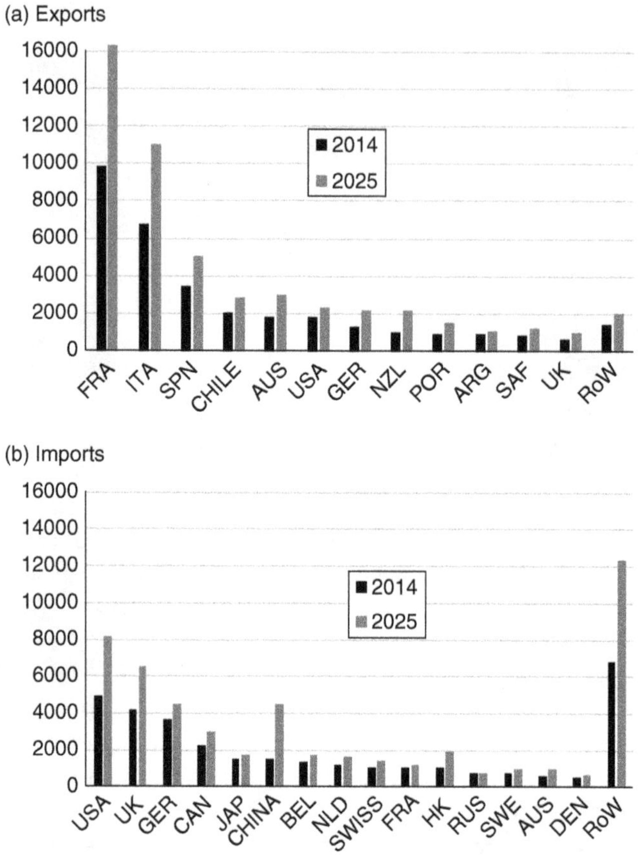

Figure 18.3 Value of wine exports and imports, key wine trading countries, 2014 and 2025 (2014 US$ million).
Source: Authors' model results.

though, it is projected that the United Kingdom will replace Germany in first place in value terms – but this baseline projection does not take account of Brexit (see the alternative scenario later in this chapter).

The increase in imports by Sub-Saharan Africa is projected to come mostly from France followed by Portugal and Spain in the case of fine wines, but overwhelmingly from South Africa (again followed by Portugal and Spain) in the case of commercial wines (Figure 18.5(a)). In value terms, France accounts for more than one-third of the projected increase over that decade, and for 70 percent when combined with Spain and Portugal, while South Africa's value share is only one-seventh and all other countries account for just one-twentieth (Figure 18.5(b)).

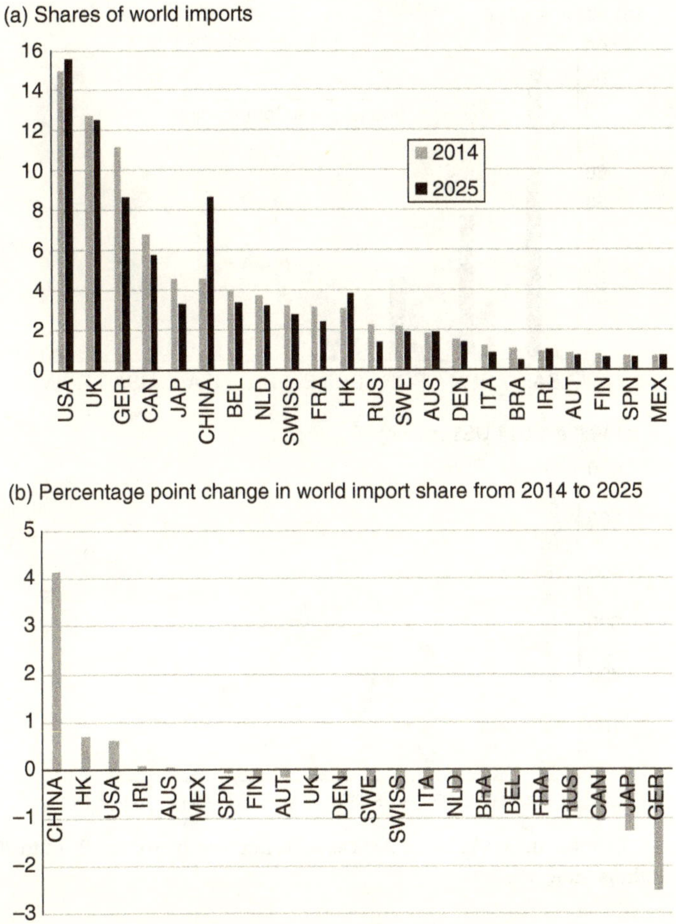

Figure 18.4 National shares of global wine import values, 2014 and 2025 (%).
Source: Authors' model results.

As for China's wine consumption increase between 2014 and 2025, according to our baseline projection almost half comes from expanded domestic production, and 70 percent of the imported volume – and most of the fine wine – comes from Europe (Figure 18.6(a)). With a proportionately larger increase in imports than in domestic production, China's self-sufficiency in wine falls from 75 percent to 64 percent over the projection period.[4]

[4] That self-sufficiency rate of 75 percent for China in 2014 is based on China's official production and import data. It may in fact have been closer to 50 percent once double-counting of production and unrecorded imports of bottled wine from Hong Kong are taken into account, according to Anderson and Harada (2017), as discussed in the previous chapter in this volume.

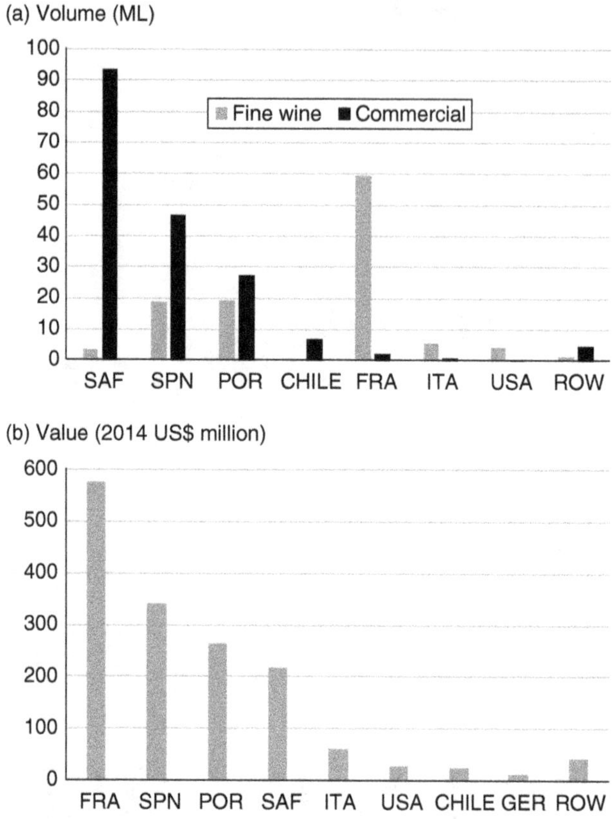

Figure 18.5 Increase in Sub-Saharan Africa's wine imports, by source, 2014 to 2025.
Source: Authors' model results.

What If the US Dollar's Real Value Was 10 Percent Higher than in the Baseline Case by 2025?

If the real value of the US dollar in 2025 was understated by one-tenth, the price of wines would be about 5 percent lower in the United States and slightly higher in all other countries in terms of their local currencies. Wine output would be about 1 percent lower in the United States and very slightly higher in other countries, while the volume of wine consumption would be 3 percent or 100 ML greater in the United States and slightly lower elsewhere such that global consumption would be about the same as in the baseline. Fine wines would account for a larger share of the volume consumed globally, though, because of the shift of gravity of the world's consumption towards the United States, which is not only the world's largest consumer of wine but also has a stronger focus on fine wine.

With US production lower but consumption higher in this scenario, its imports would be greater by about 100 ML (or $800 million). Even though the volume of world trade in wine would be only 20 ML greater, its value would be $600 million greater because so much more of it would be fine wine destined for the US market. One-third of those 100 ML extra wine imports by the United States would be from Italy, one-quarter from France and about 7 percent from each of Australia, New Zealand and Spain, with the rest of the world providing only one-seventh of that extra imported wine.

What If Incomes in China Were to Grow Slower than in the Baseline Case by 2025?

The baseline scenario assumes China's real household consumption would grow at 5.4 percent per year between 2014 and 2025. If it in fact were to grow at, say, one percentage point less per year, the country's total wine consumption would fall (and the premiumization of wine consumption in China would slow down). But other economies would suffer too, especially exporters of primary products and recipients of Chinese aid and foreign investment. Hence in this alternative scenario, we assume also that Sub-Saharan African real household consumption would grow less rapidly, at 6 percent instead of 6.9 percent per year.

In this alternative scenario, as compared with the initial baseline scenario, China's imports bear all the brunt of the slower growth in consumer demand: those imports are 350 ML or two-thirds lower than in the baseline scenario in 2025 (170ML instead of 520ML). As a consequence, China's wine self-sufficiency in this slower-growth case would be almost the same in 2025 as in 2014, at 75 percent. The reduced import growth would be felt equally by European and New World wine exporters (Figure 18.6(b)).

Wine imports would be lower in Sub-Saharan Africa too in this scenario as compared with the baseline case, by one-third or 90 ML (200 ML instead of 290 ML). The increase in global trade in wine over 2014–2025 would be 15 percent lower in volume and value terms in this scenario, but the adverse impact on exporters would vary considerably across countries. The volume of exports would increase by one-twelfth less for Italy, one-eighth less for Australia and France, one-sixth less for Spain, one-half less for South Africa and almost 90 percent less for Chile compared with the baseline case.

How Might Wine Markets Be Affected by an Exit of the United Kingdom from the EU?

As mentioned earlier, for this third alternative scenario we assume that, following the UK's exit from the EU (possibly as early as April 2019), by 2025

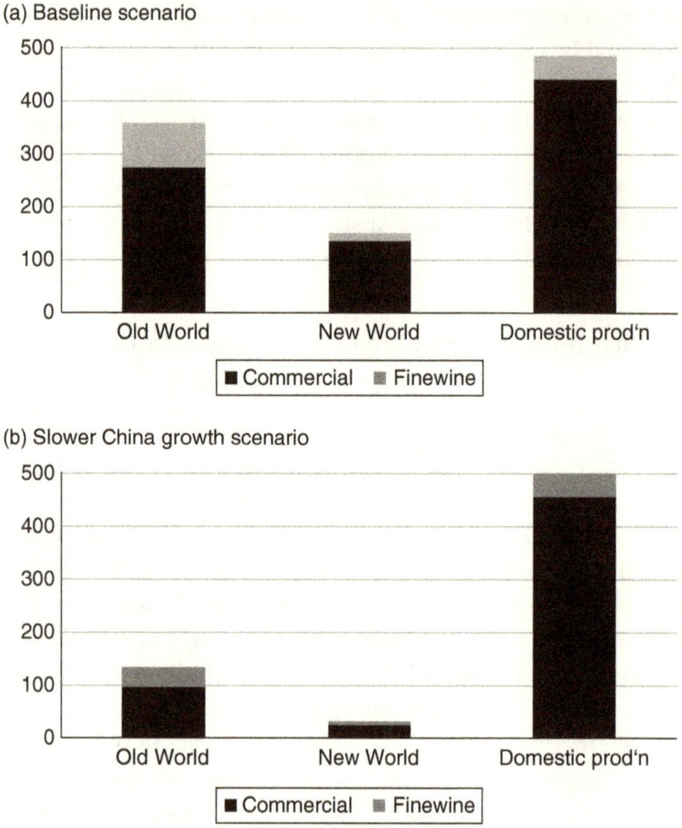

Figure 18.6 Increase in China's fine and commercial wine consumption, by source, 2014 to 2025 (ML).
Source: Authors' model results.

the UK pound would be 10 percent lower in real terms than in our model's core baseline projection; the rate of UK economic growth would halve for the period to 2025; the United Kingdom would apply the EU's external tariff on wine to imports from EU member countries; and the United Kingdom does not have enough time by 2025 to negotiate and implement FTAs with the EU27, Chile and South Africa (the latter two having preferential access to EU wine markets which would not include the United Kingdom unless or until the United Kingdom signs and implements new bilateral FTAs with them).

In this alternative scenario involving Brexit (see Anderson and Wittwer 2017), as compared with the initial baseline scenario to 2025, the consumer price of wine would be one-ninth higher in the United Kingdom in local currency terms and the volume of UK wine consumption would

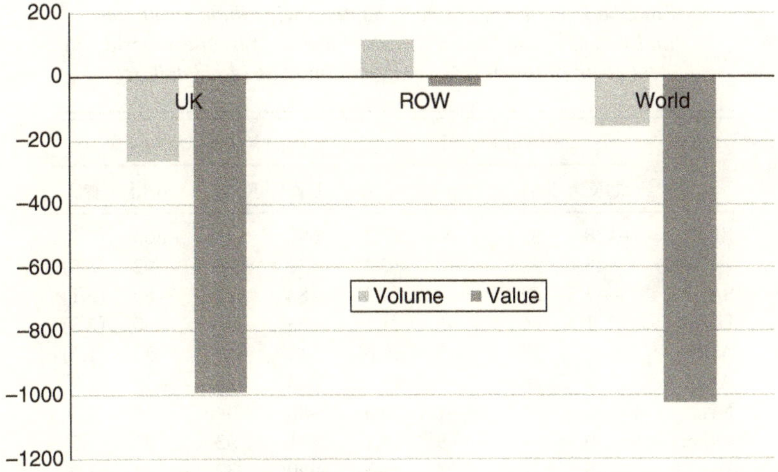

Figure 18.7 Difference in 2025 wine import volumes and values as a result of Brexit (ML and US$ million in 2014 US dollars).
Source: Authors' model results.

be 17 percent lower: 3 percent because of real depreciation of the pound; 8 percent because of slower UK economic growth; and 6 percent because of the new tariffs on EU, Chilean and South African wines. The volume of projected UK imports in 2025 is 266 ML lower in this scenario than in the baseline scenario, but world imports would be lower by just 154 ML because imports by other countries are 112 ML higher in response to the international price of wine being lower in this scenario. In value terms, UK imports are almost $1 billion lower in 2025 because of Brexit. The retail price of commercial wines relative to fine wines is higher in the United Kingdom and lower in the rest of the world, in this scenario than in the base case, thanks to the nature of the UK's new tariffs on wine imports, which are volumetric rather than *ad valorem*. A consequence of those relative price differences is that the value of the rest of the world's total wine imports also is lower in 2025 than in the base case, by $32 million (Figure 18.7).

These impacts affect bilateral wine trade patterns in varied ways (Table 18.2). European, Chilean and South African wine exports are lowered, by 96 ML or US$806 million in the case of the EU, with some of their exports diverted from the United Kingdom to EU27 and other markets in competition with other New World exporters. So while Australia, for example, sells more into the United Kingdom, it sells less to other countries

Table 18.2 *Difference in 2025 bilateral wine import volumes and values by the United Kingdom and the rest of the world as a result of Brexit (ML and $million in 2014 US dollars)*[a]

	Volume (ML)				Value (US$m)			
	UK	RoW	World	(%)	UK	RoW	World	(%)
EU27	−178	82	−96	(1.2)	−692	−114	−806	(2.3)
CHILE	−46	28	−18	(2.4)	−128	36	−92	(3.5)
SAF	−43	29	−14	(4.2)	−83	23	−60	(5.1)
USA	1	−6	−5	(1.1)	−23	−27	−50	(2.3)
AUS	5	−10	−5	(0.6)	19	−52	−33	(1.2)
ARG	0	−6	−6	(2.6)	−3	−25	−28	(2.9)
NZL	−5	4	−1	(0.6)	−80	34	−46	(2.3)
Others	0	−9	−9	(0.1)	−1	93	92	(1.5)
World	−266	112	−154	(1.3)	−990	−32	−1022	(2.0)

[a] Numbers in parentheses are the percentage difference between the projected trade volumes or values in the Brexit and baseline scenarios for 2025.

Source: Authors' model results.

and to the world in total. New Zealand, which has the highest average price of still wine exports in the world, has the opposite result to Australia: because the price of commercial wines in non-UK markets is lower relative to the price of fine wines in this scenario as compared with the base case, New Zealand is better off selling less to the United Kingdom and more to higher-priced markets for its (mostly fine) wine – but it still sells less wine overall. For Chile and South Africa, who lose their preferential access to United Kingdom (but not to EU27) markets in this scenario, some of their exports are redirected from the United Kingdom to EU27 countries, but again they are worse off overall. Global wine trade in 2025 would be less under Brexit by 154 ML or $1.02 billion. The change in relative prices also affects the *percentage* by which exporters' trade shrinks in terms of values versus volumes. Those differences are shown in the numbers in parentheses in Table 18.2.

The preceding projected effects of Brexit would be less for the EU27 if an FTA were to be signed and implemented with the United Kingdom (see extra simulations in Anderson and Wittwer 2017), but then they would be even greater for Chile and South Africa unless the United Kingdom also replicated the bilateral FTAs currently between the EU28 and those two New World wine-exporting countries.

IMPLICATIONS

The results presented in this chapter reveal a striking prospect. China has already become by far the most important wine-consuming country in Asia and, with a projected increase in its income and hence its consumption over the next decade, that dominance is expected to become even greater. Since China's domestic production is projected to increase by less than domestic demand, its net imports are projected to rise and its wine self-sufficiency to fall considerably.

This modelling exercise points to the enormous speed with which China may become a dominant market for wine exporters. While the recent and projected rates of increase in per capita wine consumption in China are no faster than what occurred in several northwestern European countries in earlier decades, it is the sheer size of China's adult population of 1.1 billion – and the fact that grape wine still accounts for only 4 percent of Chinese alcohol consumption – that makes this import growth opportunity unprecedented. It would be somewhat less if China's own winegrape production increases faster than we have assumed, but certainly in as short a period as the next decade, that is unlikely to be able to reduce the growth in China's wine imports very much, especially at the premium end of the spectrum.

Of course, these projections are not predictions. Where exchange rates move, and how fast various countries' wine producers take advantage of the projected market growth opportunities in Asia and Sub-Saharan Africa, will be key determinants of the actual changes in market shares over the coming years. Not all segments of the industry are projected to benefit, with nonpremium producers facing falling prices if demand for their product continues to dwindle as projected in this chapter. But those exporting firms willing to invest sufficiently in building relationships with their Chinese importer/distributor – or in going into grapegrowing or winemaking within China – may well enjoy long-term benefits from such investments. Meanwhile, all wine exporters and importers will be keeping a close eye on changes in the various bilateral exchange rates and on import tariffs, particularly as new preferential trade agreements come into play, perhaps most notably because of Brexit, over the next decade.

Appendix Table A18.1 *Cumulative consumption and population growth rates and changes in the real exchange rate (RER) relative to the US dollar, 2014 to 2025 (%)*

	Aggregate consumption	Pop'n	RER		Aggreg. consm	Pop'n	RER
France	18	4	−11	Australia	35	11	−17
Italy	11	2	−9	New Zealand	32	9	−26
Portugal	14	0	−9	Canada	27	8	−18
Spain	26	8	−9	United States	31	8	0
Austria	19	4	−7	Argentina	7	10	109
Belgium	20	7	−9	Brazil	16	8	−29
Denmark	22	2	−9	Chile	55	8	−2
Finland	21	3	−7	Mexico	42	12	−8
Germany	14	−2	−11	Uruguay	45	3	1
Greece	22	−1	−14	Other L. Am	60	10	−5
Ireland	42	12	−9	South Africa	36	12	−1
Netherlands	21	4	−9	Turkey	50	8	20
Sweden	24	9	−13	North Africa	53	11	0
Switzerland	18	8	−6	Other Africa	109	18	84
United Kingdom	32	6	1	Middle East	52	18	−12
Other W. Europe	21	10	−1	China	79	3	5
Bulgaria	41	−7	7	Hong Kong	42	3	2
Croatia	20	−2	−1	India	134	13	17
Georgia	35	0	23	Japan	11	−3	−24
Hungary	25	−3	−11	Korea	38	1	−9
Moldova	49	−11	13	Malaysia	62	15	−16
Romania	45	−4	22	Philippines	75	18	7
Russia	18	−2	−8	Singapore	44	21	−22
Ukraine	22	−5	14	Taiwan	29	1	−13
Other E. Europe	40	−5	48	Thailand	47	3	−9
				Other Asia	99	10	10

Source: Authors' compilation from projections by various international agencies and from global economywide modelling by Anderson and Strutt (2016).

Appendix Table A18.2 *Shares of world wine production volume and value, 2014 and projected 2025 (%)*

	2014 Volume	2014 Value	2025 Volume	2025 Value
All wine				
ITA	15.7	14.8	15.7	14.4
FRA	14.6	23.3	15.0	23.3
SPN	12.5	5.8	11.9	5.5
USA	11.6	15.0	11.5	14.7
ARG	5.2	4.1	4.1	2.8
CHINA	5.0	5.2	6.3	7.2
AUS	4.6	4.5	4.7	4.9
GER	4.2	4.8	4.5	4.7
CHILE	4.0	3.5	3.9	3.4
SAF	3.6	2.1	3.5	2.0
Rest of world	18.9	17.2	18.7	17.2
Fine wine				
FRA	26.0	31.9	26.5	31.2
USA	18.4	19.2	18.0	18.9
ITA	17.5	14.5	17.4	14.2
GER	5.5	4.4	5.5	4.1
SPN	5.1	3.7	5.2	3.7
AUS	3.0	2.9	3.1	3.4
ARG	3.0	3.0	2.5	2.1
RUS	2.9	1.7	2.9	1.5
NZL	2.6	3.0	2.7	4.0
CHINA	1.8	2.4	2.2	3.1
Rest of world	14.0	13.2	14.0	13.8
Commercial premium				
ITA	15.0	15.9	14.9	15.1
FRA	12.7	13.6	12.5	13.7
CHINA	9.5	10.7	11.1	14.4
SPN	9.2	7.1	9.3	7.0
USA	9.0	9.9	8.6	9.2
GER	6.3	6.3	6.4	6.1
CHILE	5.5	6.0	5.4	5.8
AUS	5.3	5.6	5.3	6.2
ARG	3.9	4.3	3.2	2.8
SAF	3.3	2.9	3.6	3.0
Rest of world	20.3	17.7	19.9	16.8

(*continued*)

Appendix Table A18.2 *(continued)*

	2014 Volume	2014 Value	2025 Volume	2025 Value
Nonpremium wine				
SPN	20.3	10.2	20.5	10.3
ITA	15.5	13.1	15.5	12.9
USA	10.3	11.6	10.6	11.6
FRA	9.7	14.6	9.8	14.6
ARG	8.1	7.6	6.6	6.7
SAF	5.5	4.9	5.3	5.2
AUS	4.9	7.6	5.1	8.7
CHILE	4.1	5.8	4.0	6.3
POR	2.3	2.0	2.5	2.1
CHINA	2.2	1.7	3.0	2.2
Rest of world	17.2	20.9	17.1	19.5

Source: Authors' model results.

Appendix Table A18.3 *Shares of world wine consumption volume and value, 2014 and projected 2025 (%)*

	2014 Volume	2014 Value	2025 Volume	2025 Value
All wine				
USA	13.8	19.0	14.2	19.7
FRA	10.0	11.8	8.9	10.2
GER	8.6	7.8	7.5	6.6
ITA	8.4	6.5	7.1	5.2
CHINA	6.8	7.1	10.0	11.2
UK	5.3	5.1	5.8	5.3
RUS	4.3	2.6	3.7	2.0
ARG	4.2	2.9	3.3	1.9
SPN	3.8	1.6	3.5	1.3
AUS	2.3	2.9	2.3	3.1
Rest of world	32.5	32.6	33.6	33.5
Fine wine				
USA	22.7	24.6	23.3	25.5
FRA	11.8	14.5	10.7	12.6
GER	7.4	6.8	6.5	5.7
ITA	6.7	5.6	5.7	4.6
CAN	5.0	5.7	4.4	5.3
RUS	4.7	2.5	4.2	2.0

Appendix Table A18.3 *(continued)*

	2014 Volume	2014 Value	2025 Volume	2025 Value
UK	4.0	3.8	4.2	3.8
AUS	3.5	3.2	3.4	3.6
CHINA	3.1	3.6	4.8	5.7
JAP	2.7	2.8	2.1	2.1
Rest of world	28.4	26.8	30.7	29.1
Commercial premium				
CHINA	12.3	13.8	16.9	20.7
USA	12.0	13.3	11.7	12.7
UK	8.7	7.7	9.1	7.9
GER	8.3	9.3	7.0	7.7
FRA	6.3	7.0	5.5	6.1
ITA	5.8	6.5	4.9	5.3
RUS	4.8	2.3	4.0	1.9
NLD	2.9	3.2	2.6	2.8
SPN	2.9	1.9	2.7	1.7
BRA	2.8	3.2	2.4	2.7
Rest of world	33.1	31.8	33.3	30.6
Nonpremium wine				
FRA	12.9	14.1	12.5	13.5
ITA	12.3	10.2	11.4	9.3
USA	10.3	11.6	10.6	12.0
GER	9.7	7.9	9.0	7.2
ARG	7.5	7.0	6.6	6.5
SPN	6.3	3.4	6.4	3.4
OCEF	3.8	3.0	4.5	2.9
POR	3.7	2.3	3.4	2.2
RUS	3.3	4.2	2.8	3.6
CHINA	3.1	2.9	4.4	3.9
Rest of world	27.0	33.5	28.4	35.5

Source: Authors' model results.

Appendix Table A18.4 *Shares of world wine export volume and value, 2014 and projected 2025 (%)*

	2014 Volume	2014 Value	2025 Volume	2025 Value
All wine				
SPN	20.2	10.3	18.8	9.7
ITA	19.3	20.3	20.7	21.2
FRA	17.2	29.7	18.9	31.3
CHILE	6.9	6.1	6.3	5.4
AUS	6.5	5.5	6.5	5.8
USA	4.9	5.5	4.3	4.5
SAF	4.7	2.6	4.4	2.4
GER	3.9	3.8	4.5	4.3
ARG	2.5	2.7	2.0	2.0
POR	2.4	2.8	2.6	2.9
NZL	1.6	3.1	1.7	4.1
Rest of world	10.0	7.6	9.2	6.5
Fine wine				
FRA	36.1	42.3	37.3	42.2
ITA	25.6	21.4	26.2	21.6
SPN	9.6	7.3	9.2	7.0
USA	5.9	6.4	4.7	5.2
NZL	4.3	4.7	4.5	6.6
GER	3.2	2.8	3.7	3.2
POR	2.5	2.7	2.5	3.0
AUS	2.1	1.8	2.2	2.2
UK	2.1	2.3	2.0	2.2
CHILE	1.9	2.0	1.7	1.9
Rest of world	6.7	6.3	5.9	5.1
Commercial premium				
ITA	20.4	21.6	21.4	22.3
FRA	16.5	17.7	16.8	19.2
SPN	14.3	12.3	14.3	12.2
CHILE	9.1	10.3	8.3	9.5
AUS	7.8	8.4	7.7	9.4
GER	6.3	5.6	7.0	6.2
SAF	4.2	3.6	4.8	3.7
USA	3.3	3.3	2.9	2.8
ARG	3.3	3.8	2.9	2.7
POR	2.9	3.2	2.8	3.2
Rest of world	11.9	10.3	11.0	8.8

Appendix Table A18.4 *(continued)*

	2014 Volume	2014 Value	2025 Volume	2025 Value
Nonpremium wine				
SPN	32.7	16.8	32.2	16.1
ITA	14.3	13.1	15.7	13.7
AUS	7.6	12.4	8.0	13.5
CHILE	7.4	11.3	6.9	11.1
SAF	7.4	7.4	6.6	7.3
FRA	7.3	12.0	8.1	12.6
USA	6.0	7.2	5.9	6.9
ARG	2.1	3.3	0.9	2.5
NZL	1.8	4.2	1.9	4.8
MOLD	1.7	1.0	1.6	0.8
Rest of world	11.7	11.2	12.2	10.7

Source: Authors' model results.

Appendix Table A18.5 *Shares of world wine import volume and value, 2014 and projected 2025 (%)*

	2014 Volume	2014 Value	2025 Volume	2025 Value
All wine				
GER	14.1	11.1	11.5	8.6
UK	13.2	12.7	14.0	12.5
USA	10.2	15.0	10.5	15.6
FRA	6.6	3.1	5.3	2.4
RUS	5.3	2.3	3.8	1.4
CHINA	4.3	4.5	7.9	8.7
CAN	4.0	6.8	3.5	5.7
NLD	3.8	3.7	3.4	3.2
BEL	2.9	4.0	2.5	3.4
JAP	2.9	4.5	2.2	3.3
ITA	2.5	1.2	1.8	0.8
HK	1.9	3.1	2.3	3.8
Rest of world	28.5	28.0	31.3	30.7
Fine wine				
USA	16.0	18.7	16.4	19.4
UK	9.3	8.4	9.2	8.1
CAN	8.5	9.6	6.6	7.8

(continued)

Appendix Table A18.5 *(continued)*

	2014 Volume	2014 Value	2025 Volume	2025 Value
GER	7.5	8.5	5.9	6.6
JAP	6.0	6.2	4.3	4.3
SWISS	5.3	5.3	4.6	4.5
RUS	4.2	1.8	2.9	1.0
BEL	3.9	4.6	3.3	3.8
HK	3.9	4.1	4.5	5.0
AUS	3.1	2.6	2.9	2.6
CHINA	2.9	2.7	5.8	5.5
Rest of world	29.3	27.4	33.5	31.4
Commercial premium				
UK	18.8	17.3	19.1	17.6
GER	10.7	12.4	8.4	9.7
USA	9.9	11.1	9.5	10.7
CHINA	7.2	8.1	12.9	14.9
RUS	6.9	3.0	5.0	2.0
NLD	6.3	7.3	5.4	6.3
CAN	3.1	3.7	2.6	3.0
BEL	3.1	3.5	2.5	2.9
JAP	2.5	2.9	1.6	1.8
FRA	2.5	2.6	2.0	2.1
Rest of world	29.0	28.0	31.0	28.9
Nonpremium wine				
GER	21.6	18.2	19.9	16.7
FRA	13.2	7.2	12.2	6.2
UK	9.3	17.2	10.4	19.6
USA	7.1	10.5	7.5	11.9
ITA	5.9	3.9	5.1	3.1
POR	4.4	1.8	4.0	1.5
RUS	4.2	2.0	2.8	1.1
SWE	2.4	4.5	2.3	4.2
CAN	2.4	3.7	2.5	4.0
NLD	2.2	2.7	2.0	2.4
Rest of world	27.2	28.3	31.2	29.4

Source: Authors' model results.

REFERENCES

Anderson, K. and K. Harada (2017), 'How Much Wine Is *Really* Produced and Consumed in China, Hong Kong and Japan?' Wine Economics Research Centre Working Paper 0317, University of Adelaide, November.

Anderson, K. and S. Nelgen (2011), *Global Wine Markets, 1961 to 2009: A Statistical Compendium*, Adelaide: University of Adelaide Press. Freely accessible as an e-book at www.adelaide.edu.au/press/titles/global-wine and as Excel files at www.adelaide.edu.au/wine-econ/databases/GWM

Anderson, K., S. Nelgen and V. Pinilla (2017), *Global Wine Markets, 1860 to 2016: A Statistical Compendium*, Adelaide: University of Adelaide Press. Also freely available as an e-book at www.adelaide.edu.au/press/

Anderson, K. and V. Pinilla *(with the assistance of* A. J. Holmes) (2017), *Annual Database of Global Wine Markets, 1835 to 2016*, freely available in Excel at the University of Adelaide's Wine Economics Research Centre, www.adelaide.edu.au/wine-econ/databases

Anderson, K. and A. Strutt (2016), 'Impacts of Asia's Rise on African and Latin American Trade: Projections to 2030', *World Economy* 39(2): 172–94, February.

Anderson, K. and G. Wittwer (2001), 'US Dollar Appreciation and the Spread of Pierce's Disease: Effects on the World's Wine Markets', *Australian and New Zealand Wine Industry Journal* 16(2): 70–75, March–April.

(2013), 'Modeling Global Wine Markets to 2018: Exchange Rates, Taste Changes, and China's Import Growth', *Journal of Wine Economics* 8(2): 131–58.

(2017), "The UK and Global Wine Markets by 2025, and Implications of Brexit", *Journal of Wine Economics* 12(3) (forthcoming).

Barton, D., Y. Chen and A. Jin (2013), 'Mapping China's Middle Class', *McKinsey Quarterly*, June. www.mckinsey.com/insights/consumer_and_retail/mapping_chinas_middle_class

Cavallo, A. (2013), 'Online and Official Price Indexes: Measuring Argentina's Inflation', *Journal of Monetary Economics* 60(2): 152–65. dx.doi.org/10.1016/j.jmoneco.2012.10.002

Harrison, J. and K. Pearson (1996), 'Computing Solutions for Large General Equilibrium Models Using GEMPACK', *Computational Economics* 9(1): 93–127.

Kharas, H. (2010), 'The Emerging Middle Class in Developing Countries', Working Paper 285, Organisation for Economic Cooperation and Development (OECD) Development Centre, Paris, January.

OIV (2013), *State of the Vitiviniculture World Market*, Paris: OIV, March (www.oiv.org)

Wittwer, G., N. Berger and K. Anderson (2003), 'A Model of the World's Wine Markets', *Economic Modelling* 20(3): 487–506, May.

World Bank (2016), *World Development Indicators*, Washington, DC: World Bank. Accessed online 6 November at www.worldbank.org/wdi

APPENDIX

The Global Wine Markets Database, 1835 to 2016

Kym Anderson and Vicente Pinilla

An annual database of *global wine markets from 1961* has been available from the University of Adelaide in various updated editions, the most recent covering up to 2009 (Anderson and Nelgen 2011).

As for earlier data, economic historians at the University of Zaragoza in Spain have assembled basic global wine data in order to analyse an aspect of the first wave of globalization, namely the rise and fall of Spain as a wine exporter in the century prior to World War II. That led to a paper by Pinilla and Ayuda (2002) and also the beginnings of a global wine database for that period which has since been made available as Pinilla (2014).

Meanwhile, an analysis of the economic development of Australia's wine industry from its beginning in the 1830s has been undertaken by Anderson (2015). Comprehensive though that study was, it was incomplete because at that time there was not a comparable set of pre-1961 annual data available for the other pertinent (including Southern Hemisphere) wine-producing countries, nor global wine production, consumption and trade totals, against which to compare Australian trends and industry cycles. Hence the comparative approach to economic history, as illustrated in Hatton, O'Rourke and Williamson (2007), was confined in that Australian study mostly to the years since 1960.

For the present global study, a necessary first step was to get together and entice others to join in a comparative assessment of national wine market developments over both the first and second globalization waves, as well as in the intervening 'lost' decades that included two world wars and the Great Depression. All participants agreed to contribute national data to expand on the post-1960 data previously compiled by Anderson and Nelgen (2011) and the pre-1939 data assembled by Pinilla (2014).

Data from secondary sources were added to ensure coverage of other key countries, so the database includes not only forty-seven individual countries but also five regional groups of remaining countries, so that their sum provides estimates of world totals. Those forty-seven countries account for 96 percent of global wine production and exports and over 90 percent of global wine consumption and imports since 1860.

The aim at the outset was to go back at least to 1835 when the first wave of globalization began. Some data go back as far as the 1660s for South Africa and to the 1320s in the case of Britain. But for many of the less wine-focused countries, the series do not start until the late nineteenth century, and some series had years missing, such as during the two world wars. We therefore interpolated to fill gaps in the most important series covering volumes of wine production, exports and imports so as to be able to estimate global totals for those key variables back to 1860. The interpolated data represent a small part of the world total of each variable, not usually exceeding 10 percent before 1900 and 5 percent during 1900–60. Our interpolation methodology is detailed in Anderson and Pinilla (2017a).

The time frame covered varies depending on the available data. There is comprehensive information for the whole of the world in terms of the area under vine from 1900; the volume of wine produced and exported from 1860; wine consumption and import volumes from 1925; exports in current US dollar values from 1900; and imports in current values from 1961. For previous years, data are included for those countries where they are available.

The database also includes other economic variables, such as real gross domestic product (GDP), total and adult populations, total agricultural crop area, local currency to US dollar market exchange rates and volumes of consumption of beer and spirits and hence (with wine) total consumption of alcohol. Production, exports and imports of beer also are included. So too are total values of merchandise exports and imports, allowing the calculation of 'revealed' wine comparative advantage indexes from 1900. The total trade and exchange rate data have been newly compiled for the nineteenth century by Federico and Tena-Junguito (2016). Numerous intensive indicators, such as per capita and per dollar of real GDP, also have been calculated to compensate for differences in country size. Shares of world totals are provided for each variable too.

For some countries, there are early bilateral wine trade data revealing the origins of their imports or their export destinations. For Britain, wine import data are available from 1323, with main supplying countries' shares shown from the late 1600s to 1940. The main destinations of wine exports and the principal origins of imports between 1850 and 1938 are provided also for France. For both countries, data are also included on the tariffs paid at their borders on imports of wine.

Data refer whenever possible to the named countries according to their current borders. In some cases, where there have been significant territorial changes, the various earlier national and regional statistical sources have been consulted in order to do this.

The two main international sources that provide the bulk of the national data on the area under vine and the volume of production, exports and imports of wine are the International Institute of Agriculture (IIA) and the Food and Agriculture Organization of the United Nations (FAO), both with their head offices in Rome. The IIA was founded in Rome in 1905 by David Lubin (1849–1919), an American trader and agricultural reformer of Polish origin. The objective of the IIA was to gather, classify and distribute information about crop production, product prices and international agricultural trade. It immediately began to publish international agricultural statistics. During its existence, it published six statistical compendia, starting with the data published in 1903 and ending in 1938 (IIA 1911–1939). A seventh volume with the same format as the six previous publications was published after World War II in conjunction with the recently created Food and Agriculture Organization (FAO) and covered the whole period of the Second World War. The FAO was created as a specialized agency of the United Nations and undertook the activities previously performed by the IIA, extending its objectives and aims significantly. (The ties of senior officials of the IIA with the Italian fascist regime were the reason for its dissolution and replacement by the FAO.)

The statistics of the IIA were organized into two main parts. The first provided extensive information for each country about crop area, livestock numbers, agricultural production and foreign trade. The second was according to product, and for each product the information on area, production, exports and imports was provided by country and large geographical areas. In addition, the IIA yearbooks gradually began to include complementary information about the prices of some products in certain markets, freight rates, exchange rates, fertilizer consumption and trade and so on.

The number of products for which information was provided increased significantly over the years. The first yearbook included data for fourteen products, while between 1933 and 1938 there was information for sixty-two products. The number of countries for which the information was provided also increased.

There is no information about wine before 1921. After that year, data were provided on the area under vine and production of some countries, and after 1925 data regarding trade were also included. The 1928–1929 yearbook provides information about the average annual production, area under vine and international product trade for the period 1909–1913.

When the FAO was founded to replace the IIA, it immediately began to publish more-comprehensive agricultural statistics. For our purposes, the principal publication was the *Yearbook of Food and Agricultural Statistics*, which included information about crop area, production and trade.[1] An important difference with the prewar statistics of the IIA was the substantial increase in the number of products covered. The first yearbook published in 1948 includes information for sixty-nine products, but by the 1950s the coverage had expanded to more than eighty products. Because the FAO took a few years to match the quality and exhaustiveness of the data provided by the IIA (Yates 1955), there are large gaps in the information provided during this period for many Asian and African countries and for countries of the Soviet Bloc. Data on the area under vine and the production and trade of wine are available from 1946, although they are not there for all countries.

Although the printed yearbooks of the FAO have continued to be published to the present day, for the years after 1961 we drew on the wine production and trade data published electronically by the FAOSTAT database, as they date back to 1961 and are revised periodically (FAO 2017).

All data published by the IIA and FAO are based on the national statistics of each country as reported by their government. The quality of these data depend, therefore, on the quality of the data passed on by the national statistical offices.

Some contributors to the present study chose to use national statistics directly where they offer more complete and more detailed information. For other countries, where data were required that were not included in the aforementioned sources, they were obtained from Mitchell (2007a,b,c).

The final annual database is freely available in Excel as Anderson and Pinilla (2017b), and a summary of those data together with additional data such as the volume and value of recent bilateral wine trade are available in Anderson et al. (2017).

REFERENCES

Anderson, K. (with the assistance of N. R. Aryal) (2015), *Growth and Cycles in Australia's Wine Industry: A Statistical Compendium, 1843 to 2013*, Adelaide: University of Adelaide Press. Also freely available as an e-book at www.adelaide.edu.au/press/titles/austwine and as Excel files at www.adelaide.edu.au/wine-econ/databases/winehistory

[1] In 1958 these statistics were provided in two separate publications, the *Production Yearbook* and the *Trade Yearbook*.

Anderson, K. and S. Nelgen (2011), *Global Wine Markets, 1961 to 2009: A Statistical Compendium*, Adelaide: University of Adelaide Press. Also freely available as an e-book at www.adelaide.edu.au/press/titles/global-wine and as Excel files at www.adelaide.edu.au/wine-econ/databases/GWM

Anderson, K., S. Nelgen and V. Pinilla (2017), *Global Wine Markets, 1860 to 2016: A Statistical Compendium*, Adelaide: University of Adelaide Press. Also freely available as an e-book at www.adelaide.edu.au/press/

Anderson, K. and V. Pinilla (2017a), *"Annual Database of Global Wine Markets, 1835 to 2016: Methodology and Sources"*, Wine Economics Research Centre Working Paper 0417, November.

Anderson, K. and V. Pinilla (with the assistance of A. J. Holmes) (2017b), *Annual Database of Global Wine Markets, 1835 to 2016*, freely available in Excel at the University of Adelaide's Wine Economics Research Centre, www.adelaide.edu.au/wine-econ/databases

FAO (2017), *FAOSTAT*, website at www.fao.org/faostat/en/#home

Federico, G. and A. Tena-Junguito (2016), 'World Trade, 1800–1938: A New Dataset', EHES Working Paper 93.

Hatton, T. J., K. H. O'Rourke and J. G. Williamson (eds.) (2007), 'Introduction', pp. 1–14 in *The New Comparative Economic History: Essays in Honor of Jeffrey G. Williamson*, Cambridge, MA: MIT Press.

IIA (1911–1939), *Annuaire International de Statistique Agricole*, Rome: Institut International d'Agriculture/International Institute of Agriculture.

Mitchell, B. R. (2007a), *International Historical Statistics: Europe 1750–2005* (6th Edition), New York and Basingstoke: Palgrave Macmillan.

(2007b), *International Historical Statistics: Americas 1750–2005* (6th Edition), New York and Basingstoke: Palgrave Macmillan.

(2007c), *International Historical Statistics: Africa, Asia and Oceania 1750–2005* (5th Edition), New York and Basingstoke: Palgrave Macmillan.

Pinilla, V. (2014), 'Wine Historical Statistics: A Quantitative Approach to its Consumption, Production and Trade, 1840–1938', American Association of Wine Economists (AAWE) Working Paper 167, August. Freely available at www.wine-economics.org

Pinilla, V. and M. I. Ayuda (2002), 'The Political Economy of the Wine Trade: Spanish Exports and the International Market, 1890–1935', *European Review of Economic History* 6: 51–85.

Yates, P. L. (1955), *So Bold an Aim: Ten Years of Co-operation Toward Freedom from Want*, Rome: FAO.

Index

For EU product safety concerns, contact us at Calle de José Abascal, 56–1°, 28003 Madrid, Spain or eugpsr@cambridge.org.

www.ingramcontent.com/pod-product-compliance
Lightning Source LLC
Chambersburg PA
CBHW020457210525
27036CB00001B/116
* 9 7 8 1 1 0 7 1 9 2 9 2 8 *